Principles of Business Forecasting

2ND EDITION

Keith Ord
Georgetown University

Robert Fildes
Lancaster University

Nikolaos Kourentzes
Lancaster University

Wessex Press, Inc.
www.wessexlearning.com

"In the early 1980s, two of the authors, Robert Fildes and Keith Ord, were leaders in the movement to use experiments to determine which principles led to more accurate forecasts. The experiments show that forecasting methods today are capable of providing much more accurate forecasts than they were 50 years ago. This movement was a golden age for progress in forecasting. However, this knowledge has not been widely adopted in business and government.

In recent years, Fildes and Ord have been concerned with ways of implementing new approaches. To my knowledge, *Principles of Business Forecasting* is the first textbook to include some of the new methods. It is aimed both at beginning forecasters and practitioners, so it also covers the basics. Despite the improvements in methodology, forecasting accuracy in business and government has been shown to be getting poorer. Much of the forecasting has been done by people who have no awareness of scientific forecasting methods. *Principles of Business Forecasting* is directed at this market.

Research by Kesten Green and I have found that forecasters have turned to "analytics" using "big data." This approach ignores all cumulative knowledge about forecasting methods. It also violates the Golden Rule of Forecasting and Occam's razor. In his 1972 paper "Alchemy in the Behavioral Sciences," Hillel Einhorn warned of the danger of relying on the computer. Hopefully, Ord, Fildes, and Kourentzes will bring forecasting back to the basics and convince forecasters to use more accurate methods and principles. There is profit to be made."

J. Scott Armstrong, The Wharton School, University of Pennsylvania

Library of Congress Cataloging-in-Publication Data

Ord, Keith; Fildes, Robert; Kourentzes, Nikolaos
    Principles of Business Forecasting, 2nd edition / Keith Ord, Robert Fildes, Nikolaos Kourentzes
        p. cm.

ISBN 978-0-9990649-0-0 (hardcover)
      978-0-9990649-1-7 (softcover)
      978-0-9990649-2-4 (e-book)

Editor: Tim Burgard
Design/Production: Anna Botelho
Proofreader: Miles Lott
Indexer: Judi Gibbs

Wessex Press, Inc.
www.wessexlearning.com

Founded in 2007 by Professor Capon, Wessex Press is a small publisher of marketing, account management, sales, and other higher education textbooks. Wessex's goal is to provide high quality learning materials at affordable prices. Publishing under the brands Wessex Press and AxcessCapon, Wessex offers titles in multiple printed and digital formats.

ABOUT THE AUTHORS

 Keith Ord is Professor Emeritus in the Operations and Information Management group at the McDonough School of Business at Georgetown University. He completed his graduate work at the University of London and held faculty positions at the Universities of Bristol and Warwick before moving to The Pennsylvania State University in 1980 and then to Georgetown University in 1999. His research interests include time series and forecasting, spatial modeling and the statistical modeling of business processes. He is a co-author of the 2008 research monograph *Forecasting with Exponential Smoothing: The State-Space Approach* and also co-authored Kendall's *Advanced Theory of Statistics*. He has served as an editor of the *International Journal of Forecasting* and is currently on the editorial boards of several other journals. Keith is a Fellow of the American Statistical Association and of the International Institute of Forecasters.

 Robert Fildes is Distinguished Professor of Management Science in the Management School, Lancaster University and Founding Director of the Lancaster Centre for Marketing Analytics and Forecasting. He has a mathematics degree from Oxford and a Ph.D. from the University of California in Statistics. He was co-founder in 1981 of the *Journal of Forecasting* and in 1985 of the *International Journal of Forecasting* (IJF). For ten years from 1988 he was Editor-in-Chief of the IJF and remains an associate editor. He was president of the International Institute of Forecasters between 2000 and 2004. His research interests are concerned with the comparative evaluation of different forecasting methods, the implementation of improved forecasting procedures in organizations and the design of forecasting systems. In 1976 he wrote one of the earliest business forecasting textbooks. Though long out-of-print, many of its core ideas have survived the test of time to surface again here in a more modern guise. Robert is a Fellow of the International Institute of Forecasters and of the UK Operational Research Society. In 2014 he was awarded the Beale Medal from the UK OR Society, its highest accolade.

 Nikolaos Kourentzes is an Associate Professor in the Department of Management Science at Lancaster University Management School. His background is in Strategic Management, but quickly changed his interests to Management Science, with a Ph.D. from Lancaster University in forecasting with neural networks. He is on the editorial board of the *International Journal of Forecasting* and founding member of the Forecasting Society. Nikos' primary research interest is modeling uncertainty in a business forecasting context, whether that concerns model specification and selection, or ways to make forecasts more reliable and robust. His research addresses forecasting issues of aggregation and hierarchies, model combination, promotional modeling, and supply chain collaboration. He has published multiple forecasting related open-source packages for R, in his attempt to bring current forecasting research to practice.

BRIEF CONTENTS

Topics marked with an * are advanced and may be omitted for more introductory courses.

The Appendices are located on the textbook companion website.

CONTENTS

*Topics marked with an * are advanced and may be omitted for more introductory courses.*

CHAPTER 11   **Judgment-Based Forecasting   383**

CHAPTER 12   **Putting Forecasting Methods to Work   421**

The Appendices are located on the textbook companion website.

Business forecasting is art woven into science and principle teamed with pragmatism. Virtually every manager has to make plans or decisions that depend on forecasts. Research over the past 50 years or more has shown that taking an analytical approach rather than just relying on informal intuition leads to more accurate forecasts and more effective plans and decisions. However, forecasting is often the poor relation of more theoretical material, available through courses in regression, and time series analysis. Despite our backgrounds as statisticians and management scientists we believe this to be misguided; a student leaving a business school should know how to produce a reasonable forecast and how to evaluate the forecasts of others. Forecasting is important — every day we are confronted with forecasts ranging from the weather to stock prices and the state of the economy. Our motivation in writing this book is provide students of business and management with the tools and the insight to make effective forecasts. But we are also aiming to assist the many practitioners who are working in industry or government and need guidance on how to improve their performance.

This book not only provides an introduction to both standard and advanced approaches to forecasting, but also presents general principles that underlie forecasting practice. In turn, we show how good practice can be established within a systematic framework for the forecasting enterprise. The book builds unashamedly on Scott Armstrong's reference book, *Principles of Forecasting* (2001), although our focus here is on putting these principles to work to produce forecasts. What makes this book unique is its emphasis on incorporating the latest research findings to help practicing forecasters carry out their job and to enable students to prepare for a managerial or analytical career. Ambitiously, it also aims to act as a reference book that will guide those needing to study a particular forecasting topic in depth.

As a starting point, we recognize that there can never be just one approach to forecasting that meets all needs; rather we must invest in "horses for courses". To achieve that goal we consider a series of steps summarized by the mnemonic PIVASE (pronounced 'pi-vase'). The letters stand for the six elements that must be incorporated into the forecasting task: **P**urpose, **I**nformation, **V**alue, **A**nalysis, **S**ystem, and **E**valuation. This revises and extends our ideas from the first edition to emphasize both the analysis required to make successful forecasts and the organizational system in which they are developed. Chapter 1 elaborates on these concepts.

Good forecasting is a challenge. This observation means that the reader must engage in working on real data with all its aberrations. Wherever possible, we have used series from governmental or business sources, so that it is possible to go back to the source and update the database. Not only does this activity make forecasting more realistic but we also get to see how well our forecasts did with the new "out-of-sample" data. This second edition has offered us the opportunity, as we've updated the data used in our many examples, to emphasize the importance of stability (or change) in the system being modeled: and of course to comment on how to cope with the problems that arise.

The so-called "Great Recession" which started in 2007/08 and the subsequent slow recovery have provided an unusual basis from which to accomplish these objectives. Many of the economic models analyzed in the book initially use only the data up to the end of 2008 to estimate model parameters. In this second edition, most of the data sets we provide online run through the end of 2015 so that further, detailed assessments of model stability and performance can be carried out. The end-of-chapter exercises have also been used to examine further the effects of expanding the data bases.[1]

As technology improves, databases expand exponentially and most forecasting activities become unthinkable without a computer and well-designed software. Good programs are continuously evolving and tend to focus on different aspects of the forecasting enterprise (e.g. sales, macroeconomics). Accordingly, we have made use of a variety of software in the book, so that the user can link the methodology to his or her available resources. Our only caveat is that you, the reader, should have effective forecasting software available! To make the requirement more practical we have added supplementary material from the open-source R software that makes all the models we consider freely available to the student and the practitioner.

At the end of each chapter we list a set of principles that the forecaster should keep in mind. Some of these may seem obvious, such as "Check the data for outliers" yet failure to do so has led to forecasting disasters. Just as driving an automobile requires simultaneous attention to multiple indicators, so the effective forecaster needs to internalize these principles in everyday practice.

No book can include all aspects of forecasting and answer every question. Nevertheless, we have tried to meet that challenge in several ways. We include many exercises which lead the reader from the classroom towards the role of practicing forecaster. We also include *discussion questions* that aim to stimulate thinking beyond the narrow confines of the technical issues. In addition, more references are included than is usual in a textbook so that users can quickly access the more advanced research literature. In the end, the successful forecaster has to engage with all the complexities of real data in an organizational setting. We hope that we've met the challenge of providing a set of operational principles that help in this quest.

Structure of the Book

Introduction (Chapters 1–2) Chapter 1 provides an overview of forecasting including a variety of situations where both time series and cross-sectional data can help the forecaster's understanding; then Chapter 2 introduces the basic statistical tools that are needed in later chapters. The remainder of the book falls into three component parts.

Extrapolative methods (Chapters 3–6) The focus here is upon a single time series and forecasting in the short to medium term. In Chapter 3 we consider regular (non-seasonal) time series and introduce exponential smoothing methods for series with and without a trend. Exponential smoothing was one of the first forecasting methods used extensively in industry and remains so today. We extend the discussion in Chapter 4 to include seasonal series

---

1   Many government agencies periodically update their databases and this operation may include the revision of historical data. More recent downloads may produce slightly different values for a series than those we have provided.

particularly the so-called Holt-Winters methods, but also give attention to seasonal adjustment procedures that are important for macroeconomic series.

The discussion in these two chapters is limited to forecasting *methods*, which can provide useful point forecasts but do not produce measures of uncertainty. Thus in Chapter 5 we consider the class of state-space models, which provides a natural framework for exponential smoothing and allows the creation of prediction intervals. State-space models are closely linked to the ARIMA (AutoRegressive Integrated Moving Average) models developed by George Box and Gwilym Jenkins, two of the famous names in forecasting, so Chapter 6 explores this connection and develops prediction intervals using these models. Also in Chapter 6 we consider models for changing uncertainty (ARCH/GARCH models) which are widely used in financial analysis. Just as point forecasts change, so do the related measures of uncertainty. These too need to be forecast.

Statistical model building (Chapters 7–9) Business forecasting involves both the analysis of time series and the use of cross-sectional databases (for example decisions by banks and companies on extending credit to new customers). We begin these developments by considering simple linear regression in Chapter 7, where we examine the use of a single predictor variable to assist in explaining the variations in the dependent variable to be forecast. This discussion leads naturally to multiple regression, the use of two or more predictor variables, in Chapter 8.

Although it sometimes appears that regression modeling is just a matter of downloading the database and running a suitable statistical program, genuine applications involve careful variable selection and building the database. Chapter 9 introduces various extensions to the basic linear regression model including indicator (dummy) variables, lag variables which are fundamental to time series forecasting and non-linearities. Even when the initial model is specified and estimated, the result must be checked to ensure that the final form satisfies the underlying statistical assumptions, at least approximately. These models also need to produce forecasts that are more accurate than those provided by simpler alternatives. In particular, the model should be structurally stable — that is it remains unchanging over time. The extension of the data bases in this second edition allows an extensive discussion of model stability, model development and checking: the themes of Chapter 9.

Advanced methods and forecasting practice (Chapters 10–13) The material in later parts of the book might be beyond a first course in forecasting, but it forms an essential knowledge base for the modern forecaster. As the forecasting literature expands, new methods emerge and solutions to new problems are developed. We attempt to capture these novel developments in these later chapters. Thus, Chapter 10 describes more advanced techniques including classification and regression trees, logistic regression, neural networks and vector autoregressive models. These topics have seen considerable theoretical development in the last few years and also have clear implications for improved practice.

Forecasting practice often relies heavily on subjective judgments by those who are expert (and not so expert) in the field. In Chapter 11 we consider different approaches to judgmental forecasting and discuss when judgmental inputs can add value. Like many such choices, the one between judgmental and quantitative forecasting methods is a false dichotomy and the correct answer is often to use both in combination, capitalizing on their respective strengths.

In the two final chapters we focus attention on forecasting in practice. Chapter 12 first considers the core question of how forecasts and forecasting methods should be evaluated. Procedures for comparing forecasting methods, often a "hot topic" for an organization, are fraught with difficulties. This is a core topic for any forecasting course. Section two examines how forecasts are prepared in organizations through a software-based forecasting support system. We consider what characterizes an effective support system and how such systems and the methods they contain should be evaluated. Three important application areas are then considered in more detail: operations and marketing as well as models focused on individual customer behavior. Finally, Chapter 13 examines the construction of a forecasting system within an organization with particular attention being paid to the interaction between the forecaster and the user of the forecasts. Ultimately, the purpose of forecasting is to aid planning and the reason for planning is to ensure that "things don't just happen". If the forecaster and the user are not communicating properly, the best models in the world will not help.

Use of the Book

Most readers will have had the benefit of a first course in applied statistics, or an equivalent background, although a brief refresher of key statistical methods is included in Chapter 2 (and online Appendix A). Our aim in the book is to show users how to forecast (and that forecasting is fun). In our experience forecasting is a topic that many students are interested in beyond the formulae and routines that can sometimes form the core of statistical or econometric courses. Every day there are examples in the media of important, interesting or even bizarre forecasts, which form a backdrop to the more technical material at the book's core. However, occasionally we have been forced to include material which is particularly demanding mathematically and/or statistically — we have designated such sections with '*'; similarly, more advanced exercises are labeled with '*'. Thus, we anticipate that the book might appeal to four broad groups of readers.

MBA students and advanced undergraduates in business
Chapters 1–4 and 7–9 would form the core of the course, supported by Chapters 11 and 13 to provide a more managerial focus.

Undergraduates in the management sciences and statistics
Chapters 1–9 would be the principal components of a course in this area, with the expectation that much of Chapters 2 and 7 could be omitted. Chapter 11 would offer such students (and their lecturers) light relief, but also make an important point, often omitted from more technical courses, that judgment has a key role to play. Chapter 9, on model building, would be given particular emphasis as many more technical statistical courses neglect this aspect in favor of a more mathematical approach.

Undergraduates in business analytics
Business analytics is becoming more popular as an undergraduate specialism. As yet the course content has not become established. We firmly believe that *Forecasting* is a critical component for any such course as it forms the basis of *Predictive Analytics* without which a degree in business analytics would be incomplete. Chapters 1–4, 7–9, and in particular the data mining elements of chapters 10 and 12 would provide the core material. Standardized R code for these chapters offers a major benefit.

Masters programs in applied statistics, management science and business analytics
Chapters 1–10 and 12 would be the principal components of a course in this area, with a stronger emphasis on Chapters 5 and 6 and with the expectation that Chapters 2 and 7 could be omitted.

Forecasting practitioners

The modern forecaster who wishes to be on top of the latest ideas should ultimately become familiar with all the material in the book, although we would expect him or her to chart a course like one of those just outlined, and then build on that knowledge with experience. However, some forecasters have a more limited developmental agenda focused on their particular organizational responsibilities. For an operations forecaster, chapters 1-4 should be supplemented by Chapter 7, Chapter 11 and the sections of Chapter 12 focused on evaluation and operations. Marketing forecasters also need to develop their skills in regression (Chapters 8 and 9) as well as those sections of Chapter 12 that consider marketing models. Finally, Chapter 13 provides a necessary framework for effective forecasting practice.

Additional Materials

A critical element in every good forecasting text is the provision of data sets for readers to test out their developing skills. The associated website includes all the data sets used in the book, both in the examples and the exercises. In addition we have provided basic software (The Exponential Smoothing Macro, or ESM) for carrying out the exponential smoothing methods of Chapters 3–4. This is for two good reasons: exponential smoothing software is not available (or if it is, it is not well designed) in standard statistical packages. Secondly, despite its apparent simplicity, there are a number of hazards if the student is asked to carry out the calculations relying only on Excel. In addition, a macro for analyzing non-linear trend curves is also provided and used in market modeling. But we are the first to admit these programs are not the equivalent of a professional forecasting package such as ForecastPro or an econometrics package like EViews. We discuss the important issue of computer programs to support forecasting in online Appendix B. Our basic principle is that the forecaster should use well-validated commercial packages wherever possible; many are available for regression analysis and its extensions (Chapters 7–10). Since the first edition, R has become widely available and online materials are provided in Appendix C (Forecasting in R: Tutorial and Examples) to support all the analyses we discuss.

The website resources for instructors include PowerPoint slides that may be used to develop course materials and outline solutions to many of the exercises.

Key Innovations in the Second Edition

This second edition embodies some key changes:

- R programs and tutorial material are provided so that all analyses can be carried out (for free!) wherever the user is working.
- Expanded coverage of model building in regression.
- New material on judgment to address some of the political shocks in the last few years.
- Greater coverage of data analytics, in particular neural nets together with software.
- Expanded material on applications that uniquely includes new research findings relevant and immediately applicable to operations, such as hierarchical modelling and temporal aggregation.

- A new colleague, Nikolaos Kourentzes, has joined the authoring team with complementary expertise, particularly in R.
- Updated data sets.

And of course the various minor corrections that we and others have found.

Other Resources

These days the web provides many resources to support every activity humans contemplate. Forecasting is no exception. We list here a few of the resources a practicing forecaster would wish to consider:

- Two key academic publications that an ambitious reader would need to consult (in writing a dissertation for example) are the *Journal of Forecasting* and the *International Journal of Forecasting* (*IJF*). Occasionally survey articles are written accessible to all but most of the articles published are technical in nature.
- International Institute of Forecasters (IIF) (*https://forecasters.org/*): The IIF is a non-profit organization and the publisher of the *IJF*. The Institute organizes an annual symposium that attracts a world-wide group of participants and also sponsors occasional professional workshops in various topic areas.
- *Foresight: The International Journal of Applied Forecasting:* This journal, published by the IIF aims to provide practicing forecasters with easy-to-read material on important topics that nevertheless summarize the latest research ideas.
- Principles website (*www.forecastingprinciples.com*): The Forecasting Principles site presents a personal view of developments in forecasting (some of which we agree with and some we don't). It aims to offer advice to both researchers and practitioners and is designed to make available the material in Armstrong (2001), suitably updated. It contains much that is useful from a method selection 'tree' to a dictionary.
- Online bibliography: This can be found by accessing: Fildes, R. and Allen, P.G. (2015). *Forecasting.* In Oxford Bibliographies in Management. Ed. Griffin, R.W., New York: Oxford University Press. DOI 10.1093/obo/9780199846740-0064
- Software resources (see online Appendix B): Good software for forecasting is essential but there is no perfect package. We discuss some of the best known alternatives in this appendix.
- Institute of Business Forecasting (IBF) (*https://ibf.org/*): The IBF organizes professional conferences and publishes the *Journal of Business Forecasting*. Its primary focus is on forecasting for supply chain organizations. The web site offers a job search facility.
- Applied Forecasting (*www.appliedforecasting.com*): This site provides a compendium of current news and the latest research in forecasting.
- Principal data resources are listed in Chapter 1.

Acknowledgments

In the preparation of this book we have benefitted from comments from forecasting colleagues from around the world. Particular thanks are due to Geoff Allen (University of Massachusetts, Amherst), Paul Goodwin (University of Bath), Herman Stekler (George Washington University, Washington) and the late Peg Young (from the U.S. Department of Transportation). Thanks are also due to colleagues associated with the Lancaster University Centre for Marketing Analytics and Forecasting, John Boylan, Sven Crone, Steven Finlay, Marwan Izzeldin, Fotios Petropoulos, Patrick Saoud, Oliver Schäer, and Ivan Svetunkov. However, the book would not have been conceived and developed without the research that has been stimulated by the founding of the International Institute of Forecasters and the publication of the *Journal of Forecasting* and the *International Journal of Forecasting*.

We also wish to acknowledge the support we have drawn from our families. For the first edition, both KO and RF were given support including tea, coffee, and encouragement. For this second edition, these sources have become more limited. For RF, support has consisted of putting up with the odd complaint and only occasional sustenance. For KO, both tea and coffee remained available but his clutter was moved to a separate part of the house. As for NK, he has finally started appreciating tea and coffee. Like most projects, there was considerable optimism from all parties as to its completion date, a failure to learn from the first edition: hopefully the revenue projections won't suffer the same fate. We appreciate the responsiveness of our new publishers, Wessex Press, Inc.: Paul Capon (CEO), Alisa Matlovsky (Project Manager), and Anna Botelho (Graphic Design/Production).

Reference

Armstrong, J.S. (ed.), (2001), *Principles of Forecasting*. Boston and Dordrecht: Kluwer.

CHAPTER 1

Forecasting, the Why and the How

Table of Contents

*One cannot divine nor **forecast** the conditions that will make happiness; one only stumbles upon them by chance, in a lucky hour, at the world's end somewhere, and hold fast to the days, as to fortune or fame.*

— Willa Sibert Cather (American author and winner of the Pulitzer Prize)
(http://thinkexist.com/quotes/)

Introduction

Many of us follow familiar rituals after climbing out of bed in the morning. One of these activities is to check the weather forecast. Between sips of coffee, we may scan the newspaper, listen to the TV or radio, or check an online weather service. At the simplest level, we obtain a short summary, such as, "Cloudy early in downtown Washington, some sun in the afternoon, with a high of 76°F (24°C) expected." There might also be a travelers' warning for those proposing to visit Mexico in the next couple of days, with a hurricane force 6 expected to hit land south of Cancún. More detail is often forthcoming and may include such information as:

- A summary of expected temperatures at intervals during the day.
- The probability of precipitation or of the storm.
- Summary forecasts for the next few days.

Meteorologists provide a reasonable degree of detail in their forecasts for up to 7–10 days ahead, after which broader assessments, such as "above or below average temperatures," are about as much as can be usefully provided. If we are concerned about the weather several months ahead, we rely on long-term average values for the time of year.

What does the weather report have to do with business forecasting? In fact, weather is an important factor affecting the sales of many products, such as swimsuits, fresh fruit, and barbecue food. In addition, it affects holiday and business travel.

The example also raises the most basic question of what we mean by a forecast:

FORECAST

A prediction or estimate of an actual outcome expected at a future time or for another situation.

Here we have two types of outcome: the expected temperatures over the course of the day and a predicted event, a hurricane. In this book, we will be concerned with predicting both types of outcome. When we are told the forecast, we understand it to mean the most likely outcome (e.g., that the hurricane occurs or that the temperature will reach 76°F, 24°C). Sometimes, forecasts include estimated probabilities that the outcome will happen, such as "There is a 70 percent chance of rain this evening." In the United States such probability weather forecasts are common, whereas they are absent in Great Britain. The other key feature of this weather forecast is that it is precise: It tells us where and when these events are expected to happen. So this simple example serves to illustrate a number of basic features of any forecasting problem.

We now explore these features in more detail, asking why, what, and how, as well as providing a number of examples of different forecasting issues.

DISCUSSION QUESTION: *What other forecasts are regularly included in the daily newspapers, such as the* Wall Street Journal, *the* New York Times, *or the* Times of London?

1.1 Why Forecast?

Why do we check the weather forecast? Partly, we may do so out of idle curiosity, but the information also serves to guide our planning for the days ahead. The planning activity may include such decisions as what to wear, whether to carry (and maybe lose) an umbrella, or whether to go ahead with a scheduled outdoor activity or travel plan. The forecast helps us plan, and planning, in turn, may improve our quality of life, compared with just rushing out the door. If we examine the elements of this simple vignette, we arrive at the following motivation for forecasting:

FORECASTING AND PLANNING

The purpose of forecasting is to inform the process of planning future actions.

The purpose of planning is to develop a course of action so that current activities don't "just continue" based on a no-change forecast.

Before embarking on a forecasting exercise, we should always consider the "Why?". That is, we need to specify the reasons for generating the forecast, how it fits with possible plans over the planning horizon, and the kind of forecast we need. Once the specifications are settled we must resolve the "How?" by careful analysis of the available information, its potential value in improving the planning decisions and the development of a forecasting system to implement the resulting forecasts. Indeed, "How?" is the question that we seek to answer throughout most of this book. Finally, last but by no means least, we must check whether the forecast system is doing the job for which it was designed – a question that is all too often ignored. Using the mnemonic PIVASE, we may identify these components as follows:

- Purpose
- Information
- Value
- Analysis
- System
- Evaluation.

1.1.1 Purpose

What do we hope to achieve by generating the forecast? What plans depend on the results of the forecasting exercise? The meteorologist provides information to a broad range of individuals and organizations, and they are all interested for their own reasons. For the weather service, it suffices to know that there is a demand for forecasting services. We tailor the level of detail in the forecast to satisfy our planning needs. If the weather forecast was for downtown Washington, but we were planning an outing to the nearby coast, the city forecast would give us only limited help. Similarly, the overall forecast demand for a company's cars is not sufficiently detailed to plan the production line. An integral part of this question is how far ahead do we wish to forecast? We refer to this period as the *forecasting horizon*. In turn, the horizon depends on our purpose in forecasting and will drive the choice of method. The methods we employ for short-term forecasting will consider only the factors that change rapidly, whereas longer term forecasts need to take into account a larger number of factors that may change during the time frame of interest. We also refer to the *forecast origin*, the point in time from which the forecasts start. The horizon often affects the accuracy and usefulness of a forecast. As we know, weather forecasts are quite accurate up to 7–10 days ahead, but they tend to be more like long-term seasonal averages beyond that time frame.

1.1.2 Information

What do we know that may help us in forecasting, and when will we know it? Detailed information is useful only if it is available in a timely fashion. Tomorrow's financial reports may provide an excellent explanation of today's events, but they are of no use in forecasting stock prices today. Likewise, information is of value only if it has an impact on the forecasting procedure we seek to implement. Population changes may have a major effect upon sales ten years from now, but such changes take place at a relatively slow rate and would be irrelevant to forecasting sales in the next three months.

What do we know and when will we know it? A large-scale forecasting model may take into account a broad range of key factors, but if we have to wait several months for the data to become available, the forecasts may be too dated to be useful. Thus, a forecaster often relies upon leading indicators, such as closing levels of a major stock index or a survey of consumer sentiment, to signal changes in short-term economic conditions. These factors do not provide a cause-and-effect description of what is happening, but they may well yield a timely assessment of potential changes.

An often critical factor in producing an accurate forecast is knowledge of plans made in other parts of the organization that will affect the variable to be forecast. Producing a forecast of incoming calls to a call center without information on the corporate marketing plans over the horizon will usually lead to poor forecasts. Thus, identifying potentially important drivers that will affect future outcomes is an important step in developing a forecasting system.

The distinction between forecasting and explanation is often somewhat blurred. On the one hand, we may consider so-called pure forecasts that use only currently available information. On the other hand, a detailed description of a process (e.g., a macroeconomic model of the economy or a model of the world's climate) may enable us to answer what-if questions based upon the understanding that the detailed description provides. Such models typically require more information than pure forecasting exercises. When seeking to answer what-if questions, it is entirely reasonable to use data that are available only after the fact, because they provide an indication of the likely effects of certain policy decisions. They may also provide an explanation of the forecast errors we have made. In this book, we focus primarily upon pure forecasts, although the methods discussed in later chapters are useful in both contexts.

1.1.3 Value

How valuable is the forecast? What would you pay to have perfect knowledge of a future event? For example, a weather forecast is useful to an individual in that she is better able to decide on appropriate clothing. However, most of us would not pay very much for such information, and we do not need to know exactly how much rain will fall.

In contrast, the agricultural sector is very interested in using weather forecasts to plan irrigation and the planting of crops, and it is willing to pay for more accurate location-specific forecasts. In a different context, consider a company with thousands of product lines. Although the value of forecasts for any single line may be modest, an effective forecasting system for the complete range of products is very valuable in making production and inventory decisions.

1.1.4 Analysis

Once the purpose is clear and the information has been assembled, we turn to the analysis of the data. This process includes the development of a forecasting model, which will involve the consideration of several different approaches and the final selection from within these alternatives. Once the model has been selected, we estimate any unknown model parameters and then test the model's performance using a *hold-out sample* (that is, data that are held in reserve and are separate from the information used to fit the model). For example, we might have six years of monthly sales figures and use the first four years to fit the model and keep the last two years as the hold-out sample to test performance.

1.1.5 System

Most of the examples in this book refer to a single time series or forecasting issue. However, practical applications may involve the simultaneous forecasting of thousands of items (products, stock prices, etc.). Further, an organization may generate forecasts at several different levels (e.g., individual products, distinct sales regions, weekly or monthly sales) with many people involved and these forecasts must be integrated into a consistent description of total sales as the basis for budgeting, marketing, and production planning. Thus, we must develop a forecasting system and process that is capable of meeting these needs. Such systems are usually computer based. Chapters 12 and 13 focus on these issues.

1.1.6 Evaluation

How do we know whether a particular forecasting exercise was effective? The obvious answer is that we should compare past results with the forecasts that were made, possibly comparing several different forecasting methods as we proceed. We examine several such criteria in Chapter 2, all of which are based upon the differences between forecasts and actual values. A statement about checking forecast performance might seem almost too obvious to be worth making, yet the evidence suggests that some companies never go back to check their forecasting performance. For example, an informal survey conducted by the software company Business Forecasting Systems produced the results shown in Table 1.1. Respondents *who used statistical forecasts* were asked how they did so:

Baseline: Use the statistical forecast as a baseline and then make judgmental adjustments

or

Reference: Use the statistical forecast as a reference, or "sanity check," on some other primary forecast.

Respondents were then asked whether they regularly checked the performance of the forecasts. The *percentages* in each category who said yes are given in Table 1.1. The survey was small and relied upon self-reporting, but the figures are striking nevertheless. The baseline group is making adjustments to the statistical forecasts, yet nearly half of them are not checking to see whether those adjustments improve forecast performance. Nearly one-third of the reference group do not even check their principal forecasts, and more than two-thirds fail to check the statistical forecasts.

Table 1.1 Percentages of Respondents Who Regularly Monitor Forecasting Performance

	Percentages of Respondents Who Checked	
Use Made of Statistical Forecast	**Adjusted/Principal Forecast**	**Statistical Forecast**
As a baseline	91	57
As a reference	71	29

Source: Trends Business Forecasting Systems Newsletter.

If you don't check from time to time, how do you know whether your approach is any good? Making effective forecasts is as much an art as it is a science, but asking about PIVASE before you start the exercise will help avoid expensive mistakes.

MONITORING FORECAST ERRORS

Always check on forecast performance. Checking helps you avoid repeating mistakes and leads to improved results.

■ Example 1.1: PIVASE in action

Some years ago, a US state agency asked one of the authors (KO) to develop a short-term forecasting system for state tax revenues. The author used simple extrapolative models (the details don't matter at this stage) to accomplish the job. The *purpose* was to provide the state legislators with a revenue-forecasting model that they could use to compare with the forecasts generated by the executive branch (the governor's office). Because all state representatives are up for reelection every two years, the forecast horizon was set at two years. The monthly state revenues, for each of a half dozen tax categories, were published typically within a month of the end of the collection period; because these figures are a matter of public record, the necessary *information* was freely available. Some additional information, such as upcoming changes in tax rates, was also provided. The *value* of the study lay in the provision of an independent forecasting system for the legislature to serve as a check on the executive's budgetary proposals.

The *analysis* followed the general approach laid out in Chapter 6 and the overall *system* involved monthly updates to the half-dozen series and the generation of new forecasts. As happens all too often with forecasting systems, no follow-up study was performed to *evaluate* performance. However, several years later, it was a pleasant surprise to learn that the system was still in use and that the outputs compared quite favorably with the forecasts from the state's model sponsored by the governor's office. A firm of consultants provided the state's economic statistical (econometric) model for around $100,000 per year (compared with a one-time payment of $10,000 for the short-term model). Doubtless, the econometric model is also used for other purposes, and the fees are probably well spent. ■

DISCUSSION QUESTION: *There was a two-year cycle in the tax revenues data, with a surplus in year one and a deficit in year two. Why might this be?*

1.2 What and Why Do Organizations Forecast?

Organizations — large and small, public, government or private sector — have numerous forecasting needs. To plan their operations, they need to estimate the demand they expect for their products and services. They also need to know how their actions — for example, their marketing plans, including promotions and prices — will affect demand and in turn affect revenues and costs. Figure 1.1 captures some of the complexities that organizations face. Fortunately, many of the variables can, for the most part, be ignored. In the short term, such features as the technology (used by the organization or its customers), legislation, and social trends can usually be regarded as fixed. Operational and tactical (medium term) decisions depend primarily on demand (as it is affected by competition) and the finance needed to support the organization. In the longer term, where the organization's strategy is updated, the variables in the outer box come into play; for example, social and demographic trends can change a market dramatically. In Europe, an aging population requires a different set of services (e.g., health) than a younger market. In the United States, shifts in consumer tastes relating to the changing composition of the population with regard to ethnic origin and geography also affect consumption patterns.

Figure 1.1 An Organization's Forecasting Needs

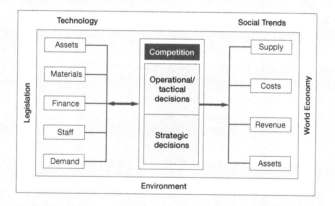

DISCUSSION QUESTIONS

What might a nuclear electricity supplier or a water company need to forecast with regard to its key assets? Why?

A state or national government provides unemployment benefits for a period of six months following a layoff (or leaving school). It continues for a further six months if the applicant attends a job training program. What variables would the government need to forecast for its annual planning?

Each of these discussion questions points up the critical linkage between forecasting and planning: If the organization or the person does not act on the forecast, it has no value beyond mere curiosity. These issues are pursued further in the end-of-chapter minicases.

1.3 Examples of Forecasting Problems

Forecasting involves using currently available data to make statements about likely future developments. Such data often arise as a time series:

TIME SERIES

A set of comparable observations ordered in time. The values may refer to either a point in time ("the current value of the Dow Jones Index is 17,000") or an aggregate over a period of time ("total sales for the last month were 350 units").

Trend: A time series contains a trend if it shows systematic movements (e.g., increase or decrease) over an extended period.

Seasonality: A time series has a seasonal component if it displays a recurrent pattern with a fixed and known duration (e.g., months of the year, days of the week).

Cycle: A time series has a cyclical component if it displays somewhat regular fluctuations about the trend but those fluctuations have a periodicity of variable and unknown duration, usually longer than one year (e.g., a business cycle).

We usually assume that the observations are equally spaced in time. On occasion, this assumption is incorrect, but we may make some adjustment to the data so that it is a closer approximation. For example, the months of the year differ in length, but we usually treat them as equally spaced. If the time series refers to data such as sales, we may use average sales per day during the month or average sales per trading day (allowing for possible closures on Sundays and public holidays). The revised time series then conforms more closely to the assumption of equal spacing.

An interesting example of such adjustments occurs with stock market data. The New York Stock Exchange (NYSE) is generally open for trading Monday through Friday, 9:30 a.m. to 4 p.m. The NYSE is closed on weekends and public holidays. Nevertheless, it is often possible to ignore the breaks in trading and to treat time series relating to the price of a stock or the trading volume (e.g., the number of shares traded per hour) as being recorded at regular equal intervals.

In the rest of this book, we typically assume that observations are recorded at equally spaced times and effectively ignore the distinction between data either recorded at a point in time or aggregated across time. Such a step poses no problems for the formal development of the forecasting methods, but it needs to be taken into account in applications.

We now examine a few series in detail. Note that we always start out with plots of the data, whether time series or cross sectional. It would be difficult to overemphasize the importance of this first step in any forecasting study. Beyond the initial benefit of identifying unusual observations (whether data entry errors or genuinely strange values), such plots serve to identify patterns in the data and to suggest possible approaches to forecasting.

1.3.1 Retail Sales

Figure 1.2 shows the monthly level of retailer sales in the United States over the period from January 2001 to December 2015 (see *US_retail_sales_2.xlsx*). The data refer to current dollars, so no allowance has been made for the effects of inflation. The series shows more or less steady growth until late 2007 when the 'Great Recession' hit; with growth resuming in mid-2009. (The National Bureau of Economic Research, NBER, officially dated the start of the recession as December 2007 and the end as June 2009.)

The growth is due to a combination of real growth in the economy and inflation. The inflationary elements could be removed by using a price index and *deflating* the current values to obtain real growth figures, but for the present we will examine the series in current dollars; see Minicase 1.4 for an example.

The second feature that is evident is a regular within-year fluctuation, which we refer to as a *seasonal pattern*. Here, it reflects high sales in December and a drop-off in January. We also observe that the fluctuations are increasing somewhat over time, indicating a proportional effect (up or down by a given percentage) rather than a fluctuation by an absolute amount.

This diagram imparts a lot of information, and it is reasonable to ask whether the different parts of the total information package can be filtered out, rather than trying to read everything from one diagram. The answer is that we can do that by identifying a separate seasonal component and then adjusting the original series by those seasonal factors to produce a seasonally adjusted series. The advantages of doing so are that we can examine not only underlying trends without being distracted by seasonal fluctuations but also the seasonal pattern to look for changes over time. This process of *decomposition* is particularly important for macroeconomic series, and most U.S. and UK government series are published in seasonally adjusted form. This topic is examined in detail in Chapter 4.

Figure 1.2 U.S. Monthly Retailers Sales

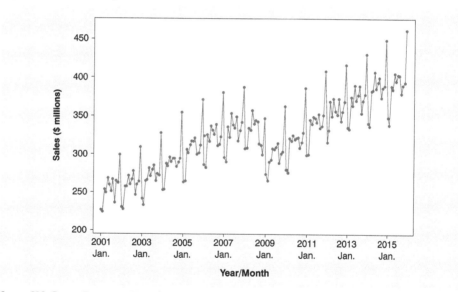

Source: U.S. Census Bureau via FRED *https://research.stlouisfed.org/fred2/*
Series ID: RETAILSMNSA; Data: US_retail_sales_2.xlsx

1.3.2 Seasonal Patterns for Retail Sales

We discuss the process of seasonal adjustment more rigorously in Chapter 4, but for purposes of the present discussion we define the seasonal factors indirectly as the ratios of actual sales to the seasonally adjusted sales, as published by the U.S. Census Bureau.

The seasonally adjusted series is shown in Figure 1.3 and provides a clear picture of the decline in sales during the recession. Such a dramatic change in the level (or trend) of a series is called a structural break. The derived seasonal patterns are shown in Figure 1.4. The December peak and subsequent drop for January and February are clearly evident. Looking more closely, we see that the seasonal pattern is fairly stable, although the holiday peaks were lower in 2007 and 2008.

DISCUSSION QUESTION: *Looking ahead two years from the present, how would you expect the series to behave?*

Figure 1.3 Seasonally Adjusted Series for U.S. Monthly Retailers Sales

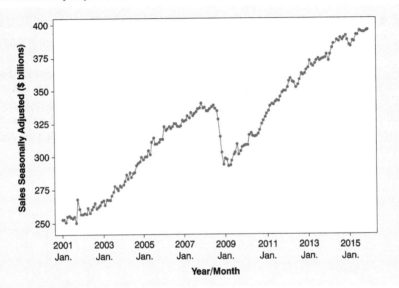

Source: U.S. Census Bureau via FRED *https://research.stlouisfed.org/fred2/*
Series ID: RETAILSMSA; Data: US_retail_sales_2_SA.xlsx

Figure 1.4 Seasonal Factors for U.S. Monthly Retailers Sales

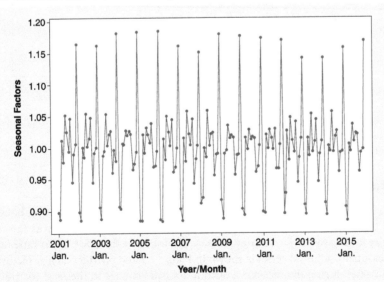

Source: U.S. Census Bureau via FRED *https://research.stlouisfed.org/fred2/*
Derived from Series RETAILSMSA and RETAILSMNSA

Another way to examine the data is to look at month-to-month changes in the seasonally adjusted series, as shown in Figure 1.5. The effect of September 11th 2001 on sales is very clear and the slide into recession at the end of 2007 is also apparent.

Figure 1.5 Month-to-Month Changes in Retailers Sales (seasonally adjusted)

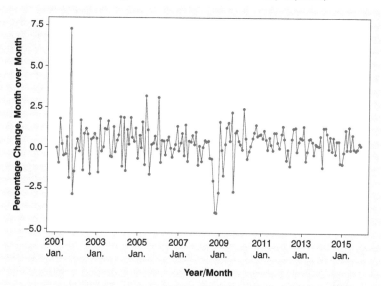

How else could we present this information? One possibility is to look at the changes in the level of sales over time. Better yet, because the retail industry talks about percentage changes for a given month from one year to the next, we can transform the data as follows:

$$\% \text{ change over the year} = \frac{100\,[(\text{Sales in year } t, \text{month } j) - (\text{Sales in year } t - 1, \text{month } j)]}{(\text{Sales in year } t - 1, \text{month } j)}$$

That is, we look at the percentage change for this month compared with that for the same month last year.

The resulting plot is shown in Figure 1.6. We can see the periods of relative growth and stagnation. Again, the sharp decline starting at the end of December 2007 is very clear, but it is also worth noting the longer periods of somewhat faster or slower growth.

The information contained in these various time series plots enables the forecaster to make statements about the potential December sales peak in conjunction with the likely change relative to the previous year. Such forecasts feed into decisions on overall inventory and staffing levels, as well as financial requirements.

1.3.3 UK Road Accidents

As an example of a series displaying both seasonal and other effects, we consider a time series on injuries caused by road accidents in the United Kingdom over the period from January 1975 to December 1984, examined in detail by Harvey and Durbin (1986). The series is shown in Figure 1.7. The seasonal peak in December is quite evident, although the pattern breaks up somewhat in the later years. The other feature worthy of note is the step-change decline in early 1983, which was when the wearing of seat belts became mandatory. Analysis of the series provides a way to determine the effectiveness of the seat belt legislation, as we shall see in Chapter 9.

Figure 1.6 Year-Over-Year Percentage Change in U.S. Monthly Retailers Sales

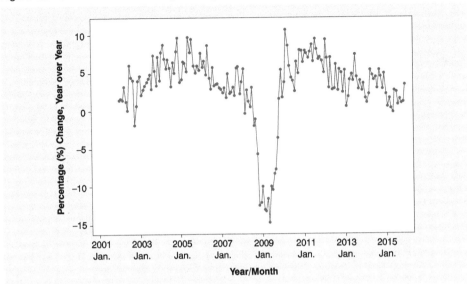

Figure 1.7 Serious Injuries and Deaths on UK Roads, January 1975–December 1984

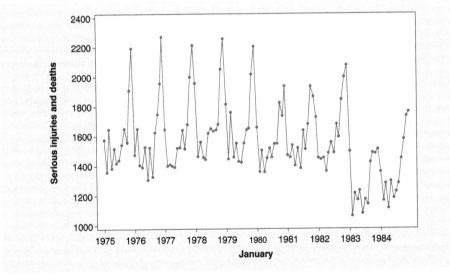

Source: Harvey and Durbin (1986); *Data: Road_accidents.xlsx*

1.3.4 Airline Travel

A major issue in time series analysis is how to deal with unusual observations or shifts (breaks) in the general level. The data on road accidents represent a series in which a change was anticipated; by contrast, an event might be totally unexpected, as with the tragic events in the United States on September 11, 2001. Figure 1.8 shows the number of revenue passenger miles traveled in the United States, by month, from January 2000 to December 2015. The impact of that day upon air travel is clearly seen; September 2001 is marked on the diagram.

Figure 1.8 Monthly U.S Air Revenue Passenger Miles (billions), January 2000–December 2015

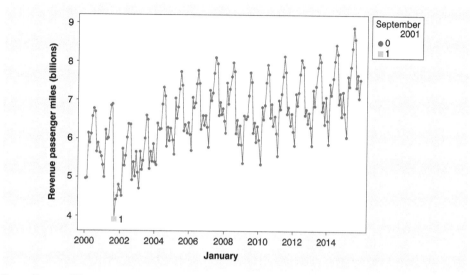

Source: Bureau of Transportation Statistics, U.S Department of Transportation via FRED
Data: Revenue_miles_2.xlsx

DISCUSSION QUESTION: *How would you estimate the effect of 9/11 upon the airline industry with respect to losses in revenue passenger miles?*

1.3.5 Sports Forecasting: Soccer (a.k.a. Football!)

Sports forecasting is big business. In many countries, betting on the outcome of a game is legal, be it American football, soccer, or tennis. In fact, gamblers go a stage further: They can and do bet on the detailed developments in a game. In soccer, this type of betting can include the number of players cautioned; in tennis, the number of games played in the longest set. Here again, the data are different. Although the outcomes (win, draw, or lose in soccer) are recorded over time, the observations are not observed at regular intervals.

Figure 1.9 shows a time series graph of the data as they fall into these three categories; they are also labeled so as to distinguish between a home game and an away game. What makes this example different from the earlier ones is that the aim here is to forecast the outcome of an event: win, draw, or lose in our example. Sports betting companies use data on events in each minute of the game to predict the outcomes. Their aim is to help set the appropriate betting odds to ensure that they make a profit (Vaughan Williams, 2005). They use the methods of Chapters 7–10 to carry out the modeling and forecasting.

Figure 1.9 The Record of English Soccer Club Manchester United During the
2014–2015 Premier League Season [38 games played, 19 home and 19 away]

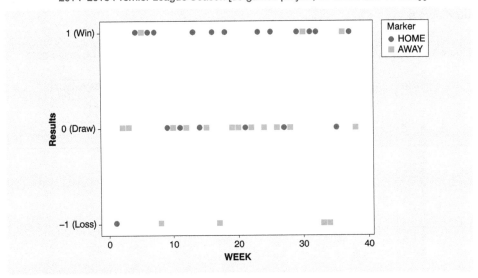

DISCUSSION QUESTION: *What conclusions can you draw from Figure 1.9 about the strength of the Manchester United team: Overall? Over time? Home and away?*

1.3.6 Sports Forecasting: A Cross-Sectional Example –
Baseball Salaries

Sports management also relies on forecasting. The manager's decisions on whom to sign, whom to release, and even whom to play, all depend on forecasts of performance. Usually, such forecasts are made intuitively on the basis of the manager's experience. However, in one now famous example, Billy Beane, general manager of the Oakland Athletics baseball team, used statistical methods to identify players who were undervalued (see Lewis, 2003, for a nontechnical description of Beane's management ideas, subsequently filmed in *Money-ball*, 2011, with Brad Pitt). In thinking about the problem of trading players, one relevant relationship is what determines their current salary. Figure 1.10 shows the relationship between salary and the years played in the major leagues. The data here are cross sectional: All observations on players and their salaries were made over the same (relatively short) period. Critically, the time the data were recorded should be irrelevant to interpreting the relationship in the near future.

Cross-sectional data are measurements on multiple units (here, players) recorded over a single period for one or more variables (salaries, years in the major leagues).

Of course, many other variables affect salary, not the least of which are the player's previous season's performance and personal characteristics, such as age. In developing an understanding of whether a player is undervalued, these factors all have to be taken into account. We discuss this question in more detail in Chapter 7.

Figure 1.10 Scatterplot of Baseball Players' Salaries Against the Number of Years Played in the Major Leagues

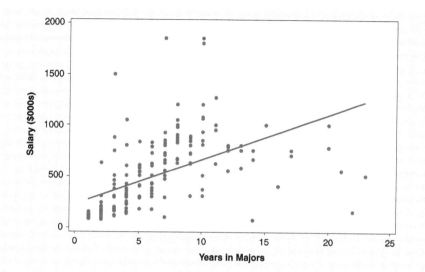

Source: We wish to acknowledge StatLib of the Department of Statistics at Carnegie Mellon University.
Data: Baseball.xlsx

1.3.7 Random (Stochastic) Processes

Observations may occur over time without forming a time series as we have defined it. For example, consider the flow of customers into and out of a supermarket. An individual customer arrives at a certain time (arrival time), spends some time selecting items for purchase (processing time), then waits in line (waiting time) before being served at the checkout (service time). If we examine the number of arrivals per unit of time or the number of customers served in a given time, we can define a time series by using successive counts. However, from the perspective of the individual customer, the elapsed waiting and service times are important. The purpose of the analysis is typically to manage the service levels cost effectively. These individual times form, not a time series, but rather outputs from a random (or *stochastic*) process. Such processes are beyond the scope of this book; for greater detail see, for example, Winston and Albright (2015).

1.4 How to Forecast

In Section 1.2, we used PIVASE to explain why we should generate forecasts. The next question is how? The how question depends heavily on the components of PIVASE. When we seek to establish a forecasting system, we first need to provide answers to the following questions:

- Do we have the necessary data to enable the use of statistical methods, or will the forecasting process be essentially judgmental? We leave the use of judgment in forecasting and its role in statistical models for later discussion (Chapters 11 and 13).

- If the process is based upon judgment, is the forecaster working alone or is a group involved?

- If the process is statistical, is the analysis to be based upon a single series or are explanatory variables to be included in the study?

The responses to these questions lead to a range of possible approaches, many of which are described in later chapters. The sequence of choices and the available methodologies are summarized briefly in Figure 1.11. A much more detailed discussion of the choice of forecasting procedures is deferred to Chapter 13, because we must first develop an understanding of each principal approach.

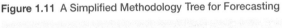

Figure 1.11 A Simplified Methodology Tree for Forecasting

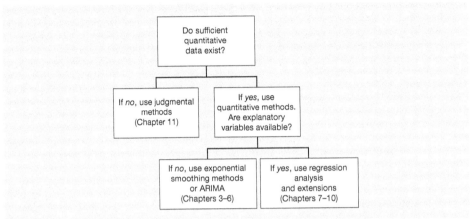

1.5 Forecasting Step by Step

On the basis of our preliminary discussion of PIVASE, we can identify seven major steps in the forecasting process:

1. Define the forecasting and planning problem, the forecast horizon and decide the value of better forecasts.
2. Determine the resources to be devoted to providing the forecasts.
3. Collect relevant information, whether from a survey, from company records, or from information generated by other agencies (e.g., government figures).
4. Conduct an initial analysis of the data.
5. Select an appropriate forecasting method.
6. Generate forecasts.
7. Evaluate the forecasting exercise by checking forecasts against actual outcomes.

Ideally, we could use these seven steps as a checklist and work our way through them. Life is not quite that simple, however. For example, we used PIVASE to discuss step 1 in Section 1.1. Although we may be comfortable with our initial definition of the problem, we may have to revisit our understanding. Step 2 is also important: The resources assigned to the forecasting exercise should be commensurate with the potential added value of improved forecasts. If there is little value in achieving improved forecast accuracy, there's no point in using scarce resources for that purpose. By contrast, if the problem is such that small improvements in accuracy have a large payoff, spending substantial sums is worthwhile. Step 3 determines whether the forecasting task is feasible: The relevant data may not be available (either at all or in a timely fashion), so we would have to go back to the drawing board.

Once we have completed steps 1–3, we need to carry out an initial analysis of the data. We describe these steps in detail in Chapter 2, but it is worth noting that the analysis serves two purposes: cleaning the data and understanding the data. *Cleaning the data* involves looking for unusual observations and perhaps correcting data-recording errors; identifying factors that need to be taken into account, such as seasonal patterns or public holidays; and making sure that the data are comparable to each other and represent the phenomenon of interest. For example, shipments to wholesalers do not truly represent sales if they are made on a sale-or-return basis. The second component, *understanding the data*, enables the choice of forecasting method, as well as providing insights about the potential reliability of the resulting forecasts. As in other endeavors, the KISS principle is valuable (keep it simple, statistician).

Once our iterations through steps 1–4 are complete, we can move on to method selection, using the refinements of Figure 1.11. Only at this stage are we in a position to generate the forecasts. Much of the remainder of this book is concerned with the technical aspects of steps 5 and 6. The final step, which must not be overlooked, is to evaluate the forecasting process by comparing actual with forecast values. At the developmental stage, this can be done by means of a so-called *hold-out sample*, in which we split the available data into two parts and then use only the first part (the *estimation sample*) to calibrate the forecasting method. Once everything is set, we use the second part (the hold-out sample) to check the performance of the forecast. When the forecasting system is up and running, periodic checks on performance are essential. Overall, the seven steps should be seen as an integrated process that operates more smoothly as the forecaster gains practical experience; that integration is the subject of the final chapter of the book.

Whenever possible, the development of a forecasting method should include the partition of the data into an *estimation sample* (used to estimate the parameters, etc.) and a *hold-out sample* (used to test the performance of the proposed forecasting method). **Once the method is selected, the entire sample should be used for future forecasting purposes.**

Finally, it must be emphasized that forecasting is not a "once and done" operation. Forecast performance should be monitored on a regular basis and changes made to the system whenever performance falls short. For a detailed discussion see Fildes and Petropoulos (2015).

1.6 Computer Packages for Forecasting

Almost all statistical packages include routines for regression analyses and for time series analysis. The basic procedures for regression are relatively standard, although the quality of the procedures for testing the adequacy of alternative models with the use of diagnostics varies considerably. Computer software for time series analysis is even more variable. Some packages include only the most basic forecasting procedures, and the types of forecast provided vary enormously. In the course of this book, the reader will observe that we have used a number of general purpose software programs: Excel (graphs and macros only), Minitab,

SAS, and SPSS. We have also used some specialized programs, notably EViews (for econometric modeling), and PcGive (both econometrics and forecasting). In particular, in this second edition we have introduced R, an open source free software that is thoroughly tested and progressively expanding as new routines become available. These routines include specialist forecasting algorithms. On the book's website, full R routines are available for most of the methods discussed in this book, notably using the forecast package developed by Rob Hyndman (*https://CRAN.R-project.org/package=forecast*), among other packages, some developed by the authors of this book. Each program has its merits, but none provides coverage of all the topics we discuss; we have tried to design the book so that it may be used compatibly with any major program. A brief summary of some of the capabilities of the major forecasting packages is available on the book website in Appendix B.

1.7 Data Sources

Thanks to the Internet, finding and downloading data are now relatively painless tasks. The data sets used in this book are all available on the website for the book (*http://www.wessexlearning. org/pobf2e/*), and they are all contained in Excel 2007 (.xlsx) files. These files may be read directly by any of the programs we have used.

All U.S. government departments have publicly available websites from which data may be downloaded; for example, two major agencies that supply economic data are the Census Bureau (*http://www.census.gov/*) and the Bureau of Labor Statistics (*http://www.bls.gov/*). In the United Kingdom, the UK National Statistics site provides similar data (*http://www. statistics.gov.uk/hub/index.html*). Also, all major companies have websites from which data on their overall operations can be obtained, although these data are not always packaged in a ready-to-download format.

Numerous specialist databases that provide downloadable data series are also available. Some are free, and others require either a personal or an institutional subscription. Following are several such sources of particular interest:

- The Federal Reserve Bank of St. Louis maintains an extensive database of U.S. and international macroeconomic series. The website is known as FRED (*https://fred. stlouisfed.org/*)
- EconStats (*http://www.econstats.com/index.htm*) contains a large amount of economic and financial data on the United States and on several other countries, including the United Kingdom, China, and Japan.
- Data.gov.uk (*http://Data.gov.uk/*) offers easy-to-access government statistical series for the United Kingdom.
- Econdata (*http://econdata.net/*) contains regional socioeconomic data for the United States.
- The Forecasting Principles website (*http://www.forecastingprinciples.com/*) provides a variety of links to other sources and data sets.

1.8 The Rest of the Book

The overall plan of the book broadly follows the different branches of the methodology tree shown in Figure 1.11. After a brief review of basic statistics and a discussion of how to measure forecast accuracy in Chapter 2, we go on to examine extrapolative (single-time-series) methods in Chapters 3 and 4. These methods are introduced in a pragmatic way as "good ideas"; the statistical underpinnings of the methods are then developed in Chapters 5 and 6. In Chapters 7–9, we develop models that may be used for either cross-sectional or time series data that can involve the inclusion of explanatory variables. Chapter 10 describes a variety of more advanced techniques, which have become an integral part of forecasting practice in recent years, while Chapter 11 discusses the role of judgment in forecasting and how it is best used. Judgmental methods are perhaps overused in modern industry, but they do have an important role to play, and it is necessary to understand how they interface with statistical procedures. With the various approaches to forecasting established, in Chapter 12 we go on to discuss their application in a variety of contexts. Finally, in Chapter 13, we examine forecasting in practice and try to provide signposts to guide the forecaster to successful applications of the tools of her trade.

Summary

In this chapter, we have discussed the reasons organizations have for forecasting, and its role in both operational and strategic planning. The why and what of forecasting have been analyzed in detail by using PIVASE: the purpose that underlies the forecasting activity, the forecast horizon, the information available, the value of the forecasting exercise, the analysis and development of a suitable method within the forecasting system, and finally, the need to evaluate forecasts. We then examined several series that showed different data patterns, including trend and seasonal components. This led to the idea of seasonal decomposition as a method for identifying the core characteristics of a time series. Other issues discussed were the examination of cross-sectional data for forecasting and the impact of unexpected events. Finally, as an introduction to the remainder of the book, we briefly explored the how of forecasting, which depends on the aims of the forecasting activity and the data available.

Minicases

Minicase 1.1 Inventory Planning

The Nuts'n'Bolts hardware store stocks some high-value items and a large number of relatively low-value components. Inventory is reviewed weekly, and orders are placed with suppliers when inventory levels indicate that current levels are "too low." Most suppliers deliver the low-value items within two weeks; some of the high-value items may take four weeks for delivery. How would you develop a forecasting system to predict the sales of such items at the individual SKU (Stock Keeping Unit) level? How would you use such forecasts to plan future purchases?

Use PIVASE to go through the necessary steps. For purposes of the discussion, assume that any historical data you might need can be made available.

Minicase 1.2 Long-Term Growth

You work for a consulting firm that is bidding on a contract to forecast the growth prospects of an electronics company over the next five years. The company has developed a specialized computer chip that is used in highly sensitive medical equipment and does not anticipate creating any new product lines, although periodic improvements to the chip are anticipated.

Write a short proposal describing how you would develop such forecasts, using PIVASE as a guide. For purposes of the assignment, assume that any historical data you might need can be made available, but describe carefully the nature of the data needed.

Minicase 1.3 Sales Forecasting

A company sells many hundreds of clothing products, historically through mail order and its own high street shops, but increasingly through the Internet. The firm also offers the customer four different purchase schemes, from pay on purchase through payment over different periods (of 6 and 12 months). The final plan allows a postponement of any payment for 12 months.

The firm has to ensure a supply of its advertised products to meet forecast demand. Adequate inventory has consequences for the distribution network. (The products need to be stocked and then shipped.) The retailer also has to decide which customers to target through mailings to stimulate further purchases.

What variables would the company need to forecast? What strategic financial decisions may need to be linked to the various customer purchase plans? Use the PIVASE framework to guide your thinking.

Minicase 1.4 Adjusting for Inflation

Use the data files for U.S. retail sales (*US_retail_sales_2.xlsx*) and for the U.S. Consumer Price Index (*US_CPI_2.xlsx*) to create a series called "real prices" by dividing sales by the *CPI*; then replicate Figures 1.2, 1.5, and 1.6 for this series. Compare your results with the three figures provided in the text, commenting on major differences.

References

Fildes, R. and Petropoulos, F. (2015). Improving forecast quality in practice. *Foresight,* 36, 5–12.

Harvey, A. C., and Durbin, J. (1986). The effects of seat belt legislation on British road casualties: A case study in structural time series modelling. *Journal of the Royal Statistical Society*, series A, 149, 187–227.

Lewis, M. (2003). *Moneyball: The Art of Winning an Unfair Game.* New York: Norton.

Vaughan Williams, L. (2005). *Information Efficiency in Financial and Betting Markets.* Cambridge, UK: Cambridge University Press,

Winston, W., and Albright, S. C. (2015). *Practical Management Science,* 5th ed. Pacific Grove, CA: Duxbury.

Appendix 1A Model-Based Probability

Forecasting by its nature involves uncertainty and we express our understanding of this uncertainty through the language of probability. The purpose of this appendix is not to provide a primer on probability as there are many sources that offer such introductions. Rather, the aim is to describe how probabilistic statements are generated in the context of time-series based forecasts.

Standard notions of probability may rest upon the notions of equally likely events, relative frequencies in repeated trials, or as a degree of belief but none of these ideas is entirely appropriate for the analysis of time series. A typical time series, such as Gross Domestic Product (*GDP*), has one observation each quarter which represents its observed value. Sampling may be involved in arriving at the final value of *GDP* in a given period but the reported number is unique and is not open to any interpretation of repeated sampling such as we employ in cross-sectional studies.

How then do we proceed? We rely on the concept of *model-based probability*. That is, we formulate a model of the process that generates the time series and derive probabilistic statements from that model. Of course, if the model is wrong, so will be the assessments of uncertainty. For that reason, throughout the book we emphasize careful model selection and checking of the underlying assumptions. For now, such issues do not concern us and we assume the model-based specification is correct. In fairly general terms we might specify a model as:

Observable variable = known component + unknown component.

Algebraically we may write this expression, at time *t* as:

$$Y_t = m_t + e_t,$$

m_t represents the known (or predictable) component or signal whereas e_t denotes the unknown component (random error or noise). Typically, it is assumed that the random error has a mean of zero so that the observable variable has mean m_t, also written as the expectation of the observable variable, or $E(Y_t) = m_t$. Thus, the *point forecast* for the series will be m_t and the uncertainty is expressed via e_t. Model-based probabilities are formulated using the assumed properties of the random error: on many occasions we will assume that the errors are normally distributed with a constant variance over time and that successive errors are independent of one another. More generally, any specification of the distribution of the errors will provide a framework for making statements about the uncertainty related to the point forecasts.

Basic Tools for Forecasting

Table of Contents

DDD: Draw the doggone diagram!

　　　　— In memory of the late David Hildebrand, who stated the matter rather more forcibly!

Introduction

In most of the chapters in this book, we assume that some kind of database is available from which to build numerical forecasts. In some situations, the data may be already available (e.g., government figures for macroeconomic forecasting); in other cases, the data may be collected directly (e.g., sales figures or purchasing behavior from scanning records). Such data may be incomplete or subject to error, they may not relate directly to the key variables of interest, and they may not be available in a timely fashion. Nevertheless, they are all we have, and we must learn to understand and respect them if not to love them. Indeed, such is the basis of any good relationship!

At a conceptual level, we need to understand how the data are compiled and how they relate to the forecasting issues we seek to address. We must establish from the outset that the data are appropriate for the *purpose* (the P in PIVASE) we have in mind, as noted in Chapter 1. Otherwise, we are only living up to the old adage "Garbage in, garbage out." Although we will not keep repeating this message in chapter after chapter, the PIVASE issues must always be examined before embarking on a forecasting project. We must then examine the data to understand their structure and main features and to summarize the available information (the I in PIVASE).

In Section 2.1, we examine the types of data that arise in practice, and then we turn to graphical summaries in Sections 2.2 and 2.3. Section 2.4 describes the basic numerical summaries that are useful, and we then move on to measures of association in Section 2.5. Sometimes the original form of the data is not appropriate, and some kind of transformation or modification is needed. This topic is the focus of Section 2.6. The steps described in all these sections are essentially those of preliminary data analysis, although similar procedures will be undertaken later in the context of model diagnostics.

Methods for the generation of forecasts are the focus of later chapters, but in this chapter we consider the evaluation of outputs from the forecasting process. Thus, in Section 2.7, we examine measures of forecasting accuracy and the evaluation of forecasting performance (the E in PIVASE), after which we turn to prediction intervals in Section 2.8. The chapter ends with a discussion of some underlying principles in Section 2.9.

2.1 Types of Data

A database may be thought of as a table with multiple dimensions, as the following examples illustrate:

- *A survey of prospective voters in an upcoming election:* The measured variables might include voting intentions, party affiliation, age, gender, and address.

- *A portfolio of stocks:* For each company, we would record contact information, market capitalization, opening and closing stock prices, dividend payments over suitable periods, and news announcements.

- *The economy of the United States:* The factors of interest would certainly include gross domestic product (*GDP*), inflation, consumer expenditures, capital investment, unemployment, government revenues and expenditures, and imports and exports.

Data may be numeric, ordered, categorical, or even text-based.

A survey of voters refers to *cross-sectional data* in that what matters is the inherent variation across respondents. For practical purposes, we view the data as being collected in the same (short) time period. Of course, voters may change their minds at a later stage, and such shifts of opinion are a major source of discrepancies between opinion polls and election outcomes.

The closing price for a particular stock or fund, recorded daily over several months or even years represents an example of *time series data*. We are interested in the movement of the price over time. The same applies if we track the movements over time of aggregate macroeconomic variables such as *GDP*; it is their development over time that is important.

TYPES OF DATA

Cross-sectional data are measurements on multiple units, recorded in a single time period.

A *time series* is a set of comparable measurements recorded on a single variable over multiple time periods.

Panel data are cross-sectional measurements that are repeated over time, such as monthly expenditures for a sample of consumers.

From these examples, we see that a database may be cross-sectional, or time-dependent, or both. (Consider tracking voting intentions over time or looking at consumer expenditures for different regions of a country). Although forecasting practice often involves multiple series, such as the sales of different product lines, the methods we examine have the common theme of using past data to predict future outcomes. Thus, our primary focus in the first part of the book is on the use of time series data. For convenience, we begin our development of these ideas in the context of a single time series, even though applications may involve a large number of such series.

As methods of data capture have become more sophisticated (e.g., scanners in supermarkets), it has become possible to develop databases that relate to individuals, be they consumers or machines. Forecasting may then involve the use of cross-sectional data to predict individual preferences or to evaluate a new customer based upon individuals with similar demographic characteristics.

By way of example, consider the data shown in Tables[1] 2.1, 2.2, and 2.3. Table 2.1 shows the weekly sales of a consumer product in a certain market area; the product is produced by a major U.S. manufacturer. This data set will be examined in greater detail in Chapter 3. The data are genuine, but we have labeled the product WFJ Sales to preserve confidentiality. Table 2.2 shows the annual numbers of domestic passengers at Washington Dulles International Airport for the years 1963–2015. Clearly, both data sets are time series, but as may be seen in the time series plots shown later in Section 2.2 in Figures 2.1 and 2.2, the sales figures are fairly level (at least after the first 12 weeks or so) whereas the passenger series shows a strong upward movement, followed by a decline in recent years. Table 2.3, appearing in Section 2.3, involves cross-sectional data on forecasts for the German economy made by different forecasting agencies.

2.1.1 Use of Large Databases

A manager responsible for a large number of product lines may well claim that "the forecasting can all be done by computer, so there is no need to waste time on model building or detailed examinations of individual series." This assertion is half right. The computer can indeed remove most of the drudgery from the forecasting exercise; see, for example, the forecasting methods described in Chapter 3. However, a computer is like a sheepdog: Properly trained, it can deliver a sound flock of forecasts; poorly trained, it can create

---

1 Here, as throughout the book, we reproduce only a few lines from each data file to illustrate the nature of the data. The complete data set is available in the cited Excel file; it is also included in the chapter data file, e.g., *Chapter2_data_xlsx*. These may be downloaded from the book's website.

mayhem. Even if the task in question involves thousands of series to be forecast, there is no substitute for understanding the general structure of the data so that we can identify appropriate forecasting procedures. The manager can then focus on the products that are providing unusual results.

Table 2.1 Value of Weekly Sales of Product WFJ Sales ($)

Week	Sales
1	23056
2	24817
3	24300
...	...
60	28155
61	28404
62	34128

Week 1 is first week of January; *Data: WFJ_sales.xlsx*

Table 2.2 Washington Dulles International Airport, Domestic Passengers, 1963–2015

Year	Passengers (000s)
1963	641
1964	728
1965	920
...	...
2013	14958
2014	14393
2015	14463

Source: U.S. Department of Transportation, Bureau of Transport Statistics
Data: Dulles_2.xlsx

To build an effective forecasting system, therefore, we need to understand the kind of data we are handling. That does not mean examining every series in detail, or even at all, but rather looking at a sample of series in order to establish a framework for effective forecasting. Thus, we need to understand when and how to use forecasting methods, how to interpret the results, and how to recognize their limitations.

2.2 Time Series Plots[2]

Our aim in the next several sections is not to provide detailed technical presentations on the construction of the various plots; rather, we indicate their application in the current context. All the major statistical and forecasting programs such as Autobox, EViews, Forecast Pro, SAS, SPSS and STATA provide detailed tutorials as well as Help commands. In this text while we use a variety of software, we provide guidance on using Excel, Minitab, SPSS, and R.

---

2 The plots in this chapter are generated by Minitab, unless stated otherwise.

As its name suggests, a time series plot shows the variable of interest on the vertical axis and time on the horizontal axis; as noted in Section 1.3, we will assume that the data relate either to equally spaced points in time (e.g. daily stock market closing prices) or to periods of equal length (e.g. weeks or months). As these examples indicate, some adjustments may be needed, such as excluding weekends and holidays for stock price series, or adjusting a monthly figure to allow for the number of days.

The time series plot for WFJ Sales is shown in Figure 2.1. Several features are immediately apparent. Sales are low for the first 12 weeks and then remain stable until week 46, when there is an increase over the Thanksgiving-to-Christmas period (weeks 48–51) followed by a peak in the last week of the year. Sales at the start of the next year are lower than for the final weeks of the previous year, but higher than for the corresponding period a year before. We should not make too much of data for one product over little more than a year, but inspection of the plot has revealed a number of interesting patterns that we might check out for similar products. If these patterns were found to persist across a number of product lines, we would need to take them into account in production planning. For example, the company might initiate extra shifts or overtime to cover peak periods and might plan to replenish inventories during slack times.

Figure 2.1 Time Series Plot of Weekly WFJ Sales

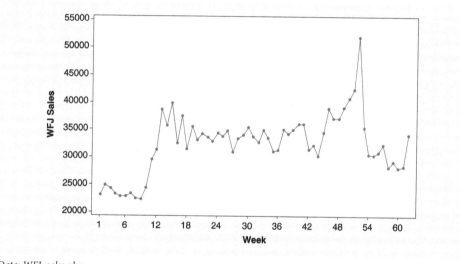

Data: WFJ_sales.xlsx

The second time plot, in Figure 2.2, presents the data from Table 2.2 on the annual number of airline passengers through Dulles Airport, Washington, DC. The figure shows steady growth from 1963 to 1979 (the airport opened in 1962), then a pause followed by rapid growth in the late eighties (after airport expansion in 1983-84). A further pause in the early nineties was followed by a long period of growth, with peaks in 1999 and 2005, and then a period of decline through to 2015. A detailed explanation of these changes lies outside the present discussion; it would require us to examine airport expansion plans, overall levels of passenger demand, the traffic at other airports in the area, and so on. The key point is that a time series plot can tell us a lot about the phenomenon under study and features that require explanation which often suggest suitable approaches to forecasting.

Figure 2.2 Time Series Plot of Domestic Passengers at Dulles, 1963–2015

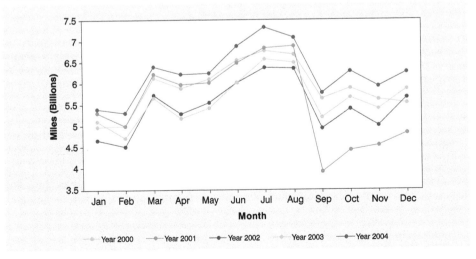

Data: Dulles_2.xlsx

2.2.1 Seasonal Plots

Figure 2.1 has some elements of a seasonal pattern (the end-of-year peak) but just over one year of data from which to identify seasonal behavior. Clearly, Figure 2.2 has no seasonal pattern, because the figures represent complete years. However, seasonal variations are often very important for planning purposes, and it is desirable to have a graphical procedure that allows us to explore whether seasonal patterns exist. For monthly data, for example, we may plot the dependent variable against the months and generate a separate, but overlaid, plot for a succession of years. In Figure 2.3A, we provide such a plot for airline revenue passenger miles (RPM). RPM measures the total number of revenue-generating miles flown by passengers of U.S. airlines, measured in billions of miles. To avoid cluttering the diagram, we use only five years of data, for 2000–2004; such a multicolored diagram that could be created online is more informative and can readily accommodate more years without confusion.

Figure 2.3 Seasonal Plots for Airline Revenue Passenger Miles for 2000-2004

A: Scatterplot by month, with years overlaid, of RPM vs. month

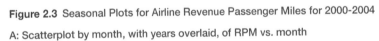

B: Time series plot of RPM, with each year identified as a subgroup

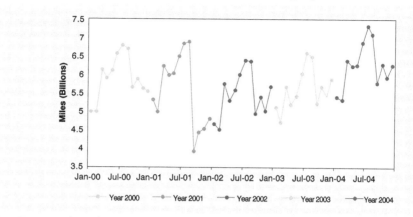

Data: *Revenue_miles_2.xlsx*

In Figure 2.3A, the line for each year lies above those for earlier years, with only rare exceptions. This configuration indicates the steady growth in airline traffic over the period shown. Figure 2.3B also shows the trend and the seasonal peaks and allows easy comparison of successive seasonal cycles. There is a major seasonal peak in the summer, as well as a lesser peak in March–April depending on the timing of Easter. These plots of the data provide considerable insight into the variations in demand for air travel. "Draw the doggone diagram" (DDD) is indeed wise counsel!

2.3 Scatterplots

The time series plots displayed so far show the evolution of a single series over time. As we saw with the seasonal plot, we can show multiple series on the same chart, although some care is required to make the axes sufficiently similar. Scatterplots may represent either cross sectional or time series data: we may plot one variable against another without any implication of causality. An alternative is to plot a variable of interest against one or more potential explanatory variables, to see how far knowledge of the explanatory variable(s) might improve the forecasts of the variable of interest.

Table 2.3 shows data from 25 forecasting organizations in Germany, each forecasting changes in eight macroeconomic variables, for year 2013. The variables of interest are Gross Domestic Product (*GDP*), Private Consumption (*Privcons*), Gross Fixed Capital Formation (*GFCF*), Exports, Imports, Government Surplus (*Govsurp*), Consumer Prices (*Consprix*) and Unemployment (*Unemp*).

In Figure 2.4, we show a cross-sectional scatterplot for the variables *GDP* and *Govsurp*. In this case, we are not attempting to impute any kind of causal relationship, but rather we seek to identify possible associations across forecasts among the different providers. For example, Figure 2.4 indicates that those organizations who predicted stronger growth in *GDP* tended to be more optimistic about the change in the government's budget surplus (or deficit).

Table 2.3 Forecasts for the German Economy for 2013 Made by
Different Forecasting Organizations

Institutions	GDP	Privcons	GFCF	Exports	Imports	Govsurp	Consprix	Unemp
Bundesbank	0.4	1	–0.1	1.9	3	–0.75	1.5	7.2
Commerzbank	0.5	1.3	0.1	2.8	4.1	–0.5	1.9	7.1
Deka	0.7	1.1	–0.3	3.3	3.3	–0.3	1.9	6.9
Deutsche Bank	0.3	0.6	1.1	3.2	4.2	–0.5	1.7	7
...	...	...	...	...	...	...	...	...
UBS	0.8	0.9	1.7	2.6	3.9	–0.2	2.1	7.2
Wirtschaftsweise	0.8	0.8	1.4	3.8	4.2	–0.5	2	6.9

Data: German_forecasts.xlsx; reproduced with permission from Müller-Dröge, Sinclair and Stekler (2016).

Figure 2.4 Scatterplot of GDP vs. Government Surplus for 25 Forecasting Organizations

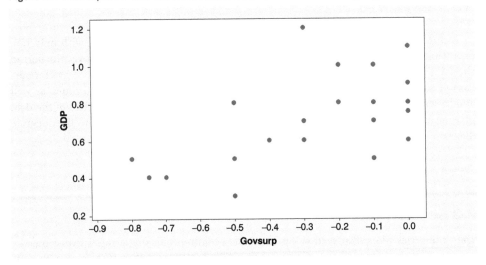

We often have multiple variables of interest and want to look for relationships among them. Rather than generate a series of separate scatterplots, we may combine them into a *matrix plot*, which is just a two-way array of plots of each variable against each of the others. The plots in the bottom left are these same as those in the top right, but with the *x*- and *y*-axes reversed. The matrix plot provides a condensed summary of the relationships among multiple variables and is a useful screening device for relevant variables in the early stages of a forecasting exercise.

Such plots can become difficult to read as the number of variables increases, so Figure 2.5 shows such a plot for just four of the variables: *GDP, GFCF, Govsurp,* and *Unemp.* The forecasts for the first three variables tend to show positive associations, and those three factors tend to be negatively associated with forecasts for unemployment, as might be expected, although the associations are rather weak in some cases.

Figure 2.5 Matrix Plot of GDP, GFCF, Govsurp and Unemp for 25 Forecasting Organizations

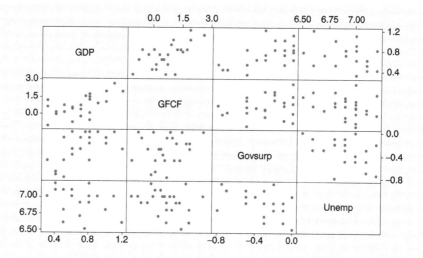

2.4 Summarizing the Data

Graphical summaries provide invaluable insights. Time plots and scatterplots should always be used in the early stages of a forecasting study to aid understanding. Furthermore, as we will see in later chapters, such diagrams also play a valuable role in providing diagnostics for further model development. Even when we have a large number of items to forecast, plots for a sample from the whole set of series provide useful guidance and insights.

At the same time, we must recognize that, although graphical methods provide qualitative insights, we often need some kind of numerical summary, such as the average level of sales over time or the variability in P–E (Price-Earnings) ratios across companies. These measures are also valuable for diagnostic purposes, when we seek to summarize forecasting errors, as in Section 2.7.

2.4.1 Notational Conventions

At this stage, we need to elaborate upon some notational conventions because we will use the following framework throughout the remainder of the book:

1. *Random variables and observations:* When we speak of an *observation*, it is something we have already recorded, a specific number or category. By contrast, when we talk about *future observations*, uncertainty exists. For example, for tomorrow's closing price of the Dow Jones Index, we face a range of possibilities that can be described by a probability distribution. Such a variable, with both a set of possible values and an associated probability distribution, is known as a *random variable*. Texts with a more theoretical orientation often use uppercase letters to denote random variables and lowercase letters for observations that have already been recorded. By contrast, books that are more applied often make no distinction but rely upon the context to make the difference clear. We will not make such a distinction and generally use the same notation for both existing observations and random variables.

2. *Variables and parameters:* As just noted, *variables* are entities that we can observe, such as sales or incomes. By contrast, *parameters* contribute to the description of an underlying process (e.g., a population mean) and are typically not observable. We distinguish these concepts by using the Roman alphabet for observed variables (sample values), but Greek letters for parameters (population values). Thus, the variable we wish to forecast will always be denoted by Y and, where appropriate, the sample mean and standard deviation by $\bar{Y}$ and S. The corresponding population mean and standard deviation will be denoted by μ (mu) and σ (sigma), respectively.

3. *Probability distributions:* The concept of a probability distribution of future observations can be somewhat elusive in a time series context; we make use of model-based probabilities, as described in Appendix 1A. As an example, consider the daily closing prices for a stock such as IBM. There is only one IBM, and only one closing price each day. Nevertheless, we could define a probability distribution for future closing prices, known as a *predictive* (or *prediction*) *distribution*. That is, probabilities are associated with the set of possible future prices and formulated using a model-based description of the past behavior of IBM stock. The "population" (of possible prices) is conceptual in that only one actual value will ever be recorded from each future closing.

2.4.2 Measures of Average

By far the most important measure of average is the *arithmetic mean*, often known simply as the mean or the average.

ARITHMETIC MEAN

Given a set of n values $Y_1, Y_2. \dots. Y_n$, the arithmetic mean is

$$\bar{Y} = \frac{Y_1 + Y_2 + \dots + Y_n}{n} = \frac{1}{n} \sum_{i=1}^{i=n} Y_i. \tag{2.1}$$

That is, the sum of the observations is divided by the number of values included.

When the range of the summation is clear from the context, such as the index going from 1 to n in the formula, we often write the summation sign without including the limits.

An alternative measure of average is given by the *median*, defined as follows:

MEDIAN AND ORDER STATISTICS

Given a set of n values $Y_1, Y_2. \dots. Y_n$ we place these values in ascending order to define the *order statistics*, written as $Y_{(1)} \leq Y_{(2)} \leq \dots \leq Y_{(n)}$. Then the median is the "middle" value:

If n is odd, $n = 2m + 1$ and the *median* is $Y_{(m+1)}$.

If n is even, $n = 2m$ and the *median* is $\frac{1}{2}[Y_{(m)} + Y_{(m+1)}]$.

The median is the value where 50% of observations lie below it and 50% above – the middle "observation".

■ Example 2.1: Calculation of the mean and median

Suppose the sales of a popular book over a seven-week period are as follows:

Week	1	2	3	4	5	6	7
Sales (000s)	15	10	12	16	9	8	14

The mean is $\bar{Y} = \dfrac{(15 + 10 + 12 + 16 + 9 + 8 + 14)}{7} = 12$.

The *order statistics* are 8, 9, 10, 12, 14, 15, 16.

Hence, the median is the fourth value in the sequence, which also happens to be 12.

If data for week 8 now becomes available (sales = 16), the mean becomes 12.5 and the median is ½(12 + 14) = 13. However, suppose that sales for week 8 had been 116 (thousands), because of a sudden surge in popularity. Then the mean becomes 25, yet the median remains at 13. In general, the mean is sensitive to extreme observations but the median is not.

Which value represents the "true" average? The question cannot be answered as framed. The median provides a better view of weekly sales over the first eight weeks, but we are more interested in the numbers actually sold. The forecaster has the unenviable task of trying to decide whether future sales will continue at the giddy level of 100,000+ or whether they will revert to the earlier, more modest level. The wise forecaster would enquire into the reasons for the sudden jump, such as a rare large order or a major publicity event. ■

> **DISCUSSION QUESTION:** *How would you describe housing prices in an area if you were (a) planning to buy a home in the area and (b) seeking to forecast revenues from the local property tax?*

2.4.3 Measures of Variation

A safe investment is an investment whose value does not fluctuate much over time. Similarly, inventory planning is much more straightforward if sales are virtually the same in each period. Implicit in both of these statements is the idea that we use some measure of variability to evaluate risk, whether of losing money or of running out of stock. Three measures of variability are in common use: the *range*, the *mean absolute deviation*, and the *standard deviation*. The standard deviation is derived from the *variance*, which we also define here.

RANGE

The *range* denotes the difference between the largest and smallest values in the sample:

$$\text{Range} = Y_{(n)} - Y_{(1)}.$$

The *deviations* are defined as the differences between each observation and the mean. By construction, the mean of the deviations is zero; so, to compute a measure of variability, we use either the absolute values or the squared values. The absolute values are indicated by vertical lines on either side of the variable, such as $|d|$ for the absolute value of the deviation d.

If we use the squares, our units of measurement become squared also. For example, revenues (in \$) become (\$)^2, so we reverse the operation after computing the average by taking the square root. These various measures are defined as follows, in terms of the deviations:

MEASURES OF DISPERSION

The *mean absolute deviation* is the average of the deviations about the mean, irrespective of the sign:

$$MAD = \frac{\sum |d_i|}{n}. \tag{2.2}$$

The *variance* is an average of the squared deviations about the mean:

$$S^2 = \frac{\sum d_i^2}{(n-1)}. \tag{2.3}$$

The *standard deviation* is the square root of the variance:

$$S = \sqrt{S^2} = \sqrt{\frac{\sum d_i^2}{(n-1)}}. \tag{2.4}$$

■ Example 2.2: Calculation of measures of variation

Consider the values for the seven weeks of book sales, given in Example 2.1. From the order statistics, we immediately see that the range is

$$Range = 16 - 8 = 8.$$

However, if week 8 is entered with sales = 116, the range shoots up to 116 − 8 = 108. This simple example illustrates both the strength and the weakness of the range: It is very easy to compute, but it is severely affected by extreme values. The vulnerability of the range to extreme values makes it unsuitable for most purposes in forecasting.

The deviations for the seven weeks are as follows (the mean is 12):

Week	1	2	3	4	5	6	7	Sums
Sales (000s)	15	10	12	16	9	8	14	84
Deviation	+3	−2	0	+4	−3	−4	+2	0
$|d|$	3	2	0	4	3	4	2	18
d^2	9	4	0	16	9	16	4	58

From the table, we have MAD = 18/7 = 2.57, S^2 = 58/6 = 9.67 and S = 3.11.

Why do we use $(n-1)$ rather than n in the denominator of the variance? The reason is that, because we are using the deviations, if we had only one observation, its deviation would necessarily be zero. In other words, we have no information about the variability in the data. Likewise, in our sample of seven, if we know six of the deviations, we can work out the value of the seventh observation from the fact that they must sum to zero. In effect, by subtracting the mean from each observation, we have "lost" an observation. In statistical parlance, this is known as *losing a degree of freedom* (DF), and we say that the variance is computed under the assumption that there are $(n-1)$ degrees of freedom, which we abbreviate to $(n-1)$ DF. In later chapters, we sometimes lose several DF, and the measure of variability will change accordingly. This adjustment has the benefit of making the sample variance an unbiased estimator of the population variance. (For a more detailed discussion of unbiasedness, see Section A3 of Appendix A, available on the book's website.)

Note: S gives greater weight to the more extreme observations by squaring them, and it may be shown that S > MAD whenever MAD is greater than zero. ■

2.4.4 Assessing Variability

The statement that book sales have a standard deviation of 3.11 (thousand, remember) conveys little about the inherent variability in the data from week to week, unless, like any penniless author, we live and breathe details about the sales of that particular book. To produce a more standard frame of reference, we use *standardized scores*. Given a sample mean $\bar{Y}$ and sample standard deviation S, we define the standardized scores for the observations, also known as Z-scores, as

$$Z_i = \frac{Y_i - \bar{Y}}{S} .$$

Each deviation is divided by the standard deviation. It follows that the Z-scores have zero mean and a standard deviation equal to 1.0. Following our simple example, we obtain the following table:

Week	1	2	3	4	5	6	7
Sales (000s)	15	10	12	16	9	8	14
Deviation	+3	–2	0	+4	–3	–4	+2
Z-score	0.96	–0.64	0	1.29	–0.96	–1.29	0.64

The Z-scores still do not provide much information until we provide a frame of reference. In this book, we typically use Z-scores to examine forecast errors and proceed in three steps:

1. Check that the observed distribution of the errors is approximately normal. (For details, see Appendix A6 on the book's website.)

2. If the assumption is satisfied, relate the Z-score to the normal tables (available through any statistics textbook, e.g. Anderson *et al.*, 2014). The Excel function is called NORM.DIST (value,0,1,1), which calculates the cumulative probability that the Z-score is less than "value" drawn from a normal distribution with mean 0 and variance 1:

   • The probability that $|Z| > 1$ is about 0.32 (or about 3 in 10).
   • The probability that $|Z| > 2$ is about 0.046 (about 5 in 100).
   • The probability that $|Z| > 3$ is about 0.0027 (about 3 in 1000).

   Most software packages include similar functions.

3. Create a time series plot of the residuals (and/or Z-scores), when appropriate, to determine whether any observations appear to be extreme.

At this stage, we do not pursue the systematic use of Z-scores, except to recognize that whenever you see a Z-score whose absolute value is greater than 3, the observation is atypical, because the probability of such an occurrence is less than 3 in 1000 (if the distribution is approximately normal). Often, such large values signify that something unusual has happened, and we refer to these kinds of observations as *outliers*. In cross-sectional studies, it is sometimes admissible to just delete such observations (e.g., a report of a 280-year-old man is undoubtedly a recording error). In time series forecasting, we wish to retain the complete sequence of values and must investigate more closely, often finding special circumstances (e.g., a strike, bad weather, a special sales promotion) for which we had not allowed. Outliers indicate the need for further exploration, not routine rejection. We defer the detailed treatment of outliers to Chapter 9.

2.4.5 An Example: Forecasts for the German Economy

The default summary outputs from Excel for the data in Table 2.3 on forecasts for the German economy are shown in Table 2.4. The output from other programs may have a somewhat different format, but the summary measures included are similar and most programs allow a variety of options. Excel typically produces too many decimal places; for ease of comparison, our output has been edited to produce a reasonable number of decimal places.

Table 2.4 Descriptive Statistics for Forecasts of the German Economy

	GDP	Privcons	GFCF	Exports	Imports	Govsurp	Consprix	Unemp
Mean	0.682	0.868	0.656	3.344	3.692	-0.294	1.894	6.92
Standard Error	0.050	0.060	0.180	0.190	0.194	0.049	0.054	0.036
Median	0.7	0.9	0.7	3.5	4	-0.3	1.9	7
Mode	0.8	1	0.7	3	4.1	-0.5	2	7
Standard Deviation	0.249	0.302	0.900	0.950	0.970	0.247	0.269	0.180
Sample Variance	0.062	0.091	0.810	0.903	0.941	0.061	0.073	0.033
Kurtosis	-0.53	-0.37	-0.21	2.34	5.19	-0.70	4.26	0.17
Skewness	0.19	-0.41	0.07	-0.67	-2.03	-0.53	1.29	-0.70
Range	0.9	1.2	3.7	4.9	4.6	0.8	1.3	0.7
Minimum	0.3	0.2	-1.1	0.6	0.4	-0.8	1.5	6.5
Maximum	1.2	1.4	2.6	5.5	5	0	2.8	7.2
Count	25	25	25	25	25	25	25	25

Data: German_forecasts.xlsx

Given the mean and standard deviation, we proceed to compute the Z-scores for each variable, shown in Table 2.5. We list those institutions that have one or more Z-scores greater than 2.0 in absolute value. It is noteworthy that the forecasters tend to be relatively optimistic or pessimistic across the board. We explore this phenomenon further by computing the sum of the Z-scores for each institution and, finally, computing the Z-scores for this sum. Helaba and DIW stand out as much more optimistic than the others.

Table 2.5 Z-Scores for Forecasts of the German Economy

Institutions	GDP	Privcons	GFCF	Exports	Imports	Govsurp	Consprix	Unemp	SUM	Z
Bundesbank	-1.13	0.44	-0.84	-1.52	-0.71	-1.85	-1.46	1.55	-5.53	-2.09
DIW	0.88	0.77	0.27	0.90	0.94	1.19	3.36	0.44	8.75	3.31
Feri	2.08	1.10	1.38	0.80	0.42	-0.02	0.39	-1.78	4.37	1.65
Gemeinschafts	1.28	0.77	1.38	0.48	0.94	0.38	0.76	-0.67	5.32	2.01
Helaba	1.68	1.10	2.16	2.27	1.35	1.19	0.39	0.44	10.59	4.00
ING	0.47	-1.55	0.60	-2.89	-3.39	0.38	0.39	-0.11	-6.09	-2.30
Landesbank Berlin	-0.73	0.44	0.05	-1.20	-0.82	-2.05	-1.09	-0.67	-6.07	-2.30
MM Wartburg	-0.33	-0.56	-1.62	0.90	-2.16	1.19	-1.46	0.44	-3.59	-1.36
RWI	-1.54	-2.21	-1.95	-0.36	-0.51	-0.83	-0.72	0.44	-7.68	-2.90

2.5 Correlation

In the previous section, we produced numerical summaries to complement the graphical analysis of Section 2.2. We now develop a statistic that performs a similar function for the scatterplots of Section 2.3: the *correlation coefficient*. Before defining the coefficient, we examine Figure 2.6; in each case, the horizontal axis may be interpreted as time. The six plots suggest the following:

  $Y1$ increases with time and is perfectly related to time.

  $Y2$ decreases with time and is perfectly related to time.

  $Y3$ tends to increase with time but is not perfectly related to time.

  $Y4$ tends to decrease with time, but the relationship is weaker than that for $Y3$.

  $Y5$ shows virtually no relationship with time.

  $Y6$ is perfectly related to time, but the relationship is not linear.

Our measure should reflect these differences but not be affected by changes in the origin or changes of scale. The origins and scales of the variables are deliberately omitted from the diagrams because they do not affect the degree of association between the two variables. The most commonly used measure that satisfies these criteria is the *(Pearson) product moment correlation coefficient*, which we simply refer to as *the* correlation. We use the letter r to denote the sample coefficient and the Greek letter ρ (rho) to denote the corresponding quantity in the population. Rho is calculated by replacing the sample components by their corresponding population values.

Figure 2.6 Plots of Hypothetical Data Against Time

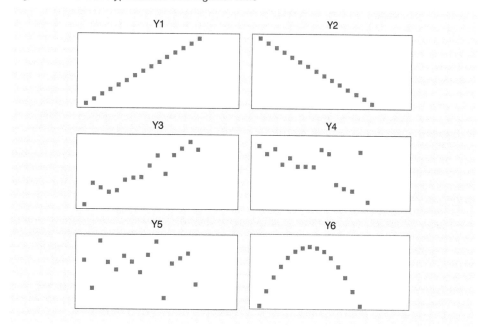

THE CORRELATION COEFFICIENT

The sample *correlation* between X and Y is defined as

$$r = \frac{\sum_{i=1}^{n}(X_i - \bar{X})(Y_i - \bar{Y})}{\sqrt{\sum_{i=1}^{n}(X_i - \bar{X})^2 \sum_{i=1}^{n}(Y_i - \bar{Y})^2}}. \tag{2.5}$$

The numerator represents the sum of cross products of the deviations, and the denominator terms are sums of squares of the two sets of deviations.

When we divide denominator by $(n-1)$, the two terms inside the square-root sign become the sample variances of X and Y, respectively; Thus, on taking the square root, the denominator represents the product of the two standard deviations S_X and S_Y. The numerator divided by $(n-1)$ is known as the sample *covariance* between X and Y, denoted by S_{XY}. Thus, the correlation may be written as

$$r = \frac{S_{XY}}{S_X S_Y}. \tag{2.6}$$

It may be shown that, for $Y1$ in Figure 2.8, $r = 1$, the maximum value possible. Similarly, $Y2$ has $r = -1$, the minimum possible. The other correlations are, 0.93, −0.66, −0.09, and 0, for $Y3$, $Y4$, $Y5$, and $Y6$, respectively. In general, we see that the *absolute* value of r declines as the relationship gets weaker. At first sight, the result for $Y6$ appears odd: There is a clear relationship with X, but the correlation is zero. The reason for this is that r measures *linear* association, but the relationship of $Y6$ with X is *quadratic* rather than linear. A good example is the relationship between total revenue and price: Charge too much or too little, and total revenue is low.

DISCUSSION QUESTION: *How would you measure the relationship between Y6 and time?*

■ Example 2.3: Calculation of the correlation

Based on the data from Example 2.1, the detailed calculations for the correlation between sales and time are shown in the table that follows. A spreadsheet could readily be set up in this format for direct calculations, but all standard software packages have a correlation function.

Week, X	1	2	3	4	5	6	7	Sums
Sales (000s), Y	15	10	12	16	9	8	14	
$X - \bar{X}$	−3	−2	−1	0	1	2	3	0
$Y - \bar{Y}$	+3	−2	0	+4	−3	−4	+2	0
$(X - \bar{X})^2$	9	4	1	0	1	4	9	28
$(Y - \bar{Y})^2$	9	4	0	16	9	16	4	58
$(X - \bar{X})(Y - \bar{Y})$	−9	4	0	0	−3	−8	6	−10

Thus, $S_{XY} = -10/6$, $S_X = \sqrt{28/6}$ and $S_Y = \sqrt{58/6}$, so $r = -0.248$.

The example shows a weak negative correlation for sales with time; that is, sales may be declining slightly over time. ■

■ Example 2.4: Correlation among forecasts for the German economy

The correlations among the eight sets of forecasts are shown in Table 2.6. The upper number in each pair is the correlation and the lower figure is the P-value, enabling a (two-sided) test of whether the coefficient is significantly different from zero. A number of the results are interesting; in particular, it is evident that forecasts of strong growth in *GDP* are associated with other aspects of economic well-being, notably *GFCF*, *Exports*, and *Govsurp*. ■

Table 2.6 Correlations Among Forecasts for the German Economy

	GDP	Privcons	GFCF	Exports	Imports	Govsurp	Consprix
Privcons	0.430						
	(0.032)						
GFCF	0.601	0.295					
	(0.001)	(0.153)					
Exports	0.459	0.262	0.192				
	(0.021)	(0.206)	(0.357)				
Imports	0.209	0.469	0.371	0.641			
	(0.315)	(0.018)	(0.068)	(0.001)			
Govsurp	0.620	0.033	0.223	0.518	0.085		
	(0.001)	(0.874)	(0.285)	(0.008)	(0.688)		
Consprix	0.317	0.192	0.336	0.210	0.382	0.179	
	(0.123)	(0.358)	(0.101)	(0.313)	(0.060)	(0.391)	
Unemp	−0.363	0.073	−0.295	−0.273	−0.087	−0.317	0.063
	(0.074)	(0.727)	(0.153)	(0.187)	(0.678)	(0.123)	(0.766)

Data: German_forecasts.xlsx

2.6 Transformations

We now examine the annual figures for the number of passengers on domestic flights out of Dulles airport for the years 1963–2015. The descriptive statistics are as follows:

Descriptive Statistics: Dulles Passengers								
Variable	N	Mean	StDev	Minimum	Q1	Median	Q3	Maximum
Passengers	53	8456	6397	641	2044	8947	14428	22129

Dulles, we have a problem! What does the average of 8456 mean? Such levels were typical of the mid-eighties, but the "average" in a strongly trending series like this one has little or no meaning. Certainly, using either the mean or the median to forecast the next year's traffic would make no sense.

How should we deal with a series that reveals a strong trend? Everyday conversation provides a clue. We talk of the return on an investment, an increase in company sales over the previous year, or the percentage change in *GDP*. This approach is partly a matter of convenience; some ideas are more readily communicated using (percentage) changes rather than raw figures. Thus, we may regard 3 percent growth in *GDP* as reasonable, 1 percent as anemic, and 7 percent as unsustainable. The same information conveyed in dollars would be hard to comprehend.

From the forecasting perspective, there are two further reasons for considering such alternatives:

- Because we are examining changes, the forecast relates directly back to the previously observed value; such forecasts are unlikely to be wildly off target
- Mean levels in terms of absolute changes or percentage changes are often more stable and more meaningful than averages computed from the original series.

We now explore these ideas in greater detail.

2.6.1 Differences and Growth Rates

The change in the absolute level of a series from one period to the next is known as the *(first) difference*[3] of the series and is written as

$$DY_t = Y_t - Y_{t-1}. \tag{2.7}$$

At time t, the previous value Y_{t-1} is already known. If the forecast for the difference is written as $\hat{D}_t$. The forecast for period t, denoted by F_t, becomes

$$F_t = Y_{t-1} + \hat{D}_t. \tag{2.8}$$

That is, the final forecast is the previous level plus the forecast of the change. Similarly, the rate of growth over time is written as[4]

$$GY_t = 100 \frac{(Y_t - Y_{t-1})}{Y_{t-1}}. \tag{2.9}$$

Expression (2.9) also defines the one-period return on an investment, given the opening price of Y_{t-1}. Once the growth rate, denoted by $\hat{G}_t$ has been predicted, the forecast for the next period is

$$F_t = Y_{t-1}\left(1 + \frac{\hat{G}_t}{100}\right). \tag{2.10}$$

The time plots for *DY* and *GY* for the Dulles passengers' series are shown in Figure 2.7A and 2.7B. Both series show a fairly stable level over time, so the mean becomes a more useful summary of the transformed series, although *GY* is trending downward, indicating a slowing in percentage growth and then a decline.

Another feature of Figure 2.7A is that the variability in *DY* is much greater at the end of the series than it is at the beginning. By contrast, the *GY* series has more consistent fluctuations. We might claim that *GY* has a stable variance over time, a claim that would be hard to make for *DY*. Which should we use? In part, the choice will depend upon the purpose behind the forecasting exercise, but an often reasonable guideline is a commonsense one: Do you naturally think of changes in the time series in absolute terms or in relative (i.e., percentage) terms? If the answer is "absolute," use *DY*; if it is "relative," use *GY*. In this case,

---

3 Some texts use the Greek capital letter Δ (delta) and others use ∇ (an inverted delta, or "del"), but the use of *D* seems a better mnemonic device for "difference."

4 The use of *G* to describe the growth rate is nonstandard; we use it here for the same reason as before: It is a convenient mnemonic device.

both transformed series show some unusual values, so further investigation is warranted. Out of interest, we note that Dulles airport underwent a significant expansion in 1984.

The summary statistics for *DY* and *GY* are as follows:

Descriptive Statistics: Difference, Growth Rate in Dulles Passengers								
Variable	N	Mean	StDev	Minimum	Q1	Median	Q3	Maximum
Difference	52	266	1463	−4342	−213	135	445	5285
Growth Rate	52	7.47	17.87	−26.99	−3.63	4.57	16.97	84.95

These figures also reflect the considerable fluctuations that appear in each series.

Figure 2.7

A: Time Series Plot for the First Differences of the Dulles Passengers Series

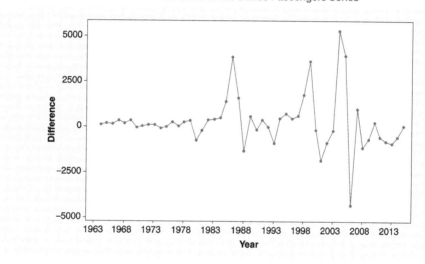

B: Time Series Plot for the Growth Rates for the Dulles Passengers Series

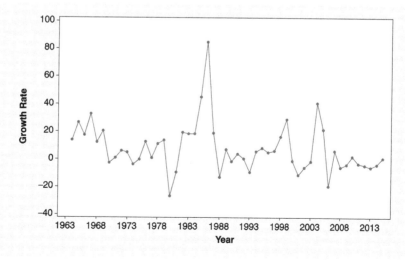

Data: Dulles_2.xlsx

2.6.2 The Log Transform

George Orwell's classic novel *1984* contains a scene in which the chocolate ration is reduced by 50 percent and then increased by 50 percent. The main character, Winston, complains that he does not have as much chocolate as before, but he is sharply rebuked for his remarks. However, Winston is right:

$$\left(1 - \frac{50}{100}\right)\left(1 + \frac{50}{100}\right) = 0.75.$$

So Winston has 25 percent less chocolate than before. To avoid this asymmetry, we may use the logarithmic (or log) transform, usually with the *natural logarithm* defined on the base $e = 2.71828 \dots$.[5] The log transform may be written as $L_t = \ln(Y_t)$ and any software package has a function such as *ln* to compute the natural logarithm. To convert back to the original units, we use an inverse function (or reverse transformation) called *exp*, the exponential function, so we have $Y_t = \exp(L_t)$. The (first) difference in logarithms represents the logarithm of the ratio:

$$DL_t = \ln(Y_t / Y_{t-1}) = \ln(Y_t) - \ln(Y_{t-1}). \qquad (2.11)$$

The primary purpose of the log transform is to convert exponential (or proportional) growth into linear growth. The transform often has the secondary benefit of stabilizing the variance, as did the use of growth rates. Indeed, the log and growth rate transforms tend to produce similar results, as can be seen by comparing the plot of the log differences for the Dulles passengers' series in Figure 2.8 with Figure 2.7B.

Figure 2.8 Time Series Plot for the First Difference of Logarithms for the Dulles Passengers Series

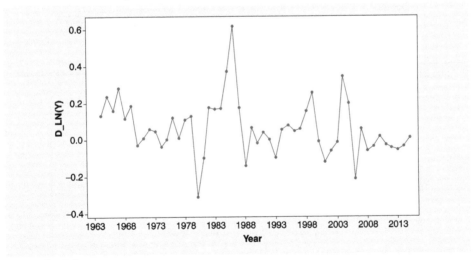

Data: Dulles_2.xlsx

If we generate a forecast of the log difference, say, $\widehat{DL}_t$, then the forecast for the original series requires that we reverse the log transform by using the exponential function. Given the previous value, Y_{t-1}, the forecast for period t becomes

$$F_t = Y_{t-1} \exp(\widehat{DL}_t). \qquad (2.12)$$

---

5 If $Y = e^X$ or $\exp(X)$, the $\log_e(Y)$ or $\ln(Y) = X$, e being the base for $\log_e Y$.

■ Example 2.5: Calculation of forecast using log differences

The actual number of passengers using Dulles International Airport in 2014 was 14393 (in thousands). To make a forecast for 2015, we might use the last value for the log difference, which is $\ln(14393) - \ln(14958) = -0.0385$. Then equation (2.12) yields

$$F_t = 14393 \times \exp(-0.0385) = 14393 \times 0.9622 = 13849.$$

This short term forecast assumes a continuing decline, whereas the passenger traffic increased slightly. This raises the question of how to measure forecast accuracy, a topic we now address. ■

Note: When x is small, $\exp(x) \approx 1 + x$, which helps to explain why the growth rate and log transform analyses often produce similar results: compare Figures 2.7B and 2.8.

2.7 How to Evaluate Forecasting Accuracy

A key question in any forecasting endeavor is how to evaluate and measure performance – the E in PIVASE. Performance measures are of particular value when we come to select a forecasting procedure, because we may compare alternatives and choose the method with the best track record. Then, once the method is being used on a regular basis, we need similar measures to tell us whether the forecasts are maintaining their historical level of accuracy. If a particular set of forecasts is not performing adequately, managerial intervention is needed to get things back on track.

The generation of forecasts and the selection of a preferred method occupy a major portion of the book. Therefore, to discuss issues of evaluating accuracy without the need to develop forecasting methods explicitly at this stage, we consider an example taken from meteorology. Weather forecasts that appear in the media are not directed at a particular audience, and there is no reason to suppose that forecasts of temperature would have any inherent bias. However, we would expect that such forecasts (and this is typically true of all forecasts) would become less accurate as the forecast horizon increases (in this case, the number of days ahead).

We consider a set of local forecasts for daily high temperatures, extracted from the *Washington Post* for the period from June 2 to July 5, 2016. The forecasts are generated by *Accuweather*, a weather-forecasting organization. The forecasts appear for 1–5 days ahead, so the initial data could be summarized as shown in Table 2.7 (first and last few days only). However, this form of presentation is not useful for the evaluation of the forecasts, because, for example, the four-day forecast made on June 2 refers to conditions to be observed on June 6. To match forecasts to actual outcomes, we must slide the columns down, as shown in Table 2.8. We may now compare forecasts along the same row.

In a general sense, it is useful to refer to a forecast for period t as F_t when the time period when the forecast is made is not an issue. However, when timing matters, we need to report both the period being forecast and the number of periods ahead of time that the forecast was made. The notation[6] must reflect this information. Accordingly, we will use $F_t(h)$ to denote the forecast for period t, made h periods previously. Thus, $F_{14}(1)$ refers to the one-step-ahead forecast made for period 14 at period 13, $F_{14}(2)$ to the two-step-ahead forecast

---

6 The notation for forecasts is not standard. Some texts use F_{t+h} to denote forecasts h steps ahead for Y_{t+h}. Although this notation is simpler than ours, the notation F_{13+2} (not equal to F_{15}!) is potentially confusing and $F_{15}(2)$ is clearer.

made for period 14 at time 12, and so on. These values will be eventually compared with the observed value in period 14, Y_{14}. The general format is shown in Table 2.9; when there is no risk of confusion, we will use F_t to represent $F_t(1)$.

Table 2.7 Temperature Forecasts for Washington, DC, June 1–July 4, 2016

Forecast Origin	Forecast Lead Time (days ahead)				
	1	2	3	4	5
1-Jun	82	82	84	81	79
2-Jun	82	81	83	80	80
3-Jun	83	85	83	82	76
4-Jun	86	86	83	74	76
5-Jun	85	84	74	75	79
6-Jun	85	74	76	75	81
7-Jun	74	78	78	85	83
...	...	...	...	...	...
30-Jun	86	84	85	85	89
1-Jul	83	82	79	84	89
2-Jul	76	78	87	92	93
3-Jul	74	89	95	93	92
4-Jul	88				

Data: DC_weather_2.xlsx
Source: Washington Post: Daily highs at Reagan National Airport

Table 2.8 Temperature Forecasts for Washington, DC, June 2–July 5, 2016

Date Corresponding to Forecast	Forecast Lead Time (days ahead)					Actual Temperature (°F)
	1	2	3	4	5	
2-Jun	82					82
3-Jun	82	82				81
4-Jun	83	81	84			82
5-Jun	86	85	83	81		85
6-Jun	85	86	83	80	79	87
7-Jun	85	84	83	82	80	87
8-Jun	74	74	74	74	76	74
...	...	...	...	...	...	...
1-Jul	86	88	88	88	88	88
2-Jul	83	84	87	87	88	80
3-Jul	76	82	85	85	86	74
4-Jul	74	78	79	85	83	73
5-Jul	88	89	87	84	89	90

Data: DC_weather_2.xlsx
Source: Washington Post: Daily highs at Reagan National Airport

Table 2.9 Structure of Forecasts for 1, 2, 3,... Periods Ahead

Period	Days Ahead that Forecasts are Made				Actual
	1	**2**	**3**	**...**	
t	$F_t(1)$	$F_t(2)$	$F_t(3)$	...	Y_t
$t + 1$	$F_{t+1}(1)$	$F_{t+1}(2)$	$F_{t+1}(3)$	...	Y_{t+1}
$t + 2$	$F_{t+2}(1)$	$F_{t+2}(2)$	$F_{t+2}(3)$	...	Y_{t+2}

2.7.1 Measures of Forecasting Accuracy for Time Series[7]

Now that we have a set of forecasts and actual values with which to compare them, how should the comparisons be made? In principle, the criteria used should reflect the decision maker's loss function (e.g., minimize cost, achieve a certain level of customer service), but such information may not be available or the forecasts might be used for multiple purposes. In these circumstances, we must develop general-purpose criteria that can be used in a variety of circumstances. A natural approach is to look at the differences between the observed values and the forecasts and to use their average as a performance measure.

ROLLING ORIGIN FORECASTS

Starting at *forecast origin t*, with $t + m$ observations available, generate forecasts successively (one-step-ahead) at time origins $t, t + 1, t + 2, ..., t + m - 1$, making m such forecasts in all. This process is known as rolling origin forecasting; an example is provided in Section 3.3.4. The one-step-ahead forecast error at time $t + i$ may be denoted by $e_{t+i} = Y_{t+i} - F_{t+i}$.

These observed error terms may be used to define performance indicators: one possibility is the mean of the errors.

THE MEAN ERROR

The *mean error (ME)* is given by

$$ME = \sum_{i=1}^{m} (Y_{t+i} - F_{t+i})/m = \sum_{i=1}^{m} e_{t+i}/m. \tag{2.13}$$

The mean error is a useful way of detecting systematic bias in a forecast; that is, *ME* will be large and positive (negative) when the actual value is consistently greater (less) than the forecast. The forecasts are then said to be biased. When the variable of interest is strictly positive, such as the number of employees or sales revenues, a percentage measure is often more useful; that is, we express the error as a percentage of the actual value and then take an average.

THE MEAN PERCENTAGE ERROR

The *mean percentage error (MPE)* is

$$MPE = \frac{100}{m} \sum_{i=1}^{m} \frac{(Y_{t+i} - F_{t+i})}{Y_{t+i}} = \frac{100}{m} \sum_{i=1}^{m} \frac{e_{t+i}}{Y_{t+i}}. \tag{2.14}$$

Note that *ME* is a useful measure for the temperature data, but *MPE* is not because the temperature can fall below zero. More importantly, temperature does not have a natural

---

7 We discuss measures of forecasting accuracy for categorical predictions in Chapter 10.

origin, so the *MPE* would give different (and equally meaningless) results, depending on whether we used the Fahrenheit or Celsius scale.

■ Example 2.6: Calculation of ME and MPE *(Data: Electricity.xlsx)*

The calculations of *ME* and *MPE* are illustrated in Table 2.10, in which the data represent the monthly electricity consumption (in KWH, kilowatt hours) in a Washington, DC, household; the column of forecasts in Table 2.10A represents the consumption in the corresponding month in the previous year. Consumption is low in the winter and high in the summer because the home uses gas heating and electric air-conditioning.

As noted, the *ME* and *MPE* are useful measures of bias. From Table 2.10A, we see that the household generally reduced its consumption relative to the previous year, so the forecasts tended to be too high. In passing, we note that the year-over-year change is given by comparing the totals for the two years — 13,190, the previous year's total (and this year's forecast), and 11,270 (this year's actual). Such a comparison indicates a 14.6 percent drop. The 18.7 percent average given by the *MPE* reflects month-by-month forecasting performance, not the change in the totals.

A limitation of these measures is that they do not reflect variability. Positive and negative errors could virtually cancel each other out, yet substantial forecasting errors could remain. To see this effect, suppose we used the average monthly figure for the first year (that is, the forecasts in this example) to predict the usage in the second year. The average is 1099 KWH, a figure that seriously underestimates summer consumption and overestimates the rest of the year. Yet the *ME* would be unchanged. The *MPE* expands to –37.2, because the errors are larger in the months with low consumption. Such changes are largely meaningless. For example, a forecast value of 800 KWH per month is clearly not very useful, yet it reduces the *MPE* to –0.1 as we shall see later!

From this discussion, we evidently also need measures that account for the magnitude of the errors regardless of their signs. ■

Table 2.10 Analysis of Forecasting Accuracy for Electricity Consumption in a Washington, DC, Household

(A) One Year Ahead: Forecast = Actual Value for Same Month in Previous Year

Period	Actual	Forecast	Errors	Absolute Errors	Percentage Errors	Absolute Percentage Errors	Squared Errors
Jan.	790	820	–30	30	–3.8	3.8	900
Feb.	810	790	20	20	2.5	2.5	400
Mar.	680	720	–40	40	–5.9	5.9	1600
Apr.	500	640	–140	140	–28.0	28.0	19600
May	520	780	–260	260	–50.0	50.0	67600
Jun.	810	980	–170	170	–21.0	21.0	28900
Jul.	1120	1550	–430	430	–38.4	38.4	184900
Aug.	1840	1850	–10	10	–0.5	0.5	100
Sep.	1600	1880	–280	280	–17.5	17.5	78400
Oct.	1250	1600	–350	350	–28.0	28.0	122500
Nov.	740	890	–150	150	–20.3	20.3	22500
Dec.	610	690	–80	80	–13.1	13.1	6400
	Totals		ME	MAE	MPE	MAPE	MSE
	11270	13190	–160	163.3	–18.7	19.1	44483.3
						RMSE	210.9

(B) One Month Ahead: Forecast = Previous Month's Actual

Period	Actual	Forecast	Errors	Absolute Errors	Percentage Errors	Absolute Percentage Errors	Squared Errors
Jan.	790	690	100	100	12.7	12.7	10000
Feb.	810	790	20	20	2.5	2.5	400
Mar.	680	810	−130	130	−19.1	19.1	16900
Apr.	500	680	−180	180	−36.0	36.0	32400
May	520	500	20	20	3.8	3.8	400
Jun.	810	520	290	290	35.8	35.8	84100
Jul.	1120	810	310	310	27.7	27.7	96100
Aug.	1840	1120	720	720	39.1	39.1	518400
Sep.	1600	1840	−240	240	−15.0	15.0	57600
Oct.	1250	1600	−350	350	−28.0	28.0	122500
Nov.	740	1250	−510	510	−68.9	68.9	260100
Dec.	610	740	−130	130	−21.3	21.3	16900
	Totals		ME	MAE	MPE	MAPE	MSE
	11270	11350	−6.7	250.0	−5.6	25.8	101316.7
						RMSE	318.3

Data: Electricity.xlsx

2.7.2 Measures of Absolute Error

The simplest way to gauge the variability in forecasting performance is to examine the *absolute error (AE)*, defined as the value of the error regardless of its sign and expressed as

$$|e_i| = |Y_i - F_i|. \tag{2.15}$$

Thus, if we generate a forecast of $F = 100$, the absolute error is 20 whenever the actual value turns out to be either 80 or 120. As before, we may consider various averages, based upon the absolute errors. They can usefully be split into two categories. Absolute measures which are on the same scale as the measurements themselves and relative measures where the (absolute) error is measured relative to some baseline. Those in common use are summarized in the following box.

The Mean Absolute Error (*MAE*) and the Root Mean Square Error (*RMSE*) measure variability in absolute terms, whereas the Mean Absolute Percentage error (*MAPE*) does so in relative terms.

The Relative Mean Absolute Error (*RelMAE*) is the ratio of the *MAE* for the current set of one-step-ahead forecasts to the *MAE* for forecasts made with the random walk, which uses the most recent observation as the forecast for the next period. Similar comparisons for *h*-periods-ahead just involve the use of the two sets of forecasts *h* steps ahead, which we designate *RelMAE(h)*. When *RelMAE(h)* is greater than one, we may conclude that the random-walk forecasts are superior for *h* periods ahead. When *RelMAE(h)* is less than 1, the method under consideration is superior to the random walk for *h* periods ahead.

Theil's U is a long-established criterion that is widely used in econometrics; its structure is similar to that of *RelMAE*, but using squares in place of absolute values. As for the *RelMAE*, *U(h)* may be calculated using forecasts made *h* steps ahead.

ONE-STEP AHEAD ERROR MEASURES STARTING AT FORECAST ORIGIN t

Mean absolute error:

$$MAE = \sum_{i=1}^{m} |Y_{t+i} - F_{t+i}|/m = \sum_{i=1}^{m} |e_{t+i}|/m. \qquad (2.16)$$

Mean absolute percentage error:

$$MAPE = \frac{100}{m} \sum_{i=1}^{m} \frac{|Y_{t+i} - F_{t+i}|}{Y_{t+i}} = \frac{100}{m} \sum_{i=1}^{m} \frac{|e_{t+i}|}{Y_{t+i}}. \qquad (2.17)$$

Mean square error (not recommended):

$$MSE = \sum_{i=1}^{m} (Y_{t+i} - F_{t+i})^2/m = \sum_{i=1}^{m} e_{t+i}^2/m. \qquad (2.18)$$

Root mean square error:

$$RMSE = \sqrt{MSE}. \qquad (2.19)$$

Relative absolute error[8]:

$$RelMAE = \frac{\sum_{i=1}^{m} |Y_{t+i} - F_{t+i}|}{\sum_{i=1}^{m} |Y_{t+i} - Y_{t+i-1}|}. \qquad (2.20)$$

Theil's U:

$$U = \frac{\left(\sum_{i=1}^{m} [Y_{t+i} - F_{t+i}]^2\right)^{1/2}}{\left(\sum_{i=1}^{m} [Y_{t+i} - Y_{t+i-1}]^2\right)^{1/2}}. \qquad (2.21)$$

The following comments are in order:

1. *MAPE* should be used only when $Y > 0$; *RelMAE* and U are not so restricted.

2. The *RMSE* is used because the *MSE* involves squared errors so that the *MSE* is measured in dollars squared. Taking the square root to obtain the *RMSE* restores the original units of dollars and makes interpretation more straightforward.

3. The *RMSE* gives greater weight to large (absolute) errors. It can be shown that *RMSE* $\geq$ *MAE* for any set of m forecasts; recall the discussion in Section 2.4.3.

4. The measure using absolute values always equals or exceeds the absolute value of the measure based on the errors, so *MAE* $\geq |ME|$ and *MAPE* $\geq |MPE|$. Values that are close in magnitude suggest a systematic bias in the forecasts.

---

8 Hyndman and Koehler (2006) introduced the Mean Absolute Scaled Error (or *MASE*). *MASE* is the ratio of the average out-of-sample absolute error to the average in-sample absolute error using the random walk to make forecasts. In our present notation, this expression may be written as:

$$MASE = \frac{\sum_{i=1}^{m} |Y_{t+i} - F_{t+i}|/m}{\sum_{i=2}^{t} |Y_j - Y_{j-1}|/(t-1)}.$$

MASE may also be used to compare methods by summing across multiple series; this property is particularly useful when only a one or a small number of out-of-sample forecasts is available.

5. *MPE, MAPE, RelMAE,* and *U* are scale free and so can be used to make comparisons across multiple series by calculating the mean, first over an individual series and then averaged over a number of related series. The other measures are scale dependent and cannot be used to make such comparisons without an additional scaling. Summarizing accuracy over a number of series is helpful for many managerial decisions such as deciding which forecasting method to apply in a retail chain.

6. All these measures may be defined for more than one period ahead simply by replacing the one-step-ahead forecasts by their *h*-step-ahead counterparts, i.e. for *h*-step ahead forecast error measures, in all the above formulae, F_{t+i} is replaced by $F_{t+i}(h)$.

7. For *RelMAE* and *U* we replace the forecasts in *both* the numerator and the denominator by their *h*-step-ahead counterparts.

The mean error measures are defined above. Because errors are often non-normal or non-symmetric, the median is often used instead of or in addition to the mean. This does not change the interpretation of the measures as "the average accuracy." The median is a better measure of accuracy for the relative error measures than the mean.

■ Example 2.7: Calculation of error measures

Recall the absolute error measures computed in Table 2.10 for the electricity forecasts. The individual terms are shown in the various columns, and *MAE, MAPE,* and *MSE* are then evaluated as the column averages. *RMSE* follows directly from equation (2.18) — that is, by taking the square root of *MSE*. Table 2.10B gives the results for the random-walk (one month ahead) forecasts, so *RelMAE* is given by the ratio of the forecast *MAE* to the *MAE* of the random-walk forecasts. Relative to the random-walk method, the forecasts based upon the same month in the previous year provide a 35 percent [= $100 \times (250 - 163.3)/250$] reduction in the mean absolute error.

Table 2.11 provides a comparison of the three sets of forecasts for electricity consumption:

- Last year's value for the same month, as given in Table 2.10A
- Monthly average for the previous year (= 1099 for all 12 months)
- Forecast set at 800 for all 12 months
- Random walk (one month ahead), as given in Table 2.10B.

Table 2.11 Comparison of Forecasts for Electricity Data

Forecasting Method	Error Measure						
Means	**ME**	**MPE**	**MAE**	**MAPE**	**RMSE**	**RelMAE**	**U**
Last year's values	−160	−18.7	163	19.1	211	0.65	0.66
Monthly average	−160	−37.2	396	51.5	440	1.58	1.38
All F = 800	139	0.1	299	28.8	433	1.20	1.36
Random walk	−6.7	−5.6	250	25.8	318	1.00	1.00
Medians	**MdE**	**MdPE**	**MdAE**	**MdAPE**	**RMdSE**	**MdRelMAE**	**MdU**
Last year's values	−145	−18.9	145	18.9	145	0.69	0.69
Monthly average	−299	−37.4	389	39.7	389	1.85	1.85
All F = 800	0	0	235	29.9	235	1.12	1.12
Random walk	−55	−6.3	210	24.5	210	1.00	1.00

Data: Electricity.xlsx

From the table, we see that the forecasts based upon last year's figures are clearly more accurate. Indeed, some local utilities use this forecasting method to estimate customers' bills when no meter recordings are available. The *ME* and *MPE* values indicate that the forecasts were somewhat biased. Did the household deliberately try to conserve energy? Perhaps, but the lower figures in the summer suggest that the second year had a cooler summer; this is not something that could be reliably forecast at the beginning of January.

We have also included the median measures. Where forecasting errors are seriously asymmetric the medians (of our standard error measures) are usually a more informative measure than the mean. Although the sample size is small, there are several large absolute errors. Thus, while most of the measures are similar the *RMSE* is considerably larger than the *RMdSE*. ■

■ Example 2.8: Comparison of weather-forecasting errors

We may now use the measures we have examined to assess the performance of the various forecasts presented in Table 2.8. The results are given in Table 2.12. Note that we have used only those days for which all five forecasts are available so that comparisons are based on the same set of days. The *MPE* and the *MAPE* are not reported: they are not sensible measures in this case because the temperature scale has no natural origin and the observations can be negative. As is to be expected, the *MAE* and *RMSE* generally increase as the forecast horizon is extended; forecasts become less accurate as we get farther away from the event.

Table 2.12 Summary of Forecast Errors for Weather Data
(Values Computed Over June 6 to July 5, 2016)

Measure	Lead Time (days ahead): 30 observations				
	1	2	3	4	5
ME	0.53	0.67	0.90	1.27	1.43
MdE	0	1	0	1.5	1
MAE	2.07	3.07	3.97	4.53	4.63
MdAE	2	3	4	4	3
RMSE	2.79	4.02	5.03	5.53	5.92
RelMAE	0.46	0.46	0.66	1.01	0.97
U	0.44	0.50	0.67	0.92	1.03

Data: DC_weather_2.xlsx; calculations in Temperature_work.xlsx.

Theoretically, the *RMSE* for forecasts should increase as the lead time increases, although this characteristic may be violated in practice when a small number of observations is used to estimate the summary measures. Overall, the expert weather forecasts are clearly superior to those produced by a random walk for one to three days ahead. ■

2.8 Prediction Intervals

Thus far, our discussion has centered upon *point forecasts* — that is, future observations for which we report a single forecast value. For many purposes, managers seem to feel most comfortable with a single figure. However, such confidence in a single number is often misplaced.

Consider, for example, the generation of weekly sales forecasts. Our method might generate a forecast of 600 units for next week. The manager who plans for the sale of *exactly* 600 units and never considers the possibility of selling more or fewer units is naïve and will probably become an ex-manager fairly quickly! Why? Because the demand for most products is inherently variable! Some weeks will see sales below the forecast level, and some will see more. When sales fall short of the point forecast, the business will incur holding costs for unsold inventory or may have to destroy perishable stock. When sales would have exceeded the point forecasts, not only will the business lose sales, but disappointed customers may go elsewhere in the future. The best choice of inventory level will depend upon the relative costs of lost sales and excess inventory, which are described by the statistical distribution of possible sales — that is, the *predictive (prediction) distribution*. The selection of the best inventory level in this case is known as the *newsvendor problem*, because it was originally formulated in the context of selling newspapers. Our purpose here is not to dwell upon the details, which may be found in most management science texts, such as Winston and Albright (2016), but rather to emphasize the fundamental role that the predictive distribution plays in such cases.

If we know the (relative) magnitudes of the costs of lost sales and of excess inventory, we may define an overall cost function and then select the level of inventory to minimize cost. (See Exercise 2.16 for further details.)

Sometimes these costs are difficult to assess, and the manager will prefer to guarantee a certain level of service. For example, suppose that we wish to meet demand 95 percent of the time. We then need to add a *safety stock* to the point forecast to ensure that the probability of a stock-out is no more than 5 percent. There are two principal approaches to this issue, which we discuss in turn:

1. Assume that the predictive distribution for demand follows the normal law (although such an assumption is at best an approximation and needs to be checked.

2. Use an empirical error distribution based upon the errors already observed.

2.8.1 Using the Normal Distribution

If we assume that the standard deviation (SD) of the distribution is known and the distribution is normal, we may use the upper 95 percent point of the standard normal distribution.[9] (This value is 1.645, from Table A.1 in on-line Appendix A2; alternatively, we may use the Excel function NORM.INV.) So the appropriate stock level is

$$\text{Mean} + 1.645 \times (\text{SD}). \tag{2.22}$$

The mean in this case is the point forecast. Thus, if the point forecast is 600, with an associated SD of 25, the manager would stock $600 + 1.645 \times 25$, or 641 units to achieve the desired level of customer service.

Expression (2.22) is an example of a *one-sided prediction interval*: The probability is 0.95 that demand will be equal to or less than 641, under the assumption that our forecasting method is appropriate for the sales of that particular product. Typically, the SD is unknown and must be estimated from the sample that was used to generate the point forecast. In other words, we use the sample *RMSE* to estimate the SD.

---

9 The normal distribution is by far the most widely used distribution in the construction of prediction intervals. Hence, it is critical to check that the forecast errors are approximately normally distributed. (See on-line Appendix A6 for details on testing for normality.)

In many forecasting applications, employing two-sided prediction intervals is more common. Putting these ingredients together, we define the two-sided $100(1 - \alpha)$ percent prediction interval as

$$\text{Forecast} \pm z_{\alpha/2} \times (RMSE). \tag{2.23}$$

Here, $z_{\alpha/2}$ denotes the upper $100(1 - \alpha/2)$ percentage point of the normal distribution. At this point, although we are using the sample value of *RMSE* to estimate the SD, we are not making any allowance for this fact. In Section 5.2, we define prediction intervals more precisely.

2.8.2 Empirical Prediction Intervals

We first form the empirical distribution, derived from the observed errors. In Table 2.13, we consider the $n = 30$ observed errors for the weather forecast data and proceed as follows:

1. Rank the values from smallest to largest.

2. Assign the percentage value $100(i - 0.5)/n$ to the ith smallest observation; in this case, the percentage values are $100/60=1.67$, $300/60=5.0$, and so on.

3. Form the two-sided prediction interval by selecting an appropriate pair of percentage points. In the example, 80 percent intervals would be a natural choice using the average of the third and fourth smallest (largest) observed errors.

The empirical prediction distribution is then defined as the error distribution shifted to have the mean equal to the point forecast.

■ Example 2.9: Evaluation of prediction intervals

Table 2.13 shows the ordered error terms based upon the forecasts made one to five days ahead. Then, each of the normal ($z = 1.282$) and empirical approaches is used to create the 80 percent prediction intervals. The normal intervals use the means and standard deviations for the 30 errors for each set of forecasts. The empirical intervals use 10th percentile (average of the third and fourth observations) and 90th percentile (average of 27th and 28th observations) to provide the 80 percent coverage. In this example, the two sets of intervals are very similar, but the differences are more pronounced with higher probabilities of coverage: see Exercise 2.13. By construction, the normal intervals are symmetric about the mean whereas the empirical intervals need not be. ■

2.8.3 Prediction Intervals: Summary

The principal reason for constructing prediction intervals is to provide an indication of the reliability of the point forecasts. The limits so derived are sometimes expressed as *optimistic* and *pessimistic* forecasts. Such nomenclature is useful as a way of presenting the concept to others, but a precise formulation of the limits should be used, rather than a vague assessment of extreme outcomes. Finally, note that prediction intervals may be used for retrospective analysis as here, but their primary purpose is to provide assessments of uncertainty for future events.

A detailed discussion of prediction intervals must await the formal development of forecasting models in later chapters. The reader who wishes to preview these discussions should consult Sections 5.2 and 6.7.

Table 2.13 Comparison of 80 Percent Prediction Intervals for Weather Data

Percentile	Errors				
	1-Day	2-Day	3-Day	4-Day	5-Day
1.67	−3	−8	−11	−12	−12
5.00	−3	−5	−7	−11	−10
8.33	−3	−5	−6	−7	−8
11.67	−3	−4	−6	−4	−4
15.00	−2	−4	−4	−4	−2
...	...	...	...	...	...
85.00	2	4	6	7	8
88.33	3	4	7	7	8
91.67	5	7	7	7	9
95.00	6	9	8	8	10
98.33	9	10	11	9	13
Mean: N = 30 observations	0.53	0.67	0.90	1.27	1.43
SD	2.79	4.03	5.03	5.48	5.85
80 Percent Intervals					
Empirical					
Lower	−3.00	−4.50	−6.00	−5.50	−6.00
Upper	4.00	5.50	7.00	7.00	8.50
Normal					
Lower	−3.04	−4.50	−5.55	−5.75	−6.06
Upper	4.11	5.83	7.35	8.29	8.93

2.9 Basic Principles of Data Analysis

This book, like most other texts on business forecasting, tends to devote most of its space to discussions of forecasting methods and underlying statistical models. However, if the groundwork is not properly laid, the best methods in the world cannot save the forecaster from the effects of poor data selection and inadequate preparation. The volume[10] edited by Scott Armstrong (2001) is particularly valuable in suggesting key principles that underlie good forecasting practice. We make extensive use of this source, among others, in formulating our own sets of principles at the end of each chapter. We number these principles in the order discussed within each chapter to facilitate cross-referencing.

[2.1] Ensure that the data match the forecasting situation.
Once the underlying purpose of the forecasting exercise has been specified, the ideal data set can be identified. However, the ideal may not be available for many reasons. For example, macroeconomic data are published with a lag that may be of several months' duration and, even then, may be published only as a preliminary estimate. The forecaster needs to examine the available data with respect to the end use to which the forecasts will be put and to make sure that a match exists.

---

10 For the latest developments see *www.forecastingprinciples.com.*

[2.2] Clean the data.

Data may be omitted, wrongly recorded, or affected by changing definitions. Adjustments should be made where necessary, but a record of such changes should be kept and made available to users of the forecasts. Data cleaning can be very time consuming, although the plots and numerical summaries described in this chapter will go a long way toward identifying data errors. Failure to clean the data can lead to the familiar situation of "Garbage in, garbage out."

[2.3] Use transformations as required by the nature of the data.

We examined differences, growth rates, and log transforms in Section 2.6. The forecaster needs to consider whether the original measurements provide the most appropriate framework for generating forecasts in the problem context or whether some form of transformation is desirable. The basic pattern of no growth (use original data), linear growth (use differences), or relative growth (use growth rates or log differences) will often provide adequate guidance.

[2.4] Use graphical representations of the data. Highlight key events.

As we have seen in Sections 2.2 and 2.3, plotting the data can provide a variety of insights and may also suggest suitable transformations or adjustments. Graphical analysis should always be the first step in developing forecasting procedures, even if applied to only a small sample from a larger set of series.

[2.5] Adjust for unsystematic past events (e.g., outliers).

Data may be affected by the weather, political upheavals, supply shortages, or other events. Such factors need to be taken into account when clear reasons can be identified for the unusual observations. The forecaster should resist the temptation to give the data a "face-lift" by overadjusting for every minor event.

[2.6] Adjust for systematic events (e.g., seasonal effects).

Systematic events such as weekends, public holidays, and seasonal patterns can affect the observed process and must be taken into account. We discuss these adjustments in Chapter 9.

[2.7] Use error measures that adjust for scale in the data when comparing across series.

When comparing forecasts for a single series, scale-dependent measures such as the *MAE* or *RMSE* are useful. However, when making a comparison across different series, use scale-free measures, such as the *MAPE* (if appropriate), or relative error measures, such as the *RelMAE* or *MASE*.

[2.8] Use multiple measures of performance based upon the observed forecast errors.

If forecasters are able to use different measures to compare performance, they can better assess performance relative to their particular needs. Multiple measures allow users to focus on those attributes of a forecasting procedure which they deem most relevant and also to check on the robustness of their conclusions. For example, one user may be interested in relative reduction in accuracy compared to a more complex method. Another may wish to avoid large errors, in which case the *RMSE* becomes most relevant, because it depends upon squared errors. A third may avoid the *RMSE* purely because it gives such weight to large errors. Instead a median measure might be used.

Summary

In this chapter, we have described the basic tools of data analysis. In particular, we examined the following topics:

- Scatterplots and time series plots for preliminary analysis of the data (Sections 2.2 and 2.3).
- Basic summary statistics for individual variables (Section 2.4).
- Correlation as a measure of association for cross-sectional data (Section 2.5).
- Transformations of the data (Section 2.6).
- Measures of forecasting accuracy (Section 2.7).
- Prediction intervals as a measure of the uncertainty related to point forecasts (Section 2.8).

Finally, in Section 2.9, we briefly examined some of the underlying principles that should be kept in mind when starting out on a forecasting exercise.

Exercises

Time series data in books do not necessarily reflect the latest figures. When it is appropriate, readers are encouraged to go to the original sources quoted in the text and download the latest figures. Readers may then use the extended data sets to redo the exercises, and the two sets of results may be compared.

2.1 The average monthly temperatures for Boulder, Colorado, from January 1991 to December 2015 are given in *Boulder_2.xlsx* (*Source:* U.S. Department of Commerce, National Oceanic and Atmospheric Administration). Plot the time series, and create a seasonal plot for the last four years of the series. Comment on your results.

2.2 The monthly figures for US Retail Sales, from January 2001 to December 2015 are given in *US_retail_sales_2.xlsx*. Plot the time series, and create a seasonal plot for the last four years of the series. Comment on your results.

2.3 The following table contains data on railroad passenger injuries in the United States (*Rail_safety.xlsx*) from 1991 to 2007. "Injuries" represents the number of persons injured in the given year, "train-miles" denotes the millions of miles traveled by trains, and the final column is the ratio that defines the number of injuries per 100 million miles traveled.

a. Create a scatterplot for injuries against train-miles.

b. Plot each of the three time series.

c. Does the level of injuries appear to be changing over time? If so, in what way?

Year	Injuries	Train-Miles	Injuries per Train-Mile
1990	473	72	657
1991	382	74	516
1992	411	74	555
.....	....	....	....
2005	935	90	1,040
2006	761	92	828
2007	938	95	990

Source: U.S. Department of Transportation, Federal Railroad Administration

2.4   An investor has a portfolio consisting of holdings in nine stocks (*Returns.xlsx*). The end-of-year returns over the previous year are, in increasing order,

$$-5.0, -3.7, 0.9, 4.8, 6.2, 8.9, 11.2, 18.6, 25.4.$$

   a. Compute the summary statistics (mean, median, *MAD*, and *S*).

   b. Just before the close of business in the last trading session of the year, the company that had reported the 5.0 percent drop declares bankruptcy, so the return becomes −100 percent. Recompute the results, and comment on your findings.

   c. Are simple summary statistics relevant to this investor? How would you modify the calculations, if at all?

2.5   For the temperature data (*Boulder_2.xlsx*) in Exercise 2.1, compute the summary statistics (mean, median, *MAD*, and *S*) overall and for each month. Comment on your results. Does it make sense to compute summary statistics across all values, rather than month by month? Explain why or why not.

2.6   Compute the summary statistics (mean, median, *MAD*, and *S*) for each of the variables listed in Exercise 2.3 (*Rail_safety.xlsx*). Are these numbers a sensible summary of safety conditions? Explain why or why not.

2.7   Calculate the correlations among the three variables listed in Exercise 2.3. Also compute the correlation of each variable with time. Interpret the results.

2.8   Calculate the correlation between the monthly values of electricity consumption (*Electricity.xlsx*) for year 1 (listed as forecasts in the table) and year 2 (actual) in Table 2.10A. Interpret the result.

2.9   Compute the correlations among the eight variables listed in Table 2.3 using the data provided in *German_forecasts.xlsx*. Identify those coefficients that are statistically significant (different from zero) and discuss why such associations might exist.

2.10 The quarterly revenues and percentage growth figures for Netflix are given in *Netflix_2.xlsx* and illustrated in the table that follows. Produce a time series plot for each of these variables.

   a. Are the mean and median useful in this case? Explain why or why not.

   b. Calculate the growth rate for each quarter relative to the same quarter in the previous year; that is, for quarter 1 of 2001, we have 100(17.06 − 5.17)/5.17 = 230. After allowing for the start-up phase of the company, do sales show signs of leveling off?

Year	Quarter	Quarterly Revenues	Growth: Absolute	Growth: Percent
2000	1	5.17	•	•
2000	2	7.15	1.97	38.1
2000	3	10.18	3.04	42.5
2000	4	13.39	3.21	31.5
2001	1	17.06	3.67	27.4
....	....	....	....	....
2015	1	1573.13	88.40	6.0
2015	2	1644.69	71.56	4.5
2015	3	1738.36	93.67	5.7
2015	4	1823.33	84.97	4.9

Data: Netflix_2.xlsx; Source: Netflix Annual Reports

2.11 Use the data in *Boulder_2.xlsx* to generate forecasts 12-months ahead; that is, the forecast corresponds to the value for the same month in the previous year, for 1992–2015. Compute the *ME*, *MAE*, *RMSE*, and *RelMAE* for these forecasts as well as the corresponding medians. Repeat the analysis, this time using the monthly averages calculated in Exercise 2.5.

   a. Which set of forecasts appears to work better?

   b. Is the comparison fair? (*Hint:* What do you know and when do you know it?)

   c. Do you see any consistent differences between the mean and median error measures?

   d. What conclusions would you draw about the choice between the two methods?

2.12 The average temperatures (in °F) on the day (January 20) of the president's inauguration in Washington, DC (*Inauguration.xlsx*) are shown in the following table:

Year	1937	1941	1945	1949	1953	1957	1961	1965	1969
Temperature	33	29	35	38	49	44	22	38	35
Year	1973	1977	1981	1985	1989	1993	1997	2001	2005
Temperature	42	28	55	7	51	40	34	35	35

Source: www.inaugural.senate.gov/swearing-in/weather

   a. Summarize the data numerically and graphically.

   b. Create a 95 percent prediction interval for the inaugurations of President Obama in 2009 and in 2013

   c. The actual values were 28° and 40°. Does that come as a surprise, given the width of the prediction interval?

2.13 Compute the 90 percent and 95 percent prediction intervals for the weather data (*DC_weather_2.xlsx*), using Table 2.13. How do the normal and empirical intervals compare at these higher levels of coverage?

2.14 Compute 95 percent prediction intervals for the 12-month forecasts for temperature (*Boulder_2.xlsx*) generated in Exercise 2.11, using (a) the normal distribution with the estimated *RMSE* and (b) the empirical distribution with all the observed errors. Find the percentage of the observations that lies outside the limits in each case. Are these figures close to 95 percent?

2.15 Use the data in Table 2.10A (*Electricity.xlsx*) to generate forecasts for electricity consumption for the household in year 3, based on the end of year 2 as the forecast origin. Use the normal distribution to generate 90 percent prediction intervals for these forecasts.

2.16 Following the discussion in Section 2.8 on inventory management, construct a cost function, assuming that the cost of lost sales is C times that of the cost of holding unsold stock. Past records show that the prediction distribution for future sales is

$$P\,(\text{sales} = x) = \frac{1}{21}, x = 90, 91, \dots, 109, 110$$

$$P\,(\text{sales} = x) = 0,\ otherwise.$$

Find the optimal inventory level, in the sense of minimizing overall cost, when $C = 1$ and when $C = 3$. What should the safety stock be to guarantee a service level of 90 percent?

Minicases

Minicase 2.1 Baseball Salaries

As part of a project with the Graphics Section of the American Statistical Association, Dr. Lorraine Denby compiled data on baseball salaries. We focus on the data that relate only to pitchers and their salaries for the 1986 season. The data are included in the file *Baseball.xlsx*, and we wish to acknowledge StatLib of the Department of Statistics at Carnegie Mellon University for access to these data.

1. Summarize the data on salaries, using the measures discussed in Section 2.4.

2. The data file also includes information on the number of years a player has spent in the major leagues, his career earned run average (ERA), the number of innings he has pitched, and his career wins and losses. Generate scatterplots of these variables with salary, and examine their correlations.

3. Older players often accept short-term lower paid contracts toward the end of their playing careers. To allow for this feature of the data, eliminate players with 12 or more years of experience from the data set and rerun the analysis.

Summarize your conclusions.

MiniCase 2.2 Whither Walmart?

As Walmart has grown, its stock has proved to be a solid investment in both good times and bad. To determine whether a future investment in the stock is worthwhile, we need to consider the plans the company has for future growth. The annual reports provide a considerable amount of information (see *http://walmartstores.com/investors/*).

One aspect of Walmart's future strategy is its investment in different types of retail outlets, known as Walmart stores, Superstores, and Sam's Clubs. As the name suggests, the Superstore may be thought of as an upgrade of the Walmart store, being generally larger in size and carrying a wider range of merchandise. The Sam's Clubs are more oriented toward bulk purchasing. The spreadsheet *Walmart_2.xlsx* provides annual data on the numbers of each type of store in the United States on March 31, the end of the fiscal year, for the period 1995–2015.

Another feature of interest to the potential investor is the growth in sales over time. The spreadsheet also provides quarterly sales figures for the period from the first quarter of 2003 through the fourth quarter of 2015. The layout of the spreadsheet *Walmart_2.xlsx* is illustrated below:

Year	Walmart Stores	Super Stores	Sam's Club	Year	Quarter	Sales ($ billion)
1995	2176	154	453	2003	1	56.7
1996	2218	255	470	2003	2	62.6
1997	1960	344	436	2003	3	62.5
...	...	...	...	...	...	...
2013	508	3288	632	2015	2	119.3
2014	470	3407	647	2015	3	116.6
2015	442	3465	655	2015	4	128.7

Data: *Walmart_2.xlsx; Source:* Walmart annual reports, 1995–2015.

1. Summarize the changes in types of store over the period. What does your summary say about Walmart's plans for the future?

2. Compute the growth in sales over time. Is there any evidence that the rate of growth is slowing or increasing?

MiniCase 2.3 Economic Recessions

The following data summarize the length of each recession in the period 1929–2015, as determined by the National Bureau of Economic Research (NBER):

Onset	Duration	End	Gap
August 1929	43	February 1933	50
May 1937	13	May 1938	80
February 1945	8	September 1945	37
November 1948	11	September 1949	45
July 1953	10	April 1954	39
August 1957	8	March 1958	24
April 1960	10	January 1961	106
December 1969	11	October 1970	36
November 1973	16	February 1975	58
January 1980	6	June 1980	12
July 1981	16	October 1982	92
July 1990	8	February 1991	120
March 2001	8	October 2001	73
December 2007	19	June 2009	

Source: National Bureau of Economic Research
Data: Recessions.xlsx

Note that the NBER defines the end of a recession as the time at which the national economy shows an upturn. It does not mean that the economy has recovered to its previous level of activity. First update the data if needed to include any recession that has commenced since June 2017.

1. Calculate the average length of a recession, and provide a 95 percent confidence interval for this quantity. Interpret the result.

2. Calculate the average time between recessions, and provide a 95 percent confidence interval for this quantity. Interpret the result.

3. Is there any correlation between the length of a recession and the period of growth immediately preceding it, referred to as "Gap" in the table?

4. Is there any correlation between the length of a recession and the period of growth immediately following a recession?

5. Comment on your findings.

References

Anderson, D. R., Sweeney, D. J., Williams, T. A., Camm, J. D. and Cochran, J. J. (2014), *Statistics for Business and Economics*, 12th ed. Mason, OH: Cengage Learning.

Armstrong, J. S. (2001). *Principles of Forecasting: A Handbook for Researchers and Practitioners.* Boston: Kluwer.

Hyndman, R. J., and Koehler, A. B. (2006). Another look at measures of forecast accuracy. *International Journal of Forecasting*, 22, 679–688.

Müller-Dröge, H-C., Sinclair, T. M. and Stekler, H. O. (2016). Evaluating forecasts of a vector of variables: A German forecasting competition. *Journal of Forecasting*, 35, 495–505.

Winston, W., and Albright, S. C. (2015). *Practical Management Science*, 5th ed. Mason, OH: Cengage Learning.

CHAPTER 3

Forecasting Non-Seasonal Series

Table of Contents

What's past is prologue.

— Shakespeare, *The Tempest*

Introduction

Forecasts may be based upon subjective judgmental assessments, numerical procedures, or some combination of the two. Judgmental procedures are valuable when we have no track record on which to base our forecasts or when circumstances appear to have undergone fundamental changes. However, such forecasts are often time consuming to generate and may be subject to a variety of conscious or unconscious biases. Often, we find that even simple analyses of available data can perform as well as judgmental procedures and that they may be much quicker and less expensive to produce. Careful subjective adjustments to quantitative forecasts may ultimately be the best combination, but we first need to develop an effective arsenal of quantitative methods. Accordingly, we now focus on quantitative methods and defer consideration of judgmental methods to Chapter 11.

We begin in Section 3.1 by drawing a distinction between *methods* and *models,* a distinction that is often ignored but that has important implications for how we approach a forecasting task. Section 3.2 then provides a general overview of extrapolation methods before we move on in Section 3.3 to the use of different weighted means as forecasts. Our aim is to balance the following potentially conflicting directives:

- Use all the data.
- Pay more attention to the recent past.

Or, to restate, "All data are important, but recent data are even more important." These ideas lead directly to the use of time-dependent averages — notably, simple moving averages and exponentially weighted moving averages (or exponential smoothing, as it is usually called).

When there are clear trends in the data, a simple averaging procedure cannot capture the trend and therefore will not work. As a consequence, we must extend our methods to incorporate such systematic movements, the subject of Section 3.4. Sections 3.5 and 3.6 consider damped smoothing methods and various other approaches to forecasting trends. Section 3.7 considers transformations of series to improve the underlying assumptions. Section 3.8 provides prediction intervals for one-step-ahead forecasts, relying implicitly upon models we develop fully in Chapter 5. Section 3.9 briefly discusses the issue of method selection, a topic that is explored more fully in Section 5.3. Finally, in Section 3.10 we explore some of the principles that underlie the use of simple extrapolation methods.

Software

Good software should provide for the automatic operation of a variety of exponential smoothing methods and ways to select from among them. We summarize some of the alternatives in Appendix B, located on the textbook companion site. At this stage, we merely note that the level of support for exponential smoothing methods varies considerably across different software providers. For example, Excel 2010 includes only simple exponential smoothing, and even then its application is far from automatic. However, exponential smoothing in Excel 2016 contains many more features. To achieve some consistency in the numerical results obtained from these methods, we provide an Excel macro, the Exponential Smoothing Macro (ESM), to carry out the estimation and forecasting procedures. The macro is available on the book's website, which also provides a User's Manual. We also provide scripts in R to carry out the smoothing procedures.

3.1 Method or Model?

The development of various quantitative approaches to forecasting occupies the next eight chapters, as we move steadily from heuristic forecasting methods to procedures that rely upon careful modeling of the process being studied. One of the pleasant discoveries we make along the way is that various heuristic forecasting methods often match up to specific statistical models of the data, even though this property was not known at the time the methods were first proposed. As in other areas of research, we often proceed by discovering what works and then try to figure out why. This chapter concentrates on what works, and we emphasize the distinction in our terminology in the text box below, even though the difference between the two terms (method and model) is sometimes ignored in discussions of forecasting.

METHOD OR MODEL

A *forecast function* is an equation for calculating the forecasts over the forecast horizon.

A *forecasting method* is a (numerical) procedure for generating a forecast. It involves the direct use of a forecast function. When such methods are not based upon an underlying statistical model, they are termed *heuristic*.

A *statistical (forecasting) model provides an approximate* description of the data-generating process. The corresponding forecasting function may then be derived from the statistical model. A statistical model is a necessary foundation for the construction of prediction intervals.

3.1.1 A Forecasting Model

We might formulate a simple trend model for a time series as

$$Y_t = \beta_0 + \beta_1 t + \varepsilon_t, \tag{3.1}$$

where Y_t denotes the time series being studied; β_0 and β_1 are the level and slope (or trend) *parameters,* respectively; and ε_t denotes a random error term corresponding to the part of the series that remains once the linear trend has been removed. If we make appropriate assumptions about the nature of the error term, we can estimate the unknown parameters β_0 and β_1. The resulting estimates are typically written as b_0 and b_1. Thus, the forecasting *model* gives rise to a forecast *function,* whose estimated version may be written as

$$F_t = b_0 + b_1 t, \tag{3.2}$$

where F_t denotes a forecast for time period t, b_0 is the (estimated) *intercept* that represents the value at time zero, and b_1 is the (estimated) *slope*, which represents the increase in forecast values from one period to the next.

Equation (3.2) is the forecast function, and the statistical model given by equation (3.1) enables the construction of prediction intervals. If we were to proceed directly to employ equation (3.2) for forecasting without such a model, we would indeed have a forecasting method, but one that suffered from two drawbacks:

1. It lacks a formal basis for choosing values for the parameters, although various ad hoc procedures could be developed.

2. There is no way to assess the uncertainty inherent in the forecasts.

Of course, if you choose a poor statistical model, you will get poor forecasts and poor assessments of uncertainty — maybe not always, but on average.

In this chapter, we focus primarily on methods. These methods will be underpinned by the statistical models we introduce in Chapter 5. On the basis of these models, we are able to consider prediction intervals, which we do in Section 3.8.

3.2 Extrapolative Methods

Extrapolative methods of forecasting focus on a single time series to identify past patterns in the historical data. These patterns are then extrapolated to map out the likely future path of the series. The overall structure is shown in Figure 3.1.

Figure 3.1 is to be interpreted as follows: We denote the particular series of interest (e.g., weekly sales) by Y. We have recorded the observations $Y_1, Y_2, \ldots, Y_t$ over t *weeks*, which represent all the data currently available. Our interest lies in forecasting sales over the next h weeks, known as the *forecasting horizon*; that is, we are interested in providing forecasts for future sales, denoted by $Y_{t+1}, Y_{t+2}, \ldots, Y_{t+h}$.

Figure 3.1 General Framework for Forecasting with a Single Series

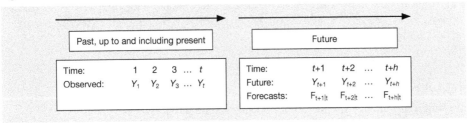

Although we use the same notation to describe past, present, and future, there is a key difference: The past and present values are already observed, whereas the future Ys represent random variables; that is, we cannot write down their values, but we can describe them in terms of a set of possible values and the associated probabilities, as discussed in Appendix A to Chapter 1. This concept is illustrated in Figure 3.2, which shows a time series observed for periods 1-12, but to be forecast for periods 13-20, typically with increasing uncertainty in the forecast as the horizon increases.

Figure 3.2 Plot of Actual Sales for Periods 1–12 and a Range of Possible Values for Periods 13–20

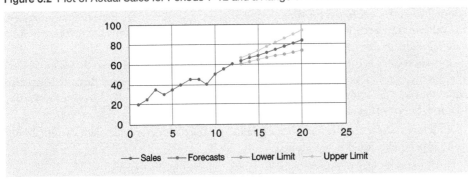

The (point) forecasts for future sales, shown in the diagram, are all made at time t (= 12 here), known as the *forecast origin*, so the first forecast (for period 13) will be made one step ahead, the second (for period 14) two steps ahead, and so on. When the results for period 13 are known, that period becomes the new forecast origin and we can compute a new forecast for period 14, which will then be only one step ahead. We need to distinguish these different forecasts, as illustrated in Table 3.1. Suppose that the initial forecast origin is week 12 and we wish to make forecasts in week 12 for weeks 13, 14, and 15. Then in week 13 we would make a new set of forecasts for weeks 14 and 15; finally, in week 14 we would make a forecast for week 15. A quick look at the table indicates that we are considering six forecasts, all of which are based upon different information or relate to different time periods. As introduced in Chapter 2 (Section 2.7.1 and Table 2.7), the notation F_{14} (2) refers to the forecast for Y_{14} made two weeks earlier in week 12. The subscript always indicates which time period is being forecast, and the term in parentheses records how far ahead the forecast is made (the forecast horizon). When no ambiguity arises, we will use F_{t+1} to represent the one-step-ahead forecast $F_{t+1}(1)$ so that $F_{13} = F_{13}(1)$ and so on.

This notation may seem a bit elaborate, but it is important to know both the forecast origin and for how many periods ahead the forecast is being made. That is, the term "forecast for period 15" is ambiguous until we know when the forecast was made, and it would be impossible to evaluate the forecast's accuracy without that information.

Table 3.1 Notation for Forecasts Made at Different Forecast Origins and for Varying Forecast Horizons

Forecast Origin	12	13	14
Forecast for period 13	$F_{13}(1)$		
Forecast for period 14	$F_{14}(2)$	$F_{14}(1)$	
Forecast for period 15	$F_{15}(3)$	$F_{15}(2)$	$F_{15}(1)$

3.2.1 Extrapolation of the Mean Value

Figure 3.3 (previously shown as Figure 2.1) shows the weekly sales figures for 62 weeks of a product line for a major U.S. manufacturer, which we continue to refer to as WFJ Sales. The series starts at the beginning of the calendar year, picks up after 12 weeks or so, and then stabilizes until a surge in the last few weeks of the year, before dropping back at the beginning of the next year (but at a higher level than a year earlier).

Suppose we traveled back in time and we were back at midyear (week 26) and wished to forecast sales for the next few weeks. A straightforward approach would be to take the average of the 26 weeks to date, which we write as

$$\bar{Y}(26) = \sum_{i=1}^{26} Y_i / 26 = 30102.$$

The bar denotes the operation of taking the mean over the 26 observations. Inspection of Figure 3.4, which shows the first 26 weeks of the series and the mean level, suggests that such a value would be too low a forecast. Somehow, we need to give less weight to the first part of the series and focus on the more recent values.

Figure 3.3 Time Series Plot of Weekly Sales for WFJ

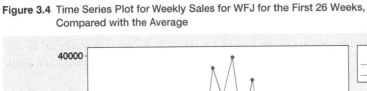

Data: WFJ_sales.xlsx

LOCALLY CONSTANT FORECASTS

A series is locally constant if the mean level changes gradually over time but there is no reason to expect a systematic increase or decrease in the future. The forecast function is

$$F_{t+h}(h) = \text{constant};$$

that is, the plot showing future forecasts is a horizontal line. When a new observation becomes available, the constant is updated.

Figure 3.4 Time Series Plot for Weekly Sales for WFJ for the First 26 Weeks, Compared with the Average

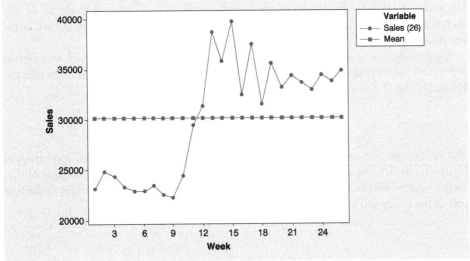

3.2.2 Use of Moving Averages

One way to proceed is to use an average of the last few values in the series. In general, we may use the last K terms of the series and update each time to include only the latest K values. We refer to the result as a moving average, which contains K terms, the most recent of which is observation t (the most recent available observation):

MOVING AVERAGE

The *moving average* of order K evaluated at time t is denoted by $MA(t\,|\,K)$:

$$MA(t\,|\,K) = \frac{Y_t + Y_{t-1} + \cdots + Y_{t-K+1}}{K}$$

We then forecast the time series at time $(t+1)$, using the formula

$$F_{t+1} = MA(t\,|\,K).$$

Suppose now that we decide to use a three-week moving average, or $K = 3$. The first such average would be $MA(3|3) = (23056 + 24817 + 24300)/3 = 24058$ as shown in Table 3.2. When a new observation becomes available, the new moving average is $MA(4|3) = (24817 + 24300 + 23242)/3 = 24120$, and so on. Each time, we drop the oldest observation and enter the new one; a slightly quicker way of doing the calculation is to write

$$New\ average = MA(t+1|K) = Old\ average + \frac{(New\ value - Oldest\ value)}{K} \tag{3.3}$$

$$= MA(t\,|\,K) + \frac{Y_{t+1} - Y_{t+1-K}}{K}$$

Table 3.2 Calculation of Moving Averages for WFJ Sales

Week	WFJ Sales	MA (3)	MA (7)
1	23056		
2	24817		
3	24300		
4	23242	24058	
5	22862	24120	
6	22863	23468	
7	23391	22989	
8	22469	23039	23504
9	22241	22908	23421
10	24367	22701	23053
...	...	...	...
...	...	...	...
25	33777	33652	33646
26	34849	33701	33975

Data: WFJ_sales_MA.xlsx

A variation of this updating mechanism will feature prominently in later developments. But now, how should we choose K? A simple comparison provides an insight. Table 3.2

illustrates the calculations for $K = 3$ and for $K = 7$, which we respectively refer to as MA(3) and MA(7), and the two averages and the original series are plotted in Figure 3.5. The first forecast that we can calculate for MA(3) is for week 4, which uses the first three observations. This forecast corresponds to the one-step-ahead forecast for week 4 made in week 3. The first forecast for MA(7) is for period 8.

Figure 3.5 WFJ Sales for First 26 Weeks, with Moving Averages of Lengths 3 and 7

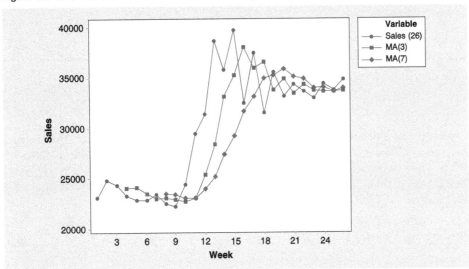

From Figure 3.5, we see that the three-term moving average adapts more quickly to movements in the series, but the seven-term average produces a greater degree of smoothing. To decide which method is preferable, we need to evaluate forecast performance, as discussed in Chapter 2. However, before we do so, we introduce another form of adaptive average.

3.3 Simple Exponential Smoothing

The simple moving average, introduced in the previous section, suffers from two drawbacks. First, the averaging process seems rather capricious in that an observation is given full weight one period and none the next, when it reaches the Kth, or "oldest," position. Second, if we use a large number of terms, we have to keep all the past values until they are finally removed from the average. This second objection is now of minor importance in practice, although it used to be critical when computer storage was much more limited or when forecasts had to be updated by hand. Ultimately, any method should be judged by its performance in forecasting, although it would be nice to have a technique that adjusted more smoothly over time. Such a method was introduced by Robert G. Brown (often referred to as the father of exponential smoothing), whose 1959 and 1963 books on forecasting are justly recognized as classics.

When a new observation is recorded, the new sample mean of the available data may be expressed as

$$New\ mean = Old\ mean + \frac{(Difference\ between\ new\ observation\ and\ old\ mean)}{New\ sample\ size\ (= old\ sample\ size\ +1)}.$$

We can see from this expression that we need only record the previous mean and the latest value, a useful feature when updating anything from sales reports to batting averages. However, as the series length increases, the mean becomes increasingly unresponsive to fluctuations in recent values because each observation has weight equal to 1/(sample size). The update of the simple MA, given in equation (3.3), avoided this problem and maintained a constant coefficient *(1/K)*, but at the cost of dumping the oldest observation completely. The aim is to construct some kind of average that describes the recent behavior of the series, but in a way that adjusts smoothly over time. We refer to such an average as the *local (mean) level*. If we use too many observations, the estimated level may be out of date, whereas if we use too few, the estimate may be inaccurate and jump around a lot. So, instead of discussing the issue in terms of a moving average, we refer to the local level at time *t* as L_t and resolve these two conflicting elements by using an updating relationship of the form

$$L_{t+1} = L_t + \alpha(Y_{t+1} - L_t). \tag{3.4}$$

That is,

New local level = Old local level + $\alpha \times$ (Difference between new observation and old local level).

EXPONENTIAL SMOOTHING

The basic equation for *exponential smoothing* is

$$L_{t+1} = L_t + \alpha(Y_{t+1} - L_t) = L_t + \alpha e_{t+1}$$

where $e_{t+1} = Y_{t+1} - F_t$ denotes the forecast error for period *t+1*.

The process involves comparing the latest observation with the previous weighted average and making a proportional adjustment, governed by the coefficient α, known as the *smoothing constant*. By convention, we constrain the coefficient to the range $0 < \alpha < 1$ so that only a part of the difference between the old level and the new observation is used in the updating. Inspection of equation (3.4) indicates that this form of average provides a constant weight (α) to the latest observation. Further, the updates require only the latest observation and the previous local level. The average in equation (3.4) is known as an *exponentially weighted moving average* (EWMA), and we now explain the origin of that name. If we start with the expression for period *(t + 1)* and substitute into it the comparable expression for time *t,* we obtain

$$L_{t+1} = (1 - \alpha)L_t + \alpha Y_{t+1} = (1 - \alpha)[(1 - \alpha)L_{t-1} + \alpha Y_t] + \alpha Y_{t+1}$$

$$= (1 - \alpha)^2 L_{t-1} + \alpha[(1 - \alpha)Y_t + Y_{t+1}].$$

Continuing to substitute the earlier smoothed means, we eventually arrive back at the start of the series with the expression

$$L_{t+1} = (1 - \alpha)^{t+1}L_0 + \alpha[Y_{t+1} + (1 - \alpha)Y_t + (1 - \alpha)^2 Y_{t-1} + \cdots + (1 - \alpha)^t Y_1]. \tag{3.5}$$

The right-hand side contains a weighted average of the observations, and the weights $\{\alpha, \alpha(1 - \alpha), \alpha(1 - \alpha)^2, ...\}$ decay steadily over time. If the weights are plotted against time and a smooth curve is drawn through the values that curve is exponential — hence the name "exponentially weighted moving average." The decay is slower for small values of α, so we can control the rate of decay by choosing α appropriately. Figure 3.6 illustrates the decay rates for $\alpha = 0.5$ and $\alpha = 0.2$. At $\alpha = 0.5$, over 99 percent of the weight falls on the first seven observations whereas the comparable figure for $\alpha = 0.2$ is only 79 percent. As α gets smaller, so does this percentage. Thus, just as we could choose K to control the rate of adjustment of the simple moving average, we may select α to achieve similar adjustments for the EWMA.

Caution: Equation (3.5) depends on a starting value L_0. When t and α are both small, the weight attached to the starting value may be high, as seen in the following table (in these circumstances, it is recommended that more sophisticated software be used to estimate the optimal value for the starting level):

α	t	Weight on Starting Value after t periods
0.50	10	0.001
	30	0.000
0.20	10	0.107
	30	0.001
0.05	10	0.599
	30	0.215

Figure 3.6 Weights on Different Lags in an Exponentially Weighted Moving Average

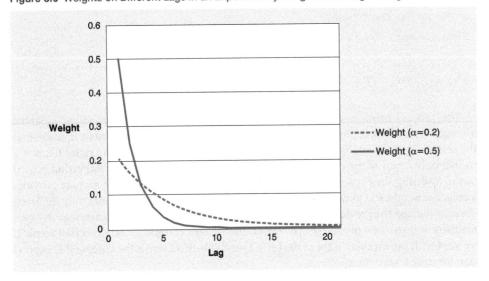

3.3.1 Forecasting with the EWMA, or Simple Exponential Smoothing

The next step is to convert these averages into forecasts. When we use the EWMA for forecasting, we refer to the method as *simple* (or *single*) *exponential smoothing* (SES).[1] The underlying logic of this process is that, although we believe that the process will fluctu-

---

1 The term is perhaps unfortunate, because "smoothing" is an overused qualifier in time series analysis. Nonetheless, "SES" is in common usage.

ate, we have no evidence to suggest that it is likely to go up, go down, or stay the same. In such circumstances, the average level for future observations is best forecast by our current estimate of the local level. Thus, forecasts made at time t for all future time periods will be the same; that is,

$$F_{t+1}(1) = F_{t+2}(2) = \cdots = F_{t+h}(h) = L_t. \tag{3.6}$$

At first sight, this equation may seem rather strange, but think of the case of stock prices. The latest price is assumed to capture all the relevant (public!) information about the value of the stock, so the current price is the best forecast for all future periods until new information comes along. We must recognize that, as the lead time increases, the forecasts will usually become less accurate.

Equation (3.4) may now be written in the terms of the forecasts as

$$F_{t+1}(1) = F_t(1) + \alpha[Y_t - F_t(1)]. \tag{3.7}$$

That is, the new one-step-ahead forecast is the previous forecast, partially adjusted by the amount the previous forecast was in error. Because this equation considers only the one-step-ahead forecasts, it may also be written as

$$F_{t+1} = F_t + \alpha(Y_t - F_t). \tag{3.8}$$

To set up the calculations that are implicit in the equation, we need to specify the value for α, as well as a starting value $F_1 = L_0$. We have already discussed the effects of different α values. Earlier literature recommended a choice in the range $0.1 < \alpha < 0.3$ to allow the EWMA to change relatively slowly, and values from that range often work well for series such as sales figures. However, relying on an arbitrary preset smoothing parameter is not advisable. Most computer programs now provide efficient estimates of the smoothing constant, based upon minimizing the mean squared error for the estimation sample (or, equivalently, the *RMSE*):

$$\text{MSE} = \frac{\sum\limits_{i=1}^{t} (Y_i - F_i)^2}{t}. \tag{3.9}$$

MSE is computed with the use of the first t values, which constitute the *estimation*, or *fitting*, sample. Forecasts may then be generated for time periods $t + 1, t + 2 \ldots$.

CHOOSING THE SMOOTHING PARAMETER

When forecasting with exponential smoothing, estimate the optimal smoothing parameters, rather than using preset values.

■ Example 3.1: Basic SES calculation

A short series of hypothetical sales data is given in Table 3.3. The first observation is used as the forecast for period 2, and the smoothing constant is set at $\alpha = 0.3$. Thus, from equation (3.7), we have, for $t = 2$,

$$F_3(1) = F_2(1) + \alpha[Y_2 - F_2(1)]$$

$$= 5.00 + 0.3 \times (6.00 - 5.00) = 5.30$$

The forecasts are computed successively in the same way. The forecast errors, their squares, their absolute values, and their absolute values as a percentage of the observed series are shown in succeeding columns. The last row of the table gives the mean error, the *MSE*, the *MAE*, and the *MAPE*, calculated over observations 2 through 12. The calculations may be checked by using the Excel spreadsheet *Table_3_3.xlsx*, available on the book's website. ∎

Table 3.3 Illustration of Spreadsheet Calculations for SES Smoothing Constant: Alpha (α) = 0.3

Time	Sales	Forecast	Error	(Error)²	Absolute Error	Absolute Percentage Error
1	5.00					
2	6.00	5.00	1.00	1.00	1.00	16.67
3	7.00	5.30	1.70	2.89	1.70	24.29
4	8.00	5.81	2.19	4.80	2.19	27.38
5	7.00	6.47	0.53	0.28	0.53	7.61
6	6.00	6.63	−0.63	0.39	0.63	10.45
7	5.00	6.44	−1.44	2.07	1.44	28.78
8	6.00	6.01	−0.01	0.00	0.01	0.12
9	7.00	6.01	0.99	0.99	0.99	14.21
10	8.00	6.30	1.70	2.88	1.70	21.21
11	7.00	6.81	0.19	0.04	0.19	2.68
12	6.00	6.87	−0.87	0.75	0.87	14.48
13		6.61				
		Means	0.49	1.46	1.02	15.26
			RMSE = 1.21			

DISCUSSION QUESTION: *If you had to make a subjective choice for the value of the smoothing constant, what value would you choose for (a) a product with long-term steady sales and (b) a stock price index?*

3.3.2 The Exponential Smoothing Macro (ESM)

The Excel macro Exponential Smoothing Macro.xlsm (or simply ESM for short), available on the book's website, provides a flexible tool for fitting SES and a variety of other exponential smoothing models. A comprehensive *Users' Manual* is also available on the website. ESM uses Solver to fit models (in this case, to select the best value for α by minimizing the *MSE*. The macro allows the user to partition the data series into estimation and hold-out samples and computes summary statistics for each subsample. For consistency, we use ESM to estimate the exponential smoothing models described in the book (except where otherwise noted), but the reader should be aware that different software programs use somewhat different fitting algorithms and results differ from one program to another. That said, the estimated values of α will usually be similar, unless we are dealing with a very short series or one that contains some unusual observations, which we will refer to as *outliers*.

Starting Values We must still resolve the choice of starting values. Two principal options are commonly used: (1) to use the first observation as F_1 or (2) to use an average of a number of initial observations; recommendations vary from the first 3 or 4 up to 6 or 12 or even the mean of the whole sample. Gardner (1985) provides a good review of the options but states, "There appears to be no empirical evidence favoring any particular method." The macro allows the choice of the first observation only or an average of the first several observations to estimate the starting value(s). When either the sample size or α is large, the choice of starting value is relatively unimportant and the different approaches yield similar results. When both the sample size and α are small, more sophisticated methods should be used.[2]

Caution: All major forecasting packages include fitting routines for SES, although the particular algorithms employed vary, especially in regard to the estimation of starting values, so the results may differ somewhat from those shown in this book. Some packages are very coy about the methods they employ.

We now explore the effects of changing α for forecasts of WFJ Sales. The macro was used in each case to generate the results.

■ Example 3.2: SES forecasts for WFJ Sales *(WFJ_sales.xlsx)*

We used the first 26 observations of the WFJ Sales series as the estimation sample. The one-step-ahead *MSE* (taken over observations 2 to 26) is minimized[3] when $\alpha = 0.728$. Table 3.4 shows the first ten one-step-ahead forecasts for WFJ sales, from week 26 as origin, using SES with $\alpha = 0.2$ and 0.5, as well as 0.728, for comparison purposes. Thus, the first out-of-sample forecast is available at week 27, and the *one-step-ahead* forecasts are listed for weeks 27-36. The starting value was taken as the first observation (the ESM default) in each case. The three sets of forecasts correspond to the following:

- SES(0.2): Simple exponential smoothing with $\alpha = 0.2$.
- SES(0.5): Simple exponential smoothing with $\alpha = 0.5$.
- SES(opt): Simple exponential smoothing with $\alpha = 0.728$.

Table 3.4 Actual and One-Step-Ahead Forecasts for WFJ Sales
(For weeks 27-36, starting from week 26 as origin and using ESM)

Week	WFJ Sales	SES (0.2)	SES (0.5)	SES (opt)
27	30986	33881	34346	34580
28	33321	33302	32666	31963
29	34003	33306	32993	32952
30	35417	33445	33498	33717
31	33822	33840	34458	34955
32	32723	33836	34140	34130
33	34925	33614	33432	33105
34	33460	33876	34178	34431
35	30999	33793	33819	33723
36	31286	33234	32409	31739

To illustrate the nature of the calculations, consider the one-step-ahead forecast for week 28 for $\alpha = 0.2$. From equation (3.7), we have

$$F_{28}(1) = 33881 + 0.2(30986 - 33881) = 33302$$

Similarly, the one-step-ahead for forecast for week 29 is $F_{29}(1) = 33306$.

---

2 In Section 5.1, we discuss fitting a complete model to estimate both the smoothing parameter and the starting value.

3 The observations over which the *MSE* is minimized also varies with the software employed.

Figure 3.7 SES Forecasts for WFJ Sales: The Effects of Different Smoothing Constants

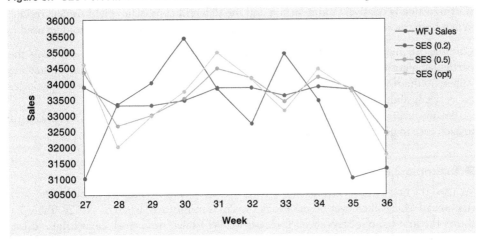

Figure 3.7 shows the one-step-ahead forecasts for weeks 27–36. The forecasts for SES(0.2) are smoother than those for SES(0.5) and SES(opt), which adapt more quickly to the latest observation. ■

3.3.3 The Use of Hold-Out Samples

Recall that in Example 3.2 we partitioned the original series into two parts. That partition provides a framework for an examination of the relative performance of alternative methods. For this purpose, we use the accuracy measures developed in Section 2.7.

When we split the series into two parts, we refer to the first part as the *estimation* sample, used to estimate the starting values and the smoothing parameters. This sample typically contains the first 75–80 percent of the observations, although the forecaster may choose to use a smaller percentage for longer series (a smaller proportion was used in our example to illustrate the results over a relatively stable part of the series). The parameters are commonly estimated by minimizing the mean squared error *(MSE)*, although the mean absolute error *(MAE)* and mean absolute percentage error *(MAPE)* can also be used; these alternatives are somewhat more robust to extreme observations, but MSE estimation combined with outlier adjustment is the path more commonly chosen (c.f. Section 9.7).

The *hold-out* sample represents the last 20–25 percent of the observations and is used to check forecasting performance. No matter how many parameters are estimated with the estimation sample, each method under consideration can be evaluated with the use of the "new" observations contained in the hold-out sample. Thus, the hold-out sample provides a level playing field for such comparisons: Relying on the estimation sample advantages more heavily parameterized methods that can overfit the data.

IN-SAMPLE AND OUT-OF-SAMPLE (HOLD-OUT) ERROR MEASURES
Measures of performance based upon the estimation sample are referred to as *in-sample*; measures based upon the *hold-out sample* are referred to as *out-of-sample*.

■ Example 3.3: Comparison of one-step-ahead forecasts

To examine the forecasting performance of the various methods discussed to date, we carried out the experiment described next, using the series WFJ Sales. Following recommended practice, we used an out-of-sample evaluation. In other words, we fit the first part of the series to the data and then examined the performance of the forecasting method by seeing how well it worked on later observations. In this example, we used a hold-out sample of more than 50 percent of the observations because our primary focus was on evaluating forecasting methods; a larger hold-out sample provides a better basis for comparisons. We compared five methods:

1. MA(3): A moving average of three terms
2. MA(8): A moving average of eight terms
3. SES(0.2): Simple exponential smoothing with $\alpha = 0.2$
4. SES(0.5): Simple exponential smoothing with $\alpha = 0.5$
5. SES(opt): Simple exponential smoothing with $\alpha = 0.728$

For each of the SES sets of forecasts, we used the first observation as the starting value, as in the previous example. We then generated the one-step-ahead forecasts for 36 weeks (weeks 27–62), starting at forecast origin $t = 26$. Only method 5 requires any parameter estimation. The summary results appear in Table 3.5. The best performance on each criterion is shown in bold. In this case, the best-fitting optimal SES scheme performs best on all counts. However, it may well happen that the different criteria lead to different conclusions. ■

Table 3.5 Summary Error Measures for One-Step-Ahead Forecasts of WFJ Sales Data *(Hold-out sample, weeks 27–62)*

Method	MAE	RMSE	MAPE
Number of Observations	36	36	36
MA(3)	3067	4320	8.9
MA(8)	3749	4865	11.0
SES(0.2)	3389	4342	9.9
SES(0.5)	2832	3980	8.2
SES(opt)	**2562**	**3915**	**7.3**

Data: WFJ_sales.xlsx

3.3.4 The Use of a Rolling Origin

Some programs allow repeated estimation and evaluation of the forecast error by advancing the estimation sample one observation at a time and repeating the error calculations, a process known as using a *rolling origin*. This process is illustrated in Figure 3.8.

The first set of forecasts is generated with time t as the forecast origin, producing forecasts at time $t+1$, $t+2$, …, $t+5$. The origin is then moved to time $t+1$ by adding the observation at time t to the estimation sample, to produce forecasts at times $t+2$, …, $t+5$. The forecast origin is then moved to time $t+2$ and the new forecasts generated.

In this schematic example, when the process is complete, we would have five one-step-ahead forecasts, four at two steps ahead and so on, up to one forecast five steps ahead.

The use of a rolling origin provides a more reliable assessment of performance (Fildes, 1992): As forecasts are produced from multiple forecast origins, we collect more evidence of the forecasting performance of a method and avoid relying solely on a single origin, or hold-out that may contain outliers or other irregularities. In addition, a rolling origin reflects practical applications because an organization typically adds the latest observations to the database and reruns the analysis. For further discussion of forecasting accuracy measures, see Tashman (2000) and Davydenko and Fildes (2013).

The ESM provides a rolling origin simulation, which is illustrated in the next example. The reader is encouraged to try the simulation on other series.

Figure 3.8 The Rolling Origin Process

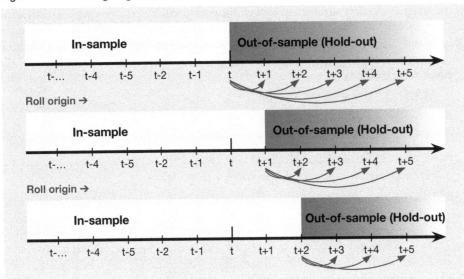

■ Example 3.4: Rolling origin forecasts for the WSJ series

An illustration of the rolling origin process is presented in Figure 3.9 using the WSJ Sales series. As before, we start with observations 1–26 as the estimation sample. Given that SES is used, the forecasts lie on a horizontal line. Nine forecast origins are shown in the plot from week 26 through week 34. Thus, the first plot, with the origin at week 26, shows forecasts equal to 34149 and the observed sales in week 27 fall to 30986, below the forecast level made in the previous week. Accordingly, the new forecasts are set at the lower level of 33200 and the observed value of sales in week 28 is 33321, producing a slight increase in the next forecast to 33236. The process continues on until week 34 becomes the origin and the forecast is 33839. ■

Figure 3.9 Rolling Origin Analysis for the WSJ Sales Series

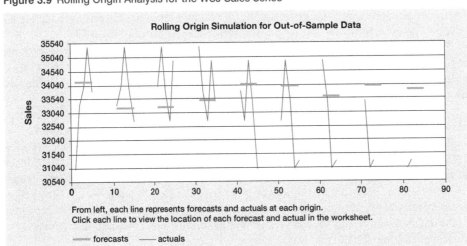

3.3.5 Some General Comments

On average, SES tends to outperform MA, as observed in an empirical comparison of their performance in the M3 forecasting competition, as reported by Makridakis and Hibon (2000) and in various other studies. In addition, as shown in Chapter 5, SES corresponds to an intuitively appealing underlying statistical model, whereas MA does not. Given the inferior properties and overall performance of moving-average-based procedures, we do not recommend their direct use for forecasting. However, moving averages have other uses, particularly in the area of seasonal adjustment, as seen in Chapter 4 (Sections 4.3-4.5).

One final question refers to the choice of fitting procedure. We could minimize the *MSE* (or, equivalently, the *RMSE)* or instead choose to minimize the *MAPE* or the *MAE*. To examine the effects of such a choice, we again use the WFJ series. The data through week 26 were used for estimation of the smoothing constant by each method in turn. Different options for the starting values (the first observation and the average of the first four observations) for the level produced essentially identical forecasts for weeks 27-62. Only the results for the starting value based upon the first observation are given in Table 3.6.

Table 3.6 Effects of Fitting SES by Minimization of RMSE, MAE, or MAPE

Estimation Criterion	RMSE		MAE		MAPE	
Sample	Estimation	Hold-Out	Estimation	Hold-Out	Estimation	Hold-Out
Error Measure						
RMSE	3030	3915	3045	3921	3045	3921
MAE	2127	2562	2012	2624	2012	2624
MAPE	6.6	7.3	6.3	7.5	6.3	7.5
Value of α	0.728		0.660		0.660	

Data: WFJ_sales.xlsx

In this example, the choice of fitting method produces only marginal differences in the results; a phenomenon that tends to happen, provided that adequate data are available for estimation. Here, the results when fitting with *MAE* and *MAPE* are identical; these two criteria produce similar results whenever the typical percentage error is small. Finally, we note that the out-of-sample error measures tend to be somewhat higher than those calculated for the estimation sample. This outcome should not come as a surprise, because the smoothing constant was chosen to minimize the appropriate criterion within the estimation sample, not the hold-out sample.

In all further analyses we choose to follow common practice and minimize the *MSE*, as do most forecasting packages.

3.4 Linear Exponential Smoothing

Figure 3.10 shows linear and quadratic trend curves fitted to the Netflix quarterly revenues data, over the period 2000Q1– 2015Q4. Plot (A) shows the linear trend, and plot (B) shows the quadratic trend.[4]

---

4 The calculations involved in creating these trend lines do not concern us here. A detailed explanation is given in Chapter 8 (Section 8.2).

Figure 3.10 Linear (A) and Quadratic (B) Trend Lines for Netflix Sales Revenues (2000Q1–2015Q4) [Time = 1, 2, ..., 64]

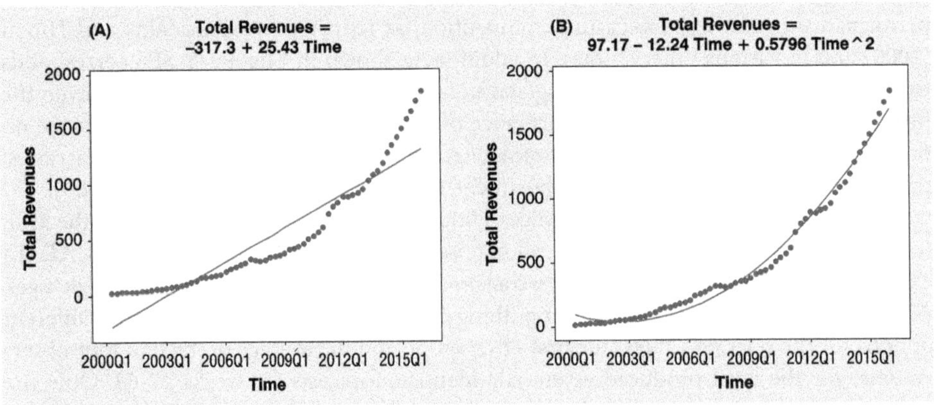

Data: Netflix_2.xlsx

The quadratic seems to provide an excellent fit, but we must be wary of such global models — that is, models which assume a never-changing trend into the far future. Indeed, the road to chapter 11 bankruptcy proceedings is littered with the remains of companies that believed such optimistic growth patterns would persist. A successful start-up company will often show dramatic growth in the early years, but the growth moderates as the company and its markets mature and competitors emerge. The Netflix record is impressive, but investors should not get too carried away: The trend is likely to change over time. Accordingly, we introduce methods with a local trend estimate in the next section.

3.4.1 Basic Structure for LES

Global trend models assume that the trend remains constant over the whole time series. Because we are reluctant to rely upon the continuation of global patterns, we now develop tools that project trends more locally, just as we looked at local levels earlier. To understand the approach, we begin with the components of a straight line: the intercept (or starting level at time zero) and the trend (or slope), which we denote by L and T, respectively. To produce forecasts that are sensitive to recent changes in the series, we now define the following variables:

$$L_t = \text{level of series at time } t$$

$$T_t = \text{trend of series at time } t.$$

The level and trend measured at time t represent our current state of knowledge about these quantities. Thus, when we seek to forecast h periods ahead, we may construct a trend line that starts at level L_t and has trend T_t. That is, the forecast function for one-step-ahead is

$$F_{t+1}(1) = F_{t+1} = (\text{level at time } t) + (\text{trend at time } t) = L_t + T_t.$$

More generally, the forecast h steps ahead is

$$F_{t+h}(h) = (\text{level at time } t) + h \times (\text{trend at time } t) = L_t + hT_t. \tag{3.10}$$

Recall that, for SES, the trend is zero, so the forecast reduces to $F_{t+h}(h) = L_t$.

> **LOCALLY LINEAR FORECASTS**
>
> A time series is said to have a local linear trend if the mean level at any point in time is expected to increase (or decrease) linearly over time. The forecast function has the general form
>
> $$F_{t+h}(h) = \text{Intercept} + h \times \text{Trend};$$
>
> that is, the plot showing future forecasts is a straight line. When a new observation is recorded, estimates of the intercept and trend are updated.

3.4.2 Updating Relationships

We now consider updating the level and the trend, using equations like those we used for SES in Section 3.3.

Given the latest observation Y_t, we update the expressions for the level and the trend by making partial adjustments:

$$L_t = L_{t-1} + T_{t-1} + \alpha e_t \qquad (3.11)$$

$$T_t = T_{t-1} + \beta(L_t - L_{t-1} - T_{t-1}).$$

As before, we define the observed error (e_t) as the difference between the newly observed value of the series and its previous one-step-ahead forecast:

$$e_t = Y_t - F_t = Y_t - (L_{t-1} + T_{t-1}).$$

Equations (3.11) may be expressed in what is known as the *error correction form* of the updating equations. The first equation is unchanged, but as may be checked by substitution (see Exercise 3.19), the update of the trend can be expressed as

$$T_t = T_{t-1} + \alpha\beta e_t. \qquad (3.12)$$

These equations may be explained as follows:

- The new level is the old level (adjusted for the increase produced by the trend) plus a partial adjustment (with weight α) for the most recent error.
- The new trend is the old trend plus a partial adjustment (with weight $\alpha\beta$) for the error.

It is apparent from equations (3.11) that a second round of smoothing is applied to estimate the trend, leading some authors to describe the method as *double exponential smoothing*. Because the forecast function (3.10) defines a straight line, we prefer the name *linear exponential smoothing (LES)*. The method is also known as *Holt's Method,* after one of its originators (Holt, 2004). If we set the trend equal to zero at all times, we are back at simple exponential smoothing; in that case, T_t vanishes and the equation for L_t reduces to equation (3.7) on identifying L_t as F_{t+1}.

3.4.3 Starting Values

To set this forecasting procedure in motion, we need starting values for the level and trend, as well as values for the two smoothing constants α and β. The smoothing constants may be specified by the user, and conventional wisdom decrees using $0.05 < \alpha < 0.3$ and $0.05 < \beta < 0.15$. These guidelines are not always appropriate, however; it is better to view them as suggesting initial values in a procedure for selecting optimal coefficients by minimizing the

MSE over some initial sample, as we did for SES. The performance of the resulting forecasting equations should be checked out of sample, as in Example 3.5.

As with SES, different programs use a variety of procedures to set starting values (Gardner, 1985). The ESM uses the starting values

$$T_3 = \frac{(Y_3 - Y_1)}{2} \text{ for the trend}$$

and

$$L_3 = \frac{(Y_1 + Y_2 + Y_3)}{3} + \frac{(Y_3 - Y_1)}{2} \text{ for the level.}$$

These values correspond to fitting a straight line to the first three observations. Once the initial values are set, equations (3.11) are used to update the level and trend as each new observation becomes available.

Caution: All major forecasting packages include fitting routines for LES, although the particular algorithms employed vary, so the results may differ somewhat from those shown in this book. Further, the use of different initial values for estimating the parameters may lead to different final values. Try several values to ensure that a global minimum of the MSE has been reached.

■ Example 3.5: Spreadsheet for LES calculations

A short series of hypothetical sales data is given in Table 3.7. The smoothing constants are set at $\alpha = 0.3$, $\beta = 0.1$, and the calculations were performed using the ESM. Thus, the first three observations were used to set initial values for the level and trend, and the forecast error measures were then computed with the use of observations 4-12, which may be regarded as the hold-out sample in this case. These values are genuine forecasts because no estimation is involved. The entries corresponding to time period 13 represent the one-step-ahead forecast and its components. The forecast errors and their squares, absolute values, and absolute percentage errors *(APEs)* are shown in succeeding columns. The last two rows of the table give the Mean Error, *ME* (as defined in Section 2.7.1), *RMSE, MAE,* and *MAPE,* calculated over the hold-out periods 4-12. ■

Table 3.7 LES Calculations for Hypothetical Sales Data [Alpha (α) = 0.3, Beta (β) = 0.1]

Period	Sales	Level	Trend	Forecast	Error	Error²	|Error|	APE
1	5.00							
2	7.00							
3	9.00							
4	10.00	9.00	2.00	11.00	−1.00	1.00	1.00	10.00
5	11.00	10.70	1.97	12.67	−1.67	2.79	1.67	15.18
6	12.00	12.17	1.92	14.09	−2.09	4.36	2.09	17.41
7	16.00	13.46	1.86	15.32	0.68	0.46	0.68	4.25
8	17.00	15.52	1.88	17.40	−0.40	0.16	0.40	2.36
9	20.00	17.28	1.87	19.15	0.85	0.73	0.85	4.27
10	17.00	19.40	1.89	21.29	−4.29	18.44	4.29	25.26
11	21.00	20.01	1.76	21.77	−0.77	0.59	0.77	3.66
12	22.00	21.54	1.74	23.28	−1.28	1.63	1.28	5.80
13		22.89	1.70	24.59				
					ME	RMSE	MAE	MAPE
					−1.11	1.83	1.45	9.80

Data: Example 3_5.xlsx. Averages taken over Periods 4-12.

■ Example 3.6: Linear exponential smoothing for WFJ sales

We now consider the use of LES for the WFJ Sales data given in *WFJ_sales.xlsx*. This table shows a number of interesting features:

- The hold-out sample produces somewhat higher values for the error measures, as would be expected.

- The estimates of β are always zero, so the trend term is not updated. Too much should not be made of a single example, but it is clear that we should retain an adequate number of observations for out-of-sample testing. If there are sufficient data, retain at least 10-12 observations for this purpose.

Finally, a comparison of Tables 3.5 and 3.8 indicates that there is no benefit to using LES in this case; indeed, SES does somewhat better, confirming our initial impression that the series did not show any marked trend, after the initial period when sales were lower. ■

Table 3.8 Estimation Sample and Hold-Out) Sample Results for WFJ Sales
(Fitted by minimizing the MSE over weeks 1–26)

Error Measure	Estimation Sample	Hold-Out Sample	Estimation Sample	Hold-Out Sample
RMSE	3030	3915	3090	4033
MAE	2128	2562	2321	2694
MAPE	6.62	7.33	7.42	7.91
Value of α	0.73		0.70	
Value of β			0.00	

Data: WFJ_sales.xlsx

■ Example 3.7: Forecasting Netflix sales with LES

The sales figures for Netflix, given in *Netflix_2.xlsx* and plotted in Figure 3.10 exhibit a very strong trend, and we would expect LES to perform much better than SES in this case. The series was fitted to observations 1-52 via the ESM, leaving the last 12 observations as a hold-out sample. From Figure 3.11A, we see that the SES forecast always undershoots the next value of the series because it fails to allow for the upward trend. By contrast, the LES does a much better job; actual and forecast values are barely distinguishable in Figure 3.11 (B).

Figure 3.11 Netflix Revenues and One-Step-Ahead Forecasts for Observations 53–64 from (A) Single Exponential Smoothing and (B) Linear Exponential Smoothing

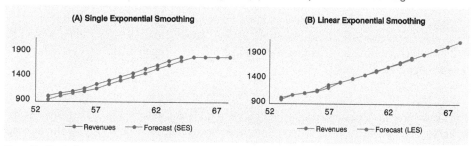

Data: Netflix_2.xlsx

The results are summarized in Table 3.9. LES is clearly much superior to SES, as we would expect. However, we observe that α is set at its upper level of 1.0, indicating that even LES may have problems capturing the pattern in the data. Again, if we step back from the technical details and look at the plot of the data in Figure 3.10, we see that the growth is exponential rather than linear. In Section 3.7, we examine the use of transformations as a way of dealing with this question. ■

Table 3.9 Summary Measures for SES and LES for Netflix Sales

Error Measure	SES		LES	
	Estimation Sample	Hold-Out	Estimation Sample	Hold-Out
RMSE	28.3	75.1	18.9	21.7
MAE	19.1	73.2	10.6	15.2
MAPE	9.5	5.3	4.3	1.2
Value of α	1.00		1.00	
Value of β			0.39	

DISCUSSION QUESTION: *How would you choose among SES, LES, or a fitted straight line for use with a given series?*

3.5 Exponential Smoothing with a Damped Trend

As we saw earlier, the growth rate for Netflix slowed as the company matured. This phenomenon is quite common in time series for sales where a product line matures and sales may then decline unless the product is upgraded in some way. Indeed, such a product life cycle is a standard expectation in marketing. We can accommodate these kinds of life-cycle effects by modifying the updating equations for the level and trend. We anticipate that, in the absence of random errors, the level should flatten out unless the process encounters some new stimulus. In turn, this expectation means that the trend should approach zero. Intuitively, we look for a means of forecasting that damps down the trend component as the forecast horizon is extended. In other words, we assume that the series will level out over time. We achieve this adjustment to our method by introducing a damping factor so that the error correction form of equations (3.11) become

$$L_t = L_{t-1} + \phi T_{t-1} + \alpha e_t \qquad (3.13)$$

$$T_t = \phi T_{t-1} + \alpha \beta e_t \, .$$

In equations (3.13), we have inserted a *damping factor* ϕ with a value between 0 and 1 in front of every occurrence of the trend term T_{t-1}. We select ϕ to be positive but less than 1 so that the effect is to shift the trend term toward zero, or to dampen it. The effect is to produce the one-step-ahead forecast

$$F_{t+1}(1) = F_{t+1} = L_t + \phi T_t \, .$$

That is, we only incorporate a proportion of the trend factor into the forecast. By feeding the forecast values for the level and trend back into this equation we can compute the forecast function for h steps ahead, which has the form

$$F_{t+h}(h) = L_t + (\phi + \phi^2 + \cdots + \phi^h) T_t \, . \qquad (3.14)$$

The derivation is left as Exercise 3.20.

This forecast levels out over time, approaching the limiting value $L_t + \phi T_t/(1 - \phi)$ because the damping factor is less than 1. This limiting value contrasts sharply with LES, where $\phi = 1$ and the forecast keeps increasing because $F_{t+h}(h) = L_t + hT_t$.

The damped trend method was introduced by Gardner and McKenzie (1985) and has proved surprisingly effective (Makridakis and Hibon, 2000).

■ Example 3.8: Forecasting Netflix sales with the damped trend method

The optimal damping factor is estimated to be $\phi = 0.94$; the results are summarized in Table 3.10 including the performance measures for the hold-out sample. The forecasts are marginally inferior to those from LES without damping, but if we believe that company expansion is slowing, the damped form may be preferable for future use: the optimal parameters for past data do not necessarily deliver the most accurate forecasts! ■

Table 3.10 One-Step-Ahead Fitted Values and Forecasts for Netflix Sales Under the Damped Trend Method

Period	Total Revenues	Level	Slope	Forecast	Forecasting Accuracy Statistics
1	5.17				
2	7.15				
3	10.18	10.01	2.50		
4	13.39	13.39	2.84	12.36	
5	17.06	17.06	3.14	16.06	
6	18.36	18.36	2.18	20.01	
...	...	...	...	...	
60	1484.73	1484.73	68.54	1472.00	RMSE = 24.90
61	1573.13	1573.13	75.69	1549.21	MAE = 18.40
62	1644.69	1644.69	71.37	1644.34	MAPE = 1.44
63	1738.36	1738.36	79.58	1711.83	
64	1823.33	1823.33	79.60	1813.22	$\alpha = 1.00$
65				1898.21	$\beta = 0.59$
66				1968.66	$\phi = 0.94$
67				2034.93	
68				2097.27	

Data: Netflix_2.xlsx

3.5.1 Choice of Method

The different forms of exponential smoothing apply to certain types of time series. Figure 3.12 shows a categorization of series by the form of the trend (no trend, additive trend, damped trend, multiplicative trend). In choosing a method, the aim is to match it with the type of data. Often, however, the form of the series is unknown. By implication in our earlier discussion, we recommend choosing the method that performs best on the hold-out sample, using one or more of the criteria discussed. When the series is too short to allow for a hold-out sample of reasonable size, we use measures defined for the estimation sample, as well as our understanding of the time series itself. This approach is developed in Chapter 5.

Figure 3.12 Possible Trend Patterns Showing Trend/No Trend and Additive/Multiplicative Trend

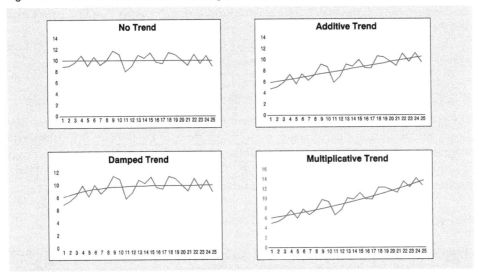

3.6 Other Approaches to Trend Forecasting

Several other methods of trend forecasting are worthy of a brief mention. For a more comprehensive review of recent developments, see the excellent review article by Gardner (2006).

3.6.1 Brown's Method of Double Exponential Smoothing (DES)

As noted earlier, Robert G. Brown was the original developer of exponential smoothing methods and his books (1959, 1963) have become classics. His initial derivation of exponential smoothing was based on minimizing the weighted sum of squared errors, where the past squared errors are discounted by α, α^2, etc. For a local linear trend, his method reduces to the use of LES with $\alpha = \beta$. Unless data are very limited, there is no particular benefit to imposing this restriction, and we do not consider it further. However, the discounted least squares approach is particularly useful when complex nonlinear functions are involved and updating equations are not readily available.

3.6.2 SES with (Constant) Drift: The Theta Method

If we set $\beta = 0$, the updated equations (3.11) become

$$L_t = L_{t-1} + T + \alpha e_t$$

$$T_t = T_{t-1} = T.$$

This version may be referred to as *SES with drift*, because the level increases by a fixed amount each period. Although the method is just a special case of LES, the simpler structure makes it easier to derive an optimal value for T by using the estimation sample, rather than the start-up values we have considered hitherto. This scheme, sometimes called the (simplified) *Theta Method* (Assimakopoulos and Nikolopoulos, 2000), is often surprisingly effective, shown by Hyndman and Billah (2003), who compared it to other methods using the data of the M3 competition (Makridakis and Hibon, 2000). An updated examination of the method with extensions is given by Fiorucci *et al.* (2016).

3.6.3 Tracking Signals

Trigg and Leach (1967) introduced the concept of a tracking signal, whereby not only the level and trend, but also the smoothing parameters, are updated each time. For example, for SES, we would use the updated value for α given by

$$\alpha_t = \frac{|E_{t-1}|}{M_{t-1}}, \tag{3.15}$$

where E_t and M_t are smoothed values of the error and the absolute error, respectively. That is,

$$E_t = \delta e_t + (1 - \delta)E_{t-1}$$
$$M_t = \delta \, | \, e_t \, | + (1 - \delta)M_{t-1}. \tag{3.16}$$

Typically, a value of δ in the range 0.1-0.2 is used. If a string of positive errors occurs, the value of α_t increases to speed up the adjustment process; the reverse occurs for negative errors. Initial values are set to zero.

Over the years, there has been considerable debate over the benefits of tracking signals; for example, Gardner (1985) found no real evidence that forecasts based upon tracking signals provided any improvements. A generally preferred approach is to update the parameter estimate regularly, which is no longer much of a computational problem even for large numbers of series. Fildes *et al.* (1998) found that regular updating produced more consistent gains over all forecast horizons. From the practical viewpoint, a forecasting system may incorporate data on a weekly or monthly basis and then the forecasting analysis rerun at regular intervals to find revised parameters. That way, updating is straightforward and should not be a problem with modern forecasting systems.

3.6.4 Linear Moving Averages

In Section 3.2, we considered a simple moving average as an alternative to SES, albeit not a recommended approach. We could also look at the successive differences in the series $Y_t - Y_{t-1}$ and take a moving average of these values to estimate the trend. The net effect is to estimate the trend by $(Y_t - Y_{t-K})/K$ for a K-term moving average, leading to the forecast function $F_{t+1}(1) = F_{t+1} = Y_t + (Y_t - Y_{t-K})/K$. Again, exponential smoothing for a trend via LES usually provides better forecasts.

3.7 The Use of Transformations

The forecasts derived from the LES method require that the series is locally linear. Intuitively, if the trend for the last few time periods in the series appears to be close to a straight line, the LES method should work well. However, in many cases this assumption is not realistic. For example, suppose we are trying to forecast the *GDP* of a country that has experienced growth of around 5 percent per year in recent years. Then, ignoring statistical variation for the moment, we might describe such growth by the expression

$$Y_t = (1.05)^t Y_0 \text{ or } Y_t = 1.05 Y_{t-1}.$$

When plotted, this function is an exponential curve, which increases at an increasing rate in monetary terms. Any linear approximation will undershoot the true function sooner or later, (This observation was first made hundreds of years ago by Malthus regarding linear growth in the world's food supply and exponential population growth, leading to starvation.) For very short-term forecasts, undershooting may not matter, but it becomes serious as the forecasting horizon increases. More complex nonlinear patterns may also exist; for example, many products have a sales history of growth, then stability, then a decline as they are superseded by new (and presumably improved) alternatives. Such series can be forecast in two ways:

1. Transform the series so that the trend becomes linear.

2. Convert the series to growth over time, forecast the growth rate, and then convert back to the original series.

We now examine each approach in turn.

3.7.1 The Log Transform

We defined the logarithmic transformation in Chapter 2 (Section 2.6.2). For the exponential growth equation just given, the log transform yields

$$\ln Y_t = \ln(1.05) + \ln Y_{t-1}.$$

If we now write $Z_t = \ln Y_t$, the reverse transformation is

$$Y_t = \exp(Z_t) = \exp[\ln (1.05) + \ln Y_{t-1}] = 1.05\ Y_{t-1}.$$

Of course, the growth rate is rarely constant. (If it were, we would estimate it by means of the averaging methods of Chapter 2.) Instead, when the log-transform produces a linear trend, we can apply LES. We must then transform back to the original series to obtain the forecasts of interest.

Typically, the effect of the log transformation process is to improve forecasting performance for exponential growth problems.

■ Example 3.9: Forecasting Netflix sales with the log transform

We applied LES to the transformed series, using the ESM. We applied the same procedures for setting starting values and estimating the parameters as before. The summary statistics are presented in Table 3.11. The table gives the results of estimating the parameters by minimizing the MSE of (a) the transformed values and (b) the original values. The summary values are computed after transforming back to the original units; otherwise comparisons between methods are not feasible. Also, we are interested in forecasting the original series, not the transformed values.

Because the original series minimizes MSE directly, whereas the minimum MSE for the transformed series relates to those transformed values, the MSE for the estimation sample will be lower for the original series than for the transformed case after transforming back to the original units; this is the case in Table 3.11. In turn, this effect stresses the importance of using a hold-out sample; the transformed series has a lower $RMSE$ for the hold-out sample, although the MAE and $MAPE$ are higher.

Whether to use LES on the original or transformed series or to use SES on growth rates remains a question for further examination in any particular study. ■

Table 3.11 Summary Measures for LES for Netflix Sales, Using Both the Original Data and a Log Transform*

Error Measures*	Original Series		Log Series	
	Estimation	Hold-Out	Estimation	Hold-Out
RMSE	18.97	21.72	20.69	20.48
MAE	10.62	15.17	12.20	16.62
MAPE	4.29	1.22	5.11	1.34
Value of α	1		1	
Value of β	0.39		0.43	

*The error measures refer to the original units of the observations.

Data: Netflix_2.xlsx

3.7.2 Use of Growth Rates

We define the growth rate as in Section 2.6.1. Assuming that the variable has a natural origin, we see that the growth rate from one time period to the next is

$$G_t = 100 \times \frac{Y_t - Y_{t-1}}{Y_{t-1}}. \tag{3.17}$$

The growth rate is approximately equal to $\ln Y_t - \ln Y_{t-1}$ as indicated in Exercise 3.18.

Note that growth, by this definition, can be negative. For example, the period-by-period returns on an investment are defined exactly as in equation (3.17). After we compute the single-period growth rates, we may use SES to predict the growth for the next period, which we denote by $g_{t+1}(1) = g_{t+1}$, following our usual convention. The one-step-ahead forecast for the original series is given by

$$F_{t+1}(1) = F_{t+1} = Y_t \times \left[1 + \frac{g_{t+1}}{100} \right]. \tag{3.18}$$

In other words, we unscramble the growth forecast to determine the forecast for the original series.

■ Example 3.10: Forecasting Netflix sales revenue data by means of the growth rate

The quarterly revenues (in $ million) for Netflix are listed in *Netflix_2.xlsx* for the first quarter of 2000 through the fourth quarter of 2015. The growth rates for one quarter over the immediately preceding quarter are then computed with equation (3.17). Selected values are listed in Table 3.12, including the summary measures for the hold-out sample (observations 53–64). The growth rates are plotted in Figure 3.13, which clearly reveals the instability in the early growth phase. The last four one-step-ahead sales forecasts are then given in the last column of Table 3.12, generated from equation (3.18), along with the 1 to 4 step-ahead forecasts for periods 65–68.

The summary measures for the hold-out sample given in Table 3.12 suggest that the log transform (recall Table 3.11) is marginally superior to the growth approach in this case. ■

Table 3.12 Growth Rate Analysis of Netflix Quarterly Sales, 2000–2015

Year	Quarter	Total Revenues	Growth Percentage	Growth Forecast	Revenues Forecast	Forecast Accuracy Statistics
2000	1	5.17				
2000	2	7.15	38.13			
2000	3	10.18	42.47	38.13	9.87	
2000	4	13.39	31.52	40.26	14.28	
2001	1	17.06	27.38	35.97	18.21	
2001	2	18.36	7.63	31.76	22.47	
...	...	...	...	...	...	For α = 0.49
2015	1	1573.13	5.95	5.49	1566.25	
2015	2	1644.69	4.55	5.72	1663.08	RMSE = 20.86
2015	3	1738.36	5.70	5.14	1729.31	MAE = 17.35
2015	4	1823.33	4.89	5.41	1832.49	MAPE = 1.40
2016	1			5.16	1917.35	
2016	2			5.16	2016.22	
2016	3			5.16	2120.19	
2016	4			5.16	2229.52	

Quarterly revenue (sales) in $ million; growth in percentages.

Data: Netflix_2 .xlsx

Figure 3.13 Netflix Growth Rates, First Quarter, 2000, Through Fourth Quarter, 2015

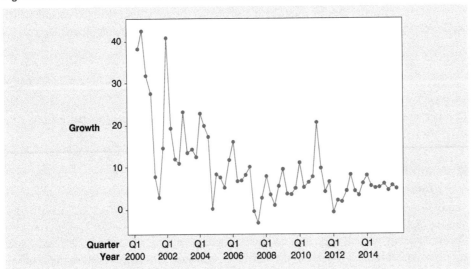

3.7.3 The Box-Cox Transformations

The logarithmic transformation is appealing because it reflects proportional rather than absolute change. For many series in business and economics, the notion of proportional, or percentage, change is a natural framework; we often encounter statements, such as "We expect *GDP* to grow by 2.5 percent next year," leading to exponential growth. However, proportional change may project future growth patterns in excess of reasonable expectations. An examination of Figure 3.13 shows that the growth rate for Netflix moderated over time, and became more stable.

How can we allow for the "irrational exuberance" sometimes shown by exponential growth but where the logarithmic transformation fails to induce linearity? We have already discussed a modification of LES to allow for a damped trend; this modification can be applied after the log transform when appropriate. A second possibility is to select a transformation that is more moderate than the logarithmic form.

Instead of restricting the choice to the original units or the logarithmic transform, Box and Cox (1964) suggested using a power transformation, of which the square root and the cube root are the most obvious cases. On occasion, such transformations may have a natural interpretation, as when one is considering the volume of a sphere; the cube root is proportional to the radius of the sphere. It is difficult, however, to find any examples in business or economics in which such transformations have intuitive appeal. Nevertheless, from a purely empirical perspective, these transforms may provide better forecasts. Given the original series Y_t we define the Box-Cox transform[5] as

$$Z_t = Y_t^c. \tag{3.19}$$

The reverse transformation is $Y_t = Z_t^{1/c}$.

The parameter c is usually restricted to the range where $-1 \leq c \leq 1$. where $c = 1$ corresponds to the original series and $c = -1$ represents the reciprocal. (Think of miles per gallon versus gallons per mile.) We use only the square and cube root as examples; in general, the choice among different values for c may be made by minimizing the MSE in the usual way; the ESM enables this option.

The transformed data values are plotted in Figure 3.14. From the plots, we can see that the log transform overcorrects, exhibiting a slight curvature or flattening out. By contrast, the cube-root plot suggests a straight-line trend.

Figure 3.14 Plots of Transformed Netflix Data

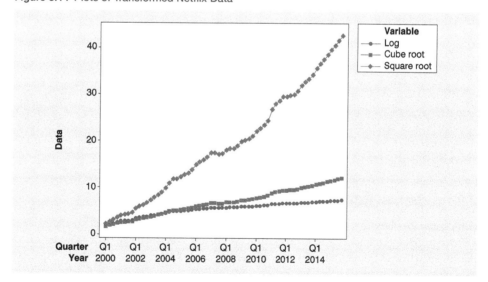

---

5   Box and Cox (1964) used the slightly more complex form $Z_t = (Y_t^c - 1)/c$, which has numerical advantages when one is seeking an optimal value for c. For our purposes, the simpler form in equation (3.19) suffices. Optimal values for c may be computed using the ESM.

■ Example 3.11: Forecasting Netflix sales by means of the Box-Cox transform

We considered the square- and cube-root transformations for the Netflix series. The results given in Table 3.13 relate to fitting by minimizing the *MSE* for the transformed series. When the *MSE* for the original data is used to estimate the parameters, the forecasting results are similar and are omitted.

When we compare the results in Table 3.13, we see that the square-root transformation seems to provide the better performance in the estimation sample, but the cube root does much better in the hold-out sample, presumably because it is produces a more linear pathway. The cube-root also outperforms the logarithm. ■

Table 3.13 LES Summary Measures for Netflix Sales, Using the Box-Cox Transform

Transform	c	α	β	RMSE	MAE	MAPE
Square root	0.50	1.00	0.05			
Estimation				19.13	10.75	4.23
Holdout				27.34	23.98	1.78
Cube root	0.33	1.00	0.09			
Estimation				19.51	11.11	4.50
Holdout				18.93	14.84	1.17

DISCUSSION QUESTION: *Suppose you carry out an extensive analysis and conclude that the best forecasting model involves a Box-Cox transform with c = ⅓. Would you feel comfortable using this transform and reporting the results to management? Why or why not?*

WHEN TO TRANSFORM

- Do not use complex transforms unless they are supported by both theory and data.
- Always compare transformed methods with a benchmark by transforming the forecasts back to the data series of interest.

3.8 Prediction Intervals

Our discussion thus far has been purely in terms of point forecasts, yet in Chapter 2 (Section 2.9) we stressed the importance of interval forecasts. At this stage, we restrict attention to the construction of prediction intervals for one-step-ahead forecasts. Intervals for forecasts made two or more periods ahead require the specification of an underlying statistical model, so we defer the formal discussion to Section 5.2. Indeed, the intervals for one-step-ahead forecasting also imply an underlying model, but we can bypass that requirement for now by using the approximate interval given in Section 2.9, based upon the normal distribution:

$$\text{Forecast} \pm z_{\alpha/2} \times (RMSE).$$

In other words, 100(1 − α)% of the time the outcome is expected to lie within the range

$$[\text{Forecast} - z_{\alpha/2} \times (RMSE), \text{Forecast} + z_{\alpha/2} \times (RMSE)].$$

We may also construct a prediction interval empirically, using the alternative approach given in Section 2.9; the interpretation is the same, but the interval need not be symmetric. When a transformation is used, the prediction interval is computed using the transformed values and then transformed back to the original units.

■ Example 3.12: Prediction interval for Netflix

From Table 3.11, the point forecast for the next period (2016.1) is 1906.8 with estimation sample $RMSE = 18.97$. The resulting (approximate) 95 percent prediction interval is

$$1906.8 \pm 1.96 \times 18.97 = 1906.8 \pm 37.0 = (1869.86, 1944.0)$$

The actual outcome is expected to lie in the interval (1870, 1944) approximately 95 percent of the time. As the forecasting horizon increases, the intervals get progressively wider, Chapter 5 (Section 5.2). ■

■ Example 3.13: Prediction interval for WFJ sales

The first 51 observations of the series are used as the estimation sample, which provides 50 observed error terms (one being lost in the initialization). To obtain empirical prediction intervals we use the pairs (3, 48), (2, 49), and (1, 50) of the 50 ranked error terms, as shown in Table 3.14A. Recall from section 2.8.3, with 50 observations, 100(1−0.5)/50, i.e. 1% are estimated as lower than the smallest observation with 1% larger than the highest giving a 98% interval. Similarly, 3% are lower (higher) than pairs (2, 49) and 5% from pair (3, 48). The half-widths of the prediction intervals (Table 3.14B) show that the distribution may be somewhat more heavy-tailed than the normal distribution. Finally, the two alternative methods of calculation, normal and empirical, for the 90 percent one-step-ahead prediction intervals for weeks 52-62 are shown in Table 3.14C, along with the actual values of the series. These ten observations occur around the year's end, when the volume of sales changes dramatically, so it comes as no surprise that the coverage of the two sets of prediction intervals is less than the nominal level. Such discrepancies would be a signal to management of changed market conditions: in this case, clearly higher sales in the holiday period. Model extensions to handle such circumstances are discussed in Section 9.1. ■

Table 3.14 One-Step-Ahead Prediction Intervals for WFJ Sales Series

(A) Smallest and largest observed errors			
Smallest Five		**Largest Five**	
Rank	**Value**	**Rank**	**Value**
1	−6378	46	3765
2	−5146	47	3801
3	−4574	48	5253
4	−3609	49	5605
5	−2715	50	8256

(B) Half-width of prediction interval			
Level	**90**	**94**	**98**
Normal	3436	4168	5506
Empirical	4913	5376	7317

(C) Normal and empirical prediction intervals for observations 51-62						
			90% Normal PI		90% Empirical PI	
Week	WFJ Sales	Point Forecast	Lower	Upper	Lower	Upper
52	51914	41801	38365	45236	36887	46714
53	35404	49329	45893	52764	44416	54242
54	30555	38963	35528	42399	34050	43877
55	30421	32704	29269	36140	27791	37617
56	30972	31005	27569	34440	26091	35918
57	32336	30981	27545	34416	26067	35894
58	28194	31990	28554	35425	27076	36903
59	29203	29164	25729	32600	24251	34077
60	28155	29193	25757	32628	24280	34106
61	28404	28420	24985	31856	23507	33334
62	34128	28408	24973	31844	23495	33321

Highlighted values fall outside one or both sets of intervals.

Data: WFJ_sales.xlsx

DISCUSSION QUESTION: *Suppose a revised forecasting method describes the WFJ Sales data for weeks 1-52 pretty well. But four actual observations fall outside the normal prediction interval for weeks 53-62. What possible explanations are there for this occurrence?*

3.9 Method Selection

In the course of this chapter, we have outlined a considerable number of forecasting methods, and more are to come in the next chapter when we discuss seasonality. For any particular forecasting task, one approach may naturally suggest itself in preference to another. For example, it is always reasonable to ask and answer the following questions:

- Does the series display a trend? Do we expect the trend to continue into the future? If so, then
  ✓ Use a method that includes a trend.
- Do the observations tend to be more (or less) variable over time? If so, then
  ✓ Transform the data to obtain roughly constant variability.

In addition, we need to check for conformity with the principles outlined in the next section. When there are a number of equally plausible methods, we usually rely on comparing their out-of-sample forecasting performance. When we are dealing with a large number of series, it is usually feasible to examine the preceding questions for a (possibly small) sample of all the series. We may overcome such obstacles by using a common estimation sample to fit each method and then generating a set of out-of-sample forecasts that can be compared with values in the hold-out sample. We then choose the method that corresponds to the best value of the selected criterion *(RMSE, MAE, MAPE, MdAPE, etc.)*, calculated over the sample of time series. We return to the issue of method selection in Chapter 5 (Section 5.3), in which the analysis is reinforced by the development of underlying statistical models.

3.10 Principles of Extrapolative Methods

To avoid undue repetition, we assume that the data series being forecast is appropriate for the problem at hand in terms of relevance, timeliness, and reporting accuracy. These assumptions are by no means trivial, but we have discussed them in the previous chapters and they remain critical to any forecasting exercise. We should always recall the maxim "Garbage in, garbage out." If the data do not satisfy the aforementioned criteria, further analysis may be useless. As before, Armstrong (2001) is a valuable resource, and many of the principles quoted reflect his ideas. A few principles are repeated from Chapter 2 because they are an integral part of the forecasting approach described in the current chapter.

[3.1] Plot the series.
Data plotting should be the first step in any analysis. If a large number of series is involved, plot a selection of them. Such plots will often serve to identify data-recording errors, missing values, and unusual events.

[3.2] Clean the data.
Data plots and simple screening procedures (checks for outliers) provide the basis for making adjustments for anomalous values. Make sure that the adjustments are for valid data-recording reasons, and keep a record of all such changes.

[3.3] Use transformations as required by expectations about the process.
Such transformations may involve a conversion of current to real-dollar values, a logarithmic transformation to reflect proportional growth, or a switch to growth rates to account for trends. The intelligent use of knowledge related to the phenomenon being studied helps to avoid "crazy" forecasts.

[3.4] Select simple methods, unless convincing empirical evidence calls for greater complexity.
The set of exponential smoothing methods described in this chapter relies upon only the past history of the series in question. Such extrapolative methods often suffice in the short to medium term, unless measurements on key explanatory variables are available.

[3.5] Evaluate alternative methods, preferably using out-of-sample data.
Methods that use more parameters or are based on a more complicated nonlinear transform often fit better within the estimation sample, but this advantage may be illusory. Out-of-sample testing provides an even playing field for comparing the performance of different methods. Note that the estimation sample can be used to make such comparisons, provided that due care is taken (see Chapter 5).

[3.6] Update the estimates frequently.
Regular updating of the parameter estimates is found to improve forecasting performance because it helps to take into account any changes in the behavior of the series. Once the database has been established and updated with the most recent information, updating the parameter estimates is straightforward.

Summary

Extrapolative forecasts are useful in the short to medium term whenever the recent behavior of the series under study is sufficient to provide a framework for forecasting. When a series does not display marked changes in level over time, simple exponential smoothing (SES), as described in Section 3.3, usually suffices. However, many series do contain systematic trends, and in such circumstances linear exponential smoothing (LES) should be considered, as described in Section 3.4. A series may display nonlinear behavior, either in the growth pattern or because of some kind of life cycle, as is the case for the sales of many products. In Section 3.5, we explored the use of damped trend methods to handle these issues. Other extrapolative methods were reviewed briefly in Section 3.6. Section 3.7 looked at different transformations. The construction of one-step-ahead prediction intervals was examined in Section 3.8. We have introduced quite a number of different variants of exponential smoothing in this chapter so in Section 3.9 we discussed method selection — how to choose among them. Finally, some basic principles for forecasting with extrapolative methods were summarized in Section 3.10.

Exercises

*Topics marked with an * are advanced and may be omitted for more introductory courses.*

3.1   The growth rate in the U.S. gross domestic product *(GDP)* for 1963–2015 is provided in *GDP_change_2.xlsx*.

    a. Use three- and seven-term moving averages to generate one-step-ahead forecasts for 2001 to the end of the series. Graph the results, and comment on the differences between the two moving averages.

    b. Compare the performance of the two procedures by calculating the *RMSE* and *MAE*. Why is the *MAPE* inappropriate in this case?

3.2   The annual percentage change in the consumer price index *(CPI)* for 1963–2015 is provided in *CPI_change_2.xlsx*.

    a. Use three- and seven-term moving averages to generate one-step-ahead forecasts for 2001 to the end of the series.

    b. Compare the performance of the two procedures by calculating the *RMSE* and *MAE*.

    c. Calculate the *RelMAE* and *MASE* for the one-step-ahead forecasts. Why is the *MAPE* inappropriate in this case?

3.3   Use the data in *GDP_change_2.xlsx* to generate forecasts for *GDP* growth by simple exponential smoothing (SES).

    a. With the observed value for 1963 as the starting value, compute the one-step-ahead SES forecasts for 2001–2015, using each of $\alpha = 0.2$, 0.5, and 0.8 in turn.

    b. Compare the forecasting performance for the given values of α by calculating the *RMSE* and *MAE* over the period 2001–2015.

    c. How does this method compare with the moving-average procedures used in Exercise 3.1? (Be careful to make comparisons over the same time periods.)

3.4 Rework the analysis in Exercise 3.3, using the optimal value of α. (Use the ESM or other suitable software.)

3.5 Use the data in *CPI_change_2.xlsx* to generate forecasts for changes in the *CPI* by means of simple exponential smoothing (SES).

a. Use the observed value for 1963 as the starting value, and compute the one-step-ahead forecasts for subsequent years for $\alpha = 0.2, 0.5,$ and 0.8 in turn.

b. Compare the performance for the given values of α by calculating the *RMSE* and *MAE* over the period 2001–2015.

c. How does this method compare with the moving-average procedures used in Exercise 3.2? (Be careful to make comparisons over the same time periods.)

3.6 Rework the analysis in Exercise 3.5, using the optimal value of α. (Use the ESM or other suitable software.)

3.7 The average annual U.S. landed cost of Saudi Arabian Light Crude Oil (in U.S. dollars per barrel) for 1978–2015 is provided in *SA_oil_prices_2.xlsx*.

a. Use the observed value for 1978 as the starting value, and compute the one-step-ahead SES forecasts for subsequent years for each of $\alpha = 0.2, 0.5,$ and 0.8 in turn.

b. With the same starting value, find the optimal level for α, using the data for the period 1978-2007 as the estimation sample. Use the ESM or other suitable software.

c. Generate the forecasts for 2008–2015.

d. Compute the out-of-sample *RMSE, MAE,* and *MAPE* for each case, and contrast the results. Does using the median rather than the mean make any difference?

3.8 Repeat the analysis in Exercise 3.7, using linear exponential smoothing. (Use the ESM or other suitable software.) Compare the forecasting performance of the two methods.

3.9 Repeat the analysis in Exercise 3.8, using 1978–2004 and then 1989–2004 as the estimation samples. Generate the 95 percent prediction intervals for the one-step-ahead forecasts in each case, using the normal approximation. Do the prediction intervals include the observed values? Interpret your results.

3.10 Evaluate the performance of SES and LES for the Netflix series *(Netflix_2.xlsx),* using different time ranges for the estimation sample, and note how the optimal values of the parameters and forecasting performance vary.

3.11 Use LES to forecast the number of domestic passengers at Dulles airport for 2004-2015 (see Table 2.2, *Dulles_2.xlsx),* with the years 1963–2003 as the estimation sample. Then use the complete data set through 2010 to make forecasts for 2011–2015. Use different time ranges for the estimation sample, and note how the optimal values of the parameters and forecasting performance vary.

3.12 Dulles Airport was greatly expanded in the mid-eighties, producing a significant increase in the number of passengers. Rerun the analyses of Exercise 3.11, using the years 1986–2010 as the estimation sample. Compare your results with those for the complete sample. What conclusions do you draw from the comparison?

3.13 Rerun the analyses of Exercise 3.9 for the damped trend and log transform versions of LES, and compare the results of the four methods, using *RMSE, MAE,* and *MAPE.*

3.14 Evaluate the approximate 95 percent prediction intervals for one-step-ahead forecasts for the hold-out sample used in Exercise 3.9.

3.15 Rerun the analyses of Exercise 3.12 for the damped trend and log transform versions of LES, and compare the results of the four methods, using *RMSE, MAE, RelMAE,* and *MAPE.* What conclusions do you draw?

3.16 Evaluate the approximate 95 percent prediction intervals for one-step-ahead forecasts for the hold-out sample used in Exercises 3.12 and 3.15.

3.17 Use the observed errors from the estimation sample in Exercise 3.12 to generate empirical 90 percent prediction intervals for the one-step-ahead forecasts for 2011–2015.

3.18* Show that $\ln(Y_t / Y_{t-1}) \approx (Y_t - Y_{t-1}) / Y_{t-1}$ when the difference between successive terms is small and, hence, that the log transform and growth rate methods often produce similar results. *(Hint:* $\ln(1 + x) \approx x$ for small x.)

3.19 Demonstrate that the trend equation in (3.11) may be rewritten as equation (3.12) by substituting the expression for the level at time *t.*

3.20* By repeated substitution of the level and trend forecasts into equations (3.13) show that the *h*-step-ahead forecast for damped trend is given by equation (3.14).

3.21 Repeat the analysis for the data on oil prices in Exercise 3.7, using the Box-Cox transform. Compare the results with the original forecasts ($c = 1.0$).

Minicases

Minicase 3.1 Job Openings

The monthly employment reports issued by the US Department of Labor are eagerly monitored by investors as indicators of the health of the overall economy. The file *Job_openings.xlsx* contains the monthly figures for total nonfarm openings, from January 2001–December 2015, seasonally adjusted.

To provide investing insights, develop a forecasting procedure for this series, using 2001–2012 as the estimation sample and 2013–2015 as the hold-out sample. You should consider all the options described in the chapter: SES, LES, damped LES, Log and Box-Cox transformations. All these options may be explored via the ESM.

Minicase 3.2 The Evolution of Walmart

Consider the data on Walmart stores described in Chapter 2 (Minicase 2.2) and available in *Walmart_2.xlsx*. In Minicase 2.2, we used basic statistical tools to examine the changing composition of store types and the company's growth. The objective now is to use exponential smoothing methods to generate the following forecasts:

1. Store composition for the next three years.

2. Sales for the next eight quarters.

In each case, plot the fitted and observed values of the series and identify any possible shortcomings in your forecasts. What steps, if any, might be taken to improve the forecasts *without collecting any new data?*

Minicase 3.3 Volatility in the Dow Jones Index

The efficient markets hypothesis (EMH) in finance embodies the notion that financial markets process new information rapidly in order that the best forecast of a stock's price in the next (short) time period be the current price. The EMH is also known as the random-walk hypothesis because any movement from the present state is essentially unpredictable. The percentage errors (or stock returns), which in this context are given by $R_t = 100(Y_t - Y_{t-1})/Y_{t-1}$, are so defined because the last period's closing price is the current forecast. The EMH corresponds to the assumption that the successive errors are independent and unpredictable from publicly available information. There is a vast literature on the EMH in its various forms (see, for example, *http://en.wikipedia.org/wiki/Efficient-market_hypothesis)*, and our purpose is not to discuss the ideas in any detail. Rather, we note that, in forecasting terms, the EMH translates into the use of SES with $\alpha = 1$, essentially of no real value to the stock trader.

Despite many efforts to the contrary, it is essentially impossible for any purely statistical forecasting method to beat the random walk for any long period of time. Insider information can, of course, be of considerable value, but those forecasters tend not to be at liberty to talk about their methods. Nevertheless, some interesting questions can be answered that relate to *volatility*. Toward that end, we can examine the pattern of the forecast errors to determine whether the inherent variability in those forecasts varies over time. When variability is high, considerable opportunities exist for traders to buy or sell options (Hull, 2002). Conversely, when variability is very low, there is little room in the market for such contracts.

We may examine the absolute values of the one-step-ahead errors $|e_t| = |R_t - R_{t-1}|$. The spreadsheet *DowJones_2.xlsx* provides daily closing prices for the period 2011–2016, along with the values of the returns and their absolute values.

1. Examine the validity of the EMH for this series.

2. Use the SES to develop a forecasting method for the absolute values of the returns. Is volatility predictable, at least to some extent?

References

Armstrong, J. S., ed. (2001). *Principles of Forecasting: A Handbook for Researchers and Practitioners.* Boston and Dordrecht: Kluwer.

Assimakopoulos, V. and Nikolopoulos, K. (2000). The theta model: a decomposition approach to forecasting. *International Journal of Forecasting,* 16, 521–530.

Box, G. E. P., and Cox, D. R. (1964). An analysis of transformations. *Journal of the Royal Statistical Society, series B,* 26, 211–252.

Brown, R. G. (1959). *Statistical Forecasting for Inventory Control.* New York: McGraw-Hill.

Brown, R. G. (1963). *Smoothing, Forecasting and Prediction of Discrete Time Series.* Englewood Cliffs, NJ: Prentice-Hall.

Davydenko, A., and Fildes, R. (2013). Measuring forecasting accuracy: The case of judgmental adjustments to SKU-level demand forecasts. *International Journal of Forecasting,* 29(3), 510–522.

Fildes, R. (1992). The evaluation of extrapolative forecasting methods. *International Journal of Forecasting,* 8, 81–98.

Fildes, R., Hibon, M., Makridakis, S., and Meade, N. (1998). Generalising about univariate forecasting methods: Further empirical evidence. *International Journal of Forecasting,* 14, 339–358.

Fiorucci, J. A., Pellegrini, T. R., Louzada, F., Petropoulos, F., and Koehler, A. B. (2016). Models for optimising the theta method and their relationship to state space models. *International Journal of Forecasting*, 32(4), 1151–1161.

Gardner, E. S., Jr. (1985). Exponential smoothing: The state of the art. *Journal of Forecasting*, 4, 1–28.

Gardner, E. S., Jr. (2006). Exponential smoothing: The state of the art — Part II. *International Journal of Forecasting*, 22, 637–677.

Gardner, E. S., Jr., and McKenzie, E. (1985). Forecasting trends in time series. *Management Science*, 31, 1237–1246.

Holt, C. C. (2004). Forecasting seasonals and trends by exponentially weighted moving averages. *International Journal of Forecasting*, 20, 5–10. Reprint of Office of Naval Research Memorandum 52/1957, Carnegie Institute of Technology.

Hull, J. C. (2002). *Fundamentals of Futures and Options Markets*, 4th ed. Upper Saddle River, NJ: Prentice-Hall.

Hyndman, R. J., and Billah, B. (2003). Unmasking the theta method. *International Journal of Forecasting*, 19, 287–290.

Makridakis, S., and Hibon, M. (2000). The M3-competition: Results, conclusions and implications. *International Journal of Forecasting*, 16, 451–76.

Tashman, J. (2000). Out-of-sample tests of forecasting accuracy: an analysis and review. *International Journal of Forecasting*, 16, 437–50.

Trigg, D. W., and Leach, D. H. (1967). Exponential smoothing with an adaptive response rate. *Operational Research Quarterly*, 18, 53–59.

Appendix 3A Excel Macro

This appendix provides a brief summary of the capabilities of the Exponential Smoothing Macro (ESM) used in this chapter. Full descriptions, along with the Excel files, are available in the Users' Manual on the book's website.

1. The parameters are estimated by minimizing the *RMSE;* the solution is obtained numerically with Solver.

2. The user may specify the estimation and hold-out samples.

3. One-step-ahead forecasts are generated for the hold-out sample and multiple step-ahead forecasts beyond the hold-out sample.

4. ESM enables consideration of SES, LES, damped LES and both logarithmic and Box-Cox transformations. The summary statistics are always reported for the original data, after inverse transformations where necessary.

CHAPTER 4

Seasonal Series: Forecasting and Decomposition

*Topics marked with an * are advanced and may be omitted for more introductory courses.*

Table of Contents

Every season has its peaks and valleys.
What you have to try to do is eliminate the Grand Canyon.

— Andy van Slyke, professional baseball player

Introduction

In the previous chapter, we examined forecasting methods for time series that contain trends. However, there are often other elements in a series that must be taken into account. In particular, the data frequently exhibit a seasonal pattern, such as sales of ice cream being higher in the summer. The term *seasonal* indicates a pattern that occurs within a *known* time frame. For example, the gross domestic product *(GDP)* is measured quarterly, so that the seasonal pattern relates to the calendar year and the series has a periodicity of 4. Likewise, unemployment is reported monthly, so that the seasonal pattern is again related to the calendar year, but now the series has a periodicity of 12. In both cases, seasonal effects arise because of the weather, so there may be lost production in the winter because of poor working and road conditions; in addition, the mix of economic activities varies as the result of more or less predictable changes, including holidays. From our perspective, it is important to emphasize that the period (such as a year) is known and that the patterns within a period (such as a year) tend to be similar from one period (or year) to the next.

However, we use the term *seasonal* more widely in this book, to refer to any pattern that occurs within a known fixed time frame. Thus, days of the week are an important seasonal effect for retail sales, because certain days (e.g., Saturdays) are known to produce higher levels of sales, whereas midweek sales tend to be lower. A further example is provided by the 24 hours within a day, which reveal a regular pattern for electricity consumption. In both these cases, seasonal effects exist in the annual cycle as well, so there are multiple seasonalities. The key feature in all these examples is that the time period(s) involved is (are) of *known and fixed* duration.

Why do we need to concern ourselves with seasonal effects? As always, forecasts underpin planning. A retailer needs to make inventory decisions and to plan deployment of the work force, whereas a utility company needs to plan for capacity that will meet peak demand, and to set lower prices for off-peak demand because the marginal cost of off-peak production is very low.

In Section 4.1, we examine the components of a time series, including trend and seasonality. Then, in Section 4.2, we look at forecasting for purely seasonal patterns — that is, for series that exhibit no trend. Series such as the average monthly temperature in a given location exhibit very little trend relative to seasonal changes (global warming notwithstanding), and such purely seasonal series represent a simple place from which to start our investigations. This starting point provides a natural progression to series that exhibit both trends and seasonal components, and we use a decomposition approach in Sections 4.3 and 4.4 to develop forecasts for such series. This approach leads to the creation of deseasonalized series — that is, series whose values have been adjusted to remove the effects of seasonal changes. Such methods are widely used in the presentation of macroeconomic data; indeed, many series produced by the United States and other governments are published only in a seasonally adjusted form. The most popular approach to the creation of such series is known as the Census X-13 ARIMA method, developed by the U.S. Bureau of the Census and described briefly in Section 4.5.

Most economic and business series display both trend and seasonal elements that evolve over time, and Sections 4.6 and 4.7 develop forecasting methods for such series. As with the exponential smoothing methods described in Chapter 3, we assume that a time series can be represented by a set of components. We then develop a forecast for each component and produce a forecast for the series that is a combination of all these elements. In the examples, the analysis uses the Exponential Smoothing Macro (ESM), so that results can be consistently replicated by the reader. However, more sophisticated programs may produce different results and this question is explored in Section 4.8 using programs available in R. The methods considered for most of the chapter are generally employed for monthly and quarterly series. Weekly series are often treated rather differently, as there may be very few years' worth of data to estimate so many (weekly) components; this issue is examined in Section 4.9. Prediction intervals for seasonal forecasts are developed in Section 4.10. The chapter concludes with a discussion of underlying principles in Section 4.11 and the chapter summary.

4.1 Components of a Time Series

We have introduced the trend and seasonal components of a time series, but there are also other components that are less regular. For example, the economy goes through business cycles of expansion and contraction; such cycles have tended to average around four years in the United States, but vary between two and ten years in duration. The duration of business cycles is not known in advance, nor is it stable from one cycle to the next. Some commentators have suggested that the business cycle is related to the four-year cycle of U.S. presidential elections, presumably on the grounds that a strong economy begets re-election! Similar suggestions apply in the United Kingdom and elsewhere. Even if successive administrations strive to induce such cycles, there is no guarantee that they will be of any predetermined length. One particularly well-established cycle occurs in the number of observed sunspots, with a mean time between peaks of around 10.7 years. The essential point is that such variations are of random duration (though with a predictable mean). We reserve the term *cyclical* for such patterns.

SEASONAL AND CYCLICAL TIME SERIES

A time series is said to have a *seasonal* component if it displays a recurrent pattern with a fixed and known duration.

A time series has a *cyclical* component if it displays somewhat regular fluctuations about the trend but those fluctuations have a periodicity of variable and unknown duration, usually longer than one year (e.g., a business cycle).

In addition to the trend and the seasonal and cyclical components, the series will contain a random error component, which, as before, represents the variations not accounted for by the other components. In common with most introductions to forecasting, we will absorb the cyclical component into the trend term and concentrate upon just three components: *trend (T), seasonal (S),* and *error (E)*. Because our current focus is upon short- to medium-term forecasts, this simplification rarely causes any problems in practice. The combination of these components is illustrated in Figure 4.1. In the example, the trend is an upward-sloping straight line and the seasonal pattern corresponds to quarterly data (of periodicity 4). The error terms do not display any regular pattern. The three components are added together to provide the plot of the complete series (series A in Figure 4.1). In any forecasting exercise, we cannot observe the separate components and must find a way to create such elements from the observed (composite) series.

Figure 4.1 The Components of a Time Series

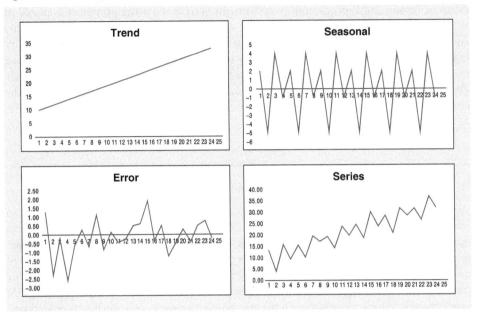

Algebraically, the three components are combined by addition to create the time series (Y):

$$Y = T + S + E. \tag{4.1}$$

Equation (4.1) is known as the *(purely) additive* model for a series. Other models are possible, of which the two best known are the *(purely) multiplicative* model,

$$Y = TSE, \tag{4.2}$$

and the *mixed additive-multiplicative* model,

$$Y = TS + E. \tag{4.3}$$

Whenever the trend and the seasonal component are multiplied together, larger levels in the series will tend to exhibit larger peaks and troughs. In addition, when the error term is also multiplicative, the magnitude of the forecast errors will tend to rise and fall with the level of the series.

Before we consider forecasts derived from these equations, we examine forecasting for purely seasonal patterns — that is, series devoid of any trend. Although this situation is uncommon for business series over periods of a year or more, for short-term forecasts (e.g., retail sales over the next month of a product in a store) such models are often more than adequate. In addition, the approach aids in understanding the methods that examine both trend and seasonality and is useful if we wish to decompose the series into deseasonalized and seasonal components. It is then possible to generate forecasts for the deseasonalized series by using the methods of Chapter 3 and to combine those values with forecasts for the purely seasonal component.

4.2 Forecasting Purely Seasonal Series

Notwithstanding the longer term effects, if any, of global warming, data relating to different aspects of the weather reflect our natural understanding of a strong seasonal pattern with little or no trend. Some other purely seasonal series are specially created, such as the seasonal index for U.S. retail sales shown earlier in Figure 1.3. Cyclical components may also exist, but these are sufficiently long term that they may often be safely ignored when forecasting in the short term.

■ Example 4.1: Temperatures in Boulder, Colorado

Figure 4.2 is a time plot of monthly average temperatures for Boulder, Colorado, over the period 1991-2015. The data are available in the file *Boulder_2.xlsx*. The seasonal pattern is very clear. Nevertheless, we may also use the seasonal plot, introduced in Chapter 2, as a useful way to detect seasonal patterns when trends also exist. In the present context, we plot temperature against the month of the year, so that there are 12 points on the x-axis; a separate but overlaid plot is then constructed for each year. The results for temperature data for the period 2012–2105 are shown in Figure 4.3; only four years of data were used to avoid cluttering up the graph. The strong seasonal pattern is clear, and the extensive overlapping indicates the absence of any marked trend. An alternative seasonal plot is obtained if we plot temperature against time but color-code each year separately. This version of a seasonal plot is examined in Exercise 4.1.

Figure 4.2 Monthly Average Temperatures (In Degrees Fahrenheit) in Boulder, Colorado, 1991–2015

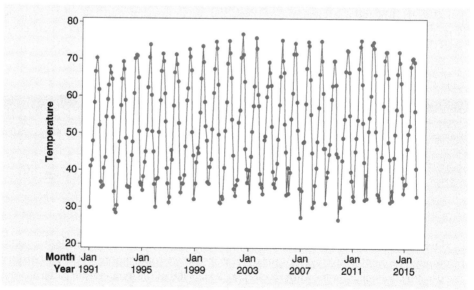

Source: Earth System Research Laboratory, Physical Sciences Division, National Oceanic and Atmospheric Administration (*www.ersl.noaa.gov/psd/boulder/Boulder.mm.html*).

Data: Boulder_2.xlsx

Figure 4.3 Seasonal Plot of Average Temperature (In Degrees Fahrenheit) in Boulder, Colorado *(2012–2015, plotted against month, partitioned by year)*

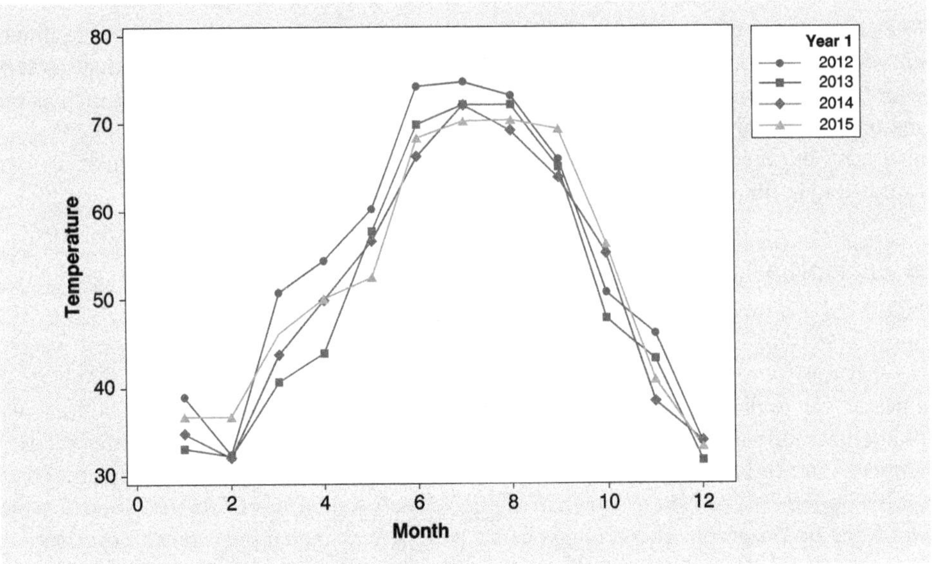

Source: Earth System Research Laboratory, Physical Sciences Division, National Oceanic and Atmospheric Administration (*www.esrl.noaa.gov/psd/boulder/Boulder.mm.html*).

Data: Boulder_2.xlsx

Suppose we wish to forecast monthly average temperatures 12 months ahead for the year 2015. The simplest approach would be to take an average for each month over the period 1991-2014 and use that as the forecast. The results are shown in Table 4.1. Over the 12 months, the mean absolute error *(MAE)* is 2.28 degrees and the root mean square error (*RMSE*) is 2.64 degrees.

Table 4.1 Actual and Forecast Values for Monthly Temperatures in Boulder, Colorado for 2015

	Jan	Feb	Mar	Apr	May	Jun	Jul	Aug	Sep	Oct	Nov	Dec
Temperature	36.5	36.6	46.1	50.1	52.4	68.3	70.3	70.5	69.4	56.2	40.8	33.1
Average	34.2	35.3	43.0	48.8	57.7	66.6	72.7	70.7	63.1	51.4	41.1	33.9
Error	2.3	1.3	3.1	1.3	−5.3	1.7	−2.4	−0.2	6.3	4.8	−0.3	−0.8
Abs Error	2.3	1.3	3.1	1.3	5.3	1.7	2.4	0.2	6.3	4.8	0.3	0.8
Sq error	5.29	1.69	9.61	1.69	28.09	2.89	5.76	0.04	39.69	23.08	0.09	0.64
ME = 0.98			MAE = 2.48			RMSE = 9.88						

Data: Boulder_2.xlsx

If we now consider forecasts for 2016 after the 2015 data become available, we could recompute the monthly averages. At the other extreme, we could ignore all the past history and use only the values for the most recent year, if we felt that the temperature patterns were changing rapidly. Both options seem rather extreme, given the discussions about smoothing in the previous chapter, so instead we adopt a seasonal smoothing procedure. ■

4.2.1 Purely Seasonal Exponential Smoothing

A seasonal version of simple exponential smoothing (SES) may be written as

New forecast for a given "month" = Old forecast for that "month" + smoothing constant × forecast error.

We use "months" within a "year" to denote the seasonal structure, but in keeping with our earlier comments, the same general idea applies to any purely seasonal series.

PURELY SEASONAL FORECASTS

The forecast for period $t + m$ made m steps earlier, denoted by $F_{t+m}(m)$, is given by the previous m-step-ahead forecast (made at time $t - m$) for period t, adjusted by the error observed for that earlier forecast. Algebraically, the updating relationship may be written as

$$F_{t+m}(m) = F_t(m) + \gamma[Y_t - F_t(m)] = F_t(m) + \gamma e_t \qquad (4.4)$$

The smoothing parameter (γ) represents the rate of adjustment to the latest error. The error term in this situation is $e_t = Y_t - F_t(m)$, which leads to the second expression in equation (4.4).

For example, the forecast for July 2016 equals the July 2015 forecast plus a partial error adjustment (based upon the difference between the observed values for July 2015 and its forecast a year earlier on the basis of the data available up to and including July 2014). Because we are focusing purely on the seasonal effects, we do not use data for any months other than previous July values. This prevents the July 2016 forecast from changing (once the July 2015 value has been observed and the forecast updated), despite our having observed August and subsequent values. Another way of looking at this situation is to think in terms of 12 separate series (one for each month) that are updated independently of each other. We update each series as soon as that monthly value is recorded, but we do not use the updated forecast until the next year. This framework is very restrictive and it is usually desirable to include information on recent trends as well. The reason for developing equation (4.4) is that it is a key element in the general framework for forecasting seasonal series, as we shall see in later sections of this chapter.

We could use equation (4.4) to forecast the average temperature but we prefer to keep the analysis within the framework of the Exponential Smoothing Macro (ESM) introduced in the previous chapter. Accordingly, the results in Table 4.1 anticipate later developments and fit a model with both level and seasonal components. The parameters are estimated using data over the period January 1991 to December 2012. The analysis in Table 4.2 considers different forecasts for January 2013 to December 2015. *MAE* and *RMSE* are used to measure forecast accuracy here. In this example, the mean absolute percentage error *(MAPE)* is not sensible, because the variable is not ratio-scaled, as it has no natural origin; consider how the *MAPE* changes if we switch from the Fahrenheit scale to Celsius!

The results are summarized in Table 4.2. The first row represents the error statistics for the estimation sample (with $\alpha = 0.015$, $\gamma = 0.189$), and the remaining rows are the results for the different forecasting methods.

For comparative purposes, we included the forecasts based only on the previous year and those based on the long run average of all years from 1991 – 2012. The results show the better performance of the monthly scheme derived using the ESM. The small value for α indicates that the carry-over from the previous month is relatively slight: the small γ suggests a slowly changing seasonal pattern.

Table 4.2 Summary Error Statistics for Forecasting Average Temperatures in Boulder, Colorado *(Hold-out sample covers from January 2013 to December 2015)*

	ME	MAE	MSE	RMSE
Estimation Sample	0.20	2.63	11.20	3.35
Hold-out Sample				
Model	−0.51	2.12	7.53	2.74
Previous Year	−0.69	3.04	15.67	3.96
Long-run Average	−2.50	3.04	13.26	3.34

Data: Boulder_2.xlsx

4.3 Forecasting Using a Seasonal Decomposition

Most of the series we are likely to encounter contain both trend and seasonal components. Because we observe only the aggregate series and not the components, one approach to forecasting is to decompose the time series into its trend, seasonal, and error components. We could remove the seasonal component and forecast the deseasonalized, or seasonally adjusted, version of the series, using the methods of Chapter 3. We may also forecast the seasonal components and then recombine the two to forecast the overall series.

Our primary interest is in forecasting, and we will approach "seasonal decomposition" from that direction, although decomposition methods are often used in the analysis of macroeconomic series, with particular interest in removing seasonal effects. Over many years, the U.S. Census Bureau has supported decomposition software, the current version of which is known as Census X-13 ARIMA. This program is applied to most major economic series, such as *GDP*, some of which are published only in seasonally adjusted form. We present a brief description of Census X-13 ARIMA in Section 4.5 and a reference to access downloadable versions. Our present focus is upon the fundamental ideas underlying seasonal adjustment. The basic steps in the process are as follows:

1. Generate estimates of the trend component by averaging out the seasonal component.

2. Estimate the seasonal component by removing the trend from the series.

3. Create a deseasonalized series.

4. Forecast the trend and the seasonal pattern separately.

5. Recombine the trend forecast with the seasonal component to produce a forecast for the original series.

DECOMPOSITION

Pure Decomposition. Use all *n* data points to estimate the fitted value at each time *t* (**two-sided** decomposition).

Forecasting Decomposition. Use only the data up to and including time *t* to predict the value at time *t* + 1 and beyond (**one-sided** decomposition).

There are two basic versions of seasonal adjustment. The first version is based upon the purely additive model, originally specified in equation (4.1) as

$$Y_t = T_t + S_t + E_{t,} \tag{4.5}$$

where T denotes the trend term, S designates the seasonal component, and E is the random error (often referred to as the *irregular component* in this context); we have added time subscripts in equation (4.5) for later use. Likewise, the mixed additive-multiplicative scheme given in equation (4.3) is represented by

$$Y_t = T_t S_t + E_t. \tag{4.6}$$

A key element in this approach is the use of moving averages, introduced in Section 3.2.2:

MOVING AVERAGE (for forecasting)

A (simple) *moving average* of order K, denoted by $MA(K)$, is the average of K successive terms in a time series, so the first average is $(Y_1 + Y_2 + \cdots + Y_K)/K$, the second is $(Y_2 + Y_3 + \cdots + Y_{K+1})/K$, and so on. The moving average taken at time t may be denoted by $MA_t(K) = (Y_{t-K+1} + Y_{t-K+2} + \cdots + Y_t)/K$.

The moving average is used to produce an average that is free of seasonal effects. That is, we might average over four consecutive quarters $(K = 4)$ or 12 consecutive months $(K = 12)$. This average provides an estimate[1] of the trend term, T_t. We use past values of the series to estimate the trend so that, for example, in a quarterly series $K = 4$ and the first trend estimate is $T_5 = (Y_1 + Y_2 + \cdots + Y_4)/4$. We then compute the detrended series Y_t^{DT} as

$$Y_t^{DT} = Y_t - T_t = S_t + E_t. \tag{4.7}$$

We now assume that the seasonal component for each period (such as summer) is stable and estimate that component by averaging Y_t^{DT} over all available observations for that period (e.g., all summers for which data are available). Often, the seasonal components are adjusted to have a zero mean, although this does not affect the forecasts. The seasonal factor for period t is denoted by $S_{(j,t)}$; the subscript indexes the seasons and is included in the parentheses to remind us that there are only 4 (quarterly), 7 (days of the week), or 12 (monthly) such factors. Finally, we produce the deseasonalized series Y_t^{DS} and the error terms:

$$Y_t^{DS} = Y_t - S_{(j,t)}$$

$$E_t = Y_t - T_t - S_{(j,t)}.$$

Now that the seasonal effects have been removed, the deseasonalized series may be forecast with SES or LES, as appropriate, as described in Sections 3.3 and 3.4. The final forecast is then obtained by adding back the seasonal component.

■ **Example 4.2:** *(Examples_chapter_4.xlsx)*

The process of additive deseasonalization is illustrated for quarterly data in Table 4.3.

In part A of the table, the third column gives the moving average of terms taken four at a time. To align the forecasts with the actual values, we place the average of the first four terms, $(115 + 90 + 65 + 135)/4 = 101.25$, in the row corresponding to observation 5, and so on. That is, we average the figures for the first year, thereby eliminating seasonal effects, and then use that average as a preliminary forecast of the level for the first period (quarter) of the second year. The fourth column contains the values of the *Detrended series*, computed with equation (4.7); that is, we subtract the initial trend values from the original observations. In part B of the table, we gather together the 12 detrended values (three observations

---

1 We are working with estimates of the components, not their actual values. This point should be kept in mind, as the distinction is not made in the notation.

for each quarter) and compute their average *(Seasonal Means)*. Next, these quarterly averages are adjusted to have zero mean, yielding the seasonal index values *(Adjusted Means)* with values (20.63, -15.21, -38.54, 33.13). The *Deseasonalized series* is then given in the sixth column of Part A by subtracting the adjusted seasonal component from each observation.

Table 4.3 Additive Deseasonalization and Its Use in Forecasting

Part A: Deseasonalized Series

Obs	Series	MA(4)	Detrended Series	Seasonal Factor	Deseasonalized Series	Deseasonalized Forecasts	Series Forecasts	Error	Error Squared	Absolute Error	Absolute Percentage Error
1	115			20.63	94.38						
2	90			-15.21	105.21						
3	65			-38.54	103.54						
4	135			33.13	101.88						
5	130	101.25	28.75	20.63	109.38	109.60	130.22	-0.22	0.05	0.22	0.17
6	95	105.00	-10.00	-15.21	110.21	111.94	96.73	-1.73	2.99	1.73	1.82
7	75	106.25	-31.25	-38.54	113.54	113.28	74.74	0.26	0.07	0.26	0.35
8	150	108.75	41.25	33.13	116.88	115.43	148.56	1.44	2.09	1.44	0.96
9	135	112.50	22.50	20.63	114.38	118.38	139.01	-4.01	16.06	4.01	2.97
10	105	113.75	-8.75	-15.21	120.21	118.30	103.09	1.91	3.64	1.91	1.82
11	85	116.25	-31.25	-38.54	123.54	120.89	82.35	2.65	7.01	2.65	3.11
12	155	118.75	36.25	33.13	121.88	124.43	157.56	-2.56	6.53	2.56	1.65
13	145	120.00	25.00	20.63	124.38	125.39	146.02	-1.02	1.03	1.02	0.70
14	110	122.50	-12.50	-15.21	125.21	126.67	111.46	-1.46	2.13	1.46	1.33
15	85	123.75	-38.75	-38.54	123.54	127.41	88.87	-3.87	14.97	3.87	4.55
16	160	123.75	36.25	33.13	126.88	126.28	159.41	0.59	0.35	0.59	0.37

Part B: Seasonal Calculations

Quarter	Year 1	Year 2	Year 3	Year 4	Seasonal Means	Adjusted Means
Q1		28.75	22.5	25	25.42	20.63
Q2		-10.00	-8.75	-12.5	-10.42	-15.21
Q3		-31.25	-31.25	-38.75	-33.75	-38.54
Q4		41.25	36.25	36.25	37.92	33.13
				Overall	4.79	0

Part C: Summary Measures

MSE	MAE	MAPE	RMSE
4.74	1.81	1.65	2.18

Data: Examples_chapter_4.xlsx

Finally, the deseasonalized series may be forecast by linear exponential smoothing (LES, described in Section 3.4, because a trend clearly exists). The resulting forecasts are shown in column seven *(Deseasonalized Forecasts)*. The starting values were specified as in Section 3.4.3, and the optimal values of the smoothing parameters turned out to be $\alpha = 0.37$ and $\beta = 0.68$. The seasonal components are then added back in to produce the final forecasts in the eighth column *(Series Forecasts)*. The error analysis then proceeds in the usual way. Note that the values given are *fitted values rather than pure forecasts*, because all the observations were used to construct the seasonal index values and to estimate the smoothing parameters. However, given these estimates, proper forecasts can be constructed for future values. ∎

Analogously to the additive model just described, we may construct a mixed additive-multiplicative scheme based upon the model given by equation (4.6). The key difference is that we must divide the original series by the moving average to obtain the detrended series (fourth column in Table 4.3) and then adjust the seasonal indexes to average 1.0 rather than zero. The deseasonalized series (column 6) follows upon dividing the original series by the seasonal indexes. After forecasting this series, we obtain forecasts for the original series (column 8) upon multiplying the deseasonalized forecasts (column 7) by the seasonal indexes. This analysis is left to the reader as Exercise 4.9.

Once the notion of decomposition is recognized, a variety of forecasting methods becomes available. The process of decomposition and the methods for forecasting the deseasonalized and seasonal components must all be determined by the forecaster. We have described two variants of one simple form, but specialized software allows a range of more sophisticated approaches, as we shall see in Section 4.6. In particular, we do not need to assume that the seasonal factors are constant over time.

4.4 Pure Decomposition

As we noted at the beginning of the previous section, time series are sometimes analyzed in order to better understand underlying trends, rather than for forecasting. This orientation is particularly strong with macroeconomic data, for which seasonally adjusted data allow a clearer picture of current developments within the economy. It is therefore worth understanding how such deseasonalized series are developed.

The first key element to recognize is that such seasonal adjustment methods may rely upon both past and future observations, as the focus now is upon understanding rather than pure forecasting. To take an obvious example, if you know the weather on Monday and Wednesday, you have a better understanding of what happened on Tuesday than if you have just Monday's weather. However, Wednesday's weather could not be available for forecasting purposes.

To make this process operational, we use moving averages as before, but now we want to align the average with the current value of the series. Thus, if we are dealing with daily sales figures, we would align the average across Sunday, Monday, ..., Saturday of a given week with Wednesday, the fourth of the seven days. However, a problem arises when the number of periods per season is even (four quarters or 12 months). If we take the average over January–December, the average is a half-period out of phase. That is, the average of the 12 months lands between June and July (the average of the numbers 1 through 12 is 6.5), so the moving-average term would not match up exactly in time with either month. To overcome this difficulty, we take a further average to produce a centered moving average.

CENTERED MOVING AVERAGES (for decomposition)

If K is odd we place $MA_t(K)$ at period $t-(K-1)/2$. For example the first value of $MA(3)$ would be placed at period $3-(3-1)/2 = 2$. With K even, the moving average falls mid-way between periods, i.e. $MA_4(4)$ would be placed at 'period' 2.5 while $MA_5(4)$ placed at 'period' 3.5.

If K is odd, the Centered Moving average, $CMA_t(K)$ is defined as equivalent to $MA_t(K)$ and placed at period $t-(K-1)/2$. If K is even, $CMA_t(K) = (MA_t(K) + MA_{t+1}(K))/2$ and placed at period $t-k/2+1$. For example the first $CMA(6)$ is calculated by averaging the first $MA(6)$ being placed at period $6-2.5=3.5$ and the second $MA(6)$ at period $7-2.5=4.5$. The $CMA(6)$ is then placed at the average of these two times: $t = 4$.

The effect of using the centered MA is to "lose" $K/2$ observations at the beginning and at the end of the series, if K is even, or $(K-1)/2$ if K is odd. Normally, this does not matter at the beginning of the series, but clearly it is critical at the end of the series, because the most recent observations are usually those of greatest interest. If the aim is only to produce a deseasonalized series, we can estimate the seasonal factors and proceed as in Table 4.3, as we show in Table 4.4. However, if we seek to identify underlying trends, we must find some way to extend the series. Earlier schemes used moving averages that assigned different weights to the last few observations in the series, but current "best practice" is to use a statistical model-based approach. The best-known such technique is Census X-13-ARIMA and is discussed briefly in the next section. A simpler method involves fitting a trend line to estimate the last $K/2$ observations (used, e.g., in the Minitab decomposition routine).

The steps that follow describe the process based upon moving averages for quarterly data, assuming t observations; a similar procedure using 12-term moving averages is followed with monthly data. The description applies to the more commonly used multiplicative scheme; modifications for the additive scheme are shown in square brackets.

1. Calculate the four-term $MA(4)$ and then the centered moving average, $CMA(4)$. The first CMA term corresponds to period 3 and the last one to period $(t - 2)$; $K = 4$, so we "lose" two values at each end of the series.

2. Divide [subtract] observations 3, ..., $(t - 2)$ by [from] their corresponding CMA to obtain a detrended series.

3. Calculate the average value (across years) of the detrended series for each quarter j ($j = 1, 2, 3, 4$) to produce the initial seasonal factors.

4. Standardize the seasonal factors by computing their average and then setting the final seasonal factor equal to the initial value divided by [minus] the overall average.

5. Estimate the error term by dividing the detrended series by the final seasonal factor [subtracting the final seasonal factor from the detrended series].

Note that this process is similar to the forecasting procedure described in the previous section. The key difference is that the moving-average values are now centered on the observations, whereas before they were used (asymmetrically) to predict future values in the forecasting framework.

■ Example 4.3: Seasonal decomposition — the calculations
(Examples_chapter_4.xlsx)

For purposes of illustration, we revisit the data set considered in Example 4.2 but now apply a multiplicative *Decomposition,* rather than generating forecasts. Following steps 1–5, we arrive at the results shown in Table 4.4. Successive columns of interest in part A show the original series, the moving average, $MA(4)$, the centered moving average, $CMA(4)$, the *Detrended series,* the *Seasonal factors,* and, finally, the *Deseasonalized series.* The final seasonal factors are calculated in part B of the table and then inserted into part A. For example, the first $CMA(4)$ value is $(101.25 + 105.00)/2 = 103.13$, where the original MA values may be obtained from Table 4.3. However, it is important to observe that the CMA values are now aligned with the corresponding time periods. In Table 4.3, the past moving averages were used to forecast. As in Table 4.3, the seasonal components are considered to be unchanging, and we can produce a deseasonalized series that covers all time periods.

The principal purpose of decomposition is to generate the deseasonalized, or seasonally adjusted, series; such series are commonly used in macroeconomic policy discussions. For example, unemployment is heavily seasonal and the focus of much political debate. Because such issues are of critical importance, the decomposition methods used in practice are much more sophisticated than the simple procedure we have just described. Accordingly, we now provide a brief outline of the most commonly used decomposition method. ■

Table 4.4 Multiplicative Decomposition for Seasonal Adjustment

Part A: Deseasonalized Series

Obs	Series	MA(4)	CMA(4)	Detrended Series	Seasonal Factors	Deseasonalized Series
1	115				1.18	97.65
2	90				0.88	102.83
		101.25				
3	65		103.13	0.630	0.67	97.64
		105.00				
4	135		105.63	1.278	1.28	105.35
		106.25				
5	130		107.50	1.209	1.18	110.39
		108.75				
6	95		110.63	0.859	0.88	108.54
		112.50				
7	75		113.13	0.663	0.67	112.66
		113.75				
8	150		115.00	1.304	1.28	117.06
		116.25				
9	135		117.50	1.149	1.18	114.64
		118.75				
10	105		119.38	0.880	0.88	119.97
		120.00				
11	85		121.25	0.701	0.67	127.68
		122.50				
12	155		123.13	1.259	1.28	120.96
		123.75				
13	145		123.75	1.172	1.18	123.13
		123.75				
14	110		124.38	0.884	0.88	125.68
		125.00				
15	85				0.67	127.68
16	160				1.28	124.86

Part B: Seasonal Calculations

Quarter	Year 1	Year 2	Year 3	Year 4	Averages	Adjusted
Q1		1.209	1.149	1.172	1.177	1.178
Q2		0.859	0.880	0.884	0.874	0.875
Q3	0.630	0.663	0.701		0.665	0.666
Q4	1.278	1.304	1.259		1.280	1.281
				Overall	**0.999**	**1.000**

Data: Examples_chapter_4.xlsx

4.5* The Census X-13 Decomposition

The original seasonal adjustment program introduced in 1965 by the U.S. Bureau of the Census was known as X-11 (Shiskin, Young, and Musgrave, 1967). The name reflects the many years of improvement and modification (from Method 1 in 1954 and onwards) that elapsed before the method reached a standard form. The X-11 method was among the first such procedures to be computerized, and it became a standard for seasonal adjustment around the world. Its successors, X-12-ARIMA and now X-13-ARIMA continue to use the smoothing operations developed in X-11 but take advantage of the ARIMA modeling framework, which we describe in Chapter 6. The ARIMA model enables us to "fill in the blanks" at the end of the series; the model also allows us to incorporate changing seasonal patterns, as in the forecasting procedures described in Sections 4.6 and 4.7. A full description of X-12-ARIMA[2] appears in Findley, Monsell, Bell, Otto, and Chen (1999) and on

---

2 A more advanced seasonal adjustment procedure, X-13-ARIMA-SEATS, is now the "gold standard." This new software embraces the modeling approach more comprehensively.

the Census Bureau website. Thus, we will summarize only a few key properties here. The detailed steps are given in appendices in Findley *et al.*

Step 1: The time series is first adjusted to take into account any anomalous observations. (An anomalous observation is an observation that stands out as incompatible with those around it.) This is begun by creating an initial time series model that provides one-step-ahead preliminary forecasts. Anomalous observations can then be identified and appropriate adjustments made to the data. For example, suppose production is interrupted by a strike or severe weather but returns to normal once the event is over. If no adjustment is made, the anomalous observation will distort future estimates of the trend and seasonal factors and so give misleading values for the seasonally adjusted series. The model is also used to extend the series for the trend and seasonal components so that standard moving averages can be applied throughout the series.

Step 2: The multiplicative (or, more rarely, the additive) version of seasonal adjustment is applied to the series, essentially as described in the previous section. However, rather than assume fixed seasonals, preliminary seasonal factors are estimated by taking a moving average of the initial seasonal estimates for each quarter or month.

Step 3: An initial set of seasonal adjustments is applied as in Table 4.4, but using more complex moving averages.

Step 4: The series is extended (using ARIMA; see Chapter 6) so that moving averages can be computed for each time period up to the end of the series, using the seasonally adjusted data. This leads to a revised estimate of the trend and seasonal factors.

Step 5: A final round of detrending is applied, and the error term is then estimated by dividing the observation by the trend and seasonal factors, to complete the decomposition.

DISCUSSION QUESTION: *In retail store sales of a product, what type of events might introduce anomalies into the observed sales figures?*

For readers wishing to conduct "industrial strength" seasonal adjustments, the X-13-ARIMA program is available free of charge from the Census Bureau; the URL is *www.census.gov/srd/www/x13as*. In both the United States and Europe, a heavily used free program is TRAMO-SEATS; the URL is *www.bde.es/bds/en/secciones/servicios/software/* under the Statistics and Econometrics heading.

4.6 The Holt-Winters Seasonal Smoothing Methods

We now examine exponential smoothing methods for forecasting series that include both trends and seasonal patterns. We focus upon two particular schemes, known as the Holt-Winters' additive and multiplicative schemes, respectively, because they were first developed by Holt (2004, original published in 1957) and Winters (1960).

4.6.1 The Additive Holt-Winters Method

We consider a forecast function that combines, by addition, the level, trend, and seasonal components. That is, we add a seasonal component to the linear exponential smoothing

(LES) scheme developed in Section 3.4. As before, we denote the level of the series by L_t, the trend by T_t, and the seasonal factor by S_t. When there are m seasons (e.g., $m = 12$ for monthly data), the forecast for one period ahead may be written as

$$F_{t+1}(1) = F_{t+1} = L_t + T_t + S_{t+1-m}.$$

For example, to forecast the sales in July 2016, we combine the level and trend elements derived up to and including June 2016 with the seasonal component from July 2015. If we wish to forecast h periods ahead, we use the more general expression

$$F_{t+h}(h) = L_t + hT_t + S_{t+h-m}. \tag{4.8}$$

Equation (4.8) takes the current local level of the series modified by h times the current trend and selects the appropriate monthly seasonal corresponding to period $(t + h)$ to estimate the h-step ahead forecast. The notation is designed to maintain the connection with exponential smoothing as developed in the previous chapter. If $h > m$, we select the appropriate seasonal index, cycling through every m periods; for example, the July index is used for future July forecasts, no matter how many years ahead.

The next step is to update these components. The new information we have is the latest observation or, equivalently, the latest error term, written as

$$e_t = Y_t - L_{t-1} - T_{t-1} - S_{t-m} = Y_t - F_t(1). \tag{4.9}$$

The updating expressions for the level and trend are the same as those used for LES in Section 3.4.2:

$$L_t = L_{t-1} + T_{t-1} + \alpha e_t$$
$$T_t = T_{t-1} + \alpha\beta e_t. \tag{4.10}$$

To complete the process, we must also update the seasonal component,[3] relative to the same period in the previous "year." That is, the seasonal update may be written as

$$S_t = S_{t-m} + \gamma e_t. \tag{4.11}$$

This expression is exactly that appearing in equation (4.4), save that we have changed the variable of interest from F to S to recognize that the seasonal component is now one part of the forecast. Each seasonal component will be updated just once per "year," when the corresponding "monthly" value has been recorded. So, if we were dealing with 12 months in a year, we would have 12 such components and each would be updated once every 12 time periods. From equations (4.10) and (4.11), we observe that each component is updated with the use of a partial adjustment for the error. As before, these equations are known as the *error correction* form. The more usual, but also more cumbersome, way of expressing these relationships is to substitute for e_t, using equation (4.9) to arrive at equations (4.12):

$$L_t = L_{t-1} + T_{t-1} + \alpha(Y_t - L_{t-1} - T_{t-1} - S_{t-m})$$
$$T_t = T_{t-1} + \beta(L_t - L_{t-1} - T_{t-1}) \tag{4.12}$$
$$S_t = S_{t-m} + \gamma(Y_t - L_{t-1} - T_{t-1} - S_{t-m}).$$

Demonstrating the equivalence between the two versions is left as an end-of-chapter exercise. At this stage, we should note that the Holt-Winters equations are often written in a slightly different form, with L_t and T_t replacing L_{t-1} and T_{t-1}, which appears in the seasonal

---

3 An alternate formulation for the seasonal components uses trigonometric functions. A description is provided in Durbin and Koopman (2012, p. 40). A thorough discussion on seasonality is given by Ghysels and Osborne (2001) with various different representations discussed in Chapters 2 and 3.

updating formulas. For the linear case, the two versions produce identical forecasts, although the parameter γ has a different value. We prefer the present formulation because it leads directly to an underlying model (see Section 5.3.2) whereas the more common version does not. The Holt-Winters method allows for a number of special cases, such as the following:

- Fixed seasonal pattern: $\gamma = 0$ (no seasonal updating)
- No seasonal pattern: $\gamma = 0$ and all initial S values are set equal to zero
- Fixed trend: $\beta = 0$
- Zero trend: $\beta = 0$ and $T_0 = 0$
- All fixed components: $\alpha = \beta = \gamma = 0$, a linear trend with fixed seasonal effects.

4.6.2* Starting Values

When the time series is seasonal with m periods, we require a total of $(m + 2)$ starting values: one each for the level and trend, as before, and one for each seasonal component. We again refer to "months" within a "year" for convenience, while recognizing that broader definitions of seasonality are also included. The Exponential Smoothing Macro (ESM) provided on the website uses starting values specified in the way we shall show here, although we should stress that a wide variety of heuristic procedures exists. We use data for the first two years, written as $Y_1, Y_2,\ldots,Y_{2m}$, to initialize the level at period m (L_m), the trend (T_m), and the first m seasonals, $S_1, S_2,\ldots S_m$. The starting values may be written as

$$L_m = \frac{1}{m}(Y_1 + Y_2 + \cdots + Y_m) + \frac{(m-1)}{2}T_m$$

$$T_m = \frac{1}{m}\left[\frac{1}{m}(Y_{m+1} + Y_{m+2} + \cdots + Y_{2m}) - \frac{1}{m}(Y_1 + Y_2 + \cdots + Y_m)\right] \qquad (4.13)$$

$$S_{(i)} = \frac{1}{2m}(Y_i + Y_{i+m}) - \frac{1}{2m}(Y_1 + Y_2 + \cdots + Y_{2m}), \; i = 1, 2, \ldots, \; m.$$

The initial value for the level is defined as the average across the first year, plus an adjustment using the estimated initial trend to allow for the difference between the middle of the year and its end. Thus, for monthly data, $m = 12$, and we add 5.5 trend increments to move from midyear to December. The trend estimate is the "monthly" average increase for the second year over the first year, and the seasonal estimates are the average value for the month in question taken over years 1 and 2 minus the average for all months taken over the first two years.

It is not too much of an exaggeration to suggest that no two statistical software packages define the start-up values in quite the same way. The net effects will be minor, provided that the series is of reasonable length and the smoothing coefficients are not too small. If greater precision is required, the starting values should be estimated from the full estimation sample; the more technically inclined reader should consult Hyndman, Koehler, Ord, and Snyder (2008, Chapter 5) for details and the software referenced in online Appendix B.

■ Example 4.4: Additive Holt-Winters forecasting — the calculations

(Examples_chapter_4.xlsx)

An illustration of the basic calculations is shown in Table 4.5. We suppose that the time series is quarterly. The first part of the table provides a schematic layout setting up the calculations. Note that these values are aligned in the table in such a way that the forecast

Table 4.5 Illustrative Calculations for the Additive Holt-Winters Scheme
(The numbers in **bold** *indicate the starting values.)*

A: Illustration of Spreadsheet Layout for Forecasting

Series	Level	Trend	Seasonal	Forecast	Error
Y1					
Y2					
Y3					
Y4					
Y5	**L4**	**B4**	**S1**		
Y6	L5	**B5**	**S2**		
Y7	L6	**B6**	**S3**		
Y8	L7	**B7**	S4	F8 = L7 + B7 + S4	Y8 – F8
Y9	L8	B8	S5	F9 = L8 + B8 + S5	Y9 – F9
Y10	L9	B9	S6	F10 = L9 + B9 + S6	Y10 – F10
Y11	L10	B10	S7	F11 = L10 + B10 + S7	Y11 – F11

B: Detailed Calculations (Alpha =0.20, Beta = 0.10, Gamma = 0.30)

Period	Series	Level	Slope	Seasonal	Forecast	Error
1	115			15.63		
2	90			–14.38		
3	65			–36.88		
4	135	105.47	2.81	35.63		
5	130	109.50	2.81	15.63	123.91	6.09
6	95	111.73	2.81	–14.38	97.94	–2.94
7	75	114.01	2.81	–36.88	77.66	–2.66
8	150	116.33	2.81	35.63	152.44	–2.44
9	135	119.19	2.82	15.70	134.77	0.23
10	105	121.48	2.76	–15.16	107.63	–2.63
11	85	123.77	2.72	–37.59	87.37	–2.37
12	155	125.06	2.57	33.49	162.11	–7.11
13	145	127.97	2.61	16.19	143.33	1.67
14	110	129.50	2.50	–16.79	115.42	–5.42
15	85	130.12	2.31	–40.41	94.41	–9.41
16	160	131.24	2.19	31.72	165.92	–5.92

Data: Examples_chapter_4.xlsx

is obtained by adding elements in the same row. Thus, the forecast for period 8 is based upon L_4, T_4, and S_{h1} all located in the row corresponding to Y_5. Part B of the table provides a numerical example. We take the smoothing parameters to be $\alpha = 0.2$, $\beta = 0.1$, and $\gamma = 0.3$. The totals for the first two years are 405 and 450 respectively, so the two-year "monthly" average is 106.875. Equations (4.13) provide the starting values:

$$T_4 = \frac{1}{4}\left[\frac{450}{4} - \frac{405}{4}\right] = 2.81$$

$$L_4 = \frac{405}{4} + 1.5 \times 2.81 = 105.47$$

$$S_1 = 0.5 \times (115 + 130) - 106.875 = 15.625$$
$$S_2 = 0.5 \times (90 + 95) - 106.875 = -14.375$$
$$S_3 = 0.5 \times (65 + 75) - 106.875 = -36.875$$
$$S_4 = 0.5 \times (135 + 150) - 106.875 = 35.625.$$

These values are shown in boldface in the table. The updating begins after the first two years. The subsequent values in the table are then calculated with the use of equations (4.8–4.11). Note that although the initial seasonal values are constrained to sum to zero, this constraint is not retained. Fortunately, this does not affect forecasting performance. The seasonal values can be adjusted to sum to zero and an exactly compensating adjustment made to the level; see Archibald and Koehler (2003) for details. ■

The table illustrates the general format used in the ESM spreadsheet and available on the book's website. The user may specify:

- The components of the model: seasonal and/or trend may be included along with the level
- Additive or multiplicative seasonality, or logarithmic transform
- Transformations: either logarithmic or Box-Cox
- The observations to be used in the estimation sample and the hold-out sample

Once we have made the selections, we can identify those values of the smoothing parameters that minimize the fitting criterion (RMSE), using Solver in Excel. In all cases, the first two "years" of data are used to establish starting values. Note that the HW models have three smoothing parameters and 6 (quarterly) or 14 (monthly) starting values: level, trend, and seasonals. Solver is not effective in optimizing over so many unknowns, so we always use heuristic starting values.

More sophisticated statistical software enables a search to determine optimal starting values for the states (level, trend and seasonals) as well as for the smoothing parameters. For example, see the R package available on CRAN-R at *https://cran.r-project.org/package=forecast* and described in our on-line supplement. It is used in section 4.8 by way of illustration. The macros provided here serve to illustrate the general principles and are not the final word in computational processes for forecasting! As noted previously, the current ad hoc starting values typically work well unless the series is short and some of the smoothing parameters are close to zero.

The next example relates to quarterly data and uses the ESM. The procedures for monthly data follow essentially the same pattern.

■ Example 4.5: Additive Holt-Winters forecasting *(Autos_index.xlsx)*

Figure 4.4 shows a plot of the total quarterly production of motor vehicles and component parts in the United States from the first quarter of 1991 (1991Q1) through the last quarter of 2015 (2015Q4), recorded as an index with the year 2012 = 100. The mean level clearly changes over time and a seasonal pattern is evident.

An additive Holt-Winters forecasting scheme was fitted using data over the period 1991Q1 to 2009Q4. The performance of the system was then checked by means of the one-step-ahead forecasts over the 24 observations from 2010Q1 to 2015Q4. The results are summarized in panel A of Table 4.6 and the components are plotted in Figure 4.5. It is interesting to note that dropping the trend component has virtually no effect upon forecast performance.

The series reflects smaller seasonal components in later years, as the drop-off in production in the third quarter gradually disappears. In Minicase 4.2, you are encouraged to explore the effects of using smaller estimation samples; recall that a longer series is preferable only if the underlying properties of the series do not change. ■

Figure 4.4 Volume of Motor Vehicles and Parts Manufacturing: Quarterly Index, 1991Q1 to 2015Q4 (2012 = 100)

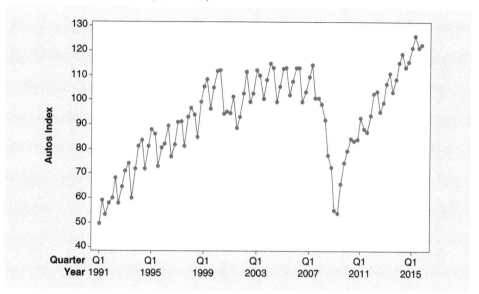

Source: U.S. Federal Reserve Bank of St. Louis (FRED) (*https://fred.stlouisfed.org*)

Data: Autos_index.xlsx

Figure 4.5 Components of the Additive Holt-Winters Scheme for the Autos_index Series

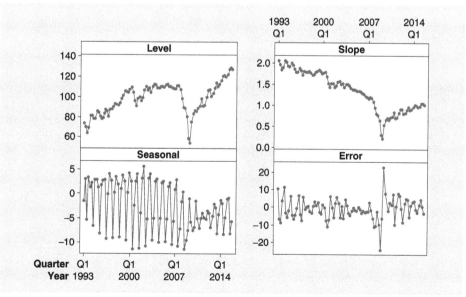

Data: Autos_index.xlsx

Table 4.6 Comparative Performance of Holt-Winters Forecasting Methods
(Autos_Index, 2010Q1–2015Q4)

	RMSE	MAE	MAPE	α	β	γ
PANEL A: Additive with Trend						
Estimation sample	6.17	4.54	5.60	1.00	0.03	0.33
Hold-out sample	5.93	4.99	4.98			
No trend						
Estimation sample	6.11	4.31	5.32	1.00		0.33
Hold-out sample	5.90	5.01	4.98			
PANEL B: Multiplicative with Trend						
Estimation sample	5.90	4.53	5.50	1.00	0.04	0.32
Hold-out sample	7.11	6.19	6.15			
No trend						
Estimation sample	5.80	4.28	5.22	1.00		0.33
Hold-out sample	6.79	5.96	5.90			
PANEL C: Logarithmic with Trend						
Estimation sample	6.05	4.69	5.70	0.98	0.06	0.32
Hold-out sample	7.12	6.09	6.05			
No trend						
Estimation sample	5.85	4.32	5.27	1.00		0.33
Hold-out sample	6.94	6.09	6.02			

Data: Autos_index.xlsx

4.7 The Multiplicative Holt-Winters Method

An examination of the time series plot sometimes reveals seasonal fluctuations that increase with the level of the series; that is, the movements are proportional rather than absolute. In these circumstances, it makes sense to combine an additive trend with a multiplicative seasonal factor to give as the forecast function

$$F_{t+1}(1) = F_{t+1} = (L_t + T_t)S_{t+1-m}. \tag{4.14}$$

Thus, the one-step-ahead error for period t becomes

$$e_t = Y_t - (L_{t-1} + T_{t-1})S_{t-m}. \tag{4.15}$$

In both equations, the seasonal component is now a multiplicative rather than an additive term. The *error correction* form of the updating equations is then

$$L_t = L_{t-1} + T_{t-1} + \alpha(e_t/S_{t-m})$$

$$T_t = T_{t-1} + \alpha\beta(e_t/S_{t-m}) \tag{4.16}$$

$$S_t = S_{t-m} + \gamma[e_t/(L_{t-1} + T_{t-1})].$$

The updating relationships involve removing the seasonal element in the error (now by division rather than by subtraction as in the additive scheme) before adjusting the level and trend. Similarly, the trend element is removed from the error before updating the seasonal component. As with the additive case, the seasonals are adjusted only once per "year," so we need $(m + 2)$ starting values in all. Exercise 4.11 provides the version of equation (4.16) that uses the observations and components in place of the error correction form. The ESM may be used to forecast using the multiplicative Holt-Winters scheme; it includes the alternative models with and without a trend term.

4.7.1* Starting Values

As with the additive case, we use data for the first two years, written as $Y_1, Y_2, \ldots, Y_{2m}$. The starting values for the level and trend are unchanged:

$$L_m = \frac{1}{m}(Y_1 + Y_2 + \cdots + Y_m) + \frac{(m-1)}{2}T_m$$

$$T_m = \frac{1}{m}\left[\frac{1}{m}(Y_{m+1} + Y_{m+2} + \cdots + Y_{2m}) - \frac{1}{m}(Y_1 + Y_2 + \cdots + Y_m)\right].$$

The seasonal values are created from the first "year's" values by division rather than subtraction:

$$S_{(i)} = \frac{1}{2} \times (Y_i + Y_{i+m}) / \left[\frac{1}{2m}(Y_1 + Y_2 + \cdots + Y_{2m})\right], \quad i = 1, 2, \ldots, m. \quad (4.17)$$

■ **Example 4.6: Multiplicative Holt-Winters** (*Autos_index.xlsx*)

For purposes of comparison, we now examine the motor vehicles series, using the multiplicative Holt-Winters scheme. The results, based upon minimizing the *MSE*, are shown in panel B of Table 4.6. The estimated smoothing parameters are similar. Plots of the components are omitted, but they again show a reduction in the magnitude of the seasonal components from the mid-1970s on. Overall, the multiplicative scheme has a better fit for the estimation sample but produces inferior results for the hold-out sample. The change is probably due to the distorting effects of the "Great Recession" in 2008-09. The results also serve to illustrate the value of the hold-out analysis. Once again, the trend component does not provide an improvement. The additive version might be a safer bet for forecasting.

Note again that the seasonal coefficients start out with an average of 1.0 but later values do not meet this constraint. Archibald and Koehler (2003) show how to adjust the seasonals to retain the average of 1.0; again, their adjustment does not affect the forecasts but makes interpretation easier. ■

4.7.2 Purely Multiplicative Schemes

A third variation is to allow both trend and seasonal components to be multiplicative. In these circumstances, we may make a (natural) logarithmic transformation, as described in Section 2.6.2, and apply the additive Holt-Winters scheme to the transformed data. The optimization step may then use either the *MSE* of the original data or the *MSE* of the transformed data. The ESM on the website uses the transformed data for estimation, but the resulting error measures are reported for the original series because it is the forecasting performance for those data that is of interest. The forecasts for the original series are found by application of the reverse transformation, or exponentiation. That is, if Z denotes the transformed variable, we make the transformation $Z = \ln(Y)$ and then, after generating the forecasts, transform the forecast F_Z back, using the inverse transform $F_Y = \exp(F_Z)$ to obtain forecasts of the original series. The subscripts have been added to the forecast variables to distinguish the transformed and original series.

■ **Example 4.7: Purely multiplicative seasonality** *(Autos_index.xlsx)*

Application of this scheme to the motor vehicles series yields the results shown in panel C of Table 4.6. The forecasting performance is similar to that of the multiplicative method. Plots of the components are omitted, but they again show a reduction in the magnitude of the seasonal components from 2007 on. Once again, the trend component does not provide an improvement. ■

4.8* Calculations Using R

From time to time we have mentioned that different programs will produce different outputs, even leading to different model choices on occasion. We now explore such differences in more detail by examining the data analysis for the automobiles data examined in the last two sections, using the R package available on CRAN-R at *https://cran.r-project.org/packages=forecast* and described in our on-line supplement. The original results were summarized in Table 4.6 and we provide comparable results in Tables 4.7 and 4.8.

First, we compare Tables 4.6 and 4.7. Both sets of results are based upon the same parameter values so the differences that arise are due to the different starting values used. In general, the R programs use more sophisticated statistical procedures to establish the starting values, so somewhat better results are to be expected.

Table 4.7 Comparative Performance of Holt-Winters Forecasting Methods, Using R Programs with Parameters Estimated by the ESM *(Autos_Index, 2010Q1–2015Q4)*

	RMSE	MAE	MAPE	α	β	γ
PANEL A: Additive with Trend						
Estimation sample	6.06	5.27	5.92	1.00	0.03	0.33
Hold-out sample	5.28	4.39	4.46			
No trend						
Estimation sample	6.13	5.53	6.22	1.00		0.33
Hold-out sample	4.95	4.08	4.13			
PANEL B: Multiplicative with Trend						
Estimation sample	9.16	7.65	8.25	1.00	0.04	0.32
Hold-out sample	8.04	7.10	7.00			
No trend						
Estimation sample	9.18	7.93	8.57	1.00		0.33
Hold-out sample	7.83	6.85	6.72			
PANEL C: Logarithmic with Trend						
Estimation sample	9.06	7.67	8.38	0.98	0.06	0.32
Hold-out sample	6.95	6.15	6.09			
No trend						
Estimation sample	9.41	8.45	9.23	1.00		0.33
Hold-out sample	6.99	5.92	5.82			

Data: Autos_index.xlsx

The results in Table 4.7 are mixed. We are using "R-based" starting values with "ESM-based" parameter estimates, which leads to inferior results for the estimation samples of the multiplicative and log-transform schemes. As might be expected, the results for the hold-out samples are much closer to each other, because the impact of the initial conditions is gradually reduced. Both sets of results point to the additive scheme without trend, although the margin of superiority is greater in Table 4.7.

We now compare Table 4.6 and 4.8. The effect of more careful estimation of the starting values is clearly seen in smaller error measures across the board. The superior performance of models developed using the R programs is evident and carries over to the hold-out samples. The results in Table 4.8 suggest that the best model is now multiplicative without trend. It is also noteworthy that the estimated trend and seasonal parameters are close to zero, but the reasons are rather different. The trend coefficient is small because the trend term does not add value to the analysis. By contrast, the seasonal pattern is important but it is also very stable, so that the updating parameter is small.

The results in Tables 4.7 and 4.8 show the importance of good estimates for the starting values, particularly for models with multiplicative components.

Table 4.8 Comparative Performance of Holt-Winters Forecasting Methods with Parameter Estimation Based Upon R Programs (Autos_Index, 2010Q1–2015Q4)

	RMSE	MAE	MAPE	α	β	γ
PANEL A: Additive with Trend						
Estimation sample	5.20	3.60	4.50	1.00	0.00*	0.00*
Hold-out sample	4.42	3.67	3.73			
No trend						
Estimation sample	5.49	3.82	4.84	1.00		0.00*
Hold-out sample	4.77	4.01	4.07			
PANEL B: Multiplicative with Trend						
Estimation sample	5.29	3.80	4.71	0.81	0.00*	0.19
Hold-out sample	4.51	3.78	3.77			
No trend						
Estimation sample	5.28	3.81	4.72	0.88		0.12
Hold-out sample	3.87	3.27	3.31			
PANEL C: Logarithmic with Trend						
Estimation sample	5.19	3.84	4.72	1.00	0.01	0.00*
Hold-out sample	5.15	4.25	4.24			
No trend						
Estimation sample	5.12	3.80	4.64	1.00		0.00*
Hold-out sample	5.42	4.54	4.53			

* Coefficient is non-zero but less than 0.005

Data: Autos_index.xlsx

4.9 Weekly Data

Business time series based upon weekly observations have four distinctive features:

- They are often short, in the sense that each week of the year may be represented only a few times (e.g., two years of data provides 104 observations, but each week appears only twice).
- Key features of the series may fall into different weeks from year to year (e.g., Easter, Thanksgiving).
- There are often a large number of series to be forecast (e.g., stock-keeping units (SKUs) for a retail company or a manufacturer).

- Totals of forecasts for individual items should match up to aggregate forecasts for product groups.

We defer a detailed discussion of forecasting support systems to Chapter 12, but address some of the technical issues here. Figure 4.6 shows the sales figures for five bracelets of a particular line of bracelets sold by a leading costume jewelry company. These data are described and examined in detail in Minicase 12.2 in Chapter 12; the observations run from week 5 in year 1 through week 24 in year 3. The Christmas sales peaks are easy to recognize, and the seasonal patterns are similar for all five products even though the sales volumes differ.

Figure 4.6 Weekly Sales Figures for Five Bracelets *(Year 1, Week 5 – Year 3, Week 24)*

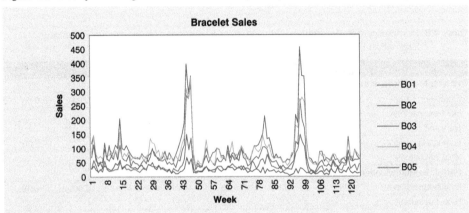

Data: Bracelet_5.xlsx

Clearly, if we are to forecast such series, we must take the seasonal patterns into account. A single series will not provide very reliable information about seasonal patterns, but a well-defined cluster of these series (e.g., all bracelets with Christmas designs) will provide a strong indication of such shifts in sales. Further, we can see that although the sales volumes may change, the seasonal patterns are remarkably consistent. These two features are combined to provide users with a framework for dealing with weekly series; the ideas may apply equally well in other cases where there are a large number of "seasons" but relatively short series.

We adapt the multiplicative Holt-Winters scheme to allow for fixed seasonals, but we calculate the seasonals from the aggregate sales data. This approach has the effect of reducing the randomness in our estimates compared with what would happen if we had just used the individual SKU data. We can drop the trend term because it appears from the data that simple exponential smoothing will suffice once we have taken care of seasonality. Again, it is possible to retain the trend component, but for many series SES will suffice. Particularly in short-term forecasting at an SKU level, the trend has little relevance. Thus, we arrive at the scheme

$$F_{t+1}(1) = L_t S_{t+1-m}$$

$$L_t = L_{t-1} + \alpha(e_t/S_{t-m})$$

$$S_t = S_{t-m}.$$

Further, because the seasonal factors are fixed and prespecified, we may produce a deseasonalized series (Y_t/S_{t-m}), forecast this series by means of SES, and then multiply the results by the seasonal factors to obtain the final forecasts. The detailed calculations are illustrated on hypothetical data in Table 4.9.

Table 4.9 Adjusting for Weekly Seasonality

A	B	C	D	E	F	G	H	I	J	K	L
Week	SKU1 Sales	Group Sales (previous year)	Seasonal Factor	Adjusted SKU1 Sales	One-step-ahead forecasts	SKU1 forecasts	Errors	Absolute Errors	Forecast (no adjustment)	Errors	Absolute errors
1	54	557	0.87	62.2	62.1	53.9	0.1	0.1	54	0.0	0.0
2	29	533	0.83	34.9	62.1	51.6	−22.6	22.6	54	−25.0	25.0
3	51	539	0.84	60.7	55.4	46.6	4.4	4.4	46.5	4.5	4.5
4	52	700	1.09	47.6	56.7	61.9	−9.9	9.9	47.9	4.1	4.1
5	113	1100	1.72	65.9	53.9	92.5	20.5	20.5	49.2	63.8	63.8
6	58	672	1.05	55.3	59.9	62.8	−4.8	4.8	68.2	−10.2	10.2
7	79	602	0.94	84.1	58.6	55.0	24.0	24.0	65.3	13.7	13.7
8	48	603	0.94	51.0	65.8	61.9	−13.9	13.9	69.4	−21.4	21.4
9	76	598	0.93	81.5	61.6	57.4	18.6	18.6	63	13.0	13.0
10	32	508	0.79	40.4	67.1	53.2	−21.2	21.2	66.8	−34.8	34.8
Averages		**641.2**	**1.00**	**58.4**	**60.3**	**59.7**	**−0.5**	**14.0**	**58.4**	**0.77**	**19.05**

Data: Table_4_9.xlsx

■ Example 4.8: Forecasting weekly sales

We consider a single-item *SKU1,* which is part of a larger product group. The sales for *SKU1* are given in column B of Table 4.9, and last year's sales for the entire product group are given in column C. We assume a seasonality of ten weeks. The seasonal factors in column D are created by dividing the total product sales in column C by the weekly average of 609. The adjusted *SKU1* sales are then given by the SKU1 Sales divided by the seasonal factor. Next, these adjusted sales are forecast one step ahead with SES. The one-step-ahead forecasts in column F are then multiplied by the seasonal factors to produce the *SKU1* forecasts in column G, with the corresponding errors shown in column H. The rest of the table provides forecasts based upon SES without any seasonal adjustment and compares the forecast errors.

The data were constructed to show peak sales in week 5; as it happens, both forecasts undershoot, but the error is much more serious when the seasonal pattern is not taken into account. The week-5 error would increase from 20 to 63 units; the overall *MAE* is 15.3 for the adjusted forecasts, as against 21.0 when the seasonal effects are ignored. Further, if seasonal effects appear in different weeks, as in Easter, it is a simple matter to shuffle the seasonal factors accordingly. ■

One final point is worth noting. If we use this approach on a group of individual (sales) series with the same seasonal coefficients and a common value for α, the forecasts for the total group sales will be the same whether we sum the forecasts for the individual items (the so-called bottom-up approach) or whether we forecast the total sales directly. If only the total sales are forecast, it is then necessary to produce forecasts for individual items by partitioning the total (the so-called top-down approach). These ideas are explored further in Chapter 12.

With weekly data, the extension of Holt-Winters exponential smoothing is not straightforward because of initialization. Software has become available in R from *https://cran.r-project.org/package=smooth.*

4.9.1 Multiple Seasonalities

At various places in this chapter we have mentioned weekly, monthly and quarterly seasonal patterns. In forecasting electricity consumption and similar phenomena, time-of-day patterns are also extremely important. Such multiple seasonalities are becoming increasingly common as forecasting methods are extended to cover new situations with more frequently collected data.

We do not have space in this volume to discuss details, save to note that the general principles remain the same: we formulate an equation to describe each seasonal component such as hours within days, days within weeks and weeks within years. More detailed accounts are available in Taylor (2003) and Gould *et al.* (2008).

4.10 Prediction Intervals

The structure of prediction intervals for series with a seasonal component is essentially the same as that of the nonseasonal series discussed in Section 3.8. As in that discussion, we restrict attention, for the time being, to the construction of prediction intervals for one-step-ahead forecasts. (Intervals for forecasts made two or more periods ahead are considered in Chapter 5.) As in Section 2.8, an approximate interval is given by

$$\text{Forecast} \pm z_{\alpha/2} \times (RMSE).$$

■ Example 4.9: Prediction intervals for automobile production, one quarter ahead

As in Example 4.3, we use the Additive Holt-Winters scheme without the trend term, as this appeared to be the best option based upon the results in Table 4.6. Having made the selection of the method, we use the data through 2014Q4 and then forecast 2015 for one to four quarters ahead. Table 4.10 provides the forecasts and the 95 percent prediction intervals. The *RMSE* was estimated from the fitting sample to be 6.04 and the smoothing parameters are $\alpha = 0.93$, $\gamma = 0.26$.

Two features stand out in the table. First, the intervals appear to be very wide compared with the differences between the actual and forecast values. This discrepancy reflects the greater stability (or lower variability) of the numbers in recent years and the large errors in 2008 and 2009 that inflated the estimate of *RMSE*. At the same time, sales can be quite volatile and we should not be lulled into a false sense of security by a period of relative calm. Second, the forecast for the third quarter is well below that for the other quarters, although little variation is seen among the actual quarterly figures. As we observed earlier, the seasonal pattern has changed somewhat over time and the forecasting procedure may not fully reflect this shift.

Table 4.10 One Step-Ahead Prediction Intervals for Quarterly Autos_index for 2015
[$\alpha = 0.93$, $\gamma = 0.26$]

Quarter	Actual	Forecast	Prediction Interval
2015Q1	121.2	118.7	(106.9, 130.6)
2015Q2	126.1	117.8	(101.7, 134.0)
2015Q3	121.2	111.3	(91.8, 130.9)
2015Q4	122.5	115.2	(92.7, 137.6)

Data: *Autos_index.xlsx*

Empirical prediction intervals may also be calculated by following the approach given in Section 2.8.2. The details are left as Exercise 4.12. Note that when we use the logarithmic transform, the prediction interval should be calculated for the transformed values and only then converted back to the original series. ∎

4.11 Principles for Seasonal Methods

The six principles described in Chapter 3 are equally valid for seasonal modeling. In addition,

[4.1] Carefully examine the structure of the seasonal pattern.
The seasonal component may be additive or multiplicative, and it may also have certain biases that require systematic adjustment. Examples include Easter falling in March or April, some months having more weekend days than others, and certain days being national holidays. In each case, the resulting seasonal pattern could be distorted and preliminary adjustments to the data may be necessary prior to forecasting. Even in the absence of special holidays, some months have more weekend days than others. Programs such as Census X-13-ARIMA allow the user to make "trading day" adjustments so that the different levels of activity (e.g., higher retail sales on Saturday, stock markets closing on weekends) can be taken into account.

[4.2] When there are limited data from which to calculate seasonal components, consider using the seasonals from related data series, such as the aggregate. Alternatively, average the estimates across similar products.

Summary

In this chapter, we have considered time series that possess a seasonal component. There are two principal objectives in the analysis of such series. The first is to take account of the seasonal pattern when making forecasts. The second is seasonal adjustment, whereby we wish to estimate the seasonal effects and then remove them, to produce a seasonally adjusted series. We began by considering a purely seasonal series — that is, one without a trend. Such series are rare in business applications but serve to illustrate how we can examine seasonal patterns, either by using a method that combines trends with seasonality or by isolating the seasonal component. We then developed forecasting procedures based upon decomposition methods and explored decomposition as a tool for describing time series phenomena. The remainder of the chapter developed the Holt-Winters approach to exponential smoothing for series with additive or multiplicative seasonal components. As in Chapter 3, the seasonal and trend components are updated after each new observation is recorded. Finally, we briefly examined the construction of prediction intervals.

DISCUSSION QUESTION: *In many forecasting applications, why is forecasting seasonality critically important?*

Exercises

4.1   Create seasonal plots for the Walmart quarterly sales data *(Walmart_2.xlsx)* by plotting

a. Sales against quarter, classified by year (as in Figure 4.2)

b. Sales against time, with years classified.

4.2   The data in the spreadsheet that follows refer to a quarterly series that is purely seasonal, as in Section 4.2. The values for year 1 are used as starting values (forecasts) for year 2. Use the purely seasonal version of exponential smoothing with $\gamma = 0.5$ to generate forecasts for year 3.

Quarter	Year	Data	Forecasts
1	1	50	
2	1	30	
3	1	20	
4	1	90	
1	2	55	50
2	2	35	30
3	2	15	20
4	2	80	90
1	3		
2	3		
3	3		
4	3		

Data: Exercise_4_2.xlsx

4.3   The file *US_retail_sales_2.xlsx* includes the series *Seasonal Factors* for the monthly series on U.S. retail sales as developed by the Census Bureau. The data cover the period from January 2001 to December 2015.

a. Using the period from January 2001 to December 2013 as the estimation sample, develop a seasonal forecasting method for this series.

b. Generate one-year-ahead forecasts for the hold-out sample for the period from January 2014 through to December 2015 using December 2013 as the forecast origin.

c. Recalibrate the forecasting equation by using the data up to December 2014, and then forecast the next 12 months. Compare the results.

The following exercises may be completed using the Exponential Smoothing Macro (ESM); other software may, of course, be used but the capabilities and estimation procedures vary so that results may differ.

In each case, the aim is to fit a suitable selection of exponential smoothing schemes: with or without a trend term; with none or additive or multiplicative seasonality; with or without transformations. Initial plots help to reduce the number of possibilities that need to be considered. Then examine the performance of the model for both the estimation and hold-out samples. Specific hold-out samples are suggested but it is important to explore the effects of changing the size and coverage of the estimation and hold-out samples.

Conclude the analysis with specific recommendations for the forecasting method to be employed.

4.4   Examine the series on Job Openings (*Job_openings.xlsx*) previously considered in Minicase 3.1. Which seasonal approach works best? Does the inclusion of seasonal factors provide a useful improvement in forecast quality?

4.5   The U.S. Census records monthly Alcoholic Beverage Sales by Wholesalers (*Alcohol_sales.xlsx*). The series is recorded monthly and it is not seasonally adjusted. Sales are measured in $Millions and the series runs from January 2001 to December 2015. Develop an appropriate seasonal model using the last 36 observations as the hold-out sample.

4.6   Use the data in the file *US_retail_sales_2.xlsx* with the period from January 2001 to December 2012 as the estimation sample. Develop an appropriate forecasting method for the series.

4.7   The movie industry is naturally very interested in forecasting ticket sales. The spread-sheet *Titanic_box_office.xlsx* provides the daily figures for the number of customers per theater for the period December 19, 1997 to July 23, 1998. Given the greater attendance at weekends, this series is seasonal with a period of seven days. Develop a suitable forecasting method, using the last four weeks as a hold-out sample.

How useful is your analysis to the movie industry? Think about different movie genres and the likely length of their runs before moving to online and DVD sales.

4.8   The spreadsheet *Gas_prices_Ch4.xlsx* gives the average end of month prices "at the pump" of regular-grade gasoline for the period from January 2000 to December 2015. Use the period from January 2000 to December 2012 as the estimation sample, and develop a seasonal forecasting method.

4.9   Modify the spreadsheet corresponding to Example 4.2 in *Examples_chapter_4.xlsx* to forecast, by means of a multiplicative decomposition, the data in Table 4.3.

4.10* Use equation (4.9) to substitute for the error term in the updating equations (4.10-11). Hence, derive the alternative form of the updating equations for the additive Holt-Winters scheme as given in equations (4.12):

$$L_t = L_{t-1} + T_{t-1} + \alpha[Y_t - S_{t-m} - L_{t-1} - T_{t-1}]$$

$$T_t = T_{t-1} + \beta[L_t - L_{t-1} - T_{t-1}]$$

$$S_t = S_{t-m} + \gamma[Y_t - L_{t-1} - T_{t-1} - S_{t-m}].$$

4.11* As in Exercise 4.10, substitute for the error term in the updating equations (4.16). Hence, derive the alternative form of the updating equations for the multiplicative Holt-Winters scheme:

$$L_t = L_{t-1} + T_{t-1} + \alpha[(Y_t/S_{t-m}) - L_{t-1} - T_{t-1}]$$

$$T_t = T_{t-1} + \beta(L_t - L_{t-1} - T_{t-1})$$

$$S_t = S_{t-m} + \gamma[Y_t/(L_{t-1} + T_{t-1}) - S_{t-m}].$$

4.12   Following on from Example 4.9, develop empirical prediction intervals for the automobile data for the four quarters of 2015.

Minicases

Minicase 4.1 Walmart Sales

Consider the data on Walmart sales previously considered in Minicase 3.2 and available in *Walmart_2.xlsx*. Plot the quarterly sales data and verify that the series exhibits a seasonal element. Using the ESM or other suitable software, contrast the additive, multiplicative, and logarithmic forms for forecasting sales, using the last 12 quarters as a hold-out sample. Compare the results, using both approximate normal and empirical prediction intervals, with those obtained for Minicase 3.2.

Minicase 4.2 Automobile Production

Reexamine the automobile production series considered in Example 4.3 and later examples *(Autos_index.xlsx)*. Use the last three years (2013–2015) as the hold-out sample, but reduce the size of the estimation sample by starting in 1996 and again in 2001. Compare the results with those obtained using 1991–2012 as the estimation sample. Also, generate prediction intervals for the four quarters of 2015, using both approximate normal and empirical prediction intervals.

What are your conclusions regarding the relevance of the earlier data in the light of possible changes in production plans over time?

Minicase 4.3 U.S. Retail Sales

The spreadsheet *US_retail_sales_2.xlsx* contains the monthly values of U.S. retail sales (measured in $ billions) over the period from January 2001 to December 2016. The series was plotted in Chapter 1. The spreadsheet includes the value of sales (*Sales*), the seasonally adjusted values (*Sales_SA*) and the seasonal factors. Compare the options of

- forecasting the series by using the Holt-Winters approach,
- forecasting the components separately and then combining them.

Use period January 2001–November 2007 as the estimation sample. The onset of the "Great Recession" was determined to have occurred in December 2007 but was not officially confirmed until December 2008; would the one-step-ahead forecasts have provided earlier warning? Generate prediction intervals and see whether the actual values fall within the limits.

If you have access to suitable software, evaluate the ability of the multiple-step-ahead forecasts to predict the downturn. Conduct a rolling origin 1-12 evaluation, forecasting for the years 2008-2010. (If no suitable software is available, use just three forecast origins to compare results.)

Extend the estimation sample to December 2012 and compare the one-step-ahead forecast performance for the period 2013–2015 using the two different estimation samples. [Exercise 4.6]

Minicase 4.4 UK Retail Sales

The spreadsheet *UK_retail_sales_2.xlsx* contains the quarterly values of the UK Retail Sales Index (measured with 2010 set at 100), both unadjusted and seasonally adjusted, over the period from January 1996 to December 2014. Create a purely seasonal series by dividing the unadjusted series by the seasonally adjusted one. Using one-step-ahead forecasts, compare the options of:

- Forecasting the series by using the Holt-Winters approach.
- Forecasting the components separately and then combining them.

It is recommended that you use the period 1996-2011 for estimation and the remaining 12 quarters as the hold-out sample.

Minicase 4.5 Newspaper Sales

A small local bakery purchases a limited number of copies of the *Washington Post* on a "sale or return" basis. Sales and unsold copies were monitored over a six-week period, with the results shown in the table below. The data[4] are available in *Newspapers.xlsx*. The owner seeks advice regarding the number of copies to order in the coming week.

Week	Variable	Sun	Mon	Tue	Wed	Thu	Fri	Sat
1	Sales	15	12	10	12	13	14	16
1	Returns	0	3	1	0	2	0	6
2	Sales	16	11	10	13	14	15	15
2	Returns	5	0	0	0	6	6	5
3	Sales	15	11	13	16	14	15	14
3	Returns	8	6	3	8	2	3	1
4	Sales	15	13	13	13	16	14	13
4	Returns	3	7	3	8	7	4	5
5	Sales	14	11	12	14	13	16	12
5	Returns	1	0	0	6	3	1	2
6	Sales	13	12	16	13	12	21	12
6	Returns	6	7	0	*	4	8	0

Data: Newspapers.xlsx

What additional information would you like to see? How do you treat the days when there were no returns? Is there any seasonal structure? What do you recommend as an ordering policy?

References

Archibald, B.C., and Koehler, A.B. (2003). Normalization of seasonal factors in Winters' methods. *International Journal of Forecasting,* 19, 143–148.

Durbin, J., and Koopman, S. J. (2012). *Time Series Analysis by State Space Methods.* Oxford, U.K.: Oxford University Press, second edition.

Findley, D.F., Monsell, B.C., Bell, W.R., Otto, M.C., and Chen, B.C. (1998). New capabilities and methods of the X-12-ARIMA seasonal adjustment program (with discussion). *Journal of Business and Economic Statistics,* 16, 127–177. [For recent developments, consult the U.S. Census Bureau website for X1-13-ARIMA: *www.census. gov/srd/www/x13a*]

Ghysels, E., and Osborn, D.R., 2001. *The econometric analysis of seasonal time series.* Cambridge University Press.

Gould, P.G., Koehler, A.B., Ord, J.K., Snyder, R.D., Hyndman, R.J. and Vahid-Araghi, F. (2008). Forecasting time series with multiple seasonal patterns. *European Journal of Operational Research,* 191, 205–220.

---

4 The data are genuine, but the name of the bakery is withheld for reasons of confidentiality.

Holt, C. (2004). Forecasting seasonals and trends by exponentially weighted moving averages. *International Journal of Forecasting,* 20, 5–10. Reprint of Office of Naval Research Memorandum 52/1957, Carnegie Institute of Technology.

Hyndman, R. J., Koehler, A. B., Ord, J. K., and Snyder, R. D. (2008). *Forecasting with Exponential Smoothing.* Berlin: Springer.

Shiskin, J., Young, A.H., and Musgrave, J.C. (1967). *The X-11 variant of the Census Method II seasonal adjustment program.* Technical Paper 15, Bureau of the Census, U.S. Department of Commerce, Washington, DC.

Taylor, J.W. (2003). Short-term electricity demand forecasting using double seasonal exponential smoothing. *Journal of the Operational Research Society,* 54, 799–805.

Winters, P.R. (1960). Forecasting sales by exponentially weighted moving averages. *Management Science,* 6, 324–342.

CHAPTER 5

State-Space Models for Time Series

*Topics marked with an * are advanced and may be omitted for more introductory courses.*

Table of Contents

Our ideas must agree with realities, be such realities concrete or abstract, be they facts or be they principles, under penalty of endless inconsistency and frustration.

— William James [*Thinkexist.com*] (American philosopher and psychologist, leader of the philosophical movement of pragmatism, 1842–1910)

Introduction

In Chapters 3 and 4, we considered forecasting methods for a single time series. These methods provided forecasting flexibility by allowing the trend and seasonal components to evolve over time. Throughout that discussion, we stressed that these forecasting methods (or good intuitive approaches) lacked any theoretical statistical foundations. Such methods can, as we have seen, provide good point forecasts and may be applied without regard to the form of the data, because all we are doing is applying a numerical recipe to the observations. However, when we wish to make statements concerning the level of uncertainty in a forecast, we must turn to a statistical model with a related set of assumptions. In turn, we must validate those assumptions if our assessment of the underlying uncertainty is to offer an accurate picture of reality. In particular, a statistical *model* will enable us to construct prediction intervals. In retrospect, we cheated a bit and came up with such intervals in Sections 3.8 and 4.9 by just assuming an additive error term that was normally distributed. Our objective in this chapter and the next is to develop underlying statistical models for exponential smoothing and then to explore possible extensions of those models. In doing so, we must keep in mind that, to be useful, a model must be validated; we seek the model that best conforms to the observations and the forecasting problem we face.

There are two principal approaches to modeling a single (univariate) time series. In this chapter, we focus upon state-space modeling, because a state-space framework is a natural extension of the exponential smoothing equations that we considered in earlier chapters. The second approach to model building is best known by the label ARIMA, which stands for *AutoRegressive Integrated Moving Average*. These models are considered in Chapter 6.

State-space models are extremely flexible, and, as a result, a number of different approaches exist. Following Hyndman *et al.* (2008), we adopt an innovations state-space scheme because it provides the most transparent link between methods and models, as shown in Section 5.1. Other approaches exist that result in similar models,[1] but we do not examine them in detail.

In Sections 5.1 and 5.2, we establish a state-space model for the simple exponential smoothing method introduced in Section 3.3 and describe the assumptions underlying this model. In Section 5.3 we extend these ideas to consider a general class of state-space models and then develop prediction intervals.

Hitherto, we have chosen from among this set of forecasting methods by comparing their performance over a hold-out sample. This procedure remains perfectly valid, but it may be inefficient when the time series is short, a circumstance that tends to be all too common in our fast-changing economy. Therefore, in Section 5.4 we introduce what is known as an *information criterion* — essentially, a penalty that is assigned to each of a number of candidate models. More complex models receive a larger penalty so that the models compete on an even playing field. The information criterion may then be used to choose the best of the competing models. A brief discussion on extreme observations (known as outliers) follows in Section 5.5. The chapter ends with a discussion of some underlying principles in Section 5.6.

---

1 See, for example, the advanced discussions in Harvey (1989), West and Harrison (1997), and Durbin and Koopman (2012).

5.1 State-Space Models for Exponential Smoothing

All activities are based upon various assumptions, and forecasting is no exception. In order to forecast effectively, we must specify the underlying assumptions and verify that they hold, at least approximately. Thus, our purpose in this section is to build upon the forecasting framework developed in Chapters 3 and 4 to produce an appropriate underlying statistical model that matches the smoothing methods we described earlier. We begin by examining this process in the context of simple exponential smoothing (SES), since the same principles apply to all the forecasting methods we have so far considered.

5.1.1 The SES Forecasting Framework

To achieve our goal, we use the basic forecasting equation to suggest an appropriate statistical model. When we introduced SES in Section 3.3.1, we specified the forecast function as

$$F_{t+1}(1) = F_t(1) + \alpha[Y_t - F_t(1)]. \tag{5.1}$$

Recall that Y_t denotes the latest observation in the series and $F_t(1)$ is the forecast for period t, made one step earlier at time $t-1$. The constant α is the smoothing parameter. Because this equation considers only the one-step-ahead forecasts, we rewrote it in terms of the simpler notation as

$$F_{t+1} = F_t + \alpha(Y_t - F_t). \tag{5.2}$$

That is, we set $F_t(1) = F_t$. Expressed verbally, the equation reads:

New forecast = Old forecast + Partial adjustment to account for the observed error.

At time t, after Y_t is observed, the term inside the parentheses represents the observed forecast error, which we may write as *Error = Observed Value – Forecast*, or

$$e_t = Y_t - F_t. \tag{5.3}$$

If we substitute this value into equation (5.2) and rearrange equation (5.3), we can write down the pair of equations

$$Y_t = F_t + e_t$$
$$F_{t+1} = F_t + \alpha e_t. \tag{5.4}$$

Equations (5.4) involve the actual observation, the forecast made one step ahead (at time $(t-1)$ for period t) and the observed error, which is the difference between the two. These two equations involve *known* quantities, the previous forecast and the previous error. In order to specify a model we must recognize that future values of the series are *random variables* that will be described by a statistical distribution with a mean level (or expected value) and a random error term. The statistical model is then specified in terms of assumptions about the random error. The mean level of the series in (5.4), F_t, changes over time — precisely the local behavior we seek to describe.

5.1.2 A State-Space Model for Simple Exponential Smoothing

Suppose now that the present time is $(t-1)$, and let Y_t represent the random variable describing the possible observed values of the series in the next period, time t. The mean level is denoted by L_{t-1} where the subscript $(t-1)$ is used to indicate that the model is being formulated based upon the information available at that time. In many traditional statistical models, the mean (level) does not change and it is represented by a single parameter (say, μ). By contrast, here we make the more general assumption that the level changes over time. The level is not directly observable, but rather, is a time-dependent component that describes the nature of the process. To distinguish the unobservable level from the random variable Y_t that we do observe in due course, we refer to L_{t-1} as a *state variable*. State variables are not directly observable but describe the underlying state of the process.

STATE-SPACE MODELS

A *state-space model* consists of two parts:

- An *observation equation* that relates the random variable (Y_t) to the underlying state variable(s).
- One or more *state equations* that describe how the state variable(s) evolve(s) over time.

Starting from the first of the two expressions in (5.4), we formulate the state-space model underlying SES in the following way. The *observation equation* has the form

New observation = current mean level + random error.

That is, the observation equation is

$$Y_t = L_{t-1} + \varepsilon_t. \tag{5.5}$$

Where ε_t denotes the random error and L_{t-1} is the state variable.[2]

Equation (5.5) has a structure similar to that of the first equation in (5.4), but keep in mind that it refers to random variables (future observations), not (already) observed quantities.

We now need to make an assumption as to how the mean level changes over time. In this simplest case we assume no trend or seasonal component: the mean level changes over time by adjusting to the latest disturbance, and we may describe its development by the *state equation*

$$L_t = L_{t-1} + \alpha\varepsilon_t. \tag{5.6}$$

That is,

New mean level = Previous mean level + Partial adjustment for random error.

Equation (5.6) is known as the state equation because it describes how the underlying state (here, the mean level) changes over time. It is evident that equation (5.6) is similar in form to the second equation in equations (5.4), but again, we are dealing with unknown (random) quantities, whereas the forecasting equations dealt with observed values. Equations (5.5) and (5.6) represent the complete specification of the state-space model. If there were more states, we would have one state equation for each state as shown in Section 5.1.3.

To match up with our earlier development of SES, we impose the same standard conditions upon the smoothing parameter as before — that is, $0 < \alpha \leq 1$. When α is small, the mean level changes only slowly; for larger values, it changes more rapidly. We note in passing that the state-space model may actually be applied for any α in the range $0 < \alpha < 2$, although when $\alpha > 1$, a given error induces an even larger adjustment to the mean level.

---

2 A more formal development would use a notation such as $\hat{L}$ to distinguish estimated values from random variables. We prefer to keep the notation simple and emphasize the distinction between past (observed) and future (unknown and random).

To summarize, the complete model, known as the *local level model*, may be stated as follows:

Observation equation: $\qquad\qquad Y_t = L_{t-1} + \varepsilon_t$

State equation: $\qquad\qquad\qquad L_t = L_{t-1} + \alpha\varepsilon_t$

The one-step-ahead forecast for period $(t+1)$ is then the updated mean level **after Y_t is observed**, or

Forecast function: $\qquad\qquad F_{t+1} = L_t$

That is, the forecast function generates the SES forecasts, just as we discussed in Chapter 3.

■ Example 5.1: The random walk

When $\alpha = 1$, $L_t = L_{t-1} + \varepsilon_t$ and $Y_t = L_{t-1} + \varepsilon_t$; thus, the two right-hand sides are identical, and it follows that $L_t = Y_t$. The two equations may then be collapsed into the single equation

$$Y_t = Y_{t-1} + \varepsilon_t.$$

The preceding equation reflects a time series whose mean level is the previous observed value. This model is known as the *random walk* and is an appropriate description of short-term movements in many financial assets such as stock prices: The best predictor for tomorrow's closing price is today's closing price. If the best forecast were not today's closing price, it would be possible to predict the movement of stock prices at least to some extent and thereby make money.

The random walk model for stock prices has an interesting history. It was first proposed by Louis Bachelier in 1900, but was virtually ignored for the next 50 years. Then, in 1953, Maurice Kendall conducted extensive empirical analyses which again suggested that stock prices followed a random walk. After more time elapsed, this empirical regularity was recognized as a theoretically justified conclusion that was based on an economic model of market transactions and the random walk hypothesis is now a cornerstone of financial theory (see, e.g., Reilly and Brown, 2009, Chapter 6). Nevertheless, investors continue to believe that they can somehow beat the market, and on any given day, about half of them do! Timmermann and Granger (2004) discuss the role of forecasting in financial markets, an important topic for everyone to consider.

Historical note: One of the reasons behind the stock market upheavals starting late 2007 was the erroneous assumption that the error terms in the random walk model followed a normal distribution. In practice, large errors are more common than the normal distribution would predict, so that investors systematically underestimated the risk of large price swings.

5.1.3 A Class of State-Space Models

We may use these ideas to formulate state-space models that lead to the broader class of forecast functions described in Chapters 3 and 4. In these more general models, the trend and seasonal terms, T_t and S_t, are also state variables.

The Holt-Winters additive scheme described in Section 4.6 may be generated from the following model. As for SES the same notation has been preserved.

Forecast function: $\qquad\quad F_{t+h}(h) = L_t + hT_t + S_{t+h-m}, \quad h = 1, 2, \ldots$

Observation equation: $\qquad\quad Y_t = L_{t-1} + T_{t-1} + S_{t-m} + \varepsilon_t$

State equations:

$$L_t = L_{t-1} + T_{t-1} + \alpha\varepsilon_t$$

$$T_t = T_{t-1} + \alpha\beta\varepsilon_t$$

$$S_t = S_{t-m} + \gamma\varepsilon_t$$

Models for the various special cases discussed in Chapters 3 and 4 are derived from this model by removing the relevant state variables and setting parameters values to zero, as needed. That is, we could mix and match components, as follows:

- Trend: none (N), additive (A), multiplicative (M), or damped (D)
- Seasonal: none (N), additive (A), or multiplicative (M).

Thus, we may choose from up to 12 different models; the inclusion of damped trend is discussed in exercise 5.4. To this arrangement may be added two options for the error term: additive (A) or multiplicative (M). The additive scheme is as just defined and typically implies that the variance of the process is constant over time. By contrast, multiplicative errors imply an increase in the standard deviation of the process proportional to the mean level; the multiplicative model is discussed in Appendix 5B.

To keep track of all these possibilities we use a classification scheme introduced by Pegels (1969) and extended by several others (see, for example, Hyndman *et al.*, 2008, pp. 11–12). Each forecasting model may be coded as an ETS scheme, where ETS stands for (*Error, Trend, Seasonal*). For example, the SES scheme considered in Section 5.1.2 is ETS(A,N,N), corresponding to an additive error, no trend, and no seasonality. Likewise, ETS(A,A,A) means that the series has additive error, trend, and seasonal components, corresponding to the additive Holt-Winters model just described. Some of the most popular models are listed in Table 5.1 along with the ETS notation and names of the corresponding forecasting methods.[3]

Table 5.1 Some Standard Forecasting Methods, Listed in Accordance with Pegels' Classification

Method	ETS	Section(s)
SES	A,N,N	3.3
LES (Holt)	A,A,N	3.4
LES (log transform)	M,M,N	3.7
Damped ES	A,D,N	3.5
Seasonal SES	A,N,A	4.2
Additive Holt-Winters	A,A,A	4.6
Multiplicative Holt-Winters	M,A,M	4.7
Holt-Winters (log transform)	M,M,M	4.7.2

5.2 The Random Error Term

We have established a class of statistical models that lead to the forecast functions developed in Chapters 3 and 4. In order to complete the specification of the model, we must specify the properties of the random error term. In Table 5.2, we summarize each assumption, along with its rationale. Only when the assumptions are (at least approximately) justified can we

---

3 For the seasonal case there are variants that use the trigonometric representation of seasonality, allowing for complex seasonalities, for example see, De Livera *et al.*, 2010.

use the model to make valid inferences (such as those involving tests of hypotheses and prediction intervals).

If we make the first three assumptions, we are supposing that the random errors are independently distributed with zero means and a common variance. The fourth assumption, that the errors are normally distributed is not essential but is commonly made. We may summarize the assumptions by stating that the errors follow independent and identically normal distributions with mean zero and equal variance; this statement is summarized in the notation: $\varepsilon_t \sim IIN(0, \sigma^2)$.

These assumptions are exactly the same as those made for the ARIMA models of Chapter 6 and for regression models (Section 7.5).

So, now we have a statistical model! Rather like a paddling duck, we do not see much happening on the surface, but a lot is going on underneath. In particular, the state-space model will enable us to formulate prediction intervals, and it is to this topic that we now turn.

Table 5.2 Model Assumptions and the Underlying Rationale

Statistical Assumption	Reason for Assumption
The expected value of each error term is zero.	We need to assume that there is no bias in the measurement process; otherwise the observed values would not reflect the true value of the process (e.g., some sales might go unreported or returned items might not be added to inventory figures).
The errors for different time periods are independent of (or at least uncorrelated with) one another and also independent of past states.	If errors are related, we could improve the forecast by using this information. If we have an appropriate model, such correlations will be (close to) zero.
The variance of the errors is constant. This common variance is denoted by σ^2.	If errors are increasing (decreasing) in absolute magnitude over time, the stated prediction intervals for future time periods would become too narrow (wide).
The errors are drawn from a normal distribution.	A distributional assumption is necessary in order to make inferences. The normal distribution is by far the most common choice, but the use of an empirical distribution of the errors that is based on observed errors in the past is becoming increasingly popular (see Section 2.8.2).

5.3 Prediction Intervals from State-Space Models

In this section, we start out by developing prediction intervals for the local level model that underlies simple exponential smoothing. Later in the section, we extend the ideas to cover more general models. Given our assumptions about the random error term and the form of equation (5.5), it follows that the conditional mean of Y_t is the current mean level L_{t-1} which we write as $E(Y_t \mid L_{t-1}) = L_{t-1}$. This equation follows from the fact that for any random variables X and Y, and constants α and β, $E(\alpha X + \beta Y) = \alpha E(X) + \beta E(Y)$ and therefore

$$E(Y_t \mid L_{t-1}) = E(L_{t-1} + \varepsilon_t \mid L_{t-1}) = L_{t-1} + 0.$$

Likewise, the conditional variance of Y_t, given the mean level, may be written as

$$V(Y_t \mid L_{t-1}) = \sigma^2. \qquad \text{(see Appendix 5A)}$$

The preceding statements conform to the assumptions we have just specified; that is, we built these results into the state-space model. But what happens if we are interested in two, three, or more periods ahead? Now that we have an underlying model, we can substitute equation (5.6) into equation (5.5) to obtain

$$Y_{t+1} = L_t + \varepsilon_{t+1} = L_{t-1} + \alpha\varepsilon_t + \varepsilon_{t+1}. \tag{5.7}$$

Thus, going two steps ahead, we see that the conditional mean of Y_{t+1}, given the mean level at time $(t-1)$, is

$$E(Y_{t+1} \mid L_{t-1}) = L_{t-1},$$

which follows because the random errors have an expected value of zero.

The variance depends upon the variability of the errors at both time t and time $(t+1)$ and is given by

$$V(Y_{t+1} \mid L_{t-1}) = V(\varepsilon_{t+1}) + \alpha^2 V(\varepsilon_t) = \sigma^2(1 + \alpha^2),$$

which follows because the errors are independent and have equal variances. The details are provided in Appendix 5A. The important thing to notice is that the two-step-ahead variance is larger than that for one step ahead. The general equations for h steps ahead are

$$E(Y_{t+h-1} \mid L_{t-1}) = L_{t-1} \text{ and } V(Y_{t+h-1} \mid L_{t-1}) = \sigma^2[1 + (h-1)\alpha^2]. \tag{5.8}$$

What these equations tell us is that, for the local level model with SES, the point forecasts for periods t, $t+1$,..., $t+h-1$ made at time $(t-1)$ are all the same, equivalent to the SES forecasts observed in Chapter 3. The second term shows how the variance increases with the forecasting horizon. The increase makes intuitive sense, because we would expect forecasts to become less accurate as the horizon increases. Of course, this statement does not mean that every forecast made two steps ahead will be less accurate than the corresponding forecast made one step ahead as illustrated in Table 2.7; rather, it is an average property.

Equations (5.8), combined with the assumption of a normal distribution for the errors, provide us with the necessary information to construct a prediction interval, which may be written as

$$L_{t-1} \pm z_{\alpha/2}\sqrt{V(Y_{t+h-1} \mid L_{t-1})}. \tag{5.9}$$

In practice, the values of L and V will be unknown and must be estimated from the data; z represents the appropriate percentage point of the normal distribution, and the entire expression represents a $100(1-\alpha)$ percent prediction interval. For short series, the Student's t distribution should be used rather than the normal. The estimated value of σ^2 in (5.8) is the *MSE* calculated over the estimation sample.

There is a notational difficulty here: The α for the normal tables is the usual probability, such as 0.10 and 0.05 (with corresponding cutoff values 1.645 and 1.960, respectively), and bears no relation whatever to the smoothing constant that we estimate from the data. Something to keep in mind!

Note that this interval is strictly valid only if we are willing to assume that the random errors have zero mean and are independent and normally distributed with equal variances. Contrary to popular belief, the Central Limit Theorem[4] is no help here, because we are making statements about a single future observation. The other option, as noted in Section 2.8.2, is to use empirical prediction intervals, but these constructs also rely upon the assumptions of independent errors with equal variances. These assumptions should be checked periodically in any forecasting application.

---

4 The Central Limit Theorem states that the sampling distribution of the sample mean approaches normality as the sample size increases. In the present case, no matter how large the estimation sample, only one future observation is under consideration.

■ Example 5.2: Prediction intervals for the WFJ Sales data

As in Chapter 3, we use the first 26 observations in the series to estimate the SES parameters by ordinary least squares. We then forecast the next ten weeks with week 26 as the origin. The 90 percent prediction intervals ($z = 1.645$) were computed from expression (5.9) using the Exponential Smoothing Macro (ESM). The results are shown in Figure 5.1 and Table 5.3. The values needed for calculating the prediction intervals are $\alpha = 0.728$, $RMSE = 3030$, and $L_{26} = 34580$.

Figure 5.1 Actual Values and Prediction Intervals for Observations 27-36 of WFJ Sales

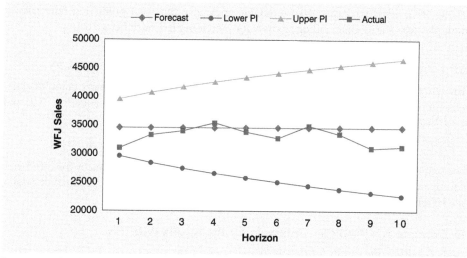

Data: WFJ_sales.xlsx

Table 5.3 90 Percent Prediction Intervals for WFJ Sales *(One to ten steps ahead from forecast origin week 26, fitted using observations 1-26 and yielding $\alpha = 0.728$)*

Forecast Horizon	Forecast	Forecast RMSE	Lower PI	Upper PI	Actual	INCLUDED
1	34580	3025	29604	39555	30986	yes
2	34580	3742	28425	40734	33321	yes
3	34580	4342	27438	41722	34003	yes
4	34580	4869	26571	42588	35417	yes
5	34580	5344	25789	43370	33822	yes
6	34580	5780	25072	44087	32723	yes
7	34580	6186	24405	44754	34925	yes
8	34580	6566	23779	45380	33460	yes
9	34580	6926	23187	45972	30999	yes
10	34580	7268	22625	46534	31286	yes

* INCLUDED = yes if Actual lies between PI Lower Limit and PI Upper Limit — that is, if the prediction interval includes the actual value. INCLUDED = no otherwise.

Data: WFJ Sales sheet in PI_exponential_smoothing.xlsx

As expected, the prediction intervals gradually widen as h is increased. The final column, INCLUDED, indicates whether the actual value fell within the prediction interval (PI); in this example, all the values fall well inside their respective intervals, suggesting that the sales in this part of the series may be more stable than in the estimation sample. This question is explored more fully in Minicase 5.2. ∎

Violations of the assumption of constant variance may have relatively little impact upon the point forecast. However, they are critical for the construction of prediction intervals. In particular, extreme observations may greatly inflate the variance and, hence, the size of the prediction interval, as we will see in Section 5.5. The establishment of good prediction intervals is a difficult, but crucial, task, and the results should be carefully scrutinized before accepting them as the basis for planning.

WARNING: Some packages, even reputable ones, give incorrect prediction intervals for multiple steps ahead, often failing to allow for increasing h. Check before using!

5.3.1 Prediction Intervals for the Additive Holt-Winters Model (A,A,A)

The same approach can be adopted to produce prediction intervals for more complex state-space models. The general form of the prediction intervals is given by equation (5.9) and uses the h-step-ahead variance expression:

$$V(Y_{t+h-1} \mid L_{t-1}, T_{t-1}, S_{t-m+h-1}) = \sigma^2[1 + (h-1)\{\alpha^2 + \alpha\beta h + \tfrac{1}{6}\beta^2 h(2h-1)\}],$$

For seasonal models, this expression applies only for $h \le m$. The variances for trend-free additive-error models listed in Table 5.1 may be obtained by setting $\beta=0$. For further details, see Hyndman *et al.*, 2008, Chapter 6.

∎ Example 5.3: Prediction intervals for the Netflix data

Table 5.4 shows the results for the Netflix data, where the series up to 2013Q4 was used as the estimation sample and then forecasts were produced for 1 – 8 periods ahead (i.e. two years). The results are also plotted in Figure 5.2 showing the 95 percent prediction intervals. The estimated parameter values are $\alpha = 1.00$, $\beta = 0.303$ and $\gamma = 0.158$. Although five of the eight observations fall within the prediction intervals, the values are very close to the upper boundary in all cases. This is a common feature: successive errors at longer horizons are correlated so that once the series drifts away from the forecasts, things tend to stay that way. ∎

Table 5.4 95 Percent Prediction Intervals for Netflix Sales
(1-8 steps ahead, from forecast origin 2013Q4)

Forecast Horizon	Forecast	Forecast RMSE	Lower PI	Upper PI	Actual	INCLUDED
1	1243	19.4	1205	1281	1270	yes
2	1284	31.9	1222	1347	1340	yes
3	1320	44.6	1233	1408	1409	no
4	1381	58.0	1267	1495	1485	yes
5	1447	73.9	1302	1592	1573	yes
6	1488	88.6	1315	1662	1645	yes
7	1524	104.1	1320	1728	1738	no
8	1585	120.5	1349	1821	1823	no

* INCLUDED = yes if Actual lies between PI Lower Limit and PI Upper Limit — that is, if the prediction interval includes the actual value. INCLUDED = no otherwise.

Data: Netflix_2.xlsx

Figure 5.2 95 Percent Prediction Intervals for Netflix Sales
(1-8 steps ahead, from forecast origin 2013Q4)

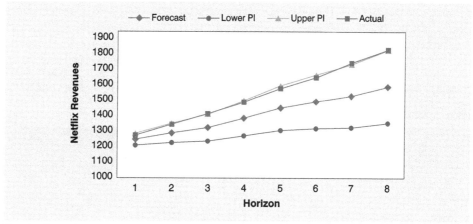

Data: Netflix_2.xlsx

5.4 Model Selection

In earlier chapters, we recommended the use of a hold-out sample as an effective way to choose among competing methods. At that time, we focused upon the simplest approach, which makes use only of the one-step-ahead forecasts. However, we may also consider forecasts over different lead times. This issue is explored in Section 5.4.1. Although such approaches have gained widespread acceptance, two concerns emerge:

- Is it feasible to use a hold-out sample when the series is short? Many series are very short — for example, after the launch of a new product.

- Can we find a criterion that uses all the data, rather than one that does not rely on excluding the most recent observations, when estimating the parameters in the alternative models?

The second question is also relevant when only a small number of observations are available. We know that it is not reasonable just to compare the *RMSE* (or a similar measure) for the estimation sample, because more complicated models involve more parameters. Given enough parameters, we can always achieve a perfect fit! So, how should we proceed? A different approach is explored in Section 5.4.2.

5.4.1 Use of a Hold-Out Sample

Suppose we hold out N observations beyond the last observation (time T, say) in the estimation sample. As we work progressively through the data, we can generate one-step-ahead forecasts for periods $T + 1$, $T + 2$,..., $T + N$; that is, we generate N one-step-ahead forecasts in all. However, we can also generate two-step-ahead forecasts for periods $T + 2$, $T + 3$, ... , $T + N$; there are $(N - 1)$ of them. We proceed in this way until we finally generate just one forecast N periods ahead. That is, we make use of rolling origin forecasts, as described in Section 3.3.4. Table 5.5 provides a detailed description of the rolling origin[5] process using the Netflix data. Panel A lists the parameter estimates for the Holt-Winters additive seasonal, or (A,A,A) model. Variation among the estimates is to be expected, especially as the newly added observation is usually the largest one to date in the series. Panel B lists the 36 error terms from which the summary statistics in Panel C are calculated. As expected the error measures increase in size as the forecast horizon is extended.

Table 5.5 The Rolling Origin Process for the Netflix Data (*The Initial Forecast Origin is 2013Q4*)

Panel A: Parameter Estimates for Each Estimation Sample

	Forecast Origin							
Parameters	2013Q4	2014Q1	2014Q2	2014Q3	2014Q4	2015Q1	2015Q2	2015Q3
alpha	1.000	1.000	1.000	1.000	1.000	1.000	1.000	1.000
beta	0.303	0.357	0.387	0.413	0.389	0.386	0.384	0.397
gamma	0.148	0.161	0.165	0.153	0.156	0.154	0.159	0.132

Panel B: Forecast Errors

	Forecast Origin							
Steps Ahead	2013Q4	2014Q1	2014Q2	2014Q3	2014Q4	2015Q1	2015Q2	2015Q3
1	26.9	18.4	17.4	−11.5	−3.5	11.9	35.9	−11.6
2	55.9	42.8	14.4	−20.0	6.9	52.0	40.6	
3	89.2	47.4	13.2	−14.3	45.7	60.8		
4	103.7	54.3	25.8	19.7	53.4			
5	126.1	77.8	70.8	20.3				
6	156.4	126.9	77.4					
7	214.3	141.1						
8	238.6							

Panel C: Summary Statistics

Steps Ahead	Number of Replicates	MAE	RMSE	MAPE
1	8	17.1	19.6	1.35
2	7	33.2	37.7	2.48
3	6	45.1	52.2	3.20
4	5	51.4	59.3	3.46
5	4	73.7	82.7	4.69
6	3	120.3	124.6	7.31
7	2	177.7	181.5	10.22
8	1	238.6	238.6	13.08

Data: Netflix_2.xlsx

---

5   There are two ways in which we may use a rolling origin. We could re-estimate the model using the data up to and including the new forecast origin (as in Table 5.5) or we could estimate the model only once and just update the forecast origin, as we did in Section 3.3.4.

Note that $\alpha = 1$ in all cases, a value that lies on the boundary of the parameter space. Allowing $\alpha > 1$ would provide a better fit but may not improve the forecast performance. Another possibility would be to consider growth rather than absolute levels, see Example 6.5.

5.4.2 Information Criteria

We need to find a balance between forecasting performance and model complexity when selecting a model. Thus far, our approach to model selection has been to partition the observed series into an estimation sample and a hold-out sample. After the parameters are estimated from the estimation sample, performance is evaluated by means of the hold-out sample. The reason for the partition is to ensure that all the models under consideration can be evaluated by using the same hold-out data on an equal footing. This approach works well when sufficient data are available, but may be problematic for short series when we have to choose between poor parameter estimates or a small hold-out sample.

DISCUSSION QUESTION: *What problems arise when a small hold-out sample based on a single forecast origin is used? After all, statistical calculations are often based on small samples.*

The concern about a small hold-out sample leads to the idea of creating a performance measure that uses all the data, with some kind of penalty function to adjust for more complex models. The argument for such an approach is as follows: When the *RMSE* or any other error measure is minimized, we recognize that a more complex model has a built-in advantage because the inclusion of extra parameters reduces the value of the error measure for the estimation sample. Thus, we seek to level the playing field by adding a penalty and then choosing the best model on the basis of the combined criterion of minimizing:

[performance measure + penalty].

The penalty function approach was introduced by Akaike (1974) and has gained widespread use in statistics generally and time series forecasting in particular.[6] The theoretical work that has been done in this area uses the *MSE* as the performance measure, so we will also follow that path, even though it entails a slight disconnect from the previous section.

Given a time series with n observations, define an Information Criterion (*IC*) that includes a penalty function $Q(n)$ weighted by p, the number of parameters fitted. That is, for the ETS(A,N,N) model leading to SES, $p = 2$ (α and σ^2); for ETS (A,A,N) leading to LES, $p = 3$ (α, β, and σ^2), where the trend is included; and for the two Holt-Winters seasonal models, (A,A,A) and (A,A,M), $p = 4$ (α, β, γ, and σ^2). If we are comparing models that are based upon series of different lengths, we must change the value of n appropriately.

MODEL SELECTION

Select the model with the minimum value of the Information Criterion:

$$IC = \ln(MSE) + pQ(n), \qquad (5.10)$$

When the model involves a transformation, we transform back to the original units before calculating the IC. This procedure is heuristic in that it is not justified theoretically, but proves to be a useful comparative measure when different transformations (or none) are to be evaluated.

---

6 Akaike used a more general version, but we use a simplified form based upon the *MSE*. For the complete version, see the online notes on R code.

How do we choose $Q(n)$? A number of alternatives have been proposed; the three best known are as follows:

Akaike's information criterion (AIC; Akaike, 1974): $Q(n) = 2/n$

Bayesian information criterion (BIC; Schwarz, 1978): $Q(n) = \ln(n)/n$

Bias corrected AIC ($AICc$; Sugiura, 1978): $Q(n) = 2/(n - p - 1)$.

The penalty in the AIC is selected so that the chosen model gives the forecasts with the minimum one-step-ahead forecast MSE, at least for large samples. That is, we might think of a very large sample, and then the AIC would select the model that had the smallest MSE in the (large) hold-out sample. The AIC has a negative bias that is more pronounced on small samples, which the $AICc$ is designed to correct. Even with the penalty, the AIC versions sometimes produce a model that seems overly complex, so the BIC is designed to avoid such extra terms. For example, when $n = 20$ and $p = 2$, the AIC has $Q(n) = 0.10$ and $AICc$ has $Q(n) = 0.18$ whereas the BIC has $Q(n) = 0.15$. When $n = 100$, the AIC has $Q(n) = 0.02$ and $AICc$ has $Q(n) = 0.021$, whereas the BIC has $Q(n) = 0.046$. Even though the formal justification relies on large samples being available, empirical studies have found that these criteria appear to do well (see, e.g., Billah, Hyndman, and Koehler, 2005).

These criteria are formulated in various ways by different authors, which leads to different numerical values but similar or identical model choices. The important thing from our perspective is that a penalty is applied to neutralize the effects of fitting extra terms. Many forecasting programs provide either the AIC or the BIC or both, and sometimes the $AICc$ as well, enabling a ready choice to be made among competing models.

■ Example 5.4: Model selection for the Netflix data

The Netflix data were fitted over the period from the first quarter of 2000 through the last quarter of 2015. We fitted the local-level, the local-trend, the level + seasonal and the two Holt-Winters models (additive and multiplicative), and included log transforms in most cases, using the ESM, as described in Chapters 3 and 4. Recall that in the ESM the MSE is calculated in the original units, after transforming back from the log transform, so the analysis tend to favor additive models, at least marginally. The results are shown in Table 5.6. The (A,A,N) model corresponding to LES fares best, even though it has a slightly higher MSE than the (A,A,A) model for additive Holt-Winters. All three criteria favor the same model, although the margin of difference is larger for BIC. The results for AIC and $AICc$ are virtually identical for a sample of this size. In conclusion, the seasonal effect appears to be slight even though we are looking at quarterly data.

Table 5.6 Values of the AIC and BIC Criteria for Different Models for the Netflix Data

Method	Model	MSE	Parameters	AIC	BIC	AICc
SES	A,N,N	1720.7	2	7.51	7.58	7.52
LES	A,A,N	379.9	3	**6.03**	**6.13**	**6.04**
LES + logs	M,M,N	417.0	3	6.13	6.23	6.13
Level + Seasonal	A,N,A	1606.1	3	7.48	7.58	7.48
Level + Seasonal + logs	M,N,M	1713.4	3	7.54	7.64	7.55
HW additive	A,A,A	375.0	4	6.05	6.19	6.06
HW additive + logs	M,M,M	686.6	4	6.66	6.79	6.67
HW multiplicative	M,A,M	567.5	4	6.47	6.60	6.48

N.B.: Minimum values in bold. *Data: Netflix_2.xlsx*

DISCUSSION QUESTION: *How might you modify AIC and BIC if you wished to select the best model for forecasting h steps ahead?*

5.4.3 Automatic Model Selection

Most leading forecasting programs include an automatic model selection procedure. Some start with a list of competing models, as we did in Table 5.6; others build a model either by starting with a simple scheme and adding components, or by starting with a very general model and simplifying. Online Appendix B provides a brief summary of some of the leading programs.

Although the *AIC* and *BIC* are now widely used, some forecasters (e.g., Armstrong, 2001) contend strongly that the use of a hold-out sample is much to be preferred. Studies are contradictory with the study by Billah *et al.* (2005) suggesting that the information criterion approach may often be preferable, while a fuller study by Fildes and Petropoulos (2015) concludes that the hold-out approaches are more flexible, and, where there is sufficient data, lead to more accurate selection. But the matter is still open for debate. We believe that the simple answer is often to use both; the hold-out sample is particularly valuable for the detection of possible changes in the series' behavior, whereas the information criteria may be preferred when the series is stable and relatively short.

DISCUSSION QUESTION: *If you were responsible for developing forecasting methods for a large number of data series (such as grocery store products), what combination of hold-out samples and information criteria would you employ?*

5.5 Outliers

OUTLIERS

An outlier is an extreme observation that, if not adjusted, may cause serious estimation and forecasting errors.

Most real series have occasional unusual observations. A sales series may have a sudden peak because of a special promotion, or a macroeconomic variable, such as employment, may be affected by severe weather. In each case, the phenomenon observed is real enough, but the values are sufficiently atypical that they may distort the model estimation process and, in turn, the derived forecasts. We cannot simply remove such observations, and we may wish to extend the model to account for such changes. However, at this stage we seek to do two things:

- Develop a way to identify such outliers
- Adjust the outliers once they have been identified

The approach we describe is rather basic as our intention is to illustrate some of the issues involved.

Outliers may take one of several forms. For example, there could be a single extreme value, after which the series reverts to its previous pattern; such an outlier is known as an *additive outlier (AO)*. Another possibility is a permanent change in the level, known as a *level shift (LS)*. Various other possibilities exist, but we will consider only the *AO* and *LS* forms. From the forecasting perspective, it is often these single unusual observations that cause the most trouble. Figure 5.3A illustrates an *AO* and Figure 5.3B an *LS*. Taking first differences of the series, we see that the *AO* and *LS* provide the patterns shown in Figures 5.3C and 5.3D, respectively. Note that an *LS* after differencing is of the same form as an *AO* without differencing. Of course, the *AO* and *LS* may be either positive or negative.

Figure 5.3 Typical Patterns for Additive Outlier and Level Shift

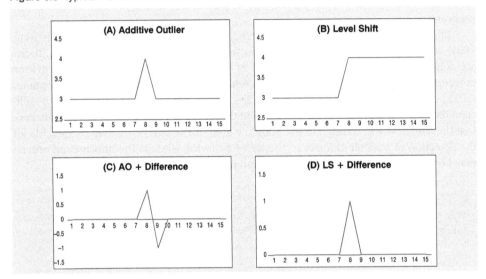

We first standardize the variables; that is, we compute the Z-scores as described in Section 2.4.4. We then compute Z-scores for the first differences. The full procedure is as follows:

1. Compute the Z-scores for the original series and for the first differences; that is,

$$Z_t = \frac{Y_t - \bar{Y}}{S(Y)}$$ and the equivalent in first differences.

   The original series is used to check for *AO* and the first differences series for *LS*.

2. Find the first absolute Z-value that exceeds 3.0. If there are no such values, end the search.

3. If the observation with the extreme Z-value suggests a pattern such as either of those shown in Figure 5.3A or 5.3C, an *AO* is suggested. If either of Figures 5.3B and 5.3D is a more appropriate match, consider an *LS*.

4. Replace the outlier by a suitable reduced value; we suggest replacing the current Z-score by 1.5, with the same sign as the original. That is, for *AO* the new value is $Y_t^* = \bar{Y} + 1.5 \times S(Y)$; replace the positive sign with a negative sign when the Z-score is negative. For *LS*, the same adjustment is applied to the first differences.

5. Return to step 1 and continue until no outliers remain.

The choice of a cutoff of 3.0 is a common one and generally viewed as reasonable, but some forecasters prefer a larger number. Likewise, the adjustment made in step 4 is one of many options that provide a compromise between the observed and fitted values. If it appears that a large number of outliers exists, a desirable extension of this approach is to refit the model after each adjustment — or even to consider a different model!

Again, we stress that the approach we have outlined is very basic and modern forecasting software systems (see online Appendix B) usually provide a much more sophisticated procedure. This involves fitting an initial model and then checking the residuals from the estimation process to determine whether any outliers exist. The model is then refitted. Outliers are modified in a sequential fashion, because earlier outliers may generate further unusual observations later in the series.

When the data are seasonal we need to develop a seasonal model and then examine the residuals from the model to see if any are outliers; our basic method can be modified to consider seasonal differences. Our primary aim is to draw attention to the problem and to provide a basic process for identifying and dealing with extreme values. By way of consolation, the very large outliers are the most important and they are usually quite easy to detect!

■ Example 5.5: Outlier detection and adjustment for Dulles domestic passengers

The number of passengers in millions per year is recorded in *Dulles_2.xlsx* and provides 53 annual observations (1963-2015). Because a log transform is clearly desirable, we analyze the transformed series. The ordered Z-scores for the first differences are summarized below:

Year	1986	1985	2004	1967	...	1988	2006	1980
Z-SCORE	3.61	2.02	1.84	1.43	...	−1.32	−1.81	−2.44

As is evident from the original plot in Figure 2.2 the airport expansion in 1986 led to a level shift.

The observed Z-score for year 1986 is 3.61 and we replace that by $Z = 1.5$ corresponding to the outlier observation 0.615 on the log scale. The mean and standard deviation are 0.060 and 0.154 respectively, so the value in the differenced series changes from 0.615 to $0.060 + 1.5 \times 0.154 = 0.290$, or about half the original value. Rather than adjust all the later observations for the level shift, we upscale all the earlier values by the multiplier $\exp(0.615 - 0.290) = \exp(0.325) = 1.384$, the proportionate amount to bring the earlier observations into line. The original and changed values for 1983-88 are shown in Table 5.7; by design, the two series match from 1986 onward. Without a log transform, the adjustment would be adding an appropriate constant rather than multiplying.

After making the adjustments to the series, we can compute the forecasts as in Chapter 3. We use ESM with the log transform and use the last six observations as a holdout sample. The results are summarized in Table 5.8.

Several points emerge from. The *RelMAE*, *RMSE*, and *MAPE* are all lower for both the estimation sample and the hold-out sample, although the parameter estimates are essentially the same.

Table 5.7 Original and Adjusted Dulles Series for 1983–8

Year	Passengers	Passengers Modified
1983	2651	3669
1984	3136	4340
1985	4538	6281
1986 (level shift)	8394	8394
1987	9980	9980
1988	8650	8650

Data: Dulles_2.xlsx

Table 5.8 Summary Results for Dulles Passengers Series, Without and With an Adjustment for the 1986 Outlier

	In Sample			Out of Sample			Parameters	
	MAE	RMSE	MAPE	MAE	RMSE	MAPE	alpha	beta
Original	1072	1728	12.9	869	985	5.56	1	0.087
Modified	1042	1652	12.0	824	943	5.27	1	0.087

Data: Dulles_2.xlsx

A check for further outliers does not reveal any values outside to 3.0 limits for the Z-scores. A word of caution is needed here: Removing all the outliers and then creating a modified prediction interval assumes that the future will be free from unusual events; the prediction intervals may be too narrow as the result of this overoptimistic assumption!

Outlier adjustment for good reason, such as the Dulles expansion in 1986, leads to model-based intervention analysis, which is explored in Section 9.8. In general, outlier adjustment needs to be approached with care, and the overzealous removal of extreme values may hurt, rather than help, the forecasting process (see Koehler, Snyder, Ord, and Beaumont, 2012).

> **DISCUSSION QUESTION:** *Suppose all the outliers in the estimation sample have been identified and adjusted. How should we construct prediction intervals to allow for the possibility of extreme observations in the future?*

5.6 State-Space Modeling Principles

The essence of model-building in a state-space context is to select states that describe the principal features of the series. The principles stated here are designed to facilitate that process. When the number of series under consideration is large, it is reasonable to select a sample stratified by key features such as length and reporting frequency and then to apply the analysis just to the sample. Automated checks for large errors may be applied to the remaining series once the general approach has been established. (For additional discussion, see Armstrong, 2001 and Section 13.1.5.)

[5.1] Plot the series (or a sample of series).
Plots of the series, augmented by seasonal plots, should be used to identify trends and seasonal patterns as well as to provide early warning of possible outliers.

[5.2] Identify all the relevant features of the series.
On the basis of the initial plots, decide whether trend and seasonal effects are important and whether the seasonal effects, if present, are additive or multiplicative. Also, consider whether a transformation is likely to be beneficial to allow for trend-dependent variation.

[5.3] Select the best performing model, using an information criterion and/or a hold-out sample.
If the series is short, an information criterion will perform better. For longer series, there is not usually a lot of difference, although some forecasters strongly prefer to use the hold-out sample as a way to detect structural changes in the series. Either way, these criteria are readily automated.

[5.4] Check the model assumptions.

This step involves plotting the observed error terms to determine whether the variance appears to be constant and whether any remaining dependence is apparent in the errors. Also, the empirical distribution of the residuals should be checked to see whether the normality assumption is appropriate.

[5.5] Check for outliers and make adjustments where appropriate.

As noted in our discussion, such action should be taken sparingly and the outlier may reflect an omitted variable rather than an aberrant observation.

[5.6] Examine the prediction intervals.

If the intervals appear much too wide or too narrow, this may suggest a change in the volatility of the series, a topic to which we return in Section 9.6.4. A transformation should be considered as a way to ameliorate the problem.

Summary

The state-space framework enables the development of underlying statistical models to support the forecasting methods discussed in Chapters 3 and 4. These models incorporate trends and seasonal components and allow for various transformations. The state-space framework describes a taxonomy of the different models that characterize time series. We also considered the selection of a suitable model, using both a hold-out sample and an information criterion.

Overall, this chapter is rather theoretical, and it might seem that the forecaster interested only in applications could pass it by. We agree that it is not necessary for every automobile driver to be a mechanic, but some knowledge of what is going on under the hood contributes to carefree driving. For the modern driver, the many displays (dare we say metrics?) on the dashboard contribute to trouble-free driving, provided that warning signs are not ignored. This chapter provides the design for a forecasting dashboard: Valid forecasts depend upon a series of assumptions, and the forecasts work best only when those assumptions are satisfied at least approximately. Good forecasting relies upon the skill and knowledge of the forecaster just as surely as good driving requires such attributes in the driver.

As elsewhere in the book, our focus is upon the development of the forecasting system. Once that step has been achieved, the system can operate more automatically, a topic to which we return in Chapter 12 when we discuss forecasting systems.

Exercises

5.1   Forecasting by means of simple exponential smoothing (SES) with $\alpha = 0.3$ produces a one-step-ahead forecast of $F_t = 100$ and an estimation sample *RMSE* of 64. Determine the point forecasts and the 95 percent prediction intervals for one through four steps ahead.

5.2   Consider the data on the change in real *GDP* (*GDP_change_2.xlsx*) previously examined in Exercises 3.1 and 3.3. Estimate the smoothing parameter and the *RMSE*, using the data from 1963 through 2007 as the estimation sample. Then determine the point forecasts and the 95 percent prediction intervals for one through six steps ahead. Repeat the exercise, using the data through 2009 as the estimation sample, and compare your results.

5.3 Consider the data on the change in the Consumer Price Index (*CPI_change_2.xlsx*), which represents the month-to-month change in the *CPI* in percentage terms, seasonally adjusted and annualized. Estimate the smoothing parameter and the *RMSE*, using the data though 2012 as the estimation sample. Then determine the point forecasts and the 95 percent prediction intervals for one through 12 steps ahead. Repeat the exercise, using the data through 2014 as the estimation sample, and compare your results.

5.4* The statistical model for damped trend may be formulated as:

Observation equation: $Y_t = L_{t-1} + \phi T_{t-1} + \varepsilon_t$

State equations: $L_t = L_{t-1} + \phi T_{t-1} + \alpha \varepsilon_t$ and $T_t = \phi T_{t-1} + \alpha \beta \varepsilon_t$

Show that the forecast function is $F_{t+h}(h) = L_t + (\phi + \phi^2 + \ldots + \phi^h) T_{t-1}$. Further show that the forecast function approaches the limiting value $L_t + (\phi/(1 - \phi)) T_{t-1}$.

5.5 An analysis of an annual sales series uses linear exponential smoothing (LES) to produce the following results:

$$L_t = 100, T_t = 4.0, \alpha = 0.3, \beta = 0.2.$$

In addition, the estimation sample produces an estimated *RMSE* of 2.5. Determine the point forecasts and the prediction intervals for one through three steps ahead.

5.6 The spreadsheet *Vix.xlsx* contains data on the monthly closing values of the VIX Index, which trades on the volatility of the S&P 500 Index, from its inception in 1990 through 2015. Use the (A,N,N) and (A,A,N) models to generate one-step-ahead forecasts for the months of 2013-2015, using the data for 1990 – 2012 as the estimation sample. Compute the one-step-ahead 95 percent prediction intervals, and check to see how many intervals include the actual values.

5.7 An analysis of an annual sales series uses linear exponential smoothing (LES) with a log transform to produce the following results:

$$L_t = 100, T_t = 4.0, \alpha = 0.3, \beta = 0.2.$$

In addition, the estimation sample produces an estimated *RMSE* (for the logarithms) of 2.5. Determine the point forecasts and the prediction intervals for the original data for one through four steps ahead.

5.8 Reexamine the VIX data described in Exercise 5.6, using a log transform. Use the (M,N,N) and (M,M,N) models to generate one-step-ahead forecasts for the months of 2013-2015, using the data for 1990–2012 as the estimation sample. Compute the one-step-ahead 95 percent prediction intervals for the transformed series and the transform back to the original series, and check to see how many intervals include the actual values. Compare the intervals given by this approach with those obtained in Exercise 5.6.

5.9 Consider the Walmart sales data stores examined in Minicase 4.1 (see the file *Walmart_2.xlsx*). Determine the most appropriate forecasting model for the quarterly sales data by (a) using the last eight quarters as a hold-out sample and (b) using information criteria. Compute the one-step-ahead prediction intervals for the original series, and check to see how many intervals include the actual values.

The following exercises relate back to Exercises 4.4–4.8 in the previous chapter. In each case, select the 'best' model using both a hold-out sample and information criteria. How does the model selected compare with your own views of what the most appropriate model would be?

5.10 Examine the series on Job Openings (*Job_openings.xlsx*) previously considered in Minicase 3.1. Does the inclusion of seasonal factors provide a useful improvement in forecast quality? Use the last 36 observations as the hold-out sample.

5.11 The U.S. Census records monthly Alcoholic Beverage Sales by Wholesalers (*Alcohol_sales.xlsx*). The series is recorded monthly and it is not seasonally adjusted. Sales are measured in $Millions and the series runs from January 2001 to December 2015. Use the last 36 observations as the hold-out sample.

5.12 Use the data in the file *US_retail_sales_2.xlsx* with the period from January 2001 to December 2012 as the estimation sample. Use the last 36 observations as the hold-out sample.

5.13 The spreadsheet *Titanic_box_office.xlsx* provides the daily figures for the number of customers per theater for the period December 19, 1997 to July 23, 1998. Use the last four weeks as a hold-out sample.

5.14 The spreadsheet *Gas_prices_Ch4.xlsx* gives the average end of month prices "at the pump" of regular-grade gasoline for the period from January 2000 to December 2015. Use the last 36 observations as the hold-out sample.

Minicases

Minicase 5.1 Analysis of UK Retail Sales

The file *UK_retail_sales_2.xlsx* contains the quarterly index for the volume of total retail trade in the UK from 1996Q1 to 2014Q4. The index is not seasonally adjusted, and the index has 2010 as the base year with the index for that year set at 100.

The file *UK_retail_sales_annual.xlsx* gives yearly figures for the same index, from 1955–2014 with an index value of 100 for 2010.

Determine the most appropriate models for forecasting both the quarterly and annual time series, and compare your forecasts from each approach for the complete years 2013 and 2014 (i.e., compare aggregate quarterly with annual).

Do the forecasts fall within appropriate prediction intervals?

Advanced: How would you generate prediction intervals for the forecasts you obtained by aggregation? Extend the data set to include the most recent data and rework the analysis for the last two years.

Minicase 5.2 Prediction Intervals for WFJ Sales

We make use of the data file *WFJ_sales.xlsx*. Around week 12, the WFJ Sales manager changed the advertising strategy for the product, which resulted in an increase in sales. To allow for this change, drop the first 12 observations and recompute the prediction intervals for weeks 27-36, using only observations 13-25 as the estimation sample. You will find that the *RMSE* is reduced and the width of the intervals increases more slowly, because α is smaller.

Repeat this analysis for other subsamples to see how the prediction intervals depend critically upon validating the assumptions listed in Table 5.2.

References

Starred items indicate more advanced reading.

*Akaike, H. (1974). A new look at the statistical model identification. *IEEE Transactions on Automatic Control*, 19, 716–723.

Armstrong, J. S. (2001). Extrapolation. In Armstrong, J.S. (ed.), *Principles of Forecasting: A Handbook for Researchers and Practitioners*. Boston and Dordrecht: Kluwer, pp. 215–243.

*Bachelier, L. (1900). Théorie de la speculation, *Annales Scientifiques de l'École Normale Supérieure*, 3, 21–86.

*Billah, B., Hyndman, R. J., and Koehler, A. B. (2005). Empirical information criteria for time series forecasting model selection. *Journal of Statistical Computation & Simulation*, 75, 831–840.

De Livera, A. M., Hyndman, R. J., and Snyder, R. D. (2011). Forecasting time series with complex seasonal patterns using exponential smoothing. *Journal of the American Statistical Association*, 106(496), 1513–1527.

*Durbin, J., and Koopman, S. J. (2012). *Time Series Analysis by State-Space Methods*. Second edition. Oxford, U.K: Oxford University Press.

Fildes, R., & Petropoulos, F. (2015). An evaluation of simple versus complex selection rules for forecasting many time series. *Journal of Business Research*, 68, 1692–1701.

*Harvey, A. C. (1989). *Forecasting, Structural Time Series Models, and the Kalman Filter*. Cambridge, U.K.: Cambridge University Press.

*Hyndman, R. J., Koehler, A. B., Ord, J. K., and Snyder, R. D. (2008). *Forecasting with Exponential Smoothing*. Berlin, Heidelberg, and New York: Springer.

Koehler, A. B., Snyder, R. D., Ord, J. K., and Beaumont, A. (2012). A study of outliers in the exponential smoothing approach to forecasting. *International Journal of Forecasting*, 28, 477–484.

Reilly, R. K., and Brown, K. C. (2012). *Investment Analysis and Portfolio Management*, 10th ed. Pacific Grove, CA: Thomson.

*Schwarz, G. (1978). Estimating the dimension of a model. *Annals of Statistics*, 6, 461–464.

Sugiura, N. (1978). Further analysis of the data by Akaike's information criterion and the finite corrections. *Communications in Statistics*, A7, 13–26.

Timmermann, A., and Granger, C. W. J. (2004). Efficient market hypothesis and forecasting. *International Journal of Forecasting*, 20, 15–27.

*West, M., and Harrison, P. J. (1997). *Bayesian Forecasting and Dynamic Models*, 2nd ed. Berlin, Heidelberg, and New York: Springer.

Appendix 5A* Derivation of Forecast Means and Variances

We consider the local-level model explored in Section 5.1.2 and rely upon the set of assumptions stated in Table 5.2. In technical terms, these assumptions about the random error terms $\varepsilon_t \sim IIN(0, \sigma^2)$ may be stated as follows:

Zero bias: $E(\varepsilon_{t+i} \mid L_{t-1}) = 0, \quad i = 0, 1, \ldots$

Constant variance: $V(\varepsilon_{t+i} \mid L_{t-1}) = \sigma^2, \quad i = 0, 1, \ldots$

Independent (strictly uncorrelated) errors: $Corr(\varepsilon_{t+i}, \varepsilon_{t+j} \mid L_{t-1}) = 0, \quad i \neq j$

Using the idea of zero bias yields (and the formulae of online Appendix A)

$$E(Y_t \mid L_{t-1}) = E(L_{t-1} + \varepsilon_t \mid L_{t-1})$$

$$= E(L_{t-1} \mid L_{t-1}) + E(\varepsilon_t \mid L_{t-1})$$

$$= L_{t-1} \text{ (since the first term is a constant).}$$

The variance for one-step-ahead forecasts may then be written as

$$V(Y_t \mid L_{t-1}) = V(L_{t-1} + \varepsilon_t \mid L_{t-1})$$
$$= V(L_{t-1} \mid L_{t-1}) + V(\varepsilon_t \mid L_{t-1})$$
$$= 0 + \sigma^2.$$

Following the same line of argument, we see that the variance for two steps ahead is given by

$$V(Y_{t+1} \mid L_{t-1}) = V(L_t + \varepsilon_{t+1} \mid L_{t-1})$$
$$= V(L_{t-1} + \alpha\varepsilon_t + \varepsilon_{t+1} \mid L_{t-1})$$
$$= V(L_{t-1} \mid L_{t-1}) + V(\alpha\varepsilon_t + \varepsilon_{t+1} \mid L_{t-1})$$
$$= 0 + V(\alpha\varepsilon_t + \varepsilon_{t+1} \mid L_{t-1}).$$

Because there is zero correlation between the two error terms, the equation becomes

$$V(Y_{t+1} \mid L_{t-1}) = V(\alpha\varepsilon_t + \varepsilon_{t+1} \mid L_{t-1})$$
$$= V(\alpha\varepsilon_t \mid L_{t-1}) + V(\varepsilon_{t+1} \mid L_{t-1})$$
$$= \alpha^2 V(\varepsilon_t \mid L_{t-1}) + V(\varepsilon_{t+1} \mid L_{t-1})$$
$$= \alpha^2\sigma^2 + \sigma^2 = \sigma^2(1 + \alpha^2).$$

Higher numbers of steps ahead are dealt with in the same way.

In the general case, the error terms in the model, for h steps ahead, may be written as

$$\varepsilon_{t+h-1} + A_1\varepsilon_{t+h-2} + \cdots + A_{h-1}\varepsilon_t.$$

By similar arguments, the variance becomes

$$V(Y_{t+h-1} \mid L_{t-1}) = V(\varepsilon_{t+h-1} + A_1\varepsilon_{t+h-2} + \cdots + A_{h-1}\varepsilon_t \mid L_{t-1})$$
$$= \sigma^2(1 + A_1^2 + \ldots + A_{h-1}^2).$$

For the model underlying SES, $A_j = \alpha$ for all values of j, so the variance is

$$V(Y_{t+h-1} \mid L_{t-1}) = \sigma^2[1 + (h-1)\alpha^2].$$

Appendix 5B The Holt-Winters Multiplicative Scheme

The multiplicative scheme follows in the way we would expect, with the seasonal term in the forecast function now involving a product in place of a sum:

Forecast function: $F_{t+h-1}(h) = (L_{t-1} + hT_{t-1})S_{t+h-1-m}, \quad h = 1, 2, \ldots$

Observation equation: $Y_t = (L_{t-1} + T_{t-1})S_{t-m}(1 + \varepsilon_t)$

State equations: $L_t = (L_{t-1} + T_{t-1})(1 + \alpha\varepsilon_t)$

$$T_t = T_{t-1} + \alpha\beta(L_{t-1} + T_{t-1})\varepsilon_t$$

$$S_t = S_{t-m}(1 + \gamma\varepsilon_t)$$

If we compare this model with that for the additive Holt-Winters scheme, we see some major differences. The forecast is now given by the product of the trend and the seasonal factor, and the state variables are updated by multiplicative factors involving the random error. In turn, when the random errors $\{\varepsilon_t\}$ have constant variance, the standard deviation of Y_t will be proportional to the current mean level rather than being constant. This idea makes sense; we have often noticed that the variability of the series increases with the mean. We note in passing that the one-step-ahead variance becomes

$$V(Y_t \,|\, L_{t-1}, T_{t-1}, S_{t-m}) = \sigma^2 F_t^2.$$

Unfortunately, the nonlinearity makes the analysis more complicated; equations for the variance for multiple steps ahead may be found in Hyndman *et al.* (2008, Chapter 4).

CHAPTER 6

Autoregressive Integrated Moving Average (ARIMA) Models

*Topics marked with an * are advanced and may be omitted for more introductory courses.*

Table of Contents

All models are wrong, but some are useful.

— George Box

Introduction

In Chapter 5, we developed state-space models that grew naturally out of the exponential smoothing methods introduced in Chapters 3 and 4. However, there are other ways to model time series, of which the most prominent is the use of the *Autoregressive Integrated Moving Average* (ARIMA) class of models. These models are often referred to as *Box-Jenkins models*, because the first systematic treatment of modeling, estimation, and forecasting with such models appeared in the seminal work of those two researchers (Box and Jenkins, 1970; the most recent edition is Box, Jenkins, Reinsel and Ljung, 2016).

In Chapter 5, we developed a state-space model by specifying components such as level, trend, and seasonality; such models are sometimes known as *structural models,* given that they are developed in terms of these intuitive components. However, once we move over to ARIMA models, the approach to model building is data driven. Rather than identify particular components, the ARIMA modeler first develops the properties of basic ARIMA models as a class. She then examines various summary statistics that characterize the time series in order to find a model that matches the data summaries. The key measures used for this purpose are the sample *Autocorrelation Function* (*ACF*), described in Section 6.1, and we also include an optional discussion of the sample *Partial Autocorrelation Function* (*PACF*) in Section 6.2.5.[1] The basic properties of ARIMA models are explored in Sections 6.1, 6.2, and 6.3, and the issue of model selection is considered in Section 6.4. Then, in Section 6.5, we examine diagnostic methods for checking whether the model selected is adequate, although an alternative approach is simply to choose the best model from a prespecified short list, as we did with state-space models. In Section 6.6, we consider the problem of outliers; we then develop forecasting procedures in Section 6.7. We consider seasonal ARIMA models in Section 6.8 and then, in Section 6.9, outline the linkages between state-space and ARIMA models. As we note, where relevant, many ARIMA models are equivalent to the state space models of Chapter 5 (and thus underlie the exponential smoothing formulations of Chapter 3).

Our analysis up to this point has always assumed that the error variance is constant. In Section 6.10, we relax that assumption and allow the variance to change over time. Finally, the section on principles provides a systematic approach to the development of ARIMA models.

The standard, albeit rather advanced, reference for ARIMA models is that of Box *et al.* (2016). A useful intermediate-level text is Cryer and Chan (2010), but both require more mathematics than is used in this chapter.

6.1 The Sample Autocorrelation Function

From Chapter 2, we are familiar with the calculation of the mean and variance of an observed time series, but we have not so far developed any direct measures of the dependence that may exist among observations. If we are to develop a data-driven framework for time series modeling, the first requirement is to provide such a measure.

Just as we used the correlation coefficient in Section 2.5 to assess the association between two variables, we now introduce the concept of *autocorrelation.* As the name suggests, auto-

---

1 We include the *PACF* in our discussion in subsequent sections, but its use is not necessary for the analysis as we make clear.

correlations measure the correlation between the current and immediate past values of a time series. We refer to Y_{t-1} as the *(first-order) lagged value* of Y_t, or just the *lag*. We then define the *(first-order) sample autocorrelation* for Y as

$$r_1 = \frac{\sum_{t=2}^{n} (Y_t - \bar{Y})(Y_{t-1} - \bar{Y})}{\sum_{t=1}^{n} (Y_t - \bar{Y})^2}. \tag{6.1}$$

There are several things to note about this expression:

- The first value, Y_1 is being compared with the second value, Y_2, so the summation starts at $t = 2$, corresponding to the first pair available.
- The two series (Y and its first-order lag) have almost the same mean, differing by only one observation out of n. So, we use a common mean taken over all n values. By the same token, we use a common variance in the denominator, also taken over all n values.
- There are $(n - 1)$ pairs in the numerator, yet n terms in the denominator. One could argue for making an adjustment, but it has generally been found useful to retain this slight bias toward zero for reasons of numerical stability in higher order autocorrelations.

■ Example 6.1: Calculation of the first-order autocorrelation

The calculations are laid out in the following table:

Week	1	2	3	4	5	6	7	Sums
Sales (000s), Y_t	15	10	12	16	9	12	10	84
Lagged values, Y_{t-1}		15	10	12	16	9	12	
$Y_t - \bar{Y}$	3	-2	0	4	-3	0	-2	0
$Y_{t-1} - \bar{Y}$		3	-2	0	4	-3	0	
$(Y_t - \bar{Y})(Y_{t-1} - \bar{Y})$		-6	0	0	-12	0	0	-18
$(Y_t - \bar{Y})^2$	9	4	0	16	9	0	4	42

Total sales over the seven weeks are 84, so the weekly average is 12.

From equation (6.1), we then have $r_1 = -18/42 = -0.429$, showing some negative autocorrelation. We interpret this as an indication that above-average sales one week tend to be followed by somewhat below-average sales the next week. We should keep in mind, however, that the autocorrelation is weak and the sample size is very small, so such a conclusion should be viewed as tentative. Like the correlation coefficient in Section 2.5, the autocorrelation can be from -1 (maximum negative) to 1 (maximum positive), with 0 signifying no linear relationship between the current and the lagged values. ■

We referred to equation (6.1) as the first-order autocorrelation because we lagged the series by one time period. In similar fashion, we could go 2, 3, ... , k steps back and define the second-, third-,..., kth-order autocorrelations. We refer to Y_{t-k} as the lag of order k, so the *sample autocorrelation of order k* for Y is defined as

$$r_k = \frac{\sum_{t=k+1}^{n} (Y_t - \bar{Y})(Y_{t-k} - \bar{Y})}{\sum_{t=1}^{n} (Y_t - \bar{Y})^2}. \tag{6.2}$$

The sample autocorrelation of order k is an estimate of the population autocorrelation of order k, which we denote by ρ_k *(Greek letter rho)*. Comments about equation (6.2) are essentially the same as those about r_1, except that we lose k terms. A good way to look for structure in a time series is to compute the first K autocorrelations, usually no further than $K = n/4$ or thereabouts. The autocorrelations are then plotted against k, and the plot is known as the *(sample) autocorrelation function,* abbreviated to *ACF*.

■ Example 6.2: The autocorrelation function for WFJ Sales

The *ACF* for WFJ Sales is shown in Figure 6.1. The broken boundary lines provide a quick visual test of the statistical significance of the autocorrelations. They are calculated in any ARIMA capable program, such as MINITAB used here. Alternatively $\pm 2/\sqrt{n}$ gives a reasonable approximation to the limits at 5% significance level. With 62 observations that gives 95% limits of ± 0.254. The computer program uses more accurate expressions for the standard error, which lead to the gradually wider limits shown in Figure 6.1. If the observed value lies outside the area enclosed by those lines, we may reject the null hypothesis that the population autocorrelation is zero (with significance level $\alpha = 0.05$ as the default value). From Figure 6.1, we can see that the first few autocorrelations are positive, indicating a carryover in sales level from one week to the next. As the lag increases, the autocorrelation dies away. ■

Figure 6.1 The *ACF* for WFJ Sales (Minitab)

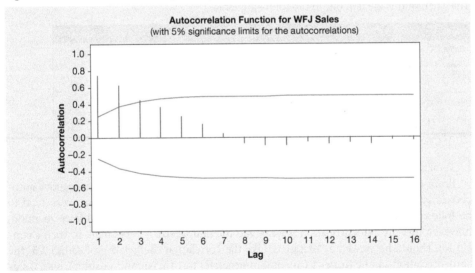

Data: WFJ_sales.xlsx

6.1.1 Model Assumptions

The pattern of association illustrated in Figure 6.1 seems quite plausible: Successive weeks show similar levels of sales, but the similarity fades as the time between weeks is increased. But how do we translate such notions into a statistical model? Recall that, to make sense of the sample mean and the sample variance, we require that the observations come from a process with a constant mean and variance. To those requirements we now add the condition that any snapshot of the time series is structurally the same as any other of the same length (whatever the starting point). Formally stated, this condition means that the theoretical autocorrelation between observations k lags apart should be the same, no matter where those two observations occur in the series; it is only their *relative* position that matters. For example, the autocorrelation between observations for the months of January and May should be the same as that for the same months the previous year. Further, they should remain the same for March and July or for August and December; all pairs are four months apart. Fortunately, this assumption is often reasonable.

Putting together these requirements for a constant mean, variance and a relative autocorrelation structure, we arrive at the concept of *stationarity.*

STATIONARITY

A time series is *stationary* if it has a constant mean and variance and its autocorrelations depend only on the relative time between the observations. Formally, we introduce the notation ω^2 for the variance of Y and ρ_k to denote the autocorrelation at lag k. Then, for stationarity, we require that

$$E(Y_t) = \mu$$
$$V(Y_t) = \omega^2$$
$$Corr(Y_t, Y_{t-k}) = \rho_k, k = 1, 2, \dots .$$

all independent of t.

Why does stationarity matter? We can always compute the sample mean, the variance, and autocorrelations from an observed time series, but the numbers make sense *only* if the assumption of stationarity holds. The following examples suggest, however, that this assumption may often be the exception, rather than the rule, for business forecasting:

- Sales of a product increase after it is introduced into the market and then flatten out as the market matures. As the product is superseded by an improved competitor, sales may begin to decline. The series is *nonstationary in the mean.*

- Gross domestic product *(GDP)* generally increases, but the fluctuations are measured in percentage terms rather than absolute terms. The series is *nonstationary in both the mean and the variance.*

- The price of a stock varies over time but does not show any tendency to fluctuate around a particular (mean) value. The series is *nonstationary in the mean, even though no systematic trend may exist.*

Fortunately, as shown later in the chapter, it is often feasible to restore stationarity by suitable transformations. For the time being, when we analyze a series, we will assume that the series is stationary and we will develop some statistical models under that assumption. We then relate these models to observed features of the data.

6.2 Autoregressive Moving Average (ARMA) Models

The models we now consider contain two components: *autoregressive (AR)* and *moving average (MA).* Just as autocorrelation is an association between past and present values, autoregression models the relationship between the current value and past values of a series. We begin by considering only the autoregressive component and then examine the moving average element before combining the two in a single model.

6.2.1 The First-Order Autoregressive Model

The simplest autoregressive model is the first-order scheme, designated AR(1) and written as

$$Y_t = \delta + \phi Y_{t-1} + \varepsilon_t, \tag{6.3}$$

where ε_t denotes the random error term, subject to the same set of assumptions as those made in Section 5.2, namely,

- The errors are independent of each other
- The errors are (normally) distributed with zero means and constant variance σ^2.

The parameter δ may be interpreted as an intercept term, whereas ϕ is a slope term. When ϕ is positive, high values in the series tend to be followed by high values (and low by low). When ϕ is negative, a pattern high-low-high-low is to be expected.

The AR(1) model is stationary if and only if $-1 < \phi < 1$. We then have

$$E(Y_t) = \mu = \delta/(1-\phi)$$

$$V(Y_t) = \omega^2 = \sigma^2/(1-\phi^2)$$

$$Corr(Y_t, Y_{t-k}) = \phi^k \quad k = 1, 2, \ldots$$

The proof is given in Appendix 6A. Note that the autocorrelations decline geometrically; for example, when $\phi = 0.8$, successive terms are 0.8, 0.64, 0.512, ... , as illustrated in Figure 6.2. Note also that when ϕ is negative, the signs alternate. Further, when $\phi = 0.4$, the values die away much more quickly. If these patterns were observed in a time series they could be used to assist in the choice of a suitable model, an approach that we discuss in Section 6.4.

Figure 6.2 *ACF* for AR(1) Scheme with $\phi = 0.8$, $\phi = -0.8$ and $\phi = 0.4$

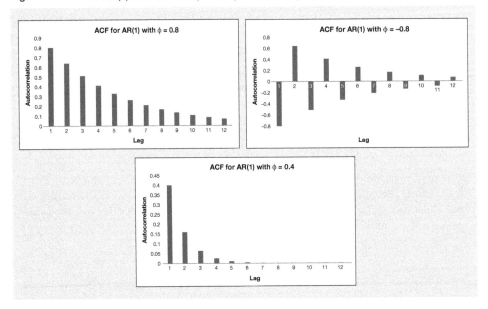

We can now gain more insight into the concept of stationarity. Suppose that $Y_1 = 120$, $\mu = 100$, and $\phi = 0.8$, and for the moment set the error terms equal to zero. Then successive terms in the series are, from equation (6.3) and the expression for μ,

$$Y_2 = 100 \times (1-0.8) + 0.8Y_1 = 20 + 0.8 \times 120 = 116$$

$$Y_3 = 20 + 0.8 \times 116 = 112.8,$$

and so on, so that the next values in the series are 110.24, 108.19, and 106.55. By time 10, we have the value $Y_{10} = 102.68$, and by time 25, $Y_{25} = 100.09$. That is, the series converges towards the mean value; the series is said to be *mean reverting*. By contrast, if we take $\phi = 1.2$, successive values are 120, 124, 128.8, and 134.56. By time 10, we have the value $Y_{10} = 203.20$, and by time 25, $Y_{25} = 1689.94$. The series is *explosive* and clearly not stationary. Negative values of ϕ would give similar results (stationary for $-1 < \phi < 0$ and explosive for $\phi < -1$). We discuss the special case of $\phi = 1$ (or $\phi = -1$) in Section 6.3.

6.2.2 Higher Order Autoregressive Models

The second-order autoregressive scheme is specified by adding a *lag-2* term:

$$Y_t = \delta + \phi_1 Y_{t-1} + \phi_2 Y_{t-2} + \varepsilon_t.$$

When $E(Y_t) = \mu$, a constant from the stationarity assumption, we can take expectations to arrive at

$$\mu = \delta + \phi_1 \mu + \phi_2 \mu$$

or

$$\delta = \mu(1 - \phi_1 - \phi_2).$$

The *ACF* now takes on a greater variety of forms, because there are two parameters to determine its shape rather than one. Some examples are shown in Figure 6.3. Note that Figures 6.3–6.7 are based upon theoretical results. The abundance of possible shapes is evident, and we need to develop further tools if we are going to match the observed patterns to their theoretical counterparts to assist in model selection (see Sections 6.2.5 and 6.2.6).

Figure 6.3 *ACFs* for an AR(2) Scheme with (A) $\phi_1 = 1.1$ and $\phi_2 = -0.5$ and (B) $\phi_1 = 0.3$ and $\phi_2 = 0.5$

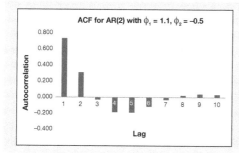
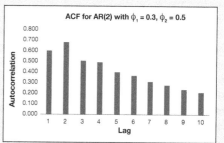

Higher order schemes follow by adding further lags. If we include p lags, we have the set of autoregressive parameters $(\phi_1, \phi_2, \ldots \phi_p)$. The general form of the model is then

$$Y_t = \delta + \phi_1 Y_{t-1} + \phi_2 Y_{t-2} + \cdots + \phi_p Y_{t-p} + \varepsilon_t$$
$$\delta = \mu(1 - \phi_1 - \phi_2 - \cdots - \phi_p). \tag{6.4}$$

The above result for the mean μ comes from taking expectations of the equation for Y_t (see Appendix 6A) and relies on stationarity. The conditions for stationarity become quite complex and we do not explore them here. Suffice it to say that these conditions are always checked in standard statistical software.

We can go as far back in time as we wish, but relatively small values of p usually suffice, unless the data are seasonal, in which case we might want to include seasonal lags [of order 4 (quarterly series) or 12 (monthly series)]. Seasonal models raise additional issues, which we address in Section 6.8.

6.2.3 Pure Moving Average (MA) Models

Pure MA models involve only lagged error terms. The simplest case is the first-order, or MA(1), scheme:

$$Y_t = \mu + \varepsilon_t - \theta\varepsilon_{t-1}. \tag{6.5}$$

No conditions are required to ensure that pure MA models are stationary. For MA(1), we have

$$E(Y_t) = \mu$$

$$V(Y_t) = \sigma^2(1 + \theta^2)$$

$$Corr(Y_t, Y_{t-1}) = -\theta/(1 + \theta^2)$$

$$Corr(Y_t, Y_{t-k}) = 0, k \geq 2.$$

The MA(1) scheme is a short-memory process in that observations two or more periods apart are uncorrelated. Accordingly, it has only a single spike on the *ACF*, as illustrated in Figure 6.4 based on simulated data. Note that $\theta = -0.6$ provides a smaller first-order autocorrelation. This is because of the expression for $Corr(Y_t, Y_{t-1})$, as example 6.3 illustrates.

Figure 6.4 *ACF* for MA(1) Scheme with (A) $\theta = -0.6$ and (B) $\theta = 0.6$

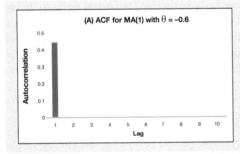
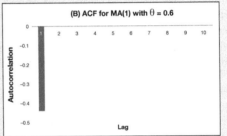

■ Example 6.3: A first-order MA scheme

Suppose that $\varepsilon_1 = 10$, $\mu = 100$ and $\theta = -0.8$. Then, given the values for period 1 and (6.5), the equation for time 2 becomes

$$Y_2 = \mu - \theta\varepsilon_1 + \varepsilon_2 = 100 + 0.8 \times 10 + \varepsilon_2 = 108 + \varepsilon_2.$$

The overall summary statistics are

$$E(Y_t) = 100$$

$$V(Y_t) = 9(1 + 0.64) = 14.76$$

$$Corr(Y_t, Y_{t-1}) = 0.8/(1 + 0.64) = 0.488$$

$$Corr(Y_t, Y_{t-k}) = 0, k \geq 2.$$

The MA(1) scheme has two other surprising properties. First of all, the maximum value of the first-order autocorrelation of MA(1) is only 0.5 when $\theta = -1$. (The minimum, –0.5, occurs at $\theta = 1$.) Intuitively, if observations *two* periods apart are uncorrelated, those values *one* period apart cannot be too closely related. The second property is that if $\theta > 1$, then the lagged error has greater weight than the current error. In turn, this state of affairs implies increasing importance for the distant past. To avoid this intuitively unattractive possibility, we make the restriction[2] that $-1 < \theta < 1$. ∎

The extension to higher order schemes, denoted by MA(q) follows directly:

$$Y_t = \mu + \varepsilon_t - \theta_1 \varepsilon_{t-1} - \cdots - \theta_q \varepsilon_{t-q}. \tag{6.6}$$

As before, μ denotes the mean of the series and the coefficients $(\theta_1, \theta_2, \ldots, \theta_q)$ are the moving average parameters. Non-zero autocorrelations exist for only the first q lags for the MA(q) scheme. As q increases, so does the maximum value of the first-order autocorrelation.

6.2.4 Mixed Autoregressive Moving Average (ARMA) Models

The mixed ARMA models follow by combining the autoregressive and moving average elements of equations (6.4) and (6.6) to produce:

$$Y_t = \delta + \phi_1 Y_{t-1} + \cdots + \phi_p Y_{t-p} + \varepsilon_t - \theta_1 \varepsilon_{t-1} - \cdots - \theta_q \varepsilon_{t-q}. \tag{6.7}$$

Equation (6.7) is referred to as the ARMA(p, q) model; the constant term is given by

$$\delta = \mu(1 - \phi_1 - \phi_2 - \cdots - \phi_p),$$

as with the AR(p) scheme.

∎ Example 6.4: An ARMA (1,1) scheme

Suppose that $p = q = 1$, $Y_1 = 120$, $\varepsilon_1 = 10$, $\mu = 100$, $\phi = 0.5$ and $\theta = -0.8$. Given these values for period 1, equation (6.7) for period 2 becomes

$$Y_2 = 100(1 - 0.5) + 0.5 \times 120 + \varepsilon_2 + 0.8 \times 10 = 118 + \varepsilon_2. ∎$$

6.2.5* Partial Autocorrelations

We have introduced a variety of possible ARMA models; how do we make an appropriate choice from among the whole set? The traditional approach has been to develop the theoretical properties of specific ARMA models and then compare the sample results with these theoretical forms. In particular, we may consider the *Partial Autocorrelation Function* (*PACF*), which highlights the autoregressive components in much the same way as the *ACF* features the MA elements. This approach is described in this section, and is still widely used although as computer speeds have increased and the demand for rapid processing of large numbers of series has grown, more automated methods have taken hold. Our preferred approach is to pre-specify a list of alternatives and try each of them, evaluating model performance using hold-out samples or information criteria, as described in Section 5.3. This is the approach we adopt in Section 6.4. However, for the sake of completeness, we outline the use of the *PACF* in this section and provide plots of both the *ACF* and *PACF* in later parts of this chapter so that the reader may also follow the more traditional path, if so desired.

When the time series seems rather complex and sufficiently important to merit careful exploration, we may seek to build a customized model. One approach would be to seek a model whose theoretical autocorrelation function matches the sample *ACF*. However, this matching process can be tricky, as suggested by the variety of shapes shown in Figures 6.2-6.4, so we now seek additional insights to assist in this task. One feature of these figures

---

2 This condition is known as the property of *invertibility*. All the standard software packages impose conditions for invertibility in their estimation procedures, and we will not comment further on this matter.

is that the *ACF* looks simpler for MA schemes than for AR schemes, so we now develop criteria that make it easier to identify AR structure. It is in this context that the *PACF* comes into its own, and we now describe the concept in detail.

We saw in Figure 6.2 that the theoretical autocorrelations for the AR(1) scheme declined geometrically. It is not easy to look at a sample *ACF* and decide when it matches up with Figure 6.2. One direct way to explore AR structure would be to estimate successively higher order AR schemes AR(1), AR(2), AR(3), ... , deciding to stop when the additional terms do not contribute to the explanatory power of the model. Box and Jenkins made use of this idea in creating the partial autocorrelation function (*PACF*), which we may define as follows:

1. For $k = 1, 2,...$, fit an AR scheme of order k to the data and record the value of the autoregressive coefficient for lag k. Denote this quantity by C_k. That is, we generate a sequence of autoregressive models as given in equation (6.4) and check the last coefficient each time. Table 6.1 illustrates the process for the WFJ Sales data.

2. Plot C_k against k (=1, 2, 3,...). For an AR(p) scheme, only the first p values will be nonzero.

Table 6.1 Estimated Coefficients for AR(*K*) Schemes for WFJ Sales, *K* = 1, 2, 3, and Resulting Values of the Partial Autocorrelations

Lag (*k*)	ϕ_1	ϕ_2	ϕ_3	C_k
1	0.787			0.787
2	0.647	0.187		0.187
3	0.674	0.281	−0.157	−0.157

Data: WFJ_sales.xlsx

The preceding statements about zero values apply to the theoretical values. In practice, sampling variation will mean that the coefficients are not exactly zero, but we can check the assumptions by setting 95 percent limits for each value (approximately $\pm 2/\sqrt{n}$). We should stress that more efficient computational methods exist than the one we have just outlined, but the foregoing definition helps to interpret the *PACF*. Intuitively the *PACF* can be interpreted as the effect of each lag, once the cumulative effect of any preceding lags is removed. The sample *PACF* for WFJ Sales is shown up to lag 16 in Figure 6.5.

Figure 6.5 The *PACF* for WFJ Sales Data

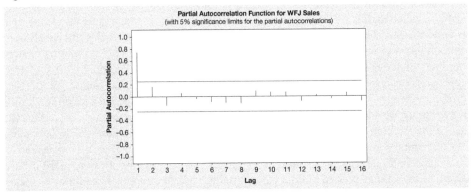

Data: WFJ_sales.xlsx

As with the sample *ACF*, we need some theoretical benchmarks for the *PACF* to guide model selection. The theoretical *PACF*s for some low-order schemes are plotted in Figures 6.6–6.8.

Figure 6.6 *PACF* for AR(1) Scheme with (A) $\phi = 0.8$ and (B) $\phi = -0.8$ and for
MA(1) Scheme with (C) $\theta = -0.6$ and (D) $\theta = 0.6$

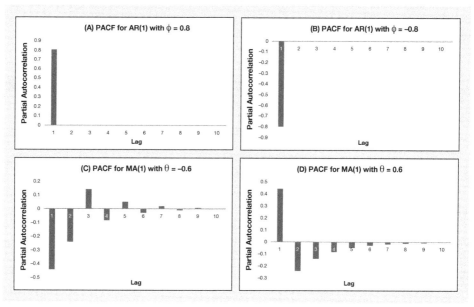

Figure 6.7 *PACF* for AR(2) Scheme with (A) $\phi_1 = 1.1$, $\phi_2 = -0.5$ and (B) $\phi_1 = 1.1$, $\phi_2 = 0.5$

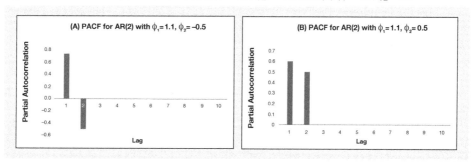

Figure 6.8 *ACF* and *PACF* for an ARMA(1,1) Scheme with $\phi = 0.8$, $\theta = -0.7$

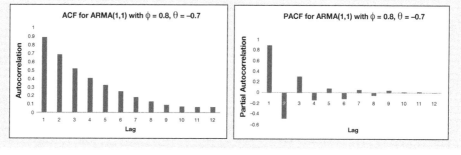

Source: Based upon a generated series of 1000 observations.

6.2.6* Model choice using the *ACF* and *PACF*

Now that we have both the *ACF* and the *PACF*, we may distinguish AR and MA components more readily. Table 6.2 summarizes typical shapes that are expected for different schemes; we use these results to suggest possible models.

Table 6.2 *ACF* and *PACF* Patterns for General AR, MA, and ARMA Schemes

Function	AR(*p*) Scheme	MA(*q*) Scheme	Mixed ARMA Scheme
ACF	Tails off as a damped wave pattern or damped exponential	Finite, *q* spikes	Tails off as a damped wave pattern or damped exponential
PACF	Finite, *p* spikes	Tails off as a damped wave pattern or damped exponential	Tails off as a damped wave pattern or damped exponential

We now examine some series to see how well they might conform to one of the ARMA schemes just described.

Figures 6.1 and 6.5 showed the sample *ACF* and *PACF*, respectively, for the WFJ Sales data; all 62 observations were used in the calculations. A comparison of these plots with Figures 6.2 and 6.6 suggests that an AR(1) model with a positive coefficient would be appropriate, rather than an AR(2) scheme (Figure 6.7) or an ARMA(1,1) scheme (Figure 6.8). Note that there will always be some sampling variation, but we can deal with that by testing whether individual coefficients differ from zero.

The test procedure contrasts the null hypothesis that the (partial) autocorrelation coefficient at a particular lag is zero against the alternative that it is nonzero. The *ACF* and *PACF* plots show the significance limits for tests at the 5 percent level. If the coefficient at a particular lag lies outside the limits, the null hypothesis is rejected for that lag.

Figure 6.5 shows that after lag 1 all the higher order partial autocorrelations lie well inside the significance limits. An examination of Figure 6.1 indicates that, although the autocorrelations lie inside the significance limits after lag 3, the systematic pattern of exponential decay in the *ACF* reinforces the AR(1) identification, as suggested by the description in Table 6.2.

Figure 6.9 shows the sample *ACF* and *PACF* for the quarterly Netflix percentage growth series (*Netflix_2.xlsx*) from 2000 to 2015. The series is fairly volatile, and the plots suggest an AR(1) (check the *PACF* in Figure 6.6) with a hint of a seasonal pattern (lag 4). The spikes in the *ACF* suggest that an MA(1) might be appropriate (check the *ACF* in Figure 6.4) although the slow rate of decay of the autocorrelations is often a signal of an inadequate model. An ARMA(1,1) scheme would be a possibility, given this slow rate of decay.

Figure 6.9 *ACF* and *PACF* for Netflix Percentage Growth

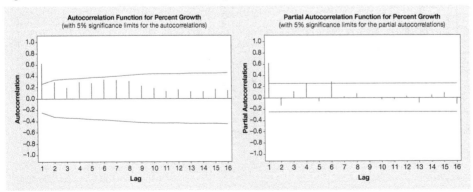

Data: Netflix_2.xlsx

6.3 An Introduction to Nonstationary Series

We have stressed the need for a series to be stationary if the selection procedures just described are to be valid. One obvious violation of stationarity arises when the series has a clear trend; however, this is not the only possibility. Stationarity implies the existence of a constant mean, therefore a series could be nonstationary because it does not revert to a known mean. The simplest example of such behavior is known as the random walk, which we now examine in detail from the ARIMA perspective.

6.3.1 The Random Walk

The random-walk model was introduced in Section 5.1.2; it is so named because successive differences are independent:

$$Y_t = Y_{t-1} + \varepsilon_t \ \text{ or } \ Y_t - Y_{t-1} = \varepsilon_t.$$

That is, ε_t is independent of ε_s for all $s \neq t$. A direct implication of the model is that the next incremental change in the series is unpredictable as it depends only on ε_t. Four examples of a random walk are shown in Figure 6.10, with $n = 50$. Each series has initial value equal to 10, and the error terms are independent and identically distributed normal variables with mean 0 and variance 1. The *ACF* and *PACF* for the first of these series are shown in Figure 6.11. Note the slow decay in the *ACF*. (For readers analyzing the *PACF*, it is very well-behaved; this is sometimes known as the Pollyanna effect, the behavior is "too good to be true".) When we take first differences we are left with only the error term, which is clearly stationary given our usual assumptions about the error process. The *ACF* (and *PACF*) for the first differences also are shown in Figure 6.11. The spike at lag 6 is statistically significant at the ten percent level, but has no real meaning; these things happen!

Figure 6.10 Four Random Walks
(with starting value equal to 10 and normal errors with mean 0 and variance 1)

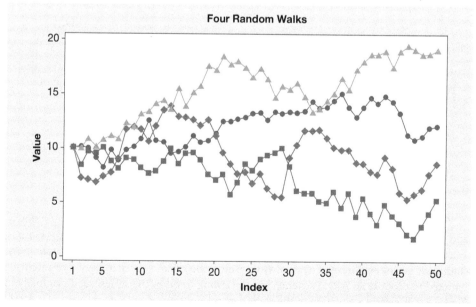

Figure 6.11 *ACF* and *PACF* for a Random Walk with *n* = 50, Before and After Differencing

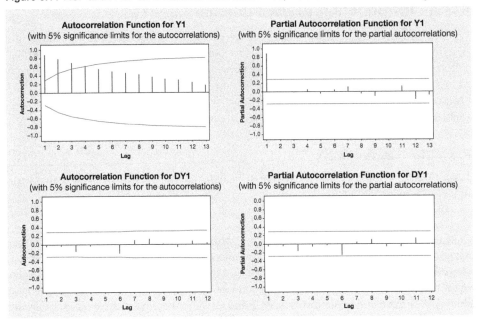

6.3.2 Nonstationary Series

What happens if the series is not stationary? The results for the random walk provide insights into more general series. Suppose we were to examine the original Netflix sales series rather than the growth figures. The resulting sample *ACF* (and *PACF*) are shown in Figure 6.12.

Figure 6.12 *ACF* and *PACF* for Netflix Quarterly Sales

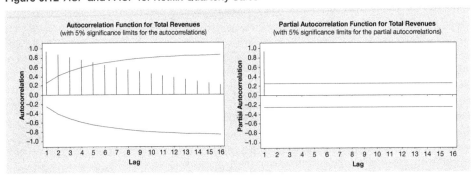

Data: Netflix_2.xlsx

The two plots are similar to those for the random walk: the *ACF* decays very slowly, and the decay is linear rather than geometric. (The first partial autocorrelation is close to 1.0, and the remaining ones are much closer to zero, just what we would expect for a non-stationary series exhibiting a very obvious Pollyanna effect.) At first sight, we might be tempted to propose an AR(1) scheme, but the strong trend in the series, seen originally in Figure 3.9, is clearly a violation of the stationarity condition of a constant mean. An AR(1) scheme proves to produce very poor forecasts.

Why does this happen? Suppose that, instead of using the Netflix series, we calculate the *ACF* and *PACF* for the sequence of numbers 1 to 32. The results are shown in Figure 6.13 and look similar to the plots in Figure 6.12. In short, whenever a series has a strong trend, the resulting plots of the *ACF* and *PACF* will tend to display the characteristics found in Figure 6.12.

Figure 6.13 *ACF* and *PACF* for the First 32 Natural Numbers

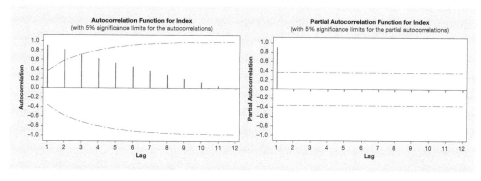

The appropriate action in these circumstances is to consider differencing the series, as discussed in Section 2.6:

DIFFERENCING A TIME SERIES

The (first) difference of the series Y_t is defined as

$$DY_t = Y_t - Y_{t-1}.$$

The second difference of the series Y_t is defined as

$$D^2 Y_t = D(DY_t) = D(Y_t - Y_{t-1})$$
$$= DY_t - DY_{t-1} = (Y_t - Y_{t-1}) - (Y_{t-1} - Y_{t-2})$$
$$= Y_t - 2Y_{t-1} + Y_{t-2}.$$

This step will often remove the trend and restore stationarity in the mean. Such a series is called "Difference stationary". If it does not suffice, a second differencing and/or a suitable transformation, such as a log transform (followed by differencing), or the use of growth rates may achieve that goal. We discuss alternatives further in Appendix 10C. Finally, we note that the original series should always be plotted, and that plot will often serve to determine whether the series needs to be differenced. The *ACF* and *PACF* for the first differences of the Netflix sales series are shown in Figure 6.14. They are similar to the plots in Figure 6.9 and suggest an AR(1) model. However, the time series plot shows much greater variability later in the series, so the assumption of constant variance is not warranted. We return to this issue in Section 6.7.2.

When a series has been differenced, the notation is changed to reflect this additional step. The model is written as ARIMA *(p, d, q)*, with *p* giving the number of autoregressive parameters included in the model, *d* the degree of differencing, and *q* the number of moving average parameters. When a series needs to be differenced *d* times to induce stationarity, we say that the series is *integrated of order d,* written as *I(d).* Thus, a stationary series is *I*(0) and a series like the Netflix sales series is probably *I*(1). Similarly, the random walk (Section 3.6.1) is ARIMA(0,1,0). Before leaving this discussion, we need to recognize that the differenced series may still exhibit both a trend and increasing variability over time, and both these issues must be taken into account. We discuss this issue further in Appendix 10B: Any model selection approach including relying on the *ACF/PACF* procedure must be supplemented to recognize such features but for the moment we will rely on differencing. Fortunately a first difference (or seasonal difference introduced in Section 6.8), possibly in logs, will usually suffice.

Figure 6.14 *ACF*, *PACF*, and Time Series Plot for Netflix Revenues, Differenced Once

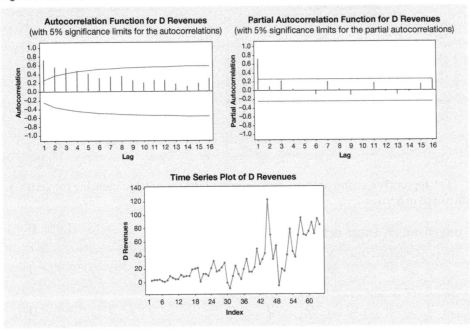

Data: Netflix_2.xlsx

6.4 Model Estimation and Differencing

Following on from the identification of the p, d and q to specify the appropriate ARIMA model for the data, we need to estimate the model's parameters. Simpler methods of estimation for ARIMA models rely upon the method of ordinary least squares, in essentially the same way as the state-space models we considered earlier. Other, more sophisticated (and somewhat statistically more efficient) estimation procedures (e.g., maximum likelihood) are available as well. Those seeking a detailed description of these procedures should consult Box *et al.* (2016, Chapter 7) or any other theoretical text. Any standard time series software will provide estimation procedures based upon either least squares or maximum likelihood or both, and we will not dwell on the theoretical details except to note that different assumptions about starting conditions may lead to somewhat different estimates, particularly in shorter series. Here we use Minitab primarily for our calculations but also from time to time include results from R (the commands can be found in the on-line appendix). Don't be too surprised if different software gives different parameter estimates and even different forecasts!

We now examine the series discussed in the previous section.

■ Example 6.5: Fitted model for Netflix percentage growth

Our discussion of this series suggested an AR(1) model or possibly an MA(1) model. We fit both and compare the results in Table 6.3.

The output suggests a simple comparison: Which model has the smaller *RMSE?* Clearly, AR(1) does better, reinforcing our initial assessment that it was the preferred scheme. Further questions remain to be answered: Is it worth including additional terms? Does the current model show any unusual features that need further consideration? We return to these questions in the next section. ■

Table 6.3 Fitted Models for Netflix Percentage Growth Series Using Minitab and R
(Note that R refers to the mean as the constant)

AR(1) Model

Type	Coefficient	Standard Errors	T-test	P-values
AR1	0.7150	0.0902	7.92	0.000
Constant	3.1261	0.8925	3.50	0.001
Mean	10.968	3.131		
Mean Square error = 50.09 with DF = 61, [RMSE = 7.08]				
R Output				
AR1	0.7017	0.0987	7.1075	0.000
Constant	10.9280	2.9409	3.7159	0.000
[RMSE = 7.22]				

NB. In R, the Constant term denotes the mean. The parameter $\delta = (1 - \phi)\,\mu = (1 - 0.7017) \times 10.9280 = 3.2598$; see equation (6.4).

MA(1) Model

Type	Coefficient	Standard Errors	T-test	P-values
MA1	−0.5237	0.1084	−4.83	0.000
Constant	10.215	1.511	6.76	0.000
Mean	10.215	1.511		
Mean Square error = 62.19 with DF = 61, [RMSE = 7.89]				
R Output				
MA1	0.5205	0.0743	7.0101	0.000
Constant	10.2220	1.4887	6.8663	0.000
[RMSE = 7.88]				

Note: The model specification in R has positive (rather than negative) signs for the MA terms in the general model given in equation (6.7). Hence the opposite sign in the output.

Data: Netflix_2.xlsx

■ Example 6.6: Fitted model for WFJ sales

Our earlier analysis using Figures 6.1 and 6.5 suggested an AR(1) model. However, further examination of Figure 6.5 suggests that the series might be nonstationary, in which case differencing would be needed. After differencing, we have the *ACF* and *PACF* shown in Figure 6.15.

The original series seemed to be AR(1), and the differenced series might reasonably be represented by either an AR(1) or an MA(1), so we have three candidate models. The summary results for each model are given in Table 6.4.

Observe that all three models have 60 DF, based on $n = 62$. The AR(1) model has three parameters: constant, AR coefficient, and variance. However, only the first two parameters involve the loss of a degree of freedom. The models for the differenced series lose one observation through differencing but have only one parameter (other than the variance), so they also have DF = 60. Typically, as here, the models for the differenced series do not include a constant term, because that would imply a fixed trend, something that is not apparent in the WFJ Sales series. Nevertheless, a constant term is sometimes useful, as we shall see in Examples 6.7 and 6.8. ∎

Figure 6.15 *ACF* and *PACF* for WFJ Sales Data, Differenced Once

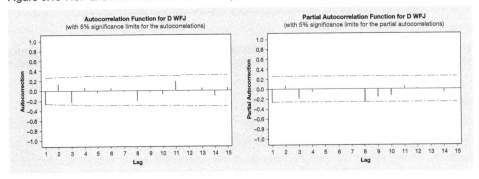

Data: WFJ_sales.xlsx

Table 6.4 Different Models for WFJ Sales Data Using Minitab

AR(1)

Type	Coefficient	Standard Errors	T-test	P-values
AR1	0.7867	0.0807	9.75	0.000
Constant	6.8382	0.4460	15.33	0.000
Mean	32.063	2.091		
Mean Square error = 12.304 with DF = 60, [RMSE = 3.51]				

ARIMA(1,1,0)

Type	Coefficient	Standard Errors	T-test	P-values
AR1	−0.2766	0.1267	−2.18	0.033
Mean Square error = 12.933 with DF = 60, [RMSE = 3.60]				

ARIMA(0,1,1)

Type	Coefficient	Standard Errors	T-test	P-values
MA1	0.2686	0.1269	2.12	0.038
Mean Square error = 13.017 with DF = 60, [RMSE = 3.61]				

Data: WFJ_sales.xlsx

On the basis of the *RMSE,* the AR(1) scheme appears to be slightly better than the other two, but we should also take into account the underlying assumptions. The AR(1) scheme implies stationarity and a fixed mean, whereas the other two are based upon nonstationary schemes. As we will discuss in Section 6.4.3 *RMSE* has some limitations and using an information criterion such as *AIC* is preferable.

6.4.1 Should We Assume Stationarity?

Are we willing to assume stationarity? We suggest that, for most business series, the volatile nature of the modern economy is such that nonstationary models are usually to be preferred. The rationale for this claim is that if a series is subject to a shift of some kind, a nonstationary scheme adapts to the changing circumstances, whereas a stationary scheme wistfully seeks to return to its original level. This is not a sterile debate based upon statistical niceties, but one that has real policy implications. For example, there is considerable debate as to whether stock prices follow a random walk with drift or are mean reverting. (The series fluctuates about a long-term trend-adjusted mean.) Forecasts made one or two periods ahead may differ little between stationary and nonstationary models, but longer term trends and associated prediction intervals become very different.

6.4.2 Examples of Nonstationary Series

We now examine the Netflix sales series in greater detail, followed by an analysis of US Retail Sales.

■ Example 6.7: Fitted model for Netflix data

We have already seen that the percentage changes in Netflix sales follow an AR(1) scheme with a constant term to allow for the steady growth. Thus, we could either work with the percentage change series as in Section 3.5.2, or consider a logarithmic transform for the original series. The best-fitting model for the Netflix sales is ARIMA(1,1,0)+C, as shown in Table 6.5, where "+C" refers to the inclusion of a constant term. A close competitor is the ARIMA(0,1,1)+C scheme, which corresponds to the Theta method described in Section 3.6.2, an example of the observation that many ARIMA models have state space (exponential smoothing) equivalents. Finally, note that failure to recognize the need to difference would carry a huge penalty in this case. ■

Table 6.5 MSE and RMSE for Different ARIMA Models for the Log Transformed Netflix Sales Series

(A) Results using Minitab

Model	MSE × 100	RMSE × 10	DF
AR(1), AR(2)	Cannot be fitted; violates stationarity assumption		
MA(1)	62.00	7.87	62
MA(2)	17.13	4.14	61
ARIMA(0,1,1)+C	0.447	0.67	61
ARIMA(1,1,0)+C	0.365	0.60	61
ARIMA(1,1,1)+C	0.370	0.61	60

(B) Results using R

Model	MSE × 100	RMSE × 10
MA(1)	63.972	7.998
MA(2)	18.939	4.352
ARIMA(0,1,1)+C	0.454	0.674
ARIMA(1,1,0)+C	0.386	0.621
ARIMA(1,1,1)+C	0.388	0.623

Data: Netflix_2.xlsx

■ **Example 6.8: Fitted model for U.S. retail sales** *(US_retail_sales_2_SA.xlsx)*

We now consider a longer series, that for monthly retail sales in the United States (deseasonalized) for the period from January 2001 to December 2015. As seen in Figure 1.3 (reproduced here), the series has a very strong upward trend, so the *ACF* and *PACF* conform to the general shapes shown in Figure 6.13. After taking first differences, we arrive at the *ACF* and *PACF* shown in Figure 6.16.

Figure 1.3 Seasonally Adjusted Series for U.S. Monthly Retailers Sales

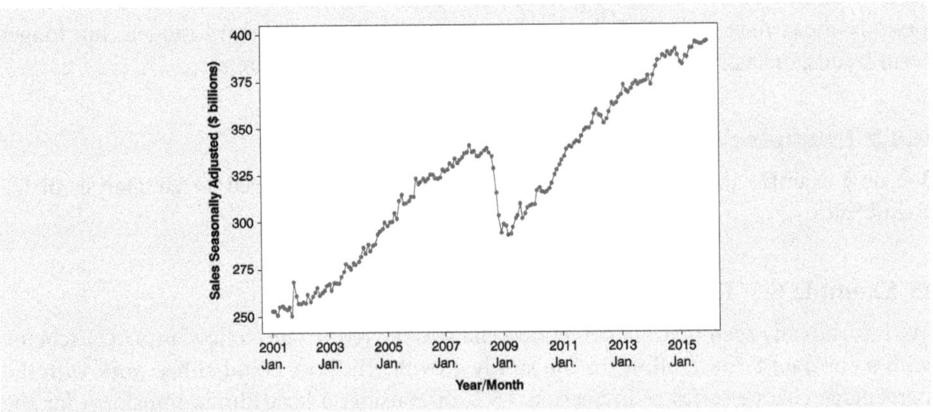

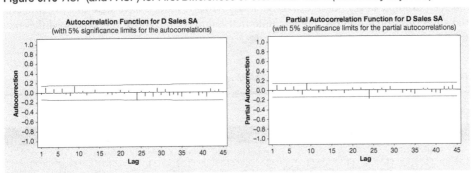

Data: US_retail_sales_2_SA.xlsx

Figure 6.16 *ACF* (and *PACF*) for First Differences of U.S. Retail Sales *(seasonally adjusted)*

Data: US_retail_sales_2_SA.xlsx

The models suggested for the differenced series by the *ACF* (supported by the *PACF*) are AR(1) and MA(1). We may or may not wish to include a constant term; these plots provide no guidance in that regard, whereas these models could be considered as natural candidates to be on the list of fitted models from which we make a selection. Before proceeding, we cannot ignore the impact of the "Great Recession" dated officially by the NBER as running from December 2007 to June 2009. To examine its effect, we fitted the models using both the series to June 2008 and the complete series up to December 2015. Following these initial choices, both models were fitted, with and without a constant term. The summary results are given in Table 6.6. In general, the need for a constant in the model may be determined with the use of the diagnostics to be developed in Section 6.5, although the results clearly indicate that the inclusion of a constant is desirable here. The results for the pre-recession data indicate that the ARIMA(0,1,1)+C model is to be preferred and indicate no advantage to adding extra terms. The ARIMA(2,2,0) model is clearly inferior and is discussed further in Section 6.5.2.

The results for the entire period are disconcerting at first sight. The ARIMA(0,1,1) model again appears to be adequate, but a check on the coefficients shows the MA term to be not significant. That is, a random walk plus drift is an adequate model based upon this analysis. The reason is not hard to find: the recession had a huge impact on the series and such effects typically lead to models that adapt rapidly to the latest information. ∎

Table 6.6 Summary Results for ARIMA Models for U.S. Retail Sales

ARIMA Model	MSE [to 06/08]	MSE [to 12/15]
(1,1,0)	12.02	13.27
(1,1,0)+C	10.34	12.69
(0,1,1)	12.22	13.27
(0,1,1)+C	9.67	12.69
(2,1,0)+C	10.16	12.60
(0,1,2)+C	9.78	12.61
(1,1,1)+C	9.78	12.65
(2,2,0)	13.47	16.30

Data: US_retail_sales_2_SA.xlsx

Final Estimates of Parameters

Period : 01/01–06/08

Type	Coefficient	Standard Errors	T-test	P-values
MA(1)	0.5648	0.0886	6.38	0.000
Constant	0.9803	0.1441	6.80	0.000

Period : 01/01–12/15

Type	Coefficient	Standard Errors	T-test	P-values
MA(1)	0.0307	0.0751	0.41	0.684
Constant	0.8003	0.2581	3.10	0.002

These results lead to three questions:

- Is it reasonable to use *MSE* or, equivalently, *RMSE* as a basis for comparison when some models contain more parameters than others?
- Are we confident that the model chosen is the best available? We need to examine diagnostics, just as we did for the state-space models in Chapter 5.
- What should be done about major dislocations to a series, such as the Great Recession?

As we observed in Section 5.4, for the state-space models, there are two ways to answer the first question. One is to use a hold-out sample in which, at each step, the next observation is included (and, on occasion, the model is re-estimated) before generating a new set of forecasts. The second possibility is to use information criteria, as introduced in Section 5.4.2. Because the two approaches use different sets of information, the conclusions may vary and both can provide useful insights.

6.4.3 Model Choice Using Information Criteria

The Akaike information criterion was defined in Section 5.4.2, as

$$AIC = \ln(MSE) + 2p/n, \tag{6.8}$$

whereas the Bayesian information criterion was given by

$$BIC = \ln(MSE) + p\ln(n)/n \tag{6.9}$$

The bias-corrected measure, $AICc$ produces results that are almost identical to those of AIC, so we have not included them here. The results for the eight models considered in Example 6.8 are summarized in Table 6.7 for the shorter series (01/01–06/08). On the basis of Figure 6.16 (and the time series plot of first differences, not shown) we conclude that differencing once is appropriate. There is no evidence to suggest that a second differencing is needed: A check of the diagnostic plots shows a strong negative first autocorrelation, which often signals over-differencing. The results for the entire series are uninteresting because everything points to the random walk plus drift model. In general, the number of parameters (NP) involved is defined as follows for ARIMA models:

> The number of parameters (NP) is
>
> NP = number of AR parameters + number of MA parameters + 1 (for the variance) + 1 (if a constant is included).

Table 6.7 Values of Information Criteria for ARIMA Models for U.S. Retail Sales

ARIMA Model	Sample Size	No. of Parameters	MSE	AIC	BIC
(1,1,0)	89	2	12.02	2.53	2.59
(1,1,0)+C	89	3	10.34	2.40	2.49
(0,1,1)	89	2	12.22	2.55	2.60
(0,1,1)+C	89	3	9.67	2.34	2.42
(2,1,0)+C	89	4	10.16	2.41	2.52
(0,1,2)+C	89	4	9.78	2.37	2.48
(1,1,1)+C	89	4	9.78	2.37	2.48

Data: US retail sales_2_SA.xlsx; Jan01–Jun08

The sample size should take account of differencing, so that although the original series contains 90 observations, we use $n = 89$ in the calculations of AIC and BIC after differencing once. Different programs vary in their exact definitions of the criteria, but the differences are typically minor in terms of how the programs rank competing models. Note that increasing the lag order also alters the sample size. Note that increasing the lag order also alters the sample size. The versions used here have the advantage that both criteria approach a stable value as the number of observations increases.

The results in Table 6.7 confirm the value of including the constant. Both criteria point to the value of the ARIMA(0,1,1)+C model, although the ARIMA(1,1,1)+C and ARIMA(0,1,2)+C also perform well. This table illustrates how the information criteria may be used to explore different models.

What should we conclude from this analysis? We would do well to recall the comment made by George Box included at the beginning of this chapter. The ARIMA system produces a rich array of possible models, and it is quite common to find that two or more such models appear to perform equally well. In fact, using the conventional route of examining the *ACF* and *PACF* is often very confusing: information criteria offer a more straightforward route for model choice. Which version *should* we choose? From the perspective of point forecasts, it probably does not matter much, provided that we have incorporated an adequate amount of differencing and a constant where needed. The situation is more complex when we turn to interval forecasts, as we shall see in Section 6.7.1. Thus, the first issue to resolve is the appropriate amount of differencing and we now examine that question.

6.4.4 How Much Differencing?

We initially decided on the degree of differencing in a heuristic fashion, but, as illustrated by Table 6.7, the information criteria also provide useful guidance in this respect.[3] Overall, the following checks are worthwhile:

1. *Plot the series.* If a pronounced trend exists, differencing is probably required.

2. *Examine the ACF (and PACF).* Slow decay in the *ACF* and a Pollyanna effect in the *PACF* are telltale signs that differencing is required, although this requirement will often be obvious without any analysis.

3. *Compare values of the MSE.* As we saw in Example 6.7 with the Netflix data, an inadequate level of differencing will usually lead to a greatly inflated value of the MSE and the information criteria. Any MSE comparisons should be made on the original data.

4. *Use a hold-out sample to compare forecasting performance.* As we have indicated throughout the book, this procedure is the ultimate test, provided that sufficient data exist.

6.4.5 Formal Tests for Differencing

A more formal approach to the decision on the degree of differencing is provided by hypothesis testing. The classical tests in this regard are known as the Dickey-Fuller tests, although several others have also been developed. For example, standard practice in modeling ARIMA models with R is to first test for the order of level and seasonal differences and once these are specified to use *AIC* or *BIC* to specify the AR and MA orders. A full description is provided by Box *et al.* (2016, pp.356-61) and Diebold (2007, pp. 297-302), among others. These tests are complicated to apply, and we are not convinced that they provide much additional value. The problem arises because the tests are not powerful at discriminating between the alternatives (e.g., $d = 0$ and $d = 1$). But for econometricians, this is a hot topic, so for completeness we have included further details in Appendix 10C to illustrate the procedure.

We must also avoid over-differencing, as this may lead to unstable estimates and inferior forecasting performance. We examine this issue in the context of diagnostic testing in Section 6.5.2.

---

3 Some care is needed when we are using information criteria to decide on the order of differencing; see Hyndman, Koehler, Ord, and Snyder (2008, Chapter 12) for details.

6.5 Model Diagnostics

One approach to improving our initial model is to use diagnostic methods based upon the residuals. (The residual plots we use here are the same as those we shall use for regression analysis in Chapter 8.) We plot four figures that directly involve the residuals, along with the *ACF* (and *PACF*) of the residuals. The plots may be used to determine the key features of the residuals, as summarized in Table 6.8.

We first consider the diagnostics for the ARIMA(0,1,1) model for U.S. retail sales, initially fitted without a constant. The plots are given in Figures 6.17 and 6.18.

Table 6.8 Interpretation of Diagnostics for Residuals from ARIMA Models

Diagnostic Plots	Issues to be Addressed	Indication of Problems	Remedial Action to Be Taken
Normal probability plot (NPP) and histogram (H)	1. The residuals may not be normally distributed.	1. The residuals do not follow a straight line (NPP), or the histogram (H) is not bell shaped.	1. Consider a transformation.
	2. Are there any outliers?	2. Individual points are far removed from the overall plot (NPP) or other observations (H).	2. Adjust outliers.
Residuals versus fitted values	1. Is there evidence of nonlinearity?	1. The plot shows curvature.	1. Consider a transformation.
	2. Are there any outliers?	2. Individual points are far removed from the overall plot.	2. Adjust outliers.
	3. Does the series show increasing or decreasing variance with the size of the observations (heteroscedasticity)?	3. The plot forms an increasing or decreasing funnel shape.	3. Consider a transformation.
	4. *(Only when the model does not contain a constant term)* Is the model consistent with a zero mean for the errors?	4. The residutals plot shows evidence of a nonzero mean.	4. Add a constant term to the model.
Residuals versus observation order	1. Is there any evidence of residual autocorrelation?	1. The plot shows long runs of residuals with the same sign (positive autocorrelation) or a zigzag pattern (negative autocorrelation).	1. Consider adding terms to the model.
	2. Are there any outliers?	2. Individual points are far removed from the overall plot.	2. Adjust outliers.
	3. Does the series show increasing or decreasing variance over time (changes in volatility)?	3. The plot forms an increasing or decreasing funnel shape.	3. Use a transformation to stabilize the variance.
Autocorrelation function (*ACF*)	1. Are additional differences required?	1. The *ACF* shows a slow linear decay.	1. Try further differencing.
	2. Should more moving average terms be added?	2. The *ACF* shows significant spikes.	2. Include further MA terms.
	3. Is there too much differencing?	3. The lag 1 autocorrelation is large and negative.	3. Reduce the amount of differencing.
Partial autocorrelation function (*PACF*)*	1. Are additional differences required?	1. A "Pollyanna" effect exists.	1. Try further differencing.
	2. Should more AR terms be added?	2. The *PACF* shows significant spikes.	2. Include further AR terms.

*The *PACF* will typically add little to the other diagnostics.

The plot of the *ACF* in Figure 6.18 indicate that the addition of further AR or MA terms is not warranted since there is little pattern to be seen. (This is confirmed by the *PACF* plot which we omit.) Figure 6.17 indicates a clear outlier in the differenced series (October sales minus September sales in 2001), an issue to which we return in Section 6.6. An outlier will often be signaled in the normal probability plot (NPP), as well as in the plots of the residuals. The remaining feature is somewhat unusual: The model under consideration does not include a constant term, and a careful viewing of the two plots of residuals reveals that most of the points lie above the horizontal axis, indicating the need for a constant in the model, as we saw from the results in Table 6.7.

When we include the constant and rerun the model, we obtain the residual plots shown in Figure 6.19. The residuals are now centered about a zero mean, but the other diagnostics are essentially the same as before. In particular, the NPP and the residual plots still signal the large outlier. As we saw in Table 6.7, adding the constant produces a sizeable reduction in the MSE.

Figure 6.17 Residual Plots for ARIMA(0,1,1) Model for U.S. Retail Sales

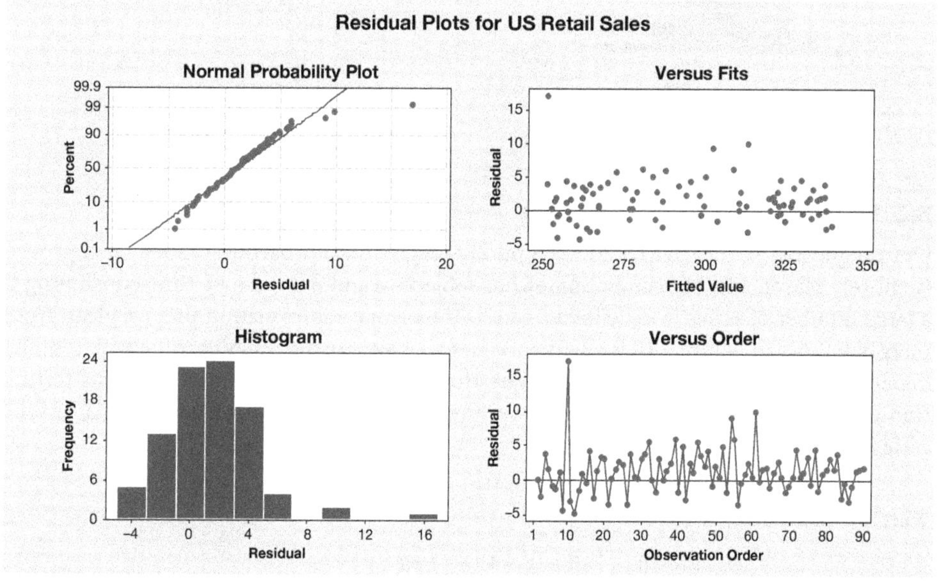

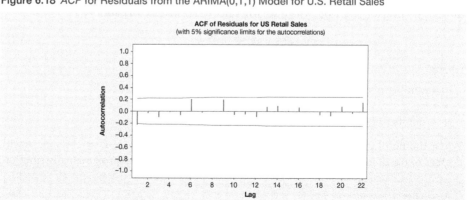

Data: US retail sales_2_SA.xlsx

Figure 6.18 *ACF* for Residuals from the ARIMA(0,1,1) Model for U.S. Retail Sales

Data: US retail sales_2_SA.xlsx

Figure 6.19 Residual Plots for ARIMA(0,1,1)+C Model for U.S. Retail Sales

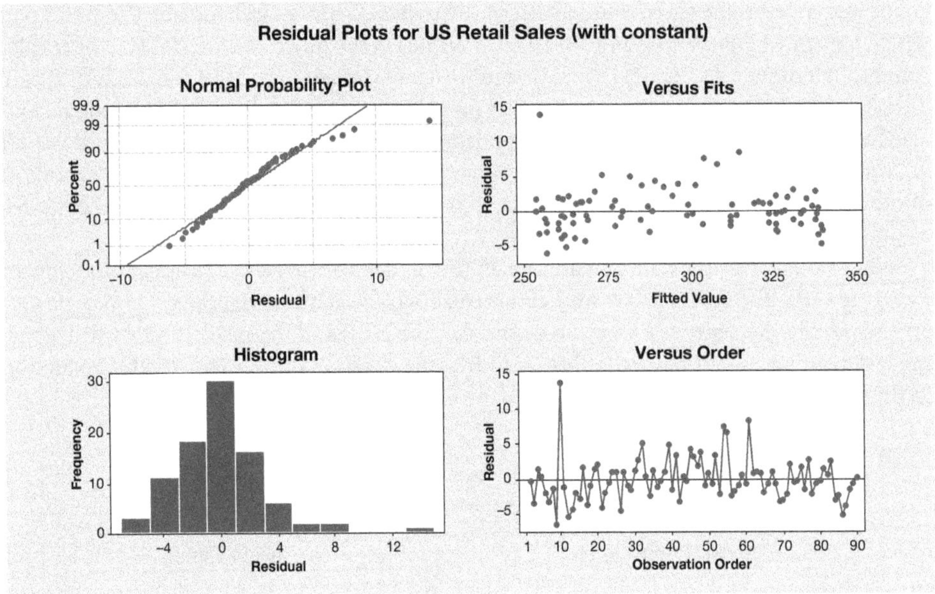

Data: US retail sales_2_SA.xlsx

6.5.1 The Ljung-Box-Pierce Test

Our diagnostics so far have been based purely on graphical procedures. Such an approach is entirely reasonable, but can be somewhat subjective and may also be time consuming if a large number of series is to be investigated. The primary information that we glean from plots like those in Figure 6.18 is whether or not we have missed a significant element of the dependence structure of the series. This question may be formulated in a hypothesis-testing framework as a comparison of the null hypothesis for the set of autocorrelations $\{\rho_k\}$ of the residuals,

$$H_0: \rho_1 = \rho_2 = \cdots = \rho_K = 0,$$

with the alternative,

$$H_A: \text{not all } \rho_k = 0, \quad k = 1, 2, ..., K$$

A test for this purpose was developed by Box and Pierce and refined by Ljung and Box; see Box *et al.,* (2016, pp. 289–90) for details. The procedure is based upon residual autocorrelations $\{r_k\}$, using the criterion, which we will refer to as the LBP statistic,[4]

$$Q = n(n + 2) \sum_{k=1}^{K} \frac{r_k^2}{n - k}, \tag{6.10}$$

where

n = number of observations in the series after any differencing
k = lag
K = number of time lags to be used in the test.

When the null hypothesis is true, the large-sample distribution of Q is chi-square with degrees of freedom $(K - p - q)$. The *P*-values are based upon this approximate distribution.

---

4 As all three authors were involved in the development of the statistic, we refer to it as the Ljung-Box-Pierce statistic; you will find a variety of names in other books and in computer programs.

■ Example 6.9: An application of the Ljung-Box-Pierce statistic to the U.S. retail sales model

It is common practice to use several values of K when testing these hypotheses: the choice will depend on the length of the time series and seasonality. Some computer programs allow for a choice of K but many do not. For example, for the ARIMA(0,1,1)+C model, Minitab considers blocks of 12 and provides the following output:

Modified Box-Pierce (Ljung-Box) Chi-Square Statistic				
Lag	12	24	36	48
Chi-Square	11.1	24.2	42.3	67.8
DF	10	22	34	46
P-Value	0.352	0.338	0.154	0.020

Using the conventional testing procedure: Reject H_0 if P-value < significance level (α), we would not reject the null hypothesis at the 5 percent level for up to 36 lags, but would reject at lag 48 (i.e., four years ahead). These results suggest that the model would be satisfactory for short to medium term forecasting but it is somewhat inadequate in the longer term, which is reasonable given the potential for structural change in the U.S. economy. ■

6.5.2 Diagnostics, Overfitting, and Model Simplification

After the preliminary identification of a suitable ARIMA model, diagnostics can point the way to a revised model. The simplest approach is to add in additional terms, say an AR or an MA term to the ARIMA(0,1,1)+C model for US retail sales where there remains some evidence of residual first order autocorrelation. With either an ARIMA (1,1,1)+C or an ARIMA(0,1,2)+C model it is easy to compare information criteria for the two models as well as the diagnostics. The results in Table 6.7 suggest that either of these steps would result in overfitting, as the AIC or BIC values become worse. If a model has an insignificant parameter it is usual to drop that parameter and re-estimate the model, aiming at the simplest (most parsimonious) model compatible with the data. Conversely, had we started with one of the more complex models, some parameter estimates would typically not be significant, pointing the way to the simpler model.

Finally, we can diagnose the effect of additional differencing. The results for the ARIMA(0,2,2) model show that the extra difference makes matters worse. The $MSE = 11.51$ and the LBP statistics also suffer even though the parameter estimates are highly significant. The results for ARIMA(2,2,0) are even worse.

Final Estimates of Parameters and LBP Statistics for ARIMA(0,2,2) Model

Type	Coefficient	Standard Errors	T-test	P-values
MA(1)	1.1498	0.0034	340.00	0.000
MA(2)	−0.1629	0.0467	−3.48	0.001

Modified Box-Pierce (Ljung-Box) Chi-Square Statistic				
Lag	12	24	36	48
Chi-Square	20.0	30.9	45.4	65.2
DF	10	22	34	46
P-Value	0.029	0.099	0.092	0.032

6.5.3* The Lag Operator

The highly significant MA estimates just shown do not appear to raise any issues. However, we can identify the issue of over-differencing by making use of a new notation, known as the *lag (or backshift) operator*, denoted by B. We may write with a similar operation for the error term. Thus, an ARIMA(0,1,1) scheme may be represented as:

$$Y_t - Y_{t-1} = (1-B)Y_t = \varepsilon_t - \theta_1\varepsilon_{t-1} = (1-\theta_1 B)\varepsilon_t.$$

Note that the backshift operator is related to the difference operator introduced in section 6.3.1 by the relationship: $D = (1-B)$: i.e. $DY_t = Y_t - Y_{t-1} = (1-B)Y_t$.

Following this approach, the ARIMA(0,2,2) scheme may be represented as:

$$Y_t - 2Y_{t-1} + Y_{t-2} = (1-B)^2 Y_t = \varepsilon_t - \theta_1\varepsilon_{t-1} - \theta_2\varepsilon_{t-2} = (1-\theta_1 B - \theta_2 B^2)\varepsilon_t.$$

We now focus attention on the quadratic at the right hand end of this equation, which we rewrite as:

$$(1 - \theta_1 B - \theta_2 B^2)\varepsilon_t = (1 - w_1 B)(1 - w_2 B).$$

Then, we may solve using the estimated values for ARIMA(0,2,2). In the present case we obtain

$$(1 - 1.1498B + 0.1629B^2)\varepsilon_t = (1 - 0.9843B)(1 - 0.1655B).$$

It is evident that one of the roots is very close to 1.0, so that we are close to having a term on either side of the model equation. If we drop that term from either side, we are back at an ARIMA(0,1,1) scheme and might reasonably suppose that little has been lost in terms of model performance.

Not all programs provide numerical values for the roots; our purpose in this section was to show how over-differencing could arise. We should always keep in mind possible over-differencing and check simpler models via hold-out samples, information criteria and the LBP statistics.

6.6 Outliers Again

The plots in Figure 6.17 reveal a large outlier. What should be done about this extreme value with respect to generating forecasts? The first point to observe is that our concern is to generate forecasts based upon what we believe to be an appropriate model or description of future events. If occasional extreme events are likely to be repeated (such as large sales of beer in the week before the Super Bowl) they can be modeled with techniques we describe in Section 9.7. However, when the events are unique, we may need to adjust the observations involved. A detailed discussion is beyond our scope, and the interested reader may consult Tsay (2010, pp. 558-565) and Koehler, Snyder, Ord, and Beaumont (2012). For the present, we resort to the simple fix of fitting the initial model and then replacing the outlier by its estimated value.

■ Example 6.10: ARIMA(0,1,1)+C model for U.S. retail sales after adjusting for an outlier

After adjusting for the outlier (October 2001, following the September terrorist attack), and keeping the same specification we may summarize the revised model as follows:

Type	Coefficient	Standard Errors	T-test	P-values
MA(1)	0.4787	0.0941	5.09	0.000
Constant	0.9761	0.1480	6.59	0.000
MSE = 7.14, DF = 87, RMSE = 2.67				

Modified Box-Pierce (Ljung-Box) Chi-Square Statistic				
Lag	12	24	36	48
Chi-Square	14.5	32.7	51.2	73.2
DF	10	22	34	46
P-Value	0.151	0.067	0.029	0.007

The parameter estimates are quite similar to those for the original series and the *MSE* is reduced from 9.67 (Table 6.7), as we would expect after removing the outlier. The LBP statistics are not so good, showing rejection at both 36 and 48 lags.

The residual plots, shown in Figure 6.20, are similar to those obtained before, as seen in Figure 6.18, apart from the removal of the outliers. The *ACF* (and *PACF*) diagnostics are little changed, so we omit them. Additional outliers might be considered for adjustment, but we do not pursue the question further. ■

Figure 6.20 Residual Plots for U.S. Retail Sales, After Adjusting for the Outlier

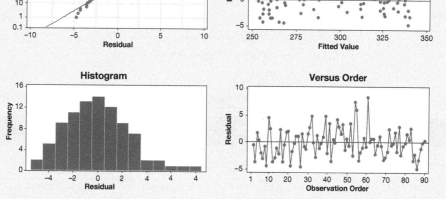

Data: US retail sales_2_SA.xlsx

We have not considered whether transformations would provide additional modeling benefits; this endeavor is left to the reader as Exercises 6.6 and 6.7.

6.6.1 Dealing with the "Great Recession"

Any analysis of macroeconomic data has to deal with the impact of the recession that ran from December 2007 to June 2009 (according to the official NBER estimates). Figure 1.3 (reproduced in Section 6.4.1) showed the dramatic nature of the economic downturn. An effective solution lies beyond the scope of this chapter; we return to the question in Chapter 9, where we make use of indicator variables to deal with the outliers.

6.7 Forecasting with ARIMA Models

Once an appropriate model has been identified, we can proceed to create forecasts. Referring back to the general form in equation (6.7) in Section 6.2.4, we observe that it is necessary to provide input values for both error terms and past values of the series. The general process is as follows:

Y_t values: Use observations already recorded where available; for values not yet recorded, insert the latest available forecast.

ε_t values: Use recorded one-step-ahead residuals where available; set future errors in the equation equal to zero (the best available forecast for future errors).

■ **Example 6.11: Forecasting for WFJ sales using AR(1) and ARIMA(0,1,1)**

From Table 6.4, the AR(1) model is

$$Y_{t+1} = 6.838 + 0.787Y_t + \varepsilon_{t+1}.$$

Applying the general process just given, we find that the one-step-ahead forecast for period 63, given period 62 as the forecast origin, is

$$F_{63} = F_{63}(1) = 6.8382 + 0.7867Y_{62}$$
$$= 6.8382 + 0.7867 \times 34.1282$$
$$= 33.69.$$

Likewise, the two-step-ahead forecast is

$$F_{64}(2) = 6.8382 + 0.7867F_{63}$$
$$= 6.8382 + 0.7867 \times 33.6878$$
$$= 33.34.$$

The forecasts for the next four weeks, with period 62 as the forecast origin, are as follows:

Period	Forecast	Lower Limit 95% PI	Upper Limit 95% PI
63	33.69	26.81	40.56
64	33.34	24.59	42.09
65	33.07	23.34	42.80
66	32.85	22.56	43.14

The lower and upper limits in the table define the 95 percent prediction intervals for the forecasts. We discuss prediction intervals in Section 6.7.1.

A similar exercise may be carried out for the ARIMA(0,1,1) model:

$$Y_{t+1} = Y_t - 0.2686\varepsilon_t + \varepsilon_{t+1}$$

$$F_{63} = Y_{62} - 0.2686e_{62}$$

$$= 34.182 - 0.2686 \times 5.7152$$

$$= 32.59.$$

The two-step-ahead forecast and all later forecasts are

$$F_{62+h}(h) = 32.59.$$

This result holds because the best forecasts for future error terms are zero. The complete summary is as follows:

Period	Forecast	Lower Limit 95% PI	Upper Limit 95% PI
63	32.59	25.52	39.67
64	32.59	23.83	41.36
65	32.59	22.42	42.77
66	32.59	21.18	44.01

In Section 6.8, we show that the ARIMA(0,1,1) model corresponds to the local-level state-space scheme, which underpins simple exponential smoothing — hence, the constant forecasts multiple steps ahead.

The two sets of point forecasts are not materially different in this case. Indeed, in the short term AR(1) and ARIMA(0,1,1) models often produce similar short-term forecasts if the estimated AR parameter is close to 1.0. In the longer term, of course, AR(1) is mean reverting (to the mean of 32.06) whereas the ARIMA(0,1,1) scheme is not. ∎

6.7.1 Prediction Intervals

The prediction intervals are evaluated by means of the same general approach that we described in Section 5.2. The intervals require calculation of the variances for forecasts one or more steps ahead. We illustrate with the AR(1) and ARIMA(0,1,1) schemes. The principles are the same for other models, although the details become more involved. We start with the AR(1) model

$$Y_{t+1} = \delta + \phi Y_t + \varepsilon_{t+1}.$$

For the time period $(t + 2)$, we can substitute the expression for Y_{t+1} to obtain

$$Y_{t+2} = \delta + \phi Y_{t+1} + \varepsilon_{t+2}$$

$$= \delta + \phi(\phi Y_t + \varepsilon_{t+1}) + \varepsilon_{t+2}$$

$$= \varepsilon_{t+2} + \phi\varepsilon_{t+1} + \text{(constant terms)}.$$

The process can be repeated successively for longer lead times. This step is achieved by substituting the model back into itself so that we need only deal with independent error terms. Just the portion of the equation involving the error terms contributes to future uncertainty, so the error component for the one-step-ahead forecast is just ε_{t+1}. Because the errors are independent with zero means and constant variance σ^2, it follows that the one-step-ahead forecast has variance σ^2. Likewise, the two-step-ahead forecast has variance $\sigma^2(1 + \phi^2)$ using the result from Appendix 6A that for independent random variables $VAR(aX + bY) = a^2VAR(X) + b^2VAR(Y)$. When we go out h steps ahead, the variance becomes $\sigma^2(1 + \phi^2 + \phi^{2h-2})$. The series is stationary, so as h increases, the variance approaches the limiting value $\sigma^2/(1 - \phi^2)$.

By similar arguments, it may be shown that the ARIMA(0,1,1) scheme has a one-step-ahead error variance equal to σ^2. Its two-step-ahead error variance is $\sigma^2/(1 + \theta^2)$, and when we go out h steps ahead, the error variance is $\sigma^2(1 + (h - 1)\theta^2)$. As h increases, the variance increases without limit. This property reflects the nonstationarity and non-mean-reverting behavior of this scheme and contrasts sharply with that of the AR(1) scheme. Thus, although the one-step-ahead forecasts may be similar and have similar prediction intervals, the long-term implications of the two models are very different, which serves to make long-term forecasting a hazardous occupation!

■ Example 6.12: Forecast RMSE for WFJ sales

We may compute the forecast *RMSE* for these two models by taking the square roots of the variances just obtained. The results for different forecasting horizons are shown in Table 6.9. ■

Table 6.9 Forecast RMSE for WFJ Sales

Horizon, h	AR(1)	ARIMA(0,1,1)
1	3.51	3.61
2	4.47	3.74
5	5.42	4.10
10	5.66	4.64
20	5.69	5.56
50	5.69	7.69
σ	3.51	3.61
ϕ	0.7867	
θ		0.2686

Data: WFJ_sales.xlsx

Note: Although we have not discussed empirical prediction intervals for ARIMA models, the approach described in Section 2.8.3 may be used.

6.7.2 Forecasting Using Transformations

The same general approach follows for all transformations:

- Transform the series.
- Generate the point forecasts and prediction intervals for the transformed series.
- Convert the point forecasts and prediction intervals back to the original units.

We use the logarithmic transform to illustrate the process:

- Convert Y_t to the new series $y_t = \ln(Y_t)$.
- Develop the model for y_t.
- Generate forecasts for future values of y_{n+h}, say, f_{n+h}, with associated lower and upper prediction limits, $l_n + h$ and $u_n + h$.
- Convert back to the original units to obtain the forecast: $F_{n+h} = \exp(f_{n+h})$, the lower limit $L_{n+h} = \exp(l_{n+h})$, and the upper limit $U_{n+h} = \exp(u_{n+h})$.

The limits for the transformed series will be symmetric about the forecasts, so the limits for the original series, after transforming back, will not be.

■ Example 6.13: Forecasting for Netflix sales using ARIMA(1,1,0)+C for the logarithms *(Adapted from Minitab Output)*

The fitted model may be summarized as follows:

Type	Coefficient	Standard Errors	T-test	P-values
AR(1)	0.7044	0.0946	7.45	0.000
Constant	0.0304	0.0081	3.74	0.000
Differencing: 1 regular difference RMSE = 0.0624, DF = 57				

Modified Box-Pierce (Ljung-Box) Chi-Square Statistic				
Lag	12	24	36	48
Chi-Square	20.9	42.3	52.2	58.8
DF	10	22	34	46
P-Value	0.022	0.006	0.024	0.098

Forecasts from Period 60 [2014Q4] for 2015

Period	Forecast	95% Limits		Actual
		Lower	Upper	
61:2015Q1	7.370	7.248	7.492	7.361
62:2015Q2	7.448	7.206	7.689	7.405
63:2015Q3	7.533	7.171	7.894	7.461
64:2015Q4	7.623	7.145	8.101	7.508

The model may be written as

$$Dy_{t+1} = 0.0304 + 0.7044 Dy_t + \varepsilon_{t+1}.$$

In turn, this expression becomes

$$y_{t+1} = y_t + 0.0304 + 0.7044(y_t - y_{t-1}) + \varepsilon_{t+1}$$
$$= 0.0304 + 1.7044 y_t - 0.7044 y_{t-1} + \varepsilon_{t+1}.$$

The computer program produces forecasts on the log scale, as shown. Applying the reverse transformation, the one-step-ahead forecasts and prediction intervals are shown in the table, along with the same items derived from the corresponding ARIMA model without the log transform. The one-step-ahead forecast (for 2015Q1) is

$$f_{n+1} = 0.0304 + 1.7044 y_n - 0.7044 y_{n-1}$$
$$= 0.0304 + 1.7044 \times 7.3030 - 0.7044 \times 7.2509$$
$$= 7.370.$$

Likewise, the two-step-ahead forecast (for 2015Q2) is

$$f_{n+2}(2) = 0.0304 + 1.7044 f_{n+1} - 0.7044 y_n$$
$$= 0.0304 + 1.7044 \times 7.3700 - 0.7044 \times 7.3030$$
$$= 7.448.$$

Forecasts from origin 2014Q4 for 2015 and the upper and lower 95 percent prediction interval limits for log sales are as follows:

Period	Quarter	Forecast	Lower Limit 95% PI	Upper Limit 95% PI
61:2015Q1	1	7.370	7.248	7.492
62:2015Q2	2	7.448	7.206	7.689
63:2015Q3	3	7.533	7.171	7.894
64:2015Q4	4	7.623	7.145	8.101

Table 6.10 shows the point forecasts and their prediction intervals, after transforming back to the original units. The final figures are rounded to a level of accuracy that is appropriate for presentation to management. ■

Table 6.10 Point Forecasts and 95 Percent Prediction Intervals for Netflix Sales for 2015

(A) Prediction Intervals Using Minitab

Quarter	Actual	Log Transform			Original Series		
		Forecast	Lower Limit	Upper Limit	Forecast	Lower Limit	Upper Limit
1	1573	1588	1405	1794	1546	1507	1585
2	1645	1716	1347	2185	1596	1519	1673
3	1738	1868	1301	2682	1640	1524	1755
4	1823	2045	1268	3296	1678	1525	1830

(B) Prediction Intervals Using R

Quarter	Actual	Log Model ARIMA (1,1,0)			ARIMA (1,1,0)+C		
		Forecast	Lower Limit	Upper Limit	Forecast	Lower Limit	Upper Limit
1	1573	1555	1364	1772	1545	1506	1584
2	1645	1619	1225	2141	1595	1518	1672
3	1738	1679	1074	2626	1637	1522	1752
4	1823	1734	926	3247	1678	1523	1826

Data: Netflix_2.xlsx

For comparison, the forecasts from the ARIMA(1,1,0)+C model without applying a transformation are shown in the right hand panel of Table 6.10; the diagnostics were similar for both models. The table reveals some interesting contrasts. Forecasts based upon the log version are consistently too optimistic and this bias becomes worse over time. By contrast, the forecasts without a transformation are pessimistic. Both sets of prediction intervals include the actual values, but those based upon the log model are about five times wider.

Which model is better? That is the wrong question to ask. Rather we need to ask what is going on. The no-transform model assumes linear growth, which we saw was inappropriate back in Section 3.4. Further this model assumes constant variance over time, so the prediction intervals for 2015 are too narrow — we got lucky in that they included the actual values. On the other hand, we saw in Section 3.8 that the rate of growth was declining, so the log transform will overestimate future revenues. In other words, neither model comes close to satisfying the stationarity assumptions.

The plot in Figure 3.14 indicated that a cube-root transform might come closer to satisfying the model assumptions. The results from this model, after completing the reverse transformations are:

Quarter	Forecast	Lower Limit	Upper Limit	Actual
1	1554	1479	1631	1573
2	1623	1497	1756	1645
3	1692	1522	1874	1738
4	1763	1555	1990	1825

These results seem more plausible and we might declare that they are just about right though a little low. However, the real conclusion is that further model development is needed and the model should be tested by proper use of a hold-out sample. Another possibility would be to drop the data for 2000 and 2001 to achieve more stable growth rates; the details are left to the reader as Exercise 6.11.

In both cases, the prediction intervals are very wide, although those for the model without the transformation are much narrower. Also, it is worth noting that the forecasts based upon the log transform are more optimistic than those based upon the untransformed data. Such forecast patterns tend to occur when strong growth has been observed in the past, given that the log model assumes a steady percentage growth. On further examination, the log model is seen to imply a steady-state $Dy_{ss} = 0.0304 / (1 - 0.7044)$ or 10.3 percent per quarter! This figure is calculated from the expression

$$Dy_{ss} = 0.0304 + 0.7044\, Dy_{ss}$$

by setting $Dy_t = Dy_{ss}$ for all t in the AR model and then solving for Dy_{ss}. Such a figure is seen to be unrealistic on the basis of recent results, where growth has been nearer to five percent per quarter. Given the start-up nature of the company, the early growth is unlikely to be sustained in later years. In other words, the assumption of stationarity (for the differences of the logarithms) is not appropriate. Dropping the data for 2000 produces more plausible results; the details are left to the reader as Exercise 6.11.

6.8 Seasonal ARIMA Models

Seasonal ARIMA models can be developed along the same lines as those developed already, but the details become quite intricate. Rather than consider the complete framework, we will examine some examples that have proved very useful in applications.

When we developed seasonal exponential smoothing methods in Chapter 4, we began with a purely seasonal scheme, and we may do the same for ARIMA modeling. Given m seasons, the purely seasonal ARIMA analogue to purely seasonal exponential smoothing is

$$D_m Y_t = Y_t - Y_{t-m} = \varepsilon_t - \theta_m \varepsilon_{t-m}. \tag{6.11}$$

We use D_m to denote the mth-order difference $Y_t - Y_{t-m}$, and the seasonal parameter is θ_m. Equation (6.11) would lead to the purely seasonal forecasting equation (4.4), with $\gamma = 1 - \theta_m$.

The question that arises is how to combine the regular and seasonal components. In the ARIMA framework this is achieved by first applying both regular and seasonal differences (note that the order in which the differences are taken does not change the result as the reader may verify):

$$DD_mY_t = D(Y_t - Y_{t-m})$$
$$= (Y_t - Y_{t-m}) - (Y_{t-1} - Y_{t-m-1})$$
$$= Y_t - Y_{t-1} - Y_{t-m} + Y_{t-m-1}$$

A full regular plus seasonal MA scheme is then obtained by superimposing first order regular and seasonal ARIMA components:

$$DD_mY_t = \varepsilon_t - \theta_1\varepsilon_{t-1} - \theta_m\varepsilon_{t-m} + \theta_1\theta_m\varepsilon_{t-m-1}. \qquad (6.12)$$

One final wrinkle to notice is that equation (6.12) has only two MA parameters rather than three. This results from the way the regular and seasonal elements have been overlaid. See Exercise 6.22 for details.

Model (6.12) is represented as an ARIMA$(0,1,1)(0,1,1)_m$ scheme to denote that we have first-order differences and MA components for both the regular and seasonal components and the seasonal element is of m periods' duration. This scheme is known as the "airline model," because the initial application by Box and Jenkins related to a time series on numbers of airline passengers. Given this notation, it is evident that we can "mix and match" regular seasonal components. For example, we could choose AR components rather than MA to produce and ARIMA$(1,1,0)(1,1,0)_m$ or we might drop one or both differences, as in ARIMA$(1,0,0)(0,1,1)_m$ or ARIMA$(1,0,0)(1,0,0)_m$. For months within a year, we rarely go more than one year back, but other seasonal patterns such as days within a week may well include additional autoregressive and moving average terms. We will not pursue that topic further here; see Box *et al.,* (2016, Chapter 9), or one of a number of other technical texts. Fortunately for us, many specialized computer programs, such as Forecast Pro, Autobox, and R will perform model selection automatically, even with seasonal models: relying on the *ACF* and *PACF* is both difficult and unnecessary. (See online Appendix B for details of the programs.)

■ Example 6.14: Seasonal model for UK retail sales

Quarterly UK retail sales for the period 1996-2014 are plotted in Figure 6.21. The quarterly airline model was fitted to the series for the period 1996Q1–2012Q4. The series shows a strong seasonal pattern with a peak in the fourth quarter, as might be expected. The results are summarized in Table 6.11. ■

Figure 6.21 UK Retail Sales Volume, 1996Q1 to 2014Q4

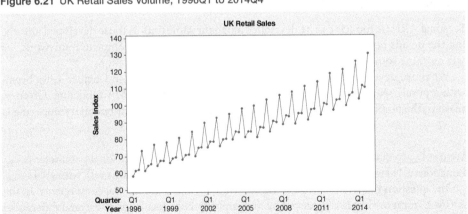

Data: UK_retail_sales_2.xlsx

Table 6.11 The Airline Model Fitted to the UK Retail Sales Series, 1996Q1–2012Q4

Type	Coefficient	Standard Errors	T-test	P-values
MA(1)	0.3153	0.1231	2.56	0.013
SMA (4)	0.3068	0.1267	2.42	0.018
Differencing: 1 regular, 1 seasonal of order 4 Number of observations: Original series 68, after differencing 63 Residuals: RMSE = 0.993, DF = 61				

Ljung-Box-Pierce Chi-Square Statistic				
Lag	12	24	36	48
Chi-Square	14.5	34.7	42.5	50.1
DF	10	22	34	46
P-Value	0.152	0.042	0.150	0.313

The test of residuals for autocorrelation indicates that there may be a pattern that is not fully accounted for (*P*-value of 0.042 at lag 24) but the plots of residuals in Figures 6.22 and 6.23 suggest that all is well. Other models could be considered, which we leave to the reader as Exercise 6.14.

Figure 6.22 Residual Plots for UK Retail Sales Volume, 1996Q1 to 2012Q4

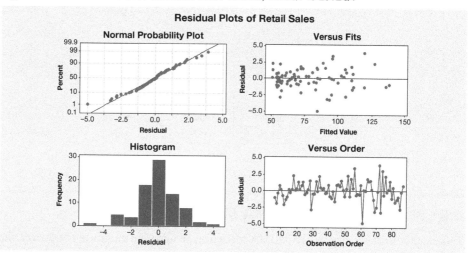

Data: UK_retail_sales_2.xlsx

Figure 6.23 *ACF* Residual Plots for UK Retail Sales Volume, 1996Q1 to 2012Q4

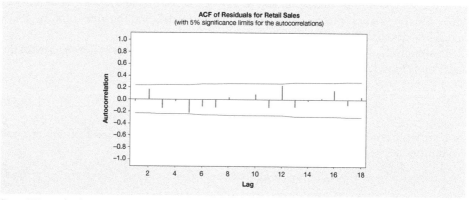

Data: UK_retail_sales_2.xlsx

6.8.1 Forecasts for Seasonal Models

The general approach is the same as that for the nonseasonal case. That is, we substitute values as follows:

Y_t values: Use observations already recorded where available; for values not yet recorded, insert the latest available forecast.

ε_t values: Use recorded one-step-ahead residuals where available; set future errors in the equation equal to zero (best available forecast).

■ Example 6.15: Forecasts for UK retail sales

When we substitute the parameter estimates into equation (6.12), we obtain

$$Y_t - Y_{t-1} - Y_{t-4} + Y_{t-5} = \varepsilon_t - 0.3153\varepsilon_{t-1} - 0.3068\varepsilon_{t-4} + 0.0967\varepsilon_{t-5}.$$

Substituting the values as before, we arrive at the one- through eight-step-ahead forecasts shown in the following table (the appropriate prediction intervals are also provided; calculations are via Minitab). ■

Quarter	Forecast	Lower Limit 95% PI	Upper Limit 95% PI	Actual	Error
2013Q1	100.16	98.22	102.11	99.63	−0.54
2013Q2	106.25	103.89	108.64	105.76	−0.49
2013Q3	106.35	103.64	109.06	107.42	1.07
2013Q4	124.01	120.99	127.03	125.99	1.98
2014Q1	103.08	99.04	107.12	103.75	0.67
2014Q2	109.17	104.54	113.79	111.58	2.41
2014Q3	109.27	104.12	114.42	110.44	1.17
2014Q4	126.92	121.30	132.54	130.60	3.68

6.9* State-Space and ARIMA Models

This chapter has been devoted to ARIMA models in an apparent complete break from the exponential smoothing methods of Chapters 3 and 4 and the state-space models developed in Chapter 5. All too often, this is how the material is treated, perhaps along with an occasional (false) statement that exponential smoothing is "just a special case of ARIMA."

We first show how the state-space and ARIMA models are related and where differences arise. The discussion is presented in terms of simple models, but the ideas carry over to a much broader class.

In Section 5.1, we introduced the local-level model for random variable Y in terms of the local level (*L*) and random error (*s*) as

$$Y_t = L_{t-1} + \varepsilon_t$$
$$L_t = L_{t-1} + \alpha\varepsilon_t \tag{6.13}$$

If we write down the observation equations for periods t and $t\text{-}1$ and then subtract one from the other, we arrive at

$$Y_t - Y_{t-1} = L_{t-1} - L_{t-2} + \varepsilon_t - \varepsilon_{t-1}. \tag{6.14}$$

We can then use the state equation to eliminate the states from the observation equation:

$$Y_t - Y_{t-1} = L_{t-1} - L_{t-2} + \varepsilon_t - \varepsilon_{t-1}$$
$$= \alpha\varepsilon_{t-1} + \varepsilon_t - \varepsilon_{t-1} \tag{6.15}$$
$$= \varepsilon_t - (1 - \alpha)\varepsilon_{t-1}$$

Equation (6.15) does not involve the state variables and so may be regarded as a *reduced form* of the state-space model (in the sense that the states have been eliminated). The left-hand side of the equation is just the difference, $DY_t = Y_t - Y_{t-1}$.

Finally, this model may be written in the standard ARIMA $(0,1,1)$ notation as

$$DY_t = \varepsilon_t - \theta\varepsilon_{t-1}, \tag{6.16}$$

where $\theta = 1 - \alpha$. So, starting with a state space model, we have found the equivalent ARIMA model, but keep in mind that the state space model relies on from different assumptions (finite start-up, no stationarity requirement). Other state-space models may be reduced to ARIMA forms by the same process of eliminating the state variables. We present two more examples and refer the reader to Hyndman *et al.* (2008, Chapter 11) for further details.

■ Example 6.16: The damped linear trend model as an ARIMA scheme

The damped linear trend model developed in Section 3.5 is underpinned by the model

$$Y_t = L_{t-1} + \phi T_{t-1} + \varepsilon_t$$
$$L_t = L_{t-1} + \phi T_{t-1} + \alpha\varepsilon_t$$
$$T_t = \phi T_{t-1} + \beta\varepsilon_t.$$

We may eliminate the local-level and trend terms to arrive at the ARIMA model:

$$DY_t - \phi DY_{t-1} = \varepsilon_t - \theta_1\varepsilon_{t-1} - \theta_2\varepsilon_{t-2}. \tag{6.17}$$

Here, $\theta_1 = 1 + \phi - \alpha - \beta\phi$, $\theta_2 = -\phi(1 - \alpha)$ and model (6.17) is an ARIMA(1,1,2) scheme, because it contains one autoregression, one difference, and two moving average terms.

The damped trend scheme includes a variety of special cases that arise for specific choices of the parameters, and we present a summary in Table 6.12. The reader is encouraged to check the details by making the appropriate substitutions. ■

Table 6.12 Equivalences Between State-Space and ARIMA Schemes

State-space form	Parameter restrictions	ARIMA
Damped linear trend	None	(1,1,2)
Local linear trend (LES)	$\phi = 1$	(0,2,2)
Local level (SES)	$\phi = 0$	(0,1,1)

■ Example 6.17: Seasonal state-space and ARIMA schemes

As before, we start out from a state-space model. The particular form we consider is the additive Holt-Winters scheme set forth in Section 5.3.2, but with the trend term and equation omitted. That is, we consider the model

$$Y_t = L_{t-1} + S_{t-m} + \varepsilon_t$$
$$L_t = L_{t-1} + \alpha\varepsilon_t$$
$$S_t = S_{t-m} + \gamma\varepsilon_t.$$

We follow the same procedure as before and eliminate the state variables. We then arrive at the reduced form

$$D_m D Y_t = Y_t - Y_{t-1} - Y_{t-m} + Y_{t-m-1}$$
$$= \varepsilon_t - (1 - \alpha)\varepsilon_{t-1} - (1 - \gamma)\varepsilon_{t-m} + (1 - \alpha - \gamma)\varepsilon_{t-m-1}.$$

The reduced model differs slightly from that given in equation (6.12). We may set $\theta_1 = 1 - \alpha$, $\theta_m = 1 - \gamma$ but the final coefficient is then $1 - \alpha - \gamma = \theta_1 + \theta_m - 1$ rather than $1 - \alpha - \gamma + \alpha\gamma = \theta_1 \theta_m$. Generally speaking, the state-space and ARIMA seasonal models that are in common use have somewhat different parameter structures. So if they are both estimated and then compared, the results will differ somewhat. ∎

EQUIVALENCE BETWEEN STATE-SPACE AND ARIMA MODELS

We can express a *linear* state-space scheme in ARIMA form if and only if we assume that the random error terms satisfy the standard assumptions being independent and distributed with a constant variance. It should be kept in mind that ARIMA schemes require stationarity (after suitable differencing) but state space models assume a set of initial conditions that does not require stationarity.

When both the error assumptions and linearity are satisfied, exponential smoothing methods do indeed correspond to an ARIMA scheme. However, methods such as the multiplicative Holt-Winters scheme have nonlinear forecast functions and cannot be represented in an ARIMA format. Further, even when the observation and state equations are linear, state-space schemes may have non-constant variances and hence are not representable as ARIMA schemes.

There is a further subtle distinction that may be illustrated by considering SES with $\alpha = 0$. In state-space format, SES then reduces to the constant-mean version

$$Y_t = L_0 + \varepsilon_t.$$

This reduction is possible because the state-space scheme has a finite starting point (time zero). By contrast, the equivalent ARIMA(0,1,1) model breaks down because stationarity implies that the starting values become irrelevant, which is not true here.

6.9.1 From ARIMA to a State-Space Form

Any ARIMA scheme may be expressed in state-space form, and a variety of state-space formulations have appeared over the years. (Again, see Hyndman *et al.*, 2008, Chapter 11, for details.)

∎ Example 6.18: The first-order autoregressive scheme, AR(1)

The AR(1) scheme is written in the ARIMA format as

$$Y_t = \delta + \phi Y_{t-1} + \varepsilon_t.$$

To show that a corresponding state-space version exists, we start from the damped local-level model:

$$Y_t = \mu + \phi L_{t-1} + \varepsilon_t$$
$$L_t = \phi L_{t-1} + \alpha \varepsilon_t$$
$$\delta = \mu(1 - \phi).$$

Here, μ denotes the mean, or expected value, of the series; that is $E(Y_t) = \mu$. After some manipulation, these equations reduce to the ARIMA form

$$Y_t = \delta + \phi Y_{t-1} + \varepsilon_t - \phi(1 - \alpha)\,\varepsilon_{t-1}.$$

The damped local-level model is represented by an ARIMA(1,0,1) scheme, and the AR(1) model results as a special case when $\alpha = 1$. The AR(1) model seems "natural," but so does the damped local-level state-space form. ∎

Two lessons emerge from this example:

1. There is a duality between the two approaches.
2. The models we select in practice may vary somewhat, depending upon whether we are working in the state-space or the ARIMA framework.

In general, the ARIMA version is obtained by eliminating the unobservable state variables.

The elimination of the state variables is both a blessing and a curse. The advantage of the state variables is that they provide insights into the structure of the model and help to guide model selection. Also, the state-space schemes can incorporate nonlinear structures such as the multiplicative Holt-Winters scheme, whereas ARIMA cannot. By contrast, the ARIMA forms are easier to link directly to functions of the data, so that model selection tends to be more data driven. Increasingly, forecasting software provides both options (see online Appendix B).

DISCUSSION QUESTION: *What factors should you consider in choosing between using a state-space approach or an ARIMA approach?*

6.10* GARCH Models

One of the standard assumptions underlying most of the models we develop is that the error terms have constant variances. In many circumstances, this assumption is manifestly false for the original series. For example, when we consider sales or GDP, we automatically think of percentage changes over time, rather than changes in absolute amounts. That thought process in turn leads naturally to looking at percentage changes (or making a logarithmic transformation), and such steps will often resolve the difficulty, at least to a reasonable degree of approximation. However, this approach will not work in other circumstances, such as the variations (or volatility) in stock prices. An individual stock, or even a whole market index, tends to show quiet times intermingled with heavy (indeed, sometimes frantic) periods of trading. Such activity does not necessarily involve major movements up or down, so simple transformations (such as differencing or logs) will not work. Rather, we must recognize that the volatility is itself a stochastic process that needs to be modeled.

This insight was first developed by Rob Engle (1982), who introduced the notion of *Autoregressive Conditional Heteroscedasticity* (ARCH), whereby the variance at time t is an autoregressive (AR) function of past variances, updated by the latest squared error term. Thus, if periods of high volatility are likely to persist, the AR structure would have a positive coefficient, just as it does in the AR models considered in Section 6.2. The heteroscedasticity is local, because it is conditional upon immediate past values. Just as AR models have been extended to ARIMA models (see Section 6.2.3), ARCH models have been extended to include moving-average-like components (Bollerslev, 1986) and given the name *generalized ARCH,* or *GARCH.* Since these models were introduced, they have become extremely popular in econometrics, especially in the financial area, where predictions of volatility are the key to the efficient design of options contracts (see Hull, 2002). The article by Engle (2001) provides a nice overview. Gonzalez-Rivera (2013) offers a full discussion including the use of EViews.

We will focus upon only one special case, the so-called GARCH (1,1) model, which has proved to be extremely popular in applications.

6.10.1 The GARCH (1,1) Model

We begin with the random variable Y_t defined in the usual way but with time-dependent mean and variance:

$$E(Y_t) = \mu_t \text{ and } V(Y_t) = \sigma_t^2.$$

Because our current interest is exclusively in the variance, we assume that the mean is known or has been estimated to a sufficiently high degree of accuracy so that we can focus upon the error process $\varepsilon_t = Y_t - \mu_t$. Such an assumption is usually appropriate for applications in finance when the random variable is defined as the return on an investment, typically over a short time period (e.g., days or even minutes). The expected value of that return would be close to zero. Accordingly, we may write

$$E(\varepsilon_t) = 0 \text{ and } E(\varepsilon_t^2) = \sigma_t^2.$$

The GARCH (1, 1) model is now defined as

$$\sigma_t^2 = \omega + \alpha\varepsilon_{t-1}^2 + \beta\sigma_{t-1}^2. \tag{6.18}$$

The variable σ_t^2 represents the *conditional variance,* defined as a function of past elements of the series. To ensure that the model gives rise to strictly positive variances, we must impose the conditions

$$\omega > 0, \alpha > 0, \text{ and } \beta > 0.$$

In addition, we impose the condition

$$\alpha + \beta < 1$$

to ensure that the long-term variance is finite. Equation (6.18) looks rather like an ARMA (1,1) scheme but with the important difference that the term on the left-hand side does not represent an observable quantity. To make the model operational, we define the new variable

$$u_t = \varepsilon_t^2 - \sigma_t^2$$

and then rewrite equation (6.18) as

$$\varepsilon_t^2 = \omega + (\alpha + \beta)\varepsilon_{t-1}^2 + u_t - \beta u_{t-1}. \tag{6.19}$$

The new "error term" u_t has a zero mean, and its autocorrelations are zero when the model is valid. However, $\{u_t\}$ are not independent and identically distributed since their *ACF* depends on the relationship between ε_t^2 and ε_{t-1}^2, so the estimation process is more complex and we will not discuss the details. Fortunately computer software will deliver the estimates automatically (see online Appendix B).

Once the model has been estimated, we may use the parameter estimates $(\hat{\omega}, \hat{\alpha}, \hat{\beta})$, the current estimate of the variance σ_t^2 and the latest sample squared error ε_t^2 to forecast future values one step ahead:

$$\hat{\sigma}_{t+1}^2(1) = \hat{\omega} + \hat{\alpha}\varepsilon_t^2 + \hat{\beta}\hat{\sigma}_t^2.$$

Beyond the first period, we update this expression step by step to forecast h-steps ahead:

$$\sigma^2_{t+h}(h) = \hat{\omega} + (\hat{\alpha} + \hat{\beta})\hat{\sigma}^2_{t+h-1}(h-1), h = 2, 3, \ldots$$

As the forecasting horizon increases, the variance approaches the limiting value

$$\frac{\omega}{1 - \alpha - \beta}.$$

From this expression, we can see that this limiting value is defined only if $\alpha + \beta < 1$.

■ Example 6.19: Variation in the Dow Jones Index

As an illustration of the GARCH methodology, we consider daily closing prices for the Dow Jones Index over the period from January 1, 2001, to September 30, 2005, a total of 1200 observations. Specialist software is needed to carry out the modeling. An advanced and widely used econometric package, EViews was used here. Routines are also available in R. The data are available in the file *DowJones.xlsx* and are plotted in Figure 6.24. The figure shows the plot of the returns data measured as $100(Y_t - Y_{t-1})/Y_{t-1}$. Volatility is clearly higher in the earlier part of the period. The summary statistics for the returns and the absolute values of the returns are shown in Table 6.13: The skewness and heavy tails in both distributions are quite evident.

Figure 6.24 Daily Returns on the Dow Jones Index, January 2001–September 2005 *(Analysis completed with EViews 9)*

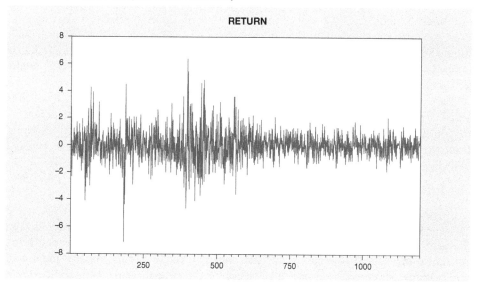

Data: *DowJones.xlsx*

DISCUSSION QUESTION: *Some investment analysts continue to operate as though returns were normally distributed with a constant variance. How do you think this approach affects measures of risk?*

Table 6.13 Summary Statistics for Returns and Absolute Returns of Dow Jones Series

	Return	Absolute Return
Mean	0.01	0.82
Median	0.02	0.61
Maximum	6.35	7.13
Minimum	–7.13	0.00
Std. Dev.	1.15	0.80
Skewness	0.15	2.31
Kurtosis	6.76	11.89
Observations	1199	1199

Data: DowJones.xlsx

The Efficient Market Hypothesis, which states that stock prices incorporate all relevant (publicly available) information, implies a random walk model for prices:

$$Y_t = Y_{t-1} + \varepsilon_t.$$

That is, the current closing price at $(t - 1)$ contains all the information which is useful in predicting the next period's price. This equation had proved extremely useful in understanding many financial markets, including stock prices and exchange rates. Broadly, such a model holds for most markets in which the instrument is widely traded. However, there are interesting exceptions that have offered valuable trading opportunities. Still, it is a hard model to beat without inside information. (See Timmermann and Granger, 2004, for an interesting discussion of where there are forecasting opportunities.) Nonetheless, the efficient market model does not suggest any constraints on the error variance. An examination of Figure 6.24 reveals that there are periods of relatively high and low volatility, so it should be possible to predict future levels of volatility to a greater degree of accuracy than is implied by a constant-variance assumption. We therefore consider a GARCH (1,1) model for the error variance.

The output from EViews for the GARCH (1, 1) model is shown in Table 6.14, which is based upon an estimation sample of the first 1160 observations (leaving aside 40 observations as a hold-out sample). The constant term (mean return) is not significantly different from zero, so the results for the variance are almost identical if it is dropped. Thus, the fitted model is

$$\hat{\sigma}^2_{t+1}(1) = 0.0095 + 0.0775\varepsilon^2_t + 0.9160\hat{\sigma}^2_t.$$

This equation was used to produce forecasts via Excel. For comparison, we computed forecasts with the use of a ten-step moving average and the unconditional variance based on the same 1160 observations. The mean absolute errors *(MAE, as defined in Section 2.7.2)* are shown in Table 6.14, computed one step ahead for the hold-out sample of the last 40 observations. For comparison, the *MAE* values for the same three methods are shown in Table 6.15 for the last 200 and the last 600 observations. The results are remarkably consistent. We conclude that it is important to obtain local forecasts of the variance, but for that purpose a suitably chosen moving average scheme may perform just as well as a GARCH model.

Exercises 6.20 and 6.21 provide opportunities for the reader to develop GARCH models and Minicase 6.2 considers GARCH modeling for a series that also includes a substantial ARIMA component.

Table 6.14 Coefficient Estimates for a GARCH (1,1) Model Using the First 1160 Observations of the Dow Jones Series *(Estimated with EViews 9)*

Variable	Coefficient	Std. Error	z-Statistic	Prob.
Mean	0.028642	0.025845	1.108225	0.2678
Variance Equation				
$\hat{\omega}$	0.009478	0.004685	2.022987	0.0431
$\hat{\alpha}$	0.077483	0.011649	6.651471	0.0000
$\hat{\beta}$	0.915981	0.012865	71.19897	0.0000

Data: DowJones.xlsx; output adapted from EViews 9

Table 6.15 Comparison of Moving Average, Unconditional Variance, and GARCH Estimates of the Variance for the Dow Jones Data

Hold-Out	MA(10)	Unconditional	GARCH
MAE last 40	0.325	1.037	0.342
MAE last 200	0.399	1.020	0.427
MAE last 600	0.511	1.018	0.532

Data: DownJones.xlsx

Exercise 6.21 considers more recent data. ■

6.11 Principles of ARIMA Modeling

One of the great strengths of the ARIMA framework is that Box and Jenkins developed a set of model-building principles. No simple summary exists beyond their injunction to "identify-estimate-test-forecast," so we have collated our own, from a variety of sources.

6.11.1 ARIMA Models

[6.1] Identify the key features of the data.
Is the series seasonal? Does it display (nonlinear) trends?

[6.2] Transform the data to stationarity.
If the series appears to be nonstationary, consider differences and/or transformations to achieve stationarity. *ACF* and statistical tests can aid in the process, while *AIC* and *BIC* can help to validate the choice.

[6.3] Consider a variety of models, compatible with the time series characteristics.
Create a list of potential models, using the sample *ACF* (and *PACF*) and keeping in mind the characteristics of the series. Alternatively, and equally valid, rely on an information criterion such as *AIC*.

[6.4] Estimate the models, using your preferred software.

[6.5] Examine the diagnostic statistics — in particular, the residual autocorrelations.
Look at the sample *ACF* (or *PACF*) for outliers and for lags that have been omitted. If the sample *ACF* shows a slow decay, consider additional differencing.

[6.6] If there is residual autocorrelation, include additional AR or MA terms in the ARIMA specification, and re-estimate, comparing results with the original model.

[6.7] Consider simplifying the model if some of the coefficients are insignificant.
Where differencing has been carried out to ensure stationarity, check for over-differencing by comparing specifications with the chosen difference *d* and difference *d-1*.

[6.8] Use an information criterion supplemented, where possible, by an out-of-sample fit to choose among models.

[6.9] Compare your ARIMA forecasts with alternative methods of forecasting — in particular, with a naïve model.

6.11.2 GARCH Models

[6.10] Start with a constant-variance model, and then examine the autocorrelation structure of the squared residuals, using the methods of this chapter.

[6.11] The GARCH(1,1) model will suffice for most purposes.
The KISS principle (keep it simple, statistician) should always be kept in mind.

Summary

We began this chapter by developing the autocorrelation function (*ACF*), which is a basic tool for describing the dependence structure of a time series. (In addition, the partial autocorrelation function (*PACF*) provides additional helpful evidence.) We developed the class of ARIMA models and showed how the *ACF* (and *PACF*) may be used to select an appropriate model from within that class. Questions of parameter estimation and model diagnostics were then explored. When the data do not conform to the underlying assumptions of a model, we may use a combination of differencing, transformation, and outlier adjustment to achieve a better description of the observed series. The initial model may be enlarged if the diagnostics suggest residual autocorrelation or simplified if any coefficient is insignificant. Alternative models can then be compared using information criteria. Once these issues have been resolved, we may generate point and interval forecasts, as in earlier chapters. These ideas were then extended to cover seasonal time series.

Although ARIMA and state-space models have a number of similarities and the two classes share a number of common models, there are some significant differences in applications and forecasters may well select different models based on the two approaches. Further, there are several approaches to the selection of ARIMA models, such as the use of the *ACF* (and *PACF*) and model simplification, or the use of information criteria. We find that both approaches can be useful. This is where the modeler's expertise becomes very important!

The discussion up to this point has assumed a constant variance over time. However, this assumption may not be true, and the final section of the chapter examined GARCH models, which enable us to consider processes whose error variances, as well as levels, change over time.

Exercises

6.1   Develop an ARIMA model for the growth rate of the U.S. gross domestic product *(GDP_change_2.xlsx)*. Compare your model with the results obtained in Exercise 3.3. Use the diagnostics discussed in Section 6.5 to guide your choice of model.

6.2   Develop an ARIMA model for changes in the Consumer Price Index *(CPI_change_2. xlsx)*. Compare your model with the results obtained in Exercise 3.5. Use the diagnostics discussed in Section 6.5 to guide your choice of model.

6.3   Develop an ARIMA model for the Saudi Arabian Light Oil spot price series *(SA_oil_ prices_2.xlsx)*. Compare your model with the results obtained in Exercises 3.7 and 3.8. Use the diagnostics discussed in Section 6.5 to guide your choice of model.

6.4   Develop an ARIMA model for the Dulles Airport passengers' series *(Dulles_2.xlsx)*. Compare your model with the results obtained in Exercises 3.11 and 3.12. Use the diagnostics discussed in Section 6.5 to guide your choice of model.

6.5   Carry out diagnostic checks for the ARIMA(2,2,0) scheme for U.S. retail sales *(US_ retail_sales_2_SA.xlsx)*, discussed in connection with Example 6.9.

6.6   Using a log transform, develop an ARIMA model for U.S. retail sales *(US_retail_ sales_2_SA.xlsx)* and carry out appropriate diagnostic tests.

6.7   Repeat the analysis of Exercise 6.6, using the Box-Cox transform.

6.8   Adjust the U.S. retail sales series for the outlier in October 2001 and rerun the analyses from Exercises 6.6 and 6.7. Compare the parameter estimates with those obtained earlier.

6.9   The actual values of the U.S. retail sales series for 2013Q1–2015Q4 are given in the file *US_retail_sales_2_SA.xlsx*. Generate the point forecasts, with 2012Q4 as origin, and compare the forecasting performance of the log transform models with and without outlier adjustments, using *MAPE* and *MAE*. Comment on your results.

6.10* Verify the two-step-ahead forecast variances for the AR(1) and MA(1) schemes given in Section 6.7.1.

6.11 Reanalyze the Netflix series *(Netflix_2.xlsx)* considered in Example 6.13 after dropping the data for 2000 and 2001. How does this change in the estimation sample affect your results? Which data set do you think is the more appropriate?

6.12 Use ARIMA models to generate point forecasts and prediction intervals for the following annual series, and compare your results with actual values obtained from the relevant data sources (United States, United Kingdom, or country of choice for the first two):

a. Changes in Gross Domestic Product *(GDP_change_2.xlsx)*
b. Changes in Consumer Price Index *(CPI_change_2.xlsx)*
c. Saudi Arabian Light Oil spot price *(SA_oil_prices_2.xlsx)*
d. Dulles Airport passengers *(Dulles_2.xlsx)*

In each case, use the last four values of the series as the hold-out sample.

6.13 Compare the point forecasts and prediction intervals for the last 12 observations for U.S. retail sales *(US_retail_sales_2_SA.xlsx)*, using both ARIMA(1,1,0)+C and ARIMA(0,2,2) models.

6.14 Develop seasonal ARIMA models for UK retail sales *(UK_retail_sales_2.xlsx)* using AR components rather than MA and compare your results with those of Example 6.14.

6.15* Show that the MA(1) scheme has $E(Y_t) = \mu$, $V(Y_t) = \sigma^2$ and $\rho_1 = -\theta/(1 + \theta^2)$. Further, show that all higher order autocorrelations are zero.

The next four exercises relate back to Exercises 4.4–4.8 and 5.10–5.13. In each case, select the "best" ARIMA model using both a hold-out sample and information criteria. How does the model selected compare with your own views of what the most appropriate model would be?

6.16 Examine the series on Job Openings *(Job_openings_xlsx)* previously considered in Minicase 3.1. Does the inclusion of seasonal factors provide a useful improvement in forecast quality? Use the last 36 observations as the hold-out sample.

6.17 The U.S. Census records monthly Alcoholic Beverage Sales by Wholesalers *(Alcohol_sales.xlsx)*. The series is recorded monthly and it is not seasonally adjusted. Sales are measured in $Millions and the series runs from January 2001 to December 2015. Use the last 36 observations as the hold-out sample.

6.18 Use the data (not seasonally adjusted) in the file *US_retail_sales_2.xlsx* with the period from January 2001 to December 2012 as the estimation sample. Use the last 36 observations as the hold-out sample.

6.19 The spreadsheet *Titanic_box_office.xlsx* provides the daily figures for the number of customers per theater for the period December 19, 1997 to July 23, 1998. Use the last four weeks as a hold-out sample.

6.20* The file *SP500_daily.xlsx* provides the daily closing prices for the S&P 500 Index for every trading day in the years 2012–2015. Conduct an analysis of the daily returns using the GARCH methodology described in Section 6.10. Is there any evidence to suggest that the series does not follow a heteroscedastic random walk?

6.21* Download the day-to-day percentage changes over the last three years for the Dow Jones Index and the FTSE 100 Index (or any other indexes in which you have an interest). These series may be found, for example, at *www.econstats.com*. Develop GARCH models for each series and compare the structures.

6.22* Reformulate equation (6.11), $D_m Y_t = \varepsilon_t - \theta_m \varepsilon_{t-m}$, as $Z_t = \delta_t$ where $Z_t = D_m Y_t$ and $\delta_t = \varepsilon_t - \theta_m \varepsilon_{t-m}$. Now consider the MA(1) scheme $Z_t = \delta_t - \theta_t \delta_{t-1}$. By substituting back in terms of (Y, δ) show that we arrive at the seasonal model shown in equation (6.12).

Minicases

Minicase 6.1 Analysis of UK Retail Sales

The file *UK_retail_sales_2.xlsx* contains the quarterly index for the volume of total retail trade in the UK from 1996Q1 to 2014Q4. The index is not seasonally adjusted, and the index has 2010 as the base year with the index for that year set at 100.

The file *UK_retail_sales_annual.xlsx* gives yearly figures for the same index, from 1955–2014 with an index value of 100 for 2010.

Use the data to develop ARIMA models for the quarterly series and for the annual series. Generate forecasts for the years 2013 and 2014 in each case, and compare the forecasts from each approach. Which forecasts would you prefer? Why?

Given that the variability of the series increases over time, rework the analyses, using a logarithmic transformation. Compare your results and comment on which model you prefer to use.

Minicase 6.2 Run Mileage

The data file *Run_miles.xlsx* records the miles run per month by a middle-aged forecaster (KO) over the period January 1981-March 2007.[5] The period from January 1981 to September 1996 shows considerably greater variability than the subsequent period from June 1997 to March 2007. The five months in between these two periods record zeros, because the runner was injured during that time. These months may be excluded from the record.

Use the observations through March 2005 as the estimation sample. After doing the usual preliminary data analyses,

1. Develop an ARIMA model, assuming a constant variance.

2. Use the model you developed to generate the one-step-ahead forecasts and corresponding prediction intervals for the next 24 months.

3. Repeat the analysis, incorporating a GARCH model for the variances.

Compare the results of the two analyses. In particular, examine the comparative widths of the prediction intervals and their coverage.

References

*Bollerslev, T. (1986). Generalized autoregressive conditional heteroskedasticity. *Journal of Econometrics*, 31, 307–327.

*Box, G. E. P., and Jenkins, G. M. (1970). *Time Series Analysis: Forecasting and Control*. Upper Saddle River, NJ: Prentice-Hall.

*Box, G. E. P., Jenkins, G. M., Reinsel, G. C., and Ljung, G.M. (2016). *Time Series Analysis: Forecasting and Control*, 5th edn. New York: Wiley.

Cryer, J.D. and Chan, K-S. (2010). *Time Series Analysis: With Applications in R*, 2nd edition. Berlin, Heidelberg, and New York: Springer.

Diebold, F. X. (2007). *Elements of Forecasting*, 4th ed. Mason, OH: Cengage (South-Western).

*Engle, R. F. (1982). Autoregressive conditional heteroscedasticity with estimates of variance of United Kingdom inflation. *Econometrica*, 50, 987–1008.

Engle, R.F. (2001). GARCH 101: The use of ARCH/GARCH models in applied econometrics. *Journal of Economic Perspectives*, 15, 157–168.

Gonzalez-Rivera, G. (2013). *Forecasting for Economics and Business*. Upper Saddle River, NJ: Pearson: Addison-Wesley.

Hull, J. C. (2002). *Fundamentals of Futures and Options Markets*, 4th edition. Upper Saddle River, NJ: Prentice Hall.

Hyndman, R. J., Koehler, A. B., Ord, J. K., and Snyder, R. D. (2008). *Forecasting with Exponential Smoothing*. Berlin, Heidelberg, and New York: Springer.

---

5 These data were originally analyzed in Ord, Koehler, Snyder, and Hyndman (2009), who used the GARCH structure within a state-space framework.

Koehler, A. B., Snyder, R. D., Ord, J. K., and Beaumont, A. (2011). A study of outliers in the exponential smoothing approach to forecasting. *International Journal of Forecasting, 28*, 477–484.

Ord, J. K., Koehler, A. B., Snyder, R. D. and Hyndman, R. J. (2009). Monitoring processes with changing variances. *International Journal of Forecasting, 25*, 518–525.

Timmermann, A., and Granger, C. W. J. (2004). Efficient market hypothesis and forecasting. *International Journal of Forecasting, 20*, 15–27.

*Tsay, R. S. (2010). *Analysis of Financial Time Series,* 3rd ed. Hoboken, NJ: Wiley.

Appendix 6A* Mean and Variance for AR(1) Scheme

We start with the AR(1) model as specified in equation (6.3):

$$Y_t = \delta + \phi Y_{t-1} + \varepsilon_t, \qquad\qquad (6A.1)$$

Taking expected values in equation (6A.1), we have

$$E(Y_t) = E(\delta + \phi Y_{t-1} + \varepsilon_t) = \delta + \phi E(Y_{t-1}) + E(\varepsilon_t). \qquad (6A.2)$$

The last result follows by the property that the mean of a sum is equal to the sum of the means and by the fact that, because δ and φ are fixed values, we can "factor" them out of the expectation sign. From the stationarity conditions, we have

$$E(\varepsilon_t) = 0, \ V(\varepsilon_t) = \sigma^2$$
$$E(Y_t) = \mu, \ V(Y_t) = \omega^2 \qquad (6A.3)$$
$$Corr(Y_t, Y_{t-k}) = \rho_k$$

for all values of t. Substituting the expected values into equation (6A.2), we arrive at

$$E(Y_t) = \mu = \delta + \phi E(Y_{t-1}) + E(\varepsilon_t) = \delta + \phi\mu + 0.$$

It then follows that $\mu = \delta/(1 - \phi)$, provided that $-1 < \phi < 1$.

To obtain the variance, we employ the following rules:

1. The variance of a constant is zero.
2. If a is a constant, then $V(aY) = a^2 V(Y)$.
3. When two variables are independent, the variance of the sum is the sum of the variances.

Because the conditions for Rule 3 hold, we can write the variance of Y_t as

$$V(Y_t) = V(\delta + \phi Y_{t-1} + \varepsilon_t) = V(\delta) + V(\phi Y_{t-1}) + V(\varepsilon_t).$$

By Rule 1, the first term is zero, and applying Rule 2 to the second term, we have

$$V(Y_t) = \phi^2 V(Y_{t-1}) + V(\varepsilon_t).$$

The values listed in equation (6A.3) reduce this equation to

$$\omega^2 = \phi^2\omega^2 + \sigma^2 \text{ or } \omega^2 = \sigma^2 / (1 - \phi^2).$$

The autocorrelation is a bit more difficult to determine. To simplify the notation, we first subtract the mean from the random variable and define

$$y_t = Y_t - \mu.$$

So (6A.1) becomes

$$Y_t - \mu = y_t = \phi y_{t-1} + \varepsilon_t. \tag{6A.4}$$

The first order autocorrelation may then be written as the autocovariance divided by the variance:

$$\rho_1 = \frac{E(y_t y_{t-1})}{\omega^2} .$$

Thus, we need to evaluate the autocovariance. We do this by the following steps:

1. Multiply the entire equation (6A.4) by y_{t-1}.
2. Take expected values:

$$E(y_t y_{t-1}) = E[y_{t-1}(\phi y_{t-1} + \varepsilon_t)] = E(\phi y_{t-1}^2) + E(y_{t-1} \varepsilon_t).$$

The second term is zero because the two components are independent and have zero means. Thus, the equation reduces to

$$E(y_t y_{t-1}) = E(\phi y_{t-1}^2) = \phi E(y_{t-1}^2) = \phi \omega^2.$$

It then follows that $\rho_1 = \phi$. By a similar approach, we may show that $\rho_k = \phi \rho_{k-1}$, $k = 2, 3, \ldots,$ from which it follows that $\rho_k = \phi^k$, $k = 1, 2, \ldots$.

The mean, the variance, and autocorrelations for more complex schemes may be derived by similar, but more involved, methods. We encourage readers to test their understanding of the arguments by deriving the expressions for the MA(1) scheme in Exercise 6.15.

CHAPTER 7

Simple Linear Regression for Forecasting

Table of Contents

Even trained statisticians often fail to appreciate the extent to which statistics are vitiated by the unrecorded assumptions of their interpreters.... It is easy to prove that the wearing of tall hats and the carrying of umbrellas enlarges the chest, prolongs life, and confers comparative immunity from disease.... A university degree, a daily bath, the owning of thirty pairs of trousers, a knowledge of Wagner's music, a pew in church, anything, in short that implies more means and better nurture... can be statistically palmed off as a magic spell conferring all sorts of privileges.... The mathematician whose correlations would fill a Newton with admiration, may, in collecting and accepting data and drawing conclusions from them, fall into quite crude errors by just such popular oversights as I have been describing.

— George Bernard Shaw, 1906, The Doctor's Dilemma[1]

---

1 As abstracted in Stuart, A., Ord, J.K. and Arnold, S.F. (1999). *Kendall's Advanced Theory of Statistics, Volume 2A*. London: Arnold, p. 467.

Introduction

So far, we have looked at models that capture patterns within a single time series. A natural next step, in both forecasting and statistical modeling generally, is to look for relationships between the variable of interest and other factors, regardless of whether the data of interest are cross-sectional or defined over time. For example, when trying to predict a company's product sales, we expect such variables as the price of the product and the level of advertising expenditures to affect sales movements. These variables come to mind when we think of consumer choice, because consumers are usually price sensitive and advertising may be needed to bring the product to consumers' attention. Probing more deeply, we recognize that such variables are not absolutes, but must be judged relative to the pricing and advertising actions of the product's principal competitors. Ah, but here lies the rub! Information on our competitors' plans would be very valuable and often helps to explain fluctuations in sales with the benefit of hindsight. However, at the time we make our production and inventory decisions, the plans of our competitors are unknown; at best, we can hope to forecast those plans or to evaluate the impact of their different possible actions. This scenario is not unusual, and it contains the essential questions that plague any forecaster: *What do you know and when will you know it?* We will return to these key questions periodically.

Similar problems arise in cross-sectional studies. We may seek to evaluate an individual's potential for purchasing a particular product, such as a new automobile. We will have demographic information on that person, plus some financial data, but we cannot measure a host of other factors, such as the importance the person attaches to having a new vehicle, other interests that may compete for his or her funds, and information obtained from friends regarding that particular model.

We are now moving away from the purely extrapolative time series methods of the earlier chapters and into the realm of economic and market modeling. Our data may be cross-sectional or time indexed, or even both. The tools we develop in this and the next two chapters are commonly referred to as methods of *regression analysis*. Because our focus is on the development of quantitative models for economic activities, we also use the term *econometric modeling*.

We continue to denote the variable of interest by Y, but now refer to it as the *dependent variable* or the *output*. Our statistical model will then depend upon one or more *inputs*, or *predictors*, or *explanatory variables*[2] that are denoted by X, with subscripts if we have two or more such variables (e.g., X_1 and X_2). In this chapter, we follow the simpler path of assuming that only one such variable is important and we proceed to develop tools for that case before extending the ideas to multiple explanatory variables in Chapter 8. We urge the reader not to be overly impatient, but to think of the chapter as training for the more realistic problems to come.

In Section 7.1, we discuss the relationship between causality and correlation. Two variables may be correlated, and that information may be useful, but it does not imply causation. This discussion serves as a lead-in to Section 7.2, in which we specify a linear relationship between the variable of interest (Y) and the explanatory variable (X) and use the method of ordinary least squares to estimate this relationship; a case study on gasoline prices follows in Section 7.3. In order to determine whether an estimated relationship is useful, we first introduce the standard error and the coefficient of determination in Section 7.4. We then provide a systematic development of statistical inference for the regression model in Sections 7.5 and 7.6, including the use of transformations. In Sections 7.7 and

---

2 Many texts use the term *independent variable* to describe the X inputs. Because we employ the term "independent" in other, more critical contexts, we will not use it here.

7.8, we discuss forecasting by means of simple linear regression. Principles of regression modeling are left to Chapter 8.

7.1 Relationships between Variables: Correlation and Causation

The ideal basis for forecasting is a *causal model*. In such a scheme, we are able to identify all the key factors that determine future values of Y and to measure them in sufficient time to generate the forecasts. In practice, at least three problems arise:

- We may not be able to identify all the causal variables (e.g., try listing all the factors that affect gasoline prices).

- We may not be able to obtain information to measure these variables (e.g., competitors' plans).

- The measurements may not be available in time to make the forecasts (e.g., measurements on macroeconomic variables such as gross domestic product (*GDP*) are not available until several weeks or even months after the forecasting horizon of interest).

The availability and timing of measurements affect the type of forecast that we can make, as we now describe.

FORECASTING WITH A REGRESSION MODEL

An *ex ante*, or *unconditional*, forecast uses only the information that would have been available at the time the forecast was made (i.e., at the forecast origin).

An *ex post*, or *conditional*, forecast uses the actual values of the explanatory variables, even if these would not have been known at the time the forecast was made.

A *what-if* forecast uses assumed values of the explanatory variables to determine the potential outcomes of different policy alternatives or different possible futures.

For example, consider the effect upon sales of the difference in price between a supplier and its competition. An *ex post conditional* analysis would use actual price differentials to review forecasting performance over past data, an exercise that is useful for the determination of price sensitivity, but does not provide genuine forecasts. An *ex ante unconditional* analysis would either forecast the price differential and use that forecast in turn to forecast sales. Alternatively, the forecasting model could be based on sufficiently distant lagged values so that all the information is available to produce the forecasts. Finally, a *what-if* analysis would use the model (previously validated by *ex post* and *ex ante* analyses of historical data) to determine the implications of different price-setting policies in the light of possible competitive prices.

Trying to track down all the causal variables in a real economic system is probably a fool's errand, but it is vital that we measure the key factors. If the measurements are not available in time for *ex ante* forecasts, we must seek appropriate substitutes. For example, the variable of interest may be the local unemployment rate, but for short-term forecasting we might use the relative numbers of "Help Wanted" advertisements on the web to gauge the health of a local labor market. Note that, in this last step, we are moving away from a causal model to a model in which an *available* input variable is substituted for the causal input variable. Of course, the available input variable may reasonably be assumed to be correlated with the input variable of interest. The apparent association may be due only to a common dependence upon other variables, but the relationship may still provide useful forecasts. Nevertheless, we will do well to heed George Bernard Shaw's warning; that is, we must beware of interpreting correlation as causation and should recognize that apparent relationships are sometimes spurious.

7.1.1 What Is Regression Analysis?

With this background in mind, we now assume that we can identify a single output variable (Y) that is related to a single input variable (X). In the simplest possible case, the value of X may completely determine the value of Y. For example, consider Figure 7.1, which shows such a *mathematical relationship* between X and Y: A single value of X produces a single value of Y. The intercept, b_0, is the value of Y when $X = 0$, and the slope, b_1 denotes the increase in Y when X is increased by 1 unit. Thus, if $b_0 = 3$ and $b_1 = 1.5$, a value of $X = 4$ yields $Y = 3 + 1.5(4) = 9.0$. Such tidy relationships do not exist in the business world, so we must allow for uncertainty in the relationship between X and Y. The methodology for establishing these relationships is known as *regression analysis*.

Figure 7.1 The Terms of the Line $Y = b_0 + b_1X$

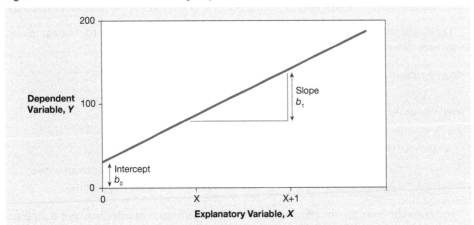

A regression line differs fundamentally from a mathematical relationship. We may observe one of many possible Y-values for a particular value of X, and the regression line reflects the *expected value of Y given X*. For a given observation, Y may be above or below our expectation. For example, in Figure 7.2 X denotes household size and Y represents monthly electricity usage (for this hypothetical data set).

The regression line indicates that the *average* household of size 4 consumes about 250 units of electricity; an individual household may consume more or less, depending on other factors such as house size, mode of heating, lifestyle, and so on. Also, it is worth noting that in this example the intercept value (the value of Y when $X = 0$) does not have any economic meaning: It does not make sense to ask about consumption for a household containing zero people. Regression lines typically have restricted ranges of application (here, $1 \leq X \leq 8$). Also in this example, non-integer values of X are not sensible, but it is still convenient to draw a straight line to represent the relationship between the expected value of Y and a given X.

In our example, the equation of the straight line is $Y = 30.0 + 5.60X$; the approach described in the next section is used to determine the slope and intercept.

Figure 7.2 Plot of Electricity Consumption Against Household Size with a Fitted Regression Line

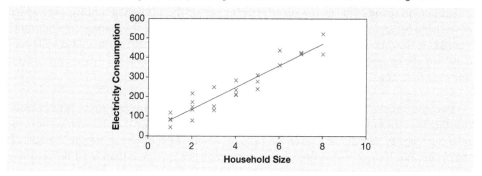

7.2 Fitting a Regression Line by Ordinary Least Squares (OLS)

After we have identified the variables of interest, we create a scatterplot, as in Figure 7.2, to determine whether the relationship between X and Y could reasonably be described by a straight line, at least over the region of interest.

■ Example 7.1: Sales versus advertising

If a company increases its advertising budget, it expects to see a higher level of sales. In any particular week, that may or may not happen, because sales will be affected by the weather, the state of the economy, and the actions of competitors. Nevertheless, we would *expect* to see an increase in sales. At the same time, there comes a point where further increases in advertising expenditures cease to have much effect. The overall relationship between expected sales and advertising may be like that shown in Figure 7.3.

Figure 7.3 Relationship Between Sales and Advertising

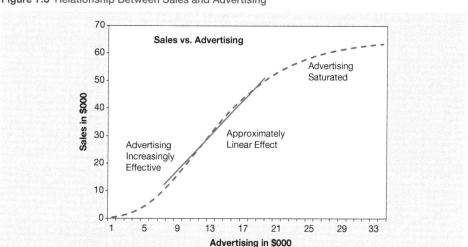

Now consider this figure from the perspective of a brand manager. On the one hand, if that person spends $8K or less on advertising, he or she is missing a range over which advertising becomes increasingly effective. On the other hand, if the manager spends more than $21K, the extra expenditures have limited impact. Accordingly, the manager will probably keep the budget in the range $8 \leq X \leq 21$, and the relationship is very close to a straight line over that range. ■

Two conclusions emerge from this example. First, it may be feasible to use a linear relationship over the range of interest, even when the true relationship is nonlinear; second, the relationship may be valid only over the range of X for which observations are available. If the brand manager estimated the relationship over $8 \leq X \leq 21$ and then used the resulting line to estimate sales at $X = 25$, he or she would be in for a rude shock! We now assume (for the moment) that a straight-line relationship is appropriate over the range of interest, and we seek to determine a (regression) line that best describes the expected relationship between Y and X. We formulate the relationship as

$$Y = b_0 + b_1 X + e = \text{Explainable pattern + Unexplained error.} \qquad (7.1)$$

The first two terms on the right-hand side of equation (7.1) show the extent to which Y can be linearly "explained" by X; the third term, e, known as the *error term*, represents the discrepancy between the observed value of Y and the corresponding Y value on the straight line. The errors are the *vertical* distances between the observed and fitted values. As is evident from the figure, we would like to choose values of the coefficients b_0 and b_1 so that the resulting line is a good representation of the relationship between Y and X. One approach would be to draw a freehand line, but this method is unreliable. An individual might draw different lines on different days, and two individuals might be quite unable to agree on whose line seemed better, as can be seen from the two lines in Figure 7.4. To resolve the argument, we must select an objective method of fitting so that, for a given set of data, everyone would arrive at the same result once the method had been agreed upon.

Figure 7.4 Two Possible Regression Lines Relating Y to X

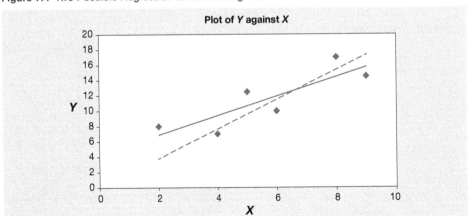

7.2.1 The Method of Ordinary Least Squares (OLS)

The technique most commonly used to estimate the regression line is the *Method of Ordinary Least Squares*, often abbreviated to OLS.[3] Once we have formulated the nature of the relationship, as in equation (7.1), we define the OLS estimates as those values of $\{b_0, b_1\}$ which minimize the *Sum of Square Errors* (SSE): Given n pairs of observed values (X_i, Y_i), we have

$$SSE = \sum_{i=1}^{n} (Observed - Fitted)^2 = \sum_{i=1}^{n} (Y_i - b_0 - b_1 X_i)^2 = \sum_{i=1}^{n} e_i^2. \tag{7.2}$$

ORDINARY LEAST SQUARES

The method of ordinary least squares determines the intercept and slope of the regression line by minimizing the sum of square errors (*SSE*).

We might compute the *SSE* for a range of values of the intercept and slope and search for the best values. Such an approach is illustrated in Figure 7.5, where we plot the *SSE* against b_0 and b_1. Given that we seek to minimize the *SSE*, inspection of that diagram suggests values in the range $2.5 < b_0 < 5.5$ and $1.0 < b_1 < 1.5$. A finer grid on the diagram would allow a more accurate determination of the best values. Such an approach is clearly tedious, but one of the nice features about the method of ordinary least squares is that we can determine exact computational formulas for the coefficients; the derivation is provided in Appendix 7A and the final formulas are presented next. Although the details of these calculations are relatively unimportant in the computer age, unless you are a programmer, details for our simple example are laid out in spreadsheet form in Table 7.1.

Figure 7.5 Minitab Plot of SSE against Different Intercept and Slope Parameters for Data in Table 7.1

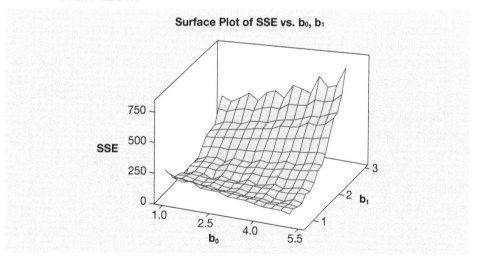

---

3 Other criteria could be — and are — applied, such as minimizing the sum of absolute errors, as defined in Section 2.7. However, the method of ordinary least squares is by far the most popular because of its numerical tractability. The method dates back to Carl Friedrich Gauss in the early nineteenth century. (For some historical insights, see the Wikipedia entry on Gauss at http://en. wikipedia.org/wiki/Carl_Friedrich_Gauss.) The method is labeled "ordinary" because there are a number of extensions, such as "generalized least squares," which we do not cover here.

Table 7.1 Spreadsheet for Regression Calculations Using Equation (7.5)

X	Y	$(X - \bar{X})$	$(X - \bar{X})^2$	$(Y - \bar{Y})$	$(X - \bar{X})(Y - \bar{Y})$	$(Y - \bar{Y})^2$
2	8	−3.67	13.44	−3.50	12.83	12.25
4	7	−1.67	2.78	−4.50	7.50	20.25
5	12.5	−0.67	0.44	1.00	−0.67	1.00
6	10	0.33	0.11	−1.50	−0.50	2.25
8	17	2.33	5.44	5.50	12.83	30.25
9	14.5	3.33	11.11	0.00	10.00	9.00
Sum	34	69	0.00	33.33	0.00	42.00	75.00
Mean	5.67	11.5	0.00	5.56	0.00	7.00	12.50
$b_0 = 4.36$ $b_1 = 1.26$						

Data: Example 7_2.xlsx. See Example 7.2 for details of calculations of intercept and slope.

The calculations may be summarized as follows; the summations are taken over all n observations. The sample means are

$$\bar{X} = \frac{\sum X_i}{n}, \quad \bar{Y} = \frac{\sum Y_i}{n}. \tag{7.3}$$

Now, denote the sum of squares for X by S_{XX} and the sum of cross products for X and Y by S_{XY}, defined respectively as

$$S_{XX} = \sum (X_i - \bar{X})^2 \quad \text{and} \quad S_{XY} = \sum (X_i - \bar{X})(Y_i - \bar{Y}). \tag{7.4}$$

OLS yields the intercept and slope as

$$b_0 = \bar{Y} - b_1\bar{X} \quad \text{and} \quad b_1 = \frac{S_{XY}}{S_{XX}}, \tag{7.5}$$

Thus, we have exact solutions and do not need to follow the search process suggested by Figure 7.5. Nevertheless, it is useful to keep the idea of a direct search in mind when models are more complex; indeed, that was the process we followed when fitting the state-space models in Chapter 5 and the ARIMA models in Chapter 6.

■ Example 7.2: Calculation of slope and intercept

From the spreadsheet given in Table 7.1, we see that

$$\bar{X} = 5.67, \ \bar{Y} = 11.50, \ S_{XX} = 33.33, \ \text{and} \ S_{XY} = 42.00,$$

and it follows that $b_1 = 42.00/33.33 = 1.26$ and $b_0 = 11.50 - (1.26)(5.67) = 4.36$.

(Note that the figures have been rounded to two decimal places, so you may get slightly different answers.)

We encourage the reader to work through the details of Table 7.1, if only this once, to aid understanding. Thereafter, we make use of one of the many statistical packages that are available for the calculation of regression lines.

We use Table 7.1 to determine the regression line for Y on X and calculate

$$\hat{Y} = 4.36 + 1.26X. \tag{7.6}$$

The "hat" notation is used to indicate that the line defined by expression (7.6) has been estimated by applying OLS to this data set. The equation refers to the fitted values of Y, not the observations. Note that the equation represents the fitted values of Y, given different values of X, and it is not appropriate to reverse the roles of X and Y. That is why we have included the "hat" only on the dependent variable. ■

Another way of thinking about this calculation is to return to Figure 7.3. The line is chosen to minimize the SSE (Sum of Square Errors), which is based upon the *vertical* distances between the observed and fitted Y values. Finally, leave the mathematics behind. What are you trying to forecast? Y! What are you using to make the forecast? X. Thus, equation (7.6) is the correct version to use.

■ Example 7.3: Baseball salaries

In 2003, a book appeared called *Moneyball: The Art of Winning an Unfair Game* (New York: W. W. Norton), written by Michael Lewis. In 2011 it was made into a film with Brad Pitt in the lead. In the book, Lewis describes how Billy Beane, general manager of the Oakland Athletics baseball team, used statistical methods to identify players who were undervalued. His teams had considerable success on the field despite having a very low budget for player salaries. The essence of Beane's approach was to identify those factors which were important to winning games but were often overlooked by other baseball managers. He then sought out players who could deliver those skills.

As a first step in such an analysis, we consider a simple regression for Y = player's salary (in thousands of dollars) on X = number of years in the major leagues.[4] The data are for the 1986 season, and in this example we use only the data relating to pitchers. The scatter-plot for the data appears in Figure 7.6.

Figure 7.6 Scatterplot of Baseball Players' Salaries Against the Number of Years Played in the Major Leagues

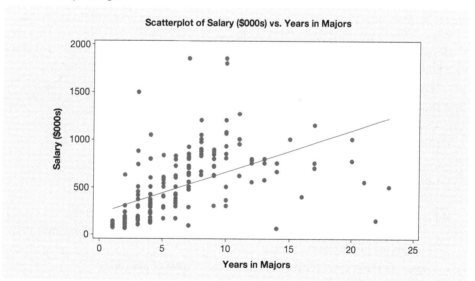

Data: Baseball.xlsx

---

4 The data are included in the file *Baseball.xlsx*, and we wish to acknowledge StatLib of the Department of Statistics at Carnegie Mellon University for allowing us access to these data. The data were originally compiled by Lorraine Denby as part of a project with the Graphics Section of the American Statistical Association.

The fitted regression line is of the form

$$Salary\ (\$000s) = 224 + 43.6 \times Years\ in\ Majors.$$

One might interpret the line as an average baseline salary of \$224K plus \$43.6K per year of service, keeping in mind that this is the expected value and that individual salaries vary considerably. Common sense suggests that players tend to become less valuable toward the end of their careers, and we can see from Figure 7.6 that a number of veteran players (say, with 12 or more years in the major leagues) have salaries well below the fitted values. Nevertheless, this simple model suggests that career length is an important determinant of salary. (We examine the model further at the end of the chapter, in Minicase 7.3.). ■

> **DISCUSSION QUESTION:** *How might you modify the analysis to allow for the lower salaries of veteran players?*

7.3 A Case Study on the Price of Gasoline

Fluctuations in gasoline prices have an impact on most sectors of the economy. Although the transportation industry is the first affected, any price increases will eventually work their way through the system to have an impact on the prices of most goods and services. At the same time, price increases in other sectors will have an effect on gasoline prices primarily by changing demand. In addition, decisions by the Organization of the Petroleum Exporting Countries (OPEC) and other world events will have an impact on supply. Our purpose in this section is to illustrate the model-building process by starting to develop a statistical model that can account for the fluctuations in retail gasoline prices. We will revisit the model from time to time and improve it as we develop our model building principles.

Where should we start? Everything seems to be related to everything else! However, recalling Principle 2.1, we start by trying to identify the key variables of interest and come up with the following (albeit incomplete) list of factors and corresponding time series:

- Price of unleaded gasoline to U.S. consumers (variable to be forecast).
- Producer price: price of crude oil
  - The major cost element in gas prices.
- Consumer prices
  - Overall price levels may affect gas prices.
- Consumer demand for gasoline
  - Higher demand leading to higher prices?
- Production, stocks and imports of crude oil
  - Higher availability may well lead to lower prices but may be a leading indicator of expected future prices.
- Consumer income: personal disposable income, total or per capita
  - Consumers with more income more likely to consume and drive.
- Level of economic activity: unemployment; retail sales; new starts in housing
  - More activity in the economy requires more driving.
- Leading indicator of economic activity: S&P 500 Index
  - Future higher levels of economic activity leads to higher prices now?

We also need to decide on the precise way to measure each variable — there are many alternative measures of consumer income and economic activity. Measures of these variables are all readily available from standard sources,[5] and monthly data for January 1996 through December 2015 are included in the file *Gas_prices_1.xlsx*.

DISCUSSION QUESTION: *What other variables might have an impact? How could they be measured effectively, and what possible sources of data might be available?*

7.3.1 Preliminary Data Analysis

Before we leap into any attempts at model building, we start out by developing a feel for the data. The first step is to take a look at a time plot of the data, as shown in Figure 7.7; prices are quoted in cents per U.S. gallon. Initially we choose to analyze only a part of the data: Observations are plotted through December 2008; January 2009 to December 2010 are used as a hold-out sample. A lot has happened to gas prices since 2008 and Minicase 7.1 explores some of these changes. More experienced automobile drivers will not need to be reminded of the wild fluctuations in gasoline prices over the years since 2008 though settling down towards the end of the time series in 2013!

Even the plot to 2008 is very revealing: Prices were reasonably steady over the first eight years of the period examined and then climbed before dropping sharply in the last six months of the period.

The next step is to think about the variables of interest and how they relate to gasoline prices. A full analysis should include an examination of each variable, using the methods of Chapter 2, plus checks for unusual observations and so on. In the interest of space, we do not report those details here, but encourage the reader to probe in greater depth. Instead, we move to the next phase and look at a matrix plot to relate gasoline prices to some of the explanatory variables. We have restricted the list to the more interesting items to make the plot more readable.

Figure 7.7 Time Plot of U.S. Gasoline Prices, in Cents per Gallon
(January 1996–December 2008)

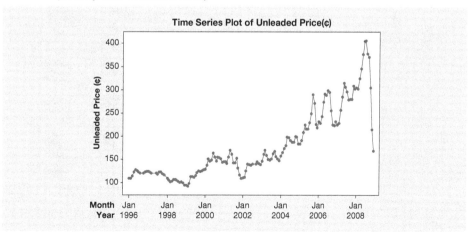

Data: Gas_Prices_1.xlsx; adapted from Minitab output.

---

5 These series are part of the library of Official Energy Statistics from the U.S. Government. They are located on the website of the Energy Information Administration: *www.eia.doe.gov* which also includes background information. The macro variables are to be found on: *https://fred.stlouisfed.org/*.

The variables plotted in Figure 7.8 are monthly average gasoline prices for the current month and the one-month lagged values for some of the explanatory variables (with unemployment omitted): we have selected various economic indicators as well as the price of the major component, crude oil. This ensures that the data would be available for forecasting at least one period ahead:

- Price of unleaded gasoline, in cents per U.S. gallon[6] (*"Unleaded"*)
- The price of crude oil, in dollars per barrel (*"L1_Crude_price"*)
- The SP500 Stock Index, end-of-month close (*"L1_SP500"*)
- Personal disposable income, in billions of current dollars (*"L1_PDI"*)
- Consumer price index for all urban consumers, indexed at 100 over 1982–1984, not seasonally adjusted (*"L1_CPI"*)
- Retail Sales: real retail sales in millions of $s, deflated by CPI (*"L1_RR_sales"*)
- Unemployment rate, not seasonally adjusted (*"L1_Unemp"*)
- Housing starts, seasonally adjusted annual rate (*"L1_Housing"*)
- Demand for gasoline, in thousands of barrels per day (*"L1_Demand"*).

The prefix *L1* is used to indicate that the variable is lagged by one month. The full data file contains additional variables.

We use the lagged values for two reasons. First, from an economic perspective, increases in production costs and other changes will take some time to pass on to consumers. Second, as forecasters, we need to make sure that the input data are available. The previous month's figures may become available relatively early in the current month, but the current month's value clearly could not be available in time for *forecasting* purposes.[7]

Figure 7.8 Matrix Plot: Gasoline Prices Against Price of Crude Oil, the S&P Index, Personal Disposable Income (current prices), the Consumer Price Index (CPI), Retail Sales (RR_sales), and Demand (all lagged one period)

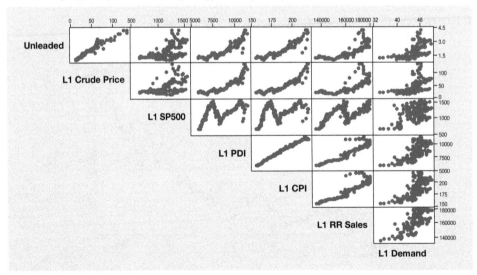

Data: Gas_Prices_1.xlsx; from the Minitab output.

---

6 In many countries, tax on gasoline prices is an important component and would have to be considered as a distinct explanatory variable. It is of limited importance in the US.

7 There are a number of different ways in which forecasts might be generated. We defer discussion of this topic until Sections 7.7 and 7.8.

The selective plots shown provide a number of insights:

- Gasoline prices appear to be most closely related to *L1_Crude_price*.
- There is a strong upward sloping relationship between gasoline prices, *PDI* and *CPI* and a somewhat weaker one between gasoline prices and real retail sales (*RR_sales*).
- The relationship with lagged *Demand* and *SP500* appears weak.
- There is an interrelationship between the different variables, perhaps because some trend together, e.g. *Crude Price* and *CPI*.

Finally, we may confirm our visual impressions by computing the correlations between each pair of variables. The full set of correlations is given in Table 7.2. Because correlations measure linear relationships, the values should accord with the intuition gained from the matrix plot, and they do.

Table 7.2 Correlations of Lagged Predictor Variables With Unleaded Price, and Intercorrelations (January 1996–December 2008)

Lagged	Unleaded	Lagged Crude Price	SP500	PDI	CPI	Retail Sales	Housing	Unemp
Crude_Price	0.971							
SP500	0.511	0.462						
PDI	0.890	0.875	0.561					
CPI	0.911	0.904	0.535	0.995				
RR_Sales	0.792	0.736	0.678	0.936	0.912			
Housing	−0.243	−0.348	−0.032	−0.085	−0.141	0.177		
Unemp	0.073	0.129	−0.592	0.197	0.212	0.039	0.006	
Demand	0.544	0.478	0.469	0.711	0.695	0.760	0.200	0.112

Data: Gas_prices_1.xlsx. P-value for testing whether the correlations differ from zero are excluded: most values are 'significant' at the 5 percent level.

On the basis of this preliminary analysis, we will focus our attention upon the relationship between gasoline prices and the lagged crude oil price. However, our preliminary investigations suffice to indicate that *L1_Crude_price* alone is unlikely to provide the whole story as both an economic analysis and the correlation matrix suggest other influences. In this chapter, we develop simple regression models, using this relationship as a running example. In Chapter 8, we return to the more general issue of developing a full model for gasoline prices that includes other variables.

Although the price of crude passes the test as the best single predictor in this case, we must recognize that forecasts based upon that model will be useful mainly in the short term. Longer term forecasts would need to capture more details about the infrastructure of the industry and proven reserves, as well as worldwide demand, which in turn affect the price of crude oil.

7.3.2 The Regression Model

Figure 7.9 shows an enlarged view of the plot for gasoline prices on *L1_Crude_price*, with the fitted regression line superimposed. The relationship appears to be linear, although there does seem to be more scatter at the upper end of the range. The fitted line has the equation

$$Unleaded_t = 68.8 + 2.71 \ L1\_Crude\_price_t. \tag{7.7}$$

W often drop subscripts when there is no ambiguity.

We may interpret equation (7.7) as stating that an increase of $1 in the price of a barrel of crude may be expected to increase the price at the pump next month by 2.7 cents per gallon. It is tempting to conclude that the intercept term represents overhead cost plus markup, but this conclusion is highly speculative, because we have no observations that correspond to X near zero. As previously noted in Section 7.1.1 such relationships should be viewed as valid only within the existing range of the explanatory variable, which is about $18 to $130 per barrel. Such a position is theoretically sound, but at times it is too restrictive. Commodity prices such as oil fluctuate dramatically as can be seen from the graph of the full data set to 2015. In addition, many economic aggregates grow over time. Thus, future values of variables such as $L1\_Crude\_price$ are likely to lie outside the "valid range" when it comes to making forecasts. The problem of *extrapolation* is not easily avoided, but we should always ask whether it makes sense to extend the relationship beyond the current range of X. Further, we must recognize that all forecasts are extrapolations, since they use the past to forecast the future. Consequently, we must assume that expressions like equation (7.7) hold both for future time periods *and* for X-values that may lie outside the current range of observations.[8] Because of the need to extrapolate, business forecasters should rightly maintain a certain degree of humility[9] about their craft: There are plenty of assumptions in their models that may well go wrong!

Figure 7.9 Plot of Unleaded Prices Against Lagged Crude Oil Prices (L1_Crude_price)

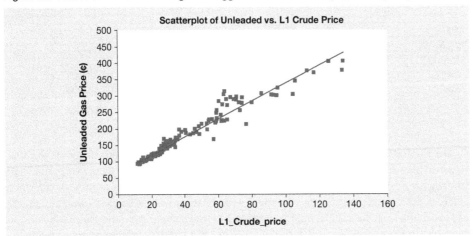

7.4 How Good Is the Fitted Line?

Once the line has been fitted, the next question is how effective is it as a basis for forecasting? In Section 7.2, we decided to fit the line by minimizing the sum of squares. That is, we

---

8 At times, we can improve matters somewhat by looking at changes rather than absolute levels (see Section 9.5.1). We should also consider whether to examine prices in real dollars (i.e., dollars adjusted for inflation) rather than current dollars; this question is explored in Minicase 7.1.

9 It is sometimes suggested that shrewd forecasters always ensure that the forecast horizon is longer than they expect to stay in their current job. That way, someone else takes the heat when the forecasts fail. Such people often run for political office.

started from the total sum of squares for Y, measured about its overall mean. We denote this sum by SST or S_{YY}:

$$SST = S_{YY} = \sum_{i=1}^{n} (Y_i - \bar{Y})^2. \tag{7.8}$$

This quantity is sometimes called the *variation in Y*. We then used OLS to choose the line in order to make the sum of the squares of the errors about the fitted line as small as possible. That sum, denoted SSE, is the variation in Y left unexplained by the model, written as

$$SSE = \sum_{i=1}^{n} (Y_i - \hat{Y}_i)^2. \tag{7.9}$$

In this equation, $\hat{Y}_i = b_0 + b_1 X_i$ denotes the fitted value for the ith observation and therefore, $Y_i - \hat{Y}_i$ estimates the error made in predicting the ith observation.

SSE represents the error sum of squares, where $Y_i - \hat{Y}_i$ is the error incurred in using the regression model to calculate the ith fitted value. Therefore, the smaller the value of SSE, the smaller is the average squared difference between the fitted and observed values. Further, we define the *sum of squares explained by the regression equation*, or the reduction in SST, as

$$SSR = SST - SSE.$$

It can be shown that

$$SSR = \sum_{i=1}^{n} (\hat{Y}_i - \bar{Y})^2.$$

These sums of squares provide a basis for examining the performance of the model, as we now explain.

7.4.1 The Standard Error of Estimate

In Section 2.4, we introduced the standard deviation as a measure of variability. The average of the squared deviations about the sample mean defined the variance, and the standard deviation is then the square root of the variance. Recall that we then defined the standardized score for an observation X, or Z-score, as

$$Z = \frac{(X - \bar{X})}{S},$$

where S is the standard deviation. Provided the distribution of X is approximately normal, we may then make probability statements such as

The probability that $|Z| > 2$ is approximately 0.046.

We now seek to make similar statements about the errors (deviations from the OLS line), and to do so we define the standard error of estimate, often just called the standard error.

THE STANDARD ERROR OF ESTIMATE

The *standard error of estimate*, denoted by S, is defined as

$$S = \frac{SSE}{\sqrt{n-2}}.$$

The standard error is a key measure of the accuracy of the model and is used in testing hypotheses and creating confidence intervals and prediction intervals.

We may define the (estimated) Z-score for the *ith* observation as

$$Z_i = \frac{Y_i - \hat{Y}_i}{S}$$

and make similar probability statements for these error terms. The assumptions necessary to justify this procedure are listed in Section 7.5.1.

The denominator in the definition of the standard error is $(n - 2)$ rather than the $(n - 1)$ that we used to define the sample variance in Section 2.4. The reason for this choice is that, from a sample of n observations or degrees of freedom (DF), we use 2 DF to specify the intercept and slope. ("A straight line is defined by two points.") Intuitively speaking, this leaves $(n - 2)$ observations from which to estimate the error variance. We say that S is based upon $(n - 2)$ degrees of freedom, or $(n - 2)$ DF. We have "lost" 2 DF in estimating the slope and intercept parameters. Another way to think about this situation is that when $n = 2$, we have a "perfect fit," so it is only with more than two observations that we can hope to estimate the residual uncertainty in the model. In the next chapter, we will use models with more parameters and lose more DF. From the computer output, we find that $S = 17.61$ (recall that the dependent variable is measured in cents).

Thus, unusual values would be about 35 cents (or two standard errors) away from the expected values. Analysis of the differences between observed and fitted values shows a period from April through July 2007 when prices were higher than expected. From August through December 2008, prices were lower than expected.

7.4.2 The Coefficient of Determination

A second measure of performance is defined as the proportion of variation accounted for by the regression line. This measure is known as the *coefficient of determination* and is denoted by R^2:

$$R^2 = \frac{SSR}{SST} = 1 - \frac{SSE}{SST}. \tag{7.10}$$

Because *SSR* and *SSE* are sums of squares, they cannot be negative. It then follows that $0 \le R^2 \le 1$.

Some of its properties are:

1. A value of $R^2 = 1$ means that the regression line fits perfectly ($SSE = 0$).

2. $R^2 = 0$ when $SSE = SST$, an equality that occurs only when every prediction $\hat{Y}_i = \bar{Y}$.

3. This condition in turn means that X is of no value in predicting Y.

4. For *simple linear regression only*, the square of the correlation (denoted by r in Section 2.5) between X and Y is equal to R^2.

5. R is known as the *coefficient of multiple correlation* and represents the correlation between Y and $\hat{Y}$. For simple regression with one explanatory variable, $R = |r|$.

In our gasoline price example, we find that $R^2 = 0.943$, or 94.3 percent. (Both formats are used and referred to as R^2, a notational quirk that needs to be remembered.) Accounting for over 90 percent of the variation seems pretty good, but how good is it? There are several parts to this question:

- Is the relationship meaningful, or could such results arise purely by chance?
- Are the assumptions underlying the model valid?

- Are the predictions from the model accurate enough to be useful?
- Are there other variables that could improve our ability to forecast Y?

R^2, THE COEFFICIENT OF DETERMINATION

R^2, the *coefficient of determination*, measures the proportion (percentage) of the variation in the dependent variable, Y, explained by the regression model.

We will defer discussion of the last three points, but even to examine the first one, we need a more formal framework than we have considered hitherto.

7.5 The Statistical Framework for Regression

In Section 7.2, we specified the fitted line in terms of an explainable (linear) pattern and an unexplained error, as given in equation (7.1). The coefficients for the fitted line were then determined with the use of OLS. No underlying theory was involved; we just applied a numerical recipe. However, in order to make statistical inferences, we must formulate an underlying statistical model, just as we did in Chapter 5 for the exponential smoothing methods developed in Chapters 3 and 4. Once the model is specified, we can use it to make probability statements about the estimated coefficients, the forecasts, and associated assessments of the accuracy of those forecasts by constructing prediction intervals. These statements are predicated on the supposition that the model is correctly and fully specified. Such an ideal state of affairs is unlikely, but we must take steps to ensure that the model we use conforms at least approximately to the assumptions we have made. Thus, statistical model building is a critical element of the forecasting process.

7.5.1 The Linear Model

The method of ordinary least squares is a pragmatic procedure for describing the relationship between variables, based upon the notion that putting a straight line through the cloud of observations provides a convenient numerical summary. We now go further and assume that there truly is an underlying linear relationship between X and Y. We recognize that different samples, or different pieces of a time series record, will lead to different OLS estimates for the slope and intercept. However, we postulate that there is a linear relationship relating the expected value of Y to X, even though individual observations will deviate from that straight line because of random errors. The structure of the assumed relationship between Y and X is illustrated in Figure 7.10.

In order to develop a statistical model and use it for data analysis, we must make a set of assumptions. We express these assumptions formally as follows:

Assumption R1: For given values of the explanatory variable X, the expected value of Y given X is written as $E(Y|X)$ and has the form

$$E(Y|X) = \beta_0 + \beta_1 X.$$

That is, $E(Y|X)$ shows how X affects Y and forms the explainable, or predictable, component of the model. Here, β_0 denotes the intercept and β_1 is the slope; the values of these parameters are unknown and must be estimated from the data. The remaining assumptions provide a framework for this estimation process.

Figure 7.10 Line Shows the Expected Value of *Y* for Each *X*
(The vertical distance from the line to the observed value denotes the error.)

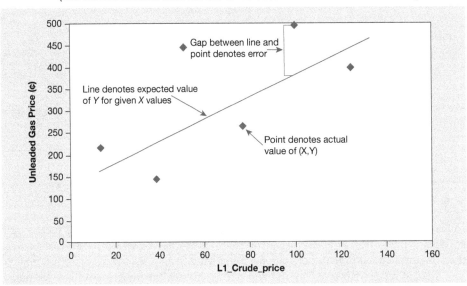

Assumption R2: The difference between an observed *Y* and its expected value is known as a *random error*, denoted by ε (epsilon). The random error represents the unexplained component of the model. Thus, the full model may be written as

$$Y = E(Y|X) + \varepsilon = \beta_0 + \beta_1 X + \varepsilon = (Expected\ value) + (Random\ error). \qquad (7.11)$$

This specification applies *before* the observations are recorded; hence, the error term is random and we can discuss its statistical properties. After the value of *Y* has been recorded for a particular value of *X*, the corresponding error may be estimated from the fitted model; this estimate is referred to as the *residual*, denoted by *e*.

Assumptions R1 and R2 constitute a *linear model*. The meaning of this term is not as obvious as would first appear. Intuitively, we would expect the adjective "linear" to indicate that the expected value of *Y* is a linear function of *X*. However, in the statistical literature, a linear model is a model that is linear *in its parameters*. We will refer to a model as being "linear in *X*" or "linear in the parameters" whenever there is any possibility of confusion. For the present, the models we examine are linear in both senses; when we consider transformations of *X* and *Y* in Section 7.6.3, the model remains linear in the parameters, but not in *X*.

The reason for specifying a formal model is to enable us to use the observed data to make *statistical inferences*. Given *n* observations $(X_1, Y_1), (X_2, Y_2),..., (X_n, Y_n)$, we wish to make probability statements concerning the values of the unknown parameters. To do so, we must make some assumptions about the nature of the corresponding random errors. These assumptions could be aggregated into a single statement, but we separate them out because we wish to check them separately later.

Assumption R3: The expected value of each error term is zero.

That is, there is no bias in the measurement process. For example, biases would arise if sales were systematically overreported by counting advance orders that later were cancelled.

Assumption R4: The errors for different observations are uncorrelated with other variables and with one another.

Thus, the errors should be uncorrelated with the explanatory variable or with other variables not included in the model. When we examine observations over time, this assumption implies no correlation between the error at time *t* and past errors. When correlation exists over time, the errors are said to be *autocorrelated.*

Assumption R5: The variance of the errors is constant.

That is, the error terms come from distributions with equal variances. This common variance is denoted by σ^2, and when the assumption is satisfied, we say that the error process is *homoscedastic.*[10] Otherwise, we say that it is *heteroscedastic.*

Assumption R6: The random errors are drawn from a normal distribution.

If we take assumptions R3-R6 together, we are making the claim that the random errors are independent and normally distributed with zero means and common variance. These four assumptions are exactly the same as those made for the state space models in Chapter 5 and the ARIMA models in Chapter 6. In the next few sections, we suppose these assumptions to be valid so that we can develop our statistical tools. However, in applications of regression analysis, each assumption must be carefully checked, and if any of them are not satisfied, corrective action must be taken. Some, of course, are more critical than others for effective forecasting. We return to the question of checking the assumptions in Chapter 8.

RANDOM ERRORS AND RESIDUALS

The *random error* represents the difference between the expected and observed values.

In a valid model, the random error for a particular observation is *completely unpredictable,* in that it is unrelated to either the explanatory variable(s) or the random errors in other observations. This is the basis of Assumption R4.

Because the intercept and slope are unknown, we must estimate the error from the fitted model; we refer to this estimate as a *residual.*

7.5.2 Parameter Estimates

In the course of our assumptions, we specified three unknown parameters: the intercept, the slope, and the error variance. The method of ordinary least squares may now be invoked in the context of our linear model. The estimates of the intercept and slope are precisely those given in equation (7.5); that is,

$$b_0 = \bar{Y} - b_1\bar{X} \quad \text{and} \quad b_1 = \frac{S_{XY}}{S_{XX}}. \tag{7.12}$$

Further, the estimate for the error variance is the square of the standard error of the estimate:
$$S^2 = SSE / (n - 2). \tag{7.13}$$

As noted earlier, the denominator in equation (7.13) reflects the loss of two *degrees of freedom* (DF), corresponding to the two parameters that must be estimated to define the regression line.

---

10 From Greek: homo = same and scedastos = scattered; similarly hetero = different.

To make the distinction clear between the unknown parameters and the sample quantities that are used to estimate them, we summarize the notation in the following table:

Term	Unknown parameter	Sample estimate
Intercept	β_0	b_0
Slope	β_1	b_1
Error variance	σ^2	S^2

So far in this section, we have introduced three new quantities and specified how to estimate them from sample data. We do not appear to have made much real progress! However, we have established a framework that will enable us to answer questions about the value of the proposed model, and it is to these questions that we now turn.

7.6 Testing the Slope

So far, using least squares, we have estimated the regression line's parameters. But these estimates are themselves random (because they are based on random data). This situation leads us back to the question raised in Section 7.4: Is the relationship that we have estimated meaningful, or could such results arise purely by chance? We are now in a position to address that question. First of all, we formulate the question in terms of two hypotheses[11]:

The *null hypothesis* is denoted by H_0 and states that the slope (β_1) in expression (7.11) is zero; that is, there is no linear relationship between X and Y.

The *alternative hypothesis* is denoted by H_A and states that the slope is not zero; that is, there is a linear relationship between X and Y.

These two hypotheses are mutually exclusive and exhaustive; that is, only one of them can be true, and exactly one of them must be true. Algebraically, we write these competing hypotheses as

$$H_0 : \beta_1 = 0 \text{ versus } H_A : \beta_1 \neq 0.$$

One-sided alternatives may also be used if there is prior information that the slope should have a particular sign. Thus, if we wish to test for a positive slope, we consider

$$H_0 : \beta_1 \leq 0 \text{ versus } H_A : \beta_1 > 0.$$

Likewise, for a negative slope we compare the hypotheses

$$H_0 : \beta_1 \geq 0 \text{ versus } H_A : \beta_1 < 0.$$

The null hypothesis always includes an equals sign, which specifies the benchmark value of the parameter to be used in the test.

We assume the null hypothesis to be true and then formulate a test based upon this assumption. We use the test statistic

$$t = b_1 / \text{SE}(b_1) \tag{7.14}$$

---

11 For a more detailed introduction to hypothesis testing, see Anderson *et al.* (2014, Chapter 9) or any other introductory statistics text.

where $SE(b_1)$ denotes the standard error of the sample slope. (Remember that our estimated regression line moves around, depending on the randomness in the data.) For simple regression, the algebraic form of the standard error is given in Appendix 7A, in equation (7A.7), but there is rarely any need to make direct use of this expression given available statistical software.

We refer to the observed value of t obtained from (7.14) as t_{obs}; this value is to be compared with the appropriate value[12] from Student's t-distribution with $(n-2)$ DF. If we set the significance level equal to α, we denote the critical value for the two-sided test as $t_{\alpha/2}(n-2)$ [and for a one-sided test by $t_{\alpha}(n-2)$ with the appropriate sign attached]. The classical decision rules for these tests are as follows:

Two sided: If $|t_{obs}| > t_{\alpha/2}(n-2)$, reject H_0; otherwise, do not reject H_0.

Positive slope: If $t_{obs} > t_{\alpha}(n-2)$, reject H_0; otherwise, do not reject H_0.

Negative slope: If $t_{obs} < -t_{\alpha}(n-2)$, reject H_0; otherwise, do not reject H_0.

Figure 7.11 shows the rejection region (shaded) for the t-distribution with DF = 15 and significance level $\alpha = 0.05$ for the two-tailed and positive-slope cases; the negative-slope case is just the mirror image of the positive-slope case.

Figure 7.11 The t-Distribution with DF=15: Shaded Areas Corresponding to $\alpha = 0.05$ for (A) A Two-Tailed Test and (B) A One-Tailed Test

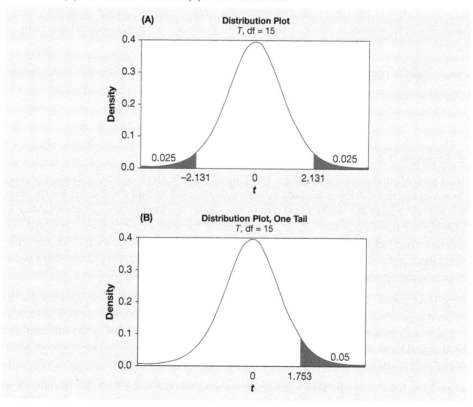

---

12 Most tests are now conducted with the use of *P*-values, which are described in Section 7.6.1. When needed, values of the percentage points of the *t*-distribution may be obtained with Excel or any statistical software (see Appendix 7B).

7.6.1 *P*-Values

An equivalent procedure and one that is more convenient for computer usage is to determine the *observed significance level*, denoted by *P*. The *P*-value denotes the probability, under H_0, of observing a value of the test statistic at least as extreme as that actually observed. Most statistical software now provides *P*-values as part of the standard output for regression analysis; see Anderson *et al.* (2014, Section 9.3) for further details. The decision rule for the two-tailed test is then written as

If $P = Prob[|t| > |t_{obs}|] < \alpha$, reject H_0; otherwise, do not reject H_0.

For a one-tailed test, the rules are also straightforward:

Upper tail: If $P = Prob[t > t_{obs}] < \alpha$ and the sign of the coefficient is compatible with H_A, reject H_0; otherwise, do not reject H_0.

Lower tail: If $P = Prob[t < t_{obs}] < \alpha$ and the sign of the coefficient is compatible with H_A, reject H_0; otherwise, do not reject H_0.

(Note that most computer programs provide only the *P*-value for the two-sided test. In such cases, when a one-sided test is used, the *P*-value in the output should be divided by 2 before making the comparison with α.)

Use of the *P*-value has two advantages; first, we can perform the test by inspecting this value without the need to enter a significance level into the program. Second, the rule just stated is "one size fits all," in that virtually all the tests we consider may be expressed in this format. In view of the importance of this result, we provide the output from both Excel, Minitab and R in the next example, by way of illustration. Other programs produce similar outputs.

HYPOTHESIS TESTING WITH *P*-VALUES

Tests based upon *P*-values are completely equivalent to those which use the same statistics with reference to tables of the *t*-distribution.

■ Example 7.4: A test of the slope

The Excel, Minitab, and R outputs for the simple example given earlier as Example 7.2 are shown in Figure 7.12. From the output, we see that $t_{obs} = 3.10$ and the *P*-value for the slope is 0.036. (The numbers in the Excel output have been rounded for ease of comparison; in addition, we never need so many decimal places in the final answer!) We set $\alpha = 0.05$ and conduct a two-tailed test. Because $P = 0.036 < \alpha = 0.05$, we reject H_0 and conclude that there is evidence in favor of a relationship between X and Y. In general, it is much easier to use *P*-values, and we shall usually do so without further comment. ■

Note 1: As may be seen from the computer output, it is also possible to set up a test for the intercept. Such tests, however, rarely provide any useful information, because the value $X = 0$ is usually well outside the range of applications. Further, the value of the intercept can be changed by shifting the origins of the X and Y measurements. Thus, an intercept test is useful *only* when we wish to test that the regression line goes through a prespecified origin.

Note 2: A $100(1 - \alpha)$ percent confidence interval for the slope may be established as $b_1 \pm t_{\alpha/2}(n - 2) \times SE(b_1)$. The t value in this expression must be obtained from the t-distribution. Thus for the data in this example, the 95 percent CI for the slope is $1.26 \pm (2.78) \times (0.4069) = [0.13, 2.39]$. Because the sample size is so small, we do not have an accurate assessment of how X affects Y, even though the test tells us that there appears to be a relationship.

Figure 7.12 Excel, Minitab, and R Outputs for Simple Example

(A) Excel Output

	A	B	C	D	E	F	G	H	I
1									
2	*Regression Statistics*								
3	Multiple R	0.84							
4	R Square	0.706							
5	Adjusted R Square	0.632							
6	Standard Error	2.349							
7	Observations	6							
8									
9									
10	ANOVA								
11						*Significance*			
12		*df*	*SS*	*MS*	*F*	*F*			
13	Regression	1	52.92	52.92	9.587	0.036			
14	Residual	4	22.08	5.52					
15	Total	5	75						
16									
17			*Standard*				*Lower*	*Upper*	
18		*Coefficients*	*Error*	*t Stat*	*P-value*		*95%*	*95%*	
19	Intercept	4.36	2.5	1.75	0.156		-2.57	11.29	
20	X	1.26	0.41	3.1	0.036		0.13	2.39	
21									
22									

(B) Minitab Output

Regressional Analysis: Y versus X

The regression equation is Y = 4.36 + 1.26X

Predictor	Coef	SE Coef	T	P
Constant	4.360	2.498	1.75	0.156
X	1.2600	0.4069	3.10	0.036

S = 2.34947   R-Sq = 70.6%   R-Sq(adj) = 63.2%

Analysis of Variance

Source	DF	SS	MS	P
Regression	1	52.920	9.59	0.036
Residual Error	4	22.080	5.520	
Total	5	75.000		

(C) R Output and Commands

The R code is as follows (see online Appendix C: *Forecasting in R: Tutorial and Examples*)

```
fit <- lm (Y ~ X)                          : #Create Regression Model
summary(fit) )$coefficients[,4]            : #View Summary Output
```

with output

```
Call:
lm(formula = Y ~ X)
Residuals:
    1        2       3       4       5       6
  1.12    -2.40    1.84   -1.92    2.56   -1.20
Coefficients:
            Estimate   Std. Error   t value   Pr(>|t|)
(Intercept)  4.3600     2.4975       1.746     0.1558
X            1.2600     0.4069       3.096     0.0364 *
---
signif. codes: 0 '***' 0.001 '**' 0.01 '*' 0.05 '.' 0.1 ' ' 1
Residual standard error: 2.349 on 4 degrees of freedom
Multiple R-squared: 0.7056,  Adjusted R-squared: 0.632
F-statistic: 9.587 on 1 and 4 DF, p-value: 0.3635
```

Note 3: For the time being, we ignore the *Analysis of Variance* (ANOVA) table. For simple regression, it provides no new information relative to the two-tailed t-test, as can be seen from the fact that the t-test and ANOVA test have the same *P*-values. We will discuss this further in Section 8.3.

> **NUMERICAL ACCURACY AND PRESENTATION OF RESULTS**
>
> Using a large number of decimal places to ensure numerical precision in the calculations is desirable. However, once the calculations are complete, we must decide how many decimal places to retain for presentation purposes.

■ Example 7.5: Test and confidence interval for gasoline prices: 1996–2008

The simple model of gasoline prices as it depends on the lagged price of crude is:

$$Y_t = \beta_0 + \beta_1 L1\_Crude\_price_t + \varepsilon_t.$$

The relevant estimates for the parameters are as follows:

Predictor	Coef	SE Coef	T	P
Constant	68.760	2.591	26.54	0.000
L1_Crude_price	2.7069	0.05367	50.44	0.000

S = 17.6121   R-Sq = 94.3%   R-Sq(adj) = 94.3%   N = 155 $\bar{Y}$ = 177.8

Note that the *P*-value is quoted to only three decimal places, so the output does not imply that *P* is exactly zero; rather, it means that $P < 0.0005$, which rounds down to 0.000 to three decimal places. Here we reproduce the computer output exactly as it appears. Elsewhere in the book for presentation purposes, we simplify the output to an appropriate number of significant figures. In this example, we expect a positive slope, so a one-sided upper-tail test is appropriate. Using $\alpha = 0.05$ (or any other plausible value!), we clearly reject H_0 and conclude that there is a strong positive relationship between the two variables, as expected. As noted earlier the intercept might conceivably be interpreted as the transport and marketing costs of gasoline, but this interpretation is a stretch when the smallest observed value of *L1_Crude_price* is so far from the origin.

To determine the 95 percent confidence interval for the slope, we first obtain the critical value from the *t*-distribution to get $t_{025}(153) = 1.975$, very close to the limiting value of 1.960 obtained from the normal distribution. The confidence interval for the slope is given by $2.7069 \pm (1.975) \times (0.05367) = [2.60, 2.81]$. That is, an increase of \$1 in the price of a barrel of crude oil produces an *expected* increase of 2.6 to 2.8 cents per gallon of gasoline at the pump. In this case, the large sample provides a clear idea of the relationship between *X* and *Y*. ■

7.6.2 Interpreting the Slope Coefficient

We have shown that when the slope coefficient is significant we can sensibly regard *X* as a suitable explanatory variable in our model. As before, suppose our linear model for the dependent variable is

$$Y = \beta_0 + \beta_1 X + \varepsilon.$$

That is, *X* has a linear impact on *Y*. Specifically, a unit change in *X* produces an impact of β_1 in *Y*. So, does the size of β_1 measure the importance of *X* in forecasting *Y*? No, because a change of units in either *Y* or *X* will affect the estimate. In our gasoline example, the price of unleaded is measured in cents. If we changed the units of measurement to dollars, this would affect β_1 and give a revised estimate of $\beta_1/100$ (and similarly with β_0). However, the tests in the previous section would again show the same P-value and R^2, and, of course, the same predictions, but this time in dollars.

> **DISCUSSION QUESTION:** *What is the impact on the standard error of a change in the units in which X is measured? In which Y is measured? Does R^2 change?*

An easily interpretable measure that eliminates the effects of the units used in measuring both X and Y is the *elasticity*, which measures the responsiveness of changes in Y to changes in X. For example, if the elasticity of the price of unleaded to the price of crude was 1, then a doubling of the price of crude would lead to a doubling of the expected price of unleaded at the pump.

ELASTICITY

The *elasticity* is defined as the proportionate change in Y relative to the proportionate change in X and is measured by

$$\frac{\Delta E(Y \mid X)}{E(Y \mid X)} \bigg/ \frac{\Delta X}{X}$$

$$\text{For the linear model} = b_1 \frac{X}{E(Y \mid X)} = \frac{b_1 X}{b_0 + b_1 X} \tag{7.15},$$

where ΔY is the change in Y and ΔX is the change in X.

In November 2008, the price of crude was \$57.31 per barrel of oil. From that dollar amount, together with the expected December price of unleaded, \$2.239, the elasticity of the price of unleaded to the price of crude is estimated to be

$$b_1 \frac{X}{E(Y \mid X)} = (2.707) \frac{57.31}{223.9} = 0.69.$$

A little mathematical manipulation shows that as X increases, the elasticity also increases, since $b_0 > 0$. This result seems counterintuitive and suggests that we should modify our analysis; accordingly, we now explore a logarithmic transformation, which leads us to a simpler, more intuitive elasticity.

7.6.3 Transformations

The increased fluctuations in the later part of the series, when the price of crude oil is higher, suggest that some kind of transformation is desirable. Two possibilities come to mind:

1. A logarithmic transformation, as in Chapters 3 and 4;

2. Conversion from current dollars to real dollars through division by a price index.

These two options are not mutually exclusive. We pursue the second option and their combination in Minicase 7.1 but now examine the first possibility, letting $\ln Y$ and $\ln X$ denote the logarithms of the two variables of interest. The output is as follows:

Predictor	Coef	SE Coef	T	P
Constant	2.8971	0.03771	76.83	0.000
ln_L1_Crude_price	0.62815	0.01056	59.46	0.000
S = 0.07631 R-Sq = 95.9% R-Sq(adj) = 95.8%				

Transforming back to the original units, we have

$$Unleaded = \exp(2.8971) \times (L1\_Crude\_price)^{0.62815}$$

Using the definition of elasticity given in Equation 7.15, the log-log model has a constant elasticity, given by the coefficient of the slope.[13] That is, the elasticity is $b_1 = 0.628$ for all values of X, implying that an increase of 1 percent in the price of crude leads to an increase of about 0.63 percent in the price at the pump. This value is somewhat lower than that obtained in the previous analysis. The key difference is that for the log transformed model, the elasticity is constant. But before we can make a reasoned choice between the two models, we need to develop diagnostic procedures, a task we defer to Section 8.5.

7.7 Forecasting Using Simple Linear Regression

Once we have established our statistical model, we are ready to use it for forecasting. With X as the explanatory variable in the model, we must first establish values of X for which the model is to be used to forecast future time periods. Similarly, when we forecast from a cross section to new members of the population, again we need to establish the relevant X values. For simplicity, we present the discussion in terms of a single future value, although multiple forecasts will often be needed. The value of X may arise in any of three ways:

  a. X is known ahead of time (e.g., the size of a sales force, or demographic details concerning a consumer).

  b. X is unknown but can still be forecast (e.g., gross domestic product).

  c. X is unknown, but we wish to make what-if forecasts (e.g., the effects of different advertising or pricing policies).

Consider the gasoline prices example that we have used throughout this chapter. We deliberately used X with a one-month lag so that the value of X would be available when we wish to make forecasts *one month ahead*. However, if we forecast gasoline prices two or more months ahead, we must either invoke case (b) and provide forecasts of the price of crude oil or construct new regression models that progressively use X lagged by two, three, or more months. For the present, we stay with forecasts one period ahead. The use of models with longer lags is explored in Section 7.7.4.

Finally, case (c) represents an important use of regression models whereby several alternative values of the input may be considered and the effects on Y examined. For example, we might specify different possible prices for a barrel of crude oil and examine the subsequent changes in price at the pump as a guide to decision making.

7.7.1 The Point Forecast

If we are given the value of the input for the next time period as X_{n+1} and we have estimated the regression line, the point forecast (F_{n+1}) is

$$F_{n+1} = b_0 + b_1 X_{n+1} \quad (7.16)$$

---

13 For the model, $\ln Y = b_0 + b_1 \ln X$, differentiating gives

$$\frac{\Delta Y}{Y} \bigg/ \frac{\Delta X}{X} = b_1$$

Many people and texts refer to equation (7.16) simply as *the* forecast. However, it is important to recognize that is the *point forecast* and that statistical models provide much more information and greater insights than just one number. In particular, the regression model may be used to generate prediction intervals, as we show in the next section.

Note: We have used $\hat{Y}$ to denote the fitted values in the regression line, as in equation (7.6), and now we use F_{n+1} to denote the forecast in equation (7.16); the two formulas are the same, so why the different notation? The reason is that the *fitted* values correspond to those observations which were used in the estimation process. By contrast, forecasts pertain to new observations that were not used to estimate the model parameters.

■ Example 7.6: Forecasting gasoline prices

The model for gasoline prices was fitted with the use of data from January 1996 through December 2008. We now generate one-step-ahead forecasts, using equation (7.16) for the 24 months from January 2009 to December 2010 so that, for example, the forecast for May 2009 uses the crude price for April 2009 and the calculation is as follows:

$$X_{n+1} = 49.65, \text{ and } F_{n+1} = 68.760 + 2.7069 \times 49.65 = 203.2$$

The first few point forecasts and the overall summary measures are given in Table 7.3. The various error measures are computed in accordance with the formulas in Section 2.7.

Table 7.3 Selected One-Step-Ahead Forecasts for Gasoline Prices, With Prediction Intervals and Overall (*24-Month*) Summary Measures (*January 2009–December 2010*)

Forecast Month	Actual Price	L1_Crude_price	Forecast	95% PI, Lower Limit	95% PI, Upper Limit
Jan-2009	178.8	41.71	180.1	145.2	215.0
Feb-2009	192.3	39.09	181.7	146.8	216.6
Mar-2009	195.9	47.97	174.6	139.7	209.5
Apr-2009	204.9	49.65	198.5	163.6	233.4
...	...	...	...	...	...
ME	1.9		RMSE	12.6	
MAE	9.2		MAPE	3.73%	

Data: Gas_prices_1.xlsx

The full set of forecast and actual values appears in Figure 7.13. The forecasts lagged the upturn in prices from March to June 2009 but otherwise did quite well. The *RMSE* over the hold-out period was 12.6, consistent with the standard error for the model ($S = 17.6$). ■

7.7.2 Prediction Intervals

Given that our forecasts are not going to be exact, what can we say about their likely accuracy? This is the critical question that arises in building a forecasting model. The random variation in the forecasts comes from three sources: the inherent variation of the process (i.e., the error term), the uncertainty caused by needing to estimate the unknown parameters, and misspecification of the model. For the time being, we assume that assumptions R3 through R6 are valid, so we focus only on the first two of these sources.

If we denote the future (unknown) value of the dependent variable by Y_{n+1} and the forecast of that value based upon the estimated regression line by F_{n+1} then the overall mean square error for the forecast in relation to the future value is

$$\text{var}(Y_{n+1} - F_{n+1}) = \sigma^2 \left[1 + \frac{1}{n} + \frac{(X_{n+1} - \bar{X})^2}{\sum_1^n (X_i - \bar{X})^2} \right]. \tag{7.17}$$

The details are given in Appendix 7A. Note that the term on the left-hand side of equation (7.17) is written as the variance rather than the mean square error because the forecast is unbiased when the linear model is correct. Given that we must estimate σ^2 by S, the estimated variance is

$$\widehat{\text{var}}(Y_{n+1} - F_{n+1}) = S^2 \left[1 + \frac{1}{n} + \frac{(X_{n+1} - \bar{X})^2}{\sum_1^n (X_i - \bar{X})^2} \right].$$

Finally, we define the standard error of the forecast as

$$SE(Y_{n+1} - F_{n+1}) = \sqrt{\widehat{\text{var}}(Y_{n+1} - F_{n+1})}.$$

Now, recall from Section 7.5 that assumptions R3-R6 combine to assert that the error terms follow a normal distribution with zero mean and variance σ^2. It can be shown that the forecast error then follows a normal distribution with variance given by equation (7.17). Because we must estimate σ by S, we replace the normal distribution by Student's t with the appropriate DF. Putting all this together, we arrive at the prediction interval:

$$F_{n+1} \pm t_{\alpha/2}(n - 2) \times SE(Y_{n+1} - F_{n+1}). \tag{7.18}$$

The $100(1 - \alpha)$ percent prediction interval is a probability statement. It says that the probability that a future observation will lie in the interval defined by equation (7.18) is $(1 - \alpha)$. For example, if we set $(1 - \alpha) = 0.95$, then, given that the price of crude (X) for April 2009 is 49.65, the prediction interval for May 2009 is $203.2 \pm 1.975 \times 17.67 = 203.2 \pm 34.9$. The detailed calculation is shown in the next example. We interpret this result as saying: With probability 0.95, the actual gasoline price will lie in the range from \$1.68 to \$2.38 per gallon when the previous month's crude price was \$49.65.

PREDICTION INTERVAL FOR THE FUTURE OBSERVATION, Y_{n+1}

The *prediction interval* for a forecast measures the range of likely outcomes for the unknown actual observation, for a specified probability and for a given X value.

■ Example 7.7: Calculation of a prediction interval

We continue our consideration of the forecasts for May 2009, begun in Example 7.6. The various numbers we need are

$$n = 155, X_{n+1} = 49.65, F_{n+1} = 203.2, S = 17.61, \bar{X} = 40.44, \sum (X_i - \bar{X})^2 = 361163.6$$

We now substitute into equation (7.16) to obtain

$$SE(Y_{n+1} - F_{n+1}) = S \left[1 + \frac{1}{n} + \frac{(X_{n+1} - \bar{X})^2}{\sum_1^n (X_i - \bar{X})^2} \right]^{1/2}$$

$$= 17.61 \left[1 + \frac{1}{155} + \frac{(49.65 - 40.44)^2}{361163.6} \right]^{1/2}$$

$$= 17.61[1 + 0.00645 + 0.000235]^{1/2}$$

$$= 17.67$$

Because the sample is large, the extra terms have a very slight effect on the SE. Returning to equation (7.18), we obtain the 95 percent prediction interval by using $t_{0.025}(153) = 1.975$:

$$203.2 \pm 1.975 \text{ x } 17.67 = 203.2 \pm 34.9 = [168.2, 238.1] \quad \blacksquare$$

In practice, the prediction intervals are evaluated with the use of standard software, which implements the analysis just described. The steps in Minitab, SPSS and R are summarized in Appendix 7C. Excel does not provide the intervals as a standard function.

The actual and one-step-ahead forecast values and the 95 percent lower and upper prediction interval limits for January 2009 through December 2010 are shown in Figure 7.13. All 24 actual values fall within the PI, which might be expected when one is using 95 percent prediction intervals. However, the intervals are of the order of ±35 cents, which is too wide to be very useful. In Chapter 8, we develop improved models that narrow the PIs.

Figure 7.13 Plot of Actual Values With One-Step-Ahead Forecasts and 95% Prediction Intervals for Price of Unleaded Gasoline (January 2009–December 2010)

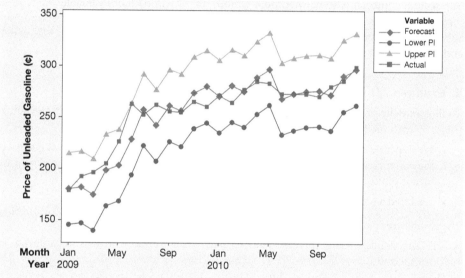

Data: Gas_prices_1.xlsx; adapted from Minitab output.

7.7.3 An Approximate Prediction Interval

The previous example suggests that when n is reasonably large, the term in square brackets in equation (7.17) is close to 1.0. This result is generally true, and as a quick calculation, the 95 percent prediction interval may be reasonably approximated by $F_{n+1} \pm 2S$. This approximation gives us an easy way of interpreting whether our predictions are useful. Effectively, the standard error S measures the predictive accuracy of our model. When $Y > 0$, as is true for most business variables, the comparison of S with $\bar{Y}$ is a rough measure of a model's accuracy. With the gasoline example

$$\frac{S}{\bar{Y}} = \frac{17.67}{177.8} = 0.099$$

which suggests a prediction interval of around 20 percent of the average price level. However, the increases in price in recent years mean that using the overall average is not as useful as relating S to the most recent data.

> **DISCUSSION QUESTION:** *Ideally, prediction intervals should be narrow. How would you decide whether a prediction interval was sufficiently narrow to be useful? How might you recognize that an interval was too narrow?*

7.7.4 Forecasting More than One Period Ahead

Suppose we were living at the end of December 2008 and wished to make forecasts further ahead than January 2009. There are two[14] possible approaches:

1. Generate forecasts for X and apply these to the original model.

2. Reformulate the model so that X is lagged as appropriate.

The first approach is more commonly applied, but suffers from the drawback that the uncertainty in X is not reflected in the prediction intervals for the forecasts. It has the advantage that different what-if paths for X can be formulated and compared using the same model. The second approach is somewhat more tedious, but it will be more valuable when good forecasts for X are unavailable. It has the advantage of providing accurate prediction intervals, especially when forecasts for X are inaccurate. However, the relationship between Y and X will be weaker for longer lags.

■ Example 7.8: Forecasting gasoline prices two periods ahead

To illustrate the preceding two points, we generated two-step-ahead forecasts for gasoline prices by each method:

- We generate one-step-ahead forecasts for the crude oil price series and then insert these forecasts into equation (7.7). The forecasts of crude prices are produced by means of the additive Holt-Winters model (see Section 4.4).

- We fitted a regression model for the crude price, lagged two periods.

The results are summarized in Table 7.4. The following points may be noted:

i. The standard error increases and R^2 falls when we move to two steps ahead, as expected.

ii. Forecast performance also falls off when we move to two steps ahead.

iii. The two sets of forecasts are broadly comparable in performance. (The second method does somewhat better here, but we should not read much into such a finding from just one example.)

iv. The prediction intervals for one step ahead and for two steps ahead with method 2 seem to provide the right level of *coverage*; that is, we would expect 95 percent of future observations to fall within the 95 percent prediction intervals. The prediction intervals for method 1 appear to be too narrow, with 4 out of 24 (16.7% instead of 5%) values lying outside the 95 percent limits for the two-step-ahead predictions.

The first two results are as expected and the third is reasonable. However, point (iv) is often overlooked in applications and can lead to overoptimistic conclusions about forecast accuracy, as assessed by the width of the prediction intervals if the uncertainty in forecasting X is not taken into account. ■

---

14 We may also use vector autoregressive (VAR) models, which we discuss in Section 10.5

Table 7.4 Summary Results for One-Step-Ahead and Two-Steps-Ahead Forecasts for Gasoline Prices

Statistic	One Step Ahead (from Table 7.3)	Two Steps Ahead	
		Lag-1 Model + Forecast	Lag-2 Model
Intercept		68.8	73.0
Slope		2.71	2.62
R²		94.3	88.6
S		17.6	25.0
ME	1.9	6.4	6.6
MAE	9.2	17.9	14.5
RMSE	12.6	23.5	20.2
MAPE	3.73%	8.64%	6.49%
MWPI	70	70	100
# outside PI	0/24	4/24	1/24

Data: Gas_prices_1.xlsx

[*Note:* MWPI = mean width of the prediction interval, the difference between the upper and lower limits in equation (7.18).]

7.8 Forecasting Using Leading Indicators

When we are developing a forecasting system, we must always ask, "What do we know and when do we know it?" An economic model would naturally relate current sales to the current value of the *gross domestic product* (GDP). However, the figure for current GDP will be available only well after the current quarter is over, so it is of limited value for *forecasting* sales over the next few weeks.

An alternative approach is to seek a suitable *leading indicator* — that is, a series produced early enough to be usable and reflective of likely future movements in sales. One such series is the Index of Consumer Sentiment, produced by the University of Michigan. A second major source of this kind of information is the Conference Board, which produces several such indexes: Consumer Confidence, CEO Confidence, U.S. Leading Indicators, and Help Wanted Advertising. (For further details, see *www.conference-board.org.*). Another natural leading indicator is the stock market, whether a general index like Dow Jones for the economy as a whole or, an industry-level index for a particular sector.

In each case, we are seeking, not a causal relationship, but rather an indicator that is published in timely fashion. Indeed, the causal pattern will often be of the form that some factor (say, Z) causes movements both in the leading indicator (LI) and in the variable of interest (Y). If Z is observed in time to make the forecast, clearly we will use it. If Z is unavailable, but LI is, we use LI. The forecasts may not be as effective as they would have been if Z were available, but LI will generally provide some improvements over forecasting with no knowledge of the inputs. We follow up on these ideas in Minicase 7.2 at the end of the chapter.

Summary

This chapter introduced the notion of modeling the relationship between two variables. After a discussion of the distinction between correlation and causation, we developed an estimation procedure by using the method of ordinary least squares and we went on to develop a statistical framework for the evaluation of regression models. We ended the chapter with a discussion of forecasting methods that provide both point and interval forecasts.

We do not discuss the relevant forecasting principles at this stage, but prefer to wait until the end of Chapter 8, when the full multiple regression model, which can include more input variables, has been developed.

Exercises

7.1   A soft-drink company monitored its television advertising over an eight-week period to evaluate the effect on sales (in millions of dollars) with respect to the number of 30-second spots aired in that week. Estimate the regression equation. The data are as follows:

Week	1	2	3	4	5	6	7	8
No. of spots	8	12	16	10	8	12	16	10
Sales	25	34	39	32	22	30	43	31

Data: Exercise_7_1.xlsx

a. Estimate the regression line for sales on spots.

b. Test whether the slope is significantly different from zero, using $\alpha = 0.10$.

c. Compute S and R^2 and interpret the results.

d. The company has reserved 20 spots for week 9. Forecast the sales and construct a 90 percent prediction interval.

e. Comment on the level of accuracy this analysis provides.

7.2   A company experiments with different price settings over a 12-week period. The weekly sales and revenue figures are shown in the following table:

Week	1	2	3	4	5	6	7	8	9	10	11	12
Price	6	8	10	6	8	10	6	8	10	6	8	10
Sales	28	30	28	30	24	22	34	26	20	36	32	26
Revenue	168	240	280	180	320	220	204	208	200	216	256	260

Data: Exercise_7_2.xlsx

a. Estimate the regression lines for sales on price and for revenues on price.

b. Test whether the slopes are significantly different from zero, using $\alpha = 0.05$.

c. Compute R^2 and interpret the results.

d. Why does the line for sales fit the data better than the line for revenues?

7.3   A linear time trend may be estimated by means of simple linear regression for Y on time.

a. Estimate the time trend for the sales data given in Exercise 7.1.

b. Compute S and R^2 and interpret the results.

    c. Test whether the slope is significantly different from zero, using $\alpha = 0.05$.

    d. Which model is more useful, the regression of sales on spots or that of sales on time? Give reasons for your answer.

7.4   Estimate a linear time trend for the Netflix data (*Netflix_2.xlsx*), using data for the period 2000Q1 to 2012Q4.

    a. Carry out a preliminary analysis of the data and interpret your results.

    b. Estimate the time trend.

    c. Test whether the slope is significantly different from zero, using $\alpha = 0.05$.

    d. Compute S and R^2 and interpret the results.

    e. Compute point forecasts for sales in each quarter of 2013 through 2015, and construct 95 percent prediction intervals.

    f. Comment upon your results.

7.5   Consider the data on rail safety previously examined in Exercise 2.2 (*Rail_safety.xlsx*).

    a. Carry out a preliminary analysis of the data and interpret your results.

    b. Estimate the regression line for injuries on train miles.

    c. Test whether the slope is significantly different from zero, using $\alpha = 0.05$.

    d. Compute S and R^2 and interpret the results.

    e. Compute a point forecast for the number of injuries, given an estimated level of train miles equal to 100. Construct a 95 percent prediction interval.

    f. Is the forecast likely to be useful? Comment upon your results.

7.6   Develop a simple linear regression model for the median price of a new home as a linear function of time, using the price data in *Housing_2.xlsx*, downloaded from FRED (*https://fred.stlouisfed.org/*) which shows monthly prices from January 1981 through December 2015. (Prices are quoted in dollars and include the price of the land.) Use the data through December 2012 to estimate the parameters and then predict monthly sales for 2013–2015. (Refer to Appendix 7C.) Generate 90 percent prediction intervals for your forecasts and compare your forecasts with the actual values. What other variables might be useful for forecasting purposes?

7.7   Develop a simple linear regression model for the number of new housing starts as a linear function of the mortgage rate, using the data on housing starts in *Housing_2.xlsx*, downloaded from FRED (*https://fred.stlouisfed.org/*). The data relate to monthly housing starts (in thousands, seasonally adjusted) and mortgage rates (end-of-month 30-year percentage rate) from January 1981 through December 2015. Using the data through December 2012, estimate the parameters and then predict monthly sales for 2013 through 2015, using the actual mortgage rates as inputs. Generate 90 percent prediction intervals for your forecasts and compare your forecasts with the actual values. Comment upon your results and then refit the model using the data through December 2015. Compare the two sets of parameters. Interpret the results.

7.8   Reanalyze the gasoline prices data, using the data in *Gas_prices_1.xlsx* after transforming both variables to logarithms, as in Section 7.6.3. Generate forecasts for the hold-out sample, and convert the point forecasts and prediction interval limits back to the original units. Compare your results with the model developed earlier that does not use any transformations. Which model would you recommend?

Minicases

Minicase 7.1 Gasoline Prices Revisited

Use the data in *Gas_prices_1.xlsx*, (or go to the U.S. Department of Energy website, *www.eia.doe.gov*, and download the data on the monthly series for retail gasoline prices and lagged crude oil prices.)

1. Using data up to December 2012, re-estimate the model, contrasting your results with those discussed in the text. Comment on your results.

2. Use the data for 2013–2015 as the hold-out sample to test the forecasting performance of your model.

3. Repeat the analysis, using the log transformed series, and compare your results.

4. Use the Consumer Price Index (*CPI*) to create real (constant-dollar) prices rather than observed prices for both variables. Repeat the analysis described in steps 1 and 2. Does this approach lead to improved forecasts? (This question is harder than it looks!) What if any economic arguments suggest using a constant-price model?

5. If you were to conduct the analysis using weekly data from the same source, how long a lag would you use?

6. In some countries, tax on fuel is a major component of the retail price of gasoline. How would you include the effects of changes in the tax?

Summarize your findings.

Minicase 7.2 Consumer Confidence and Unemployment

Measures of consumer confidence are readily available from sample surveys and often serve as useful leading indicators when data on causal macroeconomic variables are not yet available. Use the data in the spreadsheet *Unemp_conf_2.xlsx* for January 1981 to December 2012 to estimate the regression for U.S. unemployment on the University of Michigan Consumer Confidence Index. Unemployment is seasonally adjusted but the Index is not. Try the current month as the predictor variable and also try the Index of Consumer Confidence at lags one, two and three. Which model provides the best fit?

Generate forecasts for each month of 2013–2015 using each model. Compare the forecasting performance of each model, using the measures developed in Chapter 2. Summarize your findings.

Minicase 7.3 Baseball Salaries Revisited

Use the data in *Baseball.xlsx*. It is evident from Figure 7.6 that salaries start to level off or even decline once players' careers extend beyond 12 years or so. Also, the spread of salaries increases considerably as the number of years played increases. To allow for these features of the data,

1. Eliminate players with 12 or more years of experience from the data set and rerun the analysis. Compare your results with those reported in Example 7.3.

2. Transform the salaries by taking logarithms and determine whether the regression assumptions outlined in Section 7.5 seem to be better approximations to the transformed data.

3. Generate 95 percent prediction intervals for all players, and check to see how many actual salaries fall within those intervals.

What conclusion do you draw from eliminating the unusual observations?

References

Anderson, D. R., Sweeney, D. J., Williams, T. A., Camm, J. D. and Cochran, J. J. (2014), *Statistics for Business and Economics*, 12th ed. Mason, OH: Cengage Learning.

Kutner, M., Nachtsheim, C., Neter, J. and Li, W. (2005). *Applied Linear Statistical Models*, 5th ed. New York: McGraw-Hill. [Reissued as paperback in 2013]

Appendix 7A Derivation of Ordinary Least Squares Estimators[15]

In Section 7.2, we stated that the regression line relating the dependent variable Y to the explanatory variable X should be determined by the method of ordinary least squares. That is, we choose the intercept b_0 and the slope b_1 so as to minimize the quantity given in equation (7.2):

$$SSE = (Observed - Fitted)^2 = \sum_{i=1}^{n} (Y_i - b_0 - b_1 X_i)^2.$$

Here, SSE denotes the sum of squared errors, with the sum taken over all n observations. A feature of SSE is that it is quadratic in the coefficients $\{b_0, b_1\}$, so that obtaining the partial first derivatives with respect to these coefficients and setting the partial derivatives to zero yields a pair of linear equations. That is, if we set

$$\frac{\partial(SSE)}{\partial b_0} = 0 \text{ and } \frac{\partial(SSE)}{\partial b_1} = 0 \tag{7A.1}$$

we arrive at the equations

$$\sum_{i=1}^{n} (Y_i - b_0 - b_1 X_i) = 0,$$
$$\sum_{i=1}^{n} X_i(Y_i - b_0 - b_1 X_i) = 0. \tag{7A.2}$$

We now define the sample means of the two variables as

$$\bar{X} = \frac{\sum X_i}{n} \text{ and } \bar{Y} = \frac{\sum Y_i}{n} \tag{7A.3}$$

and the sums of squares and cross products as

$$S_{XX} = \sum (X_i - \bar{X})^2, \ S_{XY} = \sum (X_i - \bar{X})(Y_i - \bar{Y}), \text{ and } S_{YY} = \sum (Y_i - \bar{Y})^2. \tag{7A.4}$$

---

15 This appendix provides only a brief outline of the derivation. For a complete treatment, see a standard text on regression analysis, such as Kutner, Nachtsheim, Neter, and Li (2005).

We then simplify equation (7A.4), using equations (7A.2) and (7A.3), to arrive at

$$b_0 = \bar{Y} - b_1\bar{X} \text{ and } b_1 = \frac{S_{XY}}{S_{XX}}. \tag{7A.5}$$

The standard error is estimated as

$$S = \frac{SSE}{\sqrt{(n-2)}}. \tag{7A.6}$$

The estimated standard error of the slope is given by

$$SE(b_1) = \frac{S}{\sqrt{(S_{XX})}}. \tag{7A.7}$$

Further, it may be shown that the solution given in equation (7A.2) produces a minimum for SSE and that this minimum value is

$$SSE = S_{YY} - b_1^2 S_{XX}. \tag{7A.8}$$

Equation (7A.8) is just a restatement of the partition of the sum of squares given in Section 7.4 and may be rewritten as $SSE = (1 - R^2)S_{YY}$.

Extension to K explanatory variables

The discussion thus far relates to simple regression, with estimates given by two linear equations in two unknowns, as we can see in equation (7A.2). When we turn to multiple regression in the next chapter, we include K predictor variables in the model and SSE becomes

$$SSE = (Observed - Fitted)^2 = \sum_{i=1}^{n} (Y_i - b_0 - b_1X_{1i} - \dots - b_KX_{Ki})^2.$$

The partial first derivatives lead to the $(K + 1)$ linear equations

$$\sum_{i=1}^{n} (Y_i - b_0 - b_1X_{1i} - \dots - b_KX_{Ki}) = 0,$$
$$\sum_{i=1}^{n} X_{ji}(Y_i - b_0 - b_1X_{1i} - \dots - b_KX_{Ki}) = 0, \quad j = 1, 2, \dots, K. \tag{7A.9}$$

Equations (7A.9) reduce to equations (7A.2) when $K = 1$. However, for any value of K, we may still write

$$SSE = (1 - R^2)S_{YY}. \tag{7A.10}$$

That is, R^2 denotes the proportion of variance explained by the model. To emphasize, equations (7A.5) through (7A.8) apply only when $K = 1$, but equations (7A.9) and (7A. 10) apply for any value of K.

Prediction intervals

The uncertainty in the forecasts depends on the difference between the forecasted value (F_{n+1}) and the actual value of Y. If we knew the underlying model, a (future) new observation with the explanatory variable taking on the value X_{n+1} would be given by

$$Y_{n+1} = \beta_0 + \beta_1X_{n+1} + \varepsilon_{n+1}.$$

However, we had to estimate the intercept and slope, so the forecast is

$$F_{n+1} = b_0 + b_1 X_{n+1}.$$ (7A.11)

The difference between these two expressions is

$$Y_{n+1} - F_{n+1} = (\beta_0 + \beta_1 X_{n+1} + \varepsilon_{n+1}) - (b_0 + b_1 X_{n+1}) = \varepsilon_{n+1} - (b_0 - \beta_0) - (b_1 - \beta_1) X_{n+1}.$$

The first term in the rightmost expression represents the inherent variation in the process. Even if we knew the parameters of the model, so that the second and third terms were zero, this element would still be present. The second and third terms represent the estimation error; as the sample size increases, they will diminish in importance. Because the error term pertains to the new observation, whereas the estimates are based upon the original sample, it follows that the two terms are statistically independent when the errors are independent. Thus, the variance of the forecast error is

$$var(Y_{n+1} - F_{n+1}) = var(\varepsilon_{n+1}) + var\{(b_0 - \beta_0) + (b_1 - \beta_1) X_{n+1}\}.$$ (7A.12)

For simple linear regression, we may derive the variance of the fitted value from the variances for the intercept and slope. It can be shown that

$$var\{(b_0 - \beta_0) + (b_1 - \beta_1) X_{n+1}\} = \sigma^2 \left[\frac{1}{n} + \frac{(X_{n+1} - \bar{X})^2}{\sum (X_i - \bar{X})^2} \right].$$ (7A.13)

We substitute equation (7A.13) into equation (7A. 12) to arrive at the final expression for the *forecast variance in simple linear regression*:

$$var(Y_{n+1} - F_{n+1}) = \sigma^2 \left[1 + \frac{1}{n} + \frac{(X_{n+1} - \bar{X})^2}{\sum (X_i - \bar{X})^2} \right].$$ (7A.14)

Note that the further X_{n+1} is from the sample mean, $\bar{X}$ the larger the variance. Because the variance is unknown, we use the estimate given in equation (7A.6) to obtain

$$\widehat{var}(Y_{n+1} - F_{n+1}) = S^2 \left[1 + \frac{1}{n} + \frac{(X_{n+1} - \bar{X})^2}{\sum (X_i - \bar{X})^2} \right].$$

The second and third terms in equation (7A.14) decline as the sample size increases, but the first remains constant. Thus, in sufficiently large samples, we can approximate the forecast variance by S^2.

Appendix 7B Computing *P*-Values in Excel and R

In this appendix, we explain how to calculate *P*-values in Excel. Most statistical packages include similar procedures, and further details for select packages may be found on the book's website.

In all cases, begin by clicking on *fx* and select the *Statistical* functions. Continue using the appropriate choices for the *t* or *F* distributions as needed. The table specifies both the function to be used for each tail area and the required inputs. The final column provides numerical examples.

Distribution and Tail Area	Function	Items to Enter	Example
t: Lower tail	T.DIST	X = Observed t-value Deg. freedom = Degrees of freedom Cumulative = TRUE	X = –1.58 Deg. freedom = 20 P-value = 0.0649
t: Upper tail	T.DIST. RT	X = Observed t-value Deg. freedom = Degrees of freedom	X = 1.58 P-value = 0.0649
t: Two tails	T.DIST. 2T	X = Observed t-value Deg. freedom = Degrees of freedom	X = 1.58 Deg. freedom = 20 P-value = 0.1298
F: Upper tail	F.DIST. RT	X = Observed F-value Deg. freedom1 = Numerator degrees of freedom Deg. freedom2 = Denominator degrees of freedom	X = 2.50 Deg. freedom1 = 3 Deg. freedom2 = 25 P-value = 0.0826

The same values are provided in R as follows:

```
#Lower-Tail t-test p-value
pt(q = –1.58, df = 20, lower.tail = TRUE)
```

```
#Upper-Tail t-test p-value
pt(q = 1.58, df = 20, lower.tail = FALSE)
```

```
#Two-Tailed t-test p-value
2*pt(q = –1.58, df = 20, lower.tail = TRUE)
```

```
#Upper-Tail F-test p-value
pf(q = 2.5, df1 = 3, df2 = 25, lower.tail = FALSE)
```

Appendix 7C Computing Prediction Intervals

In practice, prediction intervals are evaluated with the use of standard software, which implements the analysis just described. The steps in Minitab, SPSS, and R are summarized in the box that follows. Excel does not provide the intervals as a standard function.

CALCULATION OF PREDICTION INTERVALS IN MINITAB

1. *Stat > Regression > Regression > Fit Regression Model*
2. Enter the Y (Response) and X (Predictor) variables.
   - e.g., *Unleaded* and *L1_Crude_price*.
3. Click OK to run the regression.
   - Enter a new column into the data matrix containing the X values to be used for forecasting, e.g., Future values of *L1_Crude_price*.
4. *Stat > Regression > Regression > Predict*
5. Specify the confidence level and type of interval (one or two sided) using *Options*.
6. Enter the name of the column with X values to be used for forecasting. These can alternatively be entered directly in the command.

Point predictions and confidence and prediction intervals are printed in the output with an option to store in the data matrix.

continues

CALCULATION OF PREDICTION INTERVALS IN SPSS

1. *Analyze > Regression > Linear*
2. Enter the *Y* (Dependent) and *X* (Independent) variables.
   - e.g., *Unleaded* and *L1_Crude_price*.
3. Click on *Save*.
4. Check *Predicted Values–Unstandardized* and *Prediction Intervals–Individual*.
   - e.g., *X* should include the out-of-sample data while *Y* should only include the observations to be used in estimating the model. The regression model is fitted on the in-sample data.
5. Specify the confidence level.

The point predictions (for *Y*, *Unleaded*) and the lower and upper prediction interval limits are saved in the data matrix.

CALCULATION OF PREDICTION INTERVALS IN R

1. Fit the regression model.
   - #Run the Regression
     fit < – lm(*Y* ~ *X*)
     fit < – lm(*Unleaded* ~ *L1_Crude_price*)
2. Store the future values of *X* in a data frame, with the name of the variables in that data frame identical to those used in the regression model.
   - #Extract Values of future *X*, *L1_Crude_price*
     e.g., *L1_Crude__price_future* < – data.frame(*L1_Crude_price* = data$*L1_Crude_price*[157:160])
3. Use the predict function, adding to its argument: (i) the name of the data frame containing the new data, (ii) interval = "prediction", and (iii) level = "0.95".
   - #Prediction Intervals
     fit.PI <- predict(fit, newdata =*X*, interval = "prediction", level = 0.95)

CHAPTER 8

Multiple Regression for Time Series

*Topics marked with an * are advanced and may be omitted for more introductory courses.*

Table of Contents

Why have you included so many variables in your regression model?

— Anonymous Statistician

Why have you included so few variables in your regression model?

— Anonymous Economist

Introduction

One of the key restrictions we faced in Chapter 7 was the inability to consider more than one explanatory variable at a time. Yet both the discussion there and basic common sense indicate that events in the business world are typically affected by multiple inputs. We may not be able to measure all of them, but we do need to identify the main factors and incorporate them into our forecasting framework. A first step toward identifying an appropriate set of variables is to consider any theoretical models of the product market. Basic economics of consumer (or business) behavior can suggest quite a catalog of possibly explanatory driving forces. The next step is to examine plots of the data, which we do in Section 8.1, although we need to proceed with caution because multiple dependencies in the data may make interpretations complex. Then, in Section 8.2, we proceed to formulate a statistical model that incorporates multiple inputs and to interpret the coefficients in that model. Estimation of the parameters follows the method of ordinary least squares developed in Section 7.2 and is extended to cover multiple regression in Section 8.2.1.

Once we have developed a model, we need to know whether it is useful. For simple linear regression, the answer to this question was straightforward. We checked to see whether or not there was a statistically meaningful relationship between X and Y, and that completed the analysis, as in Section 7.6. The question now is more complex. For example, sales of a product may depend upon both advertising expenditures and price. Either variable alone may provide only a modest description of what is going on, whereas the two taken together may give a much better level of explanation. Conversely, a model for national retail sales that includes both consumer expenditures and consumer incomes may be only marginally better than a model that includes only one of them. The reason for this apparent anomaly is that if X_1 and X_2 are highly correlated and X_1 is already in the model, X_2 will not bring much, if any, new information to the table. To resolve such questions, we need to proceed in two steps:

1. We ask, "Is the overall model useful?" If the answer is NO, we go back to the drawing board.

2. If the answer is YES, we check whether individual variables in the model are useful and the model makes sense for forecasting purposes.

These two steps are explored in Sections 8.3 and 8.4. As we explained in Section 7.5, our analysis is based upon a set of standard assumptions. In Section 8.5, we briefly revisit those assumptions and present graphical procedures to determine whether the assumptions are reasonable. Taking action to deal with failures of the assumptions is a more difficult step, which we defer to Chapter 9.

Once the model has been shown to be effective and the assumptions appear to be reasonable, we are in a position to generate forecasts. Point forecasts and prediction intervals are considered in Section 8.6. Finally, in Section 8.7, we consider some of the key principles that underlie the development of multiple regression models.

At the end of the chapter, we offer four minicases. Rather than work through "prepackaged" problem sets, these examples provide a more realistic approach to model building using multiple regression methods. The same minicases may be revisited at the end of Chapter 9, to make use of the more advanced skills developed in that chapter.

8.1 Graphical Analysis and Preliminary Model Development

We return to the study of gasoline prices, initially examined in Section 7.3 (see *Gas_prices_1.xlsx*). The matrix plot we considered there is reproduced as Figure 8.1 here for convenience and covers the period January 1996 to December 2008. The variables in the plot (unemployment has been excluded) are as follows:

- Price of unleaded gasoline, in cents per U.S. gallon (*"Unleaded"*) with potential explanatory variables:
- The price of crude oil, in dollars per barrel (*"L1_Crude_price"*)
- The SP500 Stock Index, end-of-month close (*"L1_SP500"*).
- Personal disposable income, in billions of current dollars (*"L1_PDI"*)
- Consumer price index for all urban consumers, indexed at 100 over 1982–1984, not seasonally adjusted (*"L1_CPI"*)
- Retail Sales: real retail sales in millions of $s, deflated by CPI (*"L1_RR_sales"*)
- Unemployment rate, not seasonally adjusted (*"L1_Unemp"*)
- Housing starts, seasonally adjusted annual rate (*"L1_Housing"*)
- Demand for gasoline, in thousands of barrels per day (*"L1_Demand"*).

Figure 8.1 Matrix Plot: Gasoline Prices Against Price of Crude Oil, the S&P Index, Personal Disposable Income (current prices), the Consumer Price Index (CPI), Retail Sales (RR_sales), and Demand (all lagged one period)

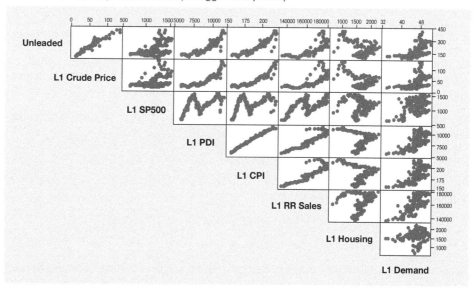

Data: Gas_Prices_1.xlsx; adapted from the Minitab output.

Examination of the plot had already revealed that the strongest linear relationship for unleaded gas price appeared to be the lagged value of the price of crude oil. However, we also see a somewhat upward-sloping relationship between price, lagged disposable income, possibly due to the effect of inflation (*CPI*) on both series. The general level of economic activity is reflected in a downward-sloping relationship with unemployment (not shown) and an upward-sloping relationship with the S&P500 Index and real retail sales. None of these last three relationships appears to be nearly as strong as that with *L1_Crude_price* (the lagged crude price); but they all make economic sense and might improve our overall ability to forecast gas prices. Also, as we noted in Table 7.2, all their correlations with gas prices are significantly different from zero, so they may add value to the model.

With this example as background, we now examine the specification of the multiple regression model.

8.2 The Multiple Regression Model

The multiple regression model is a direct extension of the simple linear regression model specified in Section 7.5. Note that we now move directly to the specification of the underlying model, having already motivated the basic ideas in Chapter 7. We consider K explanatory variables $X_1, X_2, ..., X_K$ and assume that the dependent variable Y is linearly related to them through the following model:

$$Y = \beta_0 + \beta_1 X_1 + \beta_2 X_2 + \cdots + \beta_K X_K + \varepsilon. \tag{8.1}$$

The coefficients in equation (8.1) may be interpreted as follows:

β_0 denotes the intercept, which is the *expected* value of Y when all the $\{X_j\}$ are zero, in which case the equation reduces to $Y = \beta_0$. However, this interpretation only holds *if* the model is meant to apply in such a situation.

β_j denotes the slope for X_j: When X_j increases by one unit *and all the other Xs are kept fixed*, the *expected* value of Y increases by β_j units.

Beyond the extended form of the expected value that now includes all K variables (the explained component of the model), the underlying assumptions are the same as for simple regression presented in Section 7.5.1. That is, we need only extend assumption R1 appropriately.

Assumption R1: For given values of the explanatory variables, $X = (X_1, ..., X_K)$ the expected value of Y is written as $E(Y|X)$ and has the form

$$E(Y|X) = \beta_0 + \beta_1 X_1 + \beta_2 X_2 + \cdots + \beta_K X_K.$$

Assumption R2: The difference between an observed Y and its expectation is a random error, denoted by ε. The complete model is

$$Y = E(Y|X) + \varepsilon = [Expected\ value] + [Random\ error]. \tag{8.2}$$

Assumption R3: The errors have zero means.

Assumption R4: The errors for different observations are uncorrelated with one another and with other explanatory variables.

Assumption R5: The error terms come from distributions with equal variances.

Assumption R6: The errors are drawn from a normal distribution.

As in Section 7.5, if we take assumptions R3-R6 together, we are making the claim that the random errors are independent and normally distributed with zero means and equal variances.

8.2.1 The Method of Ordinary Least Squares (OLS)

The method of ordinary least squares (OLS) may be used to estimate the unknown parameters. As with simple linear regression, we choose the sample coefficients, now $\{b_0, b_1, \dots, b_K\}$ to minimize the sum of squared errors, SSE. That is, we choose $\{b_j\}$ to minimize

$$SSE = \sum_{i=1}^{n} e_i^2 = \sum_{i=1}^{n} (Observed - Fitted)^2$$
$$= \sum_{i=1}^{n} (Y_i - b_0 - b_1 X_{1i} - b_2 X_{2i} - \dots - b_K X_{Ki})^2. \tag{8.3}$$

The technical details were summarized in Appendix 7A, and we will not consider the computational issues further.[1] After we have determined the best fitting model, we use the estimated coefficients to compute the *(least squares) residuals*, defined as

$$e_i = Y_i - b_0 - b_1 X_{1i} - b_2 X_{2i} - \dots - b_K X_{Ki}. \tag{8.4}$$

The residuals form the basis of many of the tests and diagnostic checks that we employ to validate the model, as we show in later sections.

■ **Example 8.1: Multiple regression model for unleaded gasoline prices**
   (Gas_prices_1.xlsx)

We consider a model driven by the lagged crude price, two economic indicators (Unemployment and Real Retail Sales) and an expectations indicator of future economic activity (S&P 500 Index). We have also considered the compound indicator, Personal disposable income in current prices, which includes both a general price effect and real economic activity. In the previous edition of the book this was used as an alternative to Real Retail Sales; the differences are explored in exercise 8.3. We employ the observations for January 1996–December 2008 as the estimation sample, as before. The OLS solution is

$$Unleaded = -29.0 + 2.4075\ L1\_Crude\_price$$
$$- 0.0426\ L1\_SP500 + 0.001430\ L1\_RR\_sales - 14.27\ L1\_Unemp.$$

Examination of the coefficients indicates that an increase of $1 in the price of a barrel of crude may be expected to increase the price at the pump by about 2.4 cents per gallon, somewhat lower than the figure we got with simple regression. Likewise, an increase in real retail sales (*RR_sales*) produces an increase in the expected price, whereas an increase in unemployment (*Unemp*) reduces the expected gas price. These coefficients have the signs we would expect. The coefficient for the S&P Index is also negative; initially, we might have expected an increase in the S&P to signal increased economic activity and thus exert upward pressure on gas prices. However, the issue of timing is important, and the negative sign could reflect the impact of good news in the crude oil markets, lowering pump prices and boosting the overall economy. Alternatively, the observed nonzero coefficient might have arisen due to chance alone, a topic we pick up in Section 8.4. ■

No matter how good the statistical fit, the forecaster should always check the face validity of the proposed forecasting model. By "face validity" we mean that the model's interpretation conforms to our and other experts' understanding of the product market.[2] If the

---

1 Standard texts on regression analysis provide the necessary details; see, for example, Kutner et al. (2005, pp. 15–20 and 222–227).

2 Toward that end, imagine standing in front of your boss in his or her office. Can you give a plausible justification of the model and all the coefficients? If not, develop a different model!

model passes the face-validity test, we go ahead and check to see whether it makes sense statistically.

8.3 Testing the Overall Model

We specify the null hypothesis as the claim that the overall model is of no value or, more explicitly, that none of the explanatory variables affects the expected value. Formally, this statement is written as

$$H_0 : \beta_1 = \beta_2 = \ldots = \beta_K = 0.$$

When the null hypothesis is true, none of the variables in the model contribute to explaining the variation in Y. The alternative hypothesis, H_A, states that the overall model *is* of value, in that at least one of the explanatory variables has an effect:

$$H_A : \text{Not all } \beta_1 = \beta_2 = \ldots = \beta_K = 0.$$

That is, there is some statistical relationship between Y and at least one of the Xs. If we fail to reject H_0, we conclude that the overall model is without value and we need to start over. If we reject H_0, we may still wish to eliminate those variables which do not appear to contribute, so as to arrive at a more parsimonious model.

When the model is based upon sound theoretical considerations, it makes sense to retain all the variables in it, even if some are not statistically significant, so long as the parameter estimates make sense. This is typically true in econometric modeling. By contrast, if we optimistically include variables on a "see if it flies" basis, we will usually prefer to prune the model to the smaller number of statistically significant and interpretable variables. These are critical issues in building a useful forecasting model and *should not* be resolved by statistical significance testing alone.

8.3.1 The *F*-test for Multiple Variables

The F-test is based upon partitioning the total sum of squares and is known as the *Analysis of Variance*, often referred to as ANOVA. The total sum of squares and the sums of squares resulting from the partition are as follows:

Total sum of squares: $\quad SST = S_{YY} = \sum_{1}^{n} (Y_i - \bar{Y})^2$

Sum of squared errors: $\quad SSE = \sum_{1}^{n} (Y_i - \hat{Y}_i)^2$

Sum of squares explained by the regression model: $\quad SSR = \sum_{1}^{n} (\hat{Y}_i - \bar{Y})^2$

As was true in the case of simple regression, it can be shown that

$$SST = SSR + SSE. \tag{8.5}$$

The ANOVA test is usually summarized in tabular form, and the general framework is presented in Table 8.1. Note that

- The first column describes the partition into the two sources of variation: the sums of squares explained by the regression model and the sum of squared errors.
- The second column gives the number of degrees of freedom (DF) associated with each of the sums of squares; the total DF is $(n - 1)$, because we always start out with a constant term in the model.

- The third column provides the numerical values of the sums of squares.
- Column four gives the mean squares, defined as [sum of squares/DF] for each source: MSR and MSE, respectively.
- Column five yields the test statistic $F = MSR/MSE$.

The reason for introducing the new term *Mean Square Error* is that, when the null hypothesis is true, both MSR and MSE have expected values equal to the error variance, σ^2. Thus, the test statistic[3] $F = MSR/MSE$ should have a value in the neighborhood of 1.0, if the null hypothesis is appropriate. When the regression model is useful, the amount of variation explained by the model will increase, so MSR will increase relative to MSE and F will increase. Thus, we reject H_0 for sufficiently large values of F.

We refer to the observed value of F generated from this table as F_{obs}. The decision rule becomes

$$\text{Reject } H_0 \text{ if } F_{obs} > F_\alpha(K, n - K - 1); \text{ otherwise do not reject } H_0.$$

Table 8.1 General Form of the ANOVA Table

Source	DF	Sums of Squares	Mean Squares	F
Regression	K	SSR	$MSR = SSR/K$	MSR/MSE
Residual error	$n - K - 1$	SSE	$MSE = SSE/(n - K - 1)$	
Total	$n - 1$	SST		

The critical value for F depends upon the number of degrees of freedom for both SSR (in the numerator, DF = ν_1) and the SSE (in the denominator, DF = ν_2).[4]

In keeping with our previous discussions, we use the P-value with the following decision rule:

$$\text{Reject } H_0 \text{ if } P < \alpha; \text{ otherwise do not reject } H_0.$$

Should it prove necessary to compute the P-value for some observed value of the F statistic, we follow the procedure outlined in Appendix 7A.2.

■ Example 8.2: ANOVA for unleaded gas prices *(Gas_prices_1.xlsx)*

The ANOVA table for the gas prices model given in Example 8.1 with $K = 4$ is as follows (consistent with our usual convention, we specify $\alpha = 0.05$):

Source	DF	SS	MS	F	P
Regression	4	804090	201022	1278.7	0.000
Residual error	150	32530	217		
Total	154	836620			

Because $P < 0.05$, we reject H_0. Recall that a P-value of 0.000 does not mean zero; rather, it signifies that $P < 0.0005$ and the result is rounded down. We conclude that there is strong evidence that the overall model is useful as an explanation of the price of unleaded gasoline. The next step is to determine the contribution made by each of the variables. ■

---

3 The method of analysis of variance was first derived by Sir Ronald Fisher, the father of modern inferential statistics. The ratio was labeled F in his honor.

4 Critical values can be obtained through the Excel function F.INV.RT(α,df1,df2).

The relationship between F and R^2 There is a simple relationship between F and R^2. It can be shown that

$$F = \frac{(n - K - 1)R^2}{K(1 - R^2)}. \qquad (8.6)$$

The details are left to Exercise 8.11. From inspection of equation (8.6), it is evident that an increase in R^2 leads to an increase in F, the numerator increasing while the denominator decreases, so the ANOVA test is completely equivalent to a test based upon the coefficient of determination. Either from the ANOVA table or directly from the computer output, we find that, for Example 8.2,

$$R^2 = \frac{SSR}{SST} = \frac{804090}{836620} = 0.961 \text{ or } 96.1\%.$$

Thus, the coefficient of determination shows an increase over that for the single-variable model, which had $R^2 = 94.3$ percent. Indeed, whenever we add a variable to the model, we find that R^2 increases (or, strictly speaking, cannot decrease). However, the value of the F statistic often falls because of the K in the denominator of equation (8.6). There is no inconsistency here, but we need to recognize that the decline in F does not necessarily signal a weakness in the model.

The increase in R^2 seems modest, but more important is the change in S. The single-variable model has $S = 17.61$, whereas the current model has $S = 14.73$, so the prediction interval is about six cents narrower.

8.3.2 ANOVA in Simple Regression

We did not consider the analysis of variance in Chapter 7 because it did not provide any additional information: When there is only one variable in the model, the test of the overall model is formally equivalent to the two-sided test of the single slope. Referring back to the computer output in Figure 7.12, we see that the P-value for ANOVA is identical with that for the t-test of the slope parameter. That is, in *simple linear regression*, the F-test and (two-sided) t-tests provide identical information. Another way of saying this is that, in *simple linear regression*, $F = t^2$, as can readily be verified numerically in Figure 7.12.

8.3.3 S and Adjusted R^2

The steady increase in R^2 as new variables are added is a matter for some concern: If that were all there were to model building we would just add variables! A better guide to the performance of the model is to look at S, the standard error, now defined as

$$S^2 = \frac{\sum_{i=1}^{n} e_i^2}{(n - K - 1)} = \frac{SSE}{(n - K - 1)} = MSE \qquad (8.7)$$

If S is smaller, the model has improved as the result of including the extra variable, although the improvement may be marginal. As we argued in Section 7.7.3, S has a straightforward interpretation as the accuracy of the predictions, because it is an estimate of the standard deviation of the error.

An alternative route to interpreting the overall accuracy of a multiple regression model is through the adjusted form of R^2, which we abbreviate to $R^2(adj)$. The general algebraic expression is

$$R^2(adj) = \frac{(n - 1)}{(n - K - 1)} \left[R^2 - \frac{K}{(n - 1)} \right]. \qquad (8.8)$$

The term inside the brackets removes that part of R^2 which could arise just by chance, and the ratio in front of the brackets then rescales the expression so that $R^2(adj) = 1$ when $R^2 = 1$.

The plot of $R^2(adj)$ is shown in Figure 8.2 for $n = 21$ and $K = 5$. For example, when the observed value of $R^2 = 0.20$, it follows that $R^2(adj) = -0.067$, the difference demonstrating that an apparent fit measured by R^2 can always be achieved by including sufficient (even random!) variables, but may prove illusory once adjusted for the degrees of freedom.

Figure 8.2 $R^2(adj)$ Plotted against R^2 for $n = 21, K = 5$

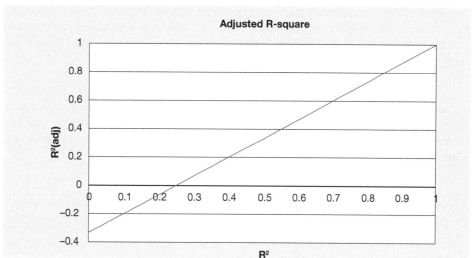

An alternative form for $R^2(adj)$ is

$$R^2(adj) = 1 - \frac{(n-1)S^2}{SST}.$$

Thus, when we add a variable to the model, $R^2(adj)$ will increase if and only if S decreases. Hence, any decisions about the choice of model that use $R^2(adj)$ or S will reach identical conclusions.

■ Example 8.3: $R^2(adj)$ and S for the gas prices model *(Gas_prices_1.xlsx)*

We have $K = 4$ and $n = 155$, so

$$S^2 = \frac{32530}{150} = 217 \text{ and it follows that } S = 14.73.$$

We then obtain $R^2(adj) = 1 - \dfrac{155 \times 217}{836620} = 0.960$ or 96.0%.

As we see in this example, when K is small relative to n, the adjusted value is only marginally less than the original R^2.

Computer programs generally provide all the information discussed in this section in summary form, such as

$$S = 14.73, R^2 = 96.11\%, R^2(adj) = 96.01\%. \blacksquare$$

8.4 Testing Individual Coefficients

Once we have established that the overall model is of value, we need to determine which variables are useful and which, if any, do not contribute. The process is similar to that described in Section 7.6, but there are some crucial differences. First, because there are K variables in the model, we will perform K separate tests. We describe the procedure for variable X_j, $j = 1, 2, ..., K$.

The null hypothesis, now denoted by $H_0(j)$, states that the theoretical slope for X_j in the regression is zero, *given that the other variables are already in the model*. We are not testing for a direct relationship between X_j and Y; rather, we seek a conditional relationship that asks the question: Given that the other variables are already in the model, does X_j add anything? This is captured by the null hypothesis

$$H_0(j) : \beta_j = 0, \text{ given that } X_i, \text{ for all } i \neq j, \text{ are in the model.}$$

The alternative hypothesis is now denoted by $H_A(j)$ and states that the slope, β_j, is not zero, again assuming that the other variables are in the model. That is, there is a relationship between X_j and Y even after accounting for the contributions of the other variables. We write the alternative hypothesis as

$$H_A(j) : \beta_j \neq 0, \text{ given that } X_i, i \neq j, \text{ are in the model.}$$

As before, we assume the null hypothesis to be true and then test this assumption. We use the test statistic

$$t = \frac{b_j}{SE(b_j)}. \tag{8.9}$$

Let t_{obs} denote the observed value of this statistic. The observed value is to be compared with the appropriate value from a table of student's t distribution with $(n - K - 1)$ DF; the number of degrees of freedom is determined by the number of observations available to estimate S. That number is now $(n - K - 1)$, as seen from Table 8.1. If we use a significance level of 100α percent, we denote the value from the t tables as $t_{\alpha/2}(n - K - 1)$. The decision rule for the test is

If $|t_{obs}| > t_{\alpha/2}(n - K - 1)$, reject $H_0(j)$; otherwise, do not reject $H_0(j)$.

As in Chapter 7, it is more convenient to use the P-value to perform the test. The decision rule is then written as

If $P < \alpha$, reject $H_0(j)$; otherwise do not reject $H_0(j)$.

A benefit of using the P-value approach is that, once the value of P is available, the decision rule always has this standard form: Reject $H_0(j)$ if $P < \alpha$.

■ Example 8.4: Testing individual coefficients *(Gas_prices_1.xlsx)*

Table 8.2 provides the output for testing the individual coefficients in the gas prices example, carrying out a test on each slope in turn. Standard computer packages typically summarize the set of K tests in a single table.

As in Chapter 7, we ignore the test for the intercept or constant because such a test is not meaningful in this case (the variables are never all zero). All four input variables have $P < 0.05$, and there is strong evidence that they should be retained in the model. Even though there are also some significant correlations among the explanatory variables (see Figure

8.3), the contribution of each variable is well defined and the signs are consistent with our previous expectations. ■

Table 8.2 Single Variable Tests for the Gas Prices Model

Predictor	Coef	SE Coef	T	P
Constant	−29.0	22.8	−1.27	0.205
L1_Crude_price	2.4075	0.0673	35.76	0.000
L1_SP500	−0.0426	0.0129	−3.30	0.001
L1_RR_sales	0.00143	0.000204	7.02	0.000
L1_Unemp	−14.27	3.37	−4.23	0.000

Figure 8.3 Correlations Between Variables in Gas Prices Model

	Crude_price	SP500	RR_sales
SP500	0.460 (0.000)		
Real Retail (RR_sales)	0.736 (0.000)	0.677 (0.000)	
Unemp	0.125 (0.120)	−0.591 (0.000)	0.031 (0.703)

Data: Gas_prices_1.xlsx. Note: *P*-values appear below the correlation coefficients.

8.4.1 Case Study: Baseball Salaries *(Baseball.xlsx)*

We now revisit the baseball salaries data and examine some other factors that might affect a player's salary. Some will have to do with his overall career performance and others with his recent results. Although baseball is arguably the most statistically oriented of all sports, a few brief explanations are in order for those who are not baseball fans:

1. A pitcher may be recorded as the winner or the loser of a game. He may also record "No decision". Thus, the numbers of wins ("*Career Wins*") and losses ("*Career Losses*") in the course of a career are important factors in a player's remuneration.

2. The quality of a pitcher's performance over the years may be assessed by the average number of runs given up in the equivalent of a full game, known as the earned run average ("*Career ERA*"); the lower the ERA, the better the pitcher is seen to be.

3. The player's recent activity level can be judged by the number of innings pitched in the previous season ("*Innings Pitched*"); the more activity, the more the team is seen to rely on the pitcher.

Baseball fans will be able to suggest a number of other criteria, and some are listed in the file *Baseball.xlsx*, but these four additional factors (wins, losses, earned run average, and innings pitched) will suffice for our purposes. The extended model is summarized in Figure 8.4(B). It is apparent that the "*Career Wins*" and "*Career Losses*" variables do not appear to add much to the overall explanation; further, "*Career Wins*" has the wrong sign. The other variables are highly significant and have the appropriate signs.

Should we drop both variables with high *P*-values? Not necessarily: Pitchers with long careers have time to accumulate a lot of wins, but also a lot of losses, so the variables may be highly correlated, as indeed can be seen from Figure 8.4(A).

Figure 8.4 Correlations and Regression Models for Baseball Players

(A) Correlation Analysis

	Salary ($000s)	Years in Majors	Career ERA	Innings Pitched	Career Wins	Career Losses
Salary ($000s)	1.00					
Years in Majors	0.53	1.00				
Career ERA	−0.34	−0.22	1.00			
Innings Pitched	0.27	0.11	0.09	1.00		
Career Wins	0.51	0.89	−0.21	0.33	1.00	
Career Losses	0.49	0.91	−0.14	0.30	0.97	1.00

(B) Regression Analysis: Five Explanatory Variables

The regression equation is

$$\text{Salary (\$000s)} = 547 + 53.6 \text{ Years in Majors} - 152 \text{ Career ERA} \\ + 171 \text{ Innings Pitched} - 0.59 \text{ Career Wins} - 1.12 \text{ Career Losses}$$

Predictor	Coef	SE Coef	T	P
Constant	547.4	167.2	3.27	0.001
Years in Majors	53.65	13.62	3.94	0.000
Career ERA	−152.37	39.81	−3.83	0.000
Innings Pitched	1.711	0.421	4.07	0.000
Career Wins	−0.590	1.846	−0.32	0.749
Career Losses	−1.123	2.400	−0.47	0.640

S = 292.804   R–Sq = 39.8%   R–Sq(adj) = 38.0%

Analysis of Variance

Source	DF	SS	MS	F	P
Regression	5	9639078	1927816	22.49	0.000
Residual error	170	14574798	85734		
Total	175	24213875			

(C) Regression Analysis: Three Explanatory Variables

The regression equation is

$$\text{Salary (\$000s)} = 620 + 36.8 \text{ Years in Majors} \\ - 154 \text{ Career ERA} + 1.42 \text{ Innings Pitched}$$

Predictor	Coef	SE Coef	T	P
Constant	620.2	150.2	4.13	0.000
Years in Majors	36.850	5.023	7.34	0.000
Career ERA	−154.21	36.88	−4.18	0.000
Innings Pitched	1.4156	0.3556	3.98	0.000

S = 292.643   R–Sq = 39.2%   R–Sq(adj) = 38.1%

Analysis of Variance

Source	DF	SS	MS	F	P
Regression	3	9483783	3161261	36.91	0.000
Residual error	172	14730092	85640		
Total	175	24213875			

Data: Baseball.xlsx; adapted from Minitab output.

One solution to the question is to drop the variables one at a time and see what happens. We leave that as an exercise for the reader. The other approach is to test the variables as a group, comparing models with and without the "*Wins*" and "*Losses*" variables. We now explore this alternative.

8.4.2 Testing a Group of Coefficients

We have seen how the *t*-test may be used to evaluate individual variables. Now, we go a step further and consider whether it is necessary to include a group of variables. The question is, "Does the group of extra variables add anything to the predictive power of the model?"

We may solve this problem by comparing two models: M_1 which contains all the variables, and M_0, which contains only a subset:

Model M_1 (with error sum of squares SSE_1)

$$Y = f(X; \beta_0, \beta_1, \beta_2, \ldots, \beta_q, \beta_{q+1}, \ldots, \beta_K),\tag{8.10}$$

and Model M_0 (with error sum of squares SSE_0),

$$Y = f(X; \beta_0, \beta_1, \beta_2, \ldots, \beta_q, 0, 0, \ldots, 0),\tag{8.11}$$

In equation (8.10), M_1 contains the $(K + 1)$ parameters $\{\beta_0, \beta_1, \ldots, \beta_q, \beta_{q+1}, \ldots, \beta_K\}$ while the simpler model M_0 in equation (8.11) contains the $(q + 1)$ parameters $\{\beta_0, \beta_1, \ldots, \beta_q\}$. In each case, the sum of squared errors is

$$SSE_j = \sum_1^n e_{ji}^2 \text{ for Model } j, j = 0, 1.$$

More formally, $(K - q)$ restrictions are placed on model M_1 to obtain the simpler model M_0, so we consider the null hypothesis

H_0: $\beta_{q+1} = \beta_{q+2} = \ldots = \beta_K = 0$, given that $X_1, \ldots, X_q$ are in the model

and the alternative hypothesis

H_A: At least one of the coefficients $\beta_{q+1}, \ldots, \beta_K$ is nonzero when $X_1, \ldots, X_q$ are in the model.

To compare the two models, we just examine their explanatory power through their residuals. We therefore estimate the sum of squared errors from both the extended model M_1 and the simpler model M_0. We define the statistic

$$F = \frac{(SSE_0 - SSE_1)/(K - q)}{SSE_1/(n - K - 1)}.$$

This statistic has an *F* distribution with $(K - q, n - K - 1)$ degrees of freedom, and the *P*-value can be found by using the Excel function FDIST.RT.

DISCUSSION QUESTION: *Why is SSE_0 always greater than SSE_1?*

■ **Example 8.5: Testing a group of coefficients** *(Baseball.xlsx)*

From Figure 8.4, $SSE_1 = 14574798$. The analysis without the two variables "*Career Wins*" and "*Career Losses*" yields $SSE_0 = 14730092$. With $n = 176$, $q = 3$, and $K = 5$, the *F* statistic has the value

$$F = \frac{(14730092 - 14574798)/2}{14574798/170} = \frac{77647}{85734} = 0.906.$$

The P-value is 0.406, so, clearly, we do not reject the null hypothesis; indeed, whenever $F < 1$, the null hypothesis will not be rejected. The two variables in question do not add to the explanatory power of the model, so we will use the three-variable model summarized in Figure 8.4(C). Tests of the residuals are deferred to Exercise 8.5. ■

The test can also be used to test for nonlinearities (of polynomial form) or any other set of parameter restrictions, so long as the simple model M_0 is a restricted version of the full model.

8.5 Checking the Assumptions

In both this chapter and the previous one we laid out a set of assumptions. However, up to now, we have not attempted to check those assumptions; rather, we have proceeded as though our model was fully and completely specified and all the assumptions were valid. In short, we have been living in a forecasting fool's paradise. In this section, we take the model for gas prices selected in Section 8.4 and try to determine how well it matches up to the assumptions stated in Section 8.2.

We examine these assumptions and devise ways to check the validity of each. Because we have available only a sample, we can never guarantee a particular assumption, but we can check whether it seems plausible. We tend to be very pragmatic: If the data suggest that a particular assumption holds, we stay with that assumption. Given a reasonably sized sample, such evidence suggests that any violation of the assumption is likely to be modest, as will be the likely impact of that violation. However, we should always keep in mind that this argument applies only if we are confident that the system will continue to operate under the same regime as in the past; if major structural changes take place, all bets are off, unless we can incorporate such changes into the model.

If a particular assumption breaks down, the nature of the breakdown will often indicate how the model might be improved. We use the residuals, as defined in equation (8.4), to develop our diagnostics. A comparison with the material in Section 6.5 serves to indicate that many of the analyses suggested here are the same as those for state-space and ARIMA models.

Assumption R1: The expected value of Y is linear in the values of the selected explanatory variables.

Potential violations: We may have missed an important variable, or the relationship may not be linear in the Xs.

Diagnostics:

1. Plot the residuals against the fitted values. Nonlinear relationships will show up as curvature in the plot.

2. Plot the residuals against potentially important Xs not currently in the model. If a particular new X has an impact on Y, it should show up as a nonzero slope on the scatterplot.

Why it matters

Using an inadequate model of the true relationship loses an important element in predicting Y.

Possible actions

1. Include omitted variables in the model.
2. Consider nonlinear models (see Section 9.6).

Assumption R2: The difference between an observed Y and its expected value is due to random error.

Discussion: The assumption states that the error is an "add-on" and serves to justify the least squares formulation for estimating the parameters. The error can always be expressed in this way, but its properties will depend critically upon the next four assumptions. Therefore, we do not check this assumption directly, but examine aspects of it as described next.

Assumption R3: The errors have zero means.

Discussion: Typically, this assumption is not testable, at least when we are looking at a single series. The inclusion of a constant term in the model ensures that the mean of the in-sample errors is zero. However, if a model is intended to apply when all explanatory variables are zero, with Y correspondingly equal to zero, then the constant term can be meaningfully tested. When the model is used for forecasting, the forecast errors may show bias.

Why it matters

Bias in the model suggests the model is missing an important variable or a variable is mis-measured. For example, many macroeconomic series are released in preliminary form and then updated. Thus, the model may have been constructed on a particular set of final figures but then used in forecasting with the preliminary data. Cross-checks between the preliminary and final versions of such variables may reveal biases.

Assumption R4: The errors associated with different observations are uncorrelated with other variables and with one another. Thus, the errors should be uncorrelated with the explanatory variable or with other variables not included in the model. In examining observations over time, this assumption implies that there is no correlation between the error at time t and past errors; otherwise, the errors are autocorrelated.

Possible violations: Assumption R4 lies at the heart of model building and boils down to the claim that the model contains all the predictable components, leaving only noise in the error term. The residuals therefore should not be related to factors omitted from the model, such as nonlinear functions of the input variables. Where the data form a time series, there should be no relationship with past values of the inputs, the dependent variable, or past errors. Such a relationship can obtain if there is a carry-over effect from one period to the next, which could be due to such factors as the weather, brand loyalty, or economic trends. Thus, a positive residual in one time period is likely to be followed by a positive residual in the next period. High-low sequences are also possible, such as a drop in sales after high volumes because of a special promotion. In cross-sectional studies, we should check whether subgroups in the population exhibit correlations, be it from locational, demographic, or other shared properties.

Diagnostics:

1. Plot the residuals against both the predicted value of Y and the input variables included in the model (as well as any other potential explanatory variables that have been excluded).
2. For time series, plot the residuals against time. If positive autocorrelation exists, lengthy sequences of values above zero and then below zero, rather than a random

scatter, will appear. If a negative autocorrelation exists, a saw-tooth pattern will prevail.

3. For time series, plot the sample autocorrelation function (*ACF*) for the residuals (see Section 6.1) and look for departures from a random series by performing tests for the presence of autocorrelation. (The *PACF* discussed in Section 6.2 may also help.) A test that is sometimes recommended for this purpose is based on the Durbin-Watson statistic, described in Appendix 8A. However, this test applies only to first-order auto-correlation so we prefer to use the *ACF* along with the Ljung-Box-Pierce statistic of Section 6.5.1 as useful overall diagnostics. In Chapter 10, we consider more efficient tests.

Why it matters

The diagnostics provide evidence of a predictable element in the error term. Its exclusion means that the error variance is larger than need be and the forecasts less accurate.

Possible actions

1. For cross-sectional data, examine the data collection process carefully. For example, check whether the sample includes multiple respondents from the same company; if it does, company affiliation could be a missing factor that explains differential (seg-mented) responses.

2. For time series, consider the use of lagged values (see Section 9.3).

Assumption R5: The error terms come from distributions with equal variances.

Possible violations: The most common pattern is that the variability increases as the mean level of Y increases. We naturally talk about percentage movements up or down in GDP, in sales, and in many other series. The implication behind such terminology is that the vari-ations are proportional to the level of the mean, rather than displaying constant variance.

Diagnostics:

1. Plot the residuals against the fitted values. If the errors are heteroscedastic, the scatter will often be greater for the larger fitted values.

2. Various test statistics are available (see Anderson *et al.*, 2014, Chapter 11), but we do not pursue that topic further here; such tests are illustrated in Chapter 10.

Why it matters and possible actions

With errors from one part of the data larger than another, the least squares procedure effec-tively gives additional weight to the former, leading to miscalibrated prediction intervals. Procedures for dealing with changing variances by transforming the raw data are discussed in Section 9.6.

Assumption R6: The errors are drawn from a normal distribution.

Possible violations: One or more outliers may render the distribution nonnormal, or the whole pattern of the residuals may suggest a nonnormal distribution.

Diagnostics:

1. Plot the histogram of the residuals, and look for a rough bell shape.

2. Use the normal probability plot. A plot that deviates significantly from a straight line indicates nonnormality.

3. Examine the plots of residuals against both time and fitted values for extreme obser-vations.

Why it matters

The normality assumption is used in calculating the prediction intervals so if the assumption fails the prediction intervals are miscalibrated.

NB. It is not needed for tests of the coefficients in a model as these can call on the Central Limit Theorem and the resulting approximately normal distribution of the estimates.

Possible actions

1. There is an interaction between normality assumption R6 and the heteroscedasticity assumption, R5. Often, correcting for extreme observations will lead to the data having an approximately constant variance.

2. Consider transformations of the dependent variable and possibly of the predictors as well (see Section 9.6).

It is evident from the preceding summary that some plots — notably, that of the residuals against fitted values — serve multiple purposes. It is important to keep these several objectives in mind in examining the plots.

8.5.1 Analysis of Residuals for Gas Price Data

Most statistical packages will generate the plots we have just discussed, some more easily than others. In particular, Minitab produces a "Four in One" plot as part of its regression component, a feature that is particularly useful for the analyses we have been discussing.

The four-variable model of unleaded gas prices was identified in Table 8.2, and the residuals are shown in Figure 8.5. We examine these plots in the order they appear in the output:

a. The probability plot (top left) shows several outliers at either end, partially a reflection of the increased volatility in the later part of the series. The histogram (bottom left) tells much the same story: The long tails shown afford some evidence of a departure from the normal curve.

b. As we noted earlier, the plot of residuals against fitted values (top right) may tell several stories. The residuals for fitted values in the range from $1 to $2 are tightly bunched, showing low variability. However, the higher fitted values show considerable variation, a clear demonstration of non-constant variances. The plot of residuals against order (bottom right) shows runs of positive values followed by runs of negative values, indicative of autocorrelation. Also, we observe that larger values are clustered together at the end of the series, suggesting a possible change in conditions that should be examined more closely.

c. Figure 8.5(B) explores possible relationships between the residuals and the price level, measured by the *CPI*. Although there is no evidence of a linear relationship, the increased fluctuations in the later part of the series suggest that constant-dollar prices might produce a better model. This figure also checks for a possible relationship with lagged demand (other variables could have been chosen such as lagged production) but there is no evidence of such dependence.

The issue of residual autocorrelation is particularly important because it indicates persistence in the time series that has not been fully captured by the current model. To investigate this phenomenon, we look at the *ACF* of the residuals, shown in Figure 8.6. This is usually done by storing the residuals from the regression command and then using a further time series command to calculate the *ACF*.

The *ACF* indicates a degree of persistence, with a significant positive autocorrelation at lag 1.[5] The spikes at lag 6 and lag 12 suggest possible seasonality, which also merits further examination. (An analysis of the Partial Autocorrelation Function — see Section 6.2.5 — gives no further information.)

Collectively, these plots provide plenty of food for thought and indicate that we have some work ahead of us before we can be satisfied with the model. We return to the model-building endeavor in Chapter 9; for now, we explore the use of such models in forecasting.

Figure 8.5(A) Residual Plots for the Four-Variable Model of Unleaded Gas Prices

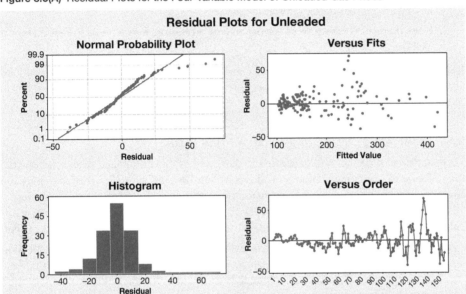

Figure 8.5(B) Residual Plots versus Possible Additional Input Variables for Unleaded Gas Prices

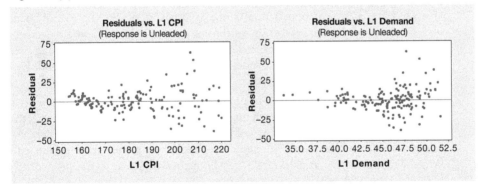

---

5   The Durbin-Watson statistic, valid for this particular model, of 0.738 is highly significant, suggesting first order autocorrelation. But the *ACF* is more informative.

Figure 8.6 ACF for the Residuals of the Four-Variable Unleaded Gas Prices Model

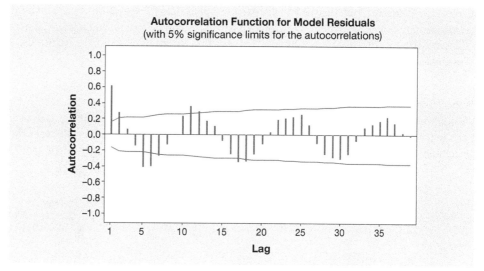

8.6 Forecasting with Multiple Regression

The general procedure for forecasting with several explanatory variables is essentially the same as that for the single-variable case described in Section 7.7. The interested reader is referred to Kutner *et al.* (2005, pp. 229–232) for further details. The first question we must answer relates to the nature of the explanatory variables. Recall that any particular X may arise in one of three ways:

a. X is known ahead of time.

b. X is unknown but can itself be forecast.

c. X is unknown but we wish to make "what-if" forecasts.

For example, consider a model for sales. Clearly, variables that designate particular seasons are known in advance, as may be substantive variables that have been sufficiently lagged in time. Policy variables — for example, price and advertising expenditures — may be explored with the model to make "what-if" forecasts so that the sensitivity of expected sales to policy changes can be explored. Finally, some variables, such as the price charged by competitors or the level of GDP, will require forecasts themselves. These forecasts are often generated by industry analysts, government sources, or macroeconomic panels (see, e.g., *www.consensuseconomics.com*). Alternatively, time series methods, such as the exponential smoothing methods discussed in Chapters 3 and 4, could be used.

8.6.1 The Point Forecast

We suppose that values for the next time period are available for each of the K variables and denote these values by $X_{n+1,1}\ X_{n+1,2},\ \dots\ X_{n+1,K}$. Given the estimated regression line, the point forecast is

$$F_{n+1} = b_0 + b_1 X_{n+1,1} + b_2 X_{n+1,2} + \dots + b_K X_{n+1,K}. \qquad (8.12)$$

As before, we need to distinguish between the fitted values Y and the forecast F_{n+1}. The two formulas are the same, but the fitted values correspond to those observations that were used in the estimation process, whereas the forecasts are based on new observations. These new values may be part of a hold-out sample or values as yet unobserved, but they are not used to estimate the model parameters.

■ Example 8.6: One-step-ahead forecasts for gas prices *(Gas_prices_1.xlsx)*

We use the four-variable model for gas prices as an illustration. One-step-ahead forecasts were generated from equation (8.12), so for example, the forecast for January 2009 uses the December 2008 values of the explanatory variables. The regression model (from Table 8.2) is

$$Unleaded = -29.0 + 2.4075 \; L1\_Crude\_price$$
$$- 0.0426 \; L1\_SP500 + 0.001430 \; L1\_RR\_sales - 14.27 \; L1\_Unemp.$$

The values of the explanatory variables for January 2009, which are of course known, are as follows:

$$L1\_Crude\_price: 41.12 \quad L1\_SP500: 903.25 \quad L1\_RR\_sales: 157080 \quad L1\_Unemp: 7.3.$$

The forecast for January 2009 is then

$$F = -29.0 + 2.4075 \times 41.12 - 0.0426 \times 903.25 + 0.001430 \times 157080 - 14.27 \times 7.3$$
$$= 152.97.$$

Rounding errors may give a slightly different answer. The forecasts for the 24 months (January 2009 to December 2010) are plotted in Figure 8.7; all the forecasts are one-step-ahead, using the previous month's values as inputs. ■

8.6.2 Prediction Intervals

We now require prediction intervals to provide an indication of the accuracy of the forecasts. We omit the technical details and simply note that, relative to the unknown future value Y_{n+1} the point forecast, when the explanatory variables are known, has an estimated standard error that we write as

$$SE(Y_{n+1} - F_{n+1}) = \sqrt{\mathrm{var}(Y_{n+1} - F_{n+1})}.$$

The prediction error falls into two parts:

$$Y_{n+1} - F_{n+1} = [Y_{n+1} - E(Y_{n+1})] - [F_{n+1} - E(Y_{n+1})].$$

The first term represents the inherent variability in the model even when the parameters are known and the second term measures the uncertainty in the forecast due to parameter estimation. The second term is small when the sample size is large but it cannot be ignored, particularly when the values of the predictor variables are not close to their respective means. (We note in passing that in Chapters 5 and 6 we followed customary procedures and ignored such terms!)

Given assumptions R3-R5, these two factors are independent and the variance of the prediction error may be written as:

$$\mathrm{var}(Y_{n+1} - F_{n+1}) = \mathrm{var}[Y_{n+1} - E(Y_{n+1})] + \mathrm{var}[F_{n+1} - E(Y_{n+1})]. \qquad (8.13)$$

This expression approaches its limiting value of σ^2 [(the first term in equation (8.13)] when the sample size is large; it does *not* reduce to zero. Given the additional assumption R6, the forecast error follows a normal distribution, and after allowing for the estimation of σ by S, we may use the Student's t distribution with the appropriate DF to specify the prediction interval.

Prediction interval for the future observation Y_{n+1}:

$$F_{n+1} \pm t_{\alpha/2}(n - K - 1) \times SE(Y_{n+1} - F_{n+1}) \qquad (8.14)$$

The $100(1 - \alpha)$ percent prediction interval is a probability statement: The probability that the future observation will lie in the interval defined by equation (8.14) is $(1 - \alpha)$.

For regression models with more than a single explanatory variable estimating the standard error requires matrix algebra. Fortunately, computer programs such as Minitab, SAS and SPSS calculate these values: they are distinct values corresponding to each individual prediction. Some programs (e.g. Minitab) provide prediction intervals directly but not the standard errors; SAS and SPSS provide both standard errors and prediction intervals.

■ Example 8.7: Construction of a prediction interval

We continue our consideration of the forecasts for January 2009, begun in Example 8.6. With $K = 4$ and $n = 155$, we have DF = 150. The standard error for the point forecast is 15.852. Using $t_{0.025}(150) = 1.976$, we find that the 95 percent prediction interval is

$$152.00 \pm (1.976) \times 15.852 = [120.7, 183.3].$$

The one-step-ahead point forecasts for January 2009 to December 2010 are plotted in Figure 8.7, along with the actual values and the 95 percent prediction intervals. From the plot, we can see that the forecasts systematically underestimated the actual values and that this error was not corrected over time.

Figure 8.7 Actual Prices for Unleaded Gasoline, Along with One-Step-Ahead Forecasts and 95 Percent Prediction Intervals (January 2009–December 2010)

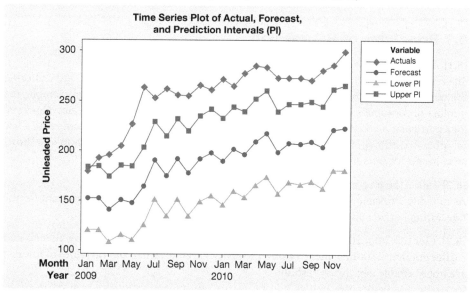

As with simple regression, when n is large, an approximate 95 percent prediction interval is given by $F \pm 2S$. From Example 8.3 with $S = 14.73$, we get an approximate prediction interval of ± 29.46, a reasonable approximation, although as the explanatory variables move away from their averages, this becomes less accurate. For multiple regression, the exact formula is complex and we rely on the programmed values from Minitab, R, or SPSS. Here, for example, the width of the exact prediction interval for 2009 Jan is ± 31.3 which increases to ± 42.3 for 2010 Dec because the values of the explanatory variables are much further from their historic mean values in 2010 Dec. Better to rely on the programmed calculations unless the sample size is very large. ■

8.6.3 Forecasting More than One Period Ahead

When we wish to forecast more than one period ahead, we must provide values for all the predictor variables over the forecasting horizon. As we discussed in Section 7.7.4, there are two possible approaches:

1. Generate forecasts for all the Xs and apply the forecasts to the original model.

2. Reformulate the model so that all unknown Xs are lagged by two (or more) periods, as appropriate.

The first approach is more commonly applied, but suffers from the drawback that the uncertainty in X is not reflected in the prediction intervals for the forecasts. This approach has the advantage that only a single model need be used to compare different "what-if" paths formulated for X. The second approach is somewhat more tedious, but it will be more valuable when good forecasts for X are unavailable and it will provide more accurate prediction intervals. However, there is the implicit assumption that as the lag order of the Xs increases there is still a useful predictive connection with Y.

As before, neither approach is necessarily better than the other. Where forecasts of the Xs are unreliable, it will usually prove better (and easier) to adopt the second approach. Exploration of the gas prices model for multiple steps ahead is left as Exercises 8.9 and 8.10.

8.7 Principles of Regression

[8.1] Aim for a relatively simple model specification.
The researcher must strike a balance between failing to include key variables and cluttering the model with variables that have very little effect upon the outcome. For example, the number of consumers in a market area clearly has an impact on the level of sales. However, for a particular market area, that figure is not going to change much over the course of a few months. Accordingly, we would not bother to include a variable for population in a short-term model for sales forecasting (Allen and Fildes, 2001).

[8.2] Tailor the forecasting model to the horizon.
As noted in Principle 8.1, we need to identify those variables which are important for the forecasting horizon under consideration (Armstrong, 2001).

[8.3] Identify important causal variables on the basis of the underlying theory and earlier empirical studies. Identify suitable proxy variables when the variables of interest are not available in a timely fashion.
Expertise and earlier research should be used to formulate a model whenever possible. Statements such as "The stock market goes up when the AFC team wins the Super Bowl" may be factually correct over a period of years, but they are not a reliable guide to investment! (Adapted from Allen and Fildes, 2001)

[8.4] If the aim of the analysis is to provide pure forecasts, you must either know the explanatory variables in advance or be able to forecast them sufficiently well to justify their inclusion in the model.

This principle is a more formal statement of the necessary response to the questions "What do you know?" and "When will you know it?" (Adapted from Allen and Fildes, 2001)

[8.5] Use the method of ordinary least squares to estimate the parameters.

The method of ordinary least squares is strictly valid only when Assumptions R3-R5 apply, but it is often a good place to start, and the basic multiple regression model presented in this chapter can be extended to deal with more complex models (Allen and Fildes, 2001).

[8.6] Update the estimates frequently.

Frequent updating involves little effort beyond recording the latest data. The new parameter estimates will better reflect the relationships among the variables and also help to alert the modeler to any lack of stability in those values (Armstrong, 2001), a point which we take up in Chapter 9.

Summary

In this chapter, we have extended regression models to multiple explanatory variables, thereby greatly increasing the range and value of models that we may use for forecasting purposes. We have also provided the basic inferential framework in terms of parameter estimation and model testing, as well as identifying the key assumptions underlying the models. This structure will enable us to check assumptions and refine the models in the next chapter.

Exercises

8.1   Exercise 7.1 (in *Exercise_7.1.xlsx*) provided data on television advertising and sales for a soft-drink company over an eight-week period. The purpose was to evaluate the effect on sales (in millions of dollars) with respect to the number of 30-second spots aired during that week. In further analysis, additional price data were collected (also in *Exercise_7_1.xlsx*). Conduct a multiple regression analysis for sales on spot and price.

   a. Carry out tests on the overall model and on the individual coefficients. Summarize your conclusions.

   b. Compare the performance of the two models. Which model would you recommend?

8.2   The file *Exercise_7_2.xlsx* contains additional data on a company's sales on advertising expenditures, beyond the data quoted in Exercise 7.2:

   a. Conduct a regression analysis of sales on advertising and price.

   b. Carry out tests on the overall model and on the individual coefficients. Summarize your conclusions.

   c. Compare the performance of the overall model and the price-only model. Which model would you recommend?

8.3   Using the unleaded gas prices data (*Gas_prices_1.xlsx*) compare the results of using Personal Disposable Income (rather than Real Retail sales) in a model of *Unleaded price*. Comment on any differences in interpretation and the one-step ahead forecasts from the two alternative models for 2009. Which one would you prefer to have used for 2008?

8.4   Create constant-dollar series for the unleaded gas prices data [*Gas_prices_1.xlsx*] by dividing *Unleaded, Crude_price, SP500,* and *PDI* by the *Consumer Price Index* (*CPI*). Repeat the analysis, using these new series and *Unemp*, and check the assumptions underlying this model. Finally, comment on the model's adequacy for explaining the price of unleaded gasoline.

8.5   Use the model developed in Exercise 8.4 to generate forecasts for the period from January 2009 through December 2010. Compare the performance of this model with that developed in Section 8.2. (This is not as easy as it looks!)

8.6   Use the file *Baseball.xlsx* to carry out the analysis of residuals for the three-variable baseball model developed in Section 8.4.1. Summarize your conclusions.

8.7   Use the file *Baseball.xlsx* and logarithms to transform the salaries data, and repeat the model development process. Compare your results with those given in Figure 8.4, and comment upon your results.

8.8   Use the file *Baseball.xlsx*. Modify the database by removing all the veterans, defined as players with ten or more years in the major leagues. Repeat the analyses of Exercises 8.5 and 8.6 and compare results.

8.9   Use the four-variable gas prices model of Example 8.1 to generate forecasts three periods ahead for the period from March 2009 to December 2010 by first generating forecasts for both the lagged crude oil price and Real Retail Sales (assume *SP500* and *Unemp* are known). Compare the estimates with those for the model developed in the chapter. Compute the forecast accuracy measures and generate the 90 percent prediction intervals, using equation (8.14) and S to estimate $SE(Y_{n+1} - F_{n+1})$. How many of the actual values fall inside these intervals?

8.10   Develop the four-variable gas prices model, using explanatory variables with lag = 3 to allow for direct prediction of the prices three periods ahead over the period from March 2009 to December 2010.

   a. Compute the forecast accuracy measures and evaluate the results.

   b. if your computer program provides them, generate the 90 percent prediction intervals. How many of the actual values fall inside these intervals? Compare the results with those obtained for Exercise 8.9.

8.11* Verify the relationship between F and R^2 given in equation (8.6).

Minicases

The purpose of these minicases is to provide opportunities for you to use data analysis to tackle important real-world problems. The format is essentially the same in each: A dependent variable of interest is identified, along with a plausible set of explanatory variables. The aim is to develop a valid forecasting model for at least one period ahead, and multiple periods ahead should also be considered. The full set of modeling steps should be examined:

- Create plots of the data to look for relationships and possible unusual observations.

- Perform basic data analysis.
- Develop a multiple regression model and check the model's adequacy with regard to the regression assumptions.
- Evaluate your chosen model's forecasting performance, preferably using a hold-out sample.

Keep in mind that there are no "right" answers, but some solutions will be more effective than others. After you complete your statistical analysis, do not fail to ask the following questions:

- Would the data be available to enable me to make timely forecasts?
- Are there other variables that should be included in the model?
- Would you feel able to justify your model to a senior manager?

If the answer to any of these questions is NO, you have more work to do!

Minicase 8.1 The Volatility of Google Stock

[Contributors: Christine Choi, Alex Dixon, Melissa Gong, Michael Neches, and Greg Thompson. Data for Minicase 8.1 can be found in file *Google_Volatility.xlsx*.]

Volatility is a measure of the uncertainty of the return realized on an asset (Hull, 2009). Applied to financial markets, the volatility of a stock price is a measure of how uncertain we are of future stock price movements. As volatility increases, the possibility that the stock price will appreciate or depreciate significantly also increases. The volatility measure has widespread implications, particularly for stock option valuation and also for volatility indices (VIX), portfolio management, and hedging strategies. Since its initial public offering, Google, Inc. (GOOG: NASDAQ), stock has become one of the most sought-after and popular investment opportunities. The search engine giant's stock price has fluctuated from an IPO price of $85/share, to a high of $741/share (adjusted close, Nov. 27, 2007), down to a low 2009 closing price of $345/share (adjusted close, Feb. 25, 2009). This fluctuation reveals the uncertainty associated with any stock especially that of high-tech companies with Web-based models for which the monetization of services can confuse even the most sophisticated investor.

The aim of the project is to develop a multiple regression model to forecast the volatility of Google's stock price over the next three months. After an initial review of Google-specific and macroeconomic data, we identified the following potential explanatory variables:

STDEV: the volatility measure for Google stock

VOLUME: amount of trading in Google shares

P/E: the price-to-earnings ratio of Google stock

GDP: quarterly growth in GDP at an annualized rate (quarterly, repeated for each month)

VIX: the market volatility index

CONF: the Conference Board Consumer Confidence Index®

JOBLESS: the number of claims posted for benefits

HOUSING: the number of new housing starts.

Monthly data are available for the period from March 2006 through January 2009 on the preceding variables. The data were downloaded from Bloomberg. A possible analysis would be to analyse the data pre-recession (through December 2007) and then check forecasting performance over the next seven months.

Minicase 8.2 Forecasting Natural Gas Consumption for the DC Metropolitan Area

[Data for Minicase 8.2 can be found in file *Natural_Gas_2.xlsx.*]

This minicase comes in two forms so that the effects of different time periods upon the modeling process can be examined.

The intent of this project was to develop a model to forecast natural gas consumption for the residential sector in the Washington, DC, metropolitan area. The level of natural gas consumption is influenced by a variety of factors, including local weather, the state of the national and the local economies, the purchasing power of the dollar (because at least some of the natural gas is imported), and the prices for other commodities.

Quarterly data
[Contributors: Sameer Aggarwal, Prashant Dhand, Yulia Egorov, and Natasha Heidenrich. Data: *Natural_Gas_2. xlsx, Sheet labelled 'Quarterly'*]

The following variables have been identified and recorded on a quarterly basis (the data cover the period 1997Q1 through 2008Q3, with all data measured quarterly); the series could be truncated at 2007Q3 to avoid the effects of the Great Recession and the last four observations used for model checking.

GASCONS: consumption of natural gas in DC metro area (million cubic feet)

AVETEMP: average temperature for the period in the DC metro area

GDP: annualized percentage change in GDP

UNEMP: percentage unemployment in the DC metro area (not seasonally adjusted)

GAS_PRICE: price of natural gas ($/100 cubic feet)

OIL_PRICE: price of crude oil ($/barrel)

RESERVES: reserves of natural gas (index, 2012 = 100)

DISTRIB: natural gas production distributed (not seasonally adjusted, index, 2012 = 100).

Monthly data
[Data: *Natural_Gas_2.xlsx, Sheet labelled 'Monthly'*]

The following variables have been identified and recorded on a monthly basis (the data cover the period January 2001–December 2015). The data may be analysed pre-recession (up to November 2007) or for the complete period.

GASCONS: consumption of natural gas in DC metro area (million cubic feet)

AVETEMP: average temperature for the period in the DC metro area

GDP: annualized percentage change in GDP

UNEMP: percentage unemployment in the DC metro area (not seasonally adjusted)

GAS_PRICE: price of natural gas ($/100 cubic feet)

CRUDE_OIL_PRICE: price of crude oil ($/barrel)

RESERVES: reserves of natural gas (index, 1972 = 100)

PRODN: natural gas production distributed (not seasonally adjusted, index, 2012 = 100).

Minicase 8.3 U.S. Retail & Food Service Sales
[Contributors: Doug Goff, Rich Marsden, Jeff Rodgers, and Masaki Takeda. Data for Minicase 8.3 can be found in file *Retail _food_sales.xlsx.*]

The purpose of this project is to forecast how U.S. retail and food sales will fare over the coming months. The variables considered include personal income and savings, consumer sentiment, and various macroeconomic variables. Because manufacturing costs and levels of activity are clearly important, these factors are also included. Considered in the analysis as well were three seasonal factors associated, respectively, with the Easter, Thanksgiving, and Christmas holidays. The data set includes monthly figures for the period January 2000–December 2008.

RSALES: U.S. retail and food service sales ($millions)

CONSENT: University of Michigan Index of U.S. Consumer Sentiment

PRICE_OIL: spot price of oil ($/barrel)

IND_PROD: Index of U.S. Industrial Production

PERSINC: U.S. personal income ($ per capita)

PERSSAV: net U.S. personal savings ($ per capita)

POPULATION: total U.S. population (thousands)

UNEMP: U.S. unemployment rate

CPI: U.S. Consumer Price Index

TGIVING:* indicator for Thanksgiving (November)

EASTER:* indicator for Easter (March or April)

XMAS:* indicator for Christmas (December).

* Denotes indicator variables, which are introduced in Section 9.1. These variables are set = 1 for the month in which the event happens, and = 0 for all other months.

Minicase 8.4 U.S. Automobile Sales

[Data for Minicase 8.4 can be found in file *Auto_sales_mc.xlsx*.]

Automobiles are regarded as essential to the American way of life, but people tend to delay replacing an older vehicle when economic conditions deteriorate, as happened most vividly during the Great Recession. Economic stress can be measured in a variety of ways including unemployment levels and declining consumer sentiment. Aside from unusual economic conditions the general state of the economy is reflected in such measures as the level of consumer expenditure, the price level and the performance of the stock market. The demand for new automobiles is also affected by the price of gasoline and the level of interest rates for auto loans.

Monthly data are available for the period January 2000–December 2011 on the following variables.

AUTO_SALES: Seasonally adjusted annual rate (millions)

CRUDE: Price of crude oil ($/barrel)

CPI: Consumer Price Index

CONSUMPTION: Personal consumer expenditures ($billions)

UNEMP: Number of people unemployed (thousands)

UNEMP_PC: Unemployment level (percentage)

UNEMP_DUR: Mean length of time unemployed (months)

CON_SENT: Consumer sentiment (index)

S&P 500: S&P 500 Index

LIBOR: One month LIBOR (London Inter-Bank Offered Rate) interest rate

TREASURY_3: Interest rate on 3-year U.S. Treasury bonds

TREASURY_10: Interest rate on 10-year U.S. Treasury bonds

RECESSION: The timing of the Great Recession, as defined by the NBER.
(This is called an indicator variable and is set = 1 during the period of the recession, and = 0 at all other times.)

Data Sources for Minicases

1. National Climatic Data Center (National Oceanic and Atmospheric Administration, Department of Commerce), *http://lwf.ncdc.noaa.gov/oa/climate/research/cag3/ md.html*

2. Bureau of Labor Statistics (U.S. Department of Labor), *www.bls.gov*

3. Energy Information Administration (U.S. Department of Energy), *www.eia.doe.gov/ overview_hd.html* and *http://tonto.eia.doe.gov/dnav/ng/ng_stor_sum_ dcu_nus_m.htm*

4. Bureau of Economic Analysis (U.S. Department of Commerce), *www.bea.gov*

5. University of Michigan Index of Consumer Sentiment, *www.sca.isr.umich.edu*

As noted previously, a valuable general source for many macroeconomic series is FRED, provided by the Economic Research Division of the Federal Reserve Bank of St. Louis, *https://fred.stlouisfed.org/*.

References

Allen, P. G., and Fildes, R. (2001). Econometric forecasting. In J. S. Armstrong (ed.) *Principles of Forecasting: A Handbook for Researchers and Practitioners*, Boston and Dordrecht: Kluwer, pp. 300–362.

Anderson, D. R., Sweeney, D. J., Williams, T. A., Camm, J. D. and Cochran, J. J. (2014), *Statistics for Business and Economics*, 12th ed. Mason, OH: Cengage Learning.

Armstrong, J. S., ed. (2001). *Principles of Forecasting: A Handbook for Researchers and Practitioners*. Boston and Dordrecht: Kluwer.

Hull, J. C. (2009). *Options, Futures, and Other Derivatives*, 7th ed. Upper Saddle River, NJ: Pearson Prentice Hall.

Kutner, M. H., Nachtsheim, C. J., Neter, J., and Li, W. (2005). *Applied Linear Statistical Models*, 5th ed. New York City: McGraw-Hill. [Re-issued as paperback in 2013]

Appendix 8A The Durbin-Watson Statistic

The Durbin-Watson test is often used to check for first-order autocorrelation in the random error terms in time series regression. The test compares the null hypothesis:

H_0: error terms are not autocorrelated

to the alternative

H_A: error terms display first order autocorrelation.

Given a sample of size n and residuals $\{e_t, t = 1, \ldots, n\}$ the Durbin-Watson statistic has the form:

$$DW = \frac{\sum_{t=2}^{n} (e_t - e_{t-1})^2}{\sum_{t=1}^{n} e_t^2} .$$

When H_0 is true, DW is close to 2.0. The minimum value is 0.0 and the maximum value is 4.0; small values indicate positive autocorrelation and large values indicate negative auto-correlation. The exact test requires detailed tables, which may be found in texts such as Kutner *et al.* (2005, pp. 1330–1331). The test is invalid when lagged values of the dependent variable are included in the regression model.

Because we use the sample autocorrelations as diagnostics and are often interested in autocorrelations at other lags as well, we prefer to use the sample *ACF* and *PACF*, as in Section 8.5. However, many software packages provide the value of the *DW* statistic but not the sample *ACF*. To make use of this information, we match up the values of *DW* with the test for first-order autocorrelation shown in Figure 8.6; this leads to the decision rule:

$$\text{Reject } H_0 \text{ with } \alpha = 0.05 \text{ if } |DW - 2.0| > \frac{3.92}{\sqrt{n}}\text{ ; do not reject otherwise.}$$

The right-hand side is $1.96 \times 2/\sqrt{n}$. The expression is based upon the assumption that DW is approximately normally distributed in large samples; the number 1.96 is the percentage point from normal tables and the other part represents the approximate standard error of DW.

Example

The gas prices model in Section 8.5.1 is found to have $DW = 0.738$. The sample size is $n = 155$ so the lower critical value is $2.0 - 3.92/\sqrt{155} = 2.0 - 0.315 = 1.685$. The observed value of 0.738 is well below this, so we reject the null hypothesis of no first order autocorrelation, reaching the same conclusion as we did from Figure 8.6.

CHAPTER 9

Model Building

Topics marked with an * are advanced and may be omitted for more introductory courses.

Table of Contents

Two hikers were walking through a forest when they were confronted by a large grizzly bear. One of the hikers promptly opened his backpack and started to lace up his running shoes. Dumbfounded, the other looked at him and said, "You can't outrun a grizzly!" "No need to," replied the first hiker, "I only need to outrun you!"

Introduction

Even the simplest business process is likely to be driven by a large number of different factors. Many of these will have only a minor impact. Our objective in statistical modeling is to identify the key elements and then to be prepared to ascribe the remaining variation to the random or unexplained error term that appears in all our models. In Chapters 7 and 8 we listed our key assumptions, and the model will be effective only if those assumptions are satisfied, at least approximately. In Section 8.5, we saw how to examine some of these assumptions by graphical means. In this chapter, guided by these diagnostic procedures, we develop more accurate forecasting models. However, we should always remember two things:

1. Our forecasts rely on the future being governed by the same rules and relationships as in the past;

2. Our conclusions about the behavior of processes are based upon sample data and can never be definitive.

The model specified in Assumptions R1 and R2 in Section 8.5 assumes that we have identified all of the relevant variables. Key variables may have been omitted, including possible changes in conditions (e.g., seasonal effects or changes in legal requirements). Some of the possible departures from the basic assumptions about the error process are the presence of (auto) correlation, the lack of constancy in the variance, and a nonnormal distribution, possibly caused by outliers. We explore each of these issues in turn. In Section 9.1, we introduce indicator (or dummy) variables and show how these tools can be used to address various problems, including seasonal patterns. In Section 9.2, we consider the introduction of lagged values of the dependent variable into the model in order to account for autocorrelation. A natural extension is to combine lagged values of the dependent variable with other variables, and this option is explored in Section 9.3.

In principle, we might consider a large number of predictor variables and incorporate lags of various orders for each of these input variables. If we are guided by strong theoretical considerations, such steps can be very valuable. More commonly, we are guided only by the vague intuition or fond hope that some of these variables might be useful. Without clear guidelines, we may arrive at a plethora of variables and no strong reason to prefer one set of inputs over another. We therefore need to develop methods that identify plausible models from among the many alternatives; we refer to these methods as variable selection methods and introduce them in Section 9.4. An additional problem arising from an increased number of inputs is that we may find that some or all of the variables are very highly correlated. This finding would have two undesirable effects: (1) our estimates of the individual slope coefficients may become highly unstable, to the point that identifying the "best" forecasting model becomes difficult, and (2) the magnitudes of the estimated effects may be unrealistic. We refer to the condition in which two or more of the input variables are highly intercorrelated as *multicollinearity* among the inputs. In Section 9.5, we consider how to check for the presence of multicollinearity and use variable selection methods as one way to handle the difficulty. An alternative is to restrict the overall absolute magnitude of the coefficients by the Lasso method.

When the level of the dependent variable increases over time (as does *GDP* or the sales of a new product), the inherent variability in the series often increases as well. Sometimes, our intuition comes to the rescue. We talk naturally about percentage changes and would expect to see greater constancy in percentage swings over time than in absolute levels. Thus, a switch (or transformation) of the dependent variable to deal with percentage changes will often take care of increasing variances. Indeed, if the "forecasting gods" are smiling on us, such a transformation may well take care of nonlinearity in the relationship as well. These issues are explored in Section 9.6.

In Section 9.7, we consider how to deal with influential observations and with outliers. Extreme observations may arise from data-recording errors or from unusual events such as a strike or a hurricane. Left alone, such items may distort model estimates and subsequent forecasts. On other occasions, process-changing events may be recognized or anticipated, such as a change in legal requirements. We usually refer to the methods for handling such events as intervention analysis, which is the subject of Section 9.8. Interventions and outliers have a close affinity in terms of the methods used to deal with them; the difference is that interventions are deliberate policy changes whereas outliers are unexpected events.

Although the chapter focuses on model building, the ultimate objective is still forecasting. To be useful, a model needs to be stable, not suffering from structural changes. In Section 9.9, we discuss how to test for their occurrence and how rolling estimation of the parameters can help in forecasting. Finally, in Section 9.10, we return to the core problem of how to produce useful forecasts. The chapter concludes with a discussion of new principles and a summary.

9.1 Indicator (Dummy) Variables

Many variables of interest are defined as (unordered) categories; gender and profession are two obvious examples. Nevertheless, such data may be valuable in building a regression model. Suppose we wish to examine a company's compensation policy in order to establish whether there is any gender bias in setting salary levels. It is certainly possible that males and females are equally recognized for such factors as years of experience, and yet a pay gap may exist. In order to allow for such a possibility in a regression model, we define an indicator variable:

INDICATOR (DUMMY) VARIABLES

When observations fall into one of two categories, we distinguish them by means of an *indicator* (or *dummy*) *variable*, defined as

   $X = 1$ if the observation falls into category A;

   $X = 0$ if the observation falls into category B.

In general, when there are H categories, we need only $(H - 1)$ indicator variables, which can be defined as follows for $i = 1, \ldots, (H - 1)$:

   $X_i = 1$ if the observation falls into the ith category;

   $X_i = 0$ otherwise.

Thus, all indicator variables have the value zero for category H.

■ Example 9.1: Use of an indicator variable

Let Y = salary (in thousands of dollars), X_1 = years of experience, and X_2 = gender (1 if female, 0 if male). Suppose that the expected salary progressions are as follows:

$$\text{Males: } E(Y) = 47 + 3X_1, \text{ Females: } E(Y) = 42 + 3X_1$$

That is, each group is expected to receive an annual increase of $3000, and males start out with a salary that is $5000 higher, as illustrated in Figure 9.1.

Figure 9.1 Expected Salaries for Each Gender, By Years of Experience

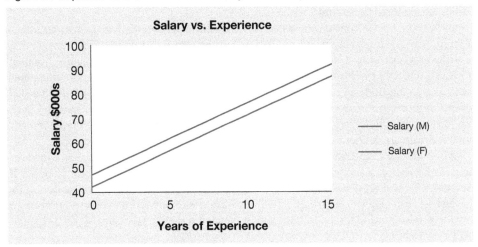

We could estimate the two relationships separately for each gender, but such a strategy may be problematic if we have to deal with small sample sizes. More generally, in time series, we may switch from one category to another and back again (e.g., weekday and weekend sales patterns). The simplest way to incorporate such differences into the statistical model is to combine the two relationships into one by using an indicator variable X_2.

In this example, we may use the indicator to combine the expectation statements into a single expression, coding $X_2 = 0$ for males and $X_2 = 1$ for females. Thus, the combined expression is

$$E(Y) = 47 + 3X_1 - 5X_2.$$

When $X_2 = 0$, we recover the expression for males, and when $X_2 = 1$, we obtain that for females. If we define $X_3 = (0$ if female, 1 if male$)$, we arrive at the formula

$$E(Y) = 42 + 3X_1 + 5X_3. \tag{9.1}$$

This relationship recovers the same initial formula, so it does not matter which of the two gender variables is used. That is, it does not matter whether we use X_2 or X_3; the two models will yield the same sets of fitted values, forecasts, and summary statistics. This equivalence continues to hold when there are more than two categories. ■

THE USE OF INDICATOR VARIABLES

All (valid) choices of indicator (dummy) variables will yield the same regression relationship, provided that a full set of $(H - 1)$ variables is included in the model. Thus, in Example 9.2, we may use any four of the five indicator variables.

■ **Example 9.2: WFJ sales and TV advertising** *(WFJ_sales_2.xlsx)*

WFJ can choose between 15-second and 30-second spots in its television advertising. In the absence of other information, we suppose that the total budget for TV advertising is fixed, so only the mix of commercials matters. WFJ employs five options: 100 percent 15-second slots, 75:25 in favor of 15- vs. 30-second slots, and then 50:50, 25:75, and 0:100 splits. These five categories may be represented by the following indicator variables that respectively identify them:

	X1	X2	X3	X4	X5
If advertising split is 100:0 for 15-second relative to 30-second commercial slots	1	0	0	0	0
If advertising split is 75:25 for 15-second relative to 30-second commercial slots	0	1	0	0	0
If advertising split is 50:50 for 15-second relative to 30-second commercial slots	0	0	1	0	0
If advertising split is 25:75 for 15-second relative to 30 second commercial slots	0	0	0	1	0
If advertising split is 0:100 for 15-second relative to 30-second commercial slots	0	0	0	0	1

We may use any four of the five indicator variables in a regression model. Using the first four (with no other variables), we have, for the fitted model,

$$WFJ\ Sales = 34488 - 8019\ X1 + 119\ X2 - 305\ X3 - 1356\ X4.$$

Predictor	Coef	SE Coef	T	P
Constant	34488	3315	10.40	0.000
X1	–8019	3564	–2.25	0.028
X2	119	3636	0.03	0.974
X3	–305	3436	–0.09	0.930
X4	–1356	3584	–0.38	0.707
S = 4688.03 R-Sq = 31.9% R-Sq(adj) = 27.1%				

If we use the last four indicators, the fitted model and summary measures are as follows:

$$WFJ\ Sales = 26470 + 8138\ X2 + 7714\ X3 + 6663\ X4 + 8019\ X5.$$

Predictor	Coef	SE Coef	T	P
Constant	26470	1309	20.23	0.000
X2	8138	2064	3.94	0.000
X3	7714	1590	4.85	0.000
X4	6663	1819	3.66	0.001
X5	8019	3564	2.25	0.028
S = 4688.03 R-Sq = 31.9% R-Sq(adj) = 27.1%				

The two models look very different at first sight. However, note that the summary measures [S, R^2, and $R^2(adj)$] are identical. Further, when we substitute a valid set of (0, 1) values into these expressions, we necessarily obtain the same fitted values and forecasts (see Exercise 9.3). It is important to recognize that the coefficients have different interpretations in the two models. In the first model, the coefficient for $X2$ measures the difference between policy 2 (75:25 in favor of 15-second slots) and policy 5 (all 30-second slots); in the second model, the coefficient for $X2$ measures the difference between policy 2 and policy 1 (all 15-second slots). Other coefficients are interpreted similarly. Although the resulting models may look different, this does not affect the fitted values or the forecasts. ∎

At this point, another question arises: Only one coefficient in the first model has a significant t-value, whereas the t-values of all four coefficients are significant in the second model, so should we drop the nonsignificant values? The short answer is *no*! The more complete answer is that the two versions indicate that the 100 percent 15-second choice is a poor one, resulting in lower sales than the other four choices, all of which yield similar results. Thus, a more parsimonious representation might be achieved by using a modified *X1* alone (100 percent 15-second slots, versus all other options), but the policy implications of that choice should be recognized first; only then should the simpler model be considered. Consequently, choosing different subsets of the indicators may provide useful insights.

INTERPRETING DUMMY VARIABLES

The coefficient of the dummy variable for a particular state measures the differential effect of being in that state compared with some baseline state (for which all the dummies equal 0).

9.1.1 Seasonal Indicators

We now introduce a data set that will be used as the running example for the next few sections of this chapter. Recall that in Minicase 4.2 we used single-series methods to explore the Walmart sales data. The series represents quarterly sales figures for Walmart from 2003Q1 through 2015Q4, with $n = 52$. We now extend that analysis to include gross domestic product (*GDP*), lagged one period, *L1_GDP*, as an explanatory variable. The measure we use is obtained from the U.S. Department of Commerce and represents *GDP* by quarter in current dollars (i.e., there is no adjustment for inflation); also, this series has been seasonally adjusted. A scatterplot of the relationship is shown in Figure 9.2.

The regression results are as follows:

Model 1: Walmart *(Walmart_2.xlsx)*

Predictor	Coef	SE Coef	T	P
Constant	−42.93	8.11	−5.30	0.000
L1_GDP	0.009642	0.0005444	17.72	0.000
S = 7.047 R-Sq = 86.50% R-Sq(adj) = 86.22%				

N.B.: We present the output as given by Minitab. To simplify the output for presentation purposes we would include fewer significant figures.

Figure 9.2 Scatterplot for Quarterly Walmart Sales on GDP, Lagged One Month
(Current Dollars, Seasonally Adjusted, 2003Q1–2015Q4)

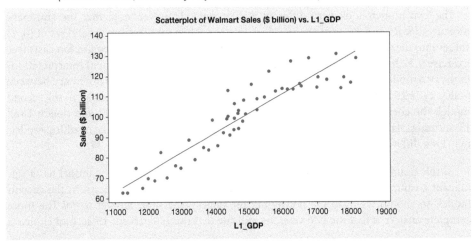

Data: Walmart_2.xlsx; adapted from Minitab output.

At first sight, the fit appears to be fairly good; but examination of the diagnostics in Figure 9.3 reveals several problems, most notably a pattern in the ordered residuals and evidence of nonnormality. To confirm the suspected seasonal pattern, we also generate the *ACF* of the residuals, shown in Figure 9.4. These autocorrelation functions show a very clear seasonal pattern (a spike at lag 4), confirming the suspicions just raised.

Figure 9.3 Residual Plots for Walmart Sales on Lagged GDP

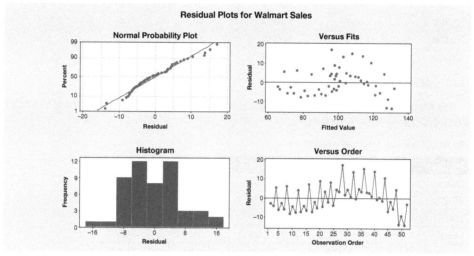

Data: Walmart_2.xlsx; adapted from Minitab output.

Figure 9.4 ACF of Residuals (*from the regression of Walmart Sales on Lagged GDP*)

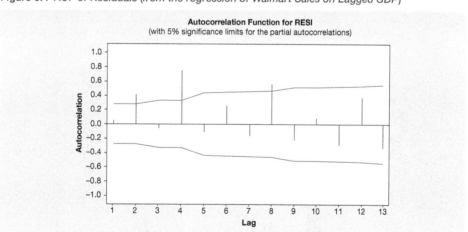

Data: Walmart_2.xlsx; adapted from Minitab output.

In order to incorporate any seasonal pattern into the model, we specify three indicator variables:

	X1	X2	X3
If the observation pertains to the first quarter	1	0	0
If the observation pertains to the second quarter	0	1	0
If the observation pertains to the third quarter	0	0	1

The fourth quarter is then identified by default as that quarter in which $X_1 = X_2 = X_3 = 0$. The first few rows of the data file are shown in Table 9.1.

Table 9.1 Data File Showing Indicator Variables for Walmart Sales

Date	Walmart Sales	L1_GDP	Quarter_1	Quarter_2	Quarter_3
2003Q1	56.7		1	0	0
2003Q2	62.6	11230.1	0	1	0
2003Q3	62.5	11370.7	0	0	1
2003Q4	74.5	11625.1	0	0	0
2004Q1	64.8	11816.8	1	0	0
2004Q2	69.7	11988.4	0	1	0
2004Q3	68.5	12181.4	0	0	1
2004Q4	82.2	12367.7	0	0	0

Data: Walmart_2.xlsx

We then rerun the regression for Walmart Sales on lagged GDP[1] and the three indicator variables. The results are as follows:

Model 2: Walmart *(Walmart_2.xlsx)*

Predictor	Coef	SE Coef	T	P
Constant	−33	5.84	−5.65	0.000
L1_GDP	0.009537	0.00038	25.11	0.000
Quarter_1	−12.94	1.97	−6.58	0.000
Quarter_2	−9.1	1.93	−4.72	0.000
Quarter_3	−11.87	1.93	−6.16	0.000
S = 4.909 R-Sq = 93.85% R-Sq(adj) = 93.31%				

Figure 9.5 Residual Plots *(From the Regression of Walmart Sales on Lagged GDP and Seasonal Indicators)*

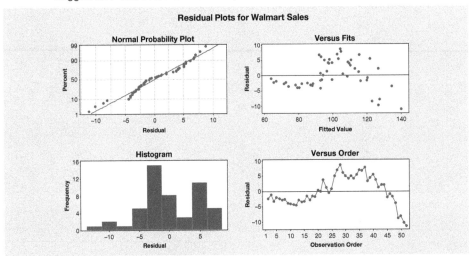

Data: Walmart_2.xlsx; adapted from Minitab output.

---

1 The official *GDP* figures differ between the data sets used in the first and second editions of this book, but the correlation between the two is 0.999. As a result, the coefficients are slightly different but the underlying relationships are essentially unchanged.

At first sight, an increase in the adjusted R^2 from 86.2 percent to 93.3 percent may not seem such a big deal, but the more important measure is S, which relates to the width of the prediction interval; S has dropped from 7.047 to 4.909, a considerable improvement in the width of the interval. When we wish to compare the fits of competing models, the standard error is a better guide than R^2. The residual plots in Figure 9.5 show that we are not yet out of the woods, because the residuals still show a systematic pattern and their *ACF* and *PACF* (not shown) still indicate some dependence over the first four lags. In order to make further progress, we need to develop additional tools, and to do so, we now turn to the use of lagged values of the dependent variable.

9.2 Autoregressive Models

Whenever the *ACF* of the residuals shows significant autocorrelation, it is worth thinking about autoregressive models — that is, models that use past values of the dependent variable to describe future developments. The general form of such models is

$$Y_t = \beta_0 + \beta_1 Y_{t-1} + \ldots + \beta_p Y_{t-p} + \varepsilon_t. \tag{9.2}$$

Equation (9.2) represents the autoregressive model of order p, written as AR(p), previously discussed in Section 6.2.2. Several points are worth noting before we proceed:

- Not all lags 1,2, … , p need to be included. This point is particularly important in dealing with seasonal series, as we shall see shortly.

- The assumptions regarding the error term are the same as those for standard regression models and need not be repeated here (see Section 8.5). The same diagnostics may be used for model checking.

- The parameters may be estimated by ordinary least squares (OLS), as before. By virtue of the central limit theorem, the estimators are approximately normally distributed, provided that the sample size is not too small. (For a detailed discussion of this issue, see Box, Jenkins, Reinsel, and Ljung, 2016, pp. 323–326.)

- OLS can be used even when the process is *nonstationary*, as defined in Section 6.1.1. For example, in the AR(1) scheme, we may allow $|\beta_1| > 1$. Nevertheless, when this occurs, the absolute values of the forecasts will increase without limit, so such models should not be used for other than short-term forecasting.

- The pure autoregressive model can be extended to also include a regression component, as we discuss in Section 9.3.

■ Example 9.3: An AR model using lags 1 and 4 *(Walmart_2.xlsx)*

The plot of the Walmart sales series clearly indicates that the final quarter of each financial year (actually, November and December of one year and January of the next year) has higher sales than the other quarters. This observation was confirmed in the previous section by our analysis using seasonal indicators. Also, the series shows a strong upward trend over time. Accordingly, lags 1 and 4 seem reasonable initial choices for modeling purposes. The resulting analysis, using a standard regression program, yields the following results:

Model 3: Walmart *(Walmart_2.xlsx)*

Predictor	Coef	SE Coef	T	P
Constant	15.55	2.19	7.09	0
L1_Sales	−0.0104	0.0416	−0.25	0.804
L4_Sales	0.8982	0.0373	24.07	0
	S = 2.577 R-Sq = 97.93% R-Sq(adj) = 97.84%			

The results provide two surprises. First of all, the model performs better than Model 2, the regression with dummy (indicator) variables. Second, lag 1 is seen to be relatively unimportant. Dropping this lag, we finish up with the following simpler model:

Model 4: Walmart *(Walmart_2.xlsx)*

Predictor	Coef	SE Coef	T	P
Constant	15.29	1.89	8.08	0.000
L4_Sales	0.8903	0.0191	46.61	0.000
	S = 2.551 R-Sq = 97.93% R-Sq(adj) = 97.88%			

Examining Walmart's sales in earlier years (prior to the recession, from 2003Q1 to 2008Q1: see *Walmart_Old.xlsx*) we find the following results:

Predictor	Coef	SE Coef	T	P
Constant	5.354	0.834	6.42	0.000
L4_Sales	1.0011	0.0126	79.72	0.000

The overall properties are similar in the two data sets, but it is worth noting that the older data set implies a constant annual increase of about $5.36 million for a given quarter over the same quarter in the previous year. Such a result suggests that the corresponding growth rate for Walmart may be slowing, and we should at least consider a log transform and the effects on the full data set to 2015; we leave this to the reader as Exercise 9.4. For the model to be stationary, we would need to restrict the lag 4 coefficient to be less than 1.0 in absolute value; such a restriction would clearly be inappropriate in this case, because the series up to 2010 has a strong upward trend. Here, the coefficient is approximately 1.0 and differencing should be considered. These issues of the stability of the model over different data bases and the use of transformations and differences are taken up in Sections 9.5 and 9.6 and exercises 9.6 and 9.7. ■

A purely autoregressive scheme will not usually be totally effective when important explanatory variables are available. Our purpose in this section has been to show how to incorporate autoregressive terms into a regression framework. We now consider a more complete model.

9.3 Models with Both Autoregressive and Regression Components

Now that we have developed a way to incorporate autoregressive terms into the model, we may combine our findings and consider a model that includes *GDP*, lagged sales for periods 1 and 4, and the three seasonal factors. It remains to be seen whether all these elements are needed, but we can start out with the six explanatory variables and then eliminate redundancies as necessary. The results for this model are as follows:

$$Walmart\ Sales = 18.27 + 0.1001\ L4\_Sales - 0.000180\ L1\_GDP + 0.870\ L1\_Sales$$
$$- 23.30\ Quarter\_1 - 7.72\ Quarter\_2 - 13.34\ Quarter\_3$$

Model 5: Walmart *(Walmart_2.xlsx)*

Predictor	Coef	SE Coef	T	P
Constant	18.27	3.19	5.73	0.000
L4_Sales	0.001	0.0940	1.06	0.293
L1_GDP	−0.000180	0.000495	−0.36	0.718
L1_Sales	0.870	0.101	8.64	0.000
Quarter_1	−23.30	2.54	−9.17	0.000
Quarter_2	−7.72	1.01	−7.65	0.000
Quarter_3	−13.34	1.51	−8.83	0.000
S = 1.534 R-Sq = 99.33% R-Sq(adj) = 99.23%				

Although all three dummy variables show small *P* values, it is evident that, in part, this reflects higher sales in the fourth quarter. Interestingly, *L1_GDP* and *L4_Sales* now appear to be relatively unimportant. The possibility of dropping variables from this model is explored in Exercise 9.8.

The residuals diagnostics are shown in Figure 9.6. These results broadly conform to the underlying assumptions, although the erratic movements in 2008 remain unaccounted for.

DISCUSSION QUESTION: *In Model 5, what are the relative advantages and disadvantages of using both the 1-period and 4-period lags for Sales, if any?*

It is always difficult to know when to stop in a model-building exercise, but we will call a halt here. The summary statistics shown in Table 9.2 indicate the progress we have made through the various stages of the model's development. Using Model 5, we find that the one-step-ahead forecast for 2016Q1 is 115.1, with 95 percent prediction interval (111.5, 118.6).

Figure 9.6 Diagnostics for the Autoregressive Regression Model for Walmart Sales (Model 5)

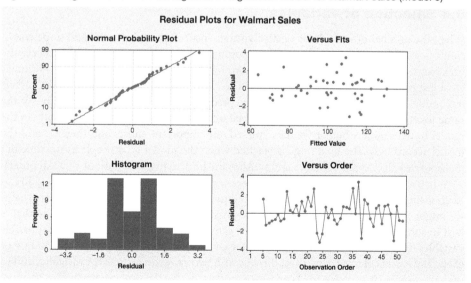

Figure 9.6 (continued)

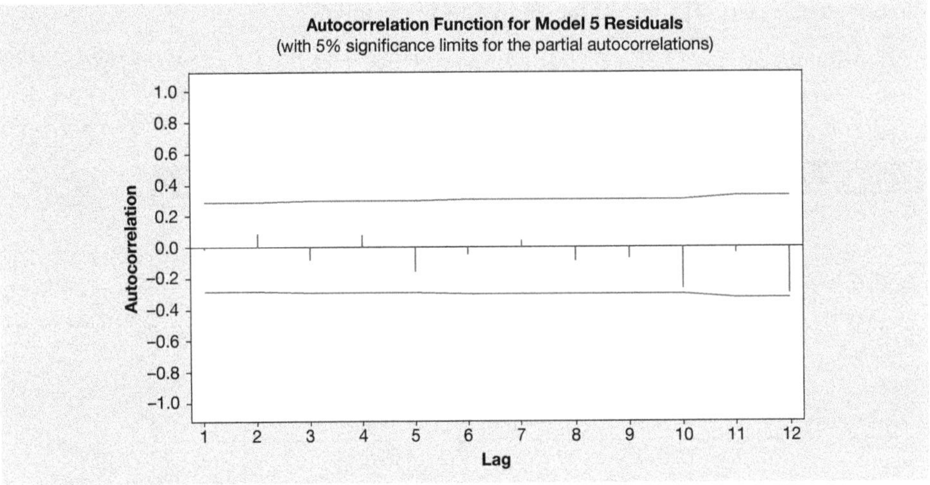

Autocorrelation Function for Model 5 Residuals
(with 5% significance limits for the partial autocorrelations)

Data: Walmart_2.xlsx; adapted from Minitab output.

Table 9.2 Summary Statistics for Different Models for Walmart Sales

Model	X Variables	R-sq(adj)	S
Model 1	L1_GDP	86.22	7.05
Model 2	L1_GDP, Seasonals	93.31	4.91
Model 3	L1_Sales, L4_Sales	97.84	2.58
Model 4	L4_Sales	97.88	2.55
Model 5	L1_GDP, Seasonals, L1 Sales, L4_Sales	99.23	1.53

Data: Walmart_2.xlsx

9.4 Selection of Variables

When the number of variables is relatively small, inspection of the individual slope coefficients is feasible and enables us to prune marginal variables from the model. These are the variables for which there are no strong reasons for their inclusion *and* their slope estimates yield insignificant *t*-values. At each step, we can check how the removal of a variable affects our model in terms of diagnostic statistics, predictive power, and interpretation. By the same token, we may plot the residuals against other variables that are not currently in the model to determine whether we have missed any important effects and then expand the model accordingly. The final stage is reached when the model is as simple as possible but incorporates all relevant variables and satisfies the underlying assumptions — a tall order!

When we have a large number of possible explanatory variables, with little to guide us in choosing one set over another, a more automated procedure is desirable. Conceptually, we might think in terms of running all the possible models and choosing the one that is best in some sense. However, such a process can be a daunting task. If we have K possible variables, there are $2^K - 1$ possible models, based upon all possible patterns of including or excluding a particular variable. (Test this out with two variables, with three variables, and so on.) When $K = 10$, we have 1023 candidate models, but by the time we reach $K = 20$, there are over a million possibilities! Such numbers for K are easy to reach when lagged variables are included in the general model. Thus, when the number of variables is large, we employ various partial searches. Standard approaches are *forward selection*, *backward selection*, and *stepwise regression*. Most statistical software, including Minitab, SAS, and SPSS, have these options. The on-line support for R illustrates these concepts.

If K is small enough (some programs have efficient search algorithms that enable them to search up to $K = 16$ or thereabouts), then we can consider all the possibilities and choose the *best subsets*. (For further details of the algorithms used, see Kutner *et al.*, 2005, pp. 361–369.)

MODEL SELECTION ALGORITHMS

Forward selection starts by including the variable that has greatest explanatory power (and most significant *t*-value). Next, those variables not yet included in the model are evaluated, and the variable that adds most to the model's explanatory power is added to the model. This step is then repeated.

Backward selection starts by including all the variables in the model and then deleting the variable with least explanatory power (and smallest absolute *t*-value). This step is then repeated for the variables remaining in the model.

Stepwise regression alternately adds a new variable to the model and then evaluates existing variables for possible deletion. When the same variable is successively deleted and immediately added back, the search considers additional variables. The aim is to achieve the highest value of R^2 (or some other preselected criterion) at each stage, but not all possibilities are considered.

Best subsets regression considers all possible subsets of the variables and so guarantees finding an optimum on whatever the preselected criterion. This approach is computationally more expensive than the other ones.

All these model selection algorithms can be implemented using an information criterion, such as *AIC*, instead of the *t*-value. This can be advantageous, as models are selected by balancing explanatory power and complexity. This is the norm in R.

9.4.1 Forward, Backward, and Stepwise Selection: Models of the Price of Gasoline

In this section, we use data on the price of unleaded gasoline to examine various model selection approaches. By way of illustration, we show only the SPSS summary printout for the different models.

As we discussed in section 7.3, a substantial number of macroeconomic variables could be considered as possible explanatory variables for movements in U.S. unleaded gasoline prices. Because we are concerned primarily with forecasting, we use only lagged variables. However, many econometricians would make use of contemporaneous observations, as well as lagged values, in model building. Minicase 9.1 encourages the exploration of model development using such an approach.

Our analyses take into account the following nine variables, all lagged by one month:

- Price of unleaded gasoline, in cents per U.S. gallon (*"L1 _Unleaded"*)
- The price of crude oil, in dollars per barrel (*"L1_Crude_price"*)
- The SP 500 Stock Index, end-of-month close (*"L1_SP500"*).
- Personal disposable income, in billions of current dollars (*"L1_PDI"*)
- Consumer price index for all urban consumers, indexed at 100 over 1982-1984, not seasonally adjusted (*"L1_CPI"*)

- Retail Sales: real retail sales in millions of $s, deflated by *CPI* (*"L1_RR_sales"*)
- Unemployment rate, not seasonally adjusted (*"L1_Unemp"*)
- Housing starts, seasonally adjusted annual rate (*"L1_Housing"*)
- Demand for gasoline, in thousands of barrels per day (*"L1_Demand"*).

These data series are contained in *Gas_prices_2.xlsx*. The data set contains additional variables on production, imports etc. which may also be relevant but we leave their analysis to the exercises. In an extension to our model developed in chapter 8 we now include additional variables, which have face validity as possible influences; critically, we have added in a one-period lag of the dependent variable which may account for the autocorrelation we observed in the diagnostic checks of Section 8.5.1. We initially start with the estimation sample the period from January 1996 to December 2008 with the hold-out sample covering the period from January 2009 to December 2010.[2]

Model Summary: Forward Selection

Model	R	R-sq	R-sq(adj)	Std. Error of the Estimate
1	.978[a]	.956	.956	15.52
2	.980[b]	.961	.960	14.70
3	.983[c]	.966	.965	13.71
4	.984[d]	.969	.968	13.23

a. Predictors: (Constant), L1_Unleaded
b. Predictors: (Constant), L1_Unleaded, L1_Crude_price
c. Predictors: (Constant), L1_Unleaded, L1_Crude_price, L1_Housing
d. Predictors: (Constant), L1_Unleaded, L1_Crude_price, L1_Housing, L1_Unemp

Data: Gas_prices_2.xlsx; adapted from SPSS output.

The selection terminates[3] when none of the excluded variables (if added) would prove significant (on the basis of the *F*-test with $\alpha = 0.05$). Does the final model (Model 4) make sense? The details are provided in Table 9.3 and the answer to the question is broadly "Yes". There is a positive autoregressive effect such that a higher past price of unleaded gasoline leads to higher current prices and previous crude prices are working through into current retail prices of unleaded gasoline with the expected positive coefficient. In addition, *Housing* has a positive sign, reflecting overall economic conditions, and the negative sign for *Unemployment* reflects the impact of reducing demand in the economy.

The backward selection method leads to a somewhat more complicated model than Forward Selection that includes the lagged *PDI*, *CPI*, and *RR_sales* but neither *Housing* nor *Unemployment* appear. The coefficients for the lagged values of *Unleaded* and *Crude_price* are broadly comparable for the two models, but certainly not the same. Such a discrepancy between the two methods is common and relates to the different criteria for adding new variables to a model or for removing existing ones. Note that, in this example, the "best" model obtained through backward selection yields a smaller standard error than forward selection does.

In this particular case, using stepwise selection (where variables can be both removed and added in) is found to give the same results as forward selection. Such differences among

---

2 In the first edition of this book we used fewer variables but included a time trend as an explanatory variable. This extended list is more economically meaningful and illustrates the same points. We go on to examine the more recent data and the changes this implies later.

3 Selection rules and cutoff values differ among programs. The user should always check the specifications before making a final choice of model.

the selection procedures may occur because of multicollinearity (see Section 9.5) but also because of outliers (a topic we discuss in Section 9.7). Also the algorithm used in the selection routine differs from software to software. Accordingly, we will defer making a choice between the models until we have examined matters further; see Section 9.5.

Table 9.3 Unleaded Price Models: Forward and Backward Selection Procedures Compared

| Model | Coefficients | | Standardized Coefficients | | |
| | Unstandardized Coefficients | | | | |
Model	B	Std. Error	Beta	T	P
4 (Forward)					
(Constant)	22.770	11.069		2.06	.041
L1_Unleaded	.540	.073	0.541	7.41	.000
L1_Crude_price	1.330	.208	0.477	6.39	.000
L1_Housing	.021	.004	0.084	5.29	.000
L1_Unemp	-5.690	1.635	-0.051	-3.48	.001
2 (Backward)					
(Constant)	344.329	126.280		2.727	.007
L1_Unleaded	0.773	0.089	0.775	8.692	.000
L1_Crude_price	1.134	0.193	0.407	5.884	.000
L1_PDI	0.033	0.013	0.729	2.638	.009
L1_CPI	-4.483	1.175	-1.094	-3.814	.000
L1_RR_sales	0.001	0.0003	0.212	4.416	.000

Note: Dependent Variable: *Unleaded*

N.B. SPSS also includes "Standardized Coefficients," which attempt to measure the importance of one explanatory variable relative to another; they represent the regression coefficients when all the variables (including the dependent variable) are standardized to have zero mean and unit variance. We omit this column in later SPSS-based tables. One simpler route to measuring the relative impact of a variable is to estimate the effect of a 10 percent change in each of them upon the expected value of the dependent variable.

Data: Gas_prices_2.xlsx; adapted from SPSS output.

Model Summary: Backward Selection

Model	R	R-sq	R-sq(adj)	Std. Error of the Estimate
1	.987[a]	.975	.973	12.124
2	.987[b]	.974	.973	12.104
3	.987[c]	.974	.973	12.113
4	.987[d]	.974	.973	12.143
5	.987[e]	.973	.973	12.211

a. Predictors: (Constant), L1_RR_sales, L1_Unemp, L1_Housing, L1_Demand, L1_Crude_price, L1_SP500_2, L1_Unleaded, L1_PDI, L1_CPI
b. Predictors: (Constant), L1_RR_sales, L1_Housing, L1_Demand, L1_Crude_price, L1_SP500_2, L1_Unleaded, L1_PDI, L1_CPI
c. Predictors: (Constant), L1_RR_sales, L1_Demand, L1_Crude_price, L1_SP500_2, L1_Unleaded, L1_PDI, L1_CPI
d. Predictors: (Constant), L1_RR_sales, L1_Crude_price, L1_SP500_2, L1_Unleaded, L1_PDI, L1_CPI
e. Predictors: (Constant), L1_RR_sales, L1_Crude_price, L1_Unleaded, L1_PDI, L1_CPI

Data: Gas_prices_2.xlsx; adapted from SPSS output.

9.4.2 Searching All Possible Models: Best Subset Regression

Alternatively, we may examine all possible regressions, using, for example, Minitab or SAS. Results are shown in Table 9.4, where we have required both lagged crude and lagged unleaded to be in the list of regressions (to reduce the computational burden).

Table 9.4 Partial Results of Best Subsets Analysis for Unleaded Prices (1996–2008)[4]

Number of Variables Selected	Best Model	R-sq(adj)	S
1	L1_Unleaded	95.6	15.5
2	L1_Unleaded, L1_Crude_price	96.0	14.7
3	L1_Unleaded, L1_Crude_price, L1_Housing	96.5	13.7
4	L1_Unleaded, L1_Crude_price, L1_RR_sales, L1_CPI	97.1	12.6
5	L1_Unleaded, L1_Crude_price, L1_CPI, L1_PDI, L1_RR_sales	97.2	12.2
6	L1_Unleaded, L1_Crude_price, L1_SP500, L1_CPI, L1_PDI, L1_RR_sales	97.2	12.14
7	L1_Unleaded, L1_Crude_price, L1_SP500, L1_CPI, L1_PDI, L1_RR_sales, L1_Demand	97.2	12.11
8	L1_Unleaded, L1_Crude_price, L1_SP500, L1_CPI, L1_PDI, L1_RR_sales, L1_Demand, L1_Unemployment,	97.2	12.13
9	L1_Unleaded, L1_Crude_price, L1_SP500, L1_CPI, L1_PDI, L1_RR_sales, L1_Demand, L1_Unemployment, L1_Housing	97.2	12.12

Data: Gas_prices_2.xlsx

The best subsets results are encouraging, in that there is a steady reduction in the value of S. But now we are faced with a second problem: How should we choose among these best subset models?

The seven-variable model has the smallest value of S, the largest value of $R^2(adj)$ and matches the choice obtained by backward selection. But we must also keep in mind that we have examined (at least implicitly) $2^9 - 1 = 511$ different models. Clearly, if we choose from among so many possibilities, we run the risk of being overoptimistic about the performance of the model selected. First off, we must look at interpretability. In fact, the coefficients (not shown here) of lagged *Demand* (with the correct sign) and *SP500* are both insignificant at the 5% level. While lagged *PDI* has a plausible positive sign, *CPI* has a negative sign raising a serious question mark as it is perhaps to be expected that general inflation carries over to the unleaded price. This argues that we should distinguish between real effects (such as real unleaded price and real *PDI*) and money effects such as general inflation (*CPI*). This is left as exercise 9.13 for the reader.

A further route to resolving the question of model choice is to split the sample: Use an estimation sample to select the preferred model, and then use the hold-out sample for final estimation of that model and for forecasting. When sufficient data exist, this is the best method, and it should be routinely applied in, for example, data-mining applications, as we discuss in Chapter 10 (see validation and cross-validation in Section 10.4). The approach is straightforward with the large cross-sectional data sets that are typically available, such as those concerned with customers' purchasing habits. With the smaller data sets that are

---

4 The results here differ in detail from the first edition due to government revisions to the data.

usual in time series, we recommend the careful use of a hold-out sample or an information criterion, as we have argued earlier.

Once satisfied with a particular specification, the usual diagnostics need to be analyzed. Figure 9.7 shows the diagnostics for the "Backward Selection" model.[5]

Figure 9.7 Residual Analysis from the 'Backward' Selection Model

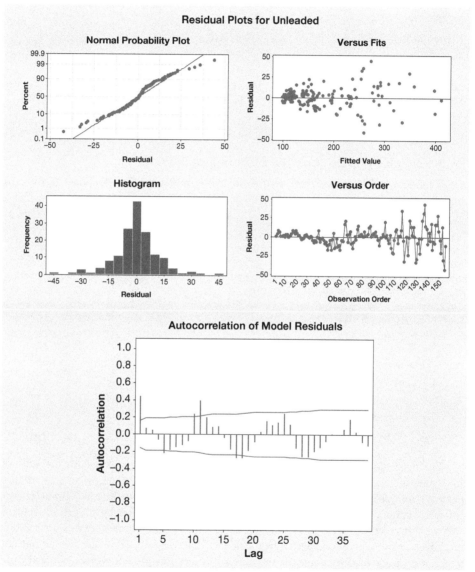

Certain issues are apparent from analyzing the residuals: in particular the increased heteroscedasticity over time. There are possible outliers (see the lack of normality and the histogram). In addition there is a significant first order autocorrelation suggesting we have

---

5 These diagnostic figures are based on fitting the five-variable "backwards" model directly. Slightly different results arise if the diagnostics are run directly after completing the model search, because additional lags and differences included in the set of possible variables, may lead to the deletion of one or more observations at the start of the series.

yet to successfully model the dynamics of the process. There is also a wave pattern in the autocorrelation function: seasonality may be suspected as the *Unleaded* price is not seasonally adjusted. We therefore should check by adding in seasonal dummies.

The seasonal dummies (with January as the base year) prove overall to be significant with the months from March to September (relative to December) proving significant with a higher price averaging 14 cents. But the autocorrelation problem remains unsolved.

MODEL SELECTION

In comparing models with reference to a hold-out sample, consider only models that are interpretable and that pass the standard diagnostic tests.

DISCUSSION QUESTION: *Why might using best subsets or stepwise regression not deliver the most accurate forecasting model?*

9.4.3 Using a Hold-Out Sample to Compare Models

Which model wins? To answer this question, we may compare the models chosen by forward and backward selection with an ARIMA(0,1,1) model by computing the mean error (*ME*), the mean absolute error (*MAE*), and the mean absolute percentage error (*MAPE*) (all introduced in Section 2.7). Our hold-out sample covers the period January 2009-December 2010. The *ME*, *MAE*, and *MAPE* for the three sets of forecasts are shown in Table 9.5.

Table 9.5 Summary Measures of One-Step-Ahead Forecast Performance for the ARIMA Scheme and the Selected Models, 2009–2010

Method of Forecasting	ME	MAE	MAPE	RelMAE
Random Walk	5.44	9.01	3.63	1.00
ARIMA(0,1,1) with $\theta = -0.564$	3.93	11.13	4.44	1.24
Forward: 2 variables	4.48	8.24	3.38	0.93
Forward: 4 variables	48.21	48.21	19.21	5.35
Forward: 4 variables plus seasonals	46.54	46.54	18.51	5.17
Backward: 5 variables	47.76	47.76	19.30	5.30
Backward: 5 variables plus seasonals	43.34	43.34	17.47	4.81

Something has gone badly wrong! Our hold-out period coincided with the start of the "Great Recession" in the United States and elsewhere. In brief, oil prices shot up, the economy slumped, and our models failed to take those possibilities into account. (Neither did most economists!) Although all the regression models included lagged price variables, both versions recorded large positive residuals in January 2009 (the forecasts were too low and never recovered, as can be seen from the fact that *ME* = *MAE*; all 24 one-step-ahead errors were positive!). By contrast, the simpler regression model, which involved only *L1_Crude_price* and *L1_Unleaded* (in Table 9.5 named as Forward: 2 variables) was the best of the bunch because it focused on market realities rather than coincidental trends with other variables. The ARIMA scheme was relatively successful because it allowed more rapid adjustments based upon recent errors. The random walk also performed quite well, an example of the common finding that the random walk is hard to beat for short-term forecasting. These results underline that forecasts rely upon the assumption that the system under study will behave as it has in the past, clearly not valid with respect to the more complex models over the period 2009–2010.

9.4.4 A Regression Model with Autoregressive Errors

The superior performance of the ARIMA model suggests that we might combine the regression terms with a component that adjusts for the errors. We set up the model as follows:

$$Y_t = \beta_0 + \beta_1 X_{1t} + \dots + \beta_K X_{Kt} + u_t$$
$$u_t = \phi\, u_{t-1} + \varepsilon_t. \tag{9.3}$$

Dropping the regression terms reduces the model to a first-order autoregressive scheme, whereas setting $\phi = 0$ reduces the model to the usual multiple regression formulation. This model is known as the *Cochrane-Orcutt scheme* (Kutner et al, 2005, pp. 492–495). Estimation of the parameters can be simultaneous but we use here an iterative solution. Conceptually, it is easiest to think of trying a range of values for ϕ and fitting a multiple regression model using OLS for each choice of ϕ. A practical approach is to use Solver in Excel, and the spreadsheet *Gas_prices_Cochrane.xlsx* is available on the website for the model we describe next. This can also be done in EViews.

■ **Example 9.4: Cochrane-Orcutt model for unleaded gas prices**
(Gas_prices_Cochrane.xlsx)

We consider model (9.3) with the two explanatory variables *L1_Unleaded* and *L1_Crude_price* and use *Solver* to estimate the model. The resulting forecast function estimated to December 2008 is

$$F_t = 42.94 + 0.371\ L1\_Unleaded + 1.704\ L1\_Crude\_price + 0.4071 u_{t-1}$$

That is $\phi = 0.407$ so that a positive residual in one time period leads to an upward adjustment for the next forecast. The standard error of estimate is $S = 14.01$. The resulting error measures for the out-of-sample forecasts are

$$ME = 4.28,\ MAE = 9.72 \text{ and } MAPE = 4.29\%.$$

These results are marginally better than those obtained with the simple ARIMA scheme. However, in this case the inclusion of the error adjustment does not appear to have improved the forecasting performance relative to the two variable model.

The latest econometric packages feature new approaches that aim to do a better job of automatic model selection as well as describing more general error structures (see, e.g., EViews 9 (available through *www.eviews.com*) or PcGive (*www.oxmetrics.net*). In this example, we have included only one-period lags, but some effects, such as those for crude oil prices, may take longer to feed through into the unleaded price as evidenced by the autocorrelation in the residuals. In addition, the specification of the error structure may be extended from an AR(1) as here to an ARMA(p, q) scheme. Exercise 9.12 explores more general structures, and other, more advanced alternatives are considered in Chapter 10. ■

9.5 Multicollinearity and Variable Selection

Model building for business processes is frequently fraught with uncertainty. We are often able to identify a considerable number of variables that may have an effect, but we lack a strong theoretical foundation for making a selection from among those variables. Further, the variables we choose may be highly correlated among themselves (different lags of the same variable, different measures of household income or various stock price indexes), or the relationships may change over time. Some of the variables we have considered in modeling unleaded gas prices fall into this category, e.g., *PDI* and *CPI* as the correlations in Table 7.2 demonstrate.

The questions we raise are similar to those posed earlier: How do we identify such problems and what do we do about them? If the explanatory variables are highly correlated with one another, there is potentially an element of redundancy and the possibility of confusing the effects of the correlated variables. Whenever such a condition arises, we say that the data display *multicollinearity* and that some of the variables *may* be superfluous. Once some of them are included in the model, it may be possible to exclude others. Conversely, a variable may be important at some times and less so at others. We first examine multicollinearity and then return to consider structural change in Section 9.8.

When we developed the multiple regression model, we used the t-test to examine the contribution of a particular variable, given that all the others were included in the model. The same idea may be exploited here: For each explanatory variable, we may perform a regression analysis on all the other explanatory variables. If a particular variable has a very high value of R^2 in such a setting, it means that most of the explanation which that variable can provide is already available from those other variables. As a consequence, it may be feasible to remove that variable from the model without any serious loss of performance.

Let R_j^2 denote the coefficient of determination for variable X_j on all the other explanatory variables. We define the *Variance Inflation Factor* (or *VIF*)

$$VIF\ (j) = \frac{1}{1 - R_j^2}.\tag{9.4}$$

If X_j is completely uncorrelated with the other variables, then $R_j^2 = 0$ $VIF = 1$, its minimum value. As the overall correlation gets higher, the coefficient of determination increases and so does *VIF*. If X_j is perfectly correlated with a linear function of the other variables, *VIF* becomes infinite, which is what happens if we try to include all four quarterly seasonal indicators in the model. That is a clear signal that we can drop one of the indicator variables without any loss of explanatory power.

In other cases, *VIF* remains finite but may be large. There are no formal rules about how large a value of *VIF* is too large, but the following guidelines are reasonable:

- If $n < 30$, consider dropping a variable if its *VIF* is greater than 5.

- If $n \geq 30$, consider dropping a variable if its *VIF* is greater than 10.

- As before, for any n, we consider dropping a variable if $P > \alpha$ (our chosen significance level).

Remember, these are guidelines, not sacred laws! A high *VIF* may be acceptable if $P < \alpha$, although such mixed signals usually mean that a more careful investigation is in order. As a practical matter, we proceed cautiously and remove variables only one at a time, to avoid casting out the baby with the bathwater. Software such as SAS, SPSS, and R provide further collinearity diagnostics for identifying which variables are highly interrelated with the potential to affect the final model selected, due to the resulting inflation in the coefficient standard errors. There is hardly any problem with dropping a variable when other variables included in the model measure much the same phenomenon (e.g., *GDP* and personal disposable income, *PDI*). However, sometimes two quite distinct variables, such as company expenditures on television advertising and in-store promotions, may be very highly (negatively) correlated because the overall marketing budget is fixed. A change in policy could lead to a very different relationship. In such a situation, the multicollinearity is *data-based*. In that case, if we think that the apparent relationship between the variables may break down during the forecast period, we really need to obtain better estimates of the slope coefficients. While this is easier said than done, the only straightforward route is to collect more relevant data to use in the model; companies sometimes do this by test marketing in restricted areas (e.g., a small number of metropolitan regions).

By contrast, when the variables are *definitionally related*, as with different measures of income, we can usually be confident that the collinearity will continue into the forecast period. In this situation, it is perfectly reasonable to drop one or more of the variables and simplify the model.

When the data are cross-sectional, the same arguments apply. Dropping variables that theory suggests are important is dangerous.

MULTICOLLINEARITY

Multicollinearity occurs when the explanatory variables are themselves strongly related.

Definitional Multicollinearity occurs when two variables are strongly related because they share a similar definition and are similarly measured; in this case, the multicollinearity will persist.

Causal Multicollinearity arises when the explanatory variables are strongly related because of the nature of the underlying phenomena: the multicollinearity can therefore be expected to persist.

Data-based Multicollinearity occurs when the relationship exists in the data being analyzed and there is no strong reason to believe that it will persist during the forecast period.

Adverse Effects of Multicollinearity are inflated standard errors of (some) slope coefficients with the potential of excluding variables that should be included in the final regression model.

■ Example 9.5: Multicollinearity in the unleaded prices data

(Gas_prices_2.xlsx)

We may examine the two previously selected models given in Table 9.3 and compute their *VIF* values. The output is given in Table 9.6. The model obtained by forward selection shows the very high correlation between the lagged values of *Unleaded* and *Crude*. This relationship is not surprising, being an example of causal multicollinearity, as there is no reason to suspect that the price of gasoline at the pump will become disconnected from crude oil prices. Also, both variables are significant with interpretable coefficients. Accordingly, we will keep both variables in the model.

The situation with the model obtained by backward selection is rather different. The *VIF*s are horrendously high, particularly *PDI* and *CPI* — they will tend to be highly correlated because of inflation: they are definitionally related. Real Retail Sales (*RR_sales*) may also be swept up into the confusion. The model is unacceptable and we must consider a reformulation. In particular, we need to consider whether some of the variables, including the unleaded price itself (as well as *PDI*), should be measured in real terms (with inflation removed) or in current dollars, as it is now measured. This question is explored in Exercise 9.13. ■

Table 9.6 VIF Values for the Gas Price Models Obtained by Forward and Backward Selection (Database: Jan1996–Dec2008)

| Model | Unstandardized Coefficients | | T | P | VIF |
	B	Std. Error			
4 (Forward)					
(Constant)	22.770	11.069	2.06	.041	
L1_Unleaded	.540	.073	7.41	.000	25.52
L1_Crude_price	1.330	.208	6.39	.000	26.63
L1_Housing	.021	.004	5.29	.000	1.21
L1_Unemp	-5.690	1.635	–3.48	.001	1.03
2 (Backward)					
(Constant)	344.329	126.280	2.727	.007	
L1_Unleaded	0.773	0.089	8.692	.000	43.43
L1_Crude_price	1.134	0.193	5.884	.000	26.12
L1_PDI	0.033	0.013	2.638	.009	417.29
L1_CPI	-4.483	1.175	–3.814	.000	449.53
L1_RR_sales	0.001	0.0003	4.416	.000	12.54

Data: Gas_prices_2.xlsx; adapted from SPSS output.

In retrospect, the poor quality of the forecasts from these models, as summarized in Table 9.5, provides additional evidence that such models are not to be trusted. *VIF* values should always be checked in multiple regression models.

9.5.1 Use of Differences

Time series often change relatively slowly over time, so we must deal with large autocorrelations as well as the high correlations that exist among some of the predictors. To keep multicollinearity in check, we need to find a way to retain the richness of the model with multiple variables and yet remove the instability caused by the high correlations. As we have seen, one solution is to use model selection procedures, but this may eliminate key variables. Another solution is to examine changes in the variables, rather than looking at their absolute levels. That is, we consider differences, as originally introduced in Section 2.6.2. As before, we define the first-order difference in the dependent variable as

$$DY_t = Y_t - Y_{t-1}.$$

with similar expressions for the differences of the explanatory variables. We continue to lag all the predictor variables by one month and explore forward and backward selection.

The model selected is summarized in Table 9.7. Now both forward and backward selection yield the same model with just the differences of lagged *Crude_price* and *SP500* included and the *VIF* values are now at acceptable levels. Depending on the significance level set in the selection options a second model can be obtained using stepwise regression that includes demand with a positive sign, higher demand leading to higher prices. However, once seasonal dummies are added in its significance is nullified. We therefore present the simpler model as well. In addition the constant term is insignificant and while it should be kept in a model formulated in levels, in differences it should be omitted, unless a constant growth in the dependent variable, here *Unleaded*, is viewed as plausible.

The much lower value for $R^2(adj)$ may come as a shock, but keep in mind that it relates to the variance explained for the *change* in the unleaded price; much of the variability has already been eliminated by using the difference rather than the original price variable. More relevant is the value of *S*, which is smaller for the case of backward selection than for any of the models discussed earlier.

DISCUSSION QUESTION: *Why can S be used to compare a model in levels with a model in differences?*

Table 9.7 Summary Results for Selection Models for Unleaded Gasoline Prices, Based Upon Differenced Series (Data: Jan1996–Dec2008)

Model	Slope	Std. Error	T	P	VIF
(Constant)	–.303	.928	–.327	.744	
DIFF(L1_Crude_price,1)	2.151	.205	10.499	.000	1.019
DIFF(L1_SP500,1)	.050	.018	2.755	.007	1.023
DIFF(L1_Demand,1)	.900	.549	1.640	.103	1.008
With DIFF(L1_Demand,1)	R-sq(adj) = 46.0% S =11.49				
With Seasonal dummies	R-sq(adj) = 54.2% S=10.58				

Notes: Dependent Variable: DY_t = DIFF(Unleaded,1). The notation DIFF(X,1) represents the first difference of *X*. The model with seasonal dummies does not included *L1_Demand*, which was not significant.

Data: Gas_prices_2.xlsx; adapted from SPSS output (with default names).

We may briefly summarize the diagnostic plots for these two differenced models (not shown). The inclusion of dummy variables and the decrease in the standard error demonstrate seasonality (though this is unclear from examination of the *ACF*), and the probability plot indicates heavier tails than for the normal distribution. Most critically, the plot of residuals against time shows increasing variability; we take up this issue again in Section 9.6.4.

Table 9.8 compares the forecasts from the models developed so far. The models incorporating differences do not appear to be as effective in adjusting for past errors as the two variables model, which includes only the first order lags for *Crude* and for *Unleaded*. However, differencing often serves to eliminate multicollinearity, and it is an important tool when we believe that changes, rather than levels, should be modeled. As is often the case, the random walk model in a period of rapid change has proved difficult to beat.

Table 9.8 Summary of One-Step Ahead Forecast Error Statistics: All Models *(based upon a hold-out sample from January 2009–December 2010)*

Model	In-sample Std. error	ME	MAE	MAPE	RelMAE
Random Walk	15.58	5.44	9.01	3.63	1.00
ARIMA (0,1,1)	12.94	3.93	11.13	4.44	1.24
Forward: 2 variable	14.70	4.48	8.24	3.38	0.93
Forward: 4 variable	13.23	48.21	48.21	19.21	5.35
Backward: 5 variable	12.21	47.76	47.76	19.30	5.30
Cochrane-Orcutt	14.01	4.28	9.72	4.29	1.08
Differenced model (with D_L1_Demand))	11.49	–6.58	14.08	5.75	1.56
Differenced model (with seasonals)	10.58	2.74	13.27	5.50	1.47

MODEL EVALUATION

When comparing a model with a differenced dependent variable with a model in the raw data,

- R^2 cannot be used to make a sensible comparison.
- The predictive accuracy of the models in forecasting the original data should be used to make the comparison.
- S is the original data or in differences is comparable, unlike R^2.

9.5.2 The Lasso Method

The Lasso method is a procedure that combines parameter shrinkage towards zero (to provide greater stability) with an element of variable selection. That is, the shrinkage process may lead to a particular coefficient being "shrunk" all the way to zero, thereby eliminating that particular variable. The benefit behind shrinkage is that it can make the parameter estimates more stable, particularly when there are high correlations among the variables. In turn, this change may produce more stable predictions. The technique was introduced by Tibshirani (1996) and although it has been applied to a variety of statistical methods, we focus upon its use in regression analysis.

We start from the usual formulation:

$$Y = \beta_0 + \beta_1 X_1 + \beta_2 X_2 + \dots + \beta_K X_K + \varepsilon.$$

In order to apply constraints to the slope coefficients in a uniform way, we first standardize all the variables:

$$Y^* = (Y - \bar{Y}) / S_Y; \quad X^*_j = (X_j - \bar{X}_j) / S_j, j = 1, \dots, K.$$

The regression equation becomes:

$$Y^* = \gamma_1 X^*_1 + \gamma_2 X^*_2 + \dots + \gamma_K X^*_K + \varepsilon^*.$$

where

$$\varepsilon^* = \varepsilon / S_Y; \gamma_j = \beta_j S_j / S_Y, j = 1, \dots, K.$$

Note that the standardization procedure ensures that $\gamma_0 = 0$. The Lasso process then involves estimating the parameters $\{\gamma_j, j = 1, \dots, K\}$ subject to the constraint:

$$|\gamma_1| + |\gamma_2| + \dots + |\gamma_K| \leq T_0.$$

The constant T_0 is chosen by the modeler (this is typically done by using cross-validation, see Section 10.4). For sufficiently large values, the OLS estimates remain optimal, but as the *Lasso* gradually tightens the coefficients reduce, to a variable extent, in absolute value. The process is most readily understood by means of an example.

■ Example 9.6: Application of Lasso to the gas prices model

We consider the nine variable model, using the data through Dec2013 as the estimation sample and one-month lags for the variables: *Crude_price, Unleaded, SP500, PDI, RR_sales, CPI, Housing, Unemp,* and *Demand.* The results are summarized in Table 9.9.

For values of $T_0 > 2.702$ the OLS results, listed in the second column are optimal. The values obtained are the same as those shown in the "Standardized coefficient" column in SPSS output. As T_0 is reduced, the coefficients are reduced; those for the highly correlated pair *PDI* and *CPI* decline the most. By the time we are down to $T_0 = 1$, *CPI* has been eliminated from the equation. Further reductions gradually squeeze out other variables but at the expense of increasing S substantially. The investigator must decide upon the appropriate degree of tightening.

Table 9.9 Results of Regular and Group *Lasso* Analyses of Unleaded Gas Prices Data

Lagged Variables		OLS	Lasso $T_0 = (2.0)$	Lasso $T_0 = (1.5)$	Lasso $T_0 = (1.0)$	Group $T_0 = (1.5)$	Group $T_0 = (1.0)$	Group $T_0 = (0.5)$
Crude_price	C1	0.263	0.265	0.265	0.218	0.264	0.265	0.267
Unleaded	C2	0.755	0.712	0.681	0.433	0.744	0.713	0.683
SP500	C3	0.012	0.011	0.010	0.011	0.012	0.011	0.011
PDI	C4	0.542	0.254	0.048	0.126	0.462	0.243	0.024
RR_sales	C5	0.148	0.147	0.146	0.118	0.147	0.146	0.144
CPI	C6	0.801	−0.456	−0.210	0.000	−0.706	−0.445	−0.185
Housing	C7	−0.056	−0.046	−0.039	−0.040	−0.053	−0.045	−0.036
Unemployment	C8	0.099	0.086	0.077	0.053	0.096	0.087	0.078
Demand	C9	−0.025	−0.024	−0.023	−0.022	−0.025	−0.023	−0.022
Sum of Squares		4.367	4.424	4.533	7.251	4.372	4.428	4.549

Data: Lasso_results.xlsx

Elsewhere, we have suggested that *Crude_price* and *Unleaded* are natural variables to include because they have a causal basis. We may use this information to good effect by applying a *Group Lasso*. That is, we apply different constraints to distinct groups of variables. We illustrate by leaving lagged *Crude_price* and *Unleaded* variables unconstrained, but imposing the constraint on the other seven. It is noticeable that preserving the two key variables allows the group lasso to tighten the coefficients of the other variables, especially *PDI* and *CPI*, with only modest increases in the sum of squares. The *Lasso* analysis may be explored using the spreadsheet *Lasso_results.xlsx*, which includes the full data set and the OLS results. The forecasting performance of the different models is explored in Exercise 9.16. ■

Lasso and its extensions are used increasingly for large data sets where there are many collinear variables to consider. Section 12.4.5 discusses an example from marketing. It is available through SAS and R, and for the latter there is example code available online at the book's website (*Appendix C: Forecasting in R: Tutorial and Examples*).

9.6 Nonlinear Models

Sometimes the response of the dependent variable (Y) to a particular input variable is unlikely to be linear *over the range of the application*. (See Figure 7.3, describing the sales-advertising relationship.) One example is the effect of temperature on the consumption of energy or foodstuffs such as beer and ice cream. Small changes from the average temperature typically have little effect on consumption, but above a certain threshold, a particularly hot day drives up air-conditioner use and people enjoy a cold drink and ice cream even more than usual.

Sometimes the data are highly suggestive of a nonlinear relationship. Figure 9.8 shows that when the price of a product is too high, the product ceases to be competitive in the marketplace and sales dwindle toward zero. If regression modeling is to capture all the possible relationships between the explanatory variables and the dependent variable, then we need to model such nonlinear relationships.

Figure 9.8 A Nonlinear Relationship Between Sales and Price

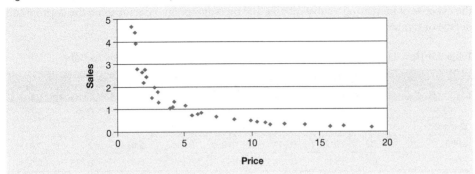

9.6.1 Polynomial Schemes

The simplest approach is to include nonlinear variables such as X^2, leaving the model still linear in the parameters. The quadratic model is

$$Y_t = \beta_0 + \beta_1 X_t + \beta_2 X_t^2 + \varepsilon_t.$$

This model can be estimated by means of the standard methods for multiple regression because it is *linear in the parameters:* You just add an additional variable, defined as the square of X, into the spreadsheet or worksheet. To see how this is done, consider Example 9.7, which shows sales as they are affected by advertising. The data set also includes a classification of the different types of advertising.

■ Example 9.7: Modeling the advertising-sales relationship

Sales	Advert	Promotion Type	AdvertSq
874.5	100.57	1	10114.3
928.1	106.80	2	11406.2
937.0	109.26	2	11937.7
928.9	121.78	1	14830.4

Data: Advert.xlsx

A graph of the data is plotted in Figure 9.9, which shows clear nonlinear effects, with sales tailing off at the higher levels of advertising but a rapid response from levels from 100 to 170. The first observation may be unusual (see Section 9.7).

Figure 9.9 The Nonlinear Relationship Between Sales and Advertising

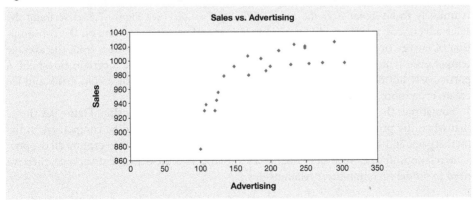

With the two input variables (*Advert* and *AdvertSq*), we can now estimate the parameters β_0, β_1, and β_2 as a standard linear model and compare it with the model that is linear in *Advert*. Results are shown in Table 9.10.

Table 9.10 Sales versus Advertising: Using SPSS to Estimate Nonlinear Effects
(*Model 1 is linear in advertising, model 2 quadratic in advertising*)

Model Summary				
Model	R	R-sq	R-sq(adj)	Std. Error of the Estimate
1	.791[a]	.626	.607	23.675
2	.909[b]	.826	.807	16.569

a. Predictors: (Constant), Advert
b. Predictors: (Constant), Advert, AdvertSq

Model	B	Std. Error	T	P
1 (Constant)	890.717	16.248	54.822	.000
Advert	.470	.081	5.780	.000
2 (Constant)	722.143	37.826	19.091	.000
Advert	2.390	.415	5.760	.000
AdvertSq	−.005	.001	4.673	.000

Data: Advert.xlsx; adapted from SPSS output.

How might we have known that there was a problem with the linear model (which included just *Advert*)? In general, we would expect a nonlinear relationship between sales and advertising; any marketing text would point this out. In addition, we should, of course, always look at the residuals, and those for Model 1 do not look at all random, showing a distinct nonlinear pattern (an exercise we leave to the reader). Because *AdvertSq* has a negative sign, the fitted value for *Sales* is now lower for higher levels of advertising; that is, the quadratic term has a damping effect on the sales response at higher advertising levels. ■

Higher order (e.g., cubic) terms could be included in the model, but this is rarely a good idea for business data because the higher order terms can create unstable models (and rarely have any theoretical justification). However, when there are two or more explanatory variables, it is often a good idea to include cross-product terms to capture interactions. (This can be particularly useful when using indicator variables, as it allows introducing logical switches in our models, for example modeling the effect of running multiple promotions at the same time, without introducing new variables.) For example, the two-variable model with quadratic and interaction terms may be written as

$$Y = \beta_0 + \beta_1 X_1 + \beta_2 X_1^2 + \beta_3 X_2 + \beta_4 X_2^2 + \beta_5 X_1 X_2 + \varepsilon.$$

As before, these kinds of models can be estimated by ordinary least squares. It should be kept in mind that quadratic models display a single turning point (maximum or minimum). If the turning point is natural in the context of the problem (e.g., profit as a function of price), all is well. If not, as in the advertising example just discussed, the model is valid only in the range of X values for which the expected values are increasing — generally, $X < -b_1/2b_2$ or $X < 2.39/0.01 = 239$ in the example. The model fits may be unreliable for $X > 239$.

9.6.2 Nonlinear Transformations

Some models are nonlinear in the parameters, not just the input variables. An example is

$$Y = \alpha X_1^{\beta_1} X_2^{\beta_2} \times (\text{error}).$$

As we discuss in Chapter 12, models such as these are needed to model a product's market share where price and promotional effects have been shown to have a multiplicative relationship. (The effect of a price change is amplified proportionately by how much the change is promoted.)

However, these models can be handled quite easily by taking natural logarithms (the function in Excel is ln) to get

$$\ln(Y) = \ln(\alpha) + \beta_1\ln(X_1) + \beta_2\ln(X_2) + \ln(\text{error}).$$

For obvious reasons, such models are often called log-log models. Of course, the preceding model does not look like a conventional regression equation, but if we set

$$Y^* = \ln(Y), \alpha^* = \ln(\alpha), X_1^* = \ln(X_1), X_2^* = \ln(X_3), \varepsilon = \ln(\text{error}).$$

we get the standard regression model

$$Y^* = \alpha^* + \beta_1 X_1^* + \beta_2 X_2^* + \varepsilon.$$

By adding the log transforms, Y^*, X_1^*, and X_2^* into the data matrix, we can use OLS to obtain estimates of the parameters, α^*, β_1, and β_2, and, therefore, an estimate of $\alpha = \exp(\alpha^*)$. The results are as shown in Table 9.11 for the advertising data (with no other input variables). The parameter $\alpha = \exp(\alpha^*)$ has the estimated value $\exp(6.392) = 597.05$.

Table 9.11 Summary Statistics and Parameter Estimates in the Log-Log Model

	Coefficients	Standard Error	T	P
Intercept	6.392	0.070	91.537	0.000
Advert	0.095	0.013	7.099	0.000

Regression Statistics	
Multiple R	0.846
R-sq	0.716
R-sq(adj)	0.702
Standard Error	0.022

Data: Advert.xlsx

Although R^2 here is less than that of the AdvertSq model, the standard error is much smaller. Have we found a particularly good model? No, we've transformed the variables into logarithms and cannot compare apples (Y) with oranges ($\ln Y$). To make an appropriate comparison, we need to take two steps. The first is to examine the residuals to see if they conform to the regression assumptions. (Here, both models have their weaknesses.) The second step is to make a quantitative comparison of the two models' predictions. This can be done by transforming the fitted values of the log model back to the original units by taking exponentials of the column labeled "Predicted LnSales" in Table 9.12. That is, we use the equation $\hat{Y}_{logmodel} = \exp(\hat{Y}^*)$, so, for example, the first observation has fitted value $\exp(6.832) = 926.59$. We can then compare the accuracy of the two models, as shown in the table.

Table 9.12 Comparing the Forecast Errors from Log Model With the AdvertSq Model

Observation	LnSales	Predicted LnSales	Ln Residuals	Sales	Predicted Sales Log Model	Residuals from Log Model	Predicted Sales AdvertSq	Residuals from AdvertSq Model
1	6.77	6.83	−0.058	874.5	926.6	−52.1	912.8	−38.3
2	6.83	6.83	−0.004	928.1	931.9	−3.8	921.4	6.7
3	6.84	6.83	0.003	937.0	933.9	13.1	924.6	12.4
4	6.83	6.85	−0.016	928.9	943.6	−14.7	940.3	−11.4
					RMSE	19.7		15.4
					MAPE	1.52		1.3

Data: Advert.xlsx

In addition to producing a model that is linear in the parameters, the logarithmic transform often helps to stabilize the variance, as we illustrate in the next section.

An easily interpretable measure of the impact of changes in the levels of the explanatory variables that eliminates the effects of the units used in measuring both X and Y is the *elasticity*, introduced in Section 7.6.2. The advantage of the log-log model just discussed is that the parameter estimates of the slope are estimates of the elasticities. In such a model, these elasticities are constant. In our example, the estimated elasticity for sales on advertising is low, only 0.095; a doubling of advertising expenditures increases expected sales by 9.5%.

9.6.3 Intrinsically Nonlinear Models

Finally, some models are intrinsically nonlinear, and no transformation will make them linear in the parameters. They can be estimated with nonlinear least squares methods (using Solver or other programs designed for nonlinear estimation). The spreadsheet program, available on the book's website, *Trend.xlsm* demonstrates how this can be done for certain non-linear models used in marketing, which we discuss further in Section 12.4. One example is the model involving unknown powers of the variables with additive errors:

$$Y_t = \alpha X_t^\delta + \beta Z_t^\gamma + \varepsilon_t.$$

DISCUSSION QUESTION: *How does this equation differ from the multiplicative model with the same variables?*

Another example is the Gompertz (S-shaped) trend curve, illustrated in Figure 9.10:

$$Y_t = ae^{-be^{-ct}} + \varepsilon_t.$$

This curve takes the limiting a when t tends to infinity and has the value ae^{-b} when $t = 0$. Larger values of c (as for the blue curve) lead to the curve flattening out more quickly. We discuss the uses of such curves and how they can be modeled in Section 12.4.

Figure 9.10 Intrinsically Nonlinear Models

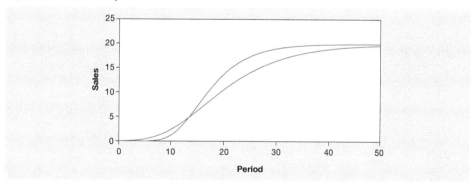

9.6.4 Changing Variances and the Use of Logarithmic Models

Many business and economic variables display growth over time, and the magnitude of the variations in the series likewise increases. There are also other reasons the variance may change over time, such as increased trading volatility in the stock market or reductions in product variability caused by improved quality assurance procedures. In this section, we address only growth-related variations, keeping in mind that this approach also encompasses negative growth (or decline). The other form of volatility was discussed in Section 6.10, where we considered GARCH models as extensions of ARIMA schemes. Similar extensions could be considered for regression models, using PcGive or EViews, but a detailed discussion lies beyond the scope of this book.

A change in the variance typically has only a modest effect upon the estimation of the intercept and slope parameters and, in turn, upon the point forecasts. However, the prediction intervals depend critically upon the estimate of the variance, which is why we seek to satisfy the assumption of a constant variance, at least approximately. Because the price series for *Unleaded* displayed increasing volatility that was somewhat related to higher prices, we continue to examine those data.

Recalling the discussion in Section 3.8, we may hope to stabilize the variance by using a transformation; a logarithmic transform is the logical choice here, because it corresponds to steady proportional growth. By way of illustration, we examine only the simple model for ln_*Unleaded* (the natural logarithm of unleaded gas prices) on the lagged variables *L1_ln_Unleaded* and ln_*L1_Crude_price*, estimated using data to Dec 2008. Forecasts derived from this model and from more extensive models based upon log transforms are left to the reader (Exercises 9.9 and 9.10). The fitted model for the estimation sample to 2008 is summarized in the following table:

Model	Unstandardized Coefficients		T	P
	B	Std. Error		
1 (Constant)	1.114	.220	5.053	.000
ln_L1_Unleaded	.620	.076	8.176	.000
ln_L1_Crude_price	.235	.049	4.812	.000

a. Dependent Variable: ln_Unleaded
In addition, *R-sq(adj)* = 97.1% and S = 0.0638.

The plot of the residuals is shown in Figure 9.11. The log transform goes some way towards stabilizing the variance although there are a number of extreme observations, an issue we address in the next section. The implication behind our discussion in this section is that nonconstant variances may not be recognized until the diagnostic stage, but the remedy is to go back to the original series and seek a suitable transformation. Generally with market models such as the oil price example, so-called log-log models (logs of both the dependent and explanatory variables) are preferred. After transforming, model building can proceed in the manner of earlier sections, with the assumption of constant variances known to be at least approximately satisfied.

Figure 9.11 Residual Plots for Ln(Unleaded) Model

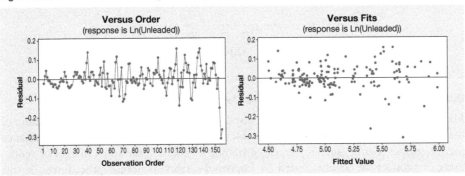

Data: Gas_prices_2.xlsx; adapted from Minitab output.

We can also use the elasticity definition given in the previous section to interpret the model: A doubling of the price of crude would lead to an expected increase of 23.5 percent in the price at the pumps in the next time period. The 23.5 percent figure represents the *short-term elasticity*, which describes the change in the price during the next time period. However, greater changes would be expected over the long term as higher prices work their way through the supply chain and refineries adapt to the new realities. We examine these longer term effects by assuming that ln_*L1_Crude_price* is increased to a new level and then is kept at this new level while the dependent variable (and hence its lagged values) updates in response to these conditions. The complete effect is known as the *long-term elasticity*. When the model is defined in terms of logarithms, as it is here, the long-term elasticity is

$$\beta_2/(1 - \beta_1)$$

where β_1 is the coefficient of the lagged dependent variable and β_2 is the coefficient of *Ln_L1_Crude_price*. In this case, the long-term elasticity becomes, $0.235/(1-0.620) = 0.618$ so that the long-term effect of a doubling of the price of crude would be to increase the price at the pump by 62 percent. As expected, prices respond more over the longer term. This formula only applies to the model specification of a one period lag in both the dependent and the explanatory variable. Exercise 9.14 examines a more general case.

9.7 Outliers and Leverage

Two further types of data characteristic may affect model building: outliers and leverage points. They affect both time series and cross-sectional data, and are illustrated in Figure 9.12. A leverage point is an observation that exerts an undue influence on the regression line (or model). Leverage points are situated far away from the average *X*-values. In Figure 9.12, we see that the point labeled as a leverage point affects the regression line quite dramatically. The line labeled "All" was estimated on the basis of all the data points, whereas the line labeled "Omit" dropped both the leverage point and the outlier. The inclusion of the leverage point has dragged the "Omit" line up toward it, relative to the position of the "All" line. An outlier in the dependent variable is an observation that is far away from its expected or forecast value. An outlier typically has less effect on the regression line, as Figure 9.12 shows: The "Omit" line has not shifted much relative to the outlier although the standard error will be larger.

Figure 9.12 Outliers and Leverage Points

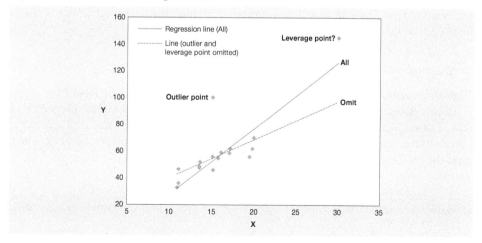

9.7.1 Leverage Points and What to Do About Them

Obviously, it is undesirable if the inclusion of a single data point dramatically affects the estimated regression line and therefore the corresponding forecasts. Often, this will occur because of a data error. Sometimes, however, the observation will be measured correctly, but no model that adequately captures the remaining observations could also describe the leverage point(s). The first step is to identify whether the data set contains such potentially influential data points. Several diagnostics can help here to come to a commonsense decision whether or not to omit the point on the basis of knowledge of the problem.

Various statistics are included in Minitab, SAS or SPSS that check whether an observation affects the regression results in a particular manner. Standardized *DFITS*[6] gives an overall measure of how unusual an observation is. The rule is that one should check an observation if *abs (Standardized DFITS)* $> 2\sqrt{p/n}$ where n is the number of observations and p is the number of explanatory variables. Alternatively, we can examine *Cook's distance D*, which is another measure of the influence of an observation. Cases with larger D values than the rest of the data are those which have unusual leverage. A cutoff for detecting influential observations is to examine values of D greater than $4/(n - p - 1)$.

Some programs allow the user to examine the effects on the individual regression coefficients. As an example, suppose the model building was focused on forecasting the effects of a promotion. Here, the sensitivity of the promotional coefficient to a particular data point could be examined through the *DFBetas* function (available in SPSS and SAS but not Minitab); this function measures the change in the individual regression coefficients when a particular observation is excluded.

These measures of leverage are not based on hard-and-fast rules. Although one measure may point to a potentially damaging observation, another may suggest that the model is just fine. What the modeler must do is check the effects both with and without the potential leverage observation, testing the resulting models by using out-of-sample data. Often, in time series forecasting, where the latest data are most relevant to producing the forecasts, these data represent exactly the points that are furthest from the center of the X observations and therefore are more likely to be leverage points.

■ Example 9.8: Effects of unusual observations on the advertising-sales relationship

We can examine the results obtained from the advertising data set *Advert.xlsx*. We use the full set of explanatory variables now, where, in addition to advertising and sales, we have included a quadratic term to capture possible saturation effects. We also use data on the promotional type. There are three types of promotion: high, low, and special. We will therefore need two dummy variables:

Newdum1 = 1 if the promotion type is high.

Newdum2 = 1 if the promotion type is special.

With all observations included, we reach the regression model shown in Table 9.13.

Cook's distance measure [with a cutoff of $4/(n - p - 1) = 0.24$] identifies observations 1 and 22 as suspect. Standardized *DFITS* (cutoff = 0.85) comes to the same conclusion, but also alerts the user to observation 6. We just omit the two common points, 1 and 22, which gives the results shown in Table 9.14.

---

6 See the HELP commands in the statistical software for further details, or see Kutner, Nachtsheim, Neter, and Li (2005, pp. 401–402).

A comparison of Tables 9.13 and 9.14 indicates that only the coefficient estimating the special promotion effect changes. Despite the fact that now other points are identified as potentially influential, we can regard the model that uses all the variables and estimates all the data as robust (apart from forecasting special promotions, where there few data points including the extreme observation 1).

Note that the summary statistics cannot readily be used to compare the two models because the data set has been changed. However, the elimination of extreme points typically leads to a reduction in S, as here. ■

Table 9.13 The Sales-Advertising Promotion Model (*all data*)

Model Summary				
Model	R	R-sq	R-sq(adj)	Std. Error of the Estimate
1	.969	.939	.925	10.37369
	Unstandardized Coefficients			
Model	B	Std. Error	T	P
1 (Constant)	755.833	30.545	24.745	.000
Advert	1.912	.325	5.886	.000
Newdum1	19.864	5.138	3.866	.001
Newdum2	−13.106	8.176	−1.603	.127
AdvertSq	−.004	.001	−4.416	.000

Note: Dependent variable: *Sales*

Data: Advert.xlsx; adapted from SPSS output.

Table 9.14 The Sales-Advertising Promotion Model With Leverage Points 1 and 22 Removed

Model Summary				
Model	R	R-sq	R-sq(adj)	Std. Error of the Estimate
1	.945	.951	.937	7.73157
	Unstandardized Coefficients			
Model	B	Std. Error	T	P
1 (Constant)	760.599	24.593	30.927	.000
Advert	1.916	.265	7.227	.000
Newdum1	20.309	3.855	5.268	.000
Newdum2	−5.791	6.700	−.864	.401
AdvertSq	−.004	.001	−5.556	.000

Note: Dependent variable: *Sales*

Data: Advert.xlsx; adapted from SPSS output.

9.7.2 The Effects of Outliers

OUTLIERS

An *outlier* is an observation (or residual from a model) that lies far away from its expected or forecast value.

To fix ideas, we again consider the basic log-log model for Unleaded Gas Prices discussed in section 9.6.4 and the residuals shown in Figure 9.11. We can see the dramatic effect of the developing recession from mid-2008 at the end of the estimation sample.

Such outliers can distort the estimates produced by a time series model with an autoregressive component, in contrast to a standard regression model where the impact is less pronounced. One solution to the problem is to use a robust estimation procedure, which gives less weight in the fitting criterion to such observations. This approach is theoretically demanding and beyond our scope; the interested reader should consult Kutner *et al.* (2005, pp. 437–449).

We have followed the second approach, which is to make use of indicator variables. We may define an indicator to capture the 'unusual' observation with *Ind*=1 for that particular observation, otherwise = 0. We then include that indicator in the regression model. The net effect is to set the residual for that observation to zero, which seems rather extreme but typically works much better than doing nothing. The analyst should not get carried away with this procedure, however: In principle, we could define an indicator for every observation and be back where we started! Rather, we follow a three-step procedure (see Section 5.4 for more details):

- Identify the outlier(s); a rough guideline is to fit an initial model and then find those residuals which lie outside the interval ±3*S*. A more sensitive statistic is the studentized deleted residual, available in most statistical packages. It removes the effect of the particular observation when estimating whether it is an outlier (see Glossary).

- Check the history of the process to see whether an omitted variable might have been important at the time in question; if so, include it in the regression.

- If not, check for unusual events around the time in question and use the indicator variable with a tentative attribution to the event(s) identified.

■ Example 9.9: Outlier effects on the crude-gasoline price relationship

To capture the effects of the Great Recession, we use an indicator variable for the second half of 2008, defined as *Change2008_7=1* for the last 6 months of 2008; this date is chosen because the price of *Unleaded* peaked in June 2008. For purposes of illustration, we consider the model discussed in Section 9.6.4 with the log of unleaded prices explained by lagged *Unleaded* and lagged *Crude_price* but extend the estimation sample to December 2013. The effect upon the model is shown in Table 9.15, and the modified residuals are plotted in Figure 9.13. The adjustment for the outlier improves the overall fit of the model but reduces the magnitude of the AR(1) coefficient.

Table 9.15 Values of Coefficients for Model for the Logarithm of Unleaded Gas Prices With Lagged Unleaded and Lagged Crude Price (Data: Jan1996–Dec2013)

Model	Unstandardized Coefficients		T	P
	B	Std. Error		
(Constant)	.814	.138	5.885	.000
L1_ln_Unleaded	.701	.049	14.236	.000
Change2008_7	−.162	.023	−7.173	.000
L1_ln_Crude_price	.206	.033	6.194	.000
a. Dependent Variable: lnUnleaded				

Data: Gas_prices_2.xlsx; adapted from SPSS output.

Figure 9.13 Residual Plots for the Logarithm of Unleaded Gas Prices, from the Model with Lagged Unleaded and Lagged Crude Price

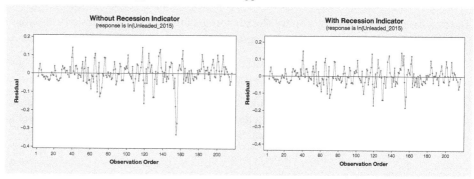

While there are still some outliers (November and December 2008 still have large negative residuals) the residuals seem better behaved with a decrease of some 10% in the standard error (of the logarithms). ■

The advertising-sales example also contains outliers — in particular, the first observation. We leave the outlier analysis by indicator variables as Exercise 9.15.

9.7.3 The Role of Outliers and Leverage Points: A Summary

Outliers and leverage points are often neglected in building a model. But both of these data characteristics can do considerable damage if they are ignored. Whether the data are cross-sectional or time series, such points should not be automatically omitted. Instead, they raise questions, both about the data (Is the suspect observation correct?) and about the model (Have we omitted a key variable from the model? Has a structural change been introduced into the problem, such as a new policy or a new competitor?) Outliers and leverage points must always be investigated.

9.8 Intervention Analysis

The outlier adjustment process described in Section 9.7 is a quick fix that is useful in circumstances in which a single aberrant observation can be identified. However, shocks to the system may produce more complex changes than a one-period outlier, so we now examine a more systematic approach to dealing with such events. Known as *intervention analysis*, this approach is often associated with ARIMA model building, but the methods are equally valuable in building standard regression models.

The goal of intervention analysis is to make adjustments to the model when the underlying structure changes, either permanently or temporarily. Consider the following interventions or changes (shocks) to the system:

a. Monthly production figures are down because of a disruption in the supply of raw materials (e.g., an industrial action, bad weather).

b. An automobile manufacturer plans to offer zero percent financing to new buyers for a four-week period.

c. A competing product is introduced into the market, affecting your own product's sales.

The first case represents what we have already termed an outlier, in that a single month is likely to be affected. Such events may be represented by an indicator variable of the form

$$X_t = 1, \text{ if } t = t_0 \tag{9.5}$$
$$= 0, \text{ otherwise.}$$

In equation (9.5), t_0 denotes the time period in which the event occurs. The special promotion in the second example extends over a finite period, and then financing plans revert to their usual form. We may represent this phenomenon by the indicator

$$X_t = 1, \text{ if } t_0 \le t \le t_0 + h \tag{9.6}$$
$$= 0, \text{ otherwise.}$$

In equation (9.6), $(h + 1)$ represents the duration of the change. This is the form adopted in the analysis just carried out for the effects of the Great Recession on the unleaded price. Finally, if the change is permanent, as in the third example, we represent the intervention by a step function:

$$X_t = 1, \text{ if } t \ge t_0 \tag{9.7}$$
$$= 0, \text{ otherwise.}$$

In all three cases, the estimated coefficient in the regression equation measures the impact of the intervention. These three examples may be viewed as basic building blocks from which more complex interventions may be constructed. For example, if lost production extends over, say, one-and-a-half months, we might use a two-period indicator weighted by the number of weeks affected in each month. Likewise, special promotions might lead to increased sales during the lifetime of the promotion, but some of those sales would be the result of consumers moving up their buying plans. Thus, post-promotion sales might be lower than normal. We could check for this possibility by using one indicator for the period of the promotion and a second for two or three weeks after the promotion. The first one would be expected to have a positive sign, demonstrating the increase in sales, whereas the second could be negative and would indicate that some sales had been shifted in time rather than being sales made to newly recruited customers.

Minicase 9.2 provides a classic example of intervention analysis related to the introduction of seat-belt requirements in the United Kingdom.

9.9 Structural Change and Model Simplification

In using a multiple regression model for forecasting, one very strong assumption is made implicitly: That the regression model and its coefficients remain constant into the forecast period.

DISCUSSION QUESTION: *If the impact of the price of Crude changes (say, doubles) during the forecast period, what would you expect to happen to the accuracy of your forecasts? If some variable, such as tax, has been omitted from the equation, what would you expect to happen?*

How might such changes affect the forecasts if they happened in the estimation sample?

A number of tests have been proposed that allow us to examine whether there have been any structural changes in the model (i.e., changes in the model's coefficients). These tests can, of course, be applied only to the available data, so there remains the judgmental question that any forecaster must ask: Do we expect stability in the forecast period? But if there has been little stability during the estimation period, we would surely be more nervous about assuming stability into the future.

We start out with a general regression model in K variables and assume that there are n_1 observations in the estimation sample:

$$Y_t = \beta_0 + \sum \beta_i X_{it} + \varepsilon_t, \; t = 1, 2, \ldots, n_1.$$

Further, we assume that n_2 observations are retained in the hold-out sample, so that there are $n = n_1 + n_2$ observations in all. If the model has undergone a structural change, the parameters for the hold-out sample will differ from those in the estimation sample. We may write the two versions as

$$Y_t = \beta_0 + \sum \beta_i X_{it} + \varepsilon_t, \text{ for } t \le n_1$$
$$Y_t = \gamma_0 + \sum \gamma_i X_{it} + \varepsilon_t, \text{ for } t > n_1. \tag{9.8}$$

A convenient way of combining these equations so that we can use standard regression software is to set

$$\gamma_i = \beta_i + \delta_i, \; i = 0, 1, \ldots, K.$$

Then the assumption of no structural change corresponds to the null hypothesis,

$$H_0 : \delta_0 = \delta_1 = \ldots = \delta_K = 0.$$

We test this null against the alternative hypothesis,

$$H_A : \text{not all } \delta_i = 0.$$

By equations (9.8), the combined equation becomes

$$Y_t = \beta_0 + \delta_0 U_t + \sum \beta_i X_{it} + \sum \delta_i U_t X_{it} + \varepsilon_t.$$

The indicator variable U serves to identify the two subsamples and is defined as

$$U_t = 0, \; t = 1, 2, \ldots, n_1$$
$$= 1, \; t = n_1 + 1, \ldots, n.$$

Under the usual assumption that the error terms are independent and identically distributed normal random variables, an F-test may be used. Let SSE_0 and SSE_i denote the sums of squared errors under the null and alternative hypotheses, respectively. Then the test statistic is

$$F = \frac{(SSE_0 - SSE_1)/(K + 1)}{SSE_1/(n - 2K - 2)}.$$

Under the null hypothesis, this statistic has an F distribution with $(K + 1, n - 2K - 2)$ DF. This test is known as the *Chow* test and is equivalent to testing whether the slopes for each variable remains the same in each period.

■ Example 9.10: Chow test for an unleaded gasoline prices model

In order to understand better why our models failed in the hold-out period, 2009–2010 we examine the structural stability. We use the model for the differenced series, including differenced lag demand, as given in Table 9.7. For the purposes of this analysis, we combine the original estimation sample covering the period up to December 2008 with the hold-out sample covering the period from January 2009 to December 2010. There are 156 observations in the first 13 years and 24 more in 2009-2010. We therefore define a variable $U=1$ in these last two years and additional variables as shown in Table 9.16. The analysis-of-variance tables for the null and alternative models are as follows:

Null Model (adapted from SPSS output)

Model	Sum of Squares	DF	Mean Square	F	P
Regression	14953.122	3	4984.374	33.923	.000
Residual	25566.395	174	146.933		
Total	40519.516	177			

Alternative Model (adapted from SPSS output)

Model	Sum of Squares	DF	Mean Square	F	P
Regression	18406.831	7	2629.547	20.216	.000
Residual	22112.685	170	130.075		
Total	40519.516	177			

The test statistic is evaluated as

$$F = \frac{(22566.4 - 22112.7)/4}{22112.7/170} = 6.64$$

with (4, 170) DF. The P-value is 0.000 to three decimal places, so, clearly, changes have taken place over the last two years. The individual coefficients are shown in the following table, where $U*Diff\_L1\_Crude\_1$ denotes the product of U with the lagged first-order difference of the crude oil price (and so on).

Table 9.16 Testing for Structural Change in 2009–2010: The Chow-Test

	Null Model Coefficients	P	Alternative Model Coefficients	P
1 (Constant)	.274		−.303	
Diff_L1_Crude_1	1.703	.000	2.151	.000
Diff(L1_SP500)	.051	.004	.050	.006
Diff(L1_Demand)	.820	.149	.900	.101
U*Diff_L1_Crude_1			−2.180	.000
U*L1_SP500			.012	.798
U*L1_Demand			−.062	.983
U			5.358	.061
	S = 12.12 R-sq(adj) = 35.8%		S = 11.41 R-sq(adj) = 43.2%	

Data: Gas_prices_2.xlsx

From the table, we see that the biggest (and statistically significant) change has been in the Crude coefficient, perhaps lending support to the popular argument that prices at the pump were set with little regard to the price at the wellhead. Further analysis of the price of unleaded gasoline needs to take this parameter shift into account. ∎

We have illustrated how the Chow test can be implemented using standard statistical software to test whether instability is the cause of forecast failure. This test and several others are included as standard outputs in various econometric packages. Key extensions include the case in which there are a number of possible structural breaks. For example, such tests are available automatically in PcGive. If we now turn to the extended data set to 2013, leaving 2014 and 2015, for out-of-sample analysis, Figure 9.14 shows its development.

Figure 9.14 Time Series Plot of Unleaded, Extended to 2015

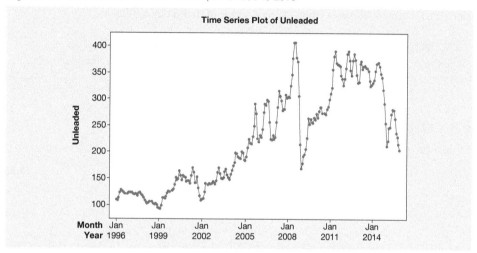

Data: Gas_Prices_Base.xlsx

We see clearly two dramatic changes in early 2009 (and in the new out-of-sample period, early 2014). For the in-sample model development we therefore add a dummy variable for this period of change defined as *Change2008_7* for the 6 months July 2008 to December 2008.

The differenced model had previously proved the most successful, however, our previous stability test showed the change in the responsiveness to *Crude_price*. In an attempt to understand how its slope coefficient is changing we will estimate a *Rolling Regression*. This estimation approach provides a recursive estimate of the coefficient(s) as the sample is updated adding one additional observation at a time. Figure 9.15 shows a graph to the coefficient of lagged crude price and lagged *SP500*, together with their standard errors. As can be seen, the responsiveness to crude price changes has declined substantially while that to stock prices through *SP500* has increased from a base of around zero.

Figure 9.15 Rolling Regression Parameter Estimate for Differenced Lagged Crude_price and Lagged SPend

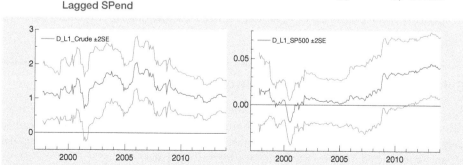

Data: Gas_Prices_Base.xlsx; output adapted from PcGive.

The graph of the coefficient of changes in lagged crude also shows quite strong oscillations with a strong effect apparent in the autumn of 2008 (as also shown by the Chow test).

Using the above model we can test for stability on the hold-out sample from 2014-5, Including seasonal dummies, the Chow test has $F(24,198) = 37.869$ (P-value is 0.0000). Yet again, we find the model suggests more changes in the out-of-sample period. In addition, the residuals are far from normal with outliers at the start of 2014. Of course, if we were sitting in December 2013 with the task of forecasting 2014 and 2015, we would not know from the data and residuals as to the forthcoming problems. But the Chow test would have alerted us to potential issues when facing periods of market instability.

> **DISCUSSION QUESTION:** *What possible approaches could be used with a model that is sometimes unstable in periods of market turmoil? In 2014 this was the collapse of the crude oil price. In 2016 this was the possible effects of Brexit.*

9.9.1 Model Simplification

In the previous section we compared two models, which we rewrite as:

$$M_0 : Y_t = \beta_0 + \sum_1^{K1} \beta_i X_{it} + \varepsilon_t \tag{9.9}$$

and

$$M_1 : Y_t = \beta_0 + \sum_1^{K} \beta_i X_{it} + \varepsilon_t \tag{9.10}$$

where $\{X_i\}_{K1+1}^{K}$ represents the variables $\{\delta_i UX_i\}$. The aim there was to decide if there was structural instability. More generally, the F test identifies whether the additional K–K variables in equation (9.10) are significantly different from zero. This is a general test for comparing two models, one of which, M_1 is more general than the other and is often referred to as the 'Extra-Sum-of-Squares' test. Alternatively, if we start from model M_1 we may view the test as a framework for model simplification. The test statistic for the null hypotheses of:

$$H_0 : \beta_{K1+1} = \beta_{K1+2} = \ldots \beta_K$$

is

$$F = \frac{(SSE_0 - SSE_1)/(K - K1)}{SSE_1 / (n - K - 1)} \text{ with } (K - K1, n - K - 1) \text{ degrees of freedom.}$$

The test is often used to simplify models such as examining whether the seasonal dummy variables in section 9.3 add anything to the model with autoregressive terms. It can also be used to test whether a model is linear or has non-linear components (by including polynomial terms in equation (9.10), as discussed in section 9.6.1). In a similar fashion it can be used to test whether an extended lag structure is needed. (As we discussed in Chapter 6, an alternative approach would be to rely on a suitable information criterion, such as AIC.)

9.10 An Update on Forecasting

This chapter has focused upon model building, and little mention has been made of forecasting, which is our ultimate objective. The emphasis is deliberate, because forecasts can be only as good as the model upon which they are based. Once we are satisfied with the model we have constructed, we must reexamine the forecasting issues.

The process of forecasting follows exactly the same steps as were laid out in Section 8.6, so we do not repeat them here. Nevertheless, prior to making forecasts, we should recall the three principal bases upon which explanatory variable values are specified. The explanatory variables may be

1. perfectly known,

2. estimated from past values for ex ante forecasting, or

3. specified hypothetically for "what-if" or policy analysis purposes.

Features of all three varieties may appear in a single model. For example, we may wish to predict seasonal sales for a company that depend upon overall economic activity levels and upon specific company policies, with the values of the seasonal variables known. The macroeconomic variables must be forecast; sometimes a company will purchase such forecasts from a specialist econometric forecaster or rely on internal expert judgment. At other times an internal model based upon either regression or exponential smoothing methods may be used. Finally, there will be some policy variables that are under the control of the company, such as prices and special promotions. These are the variables that can be set at different levels to simulate likely outcomes. Indeed, a more involved simulation may also involve varying the input values of the macroeconomic variables.

The impact of these different approaches upon the estimated prediction intervals must be recognized, always under the assumption that the model is correctly specified. When the inputs are known, the nominal coverage (90 percent or whatever) will then be correct. When the values of the variables are specified on a "what-if" basis, the coverage is correct, *conditionally upon those specified values*. Finally, when we insert forecasts for the inputs, the true prediction interval is usually wider; that is, the actual probability of coverage, i.e., the percentage of times the interval includes the actual observaton will be less than that stated.

A more detailed discussion of how to handle this problem is included in Section 13.3.1. But one simple approach that is sometimes useful is to build into the model a time delay equal to the forecasting horizon. That way, the values of the inputs will be available for forecasting purposes. This approach was considered in Section 7.7.4 and is explored in greater detail in Exercise 9.8.

9.11 Principles of Regression Model Building

The principles discussed in Chapter 8 clearly continue to apply, but the additional skills in model building that have been described in this chapter lead to some further issues that need to be addressed. These principles are based upon the work of Armstrong (2001) and Allen and Fildes (2001).

[9.1] Rely upon theory and domain expertise to select explanatory variables.
Use all important variables. The need for such care in model building has been stressed at various points in this chapter. Excessive data mining can lead to models that have no solid foundation in theory or in practice. However, it is best to start with a general model that includes all variables which have the potential to be important.

[9.2] Plot, inspect, and test the residuals for departures from the assumptions, including departures such as outliers and leverage points.
As we have seen throughout the chapter, the residual plots (including the residual *ACF*) form the most effective means to signal possible breakdowns in the assumptions. Once such

problems are identified, we can draw upon the developments in this chapter to improve the model.

[9.3] Aim for a relatively simple model specification.
But only eliminate insignificant variables if they are uninterpretable (e.g. implausible sign) or superfluous (e.g. definitional multicollinearity).

[9.4] When theory provides a guide to functional form (e.g., when you know that there is an upper limit to the market penetration level of a new technology) or when data strongly suggest a functional form that is compatible with theory, follow the theory.

[9.5] If the date of a possible structural break is known, test whether the parameters remain constant.
If key parameters are changing, include a change indicator in the model.

[9.6] Test all models for performance with data not used in the estimation process, comparing the results with baseline extrapolative or judgmental alternatives.
Criteria such as *MAPE* and *MAE* (and median measures), described in Chapter 2, are particularly useful in this context. This topic was examined in Section 9.5.1 and is also pursued in several of the end-of-chapter exercises.

[9.7] Apply the same principles to forecasts of the explanatory variables.

[9.8] Aim for an interpretable model with adequate forecasting capabilities that captures the key data characteristics and passes diagnostic tests.
Don't rely on automatic selection procedures to deliver such a model.

[9.9] Consider the use of Lasso when there are many plausible variables to consider for inclusion and data are collinear.
Group Lasso is an effective way to separate variables with a strong causal relationship from others with less strong explanatory power.

Summary

In this chapter, we have developed enhanced model-building procedures to deal with possible violations of assumptions such as autocorrelation, nonlinearity, heteroscedasticity, and the presence of outliers. Model building can be an exhausting activity — although we find it fun! The principles enunciated here and in the previous chapter, along with the examples provided, will help the modeler to arrive at a forecasting model that is grounded in both theory and empirical observation.

As regards automatic model selection, whatever approach you adopt and software you use, the final model should

- Be interpretable, making good sense in the context of the problem
- Be compatible with the data used, in that the regression assumptions should be met, at least approximately
- Have adequate forecasting accuracy for the problem under consideration, compared with benchmark alternatives.

Figure 9.16 provides a checklist of all the steps that need to be taken. As a model is developed, some of these steps will need to be performed multiple times.

Figure 9.16 Selecting a Causal Forecasting Model

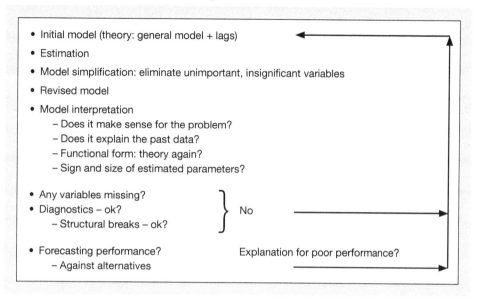

Exercises

9.1 Verify that equation (9.1) produces exactly the same regression lines as those shown in Figure 9.1.

9.2 Use your favorite software to try to fit a model containing all four seasonal indicator variables for a quarterly series, and see what happens. (Versions of Excel are particularly interesting in this regard!)

9.3 Verify that the forecasts for WFJ Sales (*WFJ_sales_2.xlsx*) will be the same, no matter which subset of four indicator variables is used.

9.4 Reanalyze the Walmart data (*Walmart_2.xlsx*), using Model 5 in Section 9.3, but keep the observations for 2014 and 2015 as a hold-out sample. Use this hold-out sample to compute *MAE* and *MAPE* for the model. Comment on your results.

9.5 Reanalyze the Walmart data (*Walmart_2.xlx*) using 2003Q1–2010Q4 as the estimation sample. Contrast the results with those discussed in this chapter. What conclusions do you reach?

9.6 Rework the analysis for Walmart outlined in Exercise 9.4, but transform the Sales and *GDP* variables to logarithms before conducting the analysis. Comment on any improvements in the regression diagnostics compared to Figure 9.6. Does the inclusion of lagged Sales improve the model(s)?

9.7 Rework the analysis for Walmart outlined in Exercises 9.4 and 9.6, but use the differences of the logarithms.

9.8 The main impact of the Great Recession is sometimes dated as starting in June 2008. Add in an Indicator (dummy) variable in Models 5 and 6 (section 9.3) to account for any structural changes in Walmart's performance. Does the recession explain the difference between the models developed to 2010 and those developed to 2013? Can the model be simplified by dropping some of the variables?

9.9   Reanalyze the unleaded gas prices data (*Gas_prices_2.xlsx*), using logarithmic transforms for all the explanatory variables included in Example 8.1 (lagged *Unleaded, Crude_price, SP500 Unemployment, RRetail_sales*). Use January 2009–December 2010 as a hold-out sample. Compute *MAE* and *MAPE* for the forecasts of the original series. Compare your results with those given in the text.

9.10   Repeat exercise 9.9, using data up to December 2013 for estimation and January 2014–December 2015 as a hold-out sample.

9.11   Re-analyze the unleaded prices data (*Gas_prices_2.xlsx*), using the model selected in Exercise 9.9 but with a sufficient number of lags to enable forecasting three months ahead. Use the same hold-out sample to check the model's forecasting performance. Compute *MAE* and *MAPE* for the forecasts, and compare your results with the one-step-ahead forecasts. Does the use of median measures make any difference? Comment on your results.

9.12* Use EViews or PcGive (or some other appropriate software) to examine a more general lag structure for the error process in the model for unleaded prices (*Gas_prices_2.xlsx*) discussed in Example 9.4. Interpret your results.

9.13   Reanalyze the unleaded prices data (*Gas_prices_2.xlsx*) after transforming all the financial variables to real terms, using *CPI* as the deflator. Consider the five models developed in the text and determine a preferred model. Use this model to generate one-step-ahead point forecasts for the months of 2014 and 2015, and compare your results with those given in the text.

9.14* Show that for the model $Y_t = \delta + \phi_1 Y_{t-1} + \phi_2 Y_{t-2} + \beta_1 X_t + \beta_2 X_{t-1} + e_t$ the expected effect of a unit increase in X at time $t+1$, increases Y in period $(t+2)$ by an amount $\beta_1/(1 - \phi_1)$ and has a long term effect of $(\beta_1 + \beta_2)/(1 - \phi_1 - \phi_2)$.

9.15   For the sales-advertising data set (*Advert.xlsx*), use the full model, as set forth in Section 9.7.1, to identify the effects of any outliers. Use indicator variables to deal with any outliers you identify. Compare your results with those given in the text. Does a model based on logarithms of advertising and sales lead to an improved description of the data?

9.16   The WFJ Sales (*WFJ_sales_2.xlsx*) series shows an extreme peak in week 52 (post-Christmas sales). Incorporate a suitable indicator variable into the model and reanalyze the data. Compare your results with the original models for WFJ Sales.

9.17* Using the data for Jan 2014–Dec 2015 as the hold-out sample, compare the forecasting performance of the full OLS model with the Lasso (1.0) model and the Group Lasso (0.5) model. Use *Lasso_results.xlsx* or other software as appropriate; the spreadsheet includes instructions for detailed use. Interpret the results.

Class Assessment

Instructor: This can be used as a take-home examination as each student will face a different data set though the essence of the problem remains the same. The code and instructions for generating the individual assessments can be downloaded by registering on the book's website: *https://wessexlearning.com/pages/principles-of-business-forecasting-2nd-ed-instructors-material.*

Assignment: You are asked to produce forecasts for the call center of a satellite broadcasting company. Calls may refer to technical support or new subscriptions, each of which is recorded separately by the company. Both series refer to daily data over a period of 7 weeks (2 May until 19 June inclusive). You are asked to produce point forecasts for each of the next 14 days (20 June until 3 July inclusive) for both technical support calls and new subscription calls. The company is interested in the effect of causal variables in forecasting new subscriptions. Owing to confidentiality reasons, these are labelled only as $X1$, $X2$, and $X3$. Data series for these three variables have been provided for you over the same 7-week period as the call data. Also, note that an international sport event is due to commence on 23 May and will finish on 26 June.

Your objective is to develop, for technical support calls and new subscription calls, the most accurate statistical forecasting models, demonstrating your modeling and forecasting skills. For both technical support and new subscription calls, you are asked to conduct an exploratory data analysis, build multiple potentially suitable forecasting models, choose what you identify as the "best" model, and, finally, produce daily forecasts for the next two weeks.

In order to obtain the data on technical support calls, new subscription calls and on the $X1$, $X2$, and $X3$ variables, download the file "call_centre_data.zip" from your course web site and select the file that is allocated to you (based on your student ID). After the headings, the files are to be read sequentially in time, with the top row referring to Day 1 and the bottom row to Day 49.

Write a technical report to document your model building skills, justify your choice of models, and discuss the findings. Include in the technical report an executive summary (of no more than a page) suitable for a non-technically trained manager to read.

Grading Scheme & Hints

Data Exploration (20% of points)

Explore the regular components and the irregular components of each time series using graphs, statistical summaries and statistical tests. Document your findings comprehensively, making adequate use of graphs, with appropriate discussion to support your arguments. Detailed evidence (e.g. the complete information from statistical tests) may be placed in the appendix, but must be referenced in the text. Conclude by recommending suitable model forms for forecasting.

Model Building (60% of points)

Build a set of potential contender models for both the technical support calls and the new subscription calls. Document the specification of each model. Document the iterative steps you took to build this particular model, including the analysis of residuals of intermediate models that have led to better ones. Document the final model form and parameters to allow a complete replication of your experiments (i.e. specify what model forms you selected, which transformations in which order and which parameters were used, so that others could reproduce what you did exactly only from your document).

For each contender model, one or more different model forms may be feasible to produce forecasts (e.g. for ARIMA you may consider models with seasonal differences or first differences or both). Where applicable, you should always consider multiple plausible candidate models, and must justify your choice of candidates in comparison to other potential models in each class of models (feel free to explicitly rule out implausible ones). To get a high score it will not be sufficient to build a single exponential smoothing model and a single ARIMA model and a single regression model, but rather you need to summarize a subset of potentially useful models. Base your justification on evidence, and document your iterative modeling process wherever applicable.

Accuracy Assessment and Recommended Forecasts (10% of points)

For each series, assess the accuracy of your models, considering a hold-out sample of appropriate size. You may use different error metrics. You should use at least two suitable error metrics for the assessment, and justify the use of each error metric you are using.

Presentation and Summary (10% of points).

Minicases

The four minicases introduced in Chapter 8 are all open to further analysis. Return to the case you examined originally and proceed as follows:

- Use a hold-out sample of the last 10-15 percent of the observations and re-run the original model.
- Check the residual plots, including the residuals *ACF*, for any departures from the assumptions: autocorrelation, heteroscedasticity, nonlinearity, and possible outliers.
- Depending upon the severity of the violations of particular assumptions, proceed in a step-by-step fashion to revise the model so as to bring it closer to the assumptions. In particular, add autoregressive structure if the diagnostics so indicate.
- When you have reached a final model, generate the one-step-ahead forecasts and associated prediction intervals. Compute the *RelMAE* and *MAPE*, and check how many of the observations lie inside the prediction intervals.
- Revise your model to make forecasts three steps ahead, and evaluate the performance. (OPTIONAL)
- Summarize your results.

Minicase 9.1 An Econometric Analysis of Unleaded Gasoline Prices

(Data for Minicase 9.1 can be found in file *Gas_prices_2.xlsx*.)

In Section 9.4 and in later sections, we developed models for the price of unleaded gasoline at the pump, but always using lagged values of the variables to enable real-time forecasting. Revisit some of these models, using the data to 2010 or a suitably extended database, but now allow for both contemporaneous values of the explanatory variables as well as longer lags (we suggest no more than two lags including for the differenced data). The possible lagged variables considered in the chapter are as follows:

- Price of unleaded gasoline, in cents per U.S. gallon (*"L1_Unleaded"*)
- The price of crude oil, in dollars per barrel (*"L1_Crude_price"*)
- The SP500 Stock Index, end-of-month close (*"L1_SP500"*).
- Personal disposable income, in billions of current dollars (*"L1_PDI"*)
- Consumer price index for all urban consumers, indexed at 100 over 1982-1984, not seasonally adjusted (*"L1_CPI"*)
- Retail Sales: real retail sales in millions of $s, deflated by *CPI* (*"L1_RR_sales"*)
- Unemployment rate, not seasonally adjusted (*"L1_Unemp"*)
- Housing starts, seasonally adjusted annual rate (*"L1_Housing"*)
- Demand for gasoline, in thousands of barrels per day (*"L1_Demand"*).

In addition the data set includes a number of variables relating to the availability of crude oil and unleaded gasoline. These are:

- Production
- Stocks
- Imports.

Do the 'supply' variables add any explanatory power to the models you propose? Does the inclusion of contemporaneous input variables provide a clearer understanding of the pricing process?

As a follow-up estimate the selected model using the data to December 2013 as the estimation sample and test its performance using the years 2012–2013 and 2014–2015 as the hold-out sample.

> **DISCUSSION QUESTION:** *Are the aims of the econometrician and the forecaster fundamentally different?*

Minicase 9.2 The Effectiveness of Seat-Belt Legislation

(Data for Minicase 9.2 can be found in file *Road_accidents.xlsx*.)

Harvey and Durbin (1986) provided a classic illustration of the value of intervention analysis to determine the effectiveness of new legislation that required drivers to wear seat belts. The data they used are plotted in Figure 9.17 and represent monthly totals of deaths and serious injuries (labeled *DSI*) on roads in the United Kingdom over the period from January 1975 to December 1984. The legislation became effective on February 1, 1983, although drivers began to comply in increasing numbers during January of that year.

Figure 9.17 Serious Injuries and Deaths on UK Roads, January 1975–December 1984

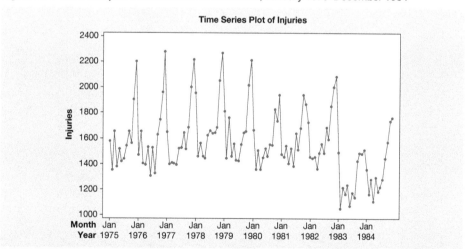

Source: Harvey and Durbin (1986): *Data: Road_accidents.xlsx*

The data clearly exhibit a strong seasonal pattern but little trend. Develop a model for this series, using only 11 seasonal indicators, plus a step function defined as

$$X_t = 1, \quad \text{if February 1983 or later}$$
$$= 0.5, \quad \text{for January 1983}$$
$$= 0, \quad \text{prior to January 1983.}$$

The value 0.5 for January 1983 is somewhat arbitrary but seems intuitively reasonable given that drivers were using seat belts in increasing numbers during that month; this was the form of step function used by Harvey and Durbin.

Because the model uses only indicator variables, forecasting is straightforward, but longer term projections would clearly need to take into account other safety measures, total traffic volumes, and similar variables. Such forecasts are clearly important in guiding policy makers.

Did the legislation achieve the desired effect of reducing deaths and serious accidents? By how much? If you were a policy maker in 1985 (when the study was conducted), would you support similar requirements for passengers? Why?

References

Allen, P. G., and Fildes, R. (2001). Econometric forecasting. In J. S. Armstrong (ed.), *Principles of Forecasting*. Boston and Dordrecht: Kluwer, pp. 300–362.

Armstrong, J. S., ed. (2001). *Principles of Forecasting: A Handbook for Researchers and Practitioners*. Boston and Dordrecht: Kluwer.

Box, G. E. P., Jenkins, G. M., Reinsel, G. C., and Ljung, G.M. (2016). *Time Series Analysis: Forecasting and Control*, 5th edn. New York: Wiley

Harvey, A. C., and Durbin, J. (1986). The effects of seat belt legislation on British road casualties: A case study in structural time series modelling. *Journal of the Royal Statistical Society*, series A, 149,187–227.

Kutner, M. H., Nachtsheim, C. J., Neter, J., and Li, W. (2005). *Applied Linear Statistical Models*, 5th ed. New York City: McGraw-Hill.

* Tibshirani, R. (1996). Regression shrinkage and selection via the lasso. *Journal of the Royal Statistical Society*, series B, 58, 267–288.

CHAPTER 10

Advanced Methods of Forecasting*

*Topics marked with an * are advanced and may be omitted for more introductory courses.*

Table of Contents

No matter how advanced your camera you still need to be responsible for getting it to the right place at the right time and pointing it in the right direction to get the photo you want.

— Ken Rockwell, *Your Camera Does Not Matter*, 2005

Introduction

In this chapter, we consider a number of advanced methods of forecasting. They are all widely used in applications. However, these methods do require the reader to work harder, because they are all more complex than those discussed so far and demand more from the user, either to get the method to work at all or to build an appropriate model and interpret the results. As a consequence, the chapter can be omitted without affecting the book's flow. (The methods are discussed further only in Chapter 12.) Still, for an "advanced forecaster," knowledge of these topics is valuable, if not essential.

We first introduce a new type of forecasting problem: predictive classification, in which the aim is to predict the probability of an event happening (or not). This question arises in many contexts: sports forecasting where the aim is to predict the winner, forecasting customer purchasing behavior, and forecasting whether a company will go bankrupt, among others. After introducing the data-mining problem of predictive classification in Section 10.1, we describe three new forecasting methods, all with the capability of predicting the outcome of a binary event: classification trees (Section 10.2), logistic regression (Section 10.3), and neural networks (Section 10.4). Neural network methods can also be used in time series forecasting when the variable of interest is continuous (see Section 10.4.2).

Econometric modeling has undergone many developments in recent years. In Section 10.5, we aim to overcome the problem of deciding which variables are determined within the system being modeled and which are determined exogenously (i.e., outside the system). Vector autoregressive models (VARs) can overcome this confusion and have delivered strong out-of-sample forecasting performance compared with standard regression methods. What is more, they have the added advantage of not relying on separate (exogenously determined) forecasts of the explanatory input variables. As usual, we conclude with some principles that aim to help the forecaster who is implementing these more complex methods.

We do not discuss software implementation details in this chapter, but we recommend exploring the online R solutions to the exercises; they are available in the folder *Forecasting in R: Tutorial and Examples*. These solutions provide examples of how to run analyses in R step by step. Specialist commercial packages are available for the three topics we cover here (Predictive Classification, Neural Nets for Time Series, and VAR Models) and these are discussed in the relevant sections.

10.1 Predictive Classification

Although many forecasting problems are concerned with predicting a continuous interval-scaled variable, such as sales, whether by value or by volume, some important forecasting problems require us to predict a binary outcome, such as whether a potential customer will purchase a product or whether a recession will happen next year. A particularly important example that has generated a major industry is predicting the outcome of a sporting event. The information in soccer as to where the match is to be played, the latest form of the teams, and the team composition will all affect the likely outcome and will form a part of a predictive (forecasting) model of the result. Such classification problems don't easily fit into the models we have developed so far because we've assumed (both in regression and in time series analysis) that the errors are unbounded and at least approximately normal.

■ Example 10.1: Computer ownership

A typical data set is illustrated in Table 10.1, in which the dependent (target) variable is whether a household owns a computer. (*Nocomp* = 1, if no computer is available in the household, and *Nocomp* = 0, if a computer is available.) The input, or predictor, variables are *Income*, *Education*, whether there are children in the household (*Kids* = 1, for households with children, and *Kids* = 0 otherwise), and, finally, a measure of the respondent's attitudes toward technology (*TAM*). The data set, created through a survey of owners and nonowners of computers in the United Kingdom, is cross-sectional (i.e., the survey was conducted over a single short time period). For ease of interpretation of British English, we have rephrased the definitions used in the survey and converted income levels to U.S. dollars. All the variables are categorical, so, for example, the income level has been broken up into five groups, with *Inc1* representing the lowest level of household income and *Inc5* the highest. Similarly, there are four education levels and a professional category (level 5). Both variables are ordinal. Panel (A) defines the variables and Panel (B) illustrates typical entries.

Table 10.1 Cross-Sectional Data for Predicting Household Ownership of Computers

Panel (A) Variables	Definition	Type
Computer user (*Nocomp*)	Do you own a computer? (*Nocomp* = 1 if no computer, *Nocomp* = 0 if own computer)	Target
Income	Ordinal: 1 (<$20K) to 5 (>$100K)	Input
Education	Ordinal: 1 (No qualifications) to 5 (Professional qualification)	Input
Kids	Binary (Yes = 1, No = 0)	Input
TAM: Attitude toward Technology	Different levels of response to technology (with dummy variables, TAM1 = 1, negative attitude, to TAM3 = 1, positive attitude)	Input

Panel (B) Household Computer Ownership (Nocomp)	Income	TAM: Attitude to Technology	Education	Kids
1	$31K ($20K–$49K): Inc2	Negative	High School: level 2	0
0	$57K ($50K–$69K): Inc3	Neutral	Degree: level 3	1
0	$95K ($70K–$99K): Inc4	Positive	Further degree: level 4	1
1	$22K ($20K–$49K): Inc2	Neutral	No qualifications/ Other: level 1	0
0	$135K (>$100K): Inc5	Positive	Professional: level 5	1

Data: Compdata.xlsx[1]

For example, the first observation shows a household that does not own a computer and has an income of $31K (which is assigned into an income class between $20K and $49K). The household has a negative attitude toward technology. Each household in the sample falls into one of five distinct income classes, thereby requiring the inclusion of four dummy variables in the regression model (see Section 9.8). The simplest model of these classifications is a regression of the form

$$Y_i = \beta_0 + \beta_1 X_{1i} + \cdots + \beta_K X_{Ki} + \varepsilon_i,$$

---

1 Our thanks for this data set are due to Alastair Robertson, who collected the data as part of his Ph.D. thesis research.

where $Y_i = Nocomp = 1$ if the ith household has no computer and $Y_i = 0$ if the ith household has at least one computer, and we include four ($K = 4$) income dummy variables as the explanatory variables. The aim of the modeling is to forecast the households that do not possess a computer in the wider population, establishing an explanatory model and this also has the potential to predict how the market develops, dependent on increasing income, education, and changing attitudes. Such a model also can be used to target non-users (with advertising for example) to persuade them of the benefits of computer ownership. More recent survey work has been used to target non-adopters of broadband.

The model can be estimated by the usual ordinary least squares method (see Chapter 8), with the data set split into an estimation data set and a test (out-of-sample) data set. The out-of-sample data is usually drawn at random from the full sample in cross-sectional studies. Where the data have a time stamp on them (i.e. observations have been taken over a period of time), there is also the need to consider whether the later cohort of data should also be used. The regression model gives a table of regression coefficients, as shown in Table 10.2, with the coefficients of the dummy variables for the different income classes all significant and increasing in absolute magnitude. Whichever computer program is used, the model will generate a set of predictions such as those labeled *PRE_1* in Table 10.3.

Table 10.2 Regression Coefficients in a Classification Problem: Household Computer Ownership as a Function of Income

	B	Std. Error	T	P
(Constant)	.436	.032	13.603	.000
Inc1	−.137	.043	−3.183	.001
Inc3	−.283	.042	−6.701	.000
Inc4	−.299	.041	−7.309	.000
Inc5	−.373	.035	−10.680	.000

Note: Dependent variable is *Nocomp*.
Data: *Compdata.xlsx*; adapted from SPSS output.

Table 10.3 Data Input and Predictions of the Probability of Household Computer Nonownership on the Estimation and Test (out-of-sample) Data

Nocomp	Inc1	Inc3	Inc4	Inc5	filter_$	PRE_1	RES_1	Prednocomp
0	0	0	0	1	1	0.063	−0.063	0.063
1	0	0	0	1	1	0.063	−0.937	0.063
0	0	0	0	1	1	0.063	−0.063	0.063
0	0	0	0	1	0			0.063
0	0	1	0	0	0			0.153
0	0	0	0	0	0			0.436
0	0	0	0	1	0			0.063
1	0	0	0	1	0			0.063
0	0	0	1	0	0			0.137

Data: *Compdata.xlsx*; the filter variable, *filter_$*, defines the estimation sample (for *filter_$ = 1*) and the test (out-of-sample) data (*filter_$ = 0*).

The regression model was fitted on the estimation data set, taken as a random sample of approximately 80 percent of the full data set. This data set is identified (in SPSS) through the *filter_$* variable, so all observations used in the estimation sample in the regression were labeled with a 1. The test data were not used in estimation ($filter_\$ = 0$), but predictions for this data set are easily calculated with the foregoing regression equation, so

$$Prednocomp = 0.436 - 0.137Inc2 - 0.283Inc3 - 0.299Inc4 - 0.373Inc5$$

gives a prediction of whether or not a household owns a computer. A high value corresponds to a high probability of nonownership, a low value to a low probability of nonownership. Not surprisingly, as income increases, so does the predicted probability of owning a computer. Note that the values calculated from the preceding formula give the same as the predictions produced automatically by SPSS on the estimation data set. Using the preceding equation allows us to calculate both the predictions and the residuals for the 20 percent sample of the data omitted in the model building. ■

To use the model in classification, a threshold value has to be chosen so that every observation above the threshold is taken as predicting nonownership = 1 and every observation below the threshold predicting that the household does in fact own a computer. There are two approaches to defining the threshold as stated in the following box:

THRESHOLD VALUES

After ranking the observations according to their fitted (or predicted) values, we may define the threshold as either

1. The top so many percent of the ranked values (the cutoff percentage),

or

2. All observations whose fitted or predicted values exceed a certain value (the cutoff value).

The two definitions will usually result in different numbers of predicted cases being assigned to a particular class or category.

For example, if the cutoff percentage is taken as 20 percent, the top 20 percent would be predicted to be nonowners. The purpose of such an exercise might be to segment the market. For example, if we were selling PC computer games, we would seek to identify the characteristics of households that already own appropriate computers. Conversely, the manufacturer of an entry-level laptop would be interested in technology-oriented nonowners.

Various error statistics may be calculated to describe the accuracy of the classifications, as we next explain.

10.1.1 Evaluating the Accuracy of the Predictive Classifications

In evaluating the accuracy of the predictive classifications, the first step is to rank the observations by the value of the predictions (scores) they receive from the model. Therefore, households that the model predicts as more likely to own a computer will fall at one end of the score distribution while those the model predicts as less likely will lie at the other end. Here, the higher values represent customers who are more likely to fall into the target event class (e.g., those who do not own a computer in the preceding example). Typically, members of the target class are often called the "bads", as they often have undesirable characteristics (as far as the analyst is concerned). Examples are mobile phone customers who are likely to churn (i.e., switch providers) and loan customers who are likely to default.

For a chosen percentage of customers predicted to fall into the target class (say, the top 50 percent of the ranked predictions), when the model is appraised on either the estimation or out-of-sample (test) data sets, its performance can be characterized by the errors made in predicting the target. This characterization, sometimes called the *Classification* (or *Confusion*) *Matrix*, may be presented in tabular form, as shown in Table 10.4.

Table 10.4 The Classification (or Confusion) Matrix

		Predicted	
		Nontarget Event	**Target Event (Nonowner)**
Actual	Nontarget = 0 (Owner)	h_{00}	h_{01}
	Target = 1 (Nonowner)	h_{10}	h_{11}

■ Example 10.1: Computer ownership *(continued)*

Table 10.5 The Classification Matrix for the Linear Regression Model for Identifying Households Not Owning Computers (*the target event*)

		Cutoff 48.9% Predicted				Cutoff 21.3% Predicted		
		0	**1**	**Row Total**		**0**	**1**	**Row Total**
Actual	0	682	537	1219	0	1018	201	1219
	1	44	158	202	1	101	101	202
	col. Total	726	695	1421	col. Total	1119	302	1421

Data: Compdata.xlsx. Cutoff percentages 48.9% and 21.3% have been used with the full data set.

Using the prediction equation (based on all the data and including just the income dummy variables) gives the following results for the five distinct income classes:

Income Class (from low to high)	Inc1	Inc2	Inc3	Inc4	Inc5
Predicted probabilities of nonownership	.436	.299	.153	.137	.063
Percentage in given class	9.6	11.7	12.7	14.9	51.1
Cumulative percentages	9.6	21.3	34.0	48.9	100

Table 10.5 shows the classification matrices for two alternative cut-off percentages of 48.9% (which predicts nonownership for all but the richest income class) and 21.3% (which predicts nonownership for the two poorest classes). Usually exact cut-off percentages can be calculated from the predicted probabilities which fall on a continuous scale (rather than into discrete classes as here).

The overall proportion classified as correct using the 48.9% cut-off is

$$\frac{(h_{00} + h_{11})}{N} = \frac{682 + 158}{1421} = 0.59.$$

$$\text{The } sensitivity = \frac{h_{11}}{(h_{10} + h_{11})} = \frac{158}{(44 + 158)} = 0.78$$

measures the proportion of target events that are correctly predicted (i.e., nonowners).

$$\text{The } specificity = \frac{h_{00}}{(h_{00} + h_{01})} = \frac{682}{(682 + 537)} = 0.56$$

measures the proportion of correctly predicted nontarget events with the 48.9% cut-off.

With the totals for target events and nontarget events (e.g., bad risks and good risks, respectively) known in the sample, once the cutoff is decided, the various percentages can be calculated.

Two examples of different cutoff percentages are shown for an extended model of computer nonownership. A cutoff of 48.9 percent (21.3 percent) assigns 48.9 percent (21.3 percent) of the scored observations to the target class, and we use these cutoff percentages in Table 10.5. The higher cutoff percentage yields more nonowners predicted (with a corresponding decrease in errors) while we predict fewer owners successfully. The 21.3 percent cutoff has sensitivity 0.50 and specificity 0.84. ■

Ideally, we would like the misclassifications, h_{01} and h_{10}, to both be zero, and our model would then correctly identify all the targets (nonowners in this case) and also all the owners. But no model has such capabilities. Moreover, as the output in Table 10.5 shows, as one type of error falls (type h_{10}, a predicted owner who turns out to be a nonowner), the other (type h_{01}, a predicted nonowner who owns a computer) increases.

The effects of the different cutoff values can be shown graphically for different cutoff percentages. By way of example, we consider a regression-type model (technically, a logistic regression, which we discuss in the Section 10.3). The result is a curve like Figure 10.1(A), which shows the cumulative percentage of the target event (the nonowners) that has been correctly predicted, that is

$$\frac{100h_{11}}{(h_{10} + h_{11})}$$

for different cut-offs.

Figure 10.1 Captured (correctly identified) Response Curves for Different Cutoff Percentages: Percentage of the Target Response, (A) Cumulative, and (B) Noncumulative

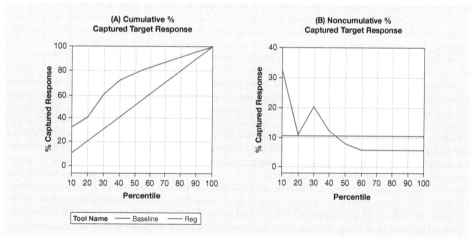

Data: Compdata.xlsx; adapted from SAS output.

Figure 10.1(A) shows the percentage of the target response (the nonowners here, often the "bads" in credit applications) that has been predicted (or captured) when the different cutoff rates are used. Thus, a random benchmark model with a 10 percent cutoff will, on average, predict 10 percent of the target population, a 20 percent cutoff will capture 20 percent, etc., as shown, labeled "Baseline". With a 20 percent cutoff, the regression model gets (approximately) 40 percent correct. Of course, with a 100 percent cutoff, because every observation is classified as a "bad," any method captures all those falling into the target class (the nonowners here) but, unfortunately, this will misclassify all the owners.

Shown in Figure 10.1(B) is the noncumulative % captured response curve, which is useful for identifying where the model is proving effective and where it is not. For each 10th percentile, a random selection would expect to capture 10 percent of the owners (or "bads"). Here, the regression model captures between 10 and 30 percent in the lower percentiles and, by way of compensation, drops below 10 percent past the 50th percentile cutoff mark.

A second tool for understanding performance is a graph of the *sensitivity* (proportion of captured target events) = versus the proportion of falsely predicted non-target events = $h_{01}/(h_{00} + h_{01})$ versus the proportion of falsely predicted non-target events = $h_{11}/(h_{10} + h_{11})$ (=1– *specificity*). This graph is called the *Receiver Operating Characteristic* curve, shown in Figure 10.2. The shape of the curve gives a visual impression of how good the classification model is: The closer the curve gets to the upper left corner [position (0, 1)], the better is the model.

Figure 10.2 The Receiver Operating Characteristic (ROC) Curve for the
Logistic Regression Model (based on the model from Section 10.3)

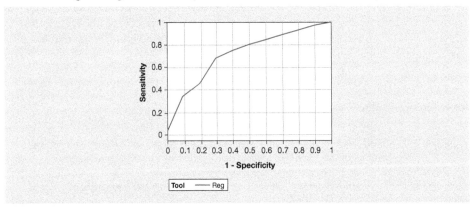

Data: Compdata.xlsx; adapted from SAS output.

In considering the benefits of a model in helping to identify the target class, it would be desirable to consider the profitability of adopting alternative cutoffs. Rather than just relying on statistical properties of the models, we can instead consider the expected profit from using a 10 percent cutoff versus, say, a 20 percent cutoff. Let us suppose that the expected profit from a "good" customer is P_G and the expected profit (typically negative) from a "bad" customer is P_B, so that the expected net profit is

$$Profit(Cutoff) = P_G h_{11} + P_B h_{01}, \tag{10.1}$$

and this quantity can be calculated for different cutoffs to give a profit curve and identify an appropriate cutoff. This approach is readily expanded to include the lost profits from failing to identify the good targets and the benefits from excluding the bad prospects.

DISCUSSION QUESTION: *For a Web-based insurance provider, what costs and profits should be considered in deciding whether to offer a policy to a new customer?*

10.1.2 A Comment

With only two possible Y values in the data, the error term cannot be normal, as we explained in Section 10.1, so other models are needed (if we are to be strict about the regression assumptions holding). In the sections that follow, we discuss three different methods for tackling the problem that do not conflict with the regression assumptions: classification trees, logistic regression, and neural networks. All are useful for predictive classification.

10.2 Classification and Regression Trees

An intuitively appealing procedure for making predictions, especially in dealing with cross-sectional data, is to divide the cases into homogeneous subgroups such that the members of a given subgroup might be expected to behave in a similar way. For example, local areas might be identified whose residents strongly favor one political party or where demographic factors might point to prospective customers for a product or service. However, such subdivisions of available data come at a cost; for example, classifying cases according to ten two-category factors produces over a thousand subclasses, too many for all but the largest databases. This realization leads to the idea that we should subdivide the data according to the most relevant factors and stop when we have reached a sufficiently fine-grained classification system. Such an approach is best represented by a *tree diagram*, which shows the successive partitions that are made in the data set to try to improve the predictions for future cases.

■ Example 10.2: Hypothetical data on bank loans

A bank that is interested in improving its ability to identify good loan customers (i.e., those who repay their loans on schedule) might select a sample of past loan histories and classify each account as "good" or "bad" according to the account history. Hopefully, the bank has made a relatively small number of bad loans, so the sample might include most, if not all, such problem cases to ensure that the model has the potential for capturing the key features of bad customers. Only a relatively small percentage of good loans would be included, so as not to overweight the good loans at the expense of the bad (see Section 12.5.2). In this example, the target class is "bad loans."

By way of illustration, we assume that the bank has selected 200 records, consisting of 150 good loans and 50 bad loans. Included in each record is information such as the customer's employment history, credit rating, home ownership, and other, similar background information. A classification tree analysis might proceed as shown in Figure 10.3. The best single variable relates to credit history (*Credit score* > 600 or *Credit score* ≤ 600), which serves to separate out most of the good cases. The employment record is found to provide useful information on those with a good credit score, but for those with a score below 600, home ownership proves the key factor. At that point, we terminate the process on the grounds that further partitions are dealing with small numbers that would produce questionable improvements.

Figure 10.3 Classification Tree Based Upon Hypothetical Data on Bank Loans

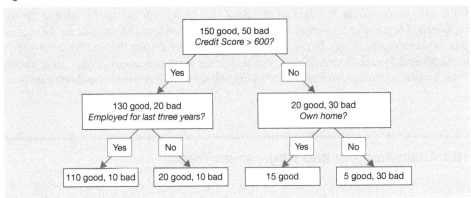

Initial screening of new applicants could then proceed, using this tree for decision-making purposes. For example if, on average, a bad loan costs five times as much as the profit from a good loan, we might approve a loan when the applicant fell into a box for which the proportion of "goods" exceeded 83 percent (when the expected profit would be positive). Thus, (*Credit score > 600 and Employed for last 3 years*) or (*Credit score ≤ 600 and Own home*) would qualify. The lowest level boxes are often called leaves on the tree's branches. ■

DISCUSSION QUESTION: *Why might a customer with (Credit score > 600 and Own home) not qualify?*

The example serves to illustrate the key issues that must be addressed in the construction of such trees:

- The process of recursive partitioning of cases
- A stopping rule that determines when the tree is sufficiently developed.

Some researchers prefer to develop a complete tree (i.e., until every last possible partition has been identified) and then to operate a *pruning rule*. This approach compares with the one we have described, which involves a *stopping rule* that comes into play when the improvements in predictive accuracy are negligible. Conceptually, the two approaches should arrive at the same final tree, although differences in detailed application may lead to differences in the final result.

10.2.1 Performance Measures: An Example

If we possess cost or profit information concerning the relative impact of wrong decisions, we can use this information to optimize the decision-making process. By way of example, suppose that granting a bad loan costs an average of $10,000 whereas granting a good one nets an average profit of $2,000. On the basis of only the first box, and making the assumption that the proportion of good and bad loans is as shown, the bank would not make any loans, because the total profit under each policy, from equation (10.1), is as follows:

No loans: *Total profit* = 0;

All loans approved: *Total profit* = (150 × $2,000 – 50 × $10,000) = –$200,000.

Using the credit rating criterion to make loans only to those with scores greater than 600 produces a *Total profit* of (130 × $2,000 – 20 × $10,000) = $60,000. Using all the criteria listed and then lending to those with a "yes" response at the second level produces a Total profit of (110 × $2,000 – 10 × $10,000 + 15 × $2,000) = $150,000.

In many circumstances, data on potential profit and costs may be either not available or not relevant and we must then employ other criteria. We will continue to employ the classification matrix introduced in Table 10.4. Using a 50 percent cutoff, Figure 10.3 produces the results shown in Table 10.6. From the latter table, with 135 loans approved, the sensitivity is 40/50 = 0.80 and the specificity is 125/150 = 0.83.

If we were to stop at the first level, we would have a sensitivity equal to 0.60 (30/50) and a specificity of 0.87 (130/150). Thus, the extension of the tree from one level to two leads to an improved sensitivity of 0.80 (40/50), although the specificity declines slightly, to 0.83 (125/150). As we have seen, the use of the second level also improves profitability.

Table 10.6 The Classification Matrix for the Hypothetical Data on Bank Loans

		Predicted		
		Good	Bad	Row Total
Actual	Nontarget = Good	125	25	150
	Target = Bad	10	40	50
	Column Total	135	65	200

10.2.2 Computer Ownership Example Revisited

We now consider a realistic example using the computer ownership data we introduced in Section 10.1. For this example, we use the same partition of the data as in Section 10.1, with approximately 80 percent of the observations in the estimation sample and the remaining 20 percent in the hold-out sample. The software employed is the SPSS add-in for classification and regression trees, evolving from the original work of Breiman, Friedman, Olshen, and Stone (1984). For ease of reproduction, the output we present is restricted to two levels of partitioning. There are several tree-building algorithms that may be employed, and we have opted for the CHAID method:

CHAID

Chi-squared Automatic Interaction Detection (CHAID). At each step, CHAID chooses the independent (predictor) variable that has the strongest interaction (as measured by a chi-squared criterion) with the dependent variable. Essentially, the aim is to identify a variable, X from the predictor variables, such that $P(Y/X)$ shows the greatest predictive power in discriminating between the different Y categories. Where X has more than one category the categories of each predictor are merged if they are not significantly different with respect to predicting the dependent variable.

This method works by splitting the data into subclasses. When the data are nominal, as in the present example, no additional splits are required, but for ordinal or interval-scaled data, the procedure involves trying multiple splits at each node and then selecting the split that provides the best partition (the highest value of the chi-squared statistic for that binary split, a value that measures the improvement in predictive power arising from the split).

■ Example 10.2: Hypothetical data on bank loans *(continued)*: Chi-squared calculations

This example illustrates the use of the chi-squared statistic and the basis of the calculations. If a split on the tree produces the same proportions of goods and bads at the next level, it has zero value as a predictor. This notion is akin to the usual use of the statistic in testing for independence. Consider the second split on the left-hand branch of the tree in Figure 10.3. The data may be summarized in the following table:

Actual	Decision (Predicted)		
	Good	Bad	Total
Good	110	20	130
Bad	10	10	20
Total	120	30	150

If there was no association between the actual classifications and the decisions made, the expected number of {Good/Good} cases would be given by

$$\frac{Predicted\ Number\ of\ Good\ Cases \times Actual\ Number\ of\ Good\ Cases}{Total\ Number} = \frac{120 \times 130}{150} = 104.$$

This result compares with the 110 of those accepted for a loan (on the basis of the prediction "Good") that actually turned out good. The other expected numbers may be calculated in the same way. The chi-squared statistic is then

$$\sum_{all\ cells} \frac{(observed - expected)^2}{expected}.$$

That is,

$$\frac{(110 - 104)^2}{104} + \frac{(20 - 26)^2}{26} + \frac{(10 - 16)^2}{16} + \frac{(10 - 4)^2}{4} = 12.98.$$

If there was no association between the two variables, this statistic would have a small value. (In a formal test, the upper 5 percent point is 3.84 and the upper 1 percent point is 6.63.) Tree development can stop when "nonsignificant" values are encountered. Because multiple classifications are attempted at each branching, the actual significance levels are larger than the nominal values cited, and the user should not rely upon them, but rather test the performance of the classification by using a hold-out sample. ■

■ Example 10.1: Computer ownership *(continued)*

An initial analysis of the computer ownership data produced a classification in which owners outnumbered nonowners in all parts of the tree. Seeking to improve the analysis, we combined the two lowest income groups (*Inc1* and *Inc2*) to form *Inc12* and repeated the analysis. The second split variable was the respondents' negative attitude to technology (*TAM1* = 1). The results proved more satisfactory, and the tree for the estimation sample is shown in Figure 10.4, in which those respondents with a negative attitude (*TAM1* = 1) who fall into the low-income group (*Inc12* = 1) were much less likely to own a computer (51/111, or 46 percent) than the respondents as a whole (85.1 percent). This model is readily interpretable, a benefit of such classification trees and a major advantage when the results need explaining. The output in Figure 10.4 includes the chi-squared statistic measuring the benefits of the split and its significance through a *P*-value. The tree for the test sample has, of course, the same structure, and the proportions assigned to each branch are similar. The

Figure 10.4 Predicting Computer Ownership: The *CHAID* Tree for 1159 Cases in the Estimation Sample (*Nocomp* = 1 *for a nonowner* and *Nocomp* = 0 *for an owner*)

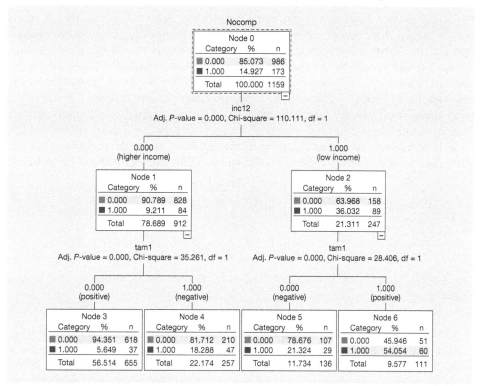

Data: Compdata.xlsx; adapted from SPSS output.

Table 10.7 Classification of Cases in the Estimation (Training) and Hold-Out (Test) Samples for the Computer Ownership Data

		Predicted			
Sample	**Observed**	**0**	**1**	**Percent Correct**	
Training	0	935	51	94.8%	Sensitivity =
	1	113	60	34.7%	60 / (113 + 60) or 35%
	Percentage of correct predictions	89.2%	54.1%	85.8%	
Test	0	221	12	94.8%	Sensitivity =
	1	22	7	24.1%	7 / (22 + 7) or 24%
	Overall Percentage	90.9%	36.8%	87.0%	

Tree Growing Method: CHAID   Dependent Variable: *Nocomp*

Data: Compdata.xlsx; adapted from SPSS output with additional calculations.

relative classifications of cases are summarized in Table 10.7. As expected, the performance on the test sample is inferior to that of the training (estimation) sample, but the overall difference is not perhaps pronounced although the sensitivity (the percentage of the target group identified correctly) drops noticeably. ■

10.3 Logistic Regression

Logistic regression employs a model that is superficially similar to the linear regression model with which we introduced the topic of classification in Section 10.1, but the model is now specified in terms of probabilities rather than a linear scale. For classification problems standard regression assumptions cannot hold, in particular normality, and logistic regression has been developed to overcome these deficiencies. The model we consider is sometimes known as *binary* logistic regression, because other versions may involve more than two categories (or classes), which, in turn may be either ordered or unordered. (For a detailed discussion of these more advanced schemes, see Kutner *et al.*, 2005, Chapter 14.)

To continue our example on computer ownership, let P_i denote the probability that the ith household does not own a computer (*Nocomp* = 1). Then the logistic model is written as

$$P_i = \frac{\exp(Q_i)}{1 + \exp(Q_i)} \tag{10.2}$$

or, equivalently, as

$$\ln\left(\frac{P_i}{1 - P_i}\right) = Q_i.$$

The quantity Q_i is known as the *log odds ratio*. Q_i contains the explanatory variables in a regression-like form, written as

$$Q_i = \beta_0 + \beta_1 X_{1i} + \cdots + \beta_K X_{Ki}. \tag{10.3}$$

Logistic regression has two advantages over linear regression: The fitted values of P_i are constrained to lie in the range (0, 1), and the observations are generated by a simple binomial (or Bernouli) distribution with parameters ($n = 1, p = P_i$). P_i represents the probability of an observation with characteristics $\{X_{1i}, X_{2i} \ldots X_{Ki}\}$ being bad: a nonowner in our example.

■ Example 10.1: Computer ownership *(continued)*

We consider the variables listed in Table 10.1, but exclude *Education*. As in linear regression, for each multiple-category indicator variable, we use one fewer indicator variable than there are categories. The estimated logistic regression model for computer ownership is summarized in Table 10.8, based upon the 1159 cases in the estimation set (approximately 80 percent of the total sample) previously selected as the estimation sample. The selected cases are identified in the data file by "*filter_$ = 1*".

Table 10.8 Logistic Regression Model for Computer Ownership Data

| | | Variables in the Equation | | | | | |
		B	S.E.	Wald	DF	P(Sig.)	Exp(B)
Step 1	Kids	−.662	.231	8.231	1	.004	.516
	Inc2	−.532	.276	3.709	1	.054	.587
	Inc3	−1.223	.307	15.847	1	.000	.294
	Inc4	−1.333	.303	19.350	1	.000	.264
	Inc5	−2.202	.265	69.163	1	.000	.111
	TAM2	−.718	.201	12.838	1	.000	.488
	TAM3	−1.453	.304	22.811	1	.000	.234
	Constant	.188	.214	.771	1	.380	1.206

Note: Variable(s) entered on step 1: *Kids, Inc2, Inc3, Inc4, Inc5, TAM2, TAM3*.
Data: Compdata.xlsx; adapted from SPSS output.

Column B lists the regression coefficient for each explanatory variable, and *S.E.* is the standard error of estimate of the coefficient. The Wald statistics, equal to $(B/S.E.)^2$ perform a role analogous to the *t* statistics in linear regression, and we may simply evaluate the contributions of the individual variables via the set of *P*-values, listed in the column marked 'Sig'.

The results presented in Table 10.8 show that the highest income level (*Inc5*) has a strong negative effect, as would be expected. The other income levels all have negative, but progressively smaller, effects relative to the lowest income level (*Inc1*, which was the omitted category). Likewise, having children (*Kids* = 1) and being pro-technology (*TAM2* and *TAM3*) both increase the probability of ownership and hence have negative signs in a prediction equation for nonownership. The final column denotes the *Odds Ratio* for each variable [exp(*Q*)] so that, for example, being technologically savvy (*TAM3*) decreases the odds in favor of nonownership by a factor of 4.28 (1/0.234) relative to someone with the same income and family structure — a considerable effect.

If we set the cutoff percentage at 50, we arrive at the classification shown in Table 10.9(A). In that table, this leads to a sensitivity of 20.2 percent, the success achieved in predicting nonowners, but a specificity of 44.6 percent. Table 10.9(B) uses the alternative classification approach of classifying an observation as "bad" if it has a fitted or projected probability higher than the cutoff value, here taken to be 0.5. This leads to many fewer observations falling into the target class, just 54 in the estimation sample. The overall percentage of correctly classified cases is 85.9 percent, but only 18.5 percent of nonowners are correctly identified (sensitivity). In the hold-out sample, only 10.3 percent of nonowners are correctly identified. By contrast, the specificity in the estimation sample is 97.8 percent, which indicates that almost all computer owners were correctly identified.

Table 10.9 Classification Tables for Logistic Regression: Estimation and Test Samples
(A) With 50% sample cutoff percentage defining the top 50% of cases to be nonowners;
(B) With those cases with a predicted probability above the cutoff value of 0.5 predicted to be nonowners (as calculated by SPSS or SAS)

(A) 50% cutoff, with approximately the top 50% predicted to be nonowners

		Predicted					
		Estimation Sample			Test Sample		
		Nocomp		Percentage	Nocomp		Percentage
Observed		0	1	Correct	0	1	Correct
Nocomp	0	549	437	55.7%	125	108	53.6%
	1	31	142	82.1%	6	23	79.3%
Overall		580	579	59.6%	131	131	56.5%

(B) Cutoff value of 0.5, classifying those cases with a predicted probability of nonownership of 0.5 or greater as nonowners

		Predicted					
		Estimation Sample			Test Sample		
		Nocomp		Percentage	Nocomp		Percentage
Observed		0	1	Correct	0	1	Correct
Nocomp	0	964	22	97.8	229	4	98.3
	1	141	32	18.5	26	3	10.3
Overall		1105	54	85.9	255	7	88.5

Data: Compdata.xlsx; adapted from SPSS output.

The 50% cutoff has been calculated by ranking the predictions and classifying the top 50% as nonowners. This assumes the observations are listed in random order with regard to ownership, which matters only if there are ties.

The figures in Table 10.9(B) are all based on the predicted probabilities. Contrasting Tables 10.9(A) and 10.9(B) demonstrates the importance of defining the cutoff procedure clearly. (See Exercise 10.5, which examines the value of additional explanatory variables in improving classification accuracy.) ■

The problem of misclassification errors is particularly acute when we seek to identify small subgroups (such as likely terrorists or those potentially suffering from a rare disease). Unless the model can be improved, the only choice is to modify the cutoff level. The appropriate choice of cutoff depends upon the objectives of the study and the relative costs of misclassification for the two categories.

> **DISCUSSION QUESTION:** *What are the pros and cons of a high cutoff when trying to identify potential terrorists? Or potential sufferers of a rare disease?*

10.3.1 Issues in Logistic Regression Modeling

A number of issues arise in logistic modeling:

1. How do we define residuals and identify outliers?
2. How do we measure overall fit?
3. Does the model work equally well across different cases, i.e., for all values of the log-odds ratio?
4. Does the hold-out sample indicate real separation between the two groups?
5. If the numbers in the target class are small, how do we improve our ability to identify them (improving the sensitivity)?
6. How does the method extend to the case where there is more than two categories of outcome?
7. What criteria should be used to compare different logistic model specifications or compared to other methods such as classification trees or neural networks (in Section 10.4)?

We provide a brief discussion here; for a more detailed account see Kutner *et al.* (2005, pp. 591-601).

1. Residuals: A number of definitions exist, but we focus on the standardized residuals

$$e_{st} = \frac{Y - \hat{P}}{\sqrt{\hat{P}(1 - \hat{P})}} \, .$$

The observed values (Y) are either 0 or 1, so although the standardized residuals have a mean close to 0 and variance close to 1, they clearly are not normally distributed. Nevertheless, large values indicate exceptional cases. For example, case #435 has kids, is in income class *Inc5*, and has a technology rating *TAM3*, yet is a nonowner. These values yield $Y = 1$, $\hat{P} = 0.016$, $e_{st} = 7.88$, indicating an unusual case (and probably a data error!).

2. **Overall Fit:** The simplest measure, known as *Efron's R*, is

$$R^2 = 1 - \frac{\sum(Y - \hat{P})^2}{\sum(Y - \bar{Y})^2}.$$

The estimation sample yields $R^2 = 0.155$. This value cannot be interpreted in the same way as the coefficient of determination in Chapter 8, but values from different models are useful for comparative purposes, with a set of perfect predictions having $R^2 = 1$.

3. **Performance Across Different Cases:** We may divide the estimation sample into G groups and then perform a chi-square-like test to determine whether the observed group sizes match predicted sizes: they should if the model is any good. The groups are defined by ordering the observations according to their fitted P_i values and then splitting them into groups by size. Ten ($G = 10$) such groups is a common choice. The average P_i is then computed for each group. If the group has N_i members, the expected number of cases with $Y = 1$ in the subgroup is $E_{i1} = N_i P_i$. Likewise, the expected number of cases with $Y = 0$ is $E_{i0} = N_i(1 - P_i)$ known as the *Hosmer-Lemeshow statistic*:

$$H = \sum_{i=1}^{G} \frac{(O_{i0} - E_{i0})^2}{N_i P_i (1 - P_i)} + \sum_{i=1}^{G} \frac{(O_{i1} - E_{i1})^2}{N_i P_i (1 - P_i)}.$$

The test statistic asymptotically follows a chi-squared distribution with $G - 2$ degrees of freedom. For $G = 10$, the results for the present example are as shown in Table 10.10.

Table 10.10 Testing Model Performance Across Sub-Groups

	Contingency Table for Hosmer-Lemeshow Test				
	Nocomp = 0; Probability = $1 - P_i$		Nocomp = 1; Probability = P_i		
Group	Observed	Expected	Observed	Expected	Total
1	160	158.78	3	4.23	163
2	97	99.45	6	3.55	103
3	116	114.55	6	7.45	122
4	117	117.53	9	8.47	126
5	38	39.61	5	3.39	43
6	132	134.10	20	17.90	152
7	99	97.92	15	16.08	114
8	100	98.54	27	28.46	127
9	72	67.09	25	29.91	97
10	55	58.43	57	53.57	112

The number of cases per group varies because of ties among the expected values. The value of the test statistic is 5.225 and with 8 DF this is insignificant at the 5% level, so the results are clearly consistent with an even performance across groups.

4. **Performance in the Hold-Out Sample:** The simplest way to examine the performance of the logistic regression in the hold-out sample is to calculate the chi-squared statistic, using the results in Table 10.9. The observed values for the test sample in panel (A) of that table are shown in Table 10.11, followed by the expected values in parentheses, for each cell under the null hypothesis of no association between the observed and predicted classifications.

Table 10.11 Classification Matrix on Hold-Out Sample

		Predicted			
		Nocomp = 0	Nocomp = 1	Total	Percentage Correct
Actual	Nocomp = 0	125 (116.5)	108 (116.5)	233	53.6
	Nocomp = 1	6 (14.5)	23 (14.5)	29	79.3
	Total	131	131	262	

The resulting value of the chi-squared statistic is 11.2, with associated *P*-value equal to 0.001. The proposed model clearly provides some separation between owners and non-owners. The same test procedure for Table 10.8(B) results in the lower value of 3.9, with *P*-value equal to 0.048. The same test procedure for the hold-out sample in Table 10.9(B) results in the slightly lower value of 7.4, with a *P*-value equal to 0.007, although the counts in the second column are very small.

5. **Small Numbers in the Target Class:** If an overall measure of performance is used, then often the best classifier is to predict all case fall in the "goods" category. But usually the primary focus is on the ability to identify the "bads" in the target class when there are few observed cases. This problem can be rectified (see Section 12.5.2) by over-sampling the target class.

6. **Dealing with More than Two Categories:** A common problem in logistic regression modeling is where there are more than two possible outcomes (e.g. in soccer, win, draw, or lose). The method may be easily extended (See Hosmer and Lemeshow, 2013). More problematic is when the different categories are nested, for example when the data represent the choice of mode of transport (bicycle, bus, car: own, shared). Here within the choice of using a car there are two alternatives nested within "car". Model building requires an extension of the basic logistic regression we have described here.

7. **Choosing Between Classification Methods:** To choose between logistic regression, regression trees and other classification methods, their comparative performance needs to be measured using a hold-out sample. The appropriate criteria need to be selected for the problem: is sensitivity the most important aspect, or can an overall measure such as the *AUC* or the *Gini* coefficient (see Section 10.4.1) be used? Interpretability of the classification rule is often a determining factor. Finally, since the model will often be used not just on cross-sectional data but for forecasting future populations, the stability of the models on different time cohorts of data needs to be considered.

10.4 Neural Network Methods

Neural network (NN) forecasting methods provide a flexible set of nonlinear forecasting tools. The methods can be used for extrapolative time series forecasting, causal modeling, or classification (where the dependent variable is categorical, most often binary, as we discussed earlier in this chapter). The initial formulation of neural networks was based on an analogy with how the brain processes information. As the literature developed separately from statistics, neural networks began to adopt their own terminology; here, we will use both sets of terms for clarity. Although neural network methods have a history that encompasses more than 50 years, it is only as increasing computer power has become available that the methods have gained wide acceptance in practical applications. Even now, however, their applications in forecasting are limited, with electricity demand being the most established. Still, research has shown neural networks to be potentially useful in a wide range of circumstances, from demand forecasting to predictions of individual consumer or business behavior.

Over the years, a large number of different types of neural network has appeared. The most common type in forecasting applications is the feedforward neural network. As the name implies, information from inputs is processed in a single direction, much like conventional linear regression. This is in contrast to recurrent neural networks that include feedback loops. Hereafter, we will always refer to feedforward networks, unless otherwise stated. Figure 10.5 illustrates such a neural network, with inputs (explanatory variables, $X_1,...,X_4$) that may be transformed to $(I_1,...,I_4)$. These transformed variables $(I_1,...,I_4)$, together with a constant (called *bias* in the neural network nomenclature), are connected through a *hidden layer* of K (here, $K = 3$) nodes (H_1, H_2, H_3) to the dependent (output) variable, Y_t. The four input variables shown are connected together with the bias term to the three nodes in the hidden layer. (There could be more or fewer than three nodes.) Each of these nodes is connected to all the inputs by producing a linear combination of inputs.

For node H_1, the input is given by

$$Z_1 = w_1 Bias + \sum_{i=1}^{4} w_{i1} I_i.$$

Figure 10.5 Schematic View of a Neural Network, Known as the Multilayer Perceptron

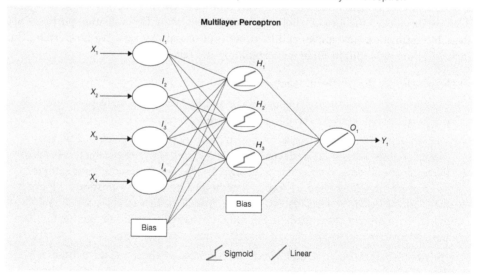

This input is then transformed by means of a nonlinear function (the *activation* function; the most common choice is the sigmoid logistic function) so that the output from node H_1 is

$$f(Z_1) = \frac{\exp(Z_1)}{[1 + \exp(Z_1)]}.$$

The final stage in the process is to take a weighted average of the outputs from the hidden layer to predict Y_1. (Alternatively, another nonlinear transform can be used.)

■ Example 10.3: Special cases of neural networks

Two special cases help to explain the general concepts underlying neural networks.

a. If the network has no hidden layer and the activation function is linear, the network corresponds to multiple linear regression.

b. If Y is binary and we use a single hidden layer with only one node and no transformations, so that

$$Z_1 = w_1 Bias + \sum_i w_{i1} I_i,$$

and then use the logistic function, we are back to logistic regression, as discussed in Section 10.3. ■

As the reader will have realized, there is a lot of flexibility in neural network modeling. In fact, it can be shown mathematically that a neural network can approximate pretty much any type of relationship between inputs and outputs, to an arbitrary degree of accuracy, depending on the number of nodes the network uses. But as with the nonlinear models we introduced in earlier chapters, such as the multiplicative seasonal models of Section 4.7, this very flexibility generates its own problems. In particular, overfitting the estimation sample ("training" is the term used by neural network specialists) results in poor performance out-of-sample, as with any other overfitted model. There are many ways to tackle the problem of overfitting, which can be broadly separated into approaches that use out-of-sample testing (the most common being to split the data into three segments: the training sample, the validation sample, and the test or hold-out sample), or shrinkage approaches, similar to the ideas introduced for Lasso regression (discussed in Section 9.5.2). In Section 3.3.3 we introduced the idea of a hold-out sample, separating for evaluation purposes our data into estimation (in-sample) and hold-out (out-of-sample) sets. We now extend this include a three-fold split to aid in model building and selection.

ESTIMATION, VALIDATION, AND HOLD-OUT SETS

- *Estimation set:* This is used to build a model and find the values of its parameters. It is also commonly known as training set or fitting sample.

- *Validation set:* This is used to select between different forecasts (such as different exponential smoothing methods) or choose the values of hyper-parameters (such as the number of hidden nodes in neural networks). We need this additional sample to avoid overfitting. If we choose a forecast method based on the estimation set it can bias our selection to models that fit best the particular characteristics of this sample, due to the flexibility of the method, but not necessarily forecast well into the future. Both estimation and validation sets constitute the in-sample data.

- *Hold-out set:* This is used to evaluate the performance of the forecasts on unseen data. We evaluate both the selection of the forecasts (validation set) and the chosen parameters (estimation set). This set is also known as the *test* data.

For time series data these sets are sequential (which we extend to include cross-validation in Section 10.4.2). For cross-sectional data the dataset is partitioned at random into the three sets.

The key decisions a neural network modeler must make are the following:

i. Which input (explanatory) variables to use;

ii. The architecture of the neural network, which implies the number of hidden nodes and type of activation functions;

iii. The approach used to ensure that the network does not overfit to the training set and forecasts well.

Before we discuss each of these steps it is useful to understand how a single neuron works (for example node H_1 in Figure 10.5). Figure 10.6 illustrates the logistic sigmoid nonlinear function that is commonly used as activation function in the hidden nodes. Observe that as the input value becomes very small or very large, the output tends towards 0 or 1 respectively. If the values are very small, close to 0, then the transformation from Z to output is almost linear, while for intermediate values the nonlinear behavior dominates. Remember that the input Z is constructed in the same way as a multiple linear regression, i.e., it is a weighted linear combination of inputs with an additive constant. For most real applications the value of an unweighted combination of Xs could result in such large values that the output of the neuron would always be very close to 1. For example, consider forecasting the UK retail sales that we analyzed earlier in Chapter 6 (Minicase 6.1), the values of which range between 51.8 and 137.5. This behavior is called saturation of the neuron, where the output always gives the same value, irrespective of the weighted (aggregate) input beyond a certain value. (The logistic sigmoid is sometimes called a squashing function as it squashes any input into the range 0 to 1). More generally, the units of measurement may be arbitrary (e.g., dollars or millions of dollars). To avoid such problems and to be able to use neural networks widely, we scale the inputs. Although the weights (w) used in the construction of Z, can also be used to scale the variables to useful ranges, this is poor practice, because in that case w has two tasks (scaling and capturing the relationship, as in multiple regression) that make estimation difficult. Instead it is good practice to first scale the inputs and then let the weights focus only on capturing the relationship between the variables. There are many ways this scaling can be performed. A common approach is to transform interval-scaled input variables by using:

$$X_i^* = (b - a)\left(\frac{X_i - Min(X_i)}{Max(X_i) - Min(X_i)}\right) + a.$$

This will result in the transformed X_i^* falling between values a and b, which typically are set to 0 and 1. Other transformations are possible, such as Z-score normalization. Dummy variables are, of course, coded as 0 or 1.

Figure 10.6 The Sigmoid Logistic Function

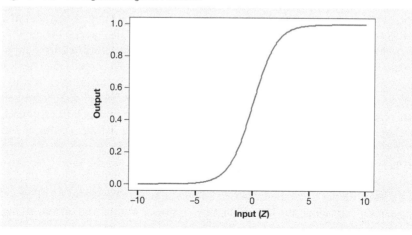

Typically such scaling is appropriate for other types of activation functions as well. Of course, if a linear activation function is used then scaling is not necessary, but as it does not harm modeling in any way, it is often done nonetheless.

As all variables are scaled, as is the target variable and therefore the output of the network is similarly scaled. To calculate the final forecast we need to reverse the transformation. In commercial neural network software, the scaling of the inputs and outputs is performed automatically.

Neural networks have been very successful in both regression and classification problems. Depending on the application the modeling process may differ. Nonetheless, both regression and classification share a number of core modeling decisions, which we discuss here.

Choosing the input variables. In contrast to variable selection for linear regression (Chapter 9), neural networks allow more flexibility. They are able to handle nonlinear interactions and multicollinearity without any special treatment of the variables. Nonetheless, careful selection of inputs has been shown to improve neural network performance greatly. For a causal (explanatory) model, the modeler should consider the guidelines given in Chapter 9 and identify possible drivers, including them all initially. However, where regression might be unable to use variables that interact nonlinearly, neural networks can capture such relationships. Therefore, relying simply on linear correlation (or regression variable selection) may exclude some useful variables. A simple way to identify such interactions is to use scatterplots. For extrapolative models or causal models with lags, there is a potentially vast number of inputs to consider. One simple, but effective, approach is to use stepwise regression to reduce the number of variables for inclusion (Crone and Kourentzes, 2010).

Specifying the architecture of the network. This step involves the selection of the number of hidden layers, the number of nodes in each and the type of activation function. Theoretical work has shown that single hidden layer networks can approximate any underlying function, given a sufficient number of nodes. In practice, with a limited training sample, this may not be achievable. Nevertheless, research has shown that a single hidden layer is adequate for most problems, particularly for regression-type problems. For classification problems, especially if the separation between the classes is highly nonlinear, one might experiment with a second hidden layer. Recently there has been a renewed interest in neural networks that have multiple hidden layers within a so-called deep learning paradigm. Although these networks have demonstrated spectacular performance in computer vision, speech recognition and natural language processing, so far there is no evidence that deep learning is beneficial for the tasks we focus on here.

There is no widely accepted approach to the specification of the number of nodes in a hidden layer and only limited guidelines from theory. In a nutshell, the greater the number of nodes the more complex processes a network can capture. On the other hand, the more nodes, the more parameters need to be estimated. Therefore the selection of the number of nodes is a compromise between model flexibility and complexity. Nonetheless, the performance of the network is not very sensitive to the number of nodes, so there is limited benefit to attempting to fine-tune the best number of nodes. The most popular approach is to search through a range of alternatives and select the one that delivers the minimum error on a validation set, or with cross-validation. Also note that information criteria, such as *AIC*, are inappropriate for choosing a specific neural network, as the same predictive accuracy can be obtained from different networks.

Last but not least, one has to specify the activation function in each layer. As we observed before, using a linear activation function will make each node a multiple regression model.

To capture nonlinear behaviors the sigmoid logistic (see Figure 10.6) or the hyperbolic tangent functions are typically used. Evidence suggests that the performance of the networks is insensitive to the choice between these two. For regression problems the output node is usually a linear function. For classification problems this is typically the sigmoid logistic or softmax (the multidimensional generalization of sigmoid logistic), both of which bound the result between 0 and 1 and allow the interpretation of the output as class membership. The latter is appropriate for solving multiple classification problems.

A final design choice is the cost function used in the training of the network. The most typical cost function is the sum of squared errors (*SSE*). In the same logic as Lasso regression (Section 9.5.2) one can use a penalized version of *SSE* that will shrink the connection weights of the network, aiding its out-of-sample performance. Specifically for classification problems a popular choice with good performance is the cross-entropy (for the binary classification problem the cross-entropy can be calculated as:

$$H = -\frac{1}{N}\sum_{i}[Y_i\ln(\hat{Y}_i) + (1 - Y_i)\ln(1 - \hat{Y}_i)],$$

where Y_i and $\hat{Y}_i$ are the actual and predicted classes).

Neural network ensembles. A final design note that is important for neural networks is how to avoid over-fitting, so as to improve out-of-sample performance. Two aspects of neural networks make them prone to over-fitting. If we compare a neural network with a linear regression with the same inputs, the former has substantially more parameters to estimate (the connection weights). This makes neural networks overly flexible, which in turn may result to over-fitting to the training sample. The second problem has to do with the estimation itself. The training of neural networks is a complex nonlinear optimization problem, which typically will not converge to the global minimum of the error function. Depending on the starting point of the optimization (affected by the initial values of the connection weights) a different local minimum may be achieved. Some of the resulting networks may perform well, while others may over- or under-fit.

To mitigate the adverse effects of either, one successful approach is to train a network multiple times with different initialization values and combine the resulting outputs. For example, suppose that our task is to produce a forecast for the next 12 months. We can train a network several times with different, e.g. random, initial values and produce forecasts from each trained network. These forecasts are then combined for each month separately to produce an ensemble forecast, see Figure 10.7. The combination is commonly done using the unweighted mean, and therefore no one single, potentially over-fit network, is preferred. This also resolves the problem of selecting a "best" network. Research has shown that for the mean combination operator to converge to a reliable ensemble forecast a large number of individual networks are needed and using the median to combine forecasts is preferable, which is immune to extreme values that over-fitted networks may produce. It has been shown that 20-30 individual networks are adequate for the median operator to converge to a robust and reliable output.

Alternatively, other more advanced combination operators can be used, such as the mode as estimated via Kernel Density Estimation, which overcomes some of the limitations of the median as a measure of central tendency. For more details, see Kourentzes, Barrow, and Crone (2014), who discuss the selection of the combination operator and the size of the ensemble. The reader should note that it is possible to construct ensembles from networks that differ in their design, in terms of inputs or architecture.

Figure 10.7 An Example of Different Forecasts from Ensemble Members and the Resulting Combination

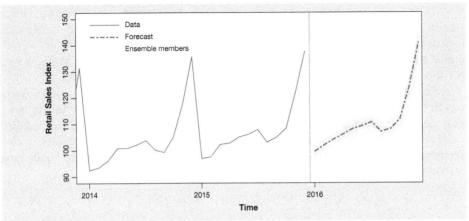

*Source: https://www.ons.gov.uk/businessindustryandtrade/retailindustryandtrade/retailindustry/datasets/
retailsalesindexreferencetables*
Data: UK_retail_sales_monthly.xlsx; adapted from *Forecasting in R: Tutorial and Examples* online materials output.

Neural network training. Although we do not intend to go into the mathematical and algorithmic details of estimating the weights of neural networks, it is useful to grasp the basic ideas behind it, as it has implications for model building and producing reliable forecasts. At its most basic form, training a neural network for predictive applications requires splitting the available fitting sample into two subsets, the training and the validation sets. We minimize the fit error in the training sample, while observing how the error evolves in the validation set. As the network "learns" the characteristics of the data, error reduces in both sets. When the network starts to overfit to the training set, the validation set error will increase, indicating that the network is no longer benefiting from training. Figure 10.8 provides such an example. For a time series the errors for the training, validation, and test sets are provided as the network trains (each epoch in the horizontal axis is a full pass using all the observations in the training set). Observe that in this example errors in all three subsets are decreasing until about epoch 250 (i.e., on each pass through the data, the revised parameter values are getting closer to the optimum values). Afterwards, the training set keeps on decreasing, while the errors for the validation and test set stabilize. These can potentially start increasing if we train the network further. This is where the network stops generalizing well to unseen data (outside of the training set) and we should stop training. The network weights that provide the minimum validation set error are selected.

Figure 10.8 Error Progression During Training

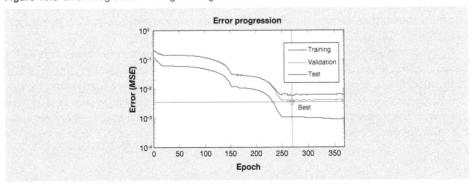

Note that Figure 10.8 corresponds to a single training initialization, and different starting weights will result in a different trajectory of errors. Furthermore, the test set error is only provided for illustrative reasons and is not used at all during training.

In a similar fashion, one could select from among different training initializations and pick a "best" network, based on the minimum error on the validation set. Nowadays, both training with two subsets and choosing a single training initialization are considered somewhat obsolete. There are several reasons for this. First, although we avoid overfitting on the training set, it is quite possible that we end up overfitting in the validation set, especially if it has limited sample size. Second, in order to devise a validation set, we sacrifice data from the training set, which more often than not is rather limited in size. Third, as computational power has increased, there is limited need to select a single network and we can afford to run multiple ones in an ensemble, as noted above. There are very efficient and robust training algorithms that do not require a validation set. This is achieved by methods similar to the penalization of the fit in Lasso regression or by smart algorithms that are resilient to the size of each residual and focus mostly on the direction of errors. Given that optimizing the weights of a neural network remains a very difficult problem, due to its dimensionality and nonlinearity, it is always recommended to use ensembles of multiple training initializations.

Given the approximation capabilities of neural networks, a newer paradigm for training, Extreme Learning Machines (ELM), assumes that in fact we do not need to train any weights in the network except for those connecting the last hidden layer to the output nodes. The training problem is now much simpler and can be solved using least squares, in the same way as in regression, resulting in almost instantaneous training. ELM can be rather sensitive to peculiarities in the data and caution should be exercised to produce robust forecasts, by using an appropriate architecture and ensemble forecasts, especially given that now the computational cost is minimal.

Different software permit different training alternatives and different training algorithms have a series of different tuning parameters. Most modern implementations are capable of adjusting the parameters during training, or are resilient enough for the user to not have to fine tune these. However, an important point to stress is that with neural networks a set of weights that would correspond to the global optimum in the training set is hardly desirable, as it will be the result of overfitting. The modeling philosophy is similar to that of Lasso regression as discussed in Section 9.5.2.

THE PROCESS OF BUILDING A NEURAL NETWORK

1. Pre-process the target variable appropriately. For time series forecasting this may involve de-trending, while for cross-sectional problems the target observations may be resampled by taking multiple samples of the target to potentially improve the sensitivity and test the effects of different re-weighting schemes (e.g., sample twice from the target population compared with once from the non-target).[2]

2. Divide the sample into training (estimation), and test (hold-out) data sets. Optionally a validation set can be used.

3. Choose the input variables.

4. Ensure that the input variables are scaled and coded appropriately (e.g., with dummy variables for categorical inputs).

5. Ensure that a number of different sets of starting values are used in estimation.

continues

---

2 For details of sample size effects and re-weighting when choosing the sample, see Crone and Finlay (2012). For an approach that focuses on re-weighting poorly explained target observations, see Barrow and Crone (2016).

THE PROCESS OF BUILDING A NEURAL NETWORK *(continued)*

6. Compare the results from using different numbers of hidden nodes.

7. Combine forecasts from multiple training initializations (and potentially architectures).

8. Use the performance on the test data to measure the likely future performance of the network.

10.4.1 A Cross-Sectional Neural Network Analysis

We return again to the data on computer usage (*Compdata.xlsx*), as described in Table 10.1. Three alternative neural networks are considered, one with three nodes, one with five nodes, and one where the size of the hidden layer is automatically specified, using a 20% validation set.

So far we have used the *ROC* curve to measure the power of a classifier and understand the impact of choosing a different threshold value. Using such curves to decide on the number of hidden nodes can be rather cumbersome. On the other hand, a simple criterion, such as *SSE*, is inadequate for the task, as it does not consider the qualitative difference of the two alternative classes. A useful alternative is the Area Under the *ROC* (referred to as *AUC* or more formally *AUROC*). Comparing the *AUC* of different network specifications can allow us to quickly identify a well performing alternative.

AREA UNDER THE *ROC*

We noted that the *ROC* of an ideal classifier would pass from $(0,1)$, covering the complete *ROC* plot. The *AUC* (or *AUROC*) summarizes that, by computing how much of the plot is under the *ROC* of that classifier, hence its name.

To calculate the *AUC*, given an *ROC*, we can use the following:

1. Take the vector that contains the sensitivity values and construct: *SensA* that contains all the sensitivities without the first value, and *SensB* that contains all the sensitivities without the last value.

2. Take the vector that contains the specificities and calculate the first differences, *SpecD*.

3. $AUC = \sum(SensA + SensB) / 2 \, SpecD$

A similar measure is the *Gini* coefficient, which is defined as $Gini = 2 \times AUC - 1$. When using *AUC* or the *Gini* coefficient, note that they do not focus on the cutoff values of interest!

■ Example 10.1: Computer ownership *(continued)*

We test from 1 to 10 hidden nodes and select the one that provides the maximum *AUC*, which is found to be a network with a single hidden node (NN.auto in Table 10.12). We proceed to build the three alternative models and the results from this analysis are given in Table 10.12. The table shows the misclassification rate and the *AUC* for the different networks for the test set. To calculate the misclassification rate a predicted output above 0.5 is taken to be a prediction for the output (target) variable of 1 (i.e., a computer nonowner), whereas a predicted value below 0.5 is taken to be a predicted output of 0 (i.e., an owner). The cutoff value can be taken to be any value between 0 and 1, as noted in Section 10.2.

Table 10.12 Summary Measures for Neural Network Analysis of Computer Ownership Data (*test data set*)

	AUC	Misclassification Rate
NN.3 (3 hidden nodes)	0.741	12.2%
NN.5 (5 hidden nodes)	0.739	13.0%
NN.auto (1 hidden node)	0.718	11.5%

Data: Compdata.xlsx

Observe that the *AUC* and the misclassification rates do not agree on which network is the best. The latter is calculated assuming a cutoff rule of assigning a case with a predicted probability of 0.5 or more to the nonowner class, while the *AUC* metric is summarizing the complete *ROC*, which are shown Figure 10.9. As we can see, for different cutoff rules we expect the ranking of the best network to change.

Also it is interesting to note that NN.auto clearly outperforms the alternative NN.3 or NN.5 when we look at the *ROC* or *AUC*. This due to potential overfit of the network to the validation set that was used to choose the number of hidden nodes. In section 10.4.2 we contrast validation with cross-validation to attempt to mitigate this potential problem.

For a particular neural network, we can examine the classification matrix, which depends on the cutoff we choose (e.g., with cutoff values of 50 percent and 20 percent, shown in Table 10.13, for NN.3). With a cut-off of 20 percent rather than 50 percent, fewer households are correctly predicted as not owning a computer. ■

Figure 10.9 *ROC* Curve for Computer Ownership Example (*test data set*)

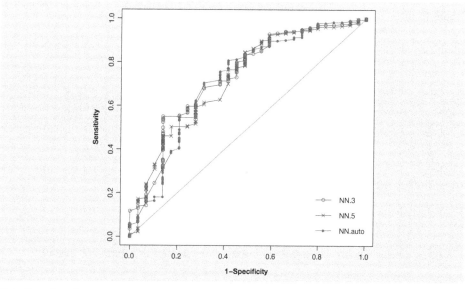

Data: Compdata.xlsx

Table 10.13 Classification Matrices for 50% and 20% Cutoffs (*test data set*)

		50% Cutoff			20% Cutoff	
		0	1		0	1
0	Frequency	223	22	Frequency	192	14
	Percent	85.11%	8.40%	Percent	73.28%	5.34%
1	Frequency	10	7	Frequency	41	15
	Percent	3.82%	2.67%	Percent	15.65%	5.73%

Data: Compdata.xlsx

10.4.2 A Time Series Neural Network Analysis: Modeling UK Retail Sales

Neural nets can equally well be used to forecast time series data. Figure 10.10 shows the time series for UK retail sales that we analyzed earlier in Chapter 6 (Minicase 6.1). We will withhold the last year as test set and use the rest to build the neural network. With 27 years of data, there should be more than enough observations to identify any non-linearities.

It is apparent that the time series has an upward changing trend, easily demonstrated through the use of a 12-period centered moving average (also shown in Figure 10.10). Neural networks of the type we have been discussing in this section, feedforward Multilayer Perceptrons (MLP), are incapable of modeling long term trends directly. The reason for this is that as the trend may go beyond the observed training set, the neurons of the network may saturate, as discussed above. Therefore, the output of the network will gradually dampen-off, to the point that it will eventually produce a flat line, once all neurons have saturated. As in the Box-Jenkins ARIMA methodology of Chapter 6, we model the trend by considering the differenced time series, which is shown in Figure 10.11. Notice that there is no trend now and only a seasonal pattern is apparent. Both Figure 10.10 and Figure 10.11 show that the seasonality is changing over time, implying some non-additive form of seasonality.

Figure 10.10 UK Retail Sales, Not Seasonally Adjusted, in Constant 2006 Prices
(*January 1988–December 2015*)

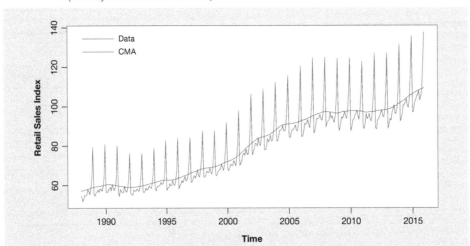

Source: https://www.ons.gov.uk/businessindustryandtrade/retailindustry/datasets/retailsalesindexreferencetables
Data: UKRetail_Sales_Monthly.xlsx; adapted from Forecasting in R: Tutorial and Examples online materials output.

Figure 10.11 Differenced UK Retail Sales Time Series

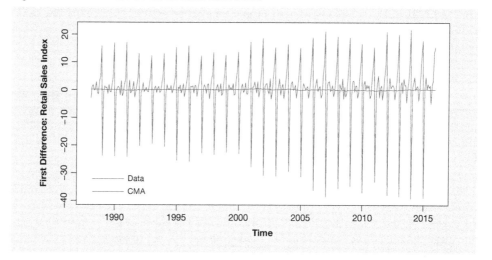

Modeling seasonality with neural networks requires some consideration. In principle they are able to model seasonality in many different ways. For example, one might use seasonal differencing or seasonal lags, as in the Box-Jenkins methodology, or could use binary dummy variables to capture seasonality. The former implies that stochastic seasonality is modeled, while the latter models deterministic seasonality. Note that one could also use trigonometric dummy variables[3] (pairs of sines-cosines of the appropriate frequency to match the time series seasonality) to model non-integer seasonality, like the number of weeks in a year (52.14) or days in a year (364.25) to account for leap years. These forms can be used separately or mixed together, but it is generally advisable to consider the problem context. For example, including binary dummies to model a weekly seasonal pattern would increase the number of weights to be estimated substantially (51 binary dummies times the number of nodes in the first hidden layer, so for instance with 10 hidden nodes we would be adding 510 weights to be estimated!) and using a seasonal autoregressive lag, or a pair of sine-cosine dummy variables would be preferable. Due to their nonlinear nature, neural networks are also able to approximate seasonal patterns in ways that are not possible with linear models. In a linear regression using a pair of sine and cosine inputs would be useless, but for a neural network this is a very efficient way to model seasonality. Similarly, both additive and multiplicative seasonal patterns can be approximated. Last but not least, it is trivial to model series with multiple seasonal patterns (for example, typical in daily and hourly time series), simply by including the relevant inputs. (For an example of the latter, as well as how to treat special days in high frequency data see Barrow and Kourentzes, 2017.)

In this application, we use a relatively simple neural network that is easy to build and replicate. A single hidden layer, together with the input and output layers, results in a standard three-layer perceptron as illustrated in Figure 10.5. In the hidden nodes, we will use the sigmoid logistic function that allows us to model flexibly any type of linear and nonlinear mapping between the inputs and the outputs of the network, given an adequate number of hidden nodes.

As discussed previously, we first scale the time series to avoid saturation of the nonlinear nodes. Although it is common practice to scale inputs between 0 and 1, often a better

---

3 These are constructed as follows: $D_s = \sin(2\pi t/T)$ and $D_c = \cos(2\pi t/T)$, where $t = 1,\dots, n$, n is the sample size and T is the seasonal period, for example $T = 12$ for monthly time series.

strategy is to modify the range of values to an interval that is symmetric about zero such as −0.8 to 0.8. This can be useful for highly erratic time series, which in the futuremay experience very high or very low values. This way such values will still remain safely away from the saturation point of neurons. We will use this range in our example.

We use 12 lags as inputs for the network, and 11 binary dummy variables for the seasonality. In fact, we pre-filter the inputs using a backward regression, but all are retained. The next design option is the size of the hidden layer. As we discussed above, there are many ways to identify this. Here we will illustrate the results of two approaches: (i) using the last 20% of the training set as validation set and comparing the performance of different numbers of hidden nodes on the validation set; and (ii) using cross-validation with 5 folds as we discuss below. We test all possible number of hidden nodes up to 10. The 5-fold cross-validation implies 5 times more computations and the network is trained in total 1000 times, 5 folds/1–10 hidden nodes/20 training replications. This comes at a substantial computation cost. Table 10.14 provides the results of the evaluation. The best error in each case is highlighted in boldface. Observe that validation and cross-validation provide different suggestions as to the best number of hidden nodes, 9 and 6 respectively. Validation is weaker, so we will prefer the cross-validation result. Nonetheless, there is an apparent trade-off in robustness of the analysis against computational cost.

Table 10.14 RMSE for Different Number of Hidden Nodes with Validation and Cross-Validation

Hidden Nodes	RMSE	
	Validation	Cross-Validation
1	0.0365	0.0423
2	0.0345	0.0406
3	0.0340	0.0438
4	0.0313	0.0370
5	0.0312	0.0365
6	0.0305	**0.0333**
7	0.0308	0.0370
8	0.0315	0.0373
9	**0.0297**	0.0369
10	0.0299	0.0364

Validation and Cross-Validation

These are two related concepts that help us to ensure that our model is not over-fitted to the training data. The validation set is used to evaluate the performance of a model, so as to tune its hyper-parameters (such as the penalty parameter in Lasso, section 9.5.2), or choose between alternative specifications. Note that the hold-out sample (or test set) should not be used for these tasks, as it is not formally part of the fitting sample, and is designed to *test* the performance of our forecasts.

The validation set is constructed by setting aside an adequate number of the later observations of the in-sample. However, if we over-rely on a specific validation sample, which is typically smaller than the training set, to decide the model specification — for neural networks this may be the number of neurons in a hidden layer — we may end up tuning the model to be appropriate for modeling only these observations, i.e., to over-fit! To mitigate this potential problem, cross-validation can help us evaluate a specification on all available data. We will explain how this is done using an example.

Suppose we want to find the number of hidden nodes for a neural network for a time series. We need to build a table similar to 10.14. If we use a validation set, we can retain the last 20% of the observations to construct it. Now only 80% of the observations are used to train the network (i.e., optimizing the values of the weights to minimize the *MSE*) and we measure its performance on the validation set. We repeat this process for different numbers of hidden nodes and pick the specification that provides the least error. However, this will be the least error for the last 20% of the in-sample, and may not be the same as if we had withheld the last 25% or any other sample. We therefore need to generate a number of alternative validation samples, each one a replication based on a different sample.

This way, all available data points have been used as validation set and the reported error is less susceptible to preferring a specification that fits well on only a small part of the data. Typical numbers of folds (replications) are 5 and 10 resulting in 5-fold and 10-fold cross-validation setups. A special case is the Leave-One-Out cross-validation, which prescribes that K matches the fitting sample size, i.e., at each iteration only a single observation is used as a validation set. For our example, using a 5-fold cross-validation, for each potential number of neurons b_1, we would fit a network 5 times (over the 5-folds) and report the cross-validation error (averaged over 5 folds) for a given number of hidden nodes.

K-FOLD CROSS-VALIDATION

In order to get more reliable errors that are not overly dependent on a specific subset, we can split the series into K parts of equal size (these are called *folds*). These are then used to calculate the validation measures (*ROC, AUC, RMSE*) as follows:

1. Split the complete training set into K equal subsets (folds). If lags of the target (or explanatory) variable are used as inputs, then use the appropriate data tuples (for example for period t a data tuple is a set of the values of the target at this period and of all the inputs corresponding to that period).

2. Choose at random a single fold that will act as a validation set. Use all remaining folds as training set.

3. Optimize the weights of the network and measure the forecast error in the fold that has been set aside as a validation set.

4. Repeat steps 2 and 3 until all folds have been used as validation sets.

5. Average the forecast error across all validation sets from step 4 and report this as the K-fold cross validation error.

The inputs and the architecture of the network are now set. We train the network 20 times and generate the forecasts. The scaling and differencing are then reversed and the resulting forecasts are combined in a single ensemble forecast using the median of the individual forecasts. To better illustrate the benefit of using the ensemble forecast instead of a single trained network, we provide in Figure 10.12 the forecasts of the ensemble and all trained networks for the next 36 periods. Observe that although most individual forecasts behave quite well, as the horizon increases they become more erratic and in particular two networks generate forecasts that are wildly different. This is due to potential overfitting in the training set or poor optimization of the weights. Nonetheless, the ensemble forecast does not exhibit these weaknesses.

Figure 10.12 Forecasts of Ensemble and Individual Networks

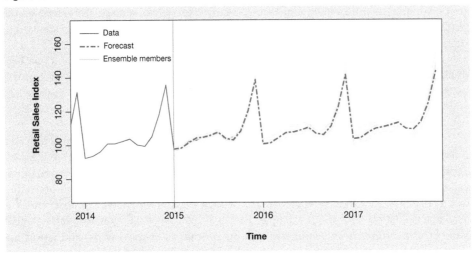

Source: https://www.ons.gov.uk/businessindustryandtrade/retailindustry/datasets/retailsalesindexreferencetables
Data: UKRetail_Sales_Monthly.xlsx; adapted from Forecasting in R: Tutorial and Examples online materials output.

Table 10.15 compares the results produced by a six-hidden-node neural network on the test data set with outputs from benchmark Holt-Winters and ARIMA methods (with the minimum values again shown in bold) and an ELM network. There are a few points to observe. First, comparing the two neural networks, the trained MLP performs better than Extreme Learning Machine (ELM), although the latter is not excessively inaccurate, highlighting the trade-off between computational speed and forecasting performance. The Holt-Winters and ARIMA forecasts are very competitive. This time series, especially at the test set does not exhibit strong nonlinearities that the neural networks could use to advantage. Despite their flexibility, neural networks do not invariably improve on simpler methods, as Crone, Hibon, and Nikolopoulos (2011) demonstrate in a wide-ranging comparison of various NN formulations with standard benchmarks. The linearity of the series is also reflected in the good performance of the additive form of Holt-Winters. The time series has leveled-off in the test data, therefore the multiplicative nature of the seasonality is not strongly evident. Finally, we find that different methods perform best depending on the different error metrics chosen and the different lead times.

Table 10.15 Forecast Comparisons on the Test Data (*Year 2015*):
Neural Networks vs. Smoothing and ARIMA Models

Forecast	Lead 1 (12 observations)			Lead 1–12 (origin Dec 2014)		
	RMSE	MAPE	MdAPE	RMSE	MAPE	MdAPE
Neural Network.MLP	1.016	0.90%	0.90%	1.189	0.92%	0.77%
Neural Network.ELM	1.373	1.18%	1.28%	1.449	1.16%	1.24%
Holt-Winters, additive	**0.919**	**0.83%**	**0.83%**	**1.034**	**0.78%**	0.74%
Holt-Winters, multiplicative	1.047	0.92%	0.92%	1.328	0.87%	**0.66%**
SARIMA(2,1,1)(0,1,1)	1.038	0.94%	0.94%	1.322	1.07%	1.00%
Holt-Winters, logarithmic	1.057	0.92%	0.92%	1.598	1.03%	0.82%
SARIMA(1,1,3)(1,1,2), logarithmic	1.030	0.90%	0.90%	1.273	0.82%	0.72%

Note: This example has been implemented in R, and the code used is downloadable from the book's website.

10.4.3 Neural Networks: A Summary

Neural network models make up a flexible class of nonlinear models that can be used for ordinary time series modeling, causal modeling, or predictive classification. An extensive literature exists, and a comprehensive discussion may be found in Haykin (2009). However, the very flexibility offered by neural network models means that there are many choices a modeler must make. Poor choices will often lead to poor results. The guidelines we have provided should be followed.

Unfortunately, although many software programs are available, they are not standardized, and some may well produce poor forecasts or misleading results due to inadequate programming. We have used R and SAS for our calculations; see *Forecasting in R: Tutorial and Examples* on the book's website. But because there are no accepted benchmarks for checking the calculations, all that can be done is to check whether the output (particularly the performance of the neural network on test data) improves on some standard classification or forecasting benchmark.

10.5 Vector Autoregressive (VAR) Models

The time series regression models we proposed in Chapter 9 typically contained a set of explanatory variables (we primarily included lagged variables but the benefits of contemporaneous variables were also considered in Minicase 9.1): such specifications are called *Autoregressive distributed lag* (ADL) models and can be written as:

$$Y_t = \beta_o + \sum_{}^{p} \phi_i Y_{t-i} + \sum_{j=1}^{K} \sum_{i=0}^{q_j} \beta_{ij} X_{jt-i} + \varepsilon_t.$$

While such an equation looks messy, it contains K explanatory variables, each lagged from 0 to q_j times together with p lags of the dependent variable, Y. An example makes it simpler: in Section 9.9 we included $K=3$ explanatory variables, *Crude_price*, *SP500*, *Demand*, and *Unleaded*, all lagged in differenced form, i.e. with one lag in the differenced explanatory variable and one lag for differenced *Unleaded*.

In regression analysis such as this, the modeler must distinguish between the explanatory input variables and the dependent variable. A major innovation in forecasting (made famous by Sims in 1980; in 2011, a Nobel Prize winner) was to argue that, in many circumstances, it is impossible to clearly distinguish between these two classes of variables, particularly in macroeconomic forecasting. Instead, he suggested that we model a set of output variables in terms of their own lagged values.

■ Example 10.4: A VAR model of Unleaded Gasoline Prices

An example is the retail price of *Unleaded* gasoline used in Chapter 9. Other key variables that might be best thought of as "jointly determined" are the Consumer Price Index (*CPI*) and the price of crude oil (*Crude_price*). A first-order vector autoregression model using these three variables is

$$Unleaded_t = \beta_{10} + \beta_{11} Unleaded_{t-1} + \beta_{12} Crude\_price_{t-1} + \beta_{13} CPI_{t-1} + \varepsilon_{1t}$$

$$Crude\_price_t = \beta_{20} + \beta_{21} Crude\_price_{t-1} + \beta_{22} Unleaded_{t-1} + \beta_{23} CPI_{t-1} + \varepsilon_{2t} \qquad (10.4)$$

$$CPI_t = \beta_{30} + \beta_{31} Crude\_price_{t-1} + \beta_{32} Unleaded_{t-1} + \beta_{33} CPI_{t-1} + \varepsilon_{3t}.$$

These equations are similar to the single-equation regression models considered in Chapter 9, but they contrast in that all the variables on the right-hand side are necessarily lagged: the models of Chapter 9 could have included contemporaneous variables. (Such a set of equations is called a VAR in standard form.) We include all variables in their log form as our earlier considerations of these series in Section 9.6.4 suggested using logarithmic transformations rather than the original series. Any standard statistical software, such as Minitab, SPSS or R, can be used to estimate the parameters, but when there are a large number of lags to include (with monthly data here, we could contemplate including 12 lags), it is easier to use an econometric package. We again use EViews (version 9)[4] to estimate the model specified in equation (10.4); the results are shown in Table 10.16.

The retail unleaded price (*Unleaded*) is strongly affected by past crude prices (*Crude_price*); the *CPI* is positively affected by past crude prices, partially balanced (with a perhaps counterintuitive negative sign) with the past unleaded price. Note that the models for *Crude_price* and *CPI* are close to an autoregressive model in first differences, given that the coefficients of their first-order lag terms are close to 1.0 (see Section 6.2). We might well choose to model *Crude_price* as a first difference. There is a positive connection between *Crude_price* and *CPI* whereas unleaded price increases apparently damp the next period's crude price.

Table 10.16 Simple Vector Autoregression of the Logs of Unleaded, Crude_price, and the Consumer Price Index (database: Jan1996–Dec2013)

Vector Autoregression Estimates
Date: 11/22/16   Time: 16:28
Sample (adjusted): 1996M02 2013M12
Included observations: 215 after adjustments
Standard errors in ( ) & t-statistics in [ ]

The notation name[−1] or more generally name[−Laglength] designates that the variable 'name' has been lagged by 1 (or Laglength), e.g., CPI[−1] represents lagged CPI.

	Log (Unleaded)	Log (Crude_price)	Log (CPI)
Log (Unleaded[−1])	0.662067	−0.175887	−0.014608
	(0.05916)	(0.08299)	(0.00352)
	[11.1915]	[−2.11949]	[−4.15460]
Log (Crude_price[−1])	0.18785	1.041692	0.010255
	(0.03693)	(0.05180)	(0.00219)
	[5.08730]	[20.1107]	[4.67241]
Log (CPI[−1])	0.186087	0.358979	0.996372
	(0.10469)	(0.14686)	(0.00622)
	[1.77743]	[2.44431]	[160.118]
C	−1.453805	−1.918457	−0.007826
	(0.52959)	(0.74289)	(0.03148)
	[−2.74518]	[−2.58243]	[−0.24864]
R-sq	0.981915	0.983884	0.999244
R-sq(adj)	0.981658	0.983655	0.999233
S.E. equation	0.059058	0.082845	0.00351
F-statistic	3818.665	4293.904	92948.39
Akaike AIC	−2.802163	−2.125261	−8.447849
Mean dependent	0.679415	3.778498	5.259851
S.D. dependent	0.436065	0.647999	0.126757

Data: *Gas_prices_base.xlsx;* output adapted from EViews 9.

Note that for presentation purposes, the number of significant figures in the table should be much smaller.

---

4 See online Appendix B for a discussion of alternatives and the rationale behind the use of specialist software.

In addition, the output includes summary statistics for each equation and the overall model. The diagnostics for the model residuals show (as before) large outliers at the onset of the Great Recession as well as possible autocorrelation. In developing this simple model, we arbitrarily chose a lag length of 1 as shown in equation (10.4). However, there are often longer lags in an economic system. We might therefore wish to select an "optimal" lag length. There are many criteria that help a user choose the maximum length. An analysis using EViews includes the results shown in Table 10.17, where we have shown just two of the available criteria for selecting the lag length. We also included an indicator dummy (an exogenous variable) for the last six months of 2008 to partially account for the recession.

Of the various selection criteria, those which aim to produce a simple model (i.e., The Schwartz information criterion (SC), previously denoted by BIC) have been shown to produce better forecasting performance: here the Schwarz criterion points to a maximum lag length of 3. Akaike's Information Criterion (the AIC) usually recommends a longer lag, as it does here. Where a lag is recommended that makes no sense in the context of the problem, it is better to use a shorter interpretable maximum lag. However, there is no strong economic reason that the maximum lag lengths of the endogenous variables should all be the same, so the criteria outlined in Table 10.17 may miss higher order terms for some of the variables. Some programs, such as PcGive (through its automatic model selection option), will simplify each individual equation automatically. The user can then choose to test or impose further constraints. As an investigative check, we provide details of the model for lags of order 3, the recommended order using Schwartz's criterion on the log transformed series, with the results shown in Table 10.18.

Table 10.17 VAR Lag Order Selection Criteria

VAR Lag Order Selection Criteria
Endogenous variables: LN_UNLEADED_ LN_CPI_ LN_CRUDE_PRICE
Exogenous variables: C CHANGE2008_7
Date: 01/23/17   Time: 15:32
Sample: 1996M01 2015M12 IF YEAR<2014
Included observations: 204

Lag	AIC	SC
0	−4.22332	−4.12573
1	−15.8045	−15.5605
2	−16.1113	−15.721
3	−16.3644	−15.82763*
4	−16.36714*	−15.684
5	−16.3567	−15.5272
6	−16.3338	−15.3579
7	−16.2775	−15.1552
8	−16.2542	−14.9855
9	−16.2484	−14.8333
10	−16.2313	−14.6698
11	−16.2248	−14.5169
12	−16.2431	−14.3888

*indicates lag order selected by the criterion AIC: Akaike information criterion, SC: Schwarz information criterion
Data: Gas_prices_base.xlsx; output adapted from EViews 9.

The extended model suggests that retail prices are also affected by a two-period lag in *Crude_price*, with a positive impact of 0.400, moderated the next period by a damping of −0.220. Again, the coefficients indicate that differencing may be appropriate (see Appendix 10A; further exploration is left to the reader).

Table 10.18 Third-Order VAR Model for the Log Transformed Unleaded, Crude_price, and CPI Series (with recession indicator); Data: 1996–2013

Standard errors in ( ) & t-statistics in [ ]

	Log (Unleaded)	Log (Crude_price)	Log (CPI)
Log (Unleaded[–1])	1.108937	–0.330929	–0.00254
	(0.14043)	(0.23318)	(0.00859)
	[7.89691]	[–1.41923]	[–0.29570]
Log (Unleaded[–2])	–1.002516	0.03797	–0.028127
	(0.2029)	(0.33691)	–0.01241
	[–4.94097]	[0.11270]	[–2.26629]
Log (Unleaded[–3])	0.578529	0.159279	0.016651
	(0.12994)	(0.21576)	(0.00795)
	[4.45224]	[0.73820]	[2.09489]
Log (Crude_price[–1])	0.254651	1.200611	0.011518
	(0.05184)	(0.08608)	(0.00317)
	[4.91228]	[13.9478]	[3.63246]
Log (Crude_price[–2])	–0.112327	–0.08268	–0.00509
	(0.07136)	(0.11848)	(0.00436)
	[–1.57419]	[–0.69781]	[–1.16618]
Log (Crude_price[–3])	0.011595	–0.106051	0.002577
	(0.05484)	(0.09106)	(0.00335)
	[0.21143]	[–1.16457]	[0.76805]
Log (CPI[–1])	–0.499385	1.367171	1.299647
	(2.16558)	(3.5959)	(0.13247)
	[–0.23060]	[0.38020]	[9.81118]
Log (CPI[–2])	9.834248	3.111399	–0.137285
	(3.39665)	(5.64008)	(0.20777)
	[2.89528]	[0.55166]	[–0.66076]
Log (CPI[–3])	–9.025087	–4.062099	–0.159744
	(2.11437)	(3.51088)	(0.12933)
	[–4.26844]	[–1.15700]	[–1.23513]
C	–0.553770	–1.526899	0.027499
	(0.38605)	(0.64103)	(0.02361)
	[–1.43445]	[–2.38194]	[1.16451]
Change2008_7_12	–0.106948	–0.180199	–0.006371
	(0.02105)	(0.03495)	(0.00129)
	[–5.08107]	[–5.15585]	[–4.94850]
R-sq	0.989544	0.986981	0.999532
R-sq(adj)	0.989026	0.986336	0.999509
Sum sq. resids	0.418567	1.154071	0.001566
S.E. equation	0.04552	0.075586	0.002784
F-statistic	1911.642	1531.36	43130.83
Log likelihood	361.4966	253.4827	956.6436
Akaike AIC	–3.291048	–2.276833	–8.879283
Schwarz SC	–3.11746	–2.103245	–8.705695
Mean dependent	0.684791	3.785764	5.261865
S.D. dependent	0.434535	0.646632	0.125622
Determinant resid covariance (dof adj.)	1.35E-11		
Determinant resid covariance	1.15E-11		
Log likelihood	1776.028		
Akaike information criterion	–16.36646		
Schwarz criterion	–15.8457		

Data: Gas_prices.xlsx; output adapted from EViews.

Another advantage of using a fully functional automatic econometric package is that a wide range of tests of the model's assumptions is usually included as standard output. As we argued in the last chapter, the in-sample residuals contain a lot of information as to whether our proposed model captures the characteristics of the data. Typical tests of the residuals include various tests for autocorrelation in the residuals, tests for heteroscedasticity and normality, and tests for outliers. An (edited) example taken from PcGive for the foregoing models with three lags included in the VAR is given in Appendix 10A. ■

10.5.1 Forecasting with a VAR Model

The final stage in the process is producing the forecasts. In a VAR model, the forecasts may be produced automatically, without any need to forecast the dependent variables *separately*. However, most programs also allow the user to include *exogenous variables*, and this avoids an excessive number of variables and parameters in the model.

The forecast origin has to be set. Here, it is 2013M12, leading to the 24 periods in 2014–2015 for which we can compare data with actual observations. The forecasts can either be rolling-origin, one-period-ahead conditional forecasts where the actual lagged values are used to produce the forecasts or fixed-origin forecasts where, for each lead time greater than 1, the lagged values are estimated (i.e., for two periods ahead), the forecast is based on the previous lagged values, which themselves have been estimated. (This type of forecasting is sometimes described as dynamic forecasting.)

FORECASTING USING VAR

Forecasts can be *dynamic* where the new forecast is based on the previous forecasts and actual values where these would be known at the forecast origin. A VAR does this automatically. For example, for the 3rd order lag model when we forecast three periods ahead $\hat{Y}_{t+3}$ depends on $\hat{Y}_{t+2}$, $\hat{Y}_{t+1}$, Y_t and Y_t is known. For more than three periods ahead the latest forecast is based on the previous (three forecasts). A conditional out-of-sample forecast uses the actual or assumed values of any exogenous variables. An unconditional forecast requires any exogenous variables to be forecast. Alternatively forecasts may be *static* (and conditional) where the new forecast assumes the past actuals and any exogenous *Xs* are known.

■ Example 10.5: Forecasting with a VAR model

The VAR model summarized in Table 10.18 was used to provide one-step-ahead forecasts for the 24 observations Jan2014–Dec2015. The results are shown in Table 10.19 along with comparative results for the random walk and two simple autoregressive models. The AR models were fitted using a regular regression program so that coefficients outside the stationary region were possible, to allow for growth; the indicator variables for the recession in 2008 was also included.

Looking at Table 10.19, we see a very substantial deterioration in the out-of-sample *RMSE* (compared to the in-sample standard error). The inclusion of an indicator variable to take into account the economic crisis starting in June 2008 developed (see Example 9.6 and Figure 10.13) cuts down the in-sample *RMSE*. The additional complexity of the three-period lag VAR system seems to offer a reasonably substantial in-sample improvement over the first-order model. However, the out-of-sample performance is more mixed, although the three-period model would appear to be somewhat more successful in forecasting some of the more extreme fluctuations in the 2014-15 data. The VAR models here outperform the univariate AR models. ■

Table 10.19 One-Step-Ahead Forecast Error Statistics for Unleaded for Out-of-Sample, 2014–2015: VAR Models vs. Benchmark Autoregression

	In-Sample		Out-of-Sample			
	Mean Absolute Error	Standard Error	RMSE	MAPE	MdAPE	RelMAE
Random Walk	9.90	15.32	18.23	5.45	4.03	1
AR(1)	9.95	15.23	18.26	5.48	3.88	1.01
AR(2)	9.32	13.47	14.52	4.50	3.90	0.94
First-order VAR	8.81	12.95	17.82	4.97	3.12	0.85
Third-order VAR(*)	7.72	10.67	15.44	4.64	3.55	0.92

(*) For the AR and VAR models in logs, fitted values and forecasts were transformed back before calculation of the error measures. The AR models and the Random Walk use the estimation sample 1996m4–2013m12 for consistency with the VAR samples.

Data: Gas_prices_base.xlsx

Figure 10.13 Time Series Plot of the Price of Unleaded Gasoline (Jan 2000 – Dec 2015)

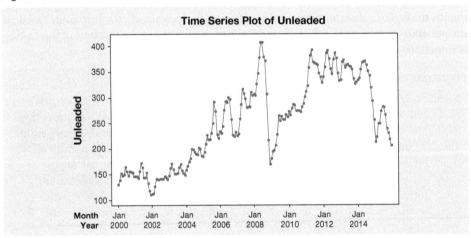

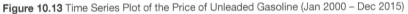

10.6 Principles: Predictive Classification, Neural Nets, and VAR Modeling

Many of the principles we have listed in earlier chapters apply to these more advanced methods, but we repeat them here to underline their importance.

Classification Methods

[10.1] Consider a variety of different classification methods, using as much data as is computationally feasible.

[10.2] Use a variety of error measures (such as the classification matrices and the *ROC* curves) to evaluate the methods.

[10.3] In developing classification models, always retain a subset of the data with which to test the effectiveness of the proposed methods.

[10.4] Always compare a proposed new method with a benchmark classification approach.

Neural Networks *(see Haykin, 2009)*

[10.5] Scale the data before estimating the neural network model.

[10.6] Use a variety of starting values (typically selected at random) to avoid local minima.

[10.7] Use techniques such ensemble forecasting to avoid overfitting.

VAR Models *(see Allen and Fildes, 2001; 2005)*

[10.8] Use a VAR model (based on lags), as opposed to a set of single equations based upon concurrent values of the explanatory variables.

[10.9] Reduce the lag length on each variable separately.

[10.10] Model the data in levels, rather than differences, initially.

[10.11] Examine all the model's variables for potential nonstationarity.
Use theoretical analysis, graphs, autocorrelations, and such tests as the augmented Dickey-Fuller test (discussed in Appendix 10C) to decide whether the variables are nonstationary. Beware: Relying on tests alone is dangerous because these tests have weak power.

[10.12] For nonstationary data, develop an Error Correction Model (ECM) and compare it with an unrestricted model and a model in differences.
As we argue in Appendixes 10D and 10E, the general VAR model can be successively constrained, first to the ECM and then to a model in differences. These constraints will generally lead to improved forecast accuracy when they are justified by the data. But it is worthwhile carrying out the straightforward comparison of the ECM model with a model in levels and a model in differences.

Summary

In this chapter, we have presented a number of new methods suitable for a wide class of forecasting problems that collectively go under the name *predictive classification*. We have also extended the range of time series methods we considered to include the relatively new approaches of neural networks and VAR models. All these methods and models are part of the required armory for a forecaster who aspires to be on top of the latest techniques. They are harder to use than the regular methods and models described in earlier chapters. But that problem arises in part because the software needed is more specialized (see online Appendix B) and in part because it is not easy for a forecaster to switch between packages. The online materials for R in *Forecasting in R: Tutorial and Examples* should help substantially. But these barriers to implementing the models in practice will still be hard to overcome, so why are the models used at all?

For classification problems, the industry-standard approach is logistic regression. Although the other methods we have described — classification trees and neural nets — have often been shown to outperform logistic regression in particular situations, the differences have not proved consistent enough to supplant the standard. One particular advantage of logistic regression compared with neural nets is that the output of the former is readily interpretable whereas neural networks act as a black box. It turns out that predictive accuracy is not the only criterion for users!

VAR models are used regularly in macroeconomic modeling but much less frequently, as far as we can tell, in industry models. Again, the software and the output are not as user friendly as they are for standard regression models. Nevertheless, the use of such software as EViews and PcGive (Oxmetrics) puts a lot of econometric power at the user's fingertips. Do these methods work better than simpler approaches? Allen and Fildes (2001) suggest that they do, but the differences are not as substantial or consistent as theory suggests.

In short, for important problems, the methods described in this chapter have the potential to improve accuracy. But success cannot be taken for granted. This tension emphasizes an important message in this book and a core forecasting principle: "Always compare your proposed model with some simple alternative."

DISCUSSION QUESTION: *Why do these advanced methods often fail to outperform simple benchmarks?*

Exercises

10.1   Using the computer owner data set (*Compdata.xlsx*) and regular regression, take a random sample of approximately 80 percent of the data. Then use the variables *Income* and *Education* to develop a linear regression model. (You should consider pooling the classes.)

a. Calculate the classification matrix on the estimation sample and compare the results, for 50 percent and 20 percent cutoffs. Does knowledge of the household's education level add anything to your ability to identify nonowners?

b. Use your preferred model to score the out-of-sample test data. Compare your results with a model that uses income only.

c. Use logistic regression to carry out the same task. Are there any substantial differences between the results of the two approaches?

10.2   Using the computer owner data set (*Compdata.xlsx*), and 80 percent of the sample, develop a classification tree. Compare the classification performance you achieve with the model given in Section 10.3. Does combining the two lowest income classes as was done in Section 10.3 still improve the model's performance?

10.3   Using a three-node neural network and the computer owner data set (*Compdata.xlsx*), compare the results obtained from using five different random starting seeds. Using the rule "classify an observation as a '1' if the average score over the five runs is above 0.8," compare the misclassification performance of this new rule with (a) the best of the five runs and (b) the average performance.

10.4   Using regression (or logistic regression) and the data set *Compdata.xlsx*, include the variable *Income* as well as the additional variables *Kids* and attitude to technology (*TAM1–TAM3*) to develop a classification model, and then compare the performance of the model at the 0.50 cutoff. What advantages do you see to adopting one cutoff approach rather than the other? Do the additional variables improve the classification performance of the models compared with the performance of the simple model that uses just *Income*?

10.5   Using the time series NN3-001 from the data set *N3.xlsx*, develop a neural network time series forecasting model. Produce forecasts for up to 18 periods ahead. Compare the out-of-sample results with benchmark models of your choosing (e.g., random walk, simple exponential smoothing). Does the choice of the best performing method depend on the error measure you have chosen or the forecast origin you have chosen?

10.6*   In the Exercise 10.5, what are the effects on the performance of the neural network, including computational times, of (a) changing the training algorithm and (b) changing its tuning parameters?

10.7   Using the data set *Gas_prices_2.xlsx* with data to Dec2013:

a. Test whether *Crude_price*, *CPI*, and *Unemployment* are stationary variables.

b. Develop a regression model for *Unleaded*, using the methods of Chapter 9.

c. Develop a three-variable VAR model that includes the price of *Unleaded*. In so doing, include only those variables you expect to have an economic impact on the unleaded price. Use a maximum of two lags.

d. Examine whether there is evidence for including lags longer than two in your model.

e. Evaluate the forecasting performance of your chosen model.

f. Develop a model in differences (for any of the nonstationary variables). Is this model a "better" model than the model developed in levels in parts (b) and (c)? Explain. Does the forecasting performance of the model improve on that of any of the earlier models?

10.8   Durkin, Ord, and Walker (2010) examined the growth of credit markets in the United States since 1946. The data file *Credit.xlsx* contains annual values for real mortgage credit (*RMC*), real consumer credit (*RCC*), and real disposable personal income (*RDPI*) for the period 1946-2006. All the observations are measured in billions of dollars, after adjustment by the Consumer Price Index (*CPI*). Develop a VAR model for these data for the period 1946-2003, and then forecast the last three years, 2004-2006. Examine the relative advantages of a logarithmic transform and the use of differences.

10.9*   Using the data set *Gas_prices_base.xlsx*, but setting aside the data for 2012 through 2015, develop an unrestricted VAR model, an ECM, and a model in stationary variables. Use appropriate error statistics to examine the residuals and test their respective forecasting performances.

a. Which of the variables *Unleaded*, *Crude_price*, and *CPI* do you regard as stationary? Justify your conclusions.

b. Do the residuals of the various models suggest any inadequacies in the model?

c. If you now consider the more recent data, from 2012 to 2015, does your chosen model show any instability in its performance?

d. If you also bring into consideration the performance of the models over the years 2014-2015, which model would you use for forecasting for the period 2016-2017? Explain your reasons.

10.10* Using the data set *Exchange_rates.xlsx*, covering data on the $US–Euro and $US–£Sterling exchange rates from June 7, 1999, to December 31, 2016,

a. Test the stationarity of each series.
   i. with the subset with data from June 7, 1999, to June 13, 2008.
   ii. with the data set to June 1, 2016.
   iii. with the data set to mid-2017.

   b. For each time series, develop an ARIMA model that produces one-step-ahead daily forecasts. Then do the same for monthly average exchange rates.

   c. Are the two series cointegrated? Consider both the full and the shorter data sets.

   d. Is there any evidence of structural breaks in the full data series?

   e. Carry out a literature review of the comparative accuracy of alternative methods of exchange rate forecasting. Do you find any evidence that any of the methods you have discovered have proved successful beyond the random-walk naïve alternative?

Minicase 10.1 KMI BioPharma, Inc.: Biocide[5]

Ed Wheeler, marketing manager for KMI BioPharma, Inc.'s (KMI's) industrial products division, was developing a marketing strategy for its first new product, a biocide for metal-working fluids. KMI was a small, but rapidly growing, biopharmaceutical firm heavily funded by venture capitalists because of its promising technologies that extracted chemical elements from exotic plants. These elements were then used to develop innovative consumer and industrial products.

Although KMI had several products in various stages of development, only one consumer product — CelluLife Body Cream — had been launched. The relatively new product had been on the market for 48 months and was considered a commercial success, becoming profitable in just the past year. CelluLife was a general-purpose skin cream which contained proprietary ingredients that promoted the healing of damaged skin cells. KMI positioned CelluLife as an all-natural product with secret healing ingredients from exotic plants. While major competitors emphasized the "skin-caring" qualities of their products, KMI focused on its powerful effectiveness.

The new biocide product was KMI's first industrial market application. Using special chemical ingredients obtained from hundreds of analyses of various kinds of plant vegetation, KMI's chemists were able to develop a product that helped solve two key problems: killing bacteria and providing a pleasant odor to a normally pungent operating environment. The new biocide product was effective in killing bacteria, fungi, and other microorganisms in metalworking fluids and promised to be useful for other applications as well.

Ed was meeting with his launch marketing team to discuss the results of a market research survey. Ed commented on the survey results: "It seems that the results and analyses may have created more problems and decisions for us than we expected." Nan Kelly, a product manager on the team, said, "These aren't really problems, but rather opportunities for us. The fact that we have four viable target market segments lets us focus our limited resources. I think we should pick one segment and go with it."

Jim Burton, the R&D manager, was quick to respond, "What's the point of picking one segment? Why don't we take the simplest approach and develop our marketing strategy to reach the entire market? We have a great product, and all of these metalworking firms are going to jump on the bandwagon once they see how effective our new product is." Art

5 We wish to acknowledge Professor Robert Thomas of Georgetown University, who developed this case and kindly consented to our reproducing it herein. Minor changes have been made to the text and to the assignment that follows to meet present needs, but the principal details and the data set *Biocide.xlsx* are entirely as originally written.

Kanjian, the controller, said, "I think you are each at the extremes. The best strategy may be to take two or three of the segments and target them accordingly."

Ed responded to the group, "Look, we need to make some decisions rather quickly. We have to make commitments soon if we want to make an April launch date. Depending on our marketing strategy, we may have to buy space in trade magazines, put together an Internet site, hire and train a sales force, or develop relationships with distributors. Furthermore, if we are really going to be successful, we have to determine how to best position this new product in the market. After all, the competition is well entrenched."

The Market

The process of working with metal generates heat and metal scraps. While the metal is ground, drilled, turned, milled, or otherwise machined, a fluid from a nozzle is directed toward the work area to cool, lubricate, and keep the metalworking surfaces clean of scraps. The metal scraps are caught in a special tray, and the fluid is filtered and returned to the work area. The fluid passes through a reservoir, or sump, the size of which depends on the application.

Several problems with such a metalworking operation are due to the bacteria and other microorganisms that grow in the warm watery mixture. First, the bacteria can breakdown the effectiveness of the basic metalworking fluid by clogging filters, flow lines, and drains. Second, the bacteria give off a foul odor that contaminates the area for workers. Third, workers often complain that, when the fluid gets on their skin, it causes dermatitis and other problems. Because of this problem, workers are reluctant to go near the reservoir to recondition the fluid as necessary. They often resort to such tactics as dumping in liquid bleach, deodorants, and other household products to reduce the smells. In many cases, this only exacerbates the problem.

To deal with these metalworking problems, the 10 major metalworking fluid formulators in the United States add a biocide to the concentrate. The concentrate is composed of emulsified oils, additives, and biocides that are mixed with 95 percent water. However, once the fluid is in place, firms rarely change it. In most cases, they add so-called maintenance biocides. Concentrate biocides accounted for about 40 percent of the market for all metalworking biocides, with maintenance biocides at 60 percent. Importantly, concentrate biocides were decreasing in sales while maintenance biocides were increasing. This trend, expected to increase over the next ten years, made the market attractive.

The market was structured such that some 300 firms with an estimated 1,500 metalworking machines used large central system reservoirs with capacities of 10,000 gallons or more. This market was well served by such firms as Rohm and Haas, with its Kathon MW product, which had a 30 percent market share. There were, however, another 140,000 firms with some 1.4 million metalworking machines. These firms were served by some 14,000 supply houses in the United States, generating, in total, about $50 billion in sales of metalworking supplies, including various fluids and biocides.

The smaller metalworking firms were not as well served in the market as the larger ones, although there were at least two major competitors that recently had developed products for stand-alone machines rather than those with large central reservoir systems.

Angus Chemical offered the so-called Tris-Nitro "Sump Saver" 2-ounce tablets. Two such tablets were required to treat a 50-gallon tank, the average size for firms with stand-alone systems. Each tablet sold for about $1.00 to distributors and $2.00 to customers. The tablets were not completely effective in eliminating bacteria, did not kill fungus, and lasted for only about a week. Nevertheless, Tris-Nitro was liked because it was easy to use. Workers had to drop the tablets into the sump only when they suspected problems. Ed Wheeler estimated that Tris-Nitro was used in about 20 percent of the market for stand-alone metalworking systems.

Dowicil 75, made by Dow Chemical, was a water-soluble package that could simply be dropped into the reservoir. Each package was about 2 pounds and sold for $10 to distributors and about $30 to customers. Dowicil 75 was quite effective for about a month against bacteria and fungi. However, it had a strong ammonia odor that occasionally released formaldehyde, which could be a safety factor with employees. Ed Wheeler estimated that, like Tris-Nitro, Dowicil 75 had about a 20 percent share of the market for stand-alone systems.

Ed saw the other 60 percent of the market as a large opportunity. Although all of the aforementioned firms adopted local solutions (such as bleach, deodorants, and disinfectants), these products were more harmful than helpful to the metalworking process — although an employee who had a hard time working with the foul odors would not agree. Ed saw the market situation as strongly motivating KMI's product development program.

The New Product

After talking with a few potential users, Ed and his team of chemists initially formulated the product into a cakelike tablet that could be dropped into the sump of metalworking machines. However, this approach proved to be problematic because tests showed that there was considerable variation in how the tablet dissolved. There were also problems in how well the tablet was dispersing the chemical in the reservoir.

The team of chemists then improved the tablet's composition and developed a system for holding the tablet just below the surface of the liquid in the sump. This adjustable and corrosion-resistant triangular frame could be hung over the edge of the sump and retrieved weekly for replacement of the dissolved cake tablets. A handgrip helped to hold the frame in place. It also facilitated the placement of a new tablet in a mesh basket at the end of the triangular arm. The tablet was sized to last about one week in a typical 50-gallon reservoir application. The cost to make each tablet averaged $1.00. The cost to make a corrosion-resistant frame was about $25.00. The frames were expected to last the lifetime of a typical reservoir.

Beta tests conducted at five sites over a three-month period revealed that the new product worked well under average operating conditions. KMI chemists visited the plant at the beginning of each week, initially to train metalworkers in the use of the new system, but later to follow up to make sure that the workers had learned how to use it most effectively.

Ed was satisfied with the product, but when he started to develop his marketing program launch decisions, he discovered that he had several unanswered questions: How should he position the new product? How should he communicate its virtues? How should he price it? Should he use distributors or go directly to customers? Most importantly, to which firms should he target his new program? To begin to answer these questions, he turned to market research.

The Market Segmentation Study

Ed retained a local market research firm to conduct a survey of the market for metalworking biocides. After hearing Ed's major questions, the research firm designed a study that included the major features or benefits of a biocide used in metalworking applications. The study also included questions about the reaction to the new KMI biocide concept, brand usage, satisfaction with the current system, media usage, the use of distributors, usage of biocides, and so on.

Data were collected via telephone contact with a random sample of customers in order to identify the survey respondent, followed by a faxed, mailed, or e-mailed questionnaire (according to the respondent's preference). A total of 130 completed surveys were obtained. Summary results for the sample (and the basic questions in the questionnaire) are presented in Exhibit 1.

Ed also asked the firm if it could segment the market. In particular, he wanted to do so on the basis of the importance of the various biocide features to respondents.

Exhibit 1 Overall Survey Findings

	N	Mean	Std. Deviation
How important are each of the following to you on a 5-point scale, with 5 = very important?			
Ease of using the biocide	130	4.48	.80
Ease of replacing the biocides	130	4.55	.68
Safety of handling the biocides	130	4.09	.92
Installation costs of the biocide system	130	3.95	1.01
Cost of replacement biocides	130	4.36	.77
Cost to maintain the system	130	4.12	.85
Biocide extends metalworking fluid life	130	3.67	1.19
Consistency of biocide dispersion in fluid reservoir	130	3.35	1.15
Stability of biocide chemicals (e.g., no formaldehyde leakage)	130	3.70	1.02
Biocide is effective over a wide pH range	130	3.72	1.19
Reducing bacteria that causes dermatitis	130	4.23	.98
Elimination of odors in machine fluid reservoir	130	4.43	.82
How effective are the following communication options to you on a 5-point scale, with 5 = very important?			
Trade shows	130	3.02	1.36
Advertising in trade media	130	3.50	1.15
Telemarketing	130	1.98	1.04
Direct mail brochures	130	3.38	1.04
Internet	130	2.94	1.41
Visit by Distributor's sales force	130	3.89	1.09
Manufacturer's sales force	130	3.75	1.14
What is your degree of satisfaction, interest, intention to buy (higher number = greater degree)?			
Satisfaction with current biocide system (scale from 1 to 5)	130	3.06	.99
Interest in changing biocide systems (scale from 1 to 5)	130	3.06	1.19
Intention to buy the new concept as pictured and described (scale from 1 to 4)	130	2.62	.90
Overall, what is your rating of the following brands of biocide?			
Dow Chemical	130	3.22	1.25
Angus Chemical	130	3.04	1.07
Biocide usage			
Average packet equivalents used	130	183.5	149.9
Use Dowicil 75 (number used and % of 130)	28	22%	
Use Tris-Nitro "Sump Saver" (number used and % of 130)	26	20%	
Use other (number used and % of 130)	76	58%	

Assignment

1. Management feels that the following features are most important to potential customers: cost, ease of replacing biocides, ease of use, and reduction in the number of bacteria. Management also feels that any potential customer recording 1 or 2 on the satisfaction scale is a likely purchaser. Define a binary variable to describe potential purchasers (*Potpurch*), and run a binary logistic regression to determine which factors should be emphasized in marketing the product.

2. To develop a market segmentation, select the appropriate variables for analysis. Generate a classification tree (as in Figure 10.4), using *Potpurch* as the dependent variable to determine an appropriate set of segments (clusters of terminal nodes). How many clusters are appropriate?

3. Use the selected clusters as the basis for analyzing the survey results to determine whether there are any advantages to taking a segmentation approach to the market. To do this, first create dummy variables to indicate cluster membership. (Remember, you need one fewer dummies than clusters.) Then, continuing to use *Potpurch* as the dependent variable, carry out logistic regression analysis on the dummy variables to determine whether the segmentation is effective for marketing purposes.

4. Complete a report to the management that summarizes your findings. In particular, you should address the following questions:

   - Should the market be segmented or treated as a whole?

   - If segmented, which segments should be targeted?

   - What additional analyses are needed with these data, and should another market research study be conducted before launching the product? If so, what information requirements are necessary in the next study?

References

*These papers are theoretical in nature and are listed for completeness and for those readers seeking an understanding of advanced topics.

Allen, P. G. and Fildes, R. (2001). Econometric forecasting, in J. S. Armstrong (ed.), *Principles of Forecasting: A Handbook for Researchers and Practitioners*. Boston and Dordrecht: Kluwer, pp. 303–362.

Allen, P. G. and Fildes, R. (2005). Levels, differences and ECMs: Principles for improved econometric forecasting. *Oxford Bulletin of Economics and Statistics*, 67, 881–904.

*Barrow, D. K., and Crone, S. F. (2016). A comparison of AdaBoost algorithms for time series forecast combination. *International Journal of Forecasting*, 32, 1103–1119.

Barrow, D. and Kourentzes, N. (2016). The impact of special days in call arrivals forecasting: a neural network approach to modelling special days. *European Journal of Operational Research*.

*Breiman, L., Friedman, J., Olshen, R., and Stone, C. (1984). *Classification and Regression Trees*. Boca Raton, FL: Chapman and Hall (CRC).

Crone, S. F., and Kourentzes, N. (2010). Feature selection for time series prediction: A combined filter and wrapper approach for neural networks. *Neurocomputing*, 73 (10-12), 1923–1936.

Crone, S. F., Hibon, M., and Nikolopoulos, K. (2011). Advances in forecasting with neural networks? Empirical evidence from the NN3 competition on time series prediction. *International Journal of Forecasting*, 27, 635–660.

Crone, S. F., and Finlay, S. (2012). Instance sampling in credit scoring: An empirical study of sample size and balancing. *International Journal of Forecasting*, 28, 224–238.

Doornik, J. A., and Hendry, D. F. (2009) *Modelling Dynamic Systems: PcGive™ 13, Vols. I and II*, London, Timberlake Consultants.

Durkin, T. A., Ord, J. K., and Walker, D. A. (2010). Long-run credit growth in the U.S. *Journal of Economics and Business*, 62, 383–400.

Elder, J., and Kennedy, P. E. (2001). Testing for unit roots: What should students be taught? *Journal of Economic Education*, 32, 137–146.

*Enders, W. (2010). *Applied Econometric Time Series*, 3rd ed. Hoboken, NJ: Wiley, 2010.

*Engle, R. E & Granger, C. W. J. (1987). Cointegration and error correction: Representation, estimation, and testing. *Econometrica*, 55 (2), 251–276.

Gonzalez-Rivera, G. (2013) *Forecasting for Economics and Business*. Boston, Pearson.

Fuller, W. A. (1996). *Introduction to Statistical Time Series*, 2nd ed. New York: Wiley.

Granger, C. W. J., and Newbold, P. (1974). Spurious regressions in econometrics. *J. Econometrics*, 2, 111–120.

Haykin, S. (2009). *Neural Networks and Learning Machines*. Vol. 3. Upper Saddle River, NJ, USA: Pearson.

*Harvey, D. I., Leybourne, S. J., and Taylor, A. M. R. (2009). Unit root testing in practice: Dealing with uncertainty over the trend and initial condition. *Econometric Theory*, 25, 587–636.

Hendry, D. F., and Mizon, G. E. (1978). Serial correlation as a convenient simplification, not a nuisance: A comment on a study of the demand for money by the Bank of England. *Economic Journal*, 88, 549–563.

Hosmer, D. W. and Lemeshow, S. (2013). *Applied Logistic Regression*. New York: Wiley

*Johansen, S. (1988). Statistical analysis of cointegration vectors. *Journal of Economic Dynamics & Control*, 12 (2-3), 231–254.

Kourentzes, N., Barrow, D. K., and Crone, S.F. (2014). Neural network ensemble operators for time series forecasting. *Expert Systems with Applications*, 41(9), 4235–4244.

Kutner, M., Nachtsheim, C., Neter, J. and Li, W. (2005). *Applied Linear Statistical Models*, 5th ed. New York: McGraw-Hill.

Murray, M. P. (1994). A drunk and her dog: An illustration of cointegration and error-correction. *American Statistician*, 48 (1), 37–39.

*Sims, C.A. (1980). Macroeconomics and reality. *Econometrica*, 48, 1–48.

Timmermann, A., and Granger, C. W. J. (2004). Efficient market hypothesis and forecasting. *International Journal of Forecasting*, 20, 15–27.

Appendix 10A PcGive Analysis of Unleaded Gasoline Price Data

We again consider the VAR model developed earlier with EViews using logs of *Unleaded*, *Crude_Price* and the *CPI* and third order lags. We also include the Great Recession indicator variable. The model is estimated on data from Jan1996–Dec2013 leaving 2014–15 for the analysis of forecast performance. A key issue in deciding whether a model is adequate is that it should capture the principal features of the data (be data congruent, as it is called) with no patterns remaining in the residuals.

In examining the residuals from the 3-lag model for the oil prices data, the residual graphs show that no residuals exceed 3.5 standard errors; therefore, outliers are unlikely to be a major problem in this model. Recall that outliers have their greatest effect on prediction intervals.

The tests that follow are automatically carried out in most econometric packages. In this appendix, we use OxMetrics™ 7.0, and in particular, PcGive 14, an advanced econometrics package, to evaluate alternative model specifications. A discussion of these tests, together with details of how the significance levels are calculated, is given in Doornik and Hendry (2009). Interpretation of the various tests is subjective: With so many tests being carried out on a system of equations such as that for the oil price model for unleaded gasoline, almost certainly some of the tests will suggest a potential problem with one or more of the model's assumptions. The aim for the forecaster is to establish whether the collective evidence points to a major misspecification and a possible improved model.

Analysis Based Upon the Estimation Sample: Jan1996–Dec2013

Individual model analysis:

Here, we include just the statistics relating to ln(*Unleaded*). Similar summary statistics are provided for all equations. There are 213 observations available up to Dec2013 with 24 observations for the years 2014-15 set aside for forecasting analysis. In all cases below, the number in square brackets represents the *P*-value for the test. We have

> ln(*Unleaded*): Portmanteau(12): x^2 (9) = 34. 665 [0.0001]**

> (This is the Ljung-Box-Pierce statistic; it tests for autocorrelation over the first 12 lags against χ^2 critical values. See Section 6.5. Results suggest autocorrelation.)

> ln(*Unleaded*): F(12,190) = 2.9430 [0.0009]** (suggesting autocorrelation)

> ln(*Unleaded*): ARCH 1-1 test: F(1,211) = 0.40337 [0.5260] (suggesting no autoregressive conditional heteroscedadasticity)

> ln(*Unleaded*): Normality test: χ^2(2) = 1.6806 [0.4316] (suggesting error distribution does not differ substantially from normality)

> ln(*Unleaded*): White's heteroscedasticity test: F(19,193) = 2.0344 [0.0085]** (suggesting some remaining heteroscedasticity despite the transform)

> ln(*Unleaded*): Hetero-X test: F(55,157) = 1.3557 [0.0753] (suggesting some remaining heteroscedasticity despite the transform)

Overall, the model seems to suffer from some residual autocorrelation.

Autocorrelation test for all equations (the residuals should not be autocorrelated):

Vector portmanteau statistic (testing all equations simultaneously with null hypothesis that there is no autocorrelation) for 12 lags and 213 observations: x^2 (108) = 179.86 [0.0000]**. This is the vector equivalent of the Ljung-Box-Pierce statistic.

> Testing for vector error autocorrelation from lags 1 to 12:

> F-form F(108,492) = 1.8113 [0.0000]**

These two tests together show evidence of residual autocorrelation.

Vector normality test for residuals:

Vector normality test: χ^2(6) = 6.5695 [0.3625] (suggesting approximately normal error distributions)

Testing for vector heteroscedasticity by using squares of the residuals:

F(114,1089) = 1.3217 [0.0171]*

Testing for vector heteroscedasticity by using squares and cross products:

F(330,916) = 1.3987 [0.0001]** (suggesting strong evidence of heteroscedasticity)

Finally, the RESET tests for functional misspecification of the model:

F-form F(9,479) = 3.1351 [0.0011]** (suggesting evidence of misspecification despite our attempt using both the log form and the Recession indicator).

Overall, this battery of tests suggests we have not identified a model that adequately characterizes the data. The final tests evaluate the model's forecasting ability and the proposed model's stability, using the out-of-sample data we set aside — here, 24 periods. A key requirement in building a successful econometric forecasting model is that the parameters remain constant. These tests use a hold-out sample to check whether this is true at least over the hold-out.

One-Step (*ex post*) Forecast Analysis
(Hold-out Sample: 2014m1-2015m12)

Three tests can be carried out, all of which examine the one-step-ahead forecast errors from the three equations. The forecaster needs to specify the data to be used — here, observations from 2014 and 2015. These errors should, of course, be compatible with the assumptions of constant parameters both within and across the hold-out sample.

Parameter constancy forecast tests (see Section 9.9):

1-step (*ex post*) forecast analysis periods 217 – 240

Parameter constancy forecast tests

using Omega 139.83 [0.0000]** F(72,202) = 1.9421 [0.0002]**

using V[e] Chi^2(72) = 125.06 [0.0001]** F(72,202) = 1.7370 [0.0014]**

using V[E] Chi^2(72) = 107.56 [0.0042]** F(72,202) = 1.4938 [0.0156]*.

These results all suggest some structural change affecting the model. We would therefore search hard to find other variables that could offer a more robust explanation of movements in the price of unleaded gasoline. Additional variables (part of the data set) include production, imports and stocks. Future expectations of world trade could also offer a fuller explanation of movements in the price of crude oil.

Parameter constancy forecast tests (including the Chow test) are conducted by PcGive when you reserve some of the observations (specifying an input in *less forecast* when you specify the range of the model, so, in the preceding example, *less forecast* = 24).

Figure 10A.1 One-Step-Ahead Forecasts of ln(*Unleaded*)

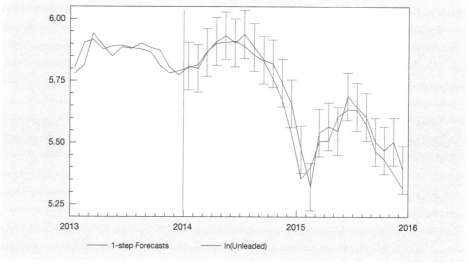

In addition, PcGive conducts another parameter instability test, testing whether the model parameters change jointly or individually on the basis of the full sample (so you don't have to reserve any observations for post-sample analysis).

Forecasting

We now use the model to produce forecasts. In estimating the model, we have set aside the last two years' data. The forecasts from the VAR model can be compared with the forecasts produced by the single-equation models we estimated in Section 9.5.1 and corresponding forecasts in Table 9.8 (though for different out-of-sample periods). A single equation ADL model if it had excluded concurrent variables would in fact produce the same forecasts. In producing forecasts from the VAR with exogenous variables or ADL models (through PcGive or EViews) there are two choices, *ex ante* and *ex post*. *Ex post* uses actual values of explanatory variables even if these would be unknown at the time the forecast is being made. *Ex ante*, more realistically, uses actual values of lagged explanatory variables when these would be known and forecasted values otherwise (see Section 8.6.3). Usually *ex post* forecasts are more accurate than *ex ante*.

By way of illustration, we fitted a model (in logarithms) for *Unleaded* using its own lags 1 and 2; lag 1 and lag 2 for *Crude_price* and current for *CPI* with lags 1 and 2 also and the recession indicator. As expected, the contemporaneous model gives much more accurate results.

The VAR model automatically produces longer lead time forecasts for the hold-out period successively substituting the latest forecast values for each variable. PcGive delivers both the *h*-step-ahead forecast based on a rolling origin and "dynamic" fixed-origin forecasts in which the unknown lagged values of the endogenous variables are replaced iteratively by the previously calculated forecasts up to the chosen lead time. The model is not re-estimated. For example, for $h = 3$-step-ahead forecasts, a model using two lags would first calculate, $\hat{Y}_{t+1}$ then $\hat{Y}_{t+2}$ using the forecast of $\hat{Y}_{t+1}$, and finally the forecast of $\hat{Y}_{t+3}$ using the previous two forecasts. If the model was based on three lags, the actual value of Y_t would be used together with the two forecast values $\hat{Y}_{t+1}$ and $\hat{Y}_{t+2}$. (In a so-called rolling regression, discussed in Section 9.8, the parameters are re-estimated each period, a useful technique to adopt when the system parameters are changing.) In Table 10A.1 the dynamic forecasts are sequentially calculated by moving the origin of the 1-12 step-ahead forecasts one period at a time until the 12 step-ahead forecast coincides with the last observation in the hold-out sample (13 1 through 12 step-ahead forecasts in all). The average forecast error is calculated for each of these sets of dynamic forecasts and the overall average across the 12 forecast origins reported in the table. The forecasts are substantially worse than the random walk, reflecting an inability to forecast *Crude_price*. Further discussion of the various forecast error statistics available through PcGive and their calculation are available on *http://www.doornik.com/pcgive/*.

Table 10A.1 Forecast Comparisons: VAR vs. Single-Equation Approaches Used in Forecasting the Price of Unleaded Gasoline (*Forecasts for 2014 and 2015*)

Model\measure	Average Across 24 One-Step-Ahead Forecasts (2014–2015)			Average 1- to-12-Step-Ahead Forecasts (2014–2015): 13 origins		
	MAPE	MdAPE	RelMAE	MAPE	MdAPE	RelMAE
Random Walk	5.453	4.034	1	23.8	26.7	1
AR(2) (with recession indicator)*	4.459	3.580	0.81	16.9	16.1	0.72
Unrestricted ex post ADL model including contemporaneous CPI	2.943	2.181	0.55	Not calculated as these require forecasting models for *CPI* and *Crude_price* for multi-step-ahead forecasts.		
VAR (3rd order)	4.147	2.552	0.77	35.7	40.0	1.50

Data: Gas_prices_2.xlsx

Note: The ARIMA(1,1,0) model is apparently the more appropriate specification though the forecasting comparison shows the AR(2) model performs better.

The estimation sample covers the period 1996m4 – 2013m12 in all cases.

Appendix 10B The Effects of Nonstationary Data

In Section 9.5.1, we noted that modeling the data in differences sometimes has the effect of removing autocorrelation and limiting multicollinearity. However, we need to be certain that the proposed model, whether in level form or in differences, makes sense. Let us suppose we include *CPI* as part of our model of unleaded prices. A graph of the two variables (after a log transform) is shown in Figure 10B.1, with the variables standardized (i.e., the mean of the series is removed and then divided by the standard deviation of the series: as $Z = (Obs - Mean)/Stddev$, introduced in Section 2.4.4).

Figure 10B.1 Time Series Plot of Unleaded Price, Price Change, and *CPI* (*Log Transformed and Standardized*)

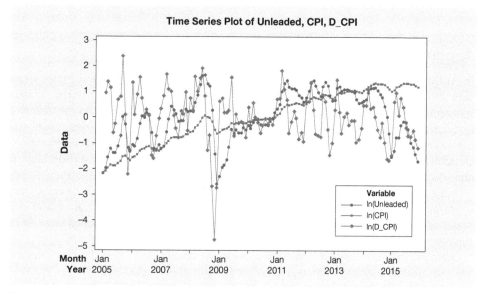

Data: Gas_prices_base.xlsx; Standardization over the period 2005-2015.

We see that, for the period from 2005, *CPI* shows steady growth (apart from the wild fluctuations of end-2008 due to the emerging recession), whereas the unleaded price fluctuates around a constant mean. With such different characteristics, there can be no sensible relationship between the *Unleaded* price and *CPI*. The *Unleaded* price is apparently a stationary variable fluctuating around a constant mean (see Chapter 5), whereas *CPI* is nonstationary. Although a regression of one on the other might lead to an apparent relationship, it could never be used successfully in forecasting. Essentially, a model of a stationary variable has to be explained by stationary variables, while a model of a nonstationary variable requires some nonstationary explanatory variables.

Historically, one suggestion for overcoming the problem of nonstationary variables has been automatic differencing. Granger and Newbold (1974) showed how easy it was to decide that two randomly chosen non-stationary variables were related. This spurious relationship is revealed by examining the residuals, which will be found to be autocorrelated. Modeling in differences was (and remains) one possible response. Here, the model explains changes in Y, rather than the actual levels of Y_t.

Note that if the theoretical model is

$$Y_t = \alpha_0 + \alpha_1 t + \alpha_2 X_t + \nu_t \tag{10B.1}$$

then

$$DY_t = \alpha_1 + \alpha_2 DX_t + \varepsilon_t. \tag{10B.2}$$

Thus, a model in differences has implications for a model in levels and vice versa.

Figure 10B.1 also shows the inflation rate (measured here by the first differences in ln(CPI)). In principle, the inflation rate, a stationary variable, could explain unleaded prices. It also makes economic sense in that the price of *Unleaded* will be determined by the price of the raw material (*Crude_price*) together with more general costs in the economy as well as various demand indicators, of which housing starts and employment are a possible measure. However, a non-stationary trending variable cannot be explained only by stationary variables and vice versa. We therefore need to establish when a variable is stationary.

Appendix 10C Differencing and Unit Roots

In ARIMA model building (see Chapter 6), it proved necessary to render the time series data stationary, usually by differencing, before the model building proper starts. Because economic data such as prices or income typically trend together, this leads to the taking of first differences, usually rendering the data stationary. As a response to the relative forecasting success of ARIMA modeling, and as a response to the pervasive autocorrelation experienced in many economic models proposed in the 1970s, economic models were developed, almost automatically, in differenced data.

But automatically differencing the data was an ad hoc procedure, and if the error term v_t in equation (10B.1) was independent, then ε_t in equation (10B.2) could not be, and vice versa, so the procedure itself might induce autocorrelation. What was needed were more rigorous procedures.

We now proceed to explain a method by which a variable can be tested for stationarity. We first consider the simple autoregressive model with a one-period lag:

$$Y_t = \gamma Y_{t-1} + \varepsilon_t \tag{10C.1}$$

Suppose for the moment that $\gamma > 0$. Then, as we discussed in Chapter 6, if the model is to make any sense, then $\gamma < 1$. Otherwise the model is explosive (i.e., $EY_{t+n} = \gamma^n EY_t$ which will increase exponentially). Two distinct alternatives now occur: $\gamma < 1$, in which case the observations tend toward zero, rapidly if γ is small and Y_t is stationary; and $\gamma = 1$ when there is no tendency to zero and the series appears to move up and down aimlessly (see Figure 6.12). This gives the equation $DY_t \equiv Y_t - Y_{t-1} = \varepsilon_t$. Y_t is then said to possess a unit root and is not stationary, whereas DY_t is. We can write equation 10A.3 as

$$DY_t = (\gamma - 1)Y_{t-1} + \varepsilon_t \tag{10C.2}$$

and a test of $\gamma - 1 = 0$, or whether Y_t possesses a unit root, was proposed by Dickey and Fuller; see Gonzalex-Rivera (2013) for more detail. The test statistic is $(\gamma - 1)/(Std.\ error\ \hat{\gamma})$ but it does not have the usual t-distribution: Special tables are available to perform the test. A key characteristic is that rejection of the null hypothesis implies that Y_t is stationary. As a consequence, failure to reject the null hypothesis tells us that the series *might* have a unit root. This in turn leads to other possibilities, involving the following equations:

Added constant: $Y_t = \alpha + \gamma Y_{t-1} + \varepsilon_t$ (10C.3)

Added constant and linear trend: $Y_t = \alpha + \beta t + \gamma Y_{t-1} + \varepsilon_t$ (10C.4)

In each equation, the test statistic looks like a t statistic based upon $(\gamma - 1)$, but it has a different non-standard distribution. Specialist software such as EViews, PcGive and R perform such tests.

Table 10C.1 The Results from an Augmented Dickey-Fuller (ADF) Test for the Stationarity of ln(Unleaded): Data: Jan1996–Dec2013

Null Hypothesis: LNUNLEADED has a unit root
Exogenous: Constant, Linear Trend
Lag Length: 1 (Automatic - based on SIC, maxlag= 14)

		t-Statistic	Prob.*
Augmented Dickey-Fuller test statistic		–3.642091	0.0286
Test critical values:	1% level	–4.001722	
	5% level	–3.431062	
	10% level	–3.139173	

*One-sided P-values (MacKinnon, 1996). *Data: Gas_prices_base.xlsx*

Why should we have to consider all three versions? The reason is that the tests are not particularly powerful (i.e., we all too often accept the null hypothesis of nonstationarity when the alternative is true). We will therefore all too rarely reject the null hypothesis of a unit root to correctly detect a stationary series.

These tests are all typically included in more advanced econometric software. For example, to test whether ln(*Unleaded*) is nonstationary (see Table 10C.1), we can use PcGive or EViews 9. The actual equations that are estimated are augmented by the addition of a user-specified number of lags. (The test is called the augmented Dickey-Fuller test.) We first need to specify which of the three tests we wish to examine.

As we see, with both a constant and a trend term included, the unit root test rejects the null hypothesis of a unit root. Testing the other two options — no constant and just a constant without any trend — suggest that the series is nonstationary. A problem arises, therefore, when, as here, the tests are contradictory. One strategy is to follow Elder and Kennedy (2001), who recommend (as we do) thinking about your data — first plotting it, but also using your knowledge of what makes the time series behave as it does. From theory and a plot of the data, three cases are possible:

a. Y_t is growing (or shrinking) in the long run. Then

  – Estimate equation (10C.4) with the trend term, and test for unit roots. Either there is a unit root $\gamma = 1$, but no time trend, but with a nonzero to create the observed growth; or there is no unit root, but there is a time trend, $\beta \neq 0$. We can use a t-test of $\gamma = 1$ to distinguish between these two alternatives.

b. Y_t is not growing (or shrinking) in the long run. Then

  – Estimate equation (10C.3), omitting the trend term. Either there is a unit root, but $\alpha = 0$; or there is no unit root and α is nonzero. Again, conduct a t-test for $\gamma = 1$ to distinguish between these two alternatives.

c. We are unclear as to Y_t's growth pattern.

  – This is a more complicated story, and if the forecaster faces such a problem, we recommend checking Elder and Kennedy (2001).

One effective and quite simple alternative implementation is due to Harvey, Leybourne, and Taylor (2009), who propose using equation (10C.2) and conducting the test (i) on the series for which the mean has been removed (i.e., where the average $\bar{Y}$ is subtracted from each observation) and (ii) on the series for which the mean and the trend have been removed (i.e., where the OLS estimates of $Y_t - (\alpha + \beta t)$ are used in the ADF test). The original series is accepted as stationary if either of these tests rejects the null hypothesis (see Exercise 10.10).

Now, how does unit root testing affect how we build econometric models? Consider the model in which both Y and X are nonstationary:

$$Y_t = \beta_0 + \beta_1 X_t + \beta_2 X_{t-1} + \gamma Y_{t-1} + \varepsilon_t. \qquad (10C.5)$$

Modeled in differences, the equation is

$$DY_t = \alpha_0 + \alpha_1 DX_t + v_t. \qquad (10C.6)$$

Note also that equation (10C.6) is a constrained dynamic regression with $\gamma = 1$ and $\alpha_2 = -\beta_2 = \beta_1$. These constraints can and should be tested for, rather than just assumed (see Hendry and Mizon, 1978).

> Do not automatically model in first differences.

Allen and Fildes (2001) give some insight into how best to carry out the tests of the constraints. The key issue is whether all this matters very much for forecasting. Here, unfortunately, the jury is still out, but we summarize the recommendations from the literature as follows:

TESTING FOR STATIONARITY AND FORECASTING

Test dependent and explanatory variables for stationarity:

- If variables are stationary, model in levels.
- Include sufficient lags to remove autocorrelation.
- If any of the variables are nonstationary, model those variables in differences, removing residual autocorrelation by including lags.
- Compare the forecasting accuracy of the model in differences with the model in levels whilst requiring interpretability of the model finally selected.

We take these recommendations further, modifying them somewhat in Appendixes 10D and 10E.

Appendix 10D Introduction to Cointegration

Consider a possible (linear) relationship between two variables X and Y: $Y = \alpha + \beta X + \varepsilon$. If X is stationary and Y is nonstationary, then ε cannot be stationary. Similarly, if X is nonstationary and Y is stationary, then ε cannot be stationary. Essentially, the equation does not "balance". Of course, if X and Y are both stationary, then ε will be stationary and the normal regression methodology can be implemented. However, there is an important fourth case: where both X and Y are nonstationary. There are then two possibilities: (i) the error is nonstationary; this is the case of spurious regressions discussed in Appendix 10B; (ii) the error is stationary (a situation that arises fairly frequently in economics). In this case, we describe the variables as *cointegrated*.

COINTEGRATION

Two nonstationary I(1) variables X and Y are said to be cointegrated if $\{Y - (\alpha + \beta X)\}$ is stationary.

N.B. An I(1) variable is stationary in its first difference (see Section 6.3.2).

Using a comparison of a drunk walking with her dog, Murray (1994) offered an intuitive explanation: Like the drunk and the dog, the variables meander about (the short-term effect), but the dog never strays too far from its mistress (the long-term effect).

Using the gas prices example, let us examine the relationship between crude oil price (*Crude_price*) and *Unleaded*. Figure 10D.1 shows a graph of the two variables, with each observation standardized (around a mean of 2).

An important point to note is that we would expect there to be a relationship between the two: Unleaded prices depend on the price the distributor must pay for the crude oil. Sure enough, a regression of the standardized variables, *Unleaded* against *Crude_price*, delivers a slope estimate of 0.98, which, based on a conventional t-test, is highly significant. (Note that such a test would most often be invalidated because the error term does not conform to the regression assumptions.) Taking logs and applying the ADF tests of Appendix 10C shows the residuals to be stationary. The two variables can therefore be considered to be cointegrated.

Figure 10D.1 An Example of Cointegrated Series: Unleaded Prices and Crude Oil Prices

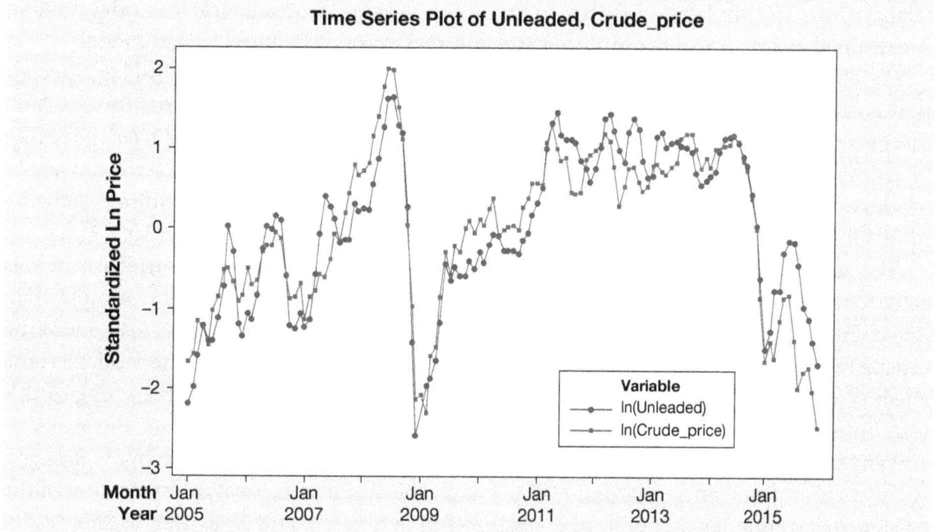

Data: Gas_prices_base.xlsx

In the previous discussions of how we might develop a model for *Unleaded*, we didn't concern ourselves directly with the stationarity or otherwise of the variables we included. However, in the discussions, we noted that a number of the first-order lagged coefficients were close to 1 (see Table 10.13) and that we should therefore consider a constrained model with some variables included in first differences. This can be best be seen by starting with the equation

$$Y_t = \alpha^* + \lambda^* Y_{t-1} + \beta_1^* X_t + \beta_2^* X_{t-1} + \varepsilon_t,$$

or, in first differences,

$$DY_t = \alpha^* - (1 - \lambda^*)Y_{t-1} + \beta_1^* DX_t - (\beta_1^* - \beta_2^*) X_{t-1} + \varepsilon_t, \qquad (10D.1)$$

We can see that the first-difference model is just a constrained form of the general model with $\lambda^* = 1$ and $\beta_1^* = \beta_2^*$.

Engle and Granger (1987) showed that when there is a cointegrating relationship between Y and X, their relationship can be expressed as

$$DY_t = \alpha + \lambda \varepsilon_{t-1} + \phi DX_t + v_t, \qquad (10D.2)$$

where

$$\varepsilon_{t-1} = Y_{t-1} - (\beta_0 + \beta_1 X_{t-1}).$$

The equilibrium value of Y (for an unchanged X with $DX_t = 0$) is $\beta_0 + \beta_1 X$. Essentially, ε_{t-1} represents the disequilibrium in the previous period between Y and its expected value. The parameter λ in (10D.2) must be negative and $\lambda^* \leq 1$, because otherwise Y_t would automatically increase above Y_{t-1} when Y_{t-1} was above its expected value (i.e., Y_t could not be stationary). It is worth noting that equation (10D.1) has four parameters whereas equation (10D.2) has only three. That is, *cointegration implies parameter constraints*. In the simplest approach, due to Engle and Granger (1987), the constrained cointegrated model is estimated by first regressing Y on X (in a separate equation) and obtaining estimates of ε_{t-1} that are used to replace Y_{t-1} and X_{t-1} in equation (10D.1) to give (10D.2).

In a vector system, X can be defined similarly to the way it is defined in equation (10D.1), which leads to equations similar to equation (10D.2) for DX and with the same long-term relationship. The implication is that in the vector system the cointegrated model leads to constrained estimators of the more general autoregressive distributed lagged model.

Equation (10D.1) usually is extended to include more than a single-period lag. Specialized computer programs are available to estimate such *Error Correction Models* (ECMs). The two programs we have considered here, PcGive and EViews 9, offer the user the ability to estimate such models as equation (10D.2) and use the resulting parameter estimates to produce forecasts. Because the equations include just lagged values, they require exactly the same inputs as do the unconstrained VAR models we considered in Section 10.5.

The same ideas apply when there are more than two nonstationary variables. In this case, Johansen (1988) developed a test that can be applied to cover the case of more than one cointegrating relationship. First, the number of cointegrating vectors is tested for. The crucial thing to remember is that including cointegrating relationships in the model has the effect of constraining its parameters. (A detailed examination is beyond the scope of this text, but see Enders (2010) for a fuller discussion.)

Why might cointegration matter in forecasting? First, the interpretation of an equation is always important, and equations (10D.1) and (10D.2) offer the neat interpretation of the existence of a long-term equilibrium relationship between Y and X, as well as short-term movements in the series. A model that is expressed just in differences cannot capture the long-term development of a series.

DISCUSSION QUESTION: *Wouldn't it be much easier and just as effective if we simply estimated the unconstrained ADL model?*

In developing an econometric forecasting model, imposing constraints justified by the data leads to a model with fewer parameters that are therefore estimated more efficiently (with tighter bounds on their standard errors). In turn, this model leads to tighter prediction intervals. So, yes, imposing justifiable constraints will theoretically lead to better forecasts. But there is always the doubt that, despite the statistical testing, the constraints aren't justified. Much of the empirical evidence (summarized by Allen and Fildes, 2005) is not strong. But overall, it seems that imposing valid constraints generally leads to improved forecasts.

Appendix 10E Modeling with Nonstationary Data: A Summary

When the variable to be forecast is nonstationary, the forecaster would benefit from having a clear path to determining the appropriate specification for the model. Current econometric textbooks are of relatively little help and often contradictory in their recommendations, as Allen and Fildes (2005) have explained. With a view to deciding among the alternative approaches, Figure 10E.1 illustrates a number of different strategies that have been recommended in various texts.

After summarizing the evidence and comparing the different strategies labeled in the diagram, Allen and Fildes argue for a strategy that first tests for stationarity and then attempts to identify cointegrating restrictions. However, for many forecasters a more empirical approach which compares an unstrestricted model (1a) with models developed after unit root tests (4), strategies (4a and 4b) should prove effective.

Figure 10E.1 Model Selection Strategies for Nonstationary Variables

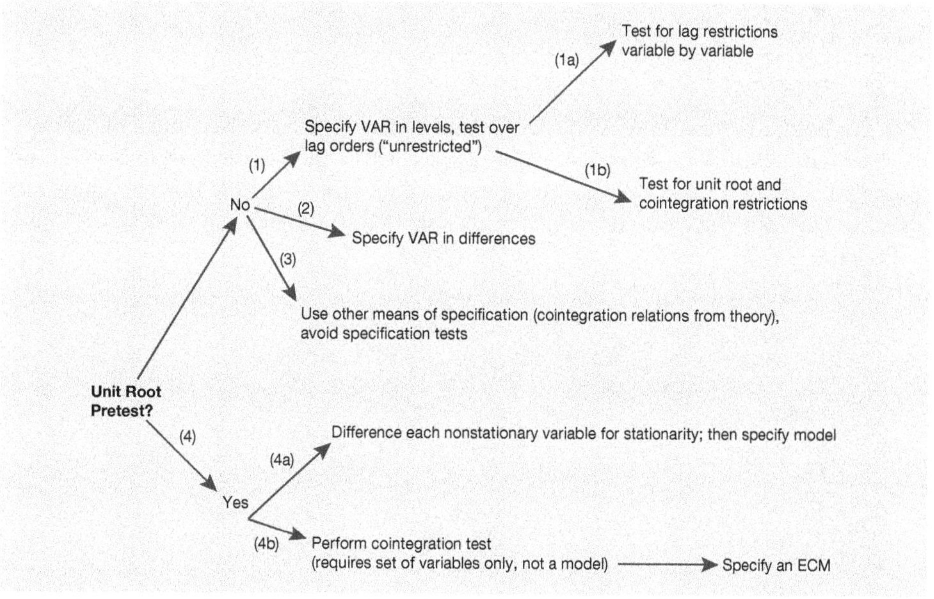

Source: From Allen and Fildes, 2005.

Here, we compare the results from the following models:

(i) An unrestricted model of *Unleaded* (with *CPI* and *Crude_price* the explanatory variables), taking logarithms of all variables. Forecasts of the *CPI* and *Crude_price* were obtained through an ARIMA model.

(ii) An unrestricted VAR model.

(iii) A VAR model with variables transformed to stationarity. *CPI* is clearly nonstationary and the Dickey-Fuller test for *Crude_price* is ambiguous. We treat both as nonstationary.

(iv) A vector ECM model with *Unleaded* and *Crude_price* cointegrated

Table 10E.1 presents only very limited results: the 1-step-ahead forecasts and 1-12-step-ahead forecasts for the years 2014–2015 with the models reestimated with a rolling origin. For the 1-12-step-ahead forecast, all the models perform worse than the benchmark random walk (and also the AR2 model results in Table 10A.1).

Table 10E.1 Forecasting Comparisons of Unleaded Prices for the ECM Model

Estimation data: 1996M01 to 2013M12; Forecast Period: 2014–2015

Model	Average Across 24 One-Step-Ahead Forecasts (2014–2015)			Average 1-12-Step-Ahead Forecasts (2014–2015): 13 origins		
	MAPE	MdAPE	RelMAE	MAPE	MdAPE	RelMAE
Unrestricted ex post ADL model including contemporaneous *CPI*	2.94	2.18	0.55	Not calculated as these require forecasting models for *CPI* and *Crude_price* for multi-step-ahead forecasts.		
Unrestricted VAR model	4.15	2.55	0.77	35.7	40.0	1.50
VAR model in stationary variables	4.20	2.70	0.78	28.7	29.3	1.20
VAR model in differences (automatic selection of lags)	4.27	2.81	0.80	28.5	30.3	1.19
VECM model	3.76	2.03	0.71	27.1	28.4	1.13

Data: Gas_prices_base.xlsx

In this particular case the VECM model outperforms the alternative (and simpler) VAR specifications. This finding has proved more generally true though the margin is small, and certainly the other models are easier to operationalize. However, note that for longer lead times we have once again been unsuccessful compared to the random walk, as measured by *RelMAE*.

CHAPTER 11

Judgment-Based Forecasting

Table of Contents

They couldn't hit an elephant at this dist. . . .

— Last words of General John B. Sedgwick at the Battle of Spotsylvania, 1864.

Introduction

In our introduction to forecasting in Chapter 1, we drew a distinction between forecasts based upon the judgments of individuals and those based upon quantitative analysis. Most of this book has been taken up with a discussion of quantitative approaches to forecasting, yet companies continue to report that the bulk of their forecasting operations are based upon judgments made by their staff.[1] Is the current emphasis by companies appropriate? Should forecasting books devote most of their pages to quantitative methods, as we and many others have done? Before rushing to answer this question, we need to look more closely at the role of judgment in forecasting. Thus, in this chapter we describe various judgmental methods and then attempt an assessment of the relative strengths of the different approaches. We should note that *all* forecasting methods contain judgmental elements, so, in some respects, the choice is one of degree rather than an absolute difference. The choice between adopting a quantitative approach or relying on judgment will also reflect the availability of data, but the choice should not be the result of managerial ignorance of the relative strengths and weaknesses of these two approaches! The forecasting literature uses various terms to describe the two basic approaches to forecasting. Forecasting based on individual judgments is also known as *managerial*, *subjective*, or *qualitative* forecasting (although researchers sometimes use these terms slightly differently). Likewise, quantitative forecasts are also labeled as *statistical*. We employ the following formal definitions:

JUDGMENTAL OR QUANTITATIVE FORECASTING

Judgmental forecasting: The process of producing forecasts based on integrating information based on subjective beliefs. The integration may be made informally or through a structured process. The forecast may also be obtained by aggregating the subjective forecasts of a number of individuals.

Quantitative forecasting: Forecasting based on the application of a prescribed explicit analysis of numerically coded data. This kind of forecasting may be *causal*, *extrapolative*, or a blend of both.

It is also useful to distinguish the *forecaster* from the *user* of the forecasts. The forecaster generates the forecasts, whereas the user employs the results in planning and decision making. The two functions may be performed by the same individual, but the distinction serves to emphasize that they are separate functions. When the same individual or group does both activities, considerable care must be taken to ensure that the resulting forecasts indicate what is *likely* to happen, not what the forecaster/user would *like* to happen. *Sales targets* describe what management would like to achieve, whereas *sales forecasts* should describe likely outcomes.[2] By contrast, when the two functions are performed by separate individuals or groups, it is important to maintain proper communication between them, a point to which we return in Chapter 13.

---

1 See, for example, the reports of surveys by Dalrymple (1987), Sanders and Manrodt (1994), and Table 13.1 taken from McCarthy, Davis, Golicic, and Mentzer (2006).

2 Every sports team or individual has the target of winning a championship. Clearly, forecasts recognize that only one winner will emerge, a reality reflected in bookmakers' odds.

FORECASTS, PLANS, AND TARGETS

Forecasts should represent the most likely (typical or expected) value of a future event.

Plans are a response by the organization to its forecasts in order to move toward its objectives.

Targets represent estimates of what might be achieved in favorable circumstances when implementing a plan. A realistic target should therefore be based on the corresponding forecast.

In Section 11.1, we consider the two approaches of judgmental and quantitative forecasting and suggest circumstances in which one may have advantages over the other. Then, in Section 11.2, we examine several judgmental methods and outline their relative strengths and weaknesses. In Section 11.3, we move on to look at the Delphi method, which overcomes some of the criticisms leveled at other judgmental methods and combines subjective judgments from groups of individuals. Prediction markets, a radically different approach to combining judgments from a group of individuals, are the topic of Section 11.4. Some problems require the assessment of probabilities, a topic that we consider in Section 11.5. On occasion, completely distinct situations may arise (e.g., war and peace) that call for quite different contingent forecasts; we may then use scenario analysis and role-playing, the subjects of Section 11.6. We conclude the chapter with a general summary and an analysis of some useful principles that underlie effective judgmental forecasting.

11.1 Judgmental or Quantitative Forecasting?

The distinction between judgmental and quantitative forecasts is perhaps most easily seen in the following example.

■ Example 11.1: Two approaches to sales forecasting

Suppose that we wish to forecast the demand for a particular type of refrigerator in a department store. A quantitative forecast might be based upon simple exponential smoothing, as introduced in Section 3.3. A judgmental forecast might be provided by the store manager, upon the basis of her past experience. Which forecast is better? The store manager may well be setting a target rather than stating a forecast, or she may be thinking about inventory levels and wishing to make sure that demand can be met. Alternatively, she may have reasons to expect higher demand because of external factors that are not reflected in the simple exponential smoothing estimate. Given sufficient time and effort, she might well arrive at accurate forecasts for every product the store has in stock, but such an activity would be very demanding of her time. ■

From this example, it is evident that a number of factors must be taken into account in deciding upon the type of forecast to use. Table 11.1 provides a summary of the pros and cons.

The weaknesses listed in the table are often captured in the phrase "heuristics and biases," due to Tversky and Kahneman (1974). The words describe the deficiencies and, to a certain extent, the strengths of judgmental forecasting. In essence, the judgmental forecaster uses various simple mental strategies or heuristics to produce the forecast, and these are often deficient in predictable ways.

Table 11.1 Comparison of Judgmental and Quantitative Forecasting

Forecasts	Strengths	Weaknesses

Judgmental	• Responsive to latest changes in environment
	• Can include inside information
	• Can compensate for one-time or unusual events
	• Forecaster "owns" the resulting forecast
		• Human cognitive limitations (e.g., limited attention span, limited memory)
		• Possible lack of consistency
		• Overresponsive to salient, easily accessed information
		• Motivational biases (e.g., the desire for a particular outcome)
		  – Affected by organizational politics and "herding"
		  – Reputational biases (e.g. adopting extreme forecasts to generate publicity)
		• Subject to optimism or wishful thinking
		• May be very costly or time consuming
		• Leads to overconfidence in forecasts

Quantitative	• Objective and consistent • Can process large amounts of data • Can consider many variables and complex relationships • Replicable by others	• May be slow to react to changing environments • Only as good as the model used and the available data • Can be costly to model soft information • Requires a technical understanding (by both forecaster and user)

Source: Adapted from Sanders, 2005.

HEURISTICS AND BIASES IN JUDGMENTAL FORECASTING

1) An *availability bias*, wherein the forecaster relies too heavily on easily available and memorable information.
   - e.g., where information is provided through a face-to-face meeting.

2) The *representativeness heuristic*, in which the forecaster matches a situation to a similar earlier event without taking into account its frequency of occurrence.
   - e.g., where apparent patterns are discerned in the latest noisy fluctuations in a time series.

3) The *anchoring and adjustment heuristic*, whereby the forecaster uses (anchors onto) an initial value such as the last observation and then adjusts the value insufficiently to give a revised forecast.
   - e.g., where the most recent observation is weighted too heavily in an extrapolation.

4) *Over-optimism* or *motivational bias* where the forecaster is motivated to bias the forecast towards a preferred state.

5) *Overconfidence* in the forecaster's own beliefs as to the accuracy of their forecasts.

How do these biases and heuristics affect judgmental forecasts? Goodwin and Wright (2014) discuss these and other heuristics in more detail. Crucially, none of the approaches we describe here to judgmental forecasting will consistently deliver unbiased and efficient forecasts that overcome these limitations. Still, despite these damaging disadvantages, judgmental forecasting can prove remarkably effective. Goldstein and Gigerenzer (2009) give a number of interesting examples of how simply selecting key plausible variables in a causal model and weighting them equally can outperform the regression methods we have discussed earlier in the book though it is doubtful that this applies to the typical time series problem. Intriguingly, they describe a heuristic (*recognition heuristic*) where identifying the best known name (e.g., a soccer team, or tennis player) as the likely winner proves most effective.

So if judgmental heuristics work well in some instances, by comparing quantitative with qualitative forecasting methods, as in the table, we see that the two approaches may be complementary: A property that is a strength in some circumstances may be a weakness in others.

As with any forecasting exercise, the PIVASE items listed back in Section 1.1 need to be considered: **P**urpose, **I**nformation, **V**alue, **A**nalysis, **S**ystem, and **E**valuation. For the present, we assume that the questions relating to purpose and value have been resolved. Typically, judgmental forecasts are most necessary when they involve "unique" forecasting assignments; this uniqueness implies past information is not directly relevant. Therefore, no summary numerical evaluation measures, as discussed in Section 2.7 are available. But few forecasting problems are wholly unique.

> **DISCUSSION QUESTION:** *What business forecasting problem seems to you to be close to "unique"?*

More typical is where a forecaster may be called upon to make a variety of judgments in somewhat similar circumstances, in which case the performance of those individuals can be tracked over time. The information we learn by such tracking may be used both to evaluate the relative performance of individuals and to provide feedback to them so that they can improve their forecasting abilities.

The preceding analysis leaves us with the following information and value questions that are pertinent to deciding whether to use judgmental or quantitative forecasting:

1. *Are quantitative data available?* If quantitative data are limited, only indirectly available, or nonexistent, a judgmental forecast will be needed, as in forecasting the sales of a new product. However, even here, it may be possible to use information on past launches of any similar products.

2. *Are data from similar forecasting situations available?* These data can be used to provide forecasts in the new situation. For example, seasonality from sales of a past fashion product can be used to estimate seasonality in the current case.

3. *How valuable is the forecast?* If the forecast has limited value, the time spent on it should be limited also: a speedy subjective assessment will generally suffice. By contrast, when a forecast relates to a major issue, we will want to devote considerable resources to the exercise, quite probably involving both judgmental and quantitative components. The final forecast will need to be "owned" by the forecaster; that is, he or she must be willing to stand by the forecast and justify it to senior staff.

4. *How many items need to be forecast?* In some applications, such as inventory management where there is typically some historical data available, the numbers of units kept in stock can run to the tens of thousands or more. The cost of subjectively assessing each product would be enormous. In that case, the effective manager can operate by using exponential smoothing methods and then looking only at those products whose recent forecasts do not match up with actual demand and which are most important: see Section 13.1.5

5. *Would the numerical data be available in a timely fashion?* Data may become available only at certain points in time (e.g., annual or quarterly macroeconomic data) and

may not be available in time to make quantitative forecasts for the next time period (e.g., a month).

6. *Are there any data that cannot be incorporated into a quantitative forecast?* For example, we may have a perfectly reasonable quantitative method that forecasts the quarterly earnings of a company on the basis of previous figures. However, by the time we get close to the next earnings announcement, there will be information available (at the company, industry, or even national level, for example, the competition announcing a new product or the government, a new tariff) that is relevant, but that cannot be incorporated directly into the model. Thus, we would start with the quantitative forecast and then adjust it upon the basis of more recent information.[3] At the company level, future promotional sales are affected by many aspects of the particular promotion which are unlikely to be part of the company's formal forecasting method, as often promotions have unique characteristics such as the back-up advertising campaign and the competitive activity that affect the outcome. This topic is discussed further in Section 12.2.1.

The issues we have just raised are illustrated in the following example.

■ Example 11.2: The U.S. Prime Rate

Table 11.2 and Figure 11.1 show the U.S. Prime Rate as reported by the *Wall Street Journal*. The data cover all changes from the beginning of January 2000 to December 2016. The rate, based upon a poll of major banks, changes when a sufficient majority of banks (currently 7 of 10 major banks) have changed their rates.

The banks will usually adjust their rates in response to a change made to the *Federal Funds Rate* (FFR), set by the Federal Reserve Board at its monthly meeting. The banks' rate is typically 3 percent above the FFR. We know the current rate and the date of the next Board meeting. The slightly bizarre scatterplot shown in Figure 11.1 enables us to see both the timing of changes and their direction. Since December 2008, the FFR has been close to zero, so any future change would be upward. Further, the Board recently made changes on the order of 0.25 percent, so we might expect the next change to be of that order of magnitude.

Are quantitative data available? Clearly the answer is yes, but the numbers need to be qualified by the background information just provided.

How valuable is the forecast? For any organization considering major investment decisions (as lender or borrower), the decision made at the next Board meeting has major implications. Getting it right is crucial.

How many items need to be forecast? Only one number is of direct interest, but the decision of the Board is based upon a balanced assessment of employment figures, economic growth, and the competing risks of deflation and inflation. Thus, we would seek to track these factors as well as the prime rate itself.

Would the numerical data be available in a timely fashion? Macroeconomic data are available only with a certain time lag and may not be published every month (e.g., the gross domestic product series is published quarterly in the U.S. and the UK). Forecasters will look for leading indicators such as stock indexes that incorporate expectations about changes in the prime rate. Typically, such activities will involve quantitative causal modeling, as we discussed in Chapter 8.

---

3 See Bandyopadhyay, Brown, and Richardson (1995) for further discussion of this topic.

Figure 11.1 Changes in the U.S. Prime Rate as Reported by the *Wall Street Journal*

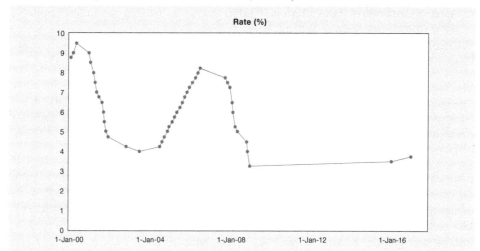

Table 11.2 Changes in the U.S. Prime Rate as Reported by the *Wall Street Journal*

Date of Rate Change	Rate (%)	Date of Rate Change	Rate (%)
3-Feb-00	8.75	3-May-05	6.00
22-Mar-00	9.00	30-Jun-05	6.25
17-May-00	9.50	9-Aug-05	6.50
4-Jan-01	9.00	21-Sep-05	6.75
1-Feb-01	8.50	1-Nov-05	7.00
21-Mar-01	8.00	13-Dec-05	7.25
19-Apr-01	7.50	31-Jan-06	7.50
16-May-01	7.00	28-Mar-06	7.75
28-Jun-01	6.75	10-May-06	8.00
22-Aug-01	6.50	29-Jun-06	8.25
18-Sep-01	6.00	18-Sep-07	7.75
3-Oct-01	5.50	31-Oct-07	7.50
7-Nov-01	5.00	11-Dec-07	7.25
12-Dec-01	4.75	22-Jan-08	6.50
7-Nov-02	4.25	30-Jan-08	6.00
27-Jun-03	4.00	18-Mar-08	5.25
1-Jul-04	4.25	30-Apr-08	5.00
11-Aug-04	4.50	8-Oct-08	4.50
22-Sep-04	4.75	29-Oct-08	4.00
10-Nov-04	5.00	16-Dec-08	3.25
14-Dec-04	5.25	17-Dec-15	3.50
2-Feb-05	5.50	15-Dec-16	3.75
22-Mar-05	5.75		

Source: http://www.fedprimerate.com/wall_street_journal_prime_rate_history.htm

Do we have data that cannot be incorporated into a quantitative forecast? Quantitative methods rely upon an assumption that the future will, in some sense, evolve in a manner that reflects the past. Although the Board considers rate changes only at its monthly meeting, there is a continuous stream of information on changing consumer confidence and financial and economic activity. A naïve extrapolation based solely upon the data in Table 11.2 that ignored the background information would be hazardous to the forecaster's health! ■

This example illustrates some of the complexities of judgmental forecasting. By going through the PIVASE steps, we can identify relevant background information and assess the importance of the task. In turn, that knowledge will guide us to a suitable choice of forecasting procedures.

11.1.1 An Appraisal

On the one hand, judgmental forecasting is often labor intensive; that is, it is likely to be an expensive proposition. On the other hand, the judgmental approach will be particularly effective when quantitative data are lacking and the decisions to be made are important such as new product launches. Also, judgmental adjustments to statistical forecasts are valuable when data on recent events cannot be directly incorporated into quantitative forecasts. From the preceding discussion, it is evident that both judgmental and quantitative forecasts are potentially valuable and that they should not be viewed as mutually exclusive.

When historical data are not directly relevant and potential effects are large, judgmental adjustments are likely to be both necessary and effective. By contrast, as Fildes and Goodwin (2007) point out, "making judgmental adjustments to statistical forecasts is not only a popular activity (75 percent of the forecasts [in their study] were adjusted), but one that is far too popular for the good of the companies." In Section 12.2.1 we discuss making such adjustments using the impact of sales promotions as an example. In the remainder of this chapter, we will focus upon how to generate purely judgmental forecasts and leave issues of adjustment until Chapter 12.

In Chapter 13, we consider good forecasting practice as an amalgam of the two approaches. That is, whenever possible, we should use the best available combination of judgment and quantitative modeling. Good judgment should inform the structure of numerical forecasts, and good numerical forecasts should provide the basis for informed judgmental adjustments.

11.2 Judgmental Methods

We now examine various judgmental forecasting methods; there are many variants on these basic themes, and some of the approaches may be used in combination. However, the basic ideas outlined here provide building blocks for more general approaches. In this section, we consider five variants: the single expert, a group of experts, sales force projections, customer surveys, and the use of analogies. We then look at the Delphi method, which is a formalized method for combining opinion, in Section 11.3.

11.2.1 The Single Expert (or Unaided Judgment)

In its simplest form, this method relies on the judgment of a single expert. If that expert is truly well qualified, the forecasts may be excellent. But such experts, if they exist, will be hard to identify. Often the single individual will have certain prejudices that lead to systematic biases in the forecasts. The problem traces back to Plato's discussion of the "philosopher-king". Who chooses the single wise leader (or forecaster) who can enlighten the rest of us? All too often, the most senior manager may be that person, and, as noted in Table 11.1, the resulting forecasts will reflect her personal biases or wishful thinking. Of course, the right person may in fact have the knowledge and insight to provide superior forecasts; the next example provides food for thought in that respect.

■ Example 11.3: The successful consultant?

Some years ago, one of us (KO) attended a seminar by a consultant whose basic forecasting methodology was to claim that everything grew at the rate of 8 percent per year. He was apparently quite a success in his job. My students gazed at him and then at me in disbelief. How could this be?

One explanation is survivor bias. Were we listening to a wild-eyed prophet who had survived by pure chance, rather like the one person who wins the lottery? Possibly not, and eventually a more cogent reason dawned. Apparently, he was advising companies whose forecasting functions resided in the sales and production departments. If forecasts and targets get confused, the sales force may understate likely sales so that it is rewarded with lower targets. The marketing team will tend to overestimate demand so that it can be sure of supplies. A third viewpoint comes from the production folks, who may instinctively tend to underestimate so that they will not be left responsible for any unsold inventory. With all this politicking going on, senior management might find the lone expert's views reasonably palatable. Indeed, an 8 percent growth forecast was probably a nice political compromise! And, of course, there was rarely a retrospective analysis of forecast errors. ■

> **DISCUSSION QUESTION:** *Identify a current "hot" topic that relies on expert forecasts. What do you think makes the forecast acceptable and convincing? What makes the forecast questionable?*

Identifying the "right" expert is far from easy, and based on an analysis of the accuracy of 284 experts and around 80 thousand political forecasts, Tetlock (2005) found the results depressing; most individual and consensus forecasts proved widely off the mark, e.g., the coming collapse of communism in 1989 was missed by almost all expert forecasters; subsequently, the recession of 2007-2009. However in amongst all the poor forecasters there emerged a group of "superforecasters" who consistently managed to outperform the rest (in the "Good Judgment" project). These forecasters understood the cognitive biases that we've been describing and the ways in part they can be overcome. They are, as Shoemaker and Tetlock (2016) describe them, "cautious, humble, openminded, analytical — and good with numbers". These judgmental skills can be identified and improved by tracking performance, auditing the process, and giving feedback.

11.2.2 Expert and Group Opinion

Expertise both actual and self-awarded can be harnessed in other ways to provide a forecast. Perhaps the betting markets provide the best example of an implicit forecast. The odds favoring one outcome rather than others provide a prediction of that outcome as well as a probability associated with the outcome (or outcomes). There is strong evidence that in established sports, where betting is widespread, the odds are close-to-efficient and therefore the predictions are hard to beat (Stekler, Sendor, and Verlander, 2011). Typically such markets, which harness a considerable number of punters, outperform other forecasting methods, in particular expert opinion such as that offered in the media. Betting markets where the numbers of participants are smaller are less efficient. The composition of the betting market may matter, a 2016 example being provided by the UK Brexit vote, where there is anecdotal evidence that the weight of money (which determines the odds) derived from the heavy participation from London, a pro-remain stronghold. If the number of bets placed (rather than the money amounts) were used to predict the outcome, they would have favored the actual vote for the UK to leave the EU. O'Leary(2017) examines aspects of the issue of the composition of the "crowd" of forecasters where he compares the "wisdom of a crowd" with expert and the betting odds. The wisdom of crowds forecast (explicit forecasts compared to the betting odds) were gathered from two sources, one with wide participation (using Yahoo!) and one more narrowly focused (on a Swiss audience). He concludes, perhaps unsurprisingly, that "the composition of the crowd characteristics such as size, location, and the information that they receive", can influence crowd choices; so only the broader based Yahoo forecasts were as accurate as the betting odds while the more constrained "Swiss" forecasts performed more poorly.

In short, the forecasts provided by the betting odds (where they are available) and those gathered from collecting individual forecasts from as wide and diverse a sample of opinion both offer alternative routes to generating aggregate forecasts. While the former have the advantage of relying on forecasters committed to the contest, the latter has the potential advantage of diversity, involving all, not merely the betting public.

11.2.3 Jury of Expert Opinion

Because of the weaknesses just noted with the single-expert approach, many organizations tend to prefer a *jury of executive opinion* that brings together leading executives with different responsibilities, such as sales, production, and finance and is the heart of the Sales and Operations Planning Process (S&OP) in companies (see for example, Chase, 2016). The advantage is that a range of managerial viewpoints can be incorporated into the discussion which has as one of its outputs an agreed upon sales forecast as well as production/ operational plans. The drawback is that forecasts (what is likely to happen) and targets (what we would like to happen) get confused and political considerations enter into the debate, a topic we return to in Chapter 13.

If a group of experts with distinct competencies is brought together to agree to a forecast, such an approach can be highly effective, although it can also be costly and slow. If the group is internal to the organization, political considerations may still prevail. Even more damaging, the group may operate to suppress dissenting viewpoints, thereby neglecting any uncertainty in the forecasts (or expected outcomes of policy decisions). Here, contradictory information is rejected in favor of information that apparently gives some support for the chosen course. A recent example is in the 2003 invasion of Iraq, in which, in both the United States and the United Kingdom, information on the low likelihood of weapons of mass destruction was discounted. Such a response, wherein the members of a group of decision makers or forecasters feel that the emerging group predictions cannot be wrong and should not be challenged, is often called *group-think*. At a less dramatic level, these kinds of political motivations may lead the organizationally based forecaster astray, as we discuss in Section 13.2.3.

Such limitations led Armstrong (2006) to argue that, for forecasting purposes, face-to-face meetings of an expert group should be avoided altogether. O'Connor (2006) suggests that the purpose of a face-to-face meeting should be to achieve management buy-in, but not to generate forecasts. Overall, the research points overwhelmingly to the conclusion that the senior management group should set the forecasting agenda and elaborate the key assumptions, but leave the actual forecasting operations to a forecasting team.

One increasingly popular method of drawing together opinion is through the use of a *focus group* (Stewart and Shamdasani, 2015). While many of the elements are common to the "jury of expert opinion" the focus of such groups is to explore the dimensions of a topic and the range of conceivable responses rather than to achieve a consensus. For example, as part of a new product forecasting task, the attributes of a new product compared to its competition could be identified through a focus group, thereby ensuring that its benefits and disadvantages are included in the comparison. Constituting an appropriate group raises many of the same issues posed in selecting a small group of experts for a forecasting task in that the participants should embrace the full range of perspectives, a requirement more easily said than achieved. However, focus groups are often used inappropriately (though sometimes just implicitly) as a forecasting tool with participants providing a group (rather than an expert) forecast while not reflecting the relevant population under study. Focus groups will also be subject to all the individual and group biases we have discussed.

11.2.4 Sales Force Projections (or Sales Force Composite)

Because a company's sales force is in regular contact with customers, its members constitute a natural source of information about prospective sales. Not only can members of the sales force provide details of likely orders in their territories, but they may also provide information on the timing of such orders. These reports may then be aggregated to produce overall forecasts for the company's operations. The method is similar to the jury of expert opinion, in that it draws upon company expertise and may be applied in situations where quantitative data are not sufficiently available (e.g., for new products). However, it usually has the advantage that the individual forecasts are independent of each other to a certain extent, because, although common information (such as the state of the economy or the company's marketing strategy) should be shared, area- or product-level forecasts are produced independently and thus with lower likelihood of common mistakes. Although members of the sales force may have similar backgrounds, their specific expertise relates to their particular sales areas.

The advantages of this approach include increased availability of timely information and tapping into an information source that would not otherwise be available. The principal weakness is that management may be tempted to use the forecasts to set sales targets; such an action would encourage biased forecasts from the sales force (by reporting a low figure in order to beat the target). This kind of procedure is poor management practice and should be avoided. In cases where the sales force survey is used on a regular basis, regression analysis (as described in Chapters 8 and 9) may be employed and the aggregate sales composite figure calibrated against actual sales so that an improved sales forecast is produced by removing any reporting bias (see Goodwin, 1996).

> **DISCUSSION QUESTION:** *Your role as the forecast manager of a company that manufactures and sells machine tools worldwide is to organize the company's forecasting process of gathering the area and regional sales forecast to produce the company's total sales by product. What considerations should you bear in mind, what information would you collect, and what information would you share? What role might quantitative methods have in this process?*

11.2.5 Customer Surveys

From the forecasting perspective, surveys of consumer (or business) intentions to buy (or use) a product or service may be treated much like the sales force figures. Data are collected directly from customers regarding their purchasing intentions, either by a survey or with some other method, such as a reply card used to register the guarantee for a newly purchased product. The question whether a potential customer intends to buy a product (such as a new car) within a given period of time can be phrased in a number of different ways. Asking respondents to estimate the probability that they will purchase the product in the future improves the accuracy of the survey (Morwitz, 2001). An example of a suitable question, taken from Morwitz, is as follows: During the next 12 months, what do you think the chances are that you will buy a new car?

1. Certain, practically certain (99 in 100)
2. Almost sure (9 in 10)
3. Possible (5 in 10)
4. Unlikely (1 in 10)
5. Definitely will not (1 in 100)

The aggregate forecast is the average probability of purchase weighted by the number of potential customers in different market segments.

The usual questions of validity related to survey work arise: Does the sample represent the population of interest (i.e., potential buyers)? Are the responses a true reflection of purchasing intentions?[4] When such surveys are conducted on a consistent basis over time, biases can be corrected by calibration; that is, we could use the regression methods described in Chapter 8 to relate data on intentions to subsequent observed sales levels. These methods have the advantage of gaining direct access to the views of the customer and can provide information on such intangibles as customer satisfaction as well as sales forecasts. A good overview of methods that use such data for forecasting is given in Morwitz (2001).

Customer surveys can also be extended to understand why people (or organizations) make the choices they do. The surveys are based on data on respondents' preferences and attitudes to the choices they face (such as whether or not to buy a new product), and these preferences and attitudes are linked to demographic characteristics as well as to factors directly characterizing the choices (such as a product's price or its brand). We expand on the advantages of *choice modeling* in Section 12.4.4.

11.2.6 Use of Analogies

One way we all make judgments is to look at the problem we face and then try to identify analogous situations in the past to help inform the current choice. A simple example of this approach is in forecasting the impact of a promotion on product sales. (We develop various statistical methods for this kind of forecasting in Section 12.2.1.) Standard industry practice is to estimate the effect by using the most recent similar promotional effect. Such reliance upon a single analogy may lead to many of the biases discussed in Section 11.1. Further, a forecaster may be tempted to rely upon on a single characteristic to identify the analogy or analogies. Green and Armstrong (2007) employ detailed case descriptions (or scenarios, see Section 11.5) to ensure that all the main characteristics of the problem are taken into

---

4 A relevant question is how people perceive probabilities, depending on way they are asked. Kent (1994) provides evidence of the variations in how people interpret probabilities. A visual summary of further results is provided in *https://github.com/zonination/perceptions*.

account. Effective use of this methodology requires that we identify a number of analogies and then attempt to capture explicitly all their similarities and differences (often called attributes) that characterize the analogous situation.

> **DISCUSSION QUESTION:** *How would you characterize the similarities and differences between various retail promotions you have experienced?*

The first issue is what attributes (of the forecasting problem) should be included in comparing two situations. If we wished to compare alternative investments, we might examine their recent returns history and their volatility as well as recent comments by financial advisers. With similar new products, experts might identify the type of product, the availability of the product, and the speed of initial uptake as appropriate similarity measures. It might also be worthwhile to include dissimilarity measures: The *absence* of some key characteristic might be important in identifying similar situations.

For most forecasting problems, there will be a range of measures with which to compare the current situation with situations in the past. Some of these measures may be subjective and rely on experts to estimate the similarity — for example, the similarity between boards of directors in two takeover situations where the aim is to decide whether a bid will be accepted. The next stage is to develop a scoring mechanism that weights the attributes to give an overall score. This technique is illustrated in Example 11.4.

■ Example 11.4: Forecasting a U.S. presidential election

The situation faced is to forecast the outcome of the next presidential election. The attributes shown in Table 11.3 were identified as potentially important. An expert panel identified the factors describing the state of the nation in an election year and assigned a weight to reflect their relative importance in presidential elections.

Table 11.3 Similarity Matrix for Estimating the Similarity between Elections

Attributes	Clinton vs Trump	Obama vs Romney	McCain vs Obama	Bush vs Kerry	Gore vs Bush & Nader	Clinton vs Dole & Perot	Bush Sr vs Clinton & Perot	Weights
Year	2016	2012	2008	2004	2000	1996	1992	
Economy	U	U	U	N	N	F	U	40%
Social Issues	F	N	F	F	U	U	N	20%
Third Party	N	N	N	N	U	N	N	10%
Outlook	N	U	U	F	F	F	F	10%
War	N	N	N	F	N	N	F	10%
Incumbency	N	F	N	F	U	F	F	10%
Unweighted		0.83	0.92	0.67	0.50	0.50	0.67	
Weighted		0.85	0.95	0.65	0.45	0.30	0.75	

1. The first named candidate represents the incumbent party and the coding is

    F = favorable to incumbent or incumbent party (scored as +1)

    N = neutral for the incumbent or incumbent party (scored as 0.5)

    U = unfavorable to incumbent or incumbent party (scored as 0)

2. Scores for 1992 – 2008 were taken from the History Central website. Those for 2012 and 2016 were assigned by the authors.

Each factor is scored as *F*, *N*, or *U* depending on whether or not it was viewed favorable, neutral, or unfavorable to the incumbent or the incumbent party. The website History Central (*www.historycentral.com/elections*) presents brief summaries of each election, thereby providing a basis for an individual wishing to generate scores independently. The last two rows of the table show the similarity between the 2016 race and the earlier campaigns.

The unweighted similarity score is defined as:

1 – [The average absolute difference in ratings for the two elections].

For example, comparing the 2016 and 1996 elections, the absolute differences in scores are 1, 1, 0, 0.5, 0, and 0.5. These values correspond to complete disagreement on *Economy* and *Social Issues*, and some disagreement on the others. Note that these ratings do not reflect similar circumstances, but rather the impact of those circumstances upon the election. It follows that the unweighted average is 3/6 = 0.50, yielding a similarity score of 0.50. Likewise, the final row shows the similarity score based upon the averages using the weights in the last column, so that the entry for 2016 relative to 1996 is:

$$1-[1 \times 0.4 + 1 \times 0.2 + 0 \times 0.1 + 0.5 \times 0.1 + 0 \times 0.1 + 0.5 \times 0.1] = 0.30.$$

Both these scores measure the similarity between the elections. Other measures are possible such as the correlation — this would be particularly appropriate if quantitative scores are assigned to the attributes.

The final step in the process is to select the closest analogy to that being forecast; here both similarity scores point to the 2016 election being most similar to McCain vs Obama, leading to the prediction that Clinton would lose. However, it is a fine line as it turned out since 2012 was almost as similar. Exercise 11.5 uses this same approach in order to make predictions for future elections. ■

DISCUSSION QUESTION: *In the 2016 presidential campaign, what attributes proved important in Donald Trump's unexpected election victory? Could these have been included in an extended similarity matrix?*

Just as with the presidential forecasting example, many attributes are relevant in identifying similar time series, from the correlation to key summary statistics such as the number of outliers and the most recent trend. Meade (2000) offers suggestions, but in addition to using statistical measures, series can often be naturally grouped by their substantive features — for example, the nature of the crime committed (crimes of violence) or the regions of the country where the product is sold (the Southwest). Then, the behavior of analogous series can be considered together, as we discuss further in Section 12.3.2.

The use of analogies in forecasting has a number of aspects which lead to its success: it decomposes the problem, the rationale behind the forecast is documented and is therefore more easily defended and audited, and the sensitivity of the forecast to the weights assigned to the attributes can be explored. Crucially, as we discuss in Section 12.4 it is often the only structured method that can be used for new products. However identifying suitable analogies is a challenge, best done through a formalized identification of attributes and similarities (Goodwin *et al.*, 2013).

11.3 The Delphi Method

The various judgmental methods described so far can all be successful under the right conditions:

- They may be used in the absence of detailed quantitative data.

- Management is more likely to buy into the forecasting process because managers can be directly involved in it.

- Forecasts can be more timely when numerical data are available only on an occasional basis.

- The forecaster has control over the resulting forecast and is therefore committed to it.

Unfortunately, this flexibility comes with some definite weaknesses:

- Some opinion leaders may exert undue influence over others in arriving at the forecasts.

- Underlying assumptions may be left unstated.

- Information may not be shared, so that forecasts are developed on the basis of incomplete knowledge (even when the relevant information is available).

- Targets and forecasts may become entwined.

- It is difficult to assess uncertainty.

Some of these problems can be addressed by good organizational practice, as noted earlier. That is, we should use judgmental forecasting only for tasks of sufficient importance and use management input primarily to formulate problems rather than to forecast outcomes. But even with these policies in place, the methods we have described may lead to biased forecasts that lack a proper evaluation of the factors affecting what might happen. In the sections that follow, we describe two different approaches that can help to overcome such problems.

The first method we examine is known as the Delphi[5] technique. This method was developed by the Rand Corporation in the 1950s and, for a long time, was used most heavily in defense-related industries. Improvements in web technology and available software have now made the method feasible for asynchronous use involving participants scattered around the world, thereby greatly increasing its appeal. We provide only a brief outline here and recommend that the reader consult Rowe and Wright (2001) and Rowe (2007) for fuller details.

A Delphi project consists of a panel of experts, along with a facilitator whose responsibilities are to manage the operation and protect the integrity of the project. The aim is to elicit the views and forecasts of the participants without any distortions resulting from personal interactions. The key difference between this approach and a group meeting of experts is that the participants' viewpoints are provided anonymously. Thus, members of the panel usually do not know who else is involved in the forecasting exercise. Inputs may be provided simultaneously by the participants, but this is not necessary. Indeed, computer-based

---

5 In ancient times, the Oracle at Delphi was famed for her cryptic predictions. For example, she advised Athenians to "defend the wooden walls" so that they might win a famous victory. The literalists built wooden fortifications and were routed by the Persian army; the more perceptive put to sea in their (wooden) ships and defeated the Persian navy. Notwithstanding this example, we urge forecasters to report their findings in a clear manner (see Chapter 13).

Delphi systems are becoming increasingly common (see Appendix 11A). The essential ingredients of the Delphi approach are as follows:

- *Anonymity and confidentiality:* Ideally, the panelists should not be aware of one another's involvement and their answers should be confidential. Thus, each panelist should be able to provide his or her views and forecasts without feeling any pressure to adopt a particular viewpoint.

- *Controlled feedback:* Panelists will have different types and degrees of background knowledge. At each stage, the project facilitator processes the inputs and sends out comments to all the other panelists. (This step may be automated.) Panelists may then revise their assessments in light of the new information and may provide further comments.

- *Repetition:* The process is repeated until the results appear to stabilize. Typically, three rounds are found to be sufficient and often only two rounds are employed.

- *Statistical summary:* The responses from the panelists are summarized in some convenient way. Numerical summaries often use the median (to avoid the effect of extreme values) and a measure of variability (e.g., a group of nine panelists might report the second smallest value and the second-largest value). Particularly with larger groups, graphical summaries are useful. Qualitative anonymized summaries of panelists' viewpoints should also be provided.

- *Consensual forecasts:* The final report is often termed a consensual forecast; this does not mean that total agreement has been reached, but rather that the variation among the respondents' answers has been reduced as far as possible.

Once the panel is established, the facilitator presents the members with the set of questions that they are to consider. These questions should be carefully framed so that their answers will provide the decision maker with the information and forecasts necessary to make an informed decision. An important aspect of the process is that a major question should be broken into parts so that assumptions are clearly stated. The next example shows how a Delphi study might work.

■ Example 11.5: Framing questions for Delphi: A new product

An automobile company is planning to launch a new vehicle. It is well known that such projects take five to seven years from drawing board to full production, but the decision on the type of automobile must be made now. We will suppose that the company definitely plans to go ahead with a new vehicle and that it has the resources to invest in only one such model at this time. The strategic question before the board of directors is whether to go for a medium-size hybrid or for an SUV. Direct questions such as "Should we go for the hybrid or the SUV?" or "Will the product be successful?" are too broad and are likely to elicit prejudices rather than any useful information.

The board of directors ultimately seeks to see how each choice might affect the company's bottom line. Forecasts in response to the following questions (among others) may be considered:

- What will be total sales of personal cars in the country over the next seven years?

- What will be the market share of hybrids and SUVs over the next seven years?

- What would be the company's share of those markets if the new product was launched?

- What are the development costs for each project?

- What profit margin is likely on individual sales of such vehicles?
- What would be the effect of a 10 percent government subsidy in the purchase price of hybrids? (Such a subsidy exists in some countries. See Section 12.4.4.)

The marketing group could provide initial inputs, such as the total current market for hybrids and SUVs, along with a summary of recent trends and the company's current share of that market. Similarly, the engineering group could provide a range of cost estimates for each project. That is, we use quantitative information wherever and whenever we can find it. The forecasting team would then need to identify the principal factors that have an impact on future demand, such as income trends, future costs of gasoline, and the development of biofuels over the next five to seven years. In each case, some quantitative data sources are available and a preliminary analysis of the data from those sources could be provided to members of a Delphi panel. From the results of this exercise, it would be possible to create different scenarios (see Section 11.5). The final steps involve an assessment of the profitability of each policy under a given scenario and the probability that scenario would come to pass. ∎

The launch of a new product is often a suitable subject for an in-house Delphi analysis. However, even the brief discussion just set forth indicates that a considerable amount of information may be available from previous launches and overall operations. The study will have a greater chance of success if the panel is provided with as much of this background information as possible. A useful start-up procedure before the Delphi analysis gets underway is to ask panelists for recommendations about the information relevant to the question so that an information pack can be produced for the panel. It is also important to note that the last element of the proposed study examines the effects of a possible policy (of subsidizing the purchase price), a slightly different style of forecasting question than the others listed, because it permits the comparison of different policies.

Classroom illustrations of the Delphi process often involve assessments of *almanac events* rather than true predictions. An almanac event is a known, but relatively obscure fact, such as a historical date. With almanac events, the "answer" is always available and the responses of the panel might be examined in light of this "truth." Another approach, illustrated in the next example, is to ask about an event that will occur in the near future. Note that each approach is only illustrative: The real purpose of the Delphi technique is to elicit views on major issues. Nevertheless, the simple example that follows provides an illustration of the Delphi process as summarized below:

KEY STEPS IN DELPHI

Key steps in a Delphi analysis (see Rowe, 2007):

1. Determine the question(s) and objectives.
2. Choose a (diverse) panel of experts.
3. Circulate an information pack of agreed trends, reports, etc.
4. Request responses to a structured questionnaire by the end of round 1.
5. Summarize responses statistically, and summarize the rationale behind the responses.
6. Update information and complete round 2 of the survey. Repeat if necessary.

■ Example 11.6: A Delphi exercise on gasoline prices

Students in an MBA class were given the current price of a gallon of regular gasoline at a local gas station and asked to predict the price a month later. Two rounds of the Delphi exercise were completed, and only limited comments were allowed. Twenty-eight students completed the first round, of whom twenty-four responded in the second round. The results are summarized in Table 11.4, where the various inputs are as follows:

Mean, *Median* of point estimates; *SD* = standard deviation of point estimates

LPL, *UPL* = average lower and upper 95 percent prediction interval limits (to be discussed in Section 11.5)

Coverage = percentage of people whose prediction interval included the actual value (again, see Section 11.5)

The price at the beginning of the study was $ 1.96 per U.S. gallon, and a month later it had risen to $2.08. (Those were the days!) One principal feature of the results is the tendency to anchor onto (or stay overly close to) the current price; this is not an unreasonable reaction but may reflect a reluctance to take into account recent events that could change the price level. Here there is little difference between the mean and median — the latter may be preferred as it is more robust to extreme individualistic opinions. A second feature is that there is a reduction in the variability of the point forecasts. (The standard deviation drops from 0.07 to 0.05.) Such a closing-in of estimates is common in Delphi studies and reflects some sharing of information. We will discuss the rest of the table in Section 11.5. ■

Table 11.4 Results of a Delphi Study on Gasoline Prices

Round	Mean	Median	SD	LPL	UPL	Coverage
One	1.96	1.96	0.07	1.86	2.08	13/28; 46%
Two	1.99	1.98	0.05	1.92	2.06	8/24; 33%

DISCUSSION QUESTION: *Demographic changes — in particular, the effects of immigration as well as an aging established population — are affecting the demand for health services, both public and private, in Miami, Florida (or, for that matter, North West England). How would you develop a Delphi study to consider the broad question of the effects of these changes? (RF was involved in just such a study.)*

ISSUES WHEN CONSIDERING A DELPHI STUDY

- Choice of participants — select a group, committed to the study question, representing a range of contrasting perspectives.
- Whether there are benefits for the participants in engaging directly with each other or is the anonymity of Delphi desirable.
- When carrying out a Delphi, minimizing drop-outs from round to round.

11.4 Forecasting Using Prediction Markets

Just as technological developments have simplified the implementation of Delphi methods, improved communications have led to other methods of data collection for judgmental forecasting. These methods are most often used to capture respondents' future intentions (as we discussed in Section 11.2.4). The most obvious source of data is the ubiquitous online survey, although this kind of instrument may be highly unreliable, unless the investigator is able to select the set of respondents.

A promising alternative that makes effective use of improved communications is to evaluate expectations by means of prediction markets. The notion of prediction markets is not new, but their implementation via electronic access provides a new tool for forecasting, as we now describe.

11.4.1 The Structure of a Prediction Market

Many structures are possible for electronic prediction markets. Our description is based upon the form used by the Iowa Electronic Market (IEM), operated by the University of Iowa and accessible on the Web at *http://tippie.biz.uiowa.edu/iem/*.

For expository purposes, we use a hypothetical two-party presidential election as a running example. An electronic market is set up by considering the following two contracts:

> *Contract A delivers $1 if the Republicans win and $0 if the Democrats win.*
>
> *Contract B delivers $1 if the Democrats win and $0 if the Republicans win.*

Depending on the purposes of the market, traders may be recruited freely or by invitation only. A would-be trader enters the market by purchasing (or being provided with) shares in multiples of, say, $1 up to a specified maximum. Each initial allocation consists of equal numbers of units of contract A and contract B. Once the market opens, a trader may act in one of several ways.[6] We consider only the simplest situation, in which a trader seeks to buy or sell shares in one of the contracts, subject to finding someone to trade with and subject to having the funds or shares available. Trading costs are zero and an individual's trades are kept confidential. Thus, in all basic respects, the market operates like a simple stock exchange, but without any brokers. Because the market defines competing choices, such as choices for presidential candidates, the value of the share may be interpreted as an estimate of the probability of that candidate winning.

Do Prices Stay Aligned? Suppose the price for each of the two contracts dropped to 40 cents. Clearly, opportunities for gain now exist. A trader could purchase both contracts for a total of 80 cents and be guaranteed $1 in return. Similarly, if both contracts then went up to 60 cents, traders would rush to cash in the guaranteed profits by selling both contracts until the total price was back in the region of $1. Thus, market forces ensure orderly operations, provided sufficient liquidity exists, and that participants can buy and sell. The issue of liquidity is not usually a problem in fast-moving markets such as those relating to elections, but can make trading difficult in other cases (e.g., in-house markets with a limited number of active participants).

---

6 For example, the guidelines for the Iowa Electronic Market state that a trader may perform one of the following actions: "place a bid (an order to buy), place an ask (an order to sell), withdraw an outstanding bid or ask, make a purchase at the current market price, and execute a sale at the market price."

Extensions to Multiple Options. The framework readily extends to multiple options. If, say, K alternatives $A_1, A_2, \ldots, A_K$ exist, we simply define contract j as

Contract j delivers $1 if the alternative A_j occurs and $0 otherwise.

New traders are then issued one each of the K contracts for each $1 invested.

The issue of *combination* is resolved by using the market mechanism. When the market is open to all comers, the question of *recruitment* is also solved, provided that participants are concerned with maximizing expected returns and are not in collusion to manipulate the results.

Readers are encouraged to visit the IEM website, both to browse historical records and, if so desired, to participate in current markets.

Payoff. When the event takes place (e.g., a Republican is elected), each share for Contract A pays out $1, whereas each share for Contract B is worthless.

11.4.2 How Might Prediction Markets Be Used in Business?

An electronic market is a suitable vehicle for forecasting when the time horizon is not too distant and the flow of information is sufficient to generate a reasonable volume of trading. The issue must also be of sufficient importance to justify the setup costs. Thus, at one extreme short-term inventory decisions can be disregarded, at the other, major issues that may be years away and have no immediate impact. Although it is not essential, a specific target event, such as the release of an earnings statement, a Treasury bond auction, or a meeting of the Federal Reserve Board (with a decision about the prime rate), will make operation of the market more straightforward.

As with the Delphi method, if participants are to be invited rather than freely recruited, it is important to ensure that a range of interests be represented. As far as possible, no restrictions should be placed upon the traders' activities, although it would be desirable to capture some feedback, such as the final dollar balance for each participant. In the Brexit betting market, the prediction in terms of money placed was that "Remain" would win. However, in terms of number of bets placed, the correct prediction was foreseen.

One last consideration is the question of who stands to benefit from the results obtained from a prediction market. For example, if political markets were found to sway voters' opinions, those markets could become corrupted; fortunately, there is scant evidence of such problems. Alternatively, if the results are made public, others may be able to make use of the conclusions. For example, at one stage, the U.S. Department of Defense proposed to use an electronic market to assess the risk of a terrorist attack. If those results were to be made public, they would provide useful insights to potential terrorists on timing their assaults to coincide with a low risk assessment. Fortunately, that proposal was abandoned.

11.4.3 Usefulness of Prediction Markets

Miles (2008) suggests that prediction markets offer the following advantages:

- Incentives to be accurate
- The elimination of bias
- Elicits (latent) views that may not otherwise be heard
- A reduction in the time spent in meetings
- Dynamic updating of the prices and forecasts each time a trade is made (although this property is somewhat questionable because not all participants may be active traders at a particular time).

Gebert (2008) describes the challenges to successful implementation in a pharmaceutical application. Berg, Nelson, and Rietz (2008) examine the forecasting accuracy of prediction markets for presidential elections and find that the market approach systematically outperforms survey methods when the forecasting horizon is relatively long (100 days or more in their study). Buckley (2016) looks at their usefulness in an organizational context and "develops a framework that can be used to identify in which situations prediction markets can be profitably deployed".

Green, Armstrong, and Graefe (2007) and Graefe and Armstrong (2011) contrast Delphi methods with prediction markets and generally come down in favor of Delphi. For the application areas they consider, this conclusion is reasonable, but our discussion suggests that the two approaches are complementary and both can produce forecasts that are relatively free from bias. However, a prediction market is no more infallible than any other forecasting method and the 2016 US presidential election proved its limitations!

11.5 Assessing Uncertainty Judgmentally

All too often, judgmental forecasting methods generate a single number that is viewed as the forecast. Managers frequently take comfort from a single point forecast, yet the failure to consider the likely inaccuracy may lead to erroneous decisions. We need to identify different possible outcomes and associate each outcome with a probability of occurrence. Quantitative methods provide such information in a standard probabilistic form, given an underlying model, as we saw in Chapters 5 and 6. The judgmental forecaster needs to build such a framework from scratch.

11.5.1 Assessing Percentage Points and Probabilities

There is a rich literature on the detailed assessment of probabilities and statistical distributions by subjective methods. We consider only a few simple methods and refer the reader to Lawrence, Goodwin, O'Connor, and Onkal (2006) for a more detailed discussion.

The simplest approach to understanding the distribution of forecast errors is to calculate a measure of uncertainty, such as the standard deviation reported in Table 11.4, from the panel responses. The theory of sampling distributions (see Anderson, Sweeney, and Williams, Chapter 7) tells us that this approach is valid for quantitative (interval scaled) data, but no such theory underpins the use of such measures for subjective assessments: the range of judgmental forecasts too often fails to capture the uncertainty in a forecasting situation. Unfortunately, most of the time forecasters (whether judgmentally based or statistical) tend to make the same mistakes based on shared and mistaken assumptions. The consensus forecast and the range of opinions around it all too often tend to miss the mark, having inadequate (too conservative) coverage. The best that can be said about such measures is that they at least reflect uncertainty among the assessors although a study of supply chain companies offers promise (Gaur *et al.*, 2007).

A second approach is to ask panelists for estimates of, say, the 5 percent and 95 percent points of the distribution. These upper and lower limits are sometimes referred to more informally as pessimistic and optimistic values, respectively. Limited empirical evidence suggests that when people are asked for pessimistic and optimistic values, the results often correspond approximately to the 5th and 95th percentage points. That is, in the terminology of Section 2.8, these assessments aim to provide, at least approximately, a 90 percent prediction interval. However, the intervals may afford less coverage than desired, as shown in the next example.

■ Example 11.6: Delphi exercise on gasoline prices *(continued)*

The panelists in the study described in Example 11.6 were also asked to provide 5 percent (*LPL*) and 95 percent (*UPL*) probability limits; the results are summarized in Table 11.4. The average levels for these probability limits are seen to be too narrow: Coverage in round one across the different groups was 46% percent. This shortfall could simply be a feature of the particular (small) study, but the same problem has been observed in other studies. A more general feature, seen in round 2, is that, as information is shared, the group becomes more confident of its predictions and the width of an average interval is further reduced. In turn, the proportion of intervals that covers the actual outcomes falls even further. Such overconfidence is a common judgmental bias but makes subjective interval estimates of questionable value. ■

A more effective way of assessing the uncertainty in the judgmental forecasts is to ask the participant to make a choice between well-defined outcomes in a hypothetical lottery to estimate the prediction intervals for different percentage points. We now illustrate one such method.

■ Example 11.7: Assessing percentage points

We continue with the gasoline example and suppose that we wish to identify the 95th percent point of the price distribution. As a comparison, we visualize drawing a ticket from a hat with 100 tickets numbered from 1 to 100. For simplicity, we phrase the questions only with respect to the upper prediction level.

Activity A: Draw a ticket from the hat; you win if it is numbered 1 through 95, and you lose if it is 96 through 100.

Activity B: Set the upper price limit, say, at $2.00 for next month; you win if the actual price is below that level, and you lose if it is at or above that level.

Next, we ask the respondent which activity she would prefer. If she selects A, her choice implies that she believes that the probability that the price will be below $2.00 is less than 0.95. Accordingly, we then select a higher value for the price limit (e.g., $2.10) and repeat the question. Had she selected B, we would have lowered the price. The process continues until our respondent is indifferent between the two bets, and that price is her estimate for the upper limit. The same process may be repeated for the lower limit. The final step is to average the results across respondents. ■

This process seems, and indeed is, rather convoluted, and getting participation from managers is difficult unless the problem is both important and relevant to them. However, such methods are more effective than straightforward questions of the "What is the 95 percent upper confidence limit" kind. Thus, on important issues, the extra effort is worthwhile. Probabilities may be assessed in a similar way. Activity B (the price of gasoline) would now be fixed, and the number of winning tickets varied. It is seldom worthwhile to try to assess probabilities on a finer scale than increments of 0.10, unless we are dealing with very rare events.

11.5.2 Decomposition

Forecasting complex and very rare events requires special treatment. Typically, the question is multifaceted and the problem should be decomposed into its simpler components, as illustrated in the next example. The benefits of decomposition are that objective information about some elements may be available and, even when such data are not available, assessments of simpler events are typically more reliable. For details, see MacGregor, 2001.

■ Example 11.8: Tornado insurance

Insurance companies often offer protection against catastrophic risks for seemingly modest premiums. Is such insurance worthwhile? A tornado strike is one example of a catastrophic event over which we have no control and might consider purchasing insurance. A decomposition of this event might involve the following steps:

1. How many tornados per year are sighted in my area (county, state)?
2. What proportion of these tornados touch down and cause damage?
3. Over what proportion of the total area is the damage severe?
4. What would the total (reimbursable) cost be to me of my business being wiped out?

Thus, the probability of your business being severely damaged by a tornado in the course of a year can be estimated approximately[7] by the formula

Expected Number × Probability (Touchdown) × Probability (Damage),

where

Number = Expected number of tornados in my area,

Touchdown = Proportion that touch down and cause damage, and

Damage = Proportion in my area resulting in severe damage, given touchdown.

Some of these estimates are available from the National Weather Service or similar sources, although the definition of "area" will be governed by the data-reporting procedures of the source. Areas with severe damage may have to be estimated from newspaper reports.

Next, this composite probability may be used together with the cost estimate of damage to those businesses which were hit to produce your expected loss for the year. The purchase of tornado insurance can then be evaluated by comparing the premium with the expected loss. Of course, any final comparison of the damage and premium costs must also take into account your level of risk aversion. Even a high premium might be worthwhile if it allows you to sleep well at night. ■

The final answer from the decomposition approach, though imprecise, will usually be more accurate than any direct attempt to answer the question "Will my business be damaged by a tornado in the coming year?" In sales forecasting, similar issues arise in estimating the impact of various marketing activities. Although such events as a promotional price change are not rare, their effects often reflect the nature of the promotional package, including the advertising, retail display, and retailer commitment. These factors can all be estimated separately to give the forecaster the information needed to produce a final sales promotion profile of incremental sales over the period of the promotion.

---

7 For commonly occurring events, more precise calculations are appropriate. For very rare events, the probability of two or more happening is exceedingly small ("lightning never strikes the same place twice") so it suffices to use the *expected number of events* and then multiply by the *touchdown* and *damage probabilities* as defined.

> **DISCUSSION QUESTION:** *How would you decompose the possible effects of global warming (a predicted increase of 0.3 degrees Fahrenheit, or 0.2 degrees Celsius, per decade) on the eastern seaboard of the United States? On the Mediterranean?*

11.5.3 Combining Judgmental Forecasts

When separate forecasts are produced by a number of experts or organizations, how should we combine the results? Table 11.5 shows results of several opinion polls taken in October 2016 regarding the level of popular support for the U.S. presidential candidates of the two major parties. What should be the final forecast as of November 6th, 2016?

Table 11.5 Results of Early Opinion Polls Regarding the 2016 U.S. Presidential Election

Polls	Dates	Type, Respondents	Democrat Clinton	Republican Trump	Margin
YouGov/Economist	11/4 – 11/7	Online 3669	45	41	Clinton +4
IBD/TIPP	11/4 – 11/7	Live Phone 1107	41	43	Trump +2
Insights West	11/4 – 11/7	Online 940	45	41	Clinton +4
Bloomberg/Selzer	11/4 – 11/6	Live Phone 799	46	43	Clinton +3
Lucid/The Times-Picayune	11/4 – 11/6	Online 931	45	40	Clinton +5
Fox News	11/3 – 11/6	Live Phone 1295	48	44	Clinton +4
Monmouth University	11/3 – 11/6	Live Phone 748	50	44	Clinton +6
ABC News/Washington Post	11/3 – 11/6	Live Phone 2220	47	43	Clinton +4
New York Times/CBS News	11/2 – 11/6	Live Phone 1426	47	43	Clinton +4
Rasmussen	11/2 – 11/6	I.V.R./Online 1500	45	43	Clinton +2

Source: http://www.nytimes.com/interactive/2016/us/elections/polls.html

Note: Republican Two-Party = Republican share of two-party vote, excluding "Don't Know" and "Refused".

Source: http://forecastingprinciples.com/Political/pollyvote2008.html

Some claims could be made for each of the following:

- The latest survey, because it captures the most recent information. This survey gives the Republican share at 41 percent compared with the Democrats at 45 percent. But we should note that such surveys are often performed over several days and may not be published immediately.

- The mean and median for the Republican share is, 42.5 and 43 percent. respectively

- The mean and median for the Democratic share is 45.9 and 45.5 percent respectively.

- An average that is weighted by the number of voters polled (provided in column 3 of the table).

- Some other weighted average that reflects the forecasting accuracy of the different organizations.

Were the polls accurate for the 2016 election? As the discussion of political analogies for elections in Section 11.2.5 makes clear, for this particular election there were many factors that hadn't formed a part of earlier elections and the outcome was unclear. The result of the nationwide popular vote favored Democrat Hillary Clinton and the percentages of 48.2% to 46.1% were close to those predicted by the polls. But Republican Donald Trump won the presidency because of the rules of the Electoral College — and the polls at state level did not prove particularly accurate, depending as they did on smaller and less frequent samples.

The issue these various polls raise is not one of selecting as if in a multiple-choice test; rather, the aim is to illustrate that even when we can obtain independent forecasts, we may not know how to put them together. Graefe, Armstrong, Jones, and Cuzán (2014) show how effective combinations can be in forecasting the outcome of elections. As ever, a simple average does well, although the forecaster should check for outliers. We return to the issue of combining forecasts in Chapter 12.

11.5.4 Assessing the Accuracy of Qualitative Predictions

The measures of forecast accuracy introduced in Section 2.7 and used repeatedly thereafter assume that the variable of interest is measured on a continuous scale. In Chapter 10 we considered the case where the prediction is a classification of a future event, whether the economy will fall into recession (or not), or whether someone will default on a loan. However, as we have seen in this chapter, the discussion may relate to the occurrence or non-occurrence of an event, when the forecast is expressed as a probability. Table 11.6 provides an example where the forthcoming event has been assigned (as in US weather forecasts) a probability of occurrence.

We begin by stating that "It rained" if more than a trace is observed; clearly other definitions are possible. We then assign a score of 1 when it rained and 0 when it did not, as shown in the last column of Table 11.6. The forecast performance is measured by the *Brier Score* (Brier, 1950), defined over n cases (here $n=5$) as:

$$B = \sum_{i=1}^{n} (P_i - O_i)^2 / n,$$

where P_i is the probability forecast and O_i is the observed outcome.

Table 11.6 The Probability of Rainfall over Five Consecutive Days in January, in the Washington, DC Area (*one day ahead forecasts*)

Day of the Week	Probability Forecast for Rain (P_i)	Actual Rainfall (inches)	Observed Score (O_i)
Wednesday	0.55	0.02	1
Thursday	0.15	0.07	1
Friday	0.10	Trace	0
Saturday	0.75	0.19	1
Sunday	0.05	0.00	0

That is,

$$B = \{(0.55 - 1)^2 + (0.15 - 1)^2 + (0.10 - 0)^2 + (0.75 - 1)^2 + (0.05 - 0)^2\} / 5$$

$$= (0.2025 + 0.7225 + 0.01 + 0.0625 + 0.0025) / 5$$

$$= 0.20$$

An uninformative forecast might assign probability 0.5 to each day's expected outcome, which would result in a Brier Score of 0.25; clearly perfect forecasting would yield a score of zero. Alternatively a forecaster who knows nothing specific about the forthcoming events apart from which is the most likely on average would accrue a similar Brier score. The extension to multiple categories is straightforward.

11.6 The Use of Scenarios

The future, particularly when we look longer-term is affected by a wide range of influences. Scenarios offer a helpful route to understanding the complexity, where a *scenario* is defined as a story that depicts possible future events. In this sense, a scenario may be used for persuasion rather than forecasting. Like any story, it needs to include the causes and interactions among its different elements. The box that follows gives a more formal definition. Our interest in scenarios lies in the elicitation and understanding of different possible outcomes as a basis for forecasting. Other uses include the development of an organizational strategy and the gaining of acceptance for a forecast or the strategy that it necessitates. (See, for example, Gregory and Duran, 2001, or Wright and Cairns, 2017, who discuss these various interpretations.)

SCENARIOS

A *scenario* is a consistent set of statements about possible future events and trends and their dependencies. A scenario traces the *progression* of the present to the future through a descriptive *narrative*.

A critical feature of scenario construction is to include the interactions among the different events and trends. With many components to the scenario and even more interactions, scenario construction, as Schoemaker (1995) remarks, aims to "simplify an avalanche of data into a limited number of possible states."

In developing scenarios, various steps need to be undertaken (adapted from Schoemaker, 1995):

1. Define the scope of the study: its horizon, decision points, geographical range, etc.
2. Identify the major stakeholders and actors. Major stakeholders are those people, groups, or organizations that are affected by the events in the scenario; major actors are those who directly affect the outcomes of the scenario.
3. Identify the basic trends (e.g., demographic changes, medical advances).
4. Identify key uncertainties, four or five in the first instance.
5. Construct initial scenario themes.
6. Check for consistency and plausibility.
7. Develop initial scenarios aimed at identifying key themes. Name the scenarios (e.g., environmental degradation, government regulations) to capture the essence of the story.
8. Fill research gaps and model (or role-play) aspects of the sub-problems to check for consistency.
9. Revise the initial scenarios to focus on key decisions being contemplated.

To be of any value, a scenario must be directly relevant to the decisions being contemplated. A scenario-building exercise should include the major internal stakeholders and actors. It should be internally consistent and plausible. The range of scenarios also needs to capture the key uncertainties being faced in the future ("archetypal" uncertainties, in Schoemaker's words). Finally, a scenario should represent a relatively stable (rather than transient) state of the envisaged future; the aim in its construction is not to capture short-term fluctuations.

It's possible to think of scenarios as the extremes and midpoint of a multivariate distribution that describes the future. Scenario analysts, however, reject such an interpretation:

There are just too many possible stories, so any individual story has close to zero probability. Nevertheless, the aim in their construction is to provide a central (archetypal) view around which a series of less compelling stories cluster. Bunn and Salo (1993) have enlarged on some of these ideas and some of the difficulties of achieving a comprehensive range with sufficient detail. The use of scenarios for dealing with uncertainty is discussed in Section 13.3.3.

The step-by-step process of constructing such scenarios is challenging, so we will pass over the topic, apart from offering Goodwin and Wright (2014) as a reference. Nevertheless, there are some pitfalls that need attention. In particular, because scenarios are constructed primarily by individuals and groups using judgment (all too often unaided judgment), the pitfalls highlighted earlier in this chapter remain dangerous. Key issues include the need to overcome cognitive biases. This need suggests that explicit justification (perhaps through Delphi-like interactions) should be required. Also, outsiders should be involved because they are less prone to *group-think*. Further, judgments tend toward the optimistic, so more time should be spent on threatening rather than nonthreatening scenarios. Finally, we know that people give more attention to stories that are vividly told. But that doesn't make those stories more likely or more important to an organization, so Bunn and Salo suggest that the various scenarios should be "balanced" and similar in format.

■ Example 11.9: Scenarios to gain acceptance of forecasts vs. scenarios as forecasts — drilling for oil

The Mammoth Oil Company [MOC] is considering whether to set up an oil rig in a deep-water location in the Arctic. The rig is expected to operate with a 20-year life-span. Several issues have already been resolved: The presence of a large oil field in the area has been established, and the depth of the water (and hence the approximate costs of the platform and pipelines) is known. We will also assume that acceptable forecasts of long term increasing crude oil prices are available (Of course the effects of stable or declining prices could also be explored.). If a scenario is used for purposes of persuasion, the CEO of MOC might paint an optimistic picture for shareholders as he describes profits gushing up from the seafloor to enhance the value of their holdings. The CEO could use the information just listed in support of the claim of increased long-term profitability. In this version of the story, the scenario is clearly being used for persuasion.

Now consider a second version, wherein the CEO is more cautious about the prospects. He might lay the available information before the MOC board and initiate a brainstorming session concerning additional factors to be considered. Factors that might emerge include the following:

- The increasing probability of severe weather in the area arising from global warming and its potential for disrupting supplies or damaging the rig
- Risks of sabotage or terrorist attacks
- The possibility of an explosion, as happened to the BP rig in the Gulf of Mexico in 2010
- Uncertain growth in the world economy following the Great Recession of 2008–2009 with knock-on effects on oil prices (see Fig. 10D.1)
- Actions by OPEC and other leading suppliers
- The cost-effectiveness of alternative energy sources
- Enhanced or reduced government environmental regulation.

The risks attributable to these factors could be reduced by building a stronger rig, including security personnel on the rig, and using more advanced technology to control the flows of oil and natural gas. Each solution clearly carries a substantial cost, as do decisions not to take action. At this stage, the board would probably pass the assignment over to an internal planning group or a group of consultants to provide a more detailed analysis.

Each potential cost needs to be identified, including the loss of operating revenues, the cost of legal actions, and compensation payouts. Risks to the company's reputation are also important, but there are advantages to be gained from the experience with new technology. The next step is to consider how likely each of the possible events is to occur. Some of these assessments will be based upon hard data, but others will depend upon subjective assessments using the methods discussed earlier in this chapter. The expected costs and benefits of different policies can then be assessed across all consequences following on the decision. Finally, the planning group can report back to the board, which will make its decisions on the strategies to adopt and, ultimately, whether to go ahead with the drilling project. In this second approach, scenarios are used to expand understanding of the forecasting issues and to identify key sources of uncertainty. Further discussion is left to Minicase 11.1. ∎

As illustrated by the example, the focused use of scenarios can enable decision makers to identify issues and key uncertainties that might otherwise be overlooked. The scenario should offer a plausible story as to how the many uncertain factors and the decisions that actors in the story might take. Minicase 11.1 provides an opportunity to explore the difficulties of their construction. Used in a structured fashion, scenarios can reduce heuristics and biases. Even in more structured modeling frameworks, the consideration of different scenarios will often be a constructive way to examine alternatives on a "what if" basis, a topic we discuss further in Chapter 13.

11.6.1 Role-Playing

The essence of role-playing is a scenario that describes a conflict among two or more interested parties. The idea is perhaps best illustrated by an example, taken from Green (2002), who describes a situation that he labels "Nurses' Dispute." Although the material was designed for a laboratory exercise, it is based upon a real conflict and the description illustrates the nature of role-playing. Green writes (p. 327):

> The situation was a dispute over pay between nursing staff and management. The nurses went on strike angry that they were being offered a much lower pay increase than management had already given to intensive care nurses and junior doctors. A mediator was appointed by a government agency.

For his experiment, Green used five participants, who were assigned the roles of government mediator, management representative (two), and union representative (two). The participants were provided with a detailed description of the dispute and were told to adopt the role that they had been assigned for the duration of the exercise. The group then negotiated until it either reached a decision or ran out of time (the time allotted to a lab exercise).

Clearly, in a genuine role-playing activity, participants would be aware of their roles, but the experimental approach allowed multiple replicates with different subjects so that the value of the role-playing could be assessed. Green reports encouraging results on the effectiveness of role-playing in this and five other situations, when compared to unaided judgment and to judgment based on a structured economic modeling approach (game theory).

From this brief summary, it is evident that a scenario can be developed which outlines various options (e.g., go on strike, tender a better offer), but the role-playing adds the dynamic of interaction among the players. Either side in such negotiations (or even the mediator) could use a role-playing exercise to evaluate the effectiveness of different approaches prior to actually making the decision. The benefit of role-playing is that participants place themselves in the situation facing the various actors in the conflict and this avoids some of the biases that arise with a more hands-off, unstructured approach.

11.7 Judgmental Forecasting Principles

The application of well-founded judgment can be a problem in any discipline and especially in forecasting. The principles we summarize next are by no means a complete guide, but adherence to these ideas will help to avoid some of the most egregious errors that can arise. (For more detailed discussions of underlying principles of judgmental forecasting, see Harvey, 2001; Stewart, 2001; MacGregor, 2001; and Rowe and Wright, 2001, all in Armstrong, 2001. A particularly interesting discussion of judgment and decision making, often focused on forecasting is given by Nobel Prize winner Kahneman, 2011).

[11.1] Identify the decision to be made and the inputs required to make that decision.
We start out with the decision to be made and then work backward to determine what information is needed in order to make that decision. As we follow this reverse process, we should identify the key variables and how to measure them. Oftentimes, we may have to modify our objectives somewhat, because either the desired variable is not measurable or the information will not be available in time. At the end of this step, we should have a clear idea of the variables whose values we need to forecast.

[11.2] Different individuals should perform the planning and forecasting tasks.
As we observed in Example 11.3, the area of responsibility of an individual manager may bias his or her assessments. Forecasts are not targets!

[11.3] In asking forecasting related questions, of individual experts or groups, develop clear wording for the questions, consider alternative versions, and always pretest.
Consider the following two questions:

- In extreme circumstances in a labor dispute, should employees have the right to withdraw their labor?
- Should employers have legal means to terminate lengthy strikes that are damaging to the economy?

The two questions could both be interpreted as asking "Do you support employees' right to strike?" yet the responses may be very different. Even the two terms "withdraw their labor" and "strike" may evoke different responses. Thus, it is important to phrase questions clearly, to avoid emotive or ambiguous terms, and to pretest with individuals who are representative of those likely to respond, in order to ensure that the results will be meaningful.

[11.4] Use multiple experts chosen for their different perspectives on the forecasting task.

[11.5] Ask experts to justify their forecasts in writing.
If some forecasts differ markedly from others, statements that justify each forecast may help to reveal hitherto unknown facts or different perceptions. Such statements may or may not reduce differences, but the increased pool of common knowledge should improve the quality of the forecasts.

[11.6] Keep records of past forecasts and use them to provide feedback.
Past records can yield insights about both the events forecast and the performance of individual experts. This second feature is particularly useful when similar situations are examined on a continuing basis (e.g., new product evaluations or investment opportunities). Confidential feedback to individuals can also help them to calibrate their own forecasting performance.

[11.7] De-bias judgmental forecasts when there is a continuous record.
When past records have been kept, they can be used to compare the actual outcomes with the forecasts. A regression of the actual outcomes on the forecasts can be run to produce an adjusted judgmental forecast with all biases removed. See Appendix 11B.

[11.8] When using analogous situations to produce a forecast, determine the attributes with respect to which the situations can be compared so that a more objective identification of relevant analogies can be made.
Analogies for most situations are easily identified, but the various biases in such judgments make them prone to error. The likelihood of error can be lessened by formalizing the comparisons made to identify analogous situations.

[11.9] When carrying out a Delphi study, use between 5 and 20 experts who possess domain knowledge yet have heterogeneous backgrounds.
The number of panelists may be determined by organizational factors such as the need to represent all departments, but such influences should be minimized. If internal politics make the subject a "hot" issue, the facilitator should seek outside expertise. There are extra costs to a large panel as it leads to slower responses and a potentially higher drop-out rate.

[11.10] Continue Delphi polling until the responses show stability; generally, three structured rounds are enough.
After a while, panelists will tend to lock into a final answer, and they are unlikely to make appreciable changes to their forecasts. At that point, the exercise should end. Most new information tends to emerge between the first and second rounds, so the changes from the second to third rounds are modest, indicating that further shifts are likely to be slight. In practice, two rounds may be all that can be executed.

[11.11] In prediction markets, the electronic predictions must be understandable, be perceived as important by the participants, and involve a choice of specific actions.
These requirements are necessary both to justify the expense and to ensure that participants are committed to achieving a valid outcome (Gebert, 2008).

[11.12] The number of participants in prediction markets need not be large, but the participants must be active. In-company markets may benefit from their competitive aspect and from personal interaction among traders. Real incentives must be provided.
Overall, participants must be convinced of the value of the exercise and must receive some kind of payoff, financial or otherwise. Also, trading volume must be sufficient to ensure timely changes as new information becomes available (Gebert, 2008).

[11.13] Use decomposition when uncertainty is high or when the task is complex; otherwise use global or holistic estimation.
Complexity and high uncertainty often go hand in hand, although not necessarily so. As we illustrated in Example 11.8, more reliable estimates may be obtainable when the project is decomposed. Indeed, it may happen that reliable estimates are already available for some parts of the problem, thereby simplifying the overall task. By contrast, simpler issues are often dealt with more expeditiously by a single estimate rather than by formulating elaborate decompositions.

[11.14] Focus scenario construction on key strategic questions and uncertainties facing the organization between now and the horizon year (rather than on general questions that fail to delineate key uncertainties).

Many scenarios are used to assess the timing of future events, such as when electric-powered automobiles will capture 25 percent of the U.S. market. Careful wording is needed to ensure that everyone is considering the same issues.

[11.15] Use multiple scenarios to focus on uncertainties.

The progress of electric vehicles will depend upon relative fuel prices, technological issues relating to the development of batteries, the provision of recharging facilities, and government subsidies. Different scenarios should emphasize particular developments.

[11.16] Develop scenarios that characterize "extreme" archetypes aimed at capturing possible diverse futures.

Using archetypal cases allows the range of possibilities to be circumscribed so that resulting scenarios will be relevant to the context of the decision.

[11.17] In constructing scenarios, follow judgmental forecasting principles to overcome the biases that occur when experts forecast.

These principles assume that the scenarios are being used for forecasting purposes. If the intent is only to persuade, these ideas remain useful but may not be essential.

Summary

Judgmental forecasting is valuable when the nature of the question under discussion does not lend itself readily to quantitative assessments, when key data are not available, or when data are available only after unacceptable delays. A variety of judgmental methods exists, including the use of customer surveys, assessments by the sales force, and expert opinions. General aspects of judgmental forecasting were presented in Section 11.1 and several methods explored in Section 11.2. The role of "experts" was critically discussed as they form an important constituent of many forecasting approaches, But it should be remembered that these methods may benefit from linkage with more quantitative analyses, a topic to which we return in the forthcoming chapters.

In Section 11.3, we explored the Delphi method in detail and found that it avoids many of the problems inherent in other techniques and is increasingly accessible now that appropriate software is available. An approach that has generated increasing interest recently is the use of (electronic) prediction markets, discussed in Section 11.4. Such markets offers an alternative way of combining judgments where participating forecasters are motivated to make an unbiased prediction. Judgmental methods were then used in Section 11.5 to provide assessments of uncertainty with the decomposition of the forecasting problem, one of the key methods to improve accuracy. One of the difficulties facing the forecaster is the identification of all the relevant issues, and we briefly examined the use of scenarios for this purpose in Section 11.6. A number of underlying principles for judgmental forecasting were laid out in Section 11.7. Our key lesson to be learned from this discussion of judgmental forecasting is that, in common with quantitative methods, a structured approach to its use delivers substantial benefits. And remember, judgment plays an often unanalyzed but important role in all forecasting, including the quantitative.

Exercises

11.1 What is your forecast for the high temperature tomorrow in the area where you currently reside, given your current state of knowledge? What limits would you place on that value, with a view to being correct 80 percent of the time; that is, you would tend to undershoot one day in ten and overshoot one day in ten. Add to your database progressively: today's high, the seasonal high temperature, and tomorrow's forecast. Then see how your forecast changes with each new piece of information.

11.2 Examine Table 2.8 to see how close forecasts tend to be to actual high temperatures (at least in Washington, DC, in winter). Modify your probability limits in light of this information.

11.3 Repeat Exercises 11.1 and 11.2 for ten days, and see whether you can do better than the meteorologist. How do you measure relative performance?

11.4 Repeat Exercises 11.1 and 11.2 for a major stock (or index) for ten days, and see whether you can outperform the simple random walk (the forecast for tomorrow's closing price is today's closing price). We recommend you read the financial pages of the *Wall Street Journal* or *The Financial Times*.

11.5 Consider predicting the results of the most recent presidential election, examine the list of attributes in Example 11.4, and add any attributes you think are important that have been missed. Estimate the weight associated with the new list of attributes (weights to add to 100 percent), and complete the missing entries for the earlier elections (justifying your estimates). Which of the past elections looks most similar to the latest election, and does this similarity successfully predict the outcome of the latest election? If not, what factors made the difference? Looking to some future election, make a prediction of the outcome. (*Hint:* Consider *www.historycentral.com/elections.*) Non-U.S. readers may prefer to consider their own national elections.

11.6 *[Group project]* Choose a high-technology consumer products (e.g., Instagram, Virtual Reality Personal Headsets, Electric cars). What attributes would you consider important in rating their similarity to their precursor generations in the context of forecasting their uptake by the China, Italy, UK, and U.S. populations? Which attribute do you regard as the most important? Assign weights (adding to 100 percent) to each of the attributes you have identified.

11.7 The numbers of medals won by the United States and by China in the summer Olympics from 1984 through 2016 are shown in the following table:

Year	United States			China			Venue
	Gold	Silver	Bronze	Gold	Silver	Bronze	
1984	83	61	30	15	8	9	Los Angeles (Russia boycotted)
1988	36	31	27	5	11	12	Seoul
1992	37	34	37	16	22	16	Barcelona
1996	44	32	25	16	22	12	Atlanta
2000	36	24	32	28	16	15	Sydney
2004	35	39	27	32	17	14	Athens
2008	36	38	36	51	21	28	Beijing
2012	46	28	29	38	29	21	London
2016	46	37	38	26	18	26	Rio (Many Russian athletes banned)

What are your estimates of the medal counts for the next Olympic Games? Expand the table to include the information on your home county's medal count and estimate the results for the next games.

11.8 The Delphi method is often illustrated by *almanac event* — that is, items which are known facts, but likely to be unknown to the panel. Cover the information in the footnote[8] at the bottom of the page so that you can add items one at a time. Update your answer to the following question, taking into account one additional piece of information each time (Do not use an internet search):

Question A: Which president and in what month and year signed into law the bill authorizing the construction of the U.S. Interstate highway system?

Question B: In what month and in what year between which warring countries did the Charge of the Light Brigade take place?

Provide both point estimates and upper and lower 10 percent points for each of "month" and "year." For reference, the answer appears at the end of this chapter. Do you think that "almanac events" provide a useful test ground for evaluating the effectiveness of judgmental forecasting procedures?

11.9 In a survey a group of economists was asked to predict the number of new jobs expected in the U.S. economy in the next month. How would you summarize the results?

Number of Jobs Gained (in thousands)	Number of Economists
Less than 100	2
101 to 125	8
126 to 150	6
151 to 175	2
176 to 200	1
201 to 225	6
226 to 250	9
241 to 275	4
276 or more	2

Examine the web site for the Survey of Professional Forecasters: *https://www.philadelphiafed.org/research-and-data/real-time-center/survey-of-professional-forecasters/* for the latest quarter. What further information would you regard as valuable as a chief executive in (i) making a short-term financial investment, (ii) an expansion of manufacturing capability with a horizon of 3 years?

11.10 A group of seven experts was asked to forecast the percentage growth in *GDP* over the next 12 months, using the Delphi approach. At the end of each round, they were asked to justify their forecasts and to provide any additional comments they could

---

8 In successive rounds, use the following information for question A:
   Round 2: Interstate highways were developed in part as a defense for the US in times of war.
   Round 3: Elvis Presley was number one in the pop charts in the same year.
   Round 4: Tom Watson, founder of IBM died this same month.

   For question B, use the following items:
   Round 2: Queen Victoria was the reigning British monarch.
   Round 3: It took place during the Crimean War which ended in 1856.
   Round 4: The Crimean harvest season was just ending.

think of. Four rounds of forecasts were generated, and the results are shown in the following table:

Expert	Round 1	Round 2	Round 3	Round 4
Alfred	1.8	2.2	2.1	2.1
Betty	2.5	2.5	2.5	2.5
Charles	2.7	3.0	2.9	3.0
Doug	2.9	2.9	2.9	2.9
Elaine	3.2	3.3	3.2	3.2
Freda	3.7	3.5	No response	No response
George	4.2	No response	3.4	No response

a. Summarize the results for each round by calculating the median, mean, range, and standard deviation.

b. Calculate the round-by-round changes made by each panelist (round 2 value minus round 1 value, etc.), and summarize the changes, using the same measures as in part (a).

c. After how many rounds would you have stopped, or would you continue? Why?

11.11 *[Group project]* Using the software described in Appendix 11A or similar software, conduct a Delphi analysis to generate forecasts for an agreed-upon event. One person should act as group administrator and the others as panelists. Go through three rounds and examine the extent to which your forecasts converge.

Minicase 11.1

Working as a group consider Example 11.9, develop two scenarios, one optimistic as far as Mammoth, the oil exploration company is concerned and one pessimistic. What additional information would be helpful in refining the scenarios to make them more plausible? Could role-playing prove useful in making the "stories" more convincing? Reflect with your group members on what have learnt in trying to develop these scenarios?

References

Anderson, D. R., Sweeney, D. J., and Williams, T. A. (2011). *Statistics for Business and Economics*, 11th ed. Mason, OH: South-Western.

Armstrong, J. S. (ed.) (2001). *Principles of Forecasting: A Handbook for Researchers and Practitioners*. Boston and Dordrecht: Kluwer.

Armstrong, J. S. (2006). How to make better forecasts and decisions: Avoid face-to-face meetings. *Foresight*, 5, 3–8.

Bandyopadhyay, S. P., Brown, L. D., and Richardson, G. D. (1995). Analysts' use of earnings forecasts in predicting stock returns: Forecast horizon effects. *International Journal of Forecasting*, 11, 429–45.

Berg, J. E., Nelson, F. D., and Rietz, T. A. (2008). Prediction market accuracy in the long run. *International Journal of Forecasting*, 24, 285–300.

Brier, G. W. (1950). Verification of Forecasts Expressed in Terms of Probability. *Monthly Weather Review*, 78: 1–3.

Buckley, P. (2016). Harnessing the wisdom of crowds: Decision spaces for prediction markets. *Business Horizons*, 59, 85–94.

Bunn, D. W., and Salo, A. A. (1993). Forecasting with scenarios. *European Journal of Operational Research*, 68 (3), 291–303.

Chase, C. W. (2016). *Next Generation Demand Management: People, Process, Analytics and Technology*. Hoboken, NJ: Wiley.

Dalrymple, D. J. (1987). Sales forecasting practices: Results from a United States survey. *International Journal of Forecasting*, 3, 379–391.

Deschamps, E. A. (2005). Six steps to overcome bias in the forecast process. *Foresight*, 2, 6–11.

Fildes, R., and Goodwin, P. (2007). Good and bad judgment in forecasting: Lessons from four companies. *Foresight*, 8, 5–10.

Galbraith, C. S., and Merrill, G. B. (1996). The politics of forecasting: Managing the truth. *California Management Review*, 38, 29–3.

Gaur, V., Kesavan, S., Raman, A., and Fisher, M. L. (2007). Estimating demand uncertainty using judgmental forecasts. *Manufacturing & Service Operations Management*, 9, 480–491.

Gebert, C. (2008). Prediction markets: A guide to practical adoption in the pharmaceutical industry. *Foresight*, 9, 25–29.

Goldstein, D. G., and Gigerenzer, G. (2009). Fast and frugal forecasting. *International Journal of Forecasting*, 25 (4), 760–772.

Goodwin, P. (1996). Statistical correction of judgmental point forecasts and decisions. *Omega: International Journal of Management Science*, 24, 551–559.

Goodwin, P., Dyussekeneva, K., and Meeran, S. (2013). The use of analogies in forecasting the annual sales of new electronics products. *IMA Journal of Management Mathematics*, 24, 407–422.

Goodwin, P., and Wright, G. (2014). *Decision Analysis for Management Judgment*, 5th ed. Chichester, U.K.: Wiley.

Graefe, A., and Armstrong, J. S. (2011). Comparing face-to-face meetings, nominal groups, Delphi and prediction markets on an estimation task. *International Journal of Forecasting*, 27 (1), 183–195.

Graefe, A., Armstrong, J. S., Jones, R. J., Jr., and Cuzan, A. G. (2014). Combining forecasts: An application to elections. *International Journal of Forecasting*, 30, 43–54.

Green, K. C. (2002). Forecasting decisions in conflict situations: A comparison of game theory, role-playing and unaided judgment. *International Journal of Forecasting*, 18, 321–344.

Green, K. C., and Armstrong, J. S. (2007). Structured analogies for forecasting. *International Journal of Forecasting*, 23, 365–376.

Green, K., Armstrong, J. S., and Graefe, A. (2007). Methods to elicit forecasts from groups: Delphi and prediction markets compared. *Foresight*, 8, 17–20.

Gregory, W L., and Duran, A. (2001). Scenarios and acceptance of forecasts. In J. S. Armstrong (ed.), *Principles of Forecasting: A Handbook for Researchers and Practitioners*. Boston and Dordrecht: Kluwer, pp. 519–540.

Harvey, N. (2001). Improving judgment in forecasting. In J. S. Armstrong (ed.), *Principles of Forecasting: A Handbook for Researchers and Practitioners*. Boston and Dordrecht: Kluwer, pp. 59–80.

Kahneman, D. (2011). *Thinking, Fast and Slow*: Macmillan.

Kent, S. (1994). Sherman Kent and the Board of National Estimates: Collected Essays. History Staff, Center for the Study of Intelligence, Central Intelligence Agency.

Lawrence, M., Goodwin, P., O'Connor, M., and Onkal, D. (2006). Judgmental forecasting: A review of progress over the last 25 years. *International Journal of Forecasting*, 22, 493–518.

MacGregor, D. G. (2001). Decomposition for judgmental forecasting and estimation. In J. S. Armstrong (ed.), *Principles of Forecasting: A Handbook for Researchers and Practitioners*. Boston and Dordrecht: Kluwer, pp. 107–123.

McCarthy, T. M., Davis, D. F., Golicic, S. L., and Mentzer, J. T. (2006). The evolution of sales forecasting management: A 20-year longitudinal study of forecasting practices. *Journal of Forecasting*, 25, 303–324.

Meade, N. (2000). Evidence for the selection of forecasting methods. *Journal of Forecasting*, 19 (6), 515–535.

Miles, J. (2008). A primer on prediction markets. *Foresight*, 9, 33–35.

Morwitz, V. G. (2001). Methods for forecasting from intentions data. In J. S. Armstrong (ed.), *Principles of Forecasting: A Handbook for Researchers and Practitioners*. Boston and Dordrecht: Kluwer, pp. 33–56.

O'Connor, M. (2006). Commentary: Forecasting meetings are really not about forecasting. *Foresight*, 5, 9–10.

O'Leary, D. E. (2017). Crowd performance in prediction of the World Cup 2014. *European Journal of Operational Research*, 260, 715–724.

Rowe, G. (2007). A guide to Delphi. *Foresight*, 8, 11–16.

Rowe, G., and Wright, G. (2001). Expert opinions in forecasting: The role of the Delphi technique. In J. S. Armstrong (ed.), *Principles of Forecasting: A Handbook for Researchers and Practitioners*. Boston and Dordrecht: Kluwer, pp. 125–144.

Sanders, N. R. (2005). When and How to Judgmentally Adjust Statistical Forecasts. *Foresight*, 1, 5–7.

Sanders, N. R., and Manrodt, K. B. (1994). Forecasting practices in U.S. corporations: Survey results. *Interfaces*, 24, 92–100.

Schoemaker, P. J. H. (1995). Scenario planning: A tool for strategic thinking. *Sloan Management Review*, 36 (2), 25–40.

Schoemaker, P. J. H., and Tetlock, P. E. (2016). Superforecasting: How to Upgrade Your Company's Judgment. *Harvard Business Review*, 94, 73–+.

Stekler, H. O., Sendor, D., and Verlander, R. (2010). Issues in sports forecasting. *International Journal of Forecasting*, 26, 606–621.

Stewart, D. W., and Shamdasani, P. N. (2015). *Focus Groups: Theory and Practice* (Vol. 20): Sage.

Stewart, T. R. (2001). Improving reliability of judgmental forecasts. In J. S. Armstrong (ed.), *Principles of Forecasting: A Handbook for Researchers and Practitioners*. Boston and Dordrecht: Kluwer, pp. 81–106.

Tetlock, P. E. (2005). *Expert Political Judgment: How Good Is It? How Can We Know?* Princeton, NJ: Princeton University Press.

Tetlock, P., and Gardner, D. (2016). *Superforecasting: The Art and Science of Prediction*. Random House.

Tversky, A., and Kahneman, D. (1974). Judgment under uncertainty: Heuristics and biases. *Science*, 185, 1124–1131.

Wright, G., and Cairns, G. (2017). *Scenario Thinking* (2nd ed.). Palgrave, Macmillan.

Appendix 11A Delphi Software

An interactive freeware program for a Delphi analysis, named Delphi Decision Aid, is available at *www.forecastingprinciples.com*. Select *Software* and then *Delphi*. We may use this software to specify the question of interest and to identify the expert panel. E-mails are then sent automatically to each panel member, indicating the name of the study, the question, the name of the study administrator (facilitator), and how to post an electronic response. The software also provides for subjective assessments of prediction intervals. Once the replies have been received by the due date, the data are analyzed. After an evaluation of the results, the facilitator may request an update from panel members, with the option to provide feedback from the previous round. Panelists might also be asked to justify earlier responses.

This implementation of the Delphi technique has a number of advantages: Anonymity is protected, a diverse panel can be assembled and may respond asynchronously, and overall costs are low because the panel does not have to be physically assembled. At the forecasting stage, the aim is to maximize agreement and understanding of the key assumptions. Based on the Delphi forecasts there can then be a debate on possible policy options.

Appendix 11B Debiasing Forecasts

A forecast is said to be biased if, in the regression:

$$Y_t - F_t = \alpha + \beta F_t + \varepsilon_t,$$

α and β are non-zero. With α non-zero it is said to be *mean biased* while with β non-zero the forecasts show *regression bias*. To remove bias, the above regression is estimated and the forecasts F_t revised to:

$$F_t^* = F_t + (\hat{\alpha} + \hat{\beta} F_t). \tag{11A.1}$$

Figure 11B.1 Bias in Forecasts

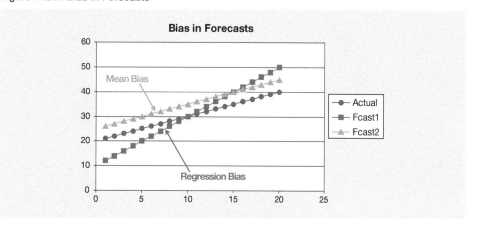

Of course, the bias can only be removed on the in-sample data leaving the possibility that the revised forecasts according to equation (11A.1) would remain biased out-of-sample. The debiasing has the effect of decreasing the *RMSE* of the forecasts.

A second aspect of evaluating a set of judgmental forecasts is to check that they have efficiently used available information. Suppose X_t is available to the forecaster at time $t-h$, h being the lead time. Then if the forecaster had used all the available information to ensure the forecast was as accurate as possible, a regression of the forecast error on X_t should lead to β being zero (apart from random variation).

$$Y_t - F_t = \alpha + \beta X_t + \varepsilon_t.$$

As in the case of adjusting for bias, the forecasts F can be adjusted in-sample to improve the *RMSE* accuracy. The original forecast F_t is said to be inefficient with regard to the information, X_t.

Answers to Exercise 11.8

Question A: U.S. Interstate construction. June 1956.

Question B: Charge of the Light Brigade. October 1854.

CHAPTER 12

Putting Forecasting Methods to Work

*Topics marked with an * are advanced and may be omitted for more introductory courses.*

Table of Contents

Production is not the application of tools to materials, but logic to work.

— Peter F. Drucker

Introduction

Forecasting applications are many and are implemented in a wide variety of organizational settings. In this chapter, we focus on how the methods we have introduced can be put to work. First, in Section 12.1, we discuss a problem that is common to any organization wishing to appraise its current forecasting methods with a view to improving those methods. We seek also to establish how such an appraisal is best carried out. Most organizations employ a forecasting support system to produce their forecasts. (Such a system is computer-based and consists of data, user interventions, and forecasting methods.) Next, in Section 12.2, we examine the characteristics of the system and how users interact with it. Then, in Section 12.3, we examine perhaps the most common applications area for quantitative forecasting methods: forecasting to support operations in manufacturing, services, government, and retail. The key features here are that the forecasts are regularly updated and that the data are readily available. Of course, judgment is also used in arriving at the final forecasts. Next, in Section 12.4 we are concerned with marketing, where there is a requirement for longer term forecasts that includes various features of the market, such as whether the product is new, the competition the product faces, and the effects of various marketing drivers, such as price. Then, Section 12.5 considers how the methods we have introduced can be applied to the choices made by individuals to predict their behavior — in particular, their behavior as consumers. We round out the chapter with a discussion of other key areas in which quantitative methods are applied, such as macroeconomic forecasting. As with Chapters 10 and 11, we include many references in order to justify or amplify our argument so that the methods we describe can be more easily operationalized by the reader.

12.1 Evaluating a Forecasting Process

In earlier chapters, we introduced a variety of different forecasting methods, both simple and complex (e.g., simple exponential smoothing models, in contrast to regression models or neural networks). How should a forecasting manager with the responsibility of maintaining and developing a forecasting process appraise its current success and its potential for improvement? To answer this question, we need to define the criteria to be used in judging success: It can't be just a question of forecasting accuracy, which we've focused on so far. Typically, the criteria will be organization specific and will certainly include accuracy, but also to be taken into account are the costs and resources needed, the availability of the data, and the speed with which the forecasts are produced. A critical issue is the impact on the organization's bottom line, be it profit, service level, etc. In addition, users often require their forecasts to be produced by a process that they understand and that captures the key features of the activity system being modeled, such as its ability to include the effects of promotional activities and special events. In sum, we need to consider all the components of PIVASE, as defined in Chapter 1.

Forecasts often have a motivational element to them. For example, when a sales force is asked to produce forecasts of its expected sales, before a figure is offered back to the head office, it will certainly be examined for its effect on the target sales that might be set by senior management and on any resulting bonuses. Similarly, the sales forecasts need to be developed prior to the annual budget and must remain distinct from budgeted figures through the year. Whereas the budgeted financial figures depend critically on sales (and associated costs), the regularly updated forecasts through the year should reflect *current* market conditions and may well be incompatible with a budget set months earlier. Budgets also tend to have a motivational aspect to them that conflicts with our concept of a forecast as our best estimate of the most likely (or expected) outcome. In appraising the forecasting process, the interaction between setting targets and budgeting within an organizational setting may lead to distorted "best estimates" that are biased, less accurate forecasts, and result in poor decisions (Galbraith and Merrill, 1996). This topic is discussed in detail in Section 13.2.3. However, it is important to put in a proviso here: In this book, we assume that the aim of forecasting is accuracy (and authors of similar books assume the same thing). However, in some forecasting situations, the aim may well be to affect policy or to motivate, when scenarios might be more effective (Section 11.6). In that case, accuracy would be subservient to these other organizational demands.

One popular route to appraising forecasting performance is through benchmarking studies, whereby an organization compares its practices with those of its peers. The Institute of Business Forecasting and Planning (*www.ibf.org*) regularly conducts surveys of attendees at the organization's training workshops. However, such benchmarks have to be accepted with a large grain of salt because they have many problems, as described by Kolassa (2008). For instance, their samples often are small and not random within any given sector, and the answers obtained from them are not based directly on empirical data and are probably biased. But if such surveys are to be distrusted, and yet benchmarking is desirable, what is the alternative? In the next section, we discuss how to carry out a benchmarking study through a so-called forecasting competition. The aim of such a competition is to use an organization's own data to compare various methods with the organization's current approach. This strategy focuses effectively on the key benchmarking question "How are we doing?" Answering this question also points a way forward toward an improved forecasting system.

Forecasting competitions are most often used in organizations that are considering replacing their current forecasting software or forecasting process. An organization seeking to embark on changes will wish to ensure that the replacement software system is at least as good as the current system in terms of forecasting accuracy.

In the next section, we will focus on just this one aspect of the appraisal: the comparison of forecasting accuracy. However, there are many other aspects that need to be taken into account, and these are discussed later, in Section 12.2.

12.1.1 Evaluating Forecasting Methods: Forecasting Competitions

Most manufacturing and retailing companies need to forecast the sales they expect of the many hundreds, if not thousands, of products they sell. Some companies, such as electricity suppliers or call center operators, focus on just the small number of variables that interest them. For government departments, there is a similar limited forecasting need, although local, regional, and national forecasts of a variable such as unemployment benefit claimants often are required. Periodically, the forecaster needs to evaluate the forecasting accuracy of the chosen method over a number of series and to compare the method with plausible alternatives. As noted earlier, the need is most acute when a new forecasting system or process is being considered.

Carrying out the Evaluation

Step 1: Specify the population of time series to be considered. For a supermarket, for example, this population could include the products sold (in stock keeping units, or SKUs — the most detailed information about a product, including brand, pack size, packaging, and more) in a number of product categories, such as fresh vegetables, beer and lagers, cleaning products, and health care. We may then need to choose a sample from various important subpopulations or segments (the whole population being too large to analyze fully in a cost-effective manner).

Step 2: Define the forecasting task precisely. We can refer back to the PIVASE framework introduced in Chapter 1. The specification includes the information that is available in producing the forecasts, whether human intervention is permitted (or whether the method should be automatic), the forecast horizon(s), whether the method's parameters (such as the smoothing parameter) are reestimated, and the frequency with which the forecasts are updated. Also, we need to consider the estimated value of improved accuracy.

Step 3: Specify the forecasting methods to be considered. The range of methods should include a standard benchmark such as damped trend smoothing (discussed in Section 3.5), as well as a naïve method (e.g., random walk). If the data may be seasonal, a simple seasonal benchmark based on decomposition (Chapter 4) should be included. Although some of the methods used in a competition might not be practical for the organization (i.e., they may be too complex), including them in the competition may give some insight into the level of improvement possible.

Step 4: Define the measures of performance to be used in the evaluation. These measures should correspond as closely as possible to those used by the organization (including measures of profitability or service level) and should incorporate both standard measures and measures that are organization specific. Sometimes however, organizational measures in use are flawed (e.g., overly influenced by outliers or they can be manipulated) so using a robust measure such as Relative Mean Absolute Error (*RelMAE*) should be also included (see Section 2.7).

Step 5: Specify the data to be used in parameterizing the methods under consideration (the fit, or in-sample, data), as well as the data to be used in the out-of-sample (or hold-out) evaluation.

Step 6: Calculate the error measures derived from the various forecasting methods for the sub-populations of time series in the study. We may then identify the best methods and the relative importance of choosing between methods rather than sticking with the benchmark.

We have already introduced various measures of accuracy in Section 2.7; in particular, mean error (*ME*) and mean percentage error (*MPE*) as measures of bias, and mean absolute error (*MAE*) and mean absolute percentage error (*MAPE*) as measures of accuracy. When we wish to measure performance across a population (or sample), we need to decide what weight to give to each of the series in the sample. Table 12.1 illustrates the problem; in the table, we examine monthly electricity consumption by two households (extending the data in *Electricity.xlsx*, analyzed in Table 2.11).

Two forecasting methods — Smooth and Random Walk — have been used to produce forecasts of the two time series on household electricity consumption. In practice, there are often many more. In household 1, Smooth outperforms Random Walk, whether measured by *MAE* or *MAPE*. For household 2, Random Walk is the consistent winner. When the two measures are averaged across households, they give conflicting results. The conflict arises because of the difference in the mean consumption level of the two households and, consequently, the difference in scale of the *MAE*: 163 compared with 6.6. Thus, household 1 counts much more in the overall comparison when the *MAE* is used. However, when *MAPE* is the chosen error measure, the two households are of almost equal importance and Random Walk is identified as the better forecasting method (although the differences are small). The electric utility company would want to use *MAE* when planning production, but might prefer *MAPE* when forecasting consumption by individual customers. (Many companies charge customers monthly on the basis of estimated consumption, but check meters only every two or three months.)

Table 12.1 Comparing Two Forecasting Methods for Two Time Series

| | Household 1 Household Mean = 939.2 | | Household 2 Household Mean = 46.3 | | Overall Overall Mean = 492.7 | |
	Smooth	Random Walk	Smooth	Random Walk	Smooth	Random Walk
Mean Error (ME)	−160.0	−149.0	2.6	0.2	−78.7	−74.5
MPE	−18.7	−17.3	3.7	−0.4	−7.4	−8.9
MAE	163.3	169.2	6.6	5.2	85.0	87.2
MAPE	19.1	19.8	13.8	11.1	16.4	15.5

Data: Competition.xlsx

This simple example, of course, generalizes: When error measures are aggregated across time series, the scale of the series might matter, implicitly affecting the weighting given to each series. So, how should a forecaster choose between conflicting measures? The differences can be substantial. In Step 4, in which we define a forecasting competition, we underlined the need to choose a measure that fits an organization's requirements such as profit or service level. In the preceding example, with the aim of forecasting overall electricity consumption, the *MAE* (or the *RMSE*) would be the more appropriate measure because the costs of generation or the marginal profit derived from selling electricity are proportional to the level of consumption. If our aim is to choose between a benchmark method and an alternative, *RelMAE* is the best choice.

Other approaches can be used to weight the individual error measures, such as weighting by product profit margin. The danger is that a forecasting method will be chosen that suits only a few products (or time series). The remedy is to segment the time series into more homogeneous subgroups and choose a (potentially different) method for each separate group (we explore this idea more fully in Section 13.1.5). As large a sample of series as is practical should be used in evaluating performance, particularly when the population being examined has to be segmented into many important subgroups.

In general, in carrying out a forecasting competition, a variety of error measures should be used. They should all conform to the requirements of a reliable and valid error measure. Key criteria to consider are the following:

  i. Sensitivity to outliers in the errors (or relative errors)

   ✓ *RMSE* is based on squared errors and therefore accentuates extreme outlying errors.

 ii. Sensitivity to performance on individual series

   ✓ *MAE* can be dominated by large errors because the data values are large, as are those in Table 12.1.

   ✓ *MAPE* can be affected by series in which the actual value is close to zero.

iii. Effect of scale

   ✓ *MAPE* and percentage errors are scale-independent.

   ✓ Relative error measures, which measure the performance of one method relative to another, are scale-independent (for example, *RelMAE*; see Section 2.7).

iv. The measure's interpretability

✓ *RMSE* is not easily interpretable unless it is translated into inventory holding. Most forecasters find that *MAPE* conveys their understanding of accuracy, although relative error measures are also easily interpretable with regard to the extent to which one method is better than another.

A number of major forecasting competitions have been described in the research literature. Notable among them are those discussed by Newbold and Granger (1974), Makridakis and Hibon (1979), and the M1 and M3 Competitions (Makridakis *et al.*, 1982; Makridakis and Hibon, 2000). All these publications have stimulated sometimes critical commentary; see, for example, the M3 Competition based on 3000 time series and 24 methods.[1] According to Fildes, Hibon, Makridakis, and Meade (1998), key conclusions coming out of this research are as follows:

a. Statistically sophisticated or complex methods do not typically produce more accurate forecasts than simpler ones.

b. The rankings of the performance of the various methods vary with the error measures used.

c. The relative performance of the various methods depends upon the length of the forecasting horizon.

d. The characteristics of the data series are important factors in determining relative performance between methods; therefore, a method designed to capture the particular characteristics of a forecasting situation may well outperform standard benchmarks.

e. The sampling variability of performance measures renders comparisons based on a single time series and a single forecast origin unreliable; thus, comparisons based on multiple time series and on multiple forecast origins are recommended.

In addition, the damped trend method of exponential smoothing (see Section 3.5) has proved to be a benchmark that is very hard to beat, so a forecaster using only time series data should always compare performances with a damped trend (as well as a naïve) benchmark. These principles for carrying out a forecasting competition and the general findings just presented suggest that a new method should be adopted (or an established method continued in use) only if, in a forecasting competition that includes standard benchmarks, its performance is no worse than the benchmarks' performance when evaluated across a wide range of series and appropriate error measures. The same principles apply in appraising a new causal method. Here, the forecaster should take care to ensure that the same data set is used in building and evaluating each model.

However, there is an alternative approach to selecting a forecasting method; we consider this approach in the next section.

12.1.2 Combining Forecasting Methods or Choosing among Methods

Suppose we have developed two separate forecasting methods, each of which delivers one-step-ahead forecasts of Y_t, which we denote F_{1t} and F_{2t}. We are faced with a choice: do we select one method to use for our data series or, instead of trying to decide which of the two methods is better, should we produce a combined forecast? The simplest method of combining the two forecasts for Y_t is by averaging the two individual forecasts:

$$F_t = 0.5F_{1t} + 0.5F_{2t}. \tag{12.1}$$

---

1 The discussion of the M3 Competition appears in the *International Journal of Forecasting*, 2001,

More generally, we can try to weight the forecasts optimally so that the combined forecast produces the best forecast of Y_t by using least squares regression to estimate the weight w in the formula

$$F_t = wF_{1t} + (1 - w)F_{2t}. \tag{12.2}$$

When there are more than two forecasts available, the formulas generalize to

$$F_t = average(F_{1t}, F_{2t}, ..., F_{Kt})$$

and

$$F_t = w_1F_{1t} + w_2F_{2t} + ... + w_KF_{Kt},$$

where it is sometimes assumed that

$$\sum_{i=1}^{K} w_i = 1.$$

In addition, some forecasters prefer to restrict attention to nonnegative weights, an approach that has some intuitive appeal.[2]

■ Example 12.1: Combining forecasts

Table 12.2 (A and B) shows four sets of out-of-sample forecasts of call center data: a random-walk benchmark (*RW*), an exponentially smoothed forecast (*Smooth*), a causal model (*Causal*), and the company's judgmental forecast (*Company*). The table shows (some of) the raw data included in spreadsheet *Combination.xlsx* and some of the corresponding error statistics.

Table 12.2(A) The Combination of Forecasts Compared
(*Absolute percentage error statistics for four forecasting methods*)

Period	Actual	Forecasts from the Forecast Methods				Absolute Percentage Error			
		RW	Smooth	Causal	Company	RW	Smooth	Causal	Company
1	32.25	25.00	35.00	44.77	30.00	22.48	8.53	38.83	6.97
2	36.62	32.25	34.45	46.70	34.45	11.93	5.92	27.55	8.92
3	50.52	36.62	34.88	48.98	60.81	27.52	30.95	3.04	20.37
4	43.43	50.52	38.01	46.98	44.26	16.32	12.48	8.19	1.92
.									
.									
18	40.38	42.90	50.45	48.39	51.00	6.24	24.94	19.83	26.30
19	50.48	40.38	48.4	54.35	44.41	20.01	4.05	7.66	12.03
20	47.70	50.48		53.00	50.92	5.84	2.41	11.10	6.75
					MAPE	11.29	12.27	9.97	11.51
					MdAPE	9.34	12.98	7.13	8.80

Data: Combination.xlsx

---

2 As for the creation of neural network ensemble forecasts, in section 10.4, when there are several forecasts available, using the median to combine them, instead of the average, can perform very well, as it eliminates the impact of potentially extreme forecasts. This has been validated for the all methods of forecasting we have discussed (see Barrow and Kourentzes, 2016).

Table 12.2(B) The Combination of Forecasts Compared
(Absolute percentage error statistics for the forecast combinations)

Period	Absolute Percentage Errors Combination			
	RW+Smooth	RW+Causal	RW+Company	All
1	6.97	8.18	14.72	4.48
2	8.92	7.81	10.42	0.20
3	29.23	15.28	3.58	10.29
4	1.92	12.26	9.12	3.49
.				
.				
18	15.59	13.04	16.27	19.33
19	12.03	6.18	16.02	7.11
20	4.12	8.47	6.30	6.53
MAPE	10.37	7.30	9.61	7.02
MdAPE	8.80	6.99	9.13	6.57

Data: Combination.xlsx

Of the four individual methods, Causal performed best (9.97 percent *MAPE*). Combining by simple averaging improves the performance when the random walk (*RW*) is combined with the causal forecasting model (*RW + Causal*), but also when it is combined with the quite inaccurate company forecasts. However, combining all four methods outperforms not only all of the individual methods, but also the paired combinations. The improvement from 7.30 percent down to 7.02 percent in *MAPE* (and also in *MdAPE*) and this improvement is probably worth the extra effort. ∎

Equation (12.2) for combining unequally weighted forecasts can be transformed to

$$Y_t - F_{2t} = w(F_{1t} - F_{2t}). \tag{12.3}$$

To estimate the unknown weight parameter w, the preceding regression is run with dependent variable $Y_t - F_{2t}$; note the constant term is suppressed. Using the regression estimate for w, however, does not improve the results much at all in the foregoing example — a finding of other researchers as well (see Exercise 12.1).

In general, the combination of a set of forecasts, based on a simple weighting scheme such as equal weights, often produces more accurate forecasts than trying to select the best individual method, series by series. This conclusion has been reached in many studies, including the competitions discussed in the previous section, as well as the many studies summarized by Clemen (1989), Armstrong (2001a) and Graefe, Armstrong, Jones and Cuzán (2014). But why should combining methods often work well when, surely, identifying the correct method would prove more accurate? The fundamental reason that combining is so effective is that all methods (and forecasts) suffer from deficiencies. Statistical approaches and judgmental approaches are all based on simplified understandings of the system being forecast, with nonlinearities and variables omitted. Even if a method is satisfactory for a period of time, the market or the economy will change, and then the method and its parameters become suboptimal. Each of the alternative methods is likely to contain some information that is helpful in improving the overall combined forecast. In addition, there is an element of insurance to using a number of methods, so that when market circumstances change, one method takes over from another as offering the best forecasts. Ord (1988) provides a simple model that explains this effect.

Intuitively, the combination will work best when the error from one method is counterbalanced by the error from another; in statistical terms, they are negatively correlated. If the errors are positively correlated, they accumulate, which is less helpful. Typically, errors from similar methods are positively correlated while errors from very different approaches have a low or even a negative correlation. Thus, an extrapolative method that exploits the autocorrelation structure in the time series can best be combined with a causal model (that includes some of the key explanatory variables) or managerial judgment. By including managerial judgment, the combination may have access to new information that could not have formed a part of the historical data. In general, however, forecast errors from different sources tend to be positively correlated, even when different methods are used (they tend to make the same mistakes), so the benefits that may be achieved from combining are sometimes limited.

In most practical situations, only a limited number of forecasting methods can contribute to the combination. When there are many alternative forecasts (see Exercise 12.2), it is often better (as in the preceding example) to use them all, although the gains from using more than five are usually limited. However, including inappropriate methods in the combination mix is not to be recommended. Therefore, benefits may be derived from excluding the extreme forecasts through trimming (removing, say, 20 percent of the extreme forecast errors in the calculation of the average; see Jose and Winkler, 2008) or using the median rather than the mean.

When forecasts are consistently biased with a nonzero mean error, combining is unlikely to prove beneficial if the foregoing formulas are used. Instead, the forecasts require modification to remove the bias; see Appendix 11B and Exercise 12.1(b).

> **DISCUSSION QUESTION:** *How is the process of combining forecasts similar to portfolio diversification in finance? Why might such procedures reduce the forecast error (or investment risk)?*

What of the alternative to combining: choosing the best performing model from the set of alternatives? This is the implicit basis of the various forecasting competitions, which aim to identify the best performer over the population under study. The 'winner' then would be the method to adopt; it is also the approach used in a variety of software packages (although the selection algorithms employed in these commercial packages often perform poorly). Fildes and Petropoulos (2015) have investigated model selection compared to combining and found that in many circumstances selection is the better option, in particular selection works best when specific sub-populations of data are considered (e.g., trended or seasonal series), but also when the alternative methods' comparative performance is stable over time. Although more demanding to implement, the idea of first segmenting the data series, examining the comparative performance of plausible methods to see if their ranked performance on the in-sample or validation data has remained much the same and then adopting the winning methods, does lead to worthwhile gains.

12.2 The Role of Forecasting Support Systems

So far, we have discussed how forecasting methods can be evaluated. But how are these forecasts produced in an organizational setting, whether for a manufacturer, in the service sector, in government, or by an economic analyst? The forecaster will often be faced with a multitude of factors that could conceivably affect the future outcomes. At the same time, the forecaster may confront the situation with very limited retrievable historical information with which to build a formal forecasting model. As a consequence, he or she often does not use a causal forecasting method, but instead adopts an approach through a forecasting support system, as shown in Figure 12.1.

Figure 12.1 The Forecasting System

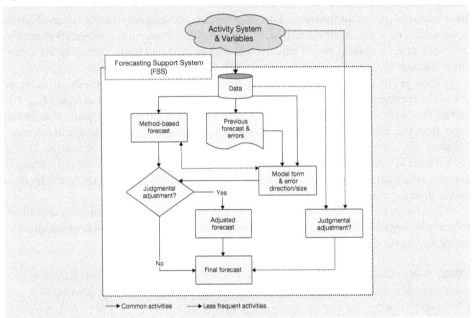

Here, the limited data on the system (within which demand is generated or other key variables are determined) is used to produce a method-based forecast. The method used is usually based on some variant of exponential smoothing, a simple causal model or a naïve method. The organizational forecasters know more (or at least think that they do) about what is going on with the focus variable being forecast, such as product demand. In forecasting demand and corresponding sales, this knowledge of factors influencing demand may often spring from a lengthy consultation process with colleagues such as account managers (who manage important customers) and brand managers (who manage the particular brand). These interactions occur as part of the Sales and Operations Planning (S&OP) process which aims to reconcile supply and demand (see for example the discussion in Chase, 2016 and in the pages of the forecasting practitioner journal, *Foresight*.)

In other areas of forecasting the gathering of information from multiple disparate sources is an important part of reaching a final forecast. In forecasting corporate earnings, the knowledge may originate in the Web or in meetings with industry specialists or company managers. Macroeconomists also gather information about the state of the economy from surveys, press reports, and other sources. In all these examples, forecasters should know how accurate their previous forecasts have been. Drawing on different sources of knowledge, they may judgmentally adjust the method-based forecasts by changing the parameters or even adopting a different method. These interactions are indicated in Figure 12.1 by the loop between the method-based forecast, the judgmental adjustment and the model form. Or they may combine the statistical forecast with judgment. More commonly, the forecaster will decide whether to adjust the statistical forecast and the size and direction of the adjustment, influenced in this decision by developments in the economic and market environment as well as past forecast errors. The result of these interactions is a *final forecast,* which, in demand forecasting, forms the input into other parts of the organization's (enterprise-wide resource planning, or ERP) information system.

Whatever the forecasting need, the data history, the algorithms, and the forecasts usually form a part of a forecasting support system.

FORECASTING SUPPORT SYSTEM (FSS)

A set of (typically computer-based) procedures that facilitate interactive forecasting of key variables in a given organizational context. An FSS enables users to combine relevant information, analytical models, and judgements, as well as visualizations, to produce (or create) the forecasts and monitor their accuracy.

Indeed, many organizations use an FSS, particularly when the forecasting problem is complex and the effects of forecast error are important. Some of these systems may cost well over a million dollars, whereas homegrown systems based upon good forecasting software may be much less expensive. Evidence from surveys (Sanders and Manrodt, 2003; Weller and Crone, 2012) suggests that the most used software in forecasting is Excel, despite its limited forecasting capability and well-documented numerical problems (McCullough, 2009). We hope that readers of this book will by now recognize that Excel is a valuable tool for data entry, manipulation and storage, but much less so for forecasting. It is therefore important to organizations that they assess the candidate systems carefully when implementing an FSS. Fildes, Goodwin, and Lawrence (2006) discuss various aspects of the design of such systems. The key dimensions that need to be considered are the following:

1. Data aspects
   a. Categorization of data (into new products, established products, etc.; we discuss this further in Section 12.3)
   b. Frequency of data and their match to the decision problem (e.g., if there is a requirement for weekly forecasts, the database and the models should operate at a weekly level)
   c. Ability to include a range of variables both hard and soft
   d. Links to other information systems (such as the transactional data storage system, the ERP or inventory systems)
   e. Common interface for the input and output (so they can be accessed by other software).

2. The forecasting methods and their accuracy
   a. Range of methods
   b. Ability to include additional variables (such as weather effects) into (some of) the methods
   c. Suitability of the methods for the organization's data
   d. Appropriate measures of accuracy of alternative methods compared with current performance.

3. User-Computer interface
   a. Ease of learning and ease of use
   b. Report-writing capabilities
   c. Support for judgmental adjustments to model-based forecasts.

4. Company characteristics
   a. Viability, history, list of clients
   b. Project team
   c. Specialist forecasting support.

5. Cost (purchase price, maintenance, and consulting/training).

One method for deciding among alternative forecasting systems would be to develop a scorecard with weights assigned to each dimension and each question within each dimension. The systems with the highest scores would be short-listed. However, some attributes of the proposed system would be absolute requirements, and those systems which failed to meet the standard would be excluded from the shortlist.

12.2.1 Forecast Adjustment

The forecaster is usually faced with many factors that influence the focus variable to be forecast. As Figure 12.1 illustrates, the initial system forecast is produced with an oversimplified model, which ignores some of this complexity. But forecasters and their colleagues know of at least some of these omitted influences, and for those series which are important to forecast accurately, they aim to improve accuracy by adjusting the statistical forecast to take the various missing factors into account.

Evidence pertaining to such judgmental adjustment is sparse, beyond the fact that manufacturing organizations will adjust up to 70-80 percent of statistical forecasts (Fildes and Goodwin, 2007; Weller and Crone, 2012; Franses, 2014). Retailers adjust proportionately fewer forecasts but have many thousands of products on their shelves, so, in total, the adjustment process is even more significant. The main reason organizational forecasters give for making adjustments is to account for promotions, but other factors they find relevant include weather effects, holidays, and price changes. Other groups of forecasters also make adjustments to their formal models: Weather forecasters and macroeconomists adjust their forecasts, often to take into account recent information not included in their formal model-based forecasts.

But do such adjustments work to the organization's benefit? The first point to make is that they allow forecasters and their colleagues to own and take responsibility for the forecasts, because the adjustments give the final revised forecast an appearance of credibility that the initial statistical forecast may have lacked. The second related aspect is that there is now a story to be told around the forecast beyond the bald statistics, and the forecaster's expert role gains credibility. However, forecasters are paid a salary, and the whole adjustment process is expensive and time consuming. There is mixed evidence on whether the adjustments do in fact achieve improved accuracy (Fildes, Goodwin, Lawrence, and Nikolopoulos, 2009; Franses, 2014). Such adjustments of course suffer from the usual problems of bias seen in judgmental forecasts, as discussed in Chapter 11. On balance, for demand forecasting, judgmental adjustments do improve accuracy, particularly in those cases where the adjustment is downward (that is to say, where it is believed that the statistical forecast is too optimistic and there are factors driving sales off course). Also, in those cases where the forecaster believes that he or she has strong evidence of a major impact on sales, judgmental adjustments lead to improved accuracy. But many small adjustments, particularly upward, are damaging. The key questions are, first, when to adjust the statistical forecast: the answer is, only when substantial new information becomes available, and, second, by how much. As usual, both the initial statistical and the judgment-adjusted forecasts should be monitored continuously, measuring the "value-added" in the judgmental adjustments appropriately (Davydenko and Fildes, 2015).

The problem of judgmentally estimating the size of the adjustment can be alleviated in a number of ways. One approach is to develop an extended database that describes the reasons an adjustment was made (e.g., a two-for-the-price-of-one promotion) and the effect on sales (e.g., sales increased 45 percent, sales of a competing product dropped 37 percent).

ADJUSTING A STATISTICAL FORECAST

- Only if the forecaster has substantial information about factors that are excluded from the statistical forecast.

Adjustments can be made more effective:

- By developing a database of their past effectiveness and the reasons the adjustments were made.

- By developing statistical summaries of past adjustments to provide advice on the size of the adjustment.

Promotions are a major reason forecasters have for making an adjustment. To estimate the effects of a promotion, a benchmark forecast needs to be developed. Figure 12.2 shows weekly sales of an SKU and typical profiles for a number of four-week promotions. Forecasting can be done in a variety of ways, and we discuss two of them here. The first and simplest approach to adjustment is to develop a baseline model using just the non-promoted periods. A simple exponential smoothing model with the smoothed value updated only in the non-promoted periods is one possibility. The results of this approach are also shown in Figure 12.2, with the baseline estimated from the exponentially smoothed non-promoted periods. This is done by developing a simple exponential smoothing model on early data with no promotions. When the forecaster is faced with a promotion, the smoothed value is just not updated until the promotion is finished. Once into the next non-promoted period, the smoothed baseline value can be updated again. (Check the calculation on the spreadsheet *Promotions.xlsx*.) The promotional effects are estimated as the difference between the baseline estimates and the observed sales.

Figure 12.2 Promotional Sales with a Baseline Forecast

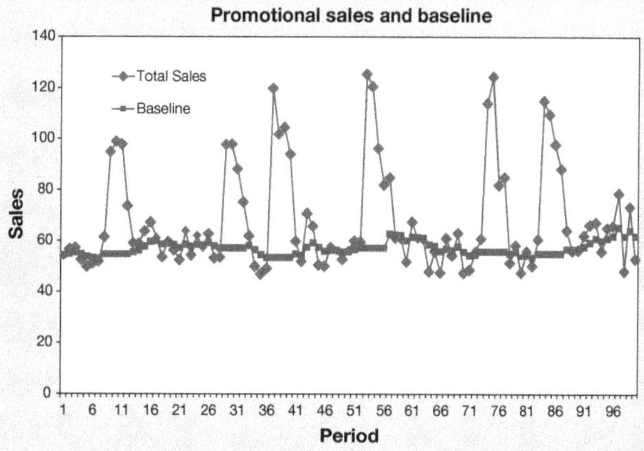

Data: Promotions.xlsx

A second method, theoretically better, but more complex, is to use the methods described in Section 9.8 to estimate a regression-based intervention model, incorporating variables to capture the marketing drivers, including promotions (see Section 12.4.5 for a fuller discussion of marketing effects). This approach may involve strong assumptions about the similarity from promotion to promotion, ignoring the possibility that each promotion has its own unique features. A simplified version of the approach is described next.

■ Example 12.2: Estimating the effects of a promotion

We can derive average promotion effects for the period of the promotion shown in Figure 12.2 (here taken as four periods and any aftermath) using an autoregressive baseline, and dummy variables. An alternative to using the autoregressive baseline is to use exponential smoothing. We have added in a dummy variable for the week beyond the promotion's end to check whether there is any carry-over (positive or negative). The forecast equation is

$$\hat{Y}_t = \alpha + \lambda Y_{t-1} + \gamma_0 D_{0t} + \gamma_1 D_{1t} + \gamma_2 D_{2t} + \gamma_3 D_{3t} + \gamma_4 D_{4t},$$

where $D_{it} = 1$ in the ith period of the promotion after the start of the promotion, $i = 0, \dots, 4$. The dummy variables indicate the difference between the promotional periods and the non-promoted baseline.

Table 12.3 shows the results from these two approaches. (The spreadsheet is *Promotions. xlsx*.) The results are similar. (For simplicity, the regression model used in this example excluded lagged sales, Y_{t-1} using only the dummy variables.) The second column shows the actual promotional effect, the third the effect calculated from the baseline approach, and the fourth the effect obtained with regression. ■

Table 12.3 Estimating Promotional Effects: Baseline vs. Regression Method

	Promotion Effect		
Period	Actual	Baseline Estimates	Regression Estimates
0	53.54	55.54	53.71
1	53.50	53.29	51.54
2	35.67	38.80	37.04
3	26.75	27.37	25.54
4	8.92	6.36	6.21

Data: Promotions.xlsx

> **DISCUSSION QUESTION:** *In forecasting sales during promotions periods, what factors might limit the effectiveness of the two approaches we have described?*

Both approaches suffer from a potential problem of seasonality. For example, many products are promoted around Christmas; therefore, it is difficult, if not impossible, to sort out the seasonal uplift from the promotional uplift. An additional complication arises when lagged sales are significant: There is a carry-over effect from one period to the next (see Exercise 12.5).

The optimal approach is also limited, because of data constraints, with different promotional types having potentially very different effects. As a consequence, there may be insufficient data to estimate the effects SKU by SKU. In part, this difficulty can be overcome by developing a database of past promotions to help the forecasters adjust their forecasts in the face of a similar forthcoming promotion. Once the promotional effects are estimated (however roughly), the information can be collated in a database that contains detailed information about the type of promotion. Then, when making a judgmental adjustment, the forecaster consults the database to identify a number of similar promotions that help guide him or her in deciding the size of the adjustment. This approach has been shown to be effective in an experimental appraisal (Lee *et al.*, 2007).

In sum, judgmental adjustments can lead to improved accuracy. To obtain the best results a well-developed FSS is needed. But the potential for bias remains high, for many of the reasons we discussed in Chapter 11. Providing the organizational forecaster with information such as base estimates of past promotional effects to guide the adjustment has been shown to improve accuracy.

DISCUSSION QUESTION: *Why might a demand forecaster or planner be biased when forecasting sales as growing compared with the baseline?*

12.3 Operations

Short-term forecasts are needed to support the operational activities of most organizations, public and private. Such forecasts are necessarily detailed so that the operational decisions that have to be made can be based on the best possible information about future requirements. For a manufacturing company, this means that demand for a particular product at the SKU level must include such details as pack size, packaging, and, sometimes, the name of the customer (or the distribution center that will store the product). The forecast horizon may be as short as a few days. For a service activity such as a call center or a government job center, forecasts of incoming calls by type of call (complaints, new business, etc.) are needed, perhaps at half-hourly intervals, to help in staff scheduling. The reason is that the number of incoming calls (or visitors) will typically depend on the time of day, as well as on the regular seasonality arising from the day of the week and the month.

DISCUSSION QUESTION: *What forecasts are needed by a chain of supermarkets to support their operations? By a criminal justice court?*

While the detailed forecasts are needed by product (or activity) and by short forecast horizon, more aggregate forecasts are also required, to support the purchase of new materials or decisions on staff numbers. At an even higher level of aggregation, overall forecasts of sales (or activities) are used for short-term financial management. In short, there is a hierarchy of forecasts needed to support operational decision making and planning in marketing. Figure 12.3 illustrates this hierarchy.

Figure 12.3 The Hierarchy of Market Drivers

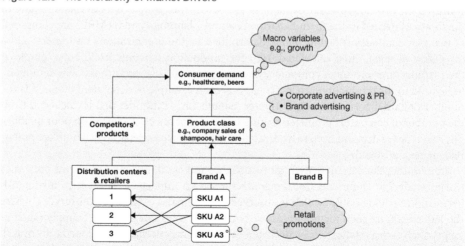

At each level of the hierarchy, various economic and market factors come into play, so, for example, the state of the economy will affect the aggregate demand for a company's products, as will the competitive products the company faces. At a product or brand level, marketing factors (such as brand advertising) are potentially important, whereas at the detailed SKU level, promotional activity by a retailer and calendar effects such as national holidays are the driving forces. The figure also shows how various SKUs are transported through distribution centers to the final clients: the retailers. The consequential demand for staff, space, and transport also needs to be forecast.

Operational forecasting with a forecast horizon beginning from a day (or less) and looking ahead three months (sometimes longer, surprisingly) is at the heart of an organization's short-term management. Most companies face a complex problem of forecasting demand (or activities) at this detailed level. Demand is affected by factors such as the economy, marketing and promotional activities, and, often, local considerations such as the weather or the local competition. In Section 12.4.5, we describe various causal models for including some of these factors. But producing the forecasts on a day-to-day basis requires considerable organization. A survey estimated the median number of data series an organization has to produce at 400; however, the range is wide. An energy supplier will have only a small number of series to focus on; a national retailer would need to make many more — in the tens or even hundreds of thousands. This effort requires databases and staff with expertise relevant to the market and an information system to integrate the sources of information and produce the forecasts — the FSSs discussed in Section 12.2. These forecasts are then used by various customers elsewhere in the organization, in their operational planning, distribution, staffing, and cash management, and often form part of an integrated ERP information system. The next three sections discuss in more detail the methods and processes used to support this expensive and important organizational activity.

12.3.1 Data Issues in Supply Chain Forecasting

Supply chain forecasting is the term we use to describe the forecasting activities of retailers, manufacturers, and their upstream suppliers. It was one of the earliest application areas and saw the development of new forecasting methods, including in particular exponential smoothing in the 1950s. Figure 12.4 presents the different levels from the retailers, directly serving customers, to the suppliers and manufacturers further upstream.

The database available to the forecaster upstream in the supply chain is often limited and confused, in that downstream demand is unknown, with only orders available. Many of the forecasts needed in the manufacturing resource planning system (MRP) are composed of two parts: an *independent demand*, determined by the organization's customers, and a *dependent demand*, often calculated from the production schedule itself. For example, if the manufacturer produces computers, the company will also require its own computers to be used in the production process itself. A second example of dependent demand is the number of hard drives needed in computer manufacture, a number that is calculated from the number of computers produced (taking into account rejections based on poor quality). The two types of demand need to be distinguished and forecast separately if both are potentially large and volatile.

In addition, the data may well not record demand at all, but instead record only sales (for a retailer) or shipments (for a manufacturer). An important aspect is to distinguish between the sales variable (which is observed) and demand (which is unobserved), where the latter includes such factors as lost or backlogged sales due to lack of supply (such as empty shelves in a retailer). In a call center, the record may exclude abandoned calls or lack a clear classification of the type of call received. All such limitations make the forecaster's

Figure 12.4 Forecasting across the Supply Chain

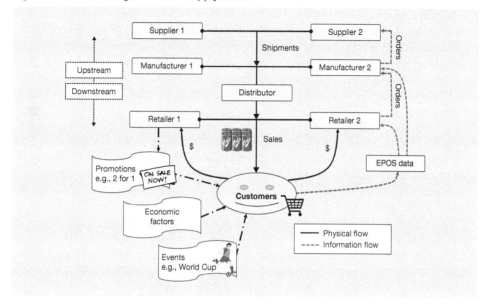

life more difficult. Essentially, the first step when one is forecasting must be to "clean" the data. In operations, the process must usually be automatic so that corrections are put in place for a retailer to take into account lost sales due to the item's being out of stock or the effect of returns. A typical correction rule is to estimate demand as

$$Demand = Sales\ if\ Demand \leq Stock.$$

But when an out-of-stock situation is observed,

$$Demand = Initial\ Stock + Expected\ (Excess\ Demand) \times P(Demand > Stock).$$

We use this revised estimate of demand to replace the raw sales figures in the forecast calculations (Lau and Hing-Ling Lau, 1996). To make this estimate, we will need to generate an estimate of the probability that demand exceeds the stock, and this requires us to assume an appropriate distribution for the demand, such as the normal or lognormal distribution, and then estimate its parameters. When the stock is unknown, this approach needs further modification (Mersereau, 2015). For a manufacturer, the sales history again does not always reflect underlying activity and the sales data may require correction once more, with distorted values corrected or replaced. For example, for shipment patterns that are unusual, the shipments may be smoothed over a number of adjacent periods. Unlike the corrections made in the case of the retailer, the ones made here are likely to be made on a case-by-case basis, using judgment.

12.3.2 Supply Chain Forecasting and the Bullwhip Effect

As data has become increasingly available supply chain forecasting has recently seen a number of innovations, focused on the demand experienced by the different participants in the supply chain and the information flows between them. Syntetos *et al.* (2016) provide a framework for understanding the interactions between the participants and the special features of the supply chain forecasting problem, summarizing the recent literature. Figure 12.4 characterizes the information flows that affect demand at each level. The retailers' sales are affected by many factors, ranging from the state of the economy, to promotional activities, holidays, sporting events, and the weather, to more localized factors (a festival or even a street closure). In response to these factors and the corresponding demand forecasts, the stock controllers (perhaps through an automated system) will take into account the stock on hand for each SKU and the orders already placed, if any. Then the controller will place a further order with the manufacturer. Fortunately, retailers will usually have up-to-date information on store SKU-level sales through their electronic point of sales (EPOS) information system.

The manufacturer suffers from a lack of knowledge, often knowing little about what's happening to the retailer's customers. The manufacturer knows only the orders placed for its own products by the retailer, the distributor, or the manufacturer. It may not even know what price is being charged or the promotional support in place, both of which affect consumer purchases. Increasingly, information may be shared on retailer sales through the retailer's EPOS data, as the figure shows.

The supplier is in an even worse situation than the manufacturer, being a further step removed from the final customer. As a consequence, the suppliers experience the effects of the downstream inventory rules used by their customers. These lead to order batching and the supplier may use a simple forecasting model of their own sales which takes no account of this downstream behavior. The interactions between sales, orders, and inventory can lead to the *bullwhip effect*, whereby the variability of sales at the retailer level is amplified by the manufacturer's response to retail orders. This variability, in turn, is amplified by the supplier in response to the manufacturer's orders. Figure 12.5 illustrates the effect. Figure 12.5A shows the hypothetical nature of the bullwhip effect and Figure 12.5B gives a real-data example.

As the figure shows, the manufacturer's orders often lag the retailer's sales: a delayed response to market changes and unexpected orders. The problem posed by the bullwhip effect is that variability and the corresponding forecast errors lead to heavy additional costs at all levels of the supply chain. The bullwhip typically becomes even more pronounced as we move upstream in the supply chain, for instance looking at parts/raw material supplier.

Various solutions have been proposed to mitigate the damaging bullwhip effects, all of which involve sharing information so that the supply chain participants know, at the very least, their retail (or downstream) customers' sales. Most large retailers collect EPOS data, which can readily be made available. In addition, some companies share inventory data and their own forecasts as part of what has become known as *Collaborative Planning, Forecasting, and Replenishment* (CPFR). The aim is to ensure the smooth, timely flow of goods throughout the supply chain by the effective use of the shared information. Lee, Padmanabhan, and Whang (1997) offer an accessible introduction to this potentially important subject. But research on how companies have operationalized these collaborative concepts suggests that their implementation is difficult: Using the downstream information requires both an effective information-sharing system through an FSS and forecasting methods that utilize the information. Software suppliers (who design the collaborative interfaces) and consultants have tended to overstate the benefits. In a real example in which the customer forecasts produced by a car manufacturer were shared, they added little to the parts manufacturer's own forecasts. So what can go wrong? Of course, the customer's own shared forecasts can be inaccurate, perhaps because they are not deemed valuable, or game playing may bias the forecasts to ensure that the manufacturer always has a readily available supply. Revealingly, survey work by Weller and Crone (2012) has shown that manufacturing companies who collaborate across the chain have greater success when forecasting, while Trapero, Kourentzes, and Fildes (2012) provide evidence of the forecast error reduction that can be achieved by sharing Point-Of-Sale information upstream.

Figure 12.5 The Bullwhip Effect across the Supply Chain: Retailer, Manufacturer, and Supplier

(A) Schematic

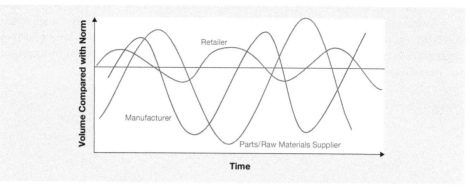

(B) Real Data Example

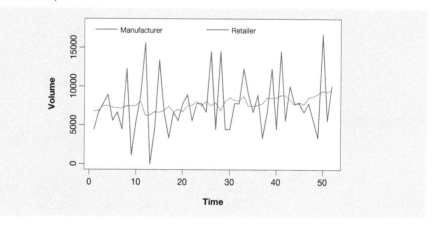

> **DISCUSSION QUESTION:** *How could a manufacturer best use a retailer's forecasts to improve the accuracy of its own forecasts?*

12.3.3 Hierarchical Forecasting

Different parts of the organization require different levels of detail in order to support planning decisions. With the focus on distribution, the manager will require sales by region (perhaps transformed into container loads). In marketing, the emphasis will be on brand sales whereas the sales department is interested in customers. In Figures 12.6 and 12.7, we show two perspectives on this problem. In the first figure, annual sales are broken down into product categories, then brands, and finally SKUs. In the second, the overall world market is decomposed into countrywide sales and then to the different within-country areas and regions so that sales can be allocated to the various distribution centers and production facilities. Both figures are abstract views of the hierarchies, which may contain many more nodes and levels. These two hierarchies can be thought of equivalently from the bottom up, equating to the same total at the highest level but following a different aggregation path. Similarly, daily SKU sales contribute to the weekly, monthly, and annual totals. From an information systems viewpoint, to carry out this aggregation, the raw data must be very detailed, by SKU, store, time period, and region at the very least.

Considering a single hierarchy (for example, either of those shown in Figure 12.6 or 12.7), we can produce forecasts by two distinct approaches. A model can be developed on the basis of past high-level aggregate data. Forecasts for lower levels may be produced by splitting proportionally the top-level forecasts. This is known as a top-down approach. Alternatively, forecasts can be produced (by whatever method) at a lower level and then aggregated to produce the high-level forecast. This second method is a bottom-up approach to forecasting.

Figure 12.6 Hierarchy of Demand Data by Product Groupings

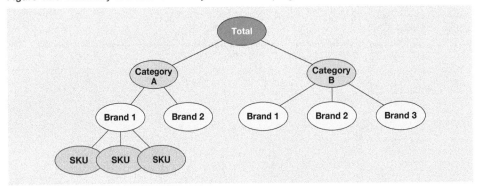

Figure 12.7 Hierarchy of Demand Data by Geographical Groupings

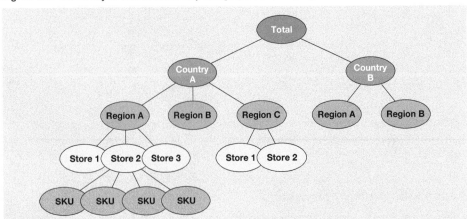

The two alternatives shown in Table 12.4 are for a two-level hierarchy. Although the notation gets more complicated for a larger number of levels, the principles remain the same. There are L_1 product groups in the first level. In the second level, each of those L_1 groups is broken down into $L_{j2}, j = 1, \ldots, L_1$ SKUs. There are therefore L_{12} SKUs in the first product group, L_{22} in the second, etc.

A top-down approach forecasts the level 1 and level 2 sales by first forecasting the top-level total and then forecasting the proportion of level 1 sales that contribute (in groups) to the total. Level 2 forecasts are calculated similarly, based on the level 1 forecasts. The historical proportions are known for the level 1 and level 2 groups, and often the historical average is used to estimate them. Alternatively, exponential smoothing can be used to forecast the proportions. The danger with using a fixed average is that this does not permit the different components of total sales to change.

The bottom-up approach first forecasts the bottom level sales for each SKU in each of the $j = 1, \ldots, L_1$ groups (level 2 in the table), with L_{j2} SKUs in each group, and these are then summed to give the level 1 sales for each of the groups S_{jt}. These level 1 sales for each group can then be summed to estimate the (top-level) total sales. A further variant is where the forecasts are made at an intermediate level and the forecasts for the levels both above and below are conditional on these middle-level forecasts — a "middle-out" approach.

Which method is better? They all have one advantage over the alternative approach of forecasting each level independently: The resulting forecasts are consistent. In effect, the organization is working with one set of numbers while other approaches can deliver conflicting forecasts. At the extreme, marketing could be working with one set of expected sales while production and distribution could be planning to produce and deliver a quite different mix of product volumes. However, there is no statistical reason that one method should be better than the other, and in fact, the empirical evidence is contradictory. The approaches may be evaluated for a given set of series using a forecast competition (see exercise 12.9). Nonetheless, the forecasting objective should guide both the evaluation metrics and the types of approaches considered: What is the level in the hierarchy where accuracy is most important?

Table 12.4 Top-Down and Bottom-Up Forecasts for a Two-Level System

	Top Down ↓	
Top	Total (T_t): The forecast is produced at this level.	$$T_t = \sum_{j=1}^{L_1} S_{jt}$$
Level 1	$P_{jt} \times T_t$, $j = 1,\ldots, L_1$, where P_{jt} is the proportion of total sales in the jth group.	Sales of the jth group $S_{jt} = \sum_{k=1}^{L_{j2}} S_{kjt}$ L_{j2} SKUs in each of the $j=1,\ldots, L_1$ groups in level 1.
Level 2	$P_{kjt} \times (P_{jt} \times T_t)$, $k = 1, \ldots, L_{j2}$, where P_{kjt} is the proportion that the kth SKU contributes to the jth group's sales.	S_{kjt}, $k=1,\ldots, L_{j2}$ where S_{kjt} = sales of the kth SKU in the jth group: The forecasts are produced at this level.
		Bottom Up ↑

DISCUSSION QUESTION: *What advantages and disadvantages do you see in adopting either a top-down approach or a bottom-up approach?*

Athanasopoulos, Ahmed, and Hyndman (2009) compare the approaches (minicase 12.2 provides the basis for a detailed example) and recommend a variant that combines them. The combination approach is built on the idea that forecasts should be constructed for each series of the hierarchy, which are subsequently combined in a way that is optimal in reducing any inconsistences between the forecasts at the different levels. The advantage of this approach is that it hedges the risk of model misspecification by the construction of multiple forecasts (in contrast with the top-down where all predictions are based on a single forecast), and it relies on forecast combinations, as the name suggests. On the other hand, it is computationally more intensive, as one needs to produce more forecasts than in the other alternatives. Nonetheless, the combination approach has one major advantage over both top-down and bottom-up approaches: it allows for "grouped" hierarchies. The hierarchies in Figures 12.6 and 12.7 are not compatible, in that forecasts that are produced to be consistent across one hierarchy (for example the one in Figure 12.6) using either top-down or bottom-up approach, will not be consistent for another hierarchy that uses the same lowest level series. The combination approach enables us to consider as many hierarchies as desired simultaneously, resulting in consistent forecasts across all. The calculations involved in the combination approach are somewhat more complicated than in the other approaches and we rely on the available software (see online R examples and exercises 12.10 and 12.11).

So far we have discussed approaches that operate solely on the forecasts within a hierarchy. Within a particular disaggregated level of the hierarchy, there are typically many similar (analogous) series — for example, for a retailer, fresh food products. Methods have been developed that use information across the series to get better estimates of the individual series sales. The most obvious feature that similar series often share is a common seasonality. This feature is particularly helpful when the data history is relatively short and seasonal estimates based on the individual series will be error prone and noisy. Seasonality for such series may be estimated by averaging the seasonal estimates of the individual series and applying the group seasonal estimates to all the series (Duncan, Gorr, and Szczypula, 2001; Leonard, 2007; Williams, 2007). An advantage of multiplicative seasonal factors is they can be used directly on each of the series (while if seasonality is additive the adjustment depends on the level of the particular series).

Applying the same logic, but this time to the trend, yields an estimate of the smoothing constant for a group of series as the average (or median) of the individually estimated series-specific constants. Such methods have generally proved more accurate than relying on the parameter estimates for individual series.

12.3.4* Forecasts and Time Aggregation

The hierarchies introduced in Figures 12.6 and 12.7 show demand at the most disaggregate lowest level, for instance SKU/store: demand is recorded at a transactional level and translated into daily demand to support operational decisions (e.g., shelf stocking at a retailer's store or patient admissions into a hospital). At higher levels of the hierarchy such as brand or product category levels, the supported decisions often have longer lead times and are based on more aggregate demand figures, such as monthly or quarterly. Similarly, forecasts can be produced at all these different time aggregation levels.

We may aggregate a series over time by summing together observations within the desired time buckets. To aggregate every k periods, given a series Y_t with n observations, into the resulting aggregate $Y_i^{[k]}$ with $i = 1, \ldots, [n/k]$ (Here the square brackets are used to denote that we round down the result to the integer part of the ratio.):

$$Y_i^{[k]} = \sum_{t=1+(i-1)k}^{ik} Y_t.$$

For example to aggregate a monthly time series with $n=120$ observations, into annual we set $k=12$ and the resulting series has 10 observations (n/k rounded down where necessary). If the remainder of the division n/k is not zero, then we remove the first $n - [n/k]$ observations from the beginning of the time series. Given that forecasting is our objective, it is important to retain the most recent information and therefore the temporal aggregation is aligned at the end of the time series.

Temporal aggregation can change the characteristics of a time series, making different aspects appear stronger or weaker. Figure 12.8 provides a plot of the weekly total emergency hospital admissions in the UK, together with a seasonal plot (multiplicative decomposition), along with aggregate 4-weekly, quarterly and annual views of the series. Observe that as we temporally aggregate the series, the seasonal signal becomes less dominant (notice how the seasonality becomes smoother) and the underlying trend becomes more apparent. At the annual level all seasonality is filtered and only the trend and irregular components of the time series are relevant. In fact, the aggregation equation is very similar to a moving average, if we would divide it by k, suggesting that temporal aggregation acts as a filter, reducing the noise of a series and masking detailed information (e.g., effect of special days, promotions, etc.). Naturally the available observations reduce as well, starting from 240 weekly observations, to only 4 annual ones. Exercise 12.12 explores the effects of temporal aggregation on model selection.

Figure 12.8 Weekly Total Emergency Admissions (UK) in 000s and Temporally Aggregated Series

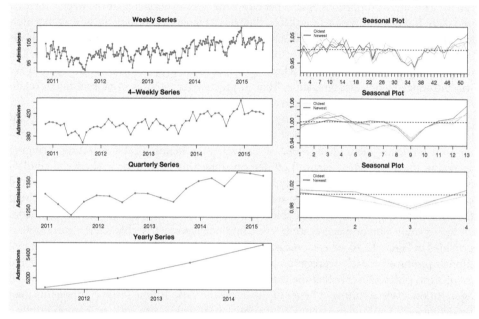

What are the implications of temporal aggregation for forecasting? To answer this, let us consider the alternative. Without temporal aggregation we would need to produce a 52-weeks ahead forecast when looking a year ahead. Forecasts for such long horizons are difficult, as we need to forecast far ahead from the last available in-sample period. If we aggregate temporally, for instance to the annual level, then we would need to forecast only one-step ahead, with the long-term trend being apparent, but we would then have to produce any forecast based on a limited number of data points. Intermediate aggregation levels would result in a mix of the above benefits and challenges. There has been substantial research dedicated to choosing the best aggregation level but so far there has been no resolution as to how to make the optimal choice.[3] Nonetheless, there are some helpful guidelines. What is the relevant forecast objective and horizon? If aggregation is too low compared to the forecast horizon (e.g., weekly data with a horizon of 5 years), then we will have to produce forecasts for too many steps-ahead. If aggregation is too high, we may filter out too much useful information and rely on very limited data points. At which level is the time series easier to forecast? This is a difficult question to answer, but the appropriate forecasting method will change as we temporally aggregate our data. In some cases the difference between levels is apparent (consider the weekly and yearly series in Figure 12.8), but in other cases this is not the case (for example, between the 4-weekly and quarterly views of the series in Figure 12.8). A forecasting competition between models built at different temporal

---

3 For a summary of the literature findings on temporal aggregation, as well as a more detailed discussion of the benefits and limitations, see Athanasopoulos *et al.*, 2017.

aggregation levels could help resolve the issue, though the comparison should be done at a common evaluation level related to the relevant forecast objective (Exercise 12.13).

One has to keep in mind that more often than not, the data available are already aggregated in some form. In some cases the decisions dependent on the forecasts may require shorter forecast horizons than the distance between two consecutive data points in the time series. For example, a retailer may use weekly data (and forecasts) to support daily stocking decisions. This would require a similar approach to top-down hierarchical forecasting. We can use a profile of proportions of sales per day of the week to disaggregate the weekly forecast into daily. If such information is available, then it is a matter of choosing the best aggregation level to model the demand. If not, then we could use simplistic heuristics to disaggregate our forecasts, such as separating a weekly forecast into days based on observed proportions. The further away in the hierarchy from where the forecasts are needed, the more uncertainty we will introduce by our disaggregation. That in practice incentivizes organizations to retain detailed data at a disaggregate level, in a similar way to the hierarchical forecasting.

Motivated by the similarities of this modeling problem to hierarchical forecasting and the difficulty in choosing a single best aggregation level, Athanasopoulos *et al.* (2017) proposed a modeling methodology that is equivalent to hierarchical forecasting, bringing several of the advantages.[4] Figure 12.9 demonstrates this equivalence, where the similarities with Figures 12.6 and 12.7 are apparent. Each complete year of the time series would constitute a "total" level in the cross-sectional hierarchical forecasting point of view. Using the combination approach to hierarchical modeling we can combine the information from all the separate temporal aggregation levels into our forecasts. A characteristic example is provided in Figure 12.10, where forecasts of both the *temporal hierarchy* and base individual models produced at each aggregation level are given for the total UK emergency hospital admissions series. Observe that the temporal hierarchy forecast borrows strength from all aggregation levels, resulting in better capturing of the various time series components than modeling each level independently (the annual and weekly series are striking examples). The forecasts at each level of the temporal hierarchy can be produced by any forecasting method or adjusted as needed by experts. That brings different information sources to bear at different levels of the hierarchy, which are subsequently transferred to the remaining aggregation levels, achieving a holistic modeling approach. Finally, only aggregation levels that result in integer seasonality, once temporally aggregated, should be used. (The online R examples, as well as exercises 12.14 and 12.15, demonstrate the use of temporal aggregation and hierarchies.)

Figure 12.9 An Example Temporal Hierarchy for Forecasting

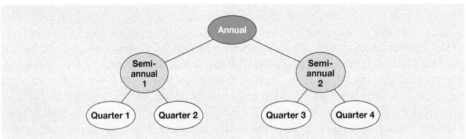

---

4 Multiple Temporal Aggregation (MTA) modeling was introduced by Kourentzes, Petropoulos, and Trapero (2014). They demonstrate the advantages of using multiple temporal aggregation levels over choosing one, which can be summarized as follows: (i) the modeling uncertainty is mitigated as multiple views of a time series are used with multiple forecasting models; (ii) the final forecast is a combination of the forecasts produced at individual levels, taking advantage of the forecast combination effects; and (iii) short and long-term dynamics are retained and strengthened across the different temporal aggregation levels, providing a holistic model of the time series.

Figure 12.10 Temporal Hierarchy and Conventional Forecasts using ARIMA for the Total Emergency Admissions (UK)

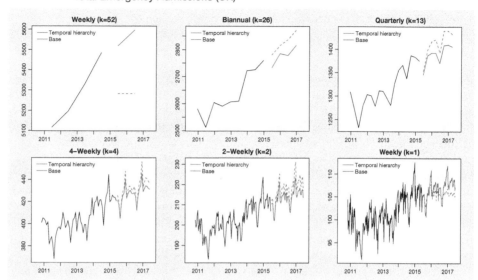

12.3.5 Demand Data and Intermittent Demand

Demand data, even after it has been cleansed, does not always fall neatly into a time series such as those described in Chapter 2. Each year, retailers stock many new products for which there is little or no history. Manufacturers face the same problem. In Section 12.4, we discuss the new-product forecasting problem from a longer term marketing perspective that delivers (usually judgmentally) a forecast of total sales for the year. Simple methods such as adopting a seasonal profile based on similar products may then be applied to estimate the period-by-period sales. A variant of this approach involves the class of fashion goods, which is a particular type of new product (e.g., sales of summer outfits). Here, there is a considerable history on the profile of sales of clothing over a season, although not on the sales of this year's latest fashions.

Other types of demand pattern that require special attention include (i) seasonal products that are unavailable through much of the year and (ii) end-of-line items that are being run down. In addition, products are usually thought about and categorized into three classes (although it might be more) in terms of their importance, from those products which are most profitable (or have the highest value, class A) to those which matter least (class C). Further, the impact of forecasting error on stock suggests an additional classification running from those with low forecast error (class X) to those exhibiting high errors (class Z). Thus, class AZ products are important products which exhibit large forecasts errors. The database will then record the fact that a particular SKU can be regarded as having regular sales, being an important class A product, being a new product, etc. Standard forecasting procedures will apply only to the "regular" SKUs, while the remainder will usually be dealt with individually. This topic is dealt with more fully in Section 13.1.5.

Intermittent Demand: One particular class of product requires more detailed discussion, because it poses a common problem and corresponding forecasting methods are included in many software products. *Intermittent-demand* SKUs frequently have zero sales, and any nonzero demand is often highly variable (so-called lumpy demand). Retailers and spare parts suppliers regularly experience this type of demand for many hundreds of SKUs, and it requires special statistical methods developed to match the data characteristics.

Accordingly, let us define two time series. The first is the history of nonzero demands, Y_t, and the second is the number of periods between successive nonzero demands, p_t. Then the h-step-ahead forecast of the demand rate made at time t is given by

$$F_{t+h}(h) = c \, \frac{Y_t'}{p_t'}$$

where p_t' denotes the exponentially smoothed inter-demand interval, and Y_t' is the exponentially smoothed (or moving-average) forecast of the size of non-zero demand. These are updated only if demand occurs in period t, otherwise the previous values are used.

This method, first proposed by Croston (and named after him), has been found to perform competitively against standard forecasting methods, such as exponential smoothing. Figure 12.11 illustrates one of the limitations of conventional time series models for intermittent time series: Croston's method forecasts are compared with exponential smoothing forecasts. Observe that exponential smoothing demand prediction always spikes after a demand event occurs, but is never on-time. This *decision-point* bias, becomes stronger as the intermittency becomes stronger. Also note that the demand drops towards zero, between demand events, due to the smoothing updating, which can result in unduly low predictions. Croston's method is designed to overcome these limitations.

Table 12.5 compares the two calculations, Croston's method and exponential smoothing, using a smoothing constant of 0.2, corresponding to the visualization of Figure 12.11. The first stage is to develop a time series of the number of periods observed between intervals of nonzero demand: 0 is observed between periods 3 and 2 because period 3 demand is 0, while period 4 has a nonzero demand of 5. Therefore, the observed interval between intervals of nonzero demand is 2. For period 11, the interval is 5. The standard exponential smoothing formula is then used to forecast the interval between nonzero demands. With smoothing parameter 0.2, the interval forecast for period 12 is $.2 \times 5 + .8 \times 2 = 2.6$. The demand size forecast is similarly calculated for period 12 as $.2 \times 6 + .8 \times 2.690 = 3.352$. The exponential smoothing parameters may be estimated for each series, in the usual way (c.f. Section 3.3).

The final Croston forecast is

Demand size forecast/Interval forecast $= 3.352/2.6 = 1.289$.

Croston's method does not always perform better than SES, whether appraised by standard error measures or by inventory cost measures. Performance depends on the coefficient of variation for demand size, as well as the expected number of periods between intervals of nonzero demand. Broadly, the less "intermittent" the time series, with smaller coefficient of variation and less time between orders, the better simple exponential smoothing performs compared with the Croston competitor (Syntetos, Boylan, and Teunter, 2011). Snyder, Ord, and Beaumont (2012) found that better results are obtained by using different smoothing constants for the order size and the period between intervals of nonzero demand. Further, they found that the benefits derived from this approach were usually in the provision of more accurate prediction distributions (required for inventory planning, etc.) than for point forecasts. Snyder, Ord, and Beaumont (2012) used a forecasting competition based upon the demand for automobile parts to validate this conclusion. Various modifications of Croston's original model have been proposed with the Syntetos and Boylan (2005) approximation demonstrating improvements. This modifies the original Croston's method as follows:

$$F_{t+h}(h) = c \, \frac{Y_t'}{p_t'},$$

where $c = 1 - \alpha_p/2$ and α_p is the smoothing parameter for the interdemand intervals (p_t). Its effect is to dampen the Croston's forecasts.

Table 12.5 Calculating Forecasts for Intermittent Demand Based on Croston's Method
(The value of the smoothing parameter is 0.2 in all cases)

Period	Actual Demand	Demand Forecast	Actual Intervals	Interval Forecast	Croston Forecast	Exponential Smoothing Forecast
1	0	No forecast	Can't be			
2	2	No forecast	calculated		No forecast	0.00
3	0	2.000	0	2.000	1.000	0.40
4	5	2.000	2	2.000	1.000	0.32
5	0	2.600	0	2.000	1.300	1.26
6	8	2.600	2	2.000	1.300	1.00
7	0	2.690	0	2.000	1.345	2.40
8	0	2.690	0	2.000	1.345	1.92
9	0	2.690	0	2.000	1.345	1.54
10	0	2.690	0	2.000	1.345	1.23
11	6	2.690	5	2.000	1.345	0.98
12	0	3.352	0	2.600	1.289	1.99

Data: Croston.xlsx

Figure 12.11 Croston's Method for Intermittent Demand Compared with Simple Exponential Smoothing

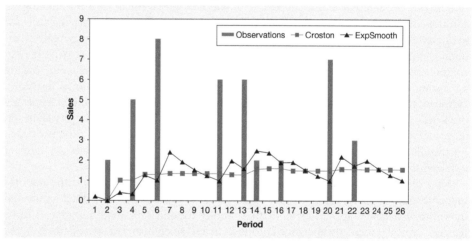

Temporal aggregation, as introduced in Section 12.3.3 can be quite useful for intermittent demand series. By temporally aggregating a time series the intermittency is reduced, making conventional forecasting models appropriate. This can be done using a single temporal aggregation level (see Nikolopoulos *et al.*, 2011) or multiple (see Petropoulos and Kourentzes, 2015), with the latter avoiding the selection of a single level and therefore simplifying the modeling setup, but being more computationally expensive. Exercises 12.17 and 12.18 explore this issue.

In general, no single method can always be relied on to produce the more accurate forecasts. In a particular application, a forecasting competition of the form described in Section 12.1.1 should be undertaken.

One potentially important issue in any FSS is how the error measures are calculated. Including intermittent demand in the calculation of the *MAPE* can lead to computational breakdowns because of the zero values in the actual observations. Such SKUs must therefore be excluded and be evaluated separately, or else a different error measure, such as the

RelMAE, should be used. However, this needs to be combined with a similar measure of bias, otherwise the forecast of zero for all future periods will often win. In appraising different methods of forecasting for intermittent demand, the recommended error measure is the percentage of time one method outperforms an alternative benchmark (such as exponential smoothing).[5] Using measures of the service level delivered for fixed inventory investment (e.g., percentage of periods in stock) is particularly valuable for applications where intermittency is important, overcoming the various limitations of forecast error metrics (though harder to calculate because it requires a simulation model to derive the estimates; see Syntetos and Boylan, 2006 and Kourentzes, 2014). A recent book (Boylan and Syntetos, 2017) covers the topic in depth.

A question that is always worth asking is "What is the cost of a stockout relative to inventory holding costs?" For major but rarely needed items the zero forecast may well be an indication that special orders as-needed are to be preferred to holding inventory.

12.3.6 Operations Forecasting: Summary

Forecasting in order to support operations remains the most common applications area for forecasting methods. The data usually fall naturally into a hierarchy, raising important questions about the level in the hierarchy at which the forecasts are needed. Considering the hierarchical nature of the data has important benefits in that this leads to consistent forecasts at the different levels, supportive of effective management decision making. In addition, information from one level of the hierarchy (such as seasonality) can be harnessed to improve forecasting at other levels. Similarly, temporal aggregation, and the implied temporal hierarchies, can aid in producing reliable long term forecasts and identifying the key components of the time series. These approaches rely on, and take advantage of, having a substantial number of time series for which we need to make operational decisions. However, they often lack richness in explanatory variables, in contrast to the forecasting problems considered in Chapter 9. On the other hand, operational forecasting is rich in soft information, which captures information from the internal and external environment of an organization. As we argued in Section 12.2, the FSS relies heavily on managerial judgment to take into account all the special circumstances that affect future demand.

Most of the methods used in operations forecasting are based on exponential smoothing, potentially adjusted by experts. However, for those products which exhibit lumpy and intermittent demand, special methods that modify exponential smoothing may well be needed. Typically, there are many such products in a retail company or spare parts supplier. In choosing between the different methods, a forecasting competition may be needed (see Section 12.1.1). But beware: In any appraisal of forecasting performance where there is intermittent demand, the most popular error measure, *MAPE*, is unusable (due to zero sales in the denominator). The performance of Croston's method is mixed, when considering point forecasts, though the inventory benefits may well be worthwhile. The method also appears to provide better prediction intervals for intermittent demands (see Snyder *et al.*, 2012) and avoids overstocking after recent sales.

Therefore, successful operations forecasting requires a mix between many elements: the correct selection and application of the appropriate forecasting methods; the use of an appropriate forecasting setup, taking advantage of any hierarchical information and temporal aggregation; providing forecasts for the multiple relevant forecast lead times to support the different operational decisions, and incorporating soft information to the statistical forecast, though the FSS. All these make operations forecasting a challenging and exciting task!

---

5   There is an active discussion in the literature on error metrics for intermittent demand. The reader can explore more in the works by Wallström and Segerstedt (2010), Kourentzes (2014), and Kolassa (2016).

12.4 Marketing

The primary reason most organizations are concerned with forecasting is that they need to forecast the demand for their products and services. Without predictions of future demand, they are unable to put capacity in place to supply potential consumers. Without understanding the factors that stimulate a consumer to buy or use the product (or service), the organization cannot influence its demand and, in particular, cannot decide on those crucial aspects of marketing, such as pricing, promotions, and product design, that lead to success. The methods suitable for forecasting demand for a product or service (from now on, we will use just "product" to include both concepts) depend quite critically on the data available, which in turn depend on the product's history and how much information has been collected from consumers. Figure 12.12 illustrates the various stages in the life cycle of an individual customer's engagement with a product or service, from the earliest stage when she is only a prospective customer, yet to decide whether to purchase. Of these prospective customers, some proportion will adopt the new product and become established users of it (and perhaps related services). Consider, for example, a fourth-generation mobile phone (such as the iPhone), offering music, Internet access, and many add-on applications. The profitability of such a phone to the telecoms supplier will depend on both the features of the new phone and the consumer's susceptibility to them (based on economic and demographic drivers such as income, age, and gender). From the perspective of telecoms suppliers the issue facing them is when and how to invest in establishing the enhanced 5th generation network and the number of customers willing to upgrade. The final stage in the consumer life cycle is retention, whereby the company competes to retain the profitable customers, rejecting those who may prove to be costly.

Figure 12.12 Prediction of Individual and Aggregate Demand in a Customer Life Cycle

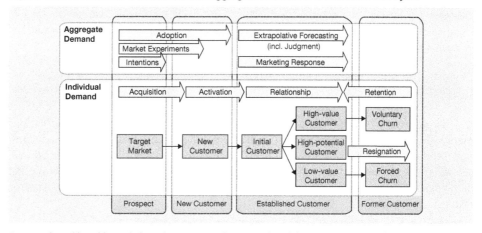

Source: Adapted by Fildes, Nikolopoulos, Crone, and Syntetos (2008) from Berry and Linoff (2004) and Olafsson, Li, and Wu (2008).

At each stage in the individual customer life cycle, more information is gathered on the customer and her behavior, adding value incrementally in the modeling of the customer's decisions. In the first stage, the market analyst aims to forecast the numbers of new customers that can be acquired, after first deciding on the target population. One of the most common applications of forecasting techniques is to decide to whom to mail promotional material, with a view toward acquiring new customers. (See Bose and Chen, 2009, for a technical survey of this area.) At this earliest stage, the analyst will know little of the target customers beyond their addresses and the demographics of the areas in which they live. At the end of the life cycle, the analyst will wish to identify those customers at risk from "churning" — that is to say, leaving their current supplier. Here the analyst should be able to access the customer's history of using the product (and the company), including such features as whether complaints have been made.

We will discuss suitable models for forecasting individual customer behavior in Section 12.5, but this is only part of the story. For market planning and related decisions, *aggregate* forecasts need to be made. For example, the capacity of the production line for a new product requires long-term forecasts of the product's potential market. Depending on the manufacturing complexity of the product, these forecasts may need to look many years ahead. As with the individual consumer, there is little, if any, history available at the earliest stages from the launch of new product. Sometimes market experiments are used, prior to the full-scale launch of the product, in order to gather data on such factors as the percentage of the target market who are willing to try the new product (if it's a fast-moving consumer product such as a new barbecue sauce). In contrast, after the product is established, the company has a time series history of sales, as well as prices and how much it spends on promoting the product. In addition, the company can buy similar information on its competition. A key issue the forecaster faces in deciding the methods to use is the availability of time series data. For example, the new-product forecasting problem must be treated differently from the situation where there is a substantial sales history.

Thus far, we have written as if the market demand we are concerned with is generated by an individual's demand for an organization's product or service (i.e., business to consumer, or B2C). However, many market forecasting problems focus on demand between businesses (B2B). Where there are many customers and little need for sustaining a relationship, the two problems are similar. Where there are few, judgment and customer information are applied to the individual purchase decisions, to estimate each customer's probability of purchase and the expected value of the purchase. The estimates obtained can then be aggregated to estimate overall demand. When the number of customers is small, information-sharing approaches to forecasting become important, as noted in Section 12.3.

> **DISCUSSION QUESTION:** *How would you go about forecasting the demand for a new airliner (e.g., Airbus 350-1000 or Boeing 787-10) over the next ten years?*

How do the techniques we have discussed so far in this book apply to these various market demand forecasting problems? In the remainder of this section, we discuss both new-product forecasting and forecasting when there is a substantial history. As we will see, the methods and the ideas all remain useful, but the special circumstances of market demand forecasting often require modifications to ensure that they match up to the specific features of the problem.

12.4.1 New Products and Services

New-product forecasting is important to organizations. The history of forecasting is full of major mistakes, usually in circumstances of over-optimism (or motivational bias), in which the company's product champion has convinced colleagues that consumers were just waiting to whip the product off the shelf (or the dealer's lot). It is estimated that between 50 and 80 percent of new products fail to establish themselves. Innovative products are particularly failure-prone. Although the failure to forecast demand is not the only reason, it is by far the most important. Goodwin, Meeran, and Dyussekeneva (2014) provide a recent review focused on consumer durables.

Sometimes the forecasting problem is one of predicting how quickly the new product replaces an existing product. This is the situation where the product is not completely new but has some of the same attributes as products already on the market (termed a *product improvement*). However, sometimes there is a key attribute in the new product — a feature which is sufficiently distinct from established alternatives — that gives it the potential to be viewed quite differently by consumers. An example is the electric car. More rarely, the product (often based on a new technology) delivers a service to the consumer that was previously unavailable (*new to the world*). An example is the personal computer, which delivered personally controlled desktop access to computing. (It could be argued that computer timesharing arrangements, popular in the 1970s, also had attributes similar to the PC, although we suggest that the issue of personal control is a critical difference.)

Numerous researchers have surveyed organizations in order to learn the techniques that are used to forecast these various types of new product or service. (See, for example, Lynn, Schnaars, and Skov, 1999, and Kahn, 2002.) Overwhelmingly, various types of judgmental forecasting are used — in particular, opinions of customers, company executives, and the sales force, which lead to an aggregate forecast. Both Lynn *et al.*'s and Kahn's surveys found that statistical models were used more rarely. However, reliance on judgment has often proved to generate overly error-prone forecasts, and as the failure history of new products makes clear, over-optimism is the typical result. We look next at models of how people (and companies) adopt a new product, for such models can be used to develop suitable benchmarks for appraising the more common judgmental approaches.

12.4.2 Long-Term Trends

For a new product that is not competing directly with others already established in the market, the question for the consumer is whether to try the product. For a frequently purchased product, the question becomes one of whether that product is sufficiently enjoyable to claim a regular spot in the consumer's shopping basket. If it is a product with a potentially long lifetime (such as a mobile phone), the decision to adopt or not to adopt is more important and so is the ultimate market size. We now consider models to describe the adoption decision. (For frequently purchased products, the frequency of purchase also needs to be considered; see Fader and Hardie, 2001, and the references therein.)

Let $N(t)$ represent the number of people (or businesses) who have adopted (or tried) the product for the first time by time period t; this is the cumulative total of adopters. What might the time path of $N(t)$ look like? Figure 12.13 shows some alternative curves.

The curves included in the figure are the linear, $N(t) = a + bt$, and four nonlinear curves:

i. the *exponential*,

$$N(t) = a\exp(bt) \text{ or } = ae^{bt}, \tag{12.5}$$

and three new nonlinear curves, all of which have an upper bound of M:

ii. the *modified exponential*,

$$N(t) = M - a\exp(-bt), \tag{12.6}$$

iii. the *Gompertz curve*, defined as

$$N(t) = M\exp(-a\exp(-bt)), \tag{12.7}$$

iv. the *extended logistic curve*, which has a shape similar to that of the Gompertz curve,

$$N(t) = M\left(\frac{1 - c\exp(-bt)}{1 + d\exp(-bt)}\right). \tag{12.8}$$

For all the curves, M, a, b, c and d are all non-negative. A fuller discussion of yet more alternative curves can be found in Meade and Islam (2006).

Figure 12.13 Various Trend Curves

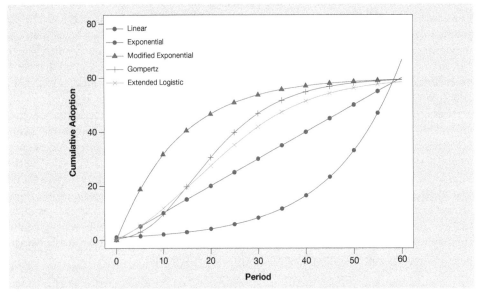

The simple logistic arises when $c = 0$. With each of the last three curves, as t gets large, $N(t)$ tends to a finite limit M (60 in the diagram). M is called the *asymptote*, the limiting value of $N(t)$ as t increases without limit. These curves are often described as S-shaped; by contrast, the linear and exponential curves increase without limit as t increases: They are unbounded. In fact, the exponential curve was the basis of one of the first forecasting models that predicted cataclysmic disaster: Malthus's prediction of the effects of an exponentially increasing population. According to Malthus, if each family has, on average, more than two children, and they in turn have more than two children, the effect is an exponentially increasing population that quickly explodes through the finite capacity of the Earth to feed itself.

DISCUSSION QUESTION: *What went wrong with Malthus's forecast of starvation for the planet? Or is the predicted catastrophe just taking longer than expected?*

When there are substantial past data, we can fit alternative curves by using an extension of the principles we introduced in Chapters 7 and 8, known as nonlinear least squares estimation. Most statistical software programs have such procedures, involving iterative solutions to obtain the parameter estimates. Also, a spreadsheet, *Trend.xlsm*, which illustrates how this analysis can be done with Excel's Solver, is available on the book's website. R code and instructions are also available on the book's web site.

Alternatively, we could linearize the exponential by taking natural logarithms to obtain

$$\ln(N(t)) = \ln(a) + bt + (error),$$

with the parameter estimated by the usual least squares procedure. However, this approach does not extend to the other models. Further, to compare the fit from a linear model with a nonlinear model, we have to make sure that the errors are in the same units; therefore, we cannot use R^2 or the standard error from the regression. As we discussed in Section 9.6 on nonlinearity, the forecasts have to be transformed back to the original units and then their *RMSE*s or other measures compared.

Are such trend curve methods useful for forecasting? As they stand, they cannot be used for new-product forecasting because they require sufficient data to estimate the parameters. Perhaps more important, forecasters would need to convince themselves and their colleagues that the trend is stable over the forecast horizon. Now, there are many reasons that a trend might persist for some considerable length of time. For example, a population may well start as Malthus feared, exponentially growing; but as the population gets richer and better educated, with a higher probability of children surviving, the growth will typically damp, leading to a modified exponential as a possibility, bounded or not. Where slow, continuous change is expected, growth curves such as these offer a benchmark with which to judge other methods. Working with Yongil Jeon, Nobel Prize winner Clive Granger (Granger and Jeon, 2007) has argued that such curves provide useful long-term forecasts. Using the growth of U.S. consumption, the two researchers compared the linear, exponential, and modified exponential curves. Their results establishing which curve provides the better forecast are left for the reader to consider in Exercise 12.20.

■ Example 12.3: The growth of Netflix

The various curves described in this section were used to fit quarterly sales figures for Netflix (see Minicase 3.1) for the period 2000Q1 through 2007Q4, and extended to 2015Q4. The results obtained from fitting each of the five models are given in Table 12.6. The *RMSE* and the first and last fitted values are included, along with the limiting values for the Gompertz and logistic curves. These two curves with finite upper limits fit much better and look similar, but show quite different asymptotic limits. The modified exponential does not have a finite upper limit because all its parameters are negative, in conflict with the original specification.

Table 12.6 Minitab Model Fits for Netflix Growth Data

Model	Upper Limit M: Models Fitted to 2007Q4	RMSE: Models Fitted to 2007Q4	2000Q1 Fit: (Period 1)	2007Q4 Fit: (Period 32)	Forecast 2015Q4 (Period 64)	RMSE: Models Fitted to 2015Q4	Upper Limit Fitted to 2015Q4	2015Q4 Fit: (Period 64)
Linear	No limit	26.4	−45.2	290	637	188.4	No limit	1310
Exponential	No limit	21.8	24.4	359	5767	42.0	No limit	1870
Modified Exponential	No limit	14.1	−9.8	339	2081	30.5	No limit	1824
Gompertz	598	9.4	2.5	323	561	32.9	212694	1805
Logistic	381	8.3	7.2	316	381	35.3	5254	1796
Corresponding Actual			5.2	302	1823			1823

Data: Netflix.xlsx

The linear model is clearly incorrect, but the Gompertz and Logistic provide the best fits up to 2007Q4. However, these two models suggest a sharp slowing of growth that results in forecasts for 2015Q4 well below what actually happened by 2015. When the models are fitted to the series using data up to 2015Q4, the fits are broadly comparable, but the limits suggested by the Gompertz and Logistic curves are very different. Clearly, the choice of model depends critically on whether we believe that Netflix sales will reach a plateau, or whether we think they will continue to grow at much the same rate. ■

DISCUSSION QUESTION: *What other information might you require before you relied on any of the models shown in Table 12.6 to forecast to 2020? Which model would you use?*

In short, growth curves offer a description of trends that are most useful with highly aggregated data. We often cite such curves colloquially, particularly the exponential curve, as we express our fear of population growth or welcome growth in world trade. But they are rarely the best forecasting tools, because long term trends tend to damp down. Thus, the S-shaped curves have more potential, and as we argue next, can form the basis of new-product forecasting methods.

12.4.3 Diffusion Curves: Modeling the Adoption of New Technologies and Products

The curves we have just described offer descriptions of past data and are not based on any model of the underlying process. (It could be argued, as Malthus did, that the exponential growth model is based on a simple biological birth-and-death process.) Models of the adoption of new technology have at their heart some simple schemes that attempt to describe how a person (or organization) comes to adopt the technology. The distinction drawn is that between consumption (of a product or service), which is potentially continuous, and adoption, which is usually thought of as a one-time irreversible choice. The most famous of the various models of adoption is due to Bass (1969). The full range of alternatives with guidelines on their use in practice is discussed in Meade and Islam (2001, 2006).

Suppose the market potential of a new product is M. The potential may be the number of individuals within some age group or income bracket, the number of households in a country, etc. Potential differs from sales in a number of important respects including the fact that it excludes replacement products and multiple purchases (e.g., a consumer owning more than a single mobile phone). Nor may the potential ever be achieved due to, for example, supply constraints.

DISCUSSION QUESTION: *What are the factors that should be considered when estimating market potential for a new high-speed rail link between San Francisco and Los Angeles (or London and Scotland)? What comparisons would you make with existing transportation systems?*

As a second example, consider the market potential of a new technological product such as an electric car.

First let us define $N(t)$ as the cumulative number of individuals (or more generally, potential adopters) who have adopted or tried the product or service by the end of time period t. Then if $n(t)$ is the number of people who adopted in period t, it follows that $n(t) = N(t) - N(t-1)$. Now, let $g(t)$ be the probability that an individual adopts a new product in period t. Then the expected number $n(t)$ of people who adopt in period t is given by the probability $g(t)$ of adopting in period t, multiplied by the number $M - N(t-1)$ of people who have not yet adopted, or

$$n(t) \equiv N(t) - N(t-1) = g(t)(M - N(t-1)). \tag{12.9}$$

Various models for $g(t)$ have been proposed. The simplest would assume that $g(t)$ is a constant; that is, there is a constant probability of someone who has not yet adopted the product trying in the next period. If we allow the model to be extended to continuous time, we can solve equation (12.9) algebraically. This assumption leads to the bounded exponential model discussed as a special case of equation (12.6). Bass (1969) proposed a more complex and more plausible model which assumes that the probability of adoption has two components: a constant probability that applies to each member of the population (sometimes called the coefficient of innovation, p) and a probability that increases with the number of people who have already adopted (a "word-of-mouth" effect proportional to those who have adopted, $qN(t-1)$, where q is the coefficient of imitation).

It follows that $g(t)=p+q(N(t)/M)$. Equation (12.9) can then be solved for $N(t)$. In continuous time the solution is a logistic curve given by equation (12.8) with $b = p + q$, $c = 1$ and $d = q/p$:

$$N(t) = M\left(\frac{1 - \exp(-(p + q)t)}{1 + \dfrac{q}{p}\exp(-(p + q)t)}\right). \tag{12.10}$$

Figure 12.14 shows how the logistic curve shifts with the values of these two coefficients. Observe that when $q = 0$ we are back to the modified exponential curve.

As the two coefficients increase, they affect how quickly the adoption reaches its potential. A larger imitation coefficient q raises the rate of adoption through an increasing probability of someone adopting as more and more of the potential market has succumbed. A larger coefficient of innovation p increases the early take-up.

Figure 12.14 The Effects of Increasing the Diffusion Parameters p and q

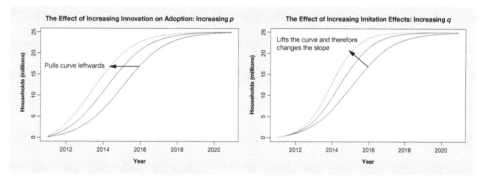

There are various ways of estimating the coefficients. A number of algorithms can be used to estimate the diffusion parameters, but nonlinear least squares estimation using Solver is usually adequate for our purposes, as demonstrated in the macro *Trend.xlsm*. The on-line R tutorials contain suitable code also. (An alternative, not recommended, however, is to estimate a linearized version of the Bass model.) The nonlinear model that is usually estimated is:

$$N(t) = M\left(\frac{1 - \exp(-(p + q)t)}{1 + \dfrac{q}{p}\exp(-(p + q)t)}\right) + \varepsilon_t. \tag{12.11}$$

But it is important to note that the error term is assumed to be additive in this model of cumulative adoption (i.e., it is equally important to minimize an error made for a large value of $N(t)$ as it is the small values in the early stages of the adoption cycle). Alternative assumptions could be made to minimize the percentage error, but for most purposes, it is the absolute value of the error that affects management decisions such as how much to invest in production capacity.

If instead of the cumulative adoption, $N(t)$, plotting the per period adoption (the change of cumulative diffusion between periods), $n(t)$, results in the familiar product life-cycle,

$$n(t) = p(m - N(t)) + q\left(\frac{N(t)}{m}\,(m - N(t))\right) + \varepsilon_t.$$

The first part of $n(t)$, $p(m - N(t))$, is dependent on p, the coefficient of innovation, and describes the number of innovative adopters, i.e., those who purchase a product on their own accord. For example, these are consumers who risk to try a new technology. The second part of $n(t)$,

$$q\left(\frac{N(t)}{m}\,(m - N(t))\right),$$

is dependent on q, the coefficient of imitation, and describes people who purchase a product, because they follow the fashion that early adopters set. For example, these are customers who wait for a technology to be proven, before purchasing a novel product. Figure 12.15 provides the two alternative views, together with the innovators and imitators. Note that in the life-cycle view the dynamics between innovators and imitators are apparent. Initially all adoption is due to innovators and gradually switches to imitators.

Figure 12.15 The Cumulative and Per Period (Life-Cycle) View of the Bass Model

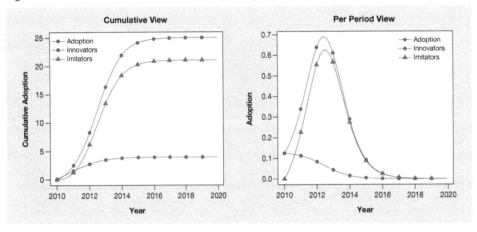

DISCUSSION QUESTION: *What makes consumers innovators or imitators? Consider the example of Virtual Reality entertainment products. What are the factors that may affect your own purchase decision?*

The life-cycle view is also helpful to understand the relative importance of the coefficients p and q. Figure 12.16 provides plots of the three possible alternatives: $p < q$ that is the vast majority of cases, $p = q$ and $p > q$. Observe that as the balance between the two parameters changes the shape of the lifecycle shifts dramatically, moving the peak of the adoptions.

With a variety of diffusion models available the question that arises here (as elsewhere in forecasting) is how to choose between the alternatives. Using a case study of mobile adoption for 25 countries, Meade and Islam (2015) develop guidelines to help in selection, concluding that the logistic model of cumulative adopters proved the most successful of their

Figure 12.16 Life-Cycles for $p < q$, $p = q$ and $p > q$: Per-Period Adoption

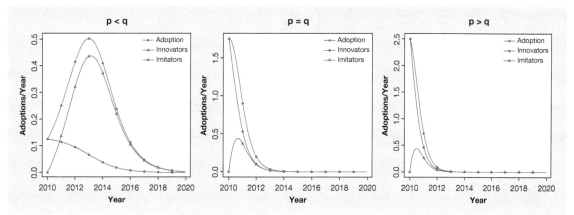

models for these markets. But how far this generalizes, they say, is unclear. Automatic use of the Bass model is therefore not recommended. With early data available, the relative performance of the models provides some evidence on which to base the choice. An illustrative example is given in Figure 12.17 (in both cumulative and per period adoption), where the adoption of a computer game series is modeled with Bass and Gompertz curves. Computer games typically follow the $p > q$ case (see Figure 12.16), where the Gompertz curve can fit better to the adoption.

Figure 12.17 Adoption of a Computer Game, Modeled with Bass and Gompertz Curves

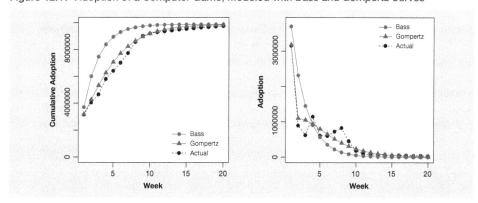

Much of the earlier research and estimation methods used assumed that substantial data were available, but that approach is of no help in new-product forecasting, where, by definition, there are few if any observations. Instead, the parameters can be estimated by analogy. In many new-product forecasting situations — even those in which the product can be thought of as being *new to the world*, there will have been examples of earlier products entering somewhat similar markets. Take the Internet as an example: In Figure 12.18, we see the various diffusion curves for radio and for both black-and-white and color television, as well as the as yet incomplete results for the Internet. Neither the average of the analogies nor the most recent example (of color TV) provide effective forecasts for the internet raising the question of the choice of analogy.

Figure 12.18 Penetration Levels, Diffusion Curves, and Parameter Estimates for
Various Media in the United States

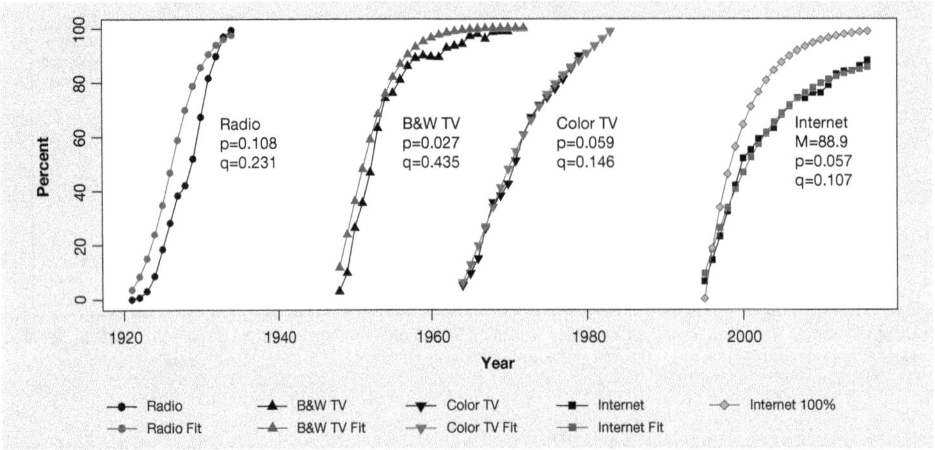

Source: Lilien, Rangaswamy, and Van den Bulte, 2000 and Pew Research Center.

To help estimate the parameters by analogy, Lilien and Rangaswamy (2004) have provided a set of historical parameter estimates with an overall median value of $p = 0.025$ and $q = 0.280$. For all these products the market potential was assumed to be 100 percent. Historical values establish a starting point that immediately provides forecasts once a group of analogous products is chosen. Because the choice of analogous products cannot be based on a similar adoption history (our focus product is new, after all), the decision must be made on the grounds of their having similar attributes and with the methods we described in Section 11.2.5. So how would we estimate the Internet diffusion parameters? The parameters from the past products we identified as similar have been estimated from the full data set (from Lilien, Rangaswamy, and Van den Bulte, 2000). Note that, for radio in the 1920s, diffusion was initially slow, but word of mouth (represented by the parameter q) proved effective. Color television, replacing an established product (black-and-white television) had a slower diffusion path, perhaps because the early availability and range of programs were both limited. There are also *network effects* whereby the attractiveness of the medium becomes higher the more people have adopted. A priori the Internet seems more like radio or black-and-white television, with a low coefficient of innovation and a high coefficient of imitation as people discover its benefits. In Figure 12.18, the forecast function shown is based on direct fitting of the data. Rather than assume a market potential of 100 percent, we obtain a fitted value of just under 90 percent. An analysis based upon 100 percent potential proved wildly optimistic about both the ceiling and the speed of diffusion.

On reflection, while the first three products are passively consumed the Internet requires active learning to be understood as valuable — it is nearer a *new to the world* product. Exercise 12.27 shows the differential figures by age and this raises the question whether the small percentage of non-users younger people will remain non-users as the older generation dies out, leaving a market saturation level less than 100%. Figure 12.18 shows both the forecasts produced both when the market potential is estimated (at a value of 89 percent) and when it is assumed to be 100%. This shows the importance of achieving a reasonable early estimate of market potential as we discuss in the next section.

Sometimes the problem of estimating the parameters for adoption in one country is helped by knowledge of the adoption path in another country, but the danger with this approach is that different countries and their populations differ in their willingness to try new products and services. Goodwin, Dyussekeneva, and Meeran (2013) discuss some of the issues surrounding selecting suitable analogies, where including a few (around six analogies) in estimating the diffusion parameters seems helpful. More recent examples of somewhat similar products based on common attributes probably lead to better accuracy; but overall accuracy is poor (with the total absolute error relative to cumulative sales) of around 50%.

In one particular situation the appropriate analogy is clear — that is when the product concerned is a follow-on from an earlier generation of the same technology. Here the diffusion parameters estimated on the first generation can be updated as sales become available for the second generation and so on (Norton and Bass, 1987). Application areas have included computers, mobile phones, pharmaceuticals and various B2B applications. In all these examples, sales from the most recent generation "steal" sales from its predecessor, but do not immediately supersede the established product.

12.4.4 Market Potential of a New Product or Technology

The Bass model and the Gompertz trend curves introduced in Section 12.4.2 both include the market potential M as a third parameter. In principle, if substantial data are available that includes peak period sales, this parameter can be estimated like any other.

■ Example 12.4: Internet adoption in the UK and Germany

Table 12.7 Diffusion Estimates: Sample Size, Model, and Country Effects for Internet Adoption
(Forecast accuracy calculated over 2014Q1 – 2016Q2, with last observation in each estimation series as fixed forecast origin)

	UK		Germany	
	(n =16) to 2007Q3	(n =41) to 2013Q4	(n =16) to 2007Q3	(n =41) to 2013Q4
Logistic/Bass				
p	0.627	0.064	0.034	0.036
q	0*	0.003	0*	0.019
M	23.57	23.18	42.47	38.11
S	0.593	0.462	1.248	1.063
Forecast Accuracy				
MAPE	7.85	8.68	28.15	12.17
MdAPE	7.77	8.60	28.29	12.29
Gompertz				
a	2.20	2.21	3.30	2.43
b	0.120	0.124	0.041	0.089
M	20.90	20.52	102.23	32.79
S	0.127	0.121	0.164	0.571
Forecast Accuracy				
MAPE	14.27	15.69	107.87	4.85
MdAPE	14.25	15.68	108.34	4.92

Data: Telecoms.xlsx
*The optimization procedure identified the boundary value $q = 0$ as optimal, leading to the modified exponential model.

One example is the level of Internet adoption likely to be achieved, information that is important to Internet service providers, retailers, and governments. Using data in *Telecoms. xlsx*, Table 12.7 shows the results obtained from estimating the Bass model and the Gompertz curve to derive the market potential M as well as the diffusion parameters p and q. Two different time spans and two different countries — the United Kingdom and Germany — were analyzed. For the United Kingdom, we are able to establish stable parameters and similar estimates of market potential for the two time periods. The same, however, is not true of Germany, for which the Gompertz curve turns out to be unstable and the choice of diffusion curve has a considerable effect on the estimates. The Gompertz models fit much better than their logistic counterparts, as the smaller values of S indicates. However, the long horizon forecasts are generally better from the logistic. Perhaps the key lesson is that estimates of M are extremely unstable when only the early part of the curve is available. All the forecasts were underestimates for the UK and all were overestimates for Germany, primarily as a consequence of the estimated values for M. ■

Market potential is a particularly important managerial variable. Whether the product is new to the world or, essentially, an improvement competing with established alternatives, its potential affects planning decisions at the earliest stage in the product's life cycle, before it is even fully designed for its market: It also influences more tactical decisions later in the product life cycle, from early adoption through growth, to saturation. After all, with a substantial market available to exploit, the managerial argument shifts from whether there are opportunities for profit to how such opportunities can be capitalized upon. In addition, the forecasts derived from the trend curve modeling exercise are often sensitive to the estimates of market potential and are themselves highly uncertain, as Table 12.7 shows for Germany. To make matters worse, the expected final penetration level itself can be increased (or decreased) by changes in the marketing of the product through pricing, distribution, and advertising, as well as by macroeconomic factors such as GDP, which change the affordability of the product.

One route to establishing the product's potential is through the use of an intentions survey, a survey that asks potential customers what their likelihood of purchase is (see Section 11.2.4; see also Morwitz, 2001). Various alternative approaches can be used to ask equivalent questions — for example, the constant-sum method, whereby potential customers are asked to allocate (or spend) part of a fixed amount among competing products, preferably in a simulated purchasing environment that is close to reality. Once the overall likelihood of purchase is calculated for different market segments, the total forecast of market potential is the product of the expected numbers of consumers falling into the segments and the estimated probability of purchase in each segment, summed over the segments.

But where a product or service has features that a purchaser must trade off against an alternative set, or where the potential customer is unfamiliar with some aspects of the product, a more complex approach is needed. The goal is to explain the choices consumers may make through various explanatory models that link the range of product attributes to the likelihood of purchasing a particular product. The core assumption is that customers value a product overall by valuing its individual attributes (or benefits), with one attribute compensating for another. (See, for instance, Table 12.8, where running costs counterbalance purchase price.)

Table 12.8 A Sample of Choice Scenarios in the Chinese Car Market

	Vehicle 1	**Vehicle 2**	**Vehicle 3**
Fuel type	Gasoline	Hybrid	Electric
Purchase price (RMB)	75000	97500	135000
Annual running cost (RMB)	15000	9000	7000
Government incentives to purchase	Not applicable	Priority lane	30,000 RMB subsidy
Availability of charging facility	Not applicable	Not applicable	40% of parking slots
Vehicle range with full charging	Not applicable	Not applicable	80 km
Your choice:	☐	☐	☐

Source: Adapted from Qian and Soopramanien (2011). NB: RMB is the Chinese currency.

Conjoint Choice Models, based on a survey of potential consumers, can be used to assess the relative value of the various attributes of the product or service that are expected to influence future intentions to purchase.

After the identification of the target population for the product, the first stage in the process is to identify the key attributes that characterize the product or service. This can be done through interviews and focus groups (as discussed in Section 11.2.2), as well as by reviewing the literature on analogous products to establish the attributes other researchers have found to be important. Then, a survey of potential customers is carried out that asks them how they value the new product concept or service (compared with a range of alternatives) on the basis of its attributes and also their likelihood of purchase (see Section 11.2.4). In so doing, the survey collects information on the characteristics of the respondent. Respondents either rank a range of alternatives or choose among them. The product attributes are often measured as dummy variables showing the presence or absence of an attribute or its level. Thus, different levels of the price of a product would each be assigned a dummy variable. For example, Qian and Soopramanien (2011) used a choice model to estimate the market potential for alternative-fuel cars (gasoline, hybrid, or electric) based on the attributes shown in Table 12.8.

CONJOINT ANALYSIS

Conjoint analysis assumes a product is made up of some key *attributes* and each attribute has a number of *levels* (options). For example, an attribute could be color and the levels could be red, green, and blue. In setting up attributes and their levels the following guidelines are important:

- Use only a few important and distinct attributes (see for example Table 12.8). Using a large number of attributes will confuse the survey respondents.

- Use only a few, easily distinguishable levels. Often the consumers' views on intermediate levels can be inferred. For example, from information on the duration of stay in a hotel: for levels of 2 days, 7 days and 14 days respondents' views could be inferred about a 10 days stay by linearly interpolating the results from 7 and 14 days.

- Use attributes and levels that are understandable to survey participants. For example, describing the level of noise in decibels will challenge even engineers to relate to, while describing noise 'like a whisper' is something that most people can relate to.

- Avoid subjective options. For example, giving the length of a conversation in minutes is more useful than describing it as 'long'. What is long for one respondent may not be for another!

DISCUSSION QUESTION: *Consider the choice you make when deciding how to communicate with someone at a distance (e.g., mobile, landline, IMS, Voice over the Internet — VoIP). What are the key attributes that affect your choice, and what circumstances affect their relative value to you?*

Where potential purchasers (respondents) choose between different products, a choice model can infer how much weight they are giving to the different attributes that distinguish between the different choices which are on offer. This same set of approaches can be used to *indirectly* estimate a consumer's preference; the approach is referred to as *self-explicated conjoint*. The first stage is to ask participants to rate the importance or value of the different attributes (using one of the different rating or ranking methods). Then they score each product or choice on these attributes. For example, a participant might rate *brand* as having a weight of 0.33 (the weights associated with the attributes should sum to 1) and then, with a new branded product in mind, could score this rating as being valued at 0.5 (compared with other products' ratings scoring higher or lower). This attribute would then contribute $0.5 \times 0.33 = 0.167$ to the overall valuation of the product. In selecting the attributes, it is important that they remain distinct, lest double counting give undue weight to both attributes taken together (Goodwin and Wright, 2014, p. 39). A second problematic issue is where consumer preferences change over time (Meeran, Jahanbin, Goodwin, and Quariguasi Frota Neto, 2017) which will often have major implications for forecasting.

What all these methods have in common is that the preference for a product is some function of a weighted sum of the value imputed to the attributes (sometimes called *part worths*), thereby providing an estimate of the overall relative value for the particular alternative under consideration. Essentially, the valuable attributes of a product compensate for weaker performance of other attributes.[6] The overall value, V_j is given by the weighted sum of the individual attributes values, $V_j = \Sigma_k w_{kj} A_{kj}$. Finally, the ith individual's preference or choice for the jth product is taken as a (sometimes linear) function of the overall value (or utility). We thus have

$$Preference_{ij} = f\left(\sum_{k=1}^{p} w_{ijk} A_{jk}\right) = f(V_{ij}),$$

where $Preference_{ij}$ is the preference of the ith respondent for the jth alternative (product) and w_{ijk} is the weight the ith respondent implicitly assigns to the kth attribute of the jth product, A_{jk}. The weights can be estimated over a group of participants in the survey. The data consists of the responses to questions "which product would you choose from the range of alternatives?" and a set of usually quantitative indicator variables that describe the alternatives. By the inclusion of sociodemographic dummy variables the preference weights for different market segments can be established. This process then leads to aggregate estimates of the potential penetration for different market segments. In a choice model, the relationship between purchase intentions and preference scores is usually assumed to be logistic (see Equation 10.2 and the accompanying discussion), with the parameters representing the odds of preferring one product to another. (Classification trees, discussed in Section 10.2, can also be used, although they are not based on a compensatory model. However, the results do lead to a ranking of the importance of the various explanatory attributes.) There are various preference or choice functions, such as assuming that each consumer chooses the alternative which maximizes his value function. For the logit model, this becomes the probability of the ith respondent choosing alternative j from J alternatives, which is

$$P_{ij} = \frac{\exp(V_{ij})}{\displaystyle\sum_j \exp(V_{ij})}.$$

As noted various demographic variables can be included in the value function to explain different levels of interest from the different market segments.

Qian and Soopramanien (2011) used this approach to derive probabilities of selecting each of the three alternative types of car, depending on the market segment into which the respondent falls. (Demographics that include variables such as family size, income, and age were added as control variables to study the differential choices made in the various market segments.) Illustrative results from estimating the logit model give weights of –1.3 for the

---

6 These values are more generally called *utilities*; see, e.g., Goodwin and Wright, 2014, which discusses the differences between the two. For our purposes here, we do not need to make the distinction.

electric car, +0.87 for the hybrid (compared with the gasoline-driven car), a price effect of –0.01, and a running cost of –0.06. As with any logit model, these weights translate into percentage increases (or decreases) in the probability of selecting the choice (e.g., $\exp(-1.3)$ = 0.27, or a 27 percent chance of choosing the electric car compared with the base choice of the gasoline-fueled car). When the attributes describing the type of car available for the respondents to buy are supplemented with the government incentives and various demographic weights, the probability of purchase for the three types can be calculated. Most statistical software provide an adequate toolset to aid in the construction of such surveys and in the estimation of values/utilities and preferences.

In the example reference, the final stage in estimating the market potential (or market share) uses simulation of the individuals or market segments, based on the probabilities (or preferences) of the individuals or segments choosing the different types of car. By knowing the combination of attributes of the focal product (and potential competitors), we identify the choices that individuals (or segments) would make, and from that calculate the market potential and share.

In sum, conjoint choice modeling (or, more generally, conjoint analysis) offers a partial solution to the difficult problem of modeling market potential and market shares for a new product or service. However, putting the approach into practice is far from straightforward, starting with the problem of identifying the target market and the attributes to consider. Wittink and Bergestuen (2001) offer a useful summary of the "major elements of a conjoint study" as well as the "conditions under which conjoint should work well" (pp. 151–152). For example, customer preferences and estimates of market potential should be mediated by variables such as the availability of the product. (If, say, only 50 percent of the potential market has access to super-fast broadband, then the current operational market potential for this product is halved.)

Accessible references that expand on the alternative approaches to estimating market potential are available through Sawtooth, one of the major suppliers of software, training, and analysis (*www.sawtoothsoftware.com/solutions/conjoint_analysis.shtml*). Marder (1999) expands on the relationship between self-explicated approaches and indirect choice models (*http://emaprinciples.com/articles/cjmr1.pdf*). Lilien and Rangaswamy (2004) offer a more detailed summary of some of these issues at a mathematical level similar to that presented in this text. More advanced references are Wind and Green (2005, Section 5) and Gustafsson, Herrmann, and Huber (2001). Conjoint suffers from one damaging weakness: there has been little research that has validated its usefulness (compared to alternative methods such as expert judgment).

The final approach in our discussion of estimating market potential is to use analogous products (with Lilien *et al.*, 2000, providing a useful database) as a basis for making a judgmental estimate of the final penetration level, as we explained in Section 11.2.5. But as we previously noted, identifying plausible analogies is not an automatic recipe for success, although there may be no other route forward without collecting survey data (Goodwin, Dyussekeneva, and Meeran, 2011).

Whichever approach is taken, it is important that the choices are contextualized as effectively as possible so that the respondent feels that the purchase situation is realistic. This requirement means that the attribute set has to include all the most important factors and that the context of the purchase (including, e.g., competitive products) should be realistic. Computer-based simulations of the shopping experience have been used to meet the requirement. Modern technology, with augmented or virtual reality, provides exciting alternatives. As ever, a combination of the applicable methods for forecasting market potential is likely to work best.

DISCUSSION QUESTION: *(1) What factors may affect the final uptake of self-drive cars in the United States? In Italy? (2) Thinking of the latest new major product or service just becoming available, write down an estimate of the percentage of the population (or households) that you expect will adopt the product or service in its final penetration level. What factors may affect its final uptake? After the class discussion of the final uptake, do you want to revise your estimate?*

While market potential is a key variable in any new product decision, on its own it is insufficient to justify investment in the product. The diffusion parameters as discussed previously remain a critical element. Methods have been developed that integrate choice-based models with the estimation of the diffusion curve (Jun and Park, 1999, analyzed successive generations of computers and DRAMS; Lee, Cho, Lee, and Lee, 2006, examined large-screen TV sets).

12.4.5 Market Response Models

Market response models are used both to forecast aggregate medium-term movements in product sales or market shares and in market planning — for example, in deciding pricing strategies. They are also at the heart of the shorter term focused promotional price optimization. Such models extend the promotional modeling framework discussed in Section 12.2.1 that considered promotional effects at the SKU level. They aim to include the key explanatory "sales driver" variables in a causal model of demand. The dependent variable modeled is sales volume, at the SKU, product, brand, or category level.

Although there seems to be no ambiguity about how sales should be measured at the dis-aggregate SKU level, in practice there are many different measures, from factory shipments to store scanner data. As ever, we need to distinguish between sales, which are observed, and demand, which is unobserved (see Section 12.3.1). Hanssens, Parsons, and Schultz (2001) provide a thorough discussion of these various sources of data and their advantages and disadvantages. A further difficulty of definition arises as we move from an individual SKU to a brand and attempt to aggregate the result (e.g., from beer in four-packs of 250 ml to cases of 330 ml bottles). More difficult still would be to measure the sales of a particular brand of detergent for use in washing machines that comes not only in powder and liquid forms, but also in different levels of concentrate. Because of these difficulties, the variables to be forecast are often best kept as disaggregated as the data permit.

WHEN MODELING DEMAND

- Use a measure of sales volume that removes the effects of price changes and package size.
- Take into account lost sales due to supply shortages.

Price and income should be among the explanatory variables typically included in market response models of sales when the focus is longer term (income doesn't change much in the short-term). Both need careful thought as to how they should be measured. Price data are collected in current money: dollars, pounds, euros, etc. In a cross-sectional study designed to explain consumer behavior, this is unproblematic, but if price data are collected over time, general inflation (the overall price movements in an economy) may affect consumer response so that a dollar in one year buys less than a dollar did the year before. The problem is overcome by measuring price (or any variable expressed in money terms, including income) in real terms by dividing money prices by a price index such as the Consumer Price Index (published monthly by the Bureau of Labor Statistics in the United States and by government statistics offices in most countries). The issue of real vs. nominal measures of money was explored briefly in Exercise 9.13, which contrasted a model of unleaded prices in money terms with one in real, or inflation-adjusted, form.

Once the effect of general inflation is taken out of the price measure, it still leaves the question of how consumers perceive price when contemplating a purchase. Often, consumers' perceptions are based on alternative purchases in the category; therefore, the appropriate measure is the brand's own price, relative to the average market price, which is an average of prices, weighted by their respective sales volumes. That is, when there are J products in a category, the relative price of the ith product is given by

$$Relative\ Price_{it} = \frac{p_{it}}{\sum_{j=1}^{J} (p_{jt} Vol_{jt}/ Total\ Vol_t)},$$

where Vol_{jt} represents the sales volume for the jth brand at time t. The denominator represents the average price in the category and this is lagged or an average taken over time, because it denotes the consumers' subjective understanding, which would affect demand. Further, Vol_{jt} would not be known during period t so must be lagged.

Income, in the aggregate or for an individual consumer, can also be measured in many ways. First, like price, it must be measured in real terms, with inflation effects removed (if a time series is being analyzed). Second, there is the question of whether any taxes paid should also be subtracted (the result of which is called *Disposable Income*). In addition, we might wish to focus on *Discretionary Income* after basic living costs, such as housing and energy, are removed as well. Finally, in considering purchases of consumer durables, it may be worth identifying *Permanent Income*, which is essentially a smoothed average of current and past income. The argument here is that major financial commitments are likely to be based on expectations that one's income will continue. A pragmatic route forward is to include current and lagged values of income in the response model.

Response models also include the price of competing products or services. For example, in models of tourism demand, the price of staying in alternative tourist destinations should be included in the initial, most general models considered (Song and Li, 2008).

Often, marketing activities — for example, advertising or a promotional mailing — have effects on sales that last over a period of time. The basic model

$$Y = \beta_0 + \beta_j X_{jt}^* + (other\ factors) + (error)$$

includes a particular marketing activity, X_j^*, that is related not only to current spending (on, say, a mail promotion) but also to past spending. For example, if effects persist for $r_j + 1$ periods, then

$$X_{jt}^* = \sum_{k=0}^{r_j} \lambda_k X_{j,t-k},$$

where $\lambda_0 = 1$. If $\lambda_k = 0$ for all $k > 0$, then there is only an immediate effect of β_j, due to X_{jt} affecting Y. Nonzero λ_k for $k > 0$ implies that past levels of X_j also affect current levels of Y. Advertising is just such an example, because it is often thought of as having just such a cumulative effect over time. X_j^* is sometimes called *Adstock*. (See the discussion in Hanssens, Parsons, and Schultz, 2001, for further details.) Similarly, in the important example of forecasting calls to a call center, the number of incoming calls is stimulated by mail promotions; however, the mailings neither go out on the same day they are scheduled nor get delivered on the same day, so the telephone response on a particular day depends on past mailings over quite a number of periods. (See Minicase 12.1.)

An important influence on current demand is the consumer's habits; that is, past behavior carries over into the present. In an extreme case, the product is addictive, as in cigarette or alcohol consumption. In essence, past demand affects current demand, so it is often natural to include lagged values of Y as one of the drivers of current consumption. The basic model then becomes

$$Y_t = \beta_0 + \gamma_1 Y_{t-1} + \beta_j X^*_{jt} + (other\ factors) + (error).$$

Additional lags beyond one may also be justified empirically, so the simple model of demand now includes lags in both the dependent variable and some of the explanatory market drivers. Seasonal lags may capture behavioral seasonal effects, so a four-period lag would be considered for quarterly data.

The opposite idea is that of the stock of a product that consumers already own. As in the example of cars, the stock of cars already on the road and the average age of that stock are likely to influence the next period's purchases. Suppose the stock at time $(t - 1)$ is S_{t-1} with Y_t the current purchases. Then the stock at time t is given by

$$S_t = S_{t-1} - \delta S_{t-1} + Y_{t-1},$$

where δS_{t-1} is the number of cars scrapped at time S_{t-1}. Thus, a demand model that explains car sales Y_t in period t, in terms of stocks, is

$$Y_t = \beta_0 + \beta_{stock} S_t + (other\ factors) + (error).$$

By substituting for S_t, the model becomes a model in lagged values of Y_t, the other factors, and the error. In the example of modeling and forecasting car demand, running costs could be included, in addition to the stock of used cars on the road (de Jong et al., 2004).

■ Example 12.5: Model for air travel demand

Various air travel models have included lag effects to take into account habit formation as well as trade growth to capture economic activities (Fildes, Wei, and Ismail, 2011). As we pointed out in Chapter 9, lags will typically account for autocorrelation. For the route between the United Kingdom and Canada, an autoregressive distributed lag model of the annual growth rate in passengers (measured in logarithms of differences) and of the form

$$Dy_t = \alpha_0 + \sum_{j=1}^{2} \alpha_j Dy_{t-j} + \sum_{k=1}^{2} \sum_{j=0}^{2} \beta_{kj} Dx_{k(t-j)} + \varepsilon_t$$

was proposed, where $t = 1, 2, \ldots, T$ (time periods); Dy_t is the growth rate of the number of passenger in year t; and Dx_{kt} is the growth rate of the 2 explanatory variables, here international trade and ticket price, in year t. A maximum lag length of 2 was needed, and the model was simplified as illustrated below. The data for a number of countries, including Canada, are given in *Air_passenger.xlsx*. The model was estimated from 1961–2002 to give

$$Dy_t = 0.0260 + 0.509^* Dy_{t-1} + 0.199^* DTrade_{t-2} - 0.196^* DTicketPrice_t;\ R^2(adj) = 42.6\%$$
$$\quad (0.013) \quad (0.125) \qquad (0.085) \qquad\qquad (0.058)$$

where the asterisks (*) denote coefficients that are significant at the 1 percent level. (Standard errors are shown in parentheses.) The model was estimated in differences in order to capture the fact that all the variables were nonstationary (see Appendix 10C). In the model, the persistence of a habit is shown by the lagged impact of the previous year's growth. In addition, both *Trade* between the two countries and the *TicketPrice* have the expected sign, although the two period lag on *Trade* is perhaps counter-intuitive. The model also passes various diagnostic tests, including autocorrelation and, in particular, parameter constancy. Extending the analysis to look across five routes from the United Kingdom, including a route to the United States, showed (unsurprisingly) that the terrorist attacks of September 11, 2001, had a significantly negative impact on travel (see Exercise 12.22). ∎

Market response models have also been developed to forecast the demand for particular brands of goods at the individual store level. A typical causal model is of the form

$$Market\ response_{ijt} = f(marketing\ instruments: price, display, feature, store, competition,$$
$$events, promotion, \dots\ ; seasonality; exogenous\ factors),$$

where i is the ith brand (or SKU) in a category of closely related products, j is the jth store, and t is time.

BUILDING MARKET RESPONSE MODELS

In building a market response model, the key decisions to make are:

(i) which explanatory variables to include in the proposed model; and

(ii) the appropriate level of aggregation at which to build the model.

∎ Example 12.6: Market response model for soft drinks

Divakar, Ratchford, and Shankar (2005) used the preceding model to examine the soft-drinks market in the United States. They considered two leading brands (Pepsi and Coke) and data on different distribution channels to market, such as grocery stores, convenience stores, gas stations, and restaurants. They considered a log-log model where sales volume and the explanatory variables that measure price have been logged. Two additional promotional variables were included: *Display* (indicating whether the product is displayed to best advantage at the point of sale), measured as percent of total volume only on display, and *Feature*, measured as percent of total volume featured without display (i.e., in a local store, leaflet advertising promoted products). Also measured was percent of total volume both featured and displayed.

Part of Divakar and colleagues' model for the grocery channel is

$$\ln(Pepsi\ volume) = 17.645 - 2.342\ln(Pepsi's\ price) + 0.583\ln(Coke's\ price)$$
$$(23.9) \qquad\qquad\qquad (5.88)$$

$$+ 0.0028(Pepsi's\ Display) + \dots + 0.0018\,Temp + (Dummies).$$
$$(3.15) \qquad\qquad\qquad (6.64)$$

t-statistics are shown in parentheses. $R^2 = 90$ percent. There is no indication of any autocorrelation in the residuals.

Estimated price and cross-price elasticities, at -2.34 and $+0.58$, respectively, accorded with other studies, so a 10 percent increase in Pepsi's price is forecast to lead to a drop of 23.4 percent in the sales volume while the impact of a 10 percent increase in Coke's price is estimated to lead to a 5.83 percent increase in Pepsi's volume.

Additional variables included in the model were dummy variables for U.S. regions, for different periods of the year, and for sporting events (e.g., the U.S. Super Bowl). Temperature (*Temp*) also had an effect, as shown in the model, with higher temperatures leading to higher sales. Because *Display* and *Feature* are measured in percentages, their impact is calculated by multiplying by 100 and taking the exponential of the result. For example, the display effect when 100 percent of volume is on display is $\exp(0.0028 \times 100) = 1.32$; that is, display increases volume by 32 percent (ranging from no store level display to 100 percent of volume being displayed).

When the model was used to forecast sales in individual regions (in the grocery channel) out of sample, *MAPE* one week ahead was around 5.5 percent, dropping to 3.1 percent when aggregated across regions.

Of course, some of the explanatory variables would be unknown when the model is put to use, so variables such as competitor price, as well as feature and display, are market drivers outside the manufacturer's control. Accordingly, models were then developed to forecast these explanatory variables, using the same variables as included in the original model. ∎

Models have been proposed to capture the relative attraction of one brand compared with that of its competitors or, more generally, one SKU within a brand. A particular SKU may compete with other *product forms* within the same brand (e.g., different pack sizes), as well as competing with other brands (and their various product forms). For a full discussion of the various forms, the reader should consult Hanssens *et al.* (2001, pp. 121–129); however, be warned that this is a demanding read. Equally demanding, Snyder *et al.* (2017) use logistic transforms to examine exponential smoothing models for market share.

A model that captures the various market complexities must include competing brands and the different product forms. Let $p = 1,\ldots, P$ represent the different product forms, and $b = 1,\ldots, B$ the different competing brands. Then if Q_{bp} represents the demand for brand b's product form p, where Q_{bp} could, in principle, depend on K variables and where each variable (e.g., price) could affect Q via all its competing products, it follows that if the price of a competing 20-oz pack goes down, then the drop in price could affect the quantity demanded of product bp (brand b in product form p). Perhaps the simplest model that captures competitive effects would be of the form

$$\ln Q_{bp,t} = \beta_{bp0} + \beta_{bp,bp} \ln X_{bp,t} + \beta_{bp,b1} \ln X_{b1,t} + \beta_{bp,1p} \ln X_{1p,t} + \beta_{bp,11} \ln X_{11,t} + \varepsilon_{bp,t}.$$

where X_{bp} represents the price of brand b (with form p), X_{1p} represents the price of brand 1 with form p, etc. Here, product form p in brand b is thought only to compete through price directly with form 1 of the same brand and competing brand 1 (also in forms 1 and p): The parameters represent the own-price elasticity ($\beta_{bp,bp}$) and cross-price elasticities (for form 1 of the same brand, $\beta_{bp,b1}$; for the competitor's form p, $\beta_{bp,1p}$, and for the competitor's form 1, $\beta_{bp,11}$). Although $\beta_{bp,bp}$ is expected to be negative, the cross-elasticities on product bp are expected to be positive. The higher price of a competing product or a competing product form, the higher are the sales of the product we focus on.

These same ideas can be used to develop market response models to capture the share of a product's sales through a market share model in which

$$Market\ Share = \frac{Our\ Sales}{Total\ Market\ Sales} \quad \text{or} \quad MS_{bp} = \frac{Q_{bp}}{\sum\limits_{i=1}^{B} \sum\limits_{j=1}^{P} Q_{ij}}.$$

An alternative multiplicative model of market share is

$$\ln (MS_{bp,t}) = \beta_0 + \sum_{k,i} \beta_{bp,ki} \ln (X^*_{bpk,t}) + \varepsilon_{bpt},$$

where $X^*_{bpk,t}$ represents the M_i competitive marketing variable, such as relative price, promotional deals, and various retail characteristics (e.g., distribution and advertising), each of which may be lagged one or more periods. (Of course, a linear version of the same model could also be used.) Market share models should be logically consistent in that, summed over the whole market, $\Sigma_{b,p}MS_{bp} = 1$. However, the multiplicative form does not have that characteristic (but this does not prevent it from being a reasonable approximation).

Models such as these are complex, with too many parameters to estimate. Alternatively, these cross-effects could all be set to zero, but doing so would often render the model unrealistic. Instead, perhaps the best approach would be to set most cross-effects to zero and consider only products that are believed by market experts to compete.

A more heuristic, but still often effective, approach is to run a stepwise regression analysis (Section 9.4) with the cutoff value $\alpha = 1/N$, where N denotes the total number of predictor variables. The use of an extreme cutoff value ensures that the risk of including spurious variables in the model is low so that most terms are excluded, but the decision is made with the use of data-driven rules rather than prior judgments. Other variables enter into such models include display (which describes how the product is displayed in the store) and feature (which describes whether the product is in retail advertisements) as well as lags in some the variables. As if this wasn't complicated enough, if we are a retailer, we may wish to understand and forecast at a store level. So the model can be extended to include store-level effects. It is unfortunate for the forecaster that stores differ in terms of their local markets and therefore experience different elasticities, depending on the preferences of their local consumers. Recent developments in analyzing large databases when there are many explanatory variables have opened up the realistic prospect of including both competitive SKUs within category as well as potentially complimentary SKUs in other categories. Lasso (see Section 9.5.2) can be used to shrink many of the parameters to zero. This has produced more accurate forecasting at store level and through an associated promotional optimization algorithm offers the realistic prospects of greater profits (estimated by Ma and Fildes, 2017, at 17%).

But with such complexities, how do practicing forecasters deal with the problem? The next section suggests some simple solutions that avoid the problems — but of course there's a cost!

12.4.6 Expert Adjustments and Promotional Effects

For most organizations, developing models of the complexity described in the previous section has historically proved just too difficult. There were probably no staff with the necessary expertise, nor were the data and the software available. Instead, forecasters resorted to taking a simple statistical approach and then would modify the baseline statistical forecast (see Section 12.2.1) to take into account the expected promotional effects. With recent improvements in data collection (e.g., point-of-sale data capture, the use of social networks) and more sophisticated models and software available, this state of affairs is beginning to change.

Returning to the question of promotional adjustments, we saw in Sections 12.2.1 and 12.4.5 how this might be done statistically. But typically, there are many different types of promotion (e.g., buy one, get one free; half price; 30 percent extra), and forecasters see their role as taking all the particular characteristics of these promotions into account by adjusting the statistical forecast. So, do they do this well?

Empirical evidence presented in Fildes *et al.* (2009) and Franses (2014) suggests that forecasters often fail quite spectacularly. In the Fildes *et al.* study an analysis of four companies revealed that all the companies typically overestimated the expected positive effects of factors such as promotions. (There was a positive bias to the adjusted forecasts.) What was worse is that often the adjustments made by the company forecasters were in the wrong direction, due perhaps to competitive factors being neglected. Franses (2014) also found similar evidence of biases and inefficiencies. There is therefore an obvious need to develop forecasting support systems (FSSs) so as to help practicing forecasters take account of promotions and other market drivers more successfully.

> **DISCUSSION QUESTION:** *How might an FSS be extended beyond the purely statistical to help forecasters take into account promotions and other market drivers?*

12.4.7 Implementation Issues

Market response modeling has been established in the research literature for many years. However, implementing the models we have examined has proved difficult for many companies, for reasons we will discuss in the last chapter of this book. In fact, Montgomery (2005) summarized the retail evidence on the practice of market modeling as follows: "the market is ready ... although widespread adoption has not happened yet" and we have no reason to believe this has changed much, more than ten years later. Occasionally, we find evidence of an advanced application; see, for example, Natter, Reutterer, Mild, and Taudes (2007), which uses the price elasticities at store level in an Austrian-German do-it-yourself chain to both forecast and price the stores' products. In recent years, software providers such as SAP have provided advanced modeling facilities, but examples of implementation are unusual. Even when a farsighted manager is successful in taking a marketing analytic view forward, it seems rare for these ideas to become embedded in the firm. All too often, the manager moves on and the system fails. It even seems rare to find companies with databases sufficiently rich to include a substantial and accessible history of their own price and promotion data, never mind that of their competition. Nor is the necessary in-house expertise available as few of the methods will run automatically. Instead, simple models are most often used, but as we have noted, new data sources are likely to drive change in this area, solving at least one part of the jigsaw. We already see dramatic changes in the analysis of web-based search data in analytical systems designed to increase customer purchases, a topic we discuss in the next section.

12.5 Forecasting Individual Behavior

In Chapter 10, we introduced various methods of mining rich databases of customer (or potential customer) characteristics in order to predict behavior. Companies want to forecast individual consumer behavior (and sometimes firm behavior) in order to gain and keep additional profitable customers. A second important application is the granting of consumer credit. Besides private companies, other organizations — for example, governments — want to forecast individual behavior for some of the same reasons, in order to predict the uptake of services. More controversially, they may wish to identify criminals who might reoffend (recidivists, who then would not be released from jail) or potential terrorists, who would undergo more intensive screening (prior to an aircraft flight, for example).

The information the organization has to help it in this regard depends on the nature of the customer relationship — in particular, whether a past history is available from a previous relationship with the organization or whether the customer is new. Figure 12.19 breaks down the process of forecasting individual behavior into four stages: (i) target marketing, in which the aim is to identify potentially profitable customers, (ii) new-customer acquisition, wherein the potential customer, having received an offer, must be accepted as a new customer (in some instances, e.g., credit granting or insurance, this may involve further information being provided by the customer before a final decision to enter into a relationship with that customer is made), (iii) maintaining a relationship, in which, after the new customer has established early patterns of behavior (e.g., through mobile calling or credit card spending), the company aims to increase the customer's profitability through cross-selling of complementary products or through promotional offers that make further spending more attractive (these are high-value customers), and (iv) churning, wherein the company loses a customer, usually because the customer has identified a better offer or because the customer is dissatisfied.

Figure 12.19 Forecasting Individual Behavior *(Adapted from Figure 12.12)*

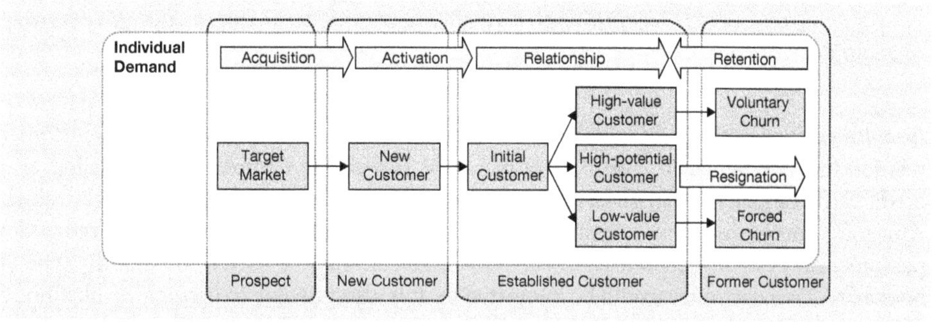

Target Marketing: Even when there has been no contact between the organization and the potential customer, some limited sociodemographic information may be readily available. This may include public social media information as well as the zip code and gender of the person in the United States or the post-code, gender, and eligibility to vote in the United Kingdom. The zip code[7] (or postcode in the United Kingdom) can be used to classify the address so that it provides proxy (indirect) information on such characteristics as income, marital status, lifestyle, and housing and this may be combined with information from a search of social media. Systems such as Mosaic, Tapestry, and Prizm are now available in much of the developed world, with Acorn in the UK, although such classifications are limited in that they associate with each person an average value for the area he or she lives in, rather than affording individual information.

GEODEMOGRAPHIC SEGMENTATION SYSTEMS (GSS)

A GSS classifies neighborhoods (e.g., census tracts) into segments (e.g., 60 or so in the United States) by grouping tracts with similar demographic characteristics. The basic premise of geodemographic segmentation is that people tend to gravitate toward communities with people of similar backgrounds, interests, and financial means.

Sociodemographic data can be enhanced by using credit agencies to add such important details as whether the person has incurred debts that have led to legal proceedings. In addition, many of the companies that provide credit pool some of their information, including such key variables as the outstanding balance on a debt and the current and his-

---

7 In the United States, there are legal restrictions on the use of information such as zip codes and ethnicity in making decisions on credit applications, etc.

torical arrears record. The dependent variable here is whether to make an offer or to target a particular customer.

New Customers: In some applications, the stage after contacting the individual through target marketing is when the potential customer responds to the offer. The additional information the company learns from a customer's response offers the opportunity for understanding the customer's characteristics. Using the credit card application as an example, we see that the additional information would include personal sociodemographic information such as marital status, length of time at the current address, and income. This additional information can then be used to accept or reject an application or, more ambitiously, to price the offer through the terms of credit offered. The dependent variable here is whether to accept the customer's application.

> **DISCUSSION QUESTION:** *Is the use of such targeting methods ethical in considering (i) credit approvals, (ii) the identification of potential tax evaders, or (iii) the identification of potential terrorists?*

Established Customers and Churning: Valuable information is collected once the customer relationship is established with the company. Be it a phone company, a bookseller, or a credit card company, it can observe how the customer uses the product or service. Taking Amazon as an example, we see that once the purchasing record has been observed and a person's tastes established at least in part, that data can then be used to predict the type of books or CDs a customer would be interested in. It is also possible to predict the likelihood of a new purchase being prompted by a mail promotion or offer, as well as the size of the likely order. Table 12.9 summarizes the types of data used in direct marketing.

Table 12.9 Types of Explanatory Data Used to Predict Response

Object	Type of Data	Significance	Accessibility	Variability
Customer	Demographic, lifestyle, sociographic	Low	External	High
Behavior	Transaction records, Web-browsing log file	High	Internal, accumulating	High
Product	Size, color, price	Low	Internal	Low
Type of Solicitation	Design style of offer	Low	Internal	Low

Source: Bose and Chen (2009).

The trouble with behavioral (transactions) data is that the database quickly gets very large. Various summary measures are used to capture the key characteristics of a customer's transactions, such as the *RFM* measures of R (recency, or the length of time since the last purchase), F (the frequency of purchase during a period), and M (monetary value of purchases over a period). Other databases beyond customer transactions are also relevant to both future purchasing behavior and whether a customer will "churn" — that is, change supplier. Here, customer satisfaction with the reliability of the service can affect the probability of churning, and companies often collect survey data on this measure. (Customer satisfaction is particularly relevant to telephone companies, Internet providers, insurance companies, etc.) What has proved even more relevant is the customer's satisfaction *after* a complaint or problem such as an interruption of service or a car accident.

In most of the applications we have described thus far, the dependent variable is categorical (0 or 1). The decision made by the credit supplier is to agree an application or to reject it on the basis of the potential customer's likelihood of default. In analyzing a consumer's propensity to churn, the aim is to classify customers into those who are loyal and those who are likely to switch. In direct marketing, the objective is to identify potential customers. We will use the methods of Chapter 10 to classify, as an example, a loan applicant. We first examine some of the practicalities of building such models using the industry standard method of logistic regression as well as the neural nets and classification trees. Once some of the problems such as missing data and sample limitations are overcome we go on to examine how such methods can be appraised. Our aim here is to show how the models we have introduced can be used in practice to forecast individual credit behavior. Thomas (2009) offers a detailed review of the topic, including an examination of the evaluation of such models, expanding on our discussion in Section 10.1.1 while Finlay (2012) gives an accessible and broad view of consumer forecasting in general.

12.5.1 Building Consumer Classification Models: The Example of Consumer Loans

In this example of consumer assessment for a housing loan, we show how the different methods of predictive classification (developed in Chapter 10) can be used. This case study in comparing models (taken with thanks to SAS for the use of its case study in its data-mining software package, Enterprise Miner; see SAS, 2013) has the objective of identifying likely defaulters for applicants for home equity credit (mortgages in the UK). The full database consists of 5960 observations with 12 predictor variables, defined in Table 12.10. The target variable, *BAD*, is whether the applicant (who had taken up a loan) subsequently defaulted on the loan, a 0/1 categorical variable.

Table 12.10 Predicting Loan Default: Explanatory (Input) Variables and Variable Type

Name	Description	Model Role	Measurement	Type
BAD	= 1 if the applicant defaulted on loan, = 0 if paid up	Target	Binary	Number
Loan	Amount of loan request	Input	Interval	Number
Mortdue	Amount due on existing mortgage	Input	Interval	Number
Value	Value of current property	Input	Interval	Number
Reason	HomeImp = Home Improvement: DebtCon=Debt consolidation	Input	Binary	Character
Job	Present job title	Input	Nominal	Character
YOJ	Years in present job	Input	Interval	Number
Derog	Number of derogatory reports	Input	Interval	Number
Delinq	Number of delinquent credit lines	Input	Interval	Number
CLAGE	Age of oldest credit line in months	Input	Interval	Number
NINQ	Number of recent credit inquiries	Input	Interval	Number
CLNO	Number of credit lines	Input	Interval	Number
Debtinc	Debt-to-income ratio	Input	Interval	Number

Source: Adapted from SAS output.

The input variables include a mixture of financial credit variables (such as *Loan, Mortdue, Delinq, CLAGE, NINQ, CLNO*) and personal finance variables (*Value, Debtinc*).

Job is a nominal variable describing the job held by the applicant. Each type of job is classified by a separate dummy variable, and there are five major job categories in all. YOJ (*years in the present job*) measures job stability (to a certain extent). *Reason* is a 0/1 binary dummy variable that describes the reason given by the applicant for applying for the loan.

The data set has initially been split into an estimation (training) subset (50 percent), a validation set (30 percent), and a test set (20 percent). If the database has been collected over a number of periods, the forecaster must consider whether a time-based sample should also be considered to identify "model drift," a condition that occurs when models change over time. Model drift is a common occurrence when economic circumstances change (as when a recession is developing).

We will first use all the variables in Table 12.10 in developing and comparing three models: a logistic regression model, a neural network, and a classification tree. The first stage in understanding the issues is to carry out some exploratory analysis, including frequency analysis and graphical analysis, missing variables, correlations, and more. We've left this as an exercise for the reader (Exercise 12.26); however, we note one important result: The percentage of defaulted loans in the sample of 5960 observations is 20 percent.

Logistic Regression: The model, including all the explanatory variables, was estimated automatically on the 50% training set giving the results shown in Table 12.11. Missing values were replaced with their mean value (see Section 12.5.2).

Table 12.11 Logistic Regression Model to Classify Potential Bad Loans: Point Estimates and Odds Ratio Estimates

Effect	Point Estimate	P-Value	Odds Ratio*
Intercept: BAD =1	−2.276	0.000	0.103
CLAGE	−0.005	0.000	0.995
CLNO	−0.023	0.000	0.977
DEBTINC	0.057	0.000	1.058
DELINQ	0.818	0.000	2.266
DEROG	0.545	0.000	1.724
JOB MGR	0.014	0.924	1.014
JOB OFFICE	−0.652	0.000	0.521
JOB OTHER	−0.126	0.260	0.882
JOB PROFEXE	−0.171	0.214	0.843
JOB SALES	0.832	0.010	2.297
LOAN	0.000	0.000	1.000
MORTDUE	0.000	0.002	1.000
NINQ	0.223	0.000	1.250
REASON DEBTCON	−0.065	0.284	0.937

* The odds ratio is not always directly available depending on the software package used. For a parameter estimate β the odds ratio is $\exp(\beta)$ and estimates the effect of the associated variable as percentage increase or decrease on the probability of a 'bad', here a defaulting loan. See Section 10.3.

Note: The dependent variable is BAD (equal to 1 if applicant defaulted on the loan, 0 if no default). Because the data are randomly sampled, exact replication of this result is not achievable.

Source: Loans.xlsx. The table is available in SAS and SPSS formats also. The SAS database from which this was taken was originally named SAMPS10.HMEQ and is used with permission of SAS.

This model, for each observation (in the training, validation, or test data sets), generates a prediction of whether the loan will prove good or bad. Each prediction whose probability is greater than 50 percent is categorized as bad and each prediction whose probability is less than 50 percent is categorized as good. For example, 53 observations fell above the 50 percent cutoff, of which 40 turned out to be correct predictions of bad performance. The parameter estimates are sensitive to the data partition, with here a random sample of 50% used for the estimation. However, the results are (usually) robust to the sign of the effect. Using alternative cutoffs generates the ROC curve as shown in Figure 12.20. Selected results are shown in Table 12.12.

Figure 12.20 Logistic Regression: ROC Curve for Validation Sample

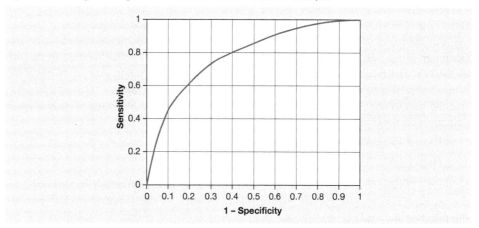

Data: Loans.xlsx or Loans.SAS7bdat

Table 12.12 Misclassification Rates for Training, Validation, and Test Data Using Various Classification Methods *(Missing values replaced)*

Description	Training: Misclassification Rate	Validation: Misclassification Rate	Test: Misclassification Rate
Logistic (50% cutoff)	0.361	0.383	0.378
Neural net: 1 hidden node	0.363	0.380	0.378
Neural net: 3 hidden nodes	0.353	0.368	0.383
Neural net: 5 hidden nodes	0.345	0.380	0.383
Classification tree	0.359	0.361	0.352

Data: Loans.xlsx or Loans.SAS7bdat

Neural Network Models: As we discussed in Section 10.4, neural nets (NN) can be used to classify a population. Following on from the first set of steps in building a NN, of selecting the training, validation and test data and coding the variables, we will carry out some exploration of the number of hidden nodes to include in a network with one hidden layer. We consider 1, 3, and 5 nodes, with the results shown in Table 12.12. (SAS that is used for this example does not offer all facilities discussed in Section 10.4, so we manually test these three potential architectures.) For NN modeling (from Section 10. 4) a number of runs with random starting values should be carried out and an ensemble/combination used to produce the final results. The comparable ROC curve shows little difference between the three alternatives on the test and validation data, and little or no benefit from increasing the number of nodes beyond 1.

We have chosen to use a 50 percent cutoff that classifies the top 50 percent of scores as defaulters (bad). SAS automatically produces a similar table, but it is based on classifying *all* cases with an estimated score of 0.50 or more (interpretable as the probability of default)

as "bads". This approach usually leads to a substantially smaller overall number of misclassified cases because most of the observations from which the model was constructed are "goods". However, the target suffers a higher level of misclassification in that the sensitivity is lower. Further testing is needed to check whether excluding some of the input variables would lead to improved classification performance on the validation data.

Classification Trees: In Chapter 10, we introduced Chi-squared Automatic Interaction Detection (CHAID) as an SPSS method for predicting categorical data such as the bad loans of the previous example. SAS has its own method of developing a classification tree (although it can be used to emulate CHAID and other variants of classification trees, such as CART). The results from all these different methods are similar, and no method has been shown to consistently outperform (or underperform) the others. We now add SAS's tree method to our predictive armory; the method delivers the following classes of likely defaulters on the training set:

   a. High *DEBTINC*, low *DELINQ*, low *CLAGE*

   b. High *DEBTINC*, high *DELINQ*.

Figure 12.21 offers the analyst an insight into how many leaves to include by showing how the misclassification rate (or alternative measures such as the sensitivity) changes with the number included on the training and validation sets. Note that this calculation is not directly comparable to the previous table as a default cut-off value of 0.5 has been used, classifying those with a score of 0.5 ore more as bad. Of course, on the training data set the rate always improves as the number of leaves (and the model's complexity) increases. But the same relationship does not hold on the validation data set, so a number between 5 and 7 seems appropriate here. (The misclassification rate shown is based on classifying those with a score of 0.5 or more as bad.)

Figure 12.21 Deciding on the Number of Leaves to Include

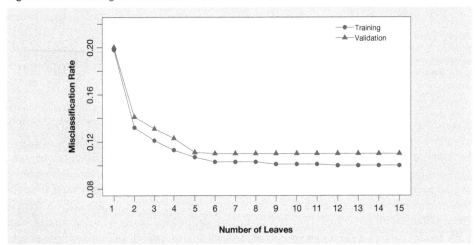

Data: Loans.xlsx or Loans.SAS7bdat

By contrast, using a model with 6 leaves and a 50 percent cutoff gives an overall misclassification rate for the training data of 0.107, on the validation data of 0.111 and the test data of 0.121. As we will see in Table 12.14 this strong performance carries over to a full comparison when using a 50% cutoff.

12.5.2 Making Customer Relationship Management Models Effective

In the last few sections, we have shown how three different methods of predictive classification can be used on the same problem. We now bring all these methods together to demonstrate their practical application. However, before the methods can deliver their best results, the data need to be preprocessed, especially given the ratio of positives and negatives (BAD) in the sample. Crone, Lessmann, and Stahlbock (2006) have shown preprocessing to be important in examining the relative performance of different methods. Key issues include the choice of sample, missing observations, and the treatment of continuous and ordered data.

Data Preprocessing

i. *Choosing the sample data:* For most applications in customer relationship marketing, the analysis focuses on a relatively small number of individuals in a much larger population. For example, the percentage of people (or firms) who respond to a direct mail promotion is around 1 percent, and the percentage of people who default on a loan is less than 10 percent. The forecaster usually tries to improve the identification of individuals falling into these target groups. The reason is that they are, respectively, more valuable and more costly to the organization than the larger population of non-respondents and non-defaulters. However, for some applications that use a method that is particularly computationally intensive, taking a very large sample is expensive or difficult. How large should the sample be? The answer depends in part on the composition of the population being modeled and, in particular, the percentage of people in the target class.

The standard approach to determining the database to employ is to first split the data at random into an estimation set, a validation set, and a test set (as we discussed in Section 10.4). However, this procedure would naturally lead to subsamples that are approximately representative of the two groups; consequently, just a small number would fall into the target group. Two alternatives spring to mind (for a fixed sample size): we can randomly oversample the target class or randomly undersample the majority class. Crone *et al.* (2006) have shown that oversampling produces better results for a number of classification methods.[8] Therefore, we should increase the number of instances of the minority class of interest so that it is approximately the same size as the majority class (e.g., with 500 in the majority class and 50 in the minority class, we should include each member of the target tenfold). Once that decision has been made, the choice of overall sample size depends on the method being employed (and other preprocessing choices).

For example, classification trees are more sensitive to sample size than is logistic regression. Critically, methods improve with increasing sample size; even with large samples, the improvements are potentially valuable. So, both the sample size and the relative size of the target class are important (Crone and Finlay, 2012).

Figure 12.22 compares ROC curves for the test set. Two sets of comparisons are shown: models in which the data set has been enhanced by replacing missing observations and models in which the "bads" have been oversampled to increase the sensitivity of the model. (This step is frequently justified because the cost of missing a "bad" may be many times higher than failing to recruit a "good".) The figure shows strong effects from oversampling and some weaker benefits from including missing observations. For any given level of the probability of rejecting a good loan applicant, i.e. (1 − specificity), there is a higher sensitivity (of correctly identifying a bad applicant) when the target is oversampled, as here.

---

8   Bootstrapping the sample can also wield substantial performance gains. A useful resource is Dietterich (2000) who discusses established ensemble based methods, such as AdaBoost and Bagging, which can be used to enhance the performance of classifiers.

Figure 12.22 ROC Curve: Test Sample Comparing Oversampling and Random Sampling With and Without Replacement of Missing Values

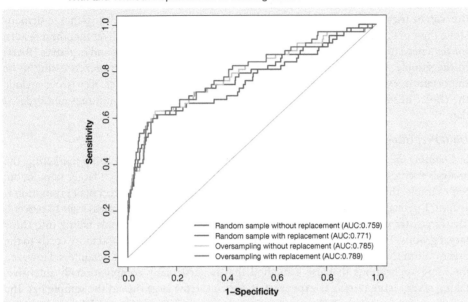

(The oversampling scheme replicated the number of bad applicants to make the two target sub-groups sizes equal.)

Data: Loans.xlsx; adapted from SAS output.

We can also compare the results on the test data set by using different cutoffs of 10 percent, 25 percent, and 40 percent, as shown in Table 12.13. (Note that this comparison is only meaningful on the original test data, as we have altered the sample composition of the training and validation sets with oversampling, making results on these non-comparable with, for instance, the original training and validation sets. In contrast, the test set has remained unchanged.)

Table 12.13 A Comparison of Misclassification Rates from Oversampling and from Replacement of Missing Observations – Test Data: Logistic Regression

Method		Misclassification Rate						AUC
		10% Cutoff		20% Cutoff		40% Cutoff		
		% Bad	% Good	% Bad	% Good	% Bad	% Good	
Random sample	Raw	38.70	16.20	46.80	4.80	72.60	1.20	0.759
	Replace	12.90	64.80	27.40	33.20	46.80	8.70	0.771
Oversampling	Raw	16.10	51.50	35.50	20.80	59.70	6.20	0.785
	Replace	3.20	94.20	8.10	72.30	27.40	32.00	0.789

Data: Loans.xlsx, based on the Test Sample.

The training set has 2979 observations, out of which 19.94% are bad (as sampled). These are replicated to bring the proportion of bad to 50% increasing the size training set to 4770.

As can easily be seen from Figure 12.22 and Table 12.13, using an oversampling scheme is beneficial if identifying the target is substantially more valuable than missing a 'good'.

ii. *Coding variables:* Many of the predictor variables in predictive classification problems are categorical (they describe a category that a customer or case belongs to, e.g., a geographical area or an occupation) or ordinal (e.g., education level). In the example examined, there are many interval-level data, such as the amount of the loan that has been requested. The advantage of recoding interval data into ordinal (dummy variable) categories is that any nonlinear effects can be easily incorporated.

> **DISCUSSION QUESTION:** *Why does coding an interval variable, such as age or income, potentially benefit predictive classification, and what are the possible problems?*

For example, in the example of computer ownership discussed in Chapter 10, *Age* and *Income* are both interval data, although in the data file they have been assigned to categories (8 for age, 5 for income), which in turn can be converted into dummy variables. Although we might expect computer ownership to increase linearly with *Income*, *Age* might have quite a different effect, with older and younger people perhaps less likely to be owners.

In the credit application example, there is no evidence of nonlinear effects in the explanatory variables (see Exercise 12.26).

iii. *Replacing missing values:* In a credit application data set such as this one, there are often many missing values for particular variables. Here, the length of the oldest credit line (i.e., the length of time the customer has held a mortgage or a loan, *CLAGE*) has many missing observations. There are numerous methods for replacing missing observations. For categorical data, a missing value can be replaced, for example, by the most common value or, more specifically, the most common value associated with the same target value. An interval-valued observation with a value missing is often replaced by the average value or the median value. Whatever the methods used (and different methods may lead to different models), it is important to replace the missing observations, because doing so can lead to a more effective model. A dummy variable has been added to identify those applications for which the missing value has been replaced (i.e., *Missing_Value* = 1 if the value of the attribute is unknown and is 0 otherwise). In the loan application data set, if logistic regression is used, these missing-value indicators prove significant and improve the misclassification rates, as shown in Table 12.13. Figure 12.22 demonstrates that the results of including both oversampling and replacement are more pronounced for higher levels of the sensitivity (i.e., where the model is capturing a greater percentage of the target variable).

Replacing the missing values and adding a missing-value indicator also changes the variables that need to be included in the model. In the loan example, the number of recent credit inquiries in the logistic model becomes insignificant.

12.5.3 Appraising Models of Individual Behavior

We have considered a number of methods for forecasting individual behavior. No single method is consistently best. The results depend on such features as the number of observations, the characteristics of the sample (in particular, the target variable), and the number of explanatory variables. As a consequence, forecasters will usually consider a number of methods and compare the results. Some software does this relatively easily, but beware: often the comparisons are not exactly as you would wish, and one method does not compare in detail exactly with another. Figure 12.23, taken from SAS's Enterprise Miner, illustrates the process of comparing models.

The first stage shown in Figure 12.23 is to partition the data into estimation (training), validation, and test data sets (*Data Partition*). *Graph* and *Stat Explorer* allow the analyst to carry out some exploratory data analysis. Missing or indeterminate values are replaced by rules set in the *Replacement* stage: A variety of methods are then considered, and then *Inputed* into the data matrix. Three core methods are considered, logistic regression, classification trees and neural nets. In addition, *Variable selection*, is used with logistic regression (which aims to cut down and simplify the variables to be considered by the *Regression* node). Two alternative *Neural Networks* (one automatic and one requiring user defined options) are also included and compared through a *Model Comparison* procedure. The last stage is to take the computer code from the final model so that it can be used in subsequent appraisals of different samples and on the test set. This is done here through the command *Score* following the model comparison. A comparison of the results from the methods is shown graphically in Figure 12.24, using the ROC curve and in Table 12.14 the effects of using variable selection are shown (compared to Table 12.12): here variable selection proved ineffective. The partition employed is 50 percent training, 30 percent validation, and 20 percent test, with no rebalancing of the sample (despite rebalancing being best practice). In addition, various misclassification matrices for different cutoffs should also be analyzed. As we see, for almost all sensitivities, the classification tree approach proved best on the validation data set and was quite substantially better on the test data set, as measured by the misclassification rate.

Figure 12.23 An Exploratory Data-Mining Process

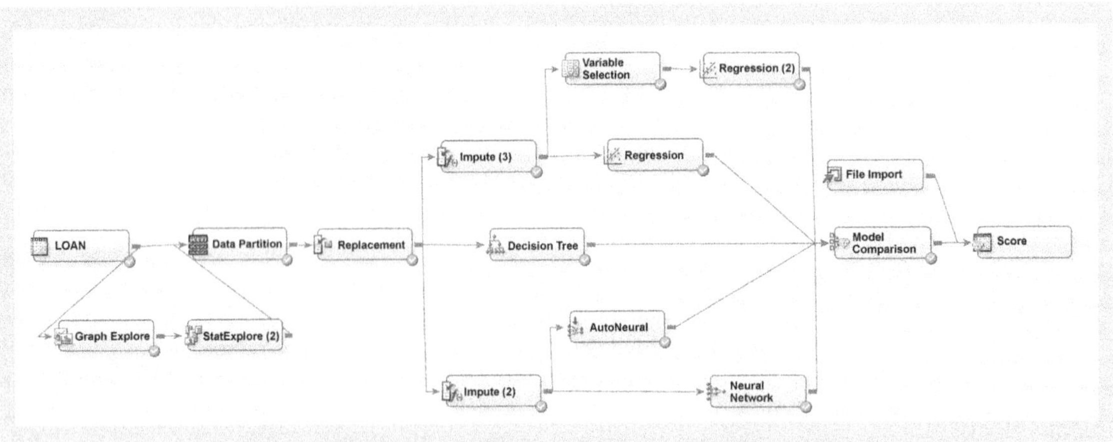

Source: Taken from SAS Enterprise Miner.

Table 12.14 Misclassification Rates for All Methods Shown in Figure 12.23
(50% Probability Cutoff)

		Misclassification Rate		
Tool	Name	Training Set	Validation Set	Test Set
Logistic regression	All var	0.361	0.383	0.378
Logistic regression	Varselect	0.376	0.386	0.390
Neural network	All var	0.363	0.380	0.378
Neural network	Automatic	0.378	0.386	0.382
Tree	All var	0.359	0.359	0.352

Figure 12.24 A Comparison of Three Data-Mining Methods: ROC Curves

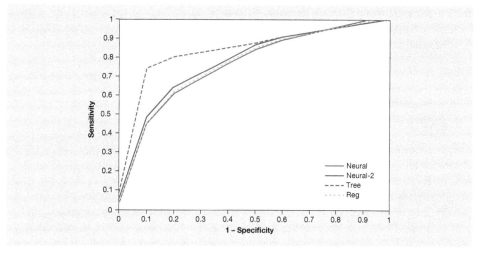

Source: Test Data Set.

In short, forecasting individual behavior is a rich topic that includes many types of forecasting problems. It poses many challenges to the forecaster, from the choice of software (see online Appendix B) to the need to come to grips with a variety of difficult techniques, all of which offer a wide variety of options that affect performance. The following box summarizes the key stages in the process:

THE PROCESS OF DEVELOPING A PREDICTIVE CLASSIFICATION MODEL

1. Use as many observations as are available and computationally tractable.
2. Segment the data into estimation (training), validation, and test subsets.
3. Examine the distribution of the variables.
4. Transform the data where necessary, coding dummy variables.
5. Replace missing and outlying observations.
6. Develop an oversampling scheme to ensure equal samples of the target and non-target subpopulations.
7. Choose a variety of plausible methods.
8. Use a procedure for eliminating insignificant variables.
9. Use an ensemble (combination) of the individual methods to overcome limitations of each method (and starting initializations in model estimation).
10. Compare performance on relevant criteria and cutoff values.
11. Evaluate performance comparatively on the test data.

There is no easy route through this complexity other than to check the effects of all these options. We've highlighted a few of the most important ones — for example, balanced sampling, replacement of outliers, and transforming interval data into groups of ordinal (dummy) variables. These problems associated with choosing a model can be resolved only through careful assessment of the results, using criteria such as the cutoff or profit-and-loss assessments (see Section 10.1.1). However, whether the application is in direct marketing, attempting to identify target consumers, in credit assessment, or in modeling consumer choice, there are major gains to be made by careful modeling and appraisal of the results. Crucially, the data set should include in the sample observations that are representative of the proposed operating environment of the model (Finlay, 2014).

12.6 Macroeconomic Forecasting

Macroeconomic (econometric) forecasting is one of the most important application areas of forecasting, although the forecasts are usually produced by economists rather than business forecasters. Before we look at the need for macroeconomic forecasts at an organizational level, we briefly discuss forecasting from a national government perspective. First, we should recognize that much macroeconometric modeling is focused upon trying to understand features of the economy, rather than making pure forecasts. That is, such models are used for "what-if" forecasting to develop policy options, because the policies chosen will have a material effect upon future outcomes.

Revisiting the earlier parts of this chapter, we see that it still makes sense to develop a national-level FSS, although this will now typically be stocked with series from government sources. Because policy decisions are the main motivation, the models used will be causal so that the effects of, say, a change in interest rates on unemployment can be followed through for several months and compared with a no-change scenario. In fact, many of the government models that form the basis of official government forecasts in the United States, the European Union, and elsewhere are based on a large, complex system of equations with many output variables affected by many other exogenous (i.e., external to the system) and policy variables. Fortunately, the available database of macroeconomic series is huge, including many of the drivers that influence such aggregate variables as national unemployment or *GDP*. Even countries as self-sufficient as the United States are affected by exchange rate movements and growth in the world economy, particularly in countries such as China and India. In Europe, the interrelationships among the major economies mean that causal forecasting models would theoretically include many variables from a range of countries. However, a standard alternative approach to such a complex set of interrelationships is to use smaller VAR models, extended to include exogenous variables such as world trade. One early example was developed by Litterman (1986). It consisted of only seven equations, for annual growth rates of real *Gross National Product (GNP)*, *Inflation*, *Unemployment*, logged levels of the *Money Supply*, logged levels of gross private domestic *Investment*, a commercial *Interest Rate*, and the change in *Business Inventories*. Six lags were included in the VAR system, which was then estimated on quarterly data. As McNees (1986) and Litterman discuss, the performance of this simple model turned out to be comparable to that of much larger systems. However, Fildes and Stekler (2002) argue that the empirical evidence does not support any particular approach being better than the rest and, in fact, the range of forecasts produced by the different models and different modeling groups often fails to encompass the actual outcome. The finding remains true 15 years later. An all-too-worrying example has been the Great Recession and the economic and financial crisis of 2007–2010, where the ad hoc rules of accuracy according to which both U.S. inflation and real *GDP* growth could be forecast with an *MAE* of around 1 percent have all too conclusively broken down.

One particular macroeconomic forecasting problem has attracted considerable attention over the years: that of predicting turning points (business cycles) in the economy. The key variable watched is real *GDP* (or *GNP*), with both governments and businesses having considerable interest in whether an expansion or a recession is coming to an end. Some of the earliest work on forecasting dealt with business cycles and the prediction of turning points. Lahiri and Moore's (1991) book covers a range of approaches, starting with the use of leading indicators, where a future turning point in an index of leading variables (such as stock prices) is claimed to predict a turning point in *GDP* in the real economy. From its earliest beginnings as a qualitative approach, such business cycle analysis uses many of the techniques we have described in this book. Logistic regression can be used to predict the probability of a turning point (moving from positive to negative growth or vice versa). The predictors used include a wide range of leading economic variables (i.e., they are lagged variables in the logistic function). But are such methods successful? As yet, a solution to the problem of predicting economic turning points — in particular, the onset of recessions — has eluded us, leaving organizations to cope as best they can with the unexpected changes in the economy.[9] As the UK Queen and many others remarked, "Why did no one notice [the coming Great Recession]?"

Many government series are available on a monthly basis (while some, such as *GDP*, only quarterly), but there is also a publication lag of several weeks. Thus, a considerable amount of economic activity may take place between the latest available figures and the present time, making adjustment by informed judgment valuable if not essential. As at the company level, the process of making adjustments enables policy makers to take ownership of the forecasts. That said, it is also often the case that political considerations may obfuscate the differences between forecasts and targets. (See Stekler, 2007, for a discussion of the process governments go through when developing macroeconomic forecasts.)

As with marketing promotions, government tax cuts or other stimuli can be evaluated after the fact by using standard regression methods with indicator variables, but forecasting the impact of future policy changes can, at best, be done only to the extent that the data series contain past examples of similar policy changes. The alternative is to make strong assumptions as to the economy's reaction to the proposed new policies (with Brexit, the UK's decision to leave the EU, providing an example).

DISCUSSION QUESTION: *Using a current example of macroeconomic policy change, how might you forecast the effects? In 2017, Brexit and President Trump's proposed initiatives provide examples.*

Considerable research has gone into improving the accuracy of macro forecasts (see Fildes and Stekler, 2002), ranging from using better and more timely data to employing increasingly complex econometric modeling. Overall, there is little evidence of accuracy improvement in the last 20 years for such key variables as *GDP* and *Inflation*, variables that often affect a firm's profitability. The only exception is that the use of current data incorporated into the macro model, "nowcasting" as it is called, has led to short-term improvements (see Kuzin, Marcellino, and Schumacher, 2011).

In general, the principles of forecasting we laid down in earlier chapters apply equally to macroeconomic forecasting; the forecasts obtained from econometric models often do not out-perform simple extrapolative alternatives. Although the primary purpose of econometric modeling is to evaluate policy options rather than to generate point forecasts, for a model to be valuable it should be capable of effective forecasting!

---

9 New research has demonstrated that using Lasso regression, and similar approaches, it is possible to identify useful leading indicators from the thousands of potentially relevant macroeconomic variables to enrich long term forecasts of aggregate company sales (see Sagaert, Aghezzaf, Kourentzes, and Desmet, 2017).

Turning now to the organizational forecaster's objective of producing more disaggregate forecasts to match the organization's decisions, we find that macroeconomic variables are often needed as explanatory variables. For example, the air passenger demand models of Section 12.4.5, which are relevant to airline and airport planners, were based on macro variables of world trade and national disposable income. Similarly, a regional government forecaster would wish to link regional forecasts to national changes. We do not recommend that the forecaster make her own macro forecasts. Instead, public and private sources are available to deliver the forecasts necessary to support the needs of an organization. For example, the organization Consensus Economics (*www.consensuseconomics.com*), which works on one of our favorite principles of combining, will deliver as accurate a forecast as any other for a wide range of variables and many countries (see Exercise 12.28).

> **DISCUSSION QUESTION:** *Why do you think that macroeconomic forecasting is often no more accurate than a naïve extrapolative model when one is looking more than 12 months out? Why do you think that most macro forecasters failed to forecast the "Great Recession" that started in 2007?*

12.7 Other Applications

The range of application areas for the forecasting methods considered in this book is extensive. We have focused on what are perhaps the organizationally most important topics of operations and marketing. However, before an organization can forecast its financial needs, it must produce cost forecasts, including the costs of raw materials, parts, and labor. Although the methods we have introduced in the earlier chapters all apply to these problems, specialist sources are available to help determine appropriate methods and explanatory variables (i.e., those which have worked in practice). For example, in forecasting production costs, one important influence is the increasing efficiency of the production process. This feature is often captured by including cumulative production in the cost forecasting model.

Within a particular industry setting, there are many specialist issues focusing on which variables to include and how they should be measured. Areas that have seen much research include telecommunications (and now more generally, ICT) forecasting (see Meade and Islam, 2015), electricity demand forecasting (see the Special *International Journal of Forecasting* Issue on Energy Forecasting, Taylor and Espasa, 2008 and subsequently, Hong and Fan, 2016), and sports forecasting (see, e.g., Williams and Stekler, 2010 and Stekler, Sendor, and Verlander, 2010). Tourism has provided an interesting comparison of both univariate and multivariate forecasting methods (Athanasopoulos, Hyndman, Song, and Wu, 2011) concluding that univariate methods were more accurate than causal (and a year ahead, naïve forecasts were hard to beat).

Financial forecasting and commodity price and agricultural forecasting are specialist areas with their own concerns. A useful summary of some of the issues in financial forecasting is given by Timmermann and Granger (2004). A key issue in forecasting financial variables and commodity and agricultural prices is whether the market is efficient (i.e., whether the current price is the best predictor of future prices or whether any inefficiencies can be capitalized on). Labys (2006) examines commodities, while Allen (1994) provides a succinct and accessible survey of agricultural forecasting. Generally, however, application areas have not developed method-specific approaches; rather, it is the features of the data that determine whether causal, extrapolative, or judgmental methods are applied and in what mix.

One final area worth remarking on is where heterogeneous individual behavior over time must be modeled to produce a forecast. For example, in governments everywhere, there is a need to model the tax take (from income tax, state sales tax, etc.) and Social Security payments (such as unemployment benefit or pension payments). One approach to this problem is through *micro simulation models* (Merz, 1991; Mitton, Shuterland, and Weeks, 2000) or, more generally, where individuals interact, *agent-based models*. Such models differ substantially from the statistical models we have discussed and are often focused on policy or planning issues rather than the forecasts themselves. An example of the use of these models in the telecommunications area is described in Fildes and Kumar (2002). The models are parameterized, often by experiments off-line; that is to say, they are not statistically estimated, but other pieces of evidence, such as market research experiments (in consumer behavior), are used to decide on the parameters to specify the model completely. In general, such models have rarely been validated in the way we have recommended in this book: by comparing their performance with that of some established benchmark. However, they are often used where the available data does not include aspects of the system being modeled (such as the policy changes discussed in the previous section) and therefore they offer valuable insight into possible futures. The value of such "scenarios" is discussed in Section 13.3.

Outside business and economics, climate is perhaps the most important and high profile application area where the forecasts of global warming have provoked a world-wide response. Here the simulation models (General Circulation Models – GCMs) are vast, consisting of many thousands of equations that aim to capture the climatic interactions between land, sea, and atmosphere in localized detail (just like a long term weather forecast). The controversy generated in the global warming debate emphasizes the importance of model validation which for these micro-simulation models, has many components. Fildes and Kourentzes (2011) describe the models non-technically and argue for a multi-faceted approach to validation. Where a model is to be used in forecasting, particularly when there are policy implications, it is incumbent on the modelers to demonstrate that the proposed, highly complex model, is more accurate than simpler statistical alternatives. At the time of writing in 2017, the jury is out as to whether these GCMs deliver more accurate forecasts looking a decade or more ahead.[10]

DISCUSSION QUESTION: *If you were to advise a funding agency on whether to support a research project on climate change, what factors would you take into account as the basis for your decision?*

12.8 Forecasting Principles in Application

Evaluation (see Armstrong, 2001 b,c; Armstrong's (2001 a, Chapter 20, Summary: also Tashman, 2010)

[12.1] Compare the current (or proposed) method against established benchmarks.
Typical benchmarks are the random walk or a similar naïve method, as well as a suitable smoothing method, such as damped trend smoothing.

[12.2] Specify the forecasting task.

---

10 However, note that the purpose of GCMs is to produce spatial forecasts of several variables of interest, rather than only aggregate temperature anomaly forecasts. A relevant concept to keep in mind both in model development and evaluate is PIVASE that we introduced in Chapter 1.

[12.3] Use error measures that are appropriate for the problem.
Use a hold-out sample calculating a variety of error measures that are suitable for comparing accuracy across a number of time series. For intermittent demand, use the costs of achieving a desired service level.

[12.4] Base comparisons on as large a sample of time series, forecast origins, and out-of-sample forecasts as possible.
Comparisons based on a small sample of forecasts are often misleading.

[12.5] When multiple forecasts are available, consider combinations of forecasts from methods that differ substantially.
A combination of quantitative and informed subjective methods can be very effective.

[12.6] Use formal procedures to combine forecasts.
In particular, consider the use of equal weights, after removing extreme forecasts from the set. Although it may seem counterintuitive, equal-weighting schemes that exclude only extreme forecasts seem to offer the most consistent performance. Don't rely on subjective weighting schemes.

[12.7] Combine models where there is substantial uncertainty.
In general, models are oversimplifications, and a combination can help to avoid bias. Using temporal hierarchies (section 12.3.3) is another way to hedge models against uncertainty.

[12.8] Select rather than combine when a particular method has consistently performed best on out-of-sample comparisons.
A consistent 'near best' method will usually outperform a broad-based combination.

Forecasting Support Systems (see Sanders, 2001, and Armstrong's (2001a) summary, Section 11)

[12.9] Structure judgmental adjustments to a statistical forecast.
Adjustments are made for any number of reasons, although promotional effects are the most important in demand forecasting. The different reasons for the adjustment should be identified separately and documented.

[12.10] Compare the system forecast with the adjusted forecast.
Records should be kept of the system forecast and the final adjusted forecast and should be used to calculate the errors made and to evaluate any biases in the two sets of forecasts.

[12.11] Base the statistical system forecast on regular time periods, not on periods during which promotions are run and not on unusual periods.
If promotional periods are run and are included in the calculation, they will bias the system forecasts upward unless appropriate adjustments are made.

[12.12] Use well-tested forecasting software.
Commercial software cannot automatically be assumed to be well designed and validated. With new software, results should be compared with some standard benchmarks and the software tuned to produce optimal forecasts.

Operations and Marketing Product Hierarchies (see Athanasopoulos et al., 2009, 2017 and Kourentzes et al, 2014)

[12.13] When product hierarchies are available, use hierarchical forecasting approaches to obtain reconciled forecasts with potential accuracy gains. When available, the combined approach is recommended.
Information that is often available at the different levels of the product hierarchy is useful when forecasting at other levels.

[12.14] Temporal aggregation can be beneficial for long-term forecasting and side-stepping intermittency. Using multiple temporal aggregation levels can offer gains in the accuracy and reliability of forecasts, mitigating modeling uncertainty.
Combining temporal and cross-section hierarchies can lead to reconciled forecasts (aligning with decisions) across the various planning levels in an organization.

New Product Diffusion Models (see Meade and Islam, 2001, 2006)

[12.15] No single diffusion model is best for all adoption processes.
A variety of curves can model the adoption process. We have discussed the Bass (logistic) curve and the Gompertz curve here. It therefore makes sense to consider alternative curves in choosing the best one for the particular problem under consideration.

[12.16] Use simpler diffusion models.
These models produce better forecasts than more complex models on the limited data that are typically available.

[12.17] Short-term forecasting ability is helpful in deciding whether a diffusion model is useful.
Although the aim of new product forecasting is to produce accurate long term forecasts, a model's short-term accuracy offers valuable information as to its usefulness in the longer term.

[12.18] Use nonlinear least squares to estimate models.
Consider how the error term should be specified in the model.

Market Potential (In estimating market potential with no historical data intentions studies (Morwitz, 2001) and conjoint choice models and its variants (Wittink and Bergestuen, 2001) offer guidance.)

[12.19] When estimating market potential, identify an appropriate sample of respondents for an intentions or choice-based conjoint study.

[12.20] Identify a meaningful set of attributes that are potentially important in a choice model of market potential.
The chosen attributes should be distinct from each other.

[12.21] Estimate market potential with intentions data that have been modified to take into account possible biases from the respondents.

[12.22] Question respondents in as realistic a choice context as possible.
Simulated environments provide respondents with information that is useful to them in making more realistic choices.

[12.23] Combine approaches with others, such as using analogous products.

Market Response Models (see Brodie, Danaher, Kumar, and Leeflang, 2001)

[12.24] Use disaggregated data.
Aggregated data make identifying marketing effects difficult because of the heterogeneity in the different market segments.

[12.25] When the sample is medium or large, use a regression model only when the current effects of the market drivers are strong.

[12.26] Use brand-specific parameters to model a competitive market.

Forecasting Individual Behavior

[12.27] Consider a variety of methods.

[12.28] Use the largest sample size possible, given the data and computer constraints, but partition into estimation, validation, and test samples whenever possible.
Often, an unnecessarily limited (but large) sample is used, rather than using all the available observations that leave the model building computationally tractable. Research has shown that including as many observations as possible produces gains. The validation sample helps avoid overfitting.

[12.29] Aim for an understandable model.
Models will frequently be rejected by users if their logic cannot be understood.

[12.30] Replace missing data, and use indicator variables to tag the replacement.

[12.31] Balance the sample of the target class with the available non-target data.
Cases of interest (e.g., poor credit risks) will often be relatively rare, so the sample of targeted cases should be oversampled to match the nontarget cases. The cutoff point for classifying the target should reflect the relative importance of the two misclassification categories.

[12.32] In the assessment of the different methods, use criteria that reflect the profit and loss in the problem.

Other Applications

[12.33] Do not try to produce your own macro forecasts.
The services that provide macro forecasts — in particular, those which provide a summary of the forecasts produced by a diversity of forecasting groups — are as accurate as you can hope for.

[12.34] In all forecasting applications, use the methods, models, and principles laid down in this text. Make sure that you understand the specific factors which are important in the particular application.

Summary

The purpose of forecasting is not just to develop models in isolation, but also to use them effectively in organizational applications. After first examining the key question of how methods should be evaluated, we considered how organizations structure their forecasting information. We found that it is often done through expensive forecasting support systems. We introduced a wide range of applications that affects most organizations, from governments to small suppliers — in particular, (1) forecasting to support operations and (2) market forecasting. Within the broad heading of market forecasting, models aimed at trying to understand and forecast individual consumer behavior have gained increasing prominence. New techniques are being applied, with the potential for substantial benefits.

In the final sections of the chapter, we touched on a whole range of additional applications. Although we were unable to discuss them in detail, such topics as sports forecasting and corporate earnings forecasting (by advisors offering advice to investors) have spawned major industries. The expert forecaster will be able to apply the methods of this book in these new contexts, but knowing the difference between a penalty in soccer (English football) and a penalty in American football will always remain important. The moral of this discussion is that the expert forecaster will know the range of techniques to be applied, but will also understand the data and the relationships specific to the application area.

Exercises

Evaluating Forecasting Methods; Forecasting Support Systems and Forecasting for Operations.

12.1   With the spreadsheet *Combine.xlsx*, calculate the *MAPE*, *MdAPE*, and *RelMAE* obtained from using optimal weights, rather than equal weights, for the three combinations of two methods.

      a. Generalize this approach to calculate the error statistics for all three methods.

      b. Does including a constant term in the regression improve the error statistics?

      c. What are the implications for choosing the weights on the basis of the whole sample of data rather than a subsample of the first 12 periods?

12.2   Earnings forecasting is one of the most important applications of forecasting and is a major industry in that the forecasts are used by investors to decide which stock they should hold. Using the file *Earnings.xlsx*, which shows the forecasts for five companies over three years, calculate combined forecasts for each year, examining the benefits of combining 3 forecast sources, 5 sources, 10 sources, and, finally, all the sources. Are there any benefits from eliminating extreme forecasts from the calculation? [*Source:* Institutional Brokers Estimate System (I/B/E/S), a service of Thomson Reuters. The data have been provided as part of a broad academic program to encourage research into earnings expectations.]

12.3   Using a forecasting support system with which you are familiar, appraise its strengths and weaknesses compared with Excel in building a forecasting system to analyze and forecast 10 products (i) with 10 years of monthly data and (ii) falling into two product groups based on 2 years of weekly data. The short report should be suitable to be presented to a non-technical senior IT manager. *Hint:* You can download a trial version of a commercial system to make the comparison more relevant.

12.4   Use the promotions sales data in *Promote1.xlsx* to estimate the promotional effects and forecast 12 periods ahead, taking into account the forthcoming promotions. The start of each promotional period is shown in the database. Does it matter (i.e., does it affect the profitability of the promotion) if you take the promotion as affecting four weeks of sales rather than five or six?

12.5*   In a two-period promotional model, the baseline sales model is of the form

$$B_t = \alpha + \lambda S_{t-1} + \varepsilon_t$$

and the sales model is:

$$S_t = B_t + \beta_0 D_{1t} + \beta_1 D_{2t},$$

where lagged sales affects promotions. B_t represents the baseline sales and $D_{1t} = 1$ if t is in the first period of the promotion, while $D_{2t} = 1$ if t is in the second period of the promotion. Show that the effect of the promotion is β_0 in the first period of the promotion and $\beta_0 + \lambda\beta_1$ in the second period.

12.6 With the data set *Bullwhip.xlsx*, use exponential smoothing to calculate the forecasting accuracy of the retailer's and the manufacturer's forecasts. Does knowledge of the retailer's sales improve the accuracy of the manufacturer's forecasts?

12.7* Using the data set *Bullwhip.xlsx*, develop a dynamic regression model of the sales of the manufacturer using lagged sales from both retailer and manufacturer. How does this compare with the exponential smoothing forecasts from 12.6?

12.8 For the data in *Lost_sales.xlsx*, estimate the demand data for the out-of-stock observations.

12.9 With the data set *HierUnemp.xlsx*, produce top-down and bottom-up hierarchical forecasts? Which approach is better for forecasting Scandinavian Unemployment?

12.10* With the data set *HierUnemp.xlsx* construct optimal combination hierarchical forecasts. How do these compare with the top-down and bottom-up forecasts? Consider different combination weighting schemes. (This requires the use of the R code provided associated with this chapter, as do questions 12.11, 12.14, 12.15, and 12.18.)

12.11* Use the multiple grouping dimensions in *HierUnempFull.xlsx*, to construct grouped hierarchy forecasts. How do these compare with the forecasts using a simple grouping dimension, as in Exercise 12.10? What are the advantages by using multiple grouping dimensions?

12.12 Aggregate the A&E admission data in *AEdata_monthly.xlsx* into quarterly and yearly time series. Carry out preliminary data analysis for each of the three series. What information does each level provide? Which exponential smoothing model would be appropriate for each temporal aggregation level?

12.13 Construct exponential smoothing forecasts for the last year (all 12 months) using the monthly, quarterly and yearly A&E admissions time series (*AEdata_monthly.xlsx*). Which forecast is more accurate? Why?

12.14* Use *AEdata_weekly.xlsx* to produce forecasts for the last 52 weeks using ARIMA and Temporal Hierarchies. Which is most accurate? Why?

12.15* Use *AEdata_monthly.xlsx* to produce exponential smoothing forecasts on a monthly level, Temporal Hierarchy forecasts and MAPA forecasts, how do these compare on a monthly level, predicting *t*+1 and a complete year? How do these compare when forecasting a complete year ahead on a yearly aggregation level?

12.16 For the data in *Intermittent.xlsx*, use first Croston's method and then simple exponential smoothing to calculate one-step-ahead forecasts. Does the choice of smoothing parameter have any impact on the results? Is the choice of error measure important in making the calculation? If being out of stock is very expensive, does this affect how you appraise the different methods?

12.17 Use temporal aggregation to produce forecasts for *Intermittent.xlsx*. Suppose that we are interested in lead times of 3, 6, and 12 periods. What are the appropriate temporal aggregation levels? Which forecasting model should we use? How do the new forecasts compare with the forecasts from Exercise 12.16?

12.18* Use either Temporal Hierarchies or MAPA to produce forecasts for *Intermittent.xlsx*. How do these compare with the forecasts developed in Exercises 12.16 and 12.17?

Market Forecasting

12.19 What variables might you include in a forecasting model for:

  i. the monthly demand for ice cream?

  ii. annual traffic fatalities?

    iii. the total U.S. market for tablets over the next five years?

    iv. the daily energy demand in a region, partitioned by the energy source?

    v. the probability of an individual defaulting on a credit card payment?

    vi. hourly calls into a credit card call center over the next week?

12.20 Download data on U.S. consumption, and then estimate various trend curve models. Select the curve that you regard as likely to provide the best forecast for consumption in 2025. Give reasons for your choice. Compare your analysis with that of Granger and Jeon (2007).

12.21 Using the data set *Telecoms_2.xlsx*, which contains data on mobile, and broadband communications for four European countries (the United Kingdom, Germany, Italy, and France), develop trend curve models for data up to 2015 and forecasts to 2022.

    a. Among Gompertz, logistic, and linear benchmark models, which do you prefer for forecasting? Give reasons for your choice.

    b. Is there any evidence of substitution between the different communications media?

12.22 Using the airline passenger data in *Air_passenger.xlsx*, estimate the passenger flows for the UK-Canada airline route for the years 1961-2000, considering all the relevant variables, including the world trade variable. Produce forecasts for 2001 and 2002. Include a dummy variable for 2001 and 2002, and estimate the effects of the September 11 terrorist attack.

12.23 The data file *Promote2.xlsx* includes sales and price data on eight competing products for 399 weeks. The file also contains promotional information. (A full description is included in it.) Using the data in *Promote2.xlsx*, estimate the effects of the promotions, including any competitive effects, and produce 1-5-week-ahead rolling forecasts for the periods 120-140 and 201-220. Is there any evidence of instability in the model? How does this model compare with alternative extrapolative models with regard to periods with and without promotions?

12.24 Evaluate the Divakar *et al.* (2005) study, focusing on the following questions:

    a. Do the models for volume and price include the key variables you would consider?

    b. What other aspects of the market would you wish to be informed about?

    c. Is the evaluation carried out in ways you find useful?

    d. Write an executive summary of the results, arguing why the model should be implemented.

Forecasting Individual Behavior

12.25 Using the data set *Loans.xlsx* and a linear regression model of the bad loans that incorporates the predictor variables *CLAGE, DEBTINC, NLINQ,* and *DELINQ*, develop an ROC operating curve. Compare this curve with the curves obtained by each of the three methods used in Section 12.5. Which method do you prefer and why? Does the inclusion of *Job* lead to any improvement in predictability?

12.26 Using the data set *Loans.xlsx*, develop a model that predicts the target variable bad loans.

    a. Carry out an exploratory analysis of the loans data, identifying any interesting features that may affect your subsequent model building.

    b. Set up suitable dummy variables to describe the variables *Job* and *DELINQ*.

c. Using step wise and backward regression, decide on a subset of potentially important explanatory variables.

d. Using the chosen subset of variables, follow the procedure set out in Section 12.5.3 and compare the methods of predictive classification with the results shown in the section.

e. Does the sample size matter in developing the predictive model and estimating the misclassification rates on the test data?

f. Using the data set *Loans.xlsx*, estimate whether there are any nonlinear effects of *MORTDUE* and *DEBTINC* on the probability of defaulting.

12.27 It is well known that younger people have become Internet users more rapidly than older segments of the population. Use the data in Table 12.15 to develop forecasts for each age group for 2020. How would you forecast the overall participation rate?

Table 12.15 Internet Participation Rates as Percentages of the Corresponding Age Cohort *(sample estimates)*

Year	18-29	30-49	50-64	65+
2000	70	61	46	14
2001	72	65	50	14
2002	76	70	54	18
2003	78	72	56	22
2004	77	75	61	24
2005	83	79	66	28
2006	86	82	70	32
2007	89	85	71	35
2008	89	84	72	38
2009	92	84	75	40
2010	92	85	74	43
2011	94	87	77	46
2012	96	91	79	54
2013	97	92	81	56
2014	97	92	81	57
2015	97	95	82	63

Source: Pew Research Center

12.28 Download macro forecasts from *www.consensuseconomics.com*, and calculate the accuracy of the consensus forecast for the two years of data that are available. (You may have to estimate the actual value for the current year.) Include a number of macro variables in this evaluation. How do the consensus forecasts compare against forecasts by the best forecasting provider, the average provider, and the worst provider? *Hint:* You will have to decide how to rank the individual macro-forecasting providers.

Minicases

Minicase 12.1 Call Center Planning[11]

InsurCo's call center performance was part of Ms. Chen's new responsibilities for operations. Accuracy, she knew, was important. Staff were usually scheduled for the next week (five days), and the operations director (to whom Ms. Chen reported) regarded service performance as very important. In emergencies, extra staff could be brought in for the next day. Although not a technical expert, Ms. Chen knew that the basic approach of the forecasting group had been to use Excel-based simple exponential smoothing in calculating the forecasts. If marketing information was available which suggested that something out of the ordinary was expected to happen, the statistical forecasts were adjusted. There was no set procedure laid down. On top of that, a standard seasonal adjustment was incorporated into the forecasts.

But Ms. Chen had looked at the past 40 days' (8 weeks') worth of data and could see that there was a problem. When questioned, the principal forecaster confirmed that his team used the system forecast and then tried to take into account any unexpected business drivers that affected call center activity. For example, the figures on mailings applied to just one day but often seemed to carry over to the next for the obvious reason that deliveries did not automatically occur the next day as planned. Ms. Chen thought that daily seasonality might be an issue, particularly after a weekend. (The data start on a Monday in period 1.) The standard seasonal adjustment seemed inadequate to account for the observed seasonality.

The previous operations manager (an accountant by training) had laid down the law that the forecasts had to be within 10 percent accuracy. Whatever that might mean, the net result was that one of the better trained junior staff members resigned, arguing that it just wasn't possible: Too many other factors affected the results. In particular, mailings were a problem not least because the data were rarely made available, and the marketing people (when they bothered to talk to you) argued that the type of mail promotion also had an effect.

The data can be found in the data set *Call_center.xlsx*.

1. What forecast horizon(s) are relevant for making the comparisons? What is an appropriate error measure?

2. How accurate were the department's forecasts? How did they compare with the automatic system forecast? Are the department's system forecasts more accurate than random-walk forecasts?

3. Could a standard extrapolative method such as exponential smoothing do any better?

4. Additional data were usually available to the forecasting team. The team used these data judgmentally. The periods affected by a mail promotion were labeled 1. Develop a regression model that explains the calls. Calculate prediction intervals for these forecasts, and calculate the forecast errors. Is the model more accurate than your best exponential smoothing model?

5. How can seasonality be incorporated into the forecast?

6. What suggestions would you make for possible changes in the operational forecasting system?

11 See Ibrahim, Ye, L'Ecuver, and Shen (2016) for a review.

Minicase 12.2 Costume Jewelry

A company that markets costume jewelry has three main product lines: bracelets, necklaces, and pins. Within each line there are several groups, and within each group a number of distinct items. The details are shown in Table 12.16.[12] Organized by calendar year, the series run from Year 1, week 5, to Year 3, week 24.

The company wishes to develop a hierarchical forecasting system by product line so that forecasts of sales of each item aggregate up to the forecasts at the group level, in turn for each product line.

a. Examine different top-down and bottom-up approaches to forecasting, using at least 30 percent of the observations as a hold-out sample. Compare the accuracy of the two approaches, considering forecasting horizons of 1 week ahead and 4 weeks ahead, and cumulative sales 1-13 weeks ahead.

b. If the jewelry data relate to a manufacturer, which do you regard as the relevant lead time(s) to focus on and why? If the data relate to a distributor, does that change your conclusions?

c. How would you identify subgroups of items that appear to have similar demand patterns?

Table 12.16 Information for Costume Jewelry Manufacturer

Product Line	Product Group	Number of Items
Bracelets	B1	5
	B2	5
Necklaces	N1	6
	N2	7
	N3	5
	N4	2
Pins	P1	4
	P2	6

Data: Jewelry.xlsx

Group Exercise

In order to understand the developing market in (choose a new product or service of interest), identify the key attributes of the market and its competition and develop a conjoint choice experimental questionnaire with the aim of estimating its long run market potential. Consider a new product or service such as the electric car or the driverless car.

---

12 These data form a subset of data on the products sold by an actual costume jewelry company. We are grateful to Dr. Hans Levenbach for providing the data.

References

Allen, P. G. (1994). Economic forecasting in agriculture. *International Journal of Forecasting*, 10, 81–135.

Armstrong, J. S. (ed.). (2001a). *Principles of Forecasting: A Handbook for Researchers and Practitioners*. Boston and Dordrecht: Kluwer.

Armstrong, J. S. (2001b). Combining forecasts. In J. S. Armstrong (ed.), *Principles of Forecasting: A Handbook for Researchers and Practitioners*. Boston and Dordrecht: Kluwer, pp. 417–439.

Armstrong, J. S. (2001c). Evaluating forecasting methods. In J. S. Armstrong (ed.), *Principles of Forecasting: A Handbook for Researchers and Practitioners*. Boston and Dordrecht: Kluwer, pp. 443–472.

Athanasopoulos, G., Ahmed, R. A., and Hyndman, R. J. (2009). Hierarchical forecasts for Australian domestic tourism. *International Journal of Forecasting*, 25, 146–166.

Athanasopoulos, G., Hyndman, R. J., Song, H., and Wu, D. C. (2011). The tourism forecasting competition. *International Journal of Forecasting*, 27, 822–844.

Athanasopoulos, G., Hyndman, R. J., Kourentzes, N. and Petropoulos, F. (2017). Forecasting with temporal hierarchies. *European Journal of Operational Research*, 262, 60–74.

Barrow, D. K., and Kourentzes N. (2016). Distributions of forecast errors of forecast combinations: Implications for inventory management. *International Journal of Production Economics*, 177, 24–33.

Bass, F. M. (1969). A new product growth model for consumer durables. *Management Science (A)*, 15, 215–227.

Berry, M. J. R., and Linoff, G. S. (2004). *Data Mining Techniques for Marketing, Sales and Customer Support*. New York: Wiley.

Bose, I., and Chen, X. (2009). Quantitative models for direct marketing: A review from systems perspective. *European Journal of Operational Research*, 195, 1–16.

Boylan, J. E., and Syntetos, A. A. (2017). *Intermittent Demand Forecasting: Context, Methods and Applications*. Chichester, UK: Wiley.

Brodie, R., Danaher, P. J., Kumar, V., and Leeflang, P. S. H. (2001). Econometric models for forecasting market share. In J. S. Armstrong (ed.), *Principles of Forecasting: A Handbook for Researchers and Practitioners*. Boston and Dordrecht: Kluwer, pp. 597–611.

Chase, C. W. (2016). *Next Generation Demand Management: People, Process, Analytics and Technology*. Hoboken, NJ: Wiley.

Clemen, R. T. (1989). Combining forecasts: A review and annotated bibliography. *International Journal of Forecasting*, 5, 559–583.

Crone, S. F., Lessmann, S., and Stahlbock, R. (2006). The impact of preprocessing on data mining: An evaluation of classifier sensitivity in direct marketing. *European Journal of Operational Research*, 173, 781–800.

de Jong, G., Fox, J., Pieters, M., Daly, A. J., and Smith, R. (2004). A comparison of car ownership models. *Transport Reviews*, 24, 379–408.

Davydenko, A., and Fildes, R. (2015). Forecast error measures: Critical review and practical recommendations. In M. Gilliland, L. Tashman and U. Sglavo (Eds.), *Business Forecasting* (pp. 238–258). Hoboken, New Jersey: Wiley.

Dietterich T. G. (2000). An experimental comparison of three methods for constructing ensembles of decision trees: bagging, boosting, and randomization. *Machine Learning*, 40(2):139–158.

Divakar, S., Ratchford, B. T., and Shankar, V. (2005). CHAN4CAST: A multichannel, multiregion sales forecasting model and decision support system for consumer packaged goods. *Marketing Science*, 24, 334–350.

Duncan, G. T., Gorr, W., and Szczypula, J. (2001). Forecasting analagous time series. In J. S. Armstrong (ed.), *Principles of Forecasting: A Handbook for Researchers and Practitioners*. Boston and Dordrecht: Kluwer, pp. 195–213.

Fader, P. S., and Hardie, B. G. S. (2001). Forecasting trial sales of new consumer packaged goods. In J. S. Armstrong (ed.), *Principles of Forecasting: A Handbook for Researchers and Practitioners*. Boston and Dordrecht: Kluwer, pp. 613–630.

Fildes, R., and Goodwin, P. (2007). Against your better judgment? How organizations can improve their use of management judgment in forecasting. *Interfaces*, 37, 570–576.

Fildes, R., Goodwin, P., and Lawrence, M. (2006). The design features of forecasting support systems and their effectiveness. *Decision Support Systems*, 42, 351–361.

Fildes, R., Goodwin, P., Lawrence, M., and Nikolopoulos, K. (2009). Effective forecasting and judgmental adjustments: An empirical evaluation and strategies for improvement in supply-chain planning. *International Journal of Forecasting*, 25, 3–23.

Fildes, R., Hibon, M., Makridakis, S., and Meade, N. (1998). Generalising about univariate forecasting methods: Further empirical evidence. *International Journal of Forecasting*, 14, 339–358.

Fildes, R. and Kourentzes, N. (2011). Validation and forecasting accuracy in models of climate change. *International Journal of Forecasting*, 27, 968–995 and Discussion 996–1005.

Fildes, R., and Kumar, V. (2002). Telecommunications demand forecasting: A review. *International Journal of Forecasting*, 18, 489–522.

Fildes, R., Nikolopoulos, K., Crone, S. F., and Syntetos, A. A. (2008). Forecasting and operational research: A review. *Journal of the Operational Research Society*, 59, 1150–1172.

Fildes, R., and Petropoulos, F. (2015). An evaluation of simple versus complex selection rules for forecasting many time series. *Journal of Business Research*, 68, 1692–1701.

Fildes, R., and Stekler, H. (2002). The state of macroeconomic forecasting. *Journal of Macroeconomics*, 24, 435–468.

Fildes, R., Wei, Y., and Ismail, S. (2011). Evaluating the forecasting performance of econometric models of air passenger traffic flows using multiple error measures. *International Journal of Forecasting*, 27, 902–922.

Finlay, S. (2012). *Credit Scoring, Response Modeling and Insurance Rating. A Practical Guide to Forecasting Consumer Behavior*, 2nd Edition. Palgrave Macmillan.

Finlay, S. (2014). *Predictive Analytics, Data Mining, and Big Data*. Basingstoke, UK, Palgrave Macmillan.

Franses, P. H. (2014). *Expert Adjustments of Model Forecasts: Theory, Practice and Strategies for Improvement*. Cambridge University Press.

Galbraith, C. S., and Merrill, G. B. (1996). The politics of forecasting: Managing the truth. *California Management Review*, 38, 29–43.

Goodwin, P., Dyussekeneva, K., and Meeran, S. (2013). The use of analogies in forecasting the annual sales of new electronics products. *IMA Journal of Management Mathematics*, 24, 407–422.

Goodwin, P., Meeran, S., and Dyussekeneva, K. (2014). The challenges of pre-launch forecasting of adoption time series for new durable products. *International Journal of Forecasting*, 30, 1082–1097.

Graefe, A., Armstrong, J. S., Jones Jr, R. J., and Cuzán, A. G. (2014). Combining forecasts: An application to elections. *International Journal of Forecasting*, 30, 43–54.

Graefe, A., Armstrong, J. S., Jones, R. J., and Cuzán, A. G. (2014). Combining forecasts: An application to elections. *International Journal of Forecasting*, 30(1), 43-54.

Granger, C. W. J., and Jeon, Y. (2007). Long-term forecasting and evaluation. *International Journal of Forecasting*, 23, 539–551.

Gustafsson, A., Herrmann, A., and Huber, F. (2001) *Conjoint Measurement: Methods and Applications* (2nd ed.), Berlin and New York: Springer.

Hanssens, D. M., Parsons, L. J., and Schultz, R. L. (2001). *Market Response Models: Econometric and Time Series Analysis*, 2nd ed. Boston and Dordrecht: Kluwer.

Hong, T., and Fan, S. (2016). Probabilistic electric load forecasting: A tutorial review. *International Journal of Forecasting*, 32, 914–938.

Ibrahim, R., Ye, H., L'Ecuyer, P., and Shen, H. P. (2016). Modeling and forecasting call center arrivals: A literature survey and a case study. *International Journal of Forecasting*, 32, 865–874.

Jose, V. R. R., and Winkler, R. L. (2008). Simple robust averages of forecasts: Some empirical results. *International Journal of Forecasting*, 24, 163–169.

Jun, D. B., and Park, Y. S. (1999). A choice-based diffusion model for multiple generations of products. *Technological Forecasting and Social Change*, 61, 45–58.

Kahn, K. B. (2002). An exploratory investigation of new product forecasting practices. *Journal of Product Innovation Management*, 19, 133–143.

Kolassa, S. (2008). Can we obtain valid benchmarks from published surveys of forecast accuracy. *Foresight*, 11, 6–14.

Kolassa, S. (2016). Evaluating predictive count data distributions in retail sales forecasting. *International Journal of Forecasting*, 32(3), 788–803.

Kourentzes, N. (2014). On intermittent demand model optimisation and selection. *International Journal of Production Economics*, 156, 180–190.

Kourentzes, N., Petropoulos F. and Trapero, J. R. (2014). Improving forecasting by estimating time series structural components across multiple frequencies. *International Journal of Forecasting*, 30(2), 291–302.

Kuzin, V., Marcellino, M., and Schumacher, C. (2011). MIDAS vs. mixed-frequency VAR: Nowcasting GDP in the euro area. *International Journal of Forecasting*, 27(2), 529–542.

Labys, W. C. (2006). *Modeling and Forecasting Primary Commodity Prices*. Aldershot, Hampshire, UK: Ashgate Publishing.

Lahiri, K., and Moore, G. H. (eds.). (1991). *Leading Economic Indicators: New Approaches and Forecasting Record*. Cambridge, UK: Cambridge University Press.

Lau, H.-S., and Hing-Ling Lau, A. (1996). Estimating the demand distributions of single-period items having frequent stockouts. *European Journal of Operational Research*, 92, 254–265.

Lee, H. L., Padmanabhan, V., and Whang, S. (1997). The bullwhip effect in supply chains. *Sloan Management Review*, 38, 93–102.

Lee, J., Cho, Y., Lee, J.-D., and Lee, C.-Y. (2006). Forecasting future demand for large-screen television sets using conjoint analysis with diffusion model. *Technological Forecasting and Social Change*, 73, 362–376.

Lee, W. Y., Goodwin, P., Fildes, R., Nikolopoulos, K., and Lawrence, M. (2007). Providing support for the use of analogies in demand forecasting tasks. *International Journal of Forecasting*, 23, 377–390.

Leonard, M. (2007). Forecasting short sesaonl time series using aggregate and analagous series. Foresight, 6, 16–20.

Lilien, G. L., and Rangaswamy, A. (2004). *Marketing Engineering: Computer-Assisted Marketing Analysis and Planning*, revised 2nd ed. Victoria, B.C.: Trafford Publishing.

Lilien, G. L., Rangaswamy, A., and Van den Bulte, C. (2000). Diffusion models: Managerial applications and software. In V. Mahajan, E. Muller, and Y. Wind (eds.), *New-Product Diffusion Models*. Boston and Dordrecht: Kluwer.

Litterman, R. B. (1986). Forecasting with Bayesian vector autoregressions: 5 years of experience. *Journal of Business and Economic Statistics*, 4, 25–38.

Lynn, G. S., Schnaars, S. P., and Skov, R. B. (1999). Survey of new product forecasting practices in industrial high technology and low technology businesses. *Industrial Marketing Management*, 28, 565–571.

Ma, S., and Fildes, R. (2017). A retail store SKU promotions optimization model for category multi-period profit maximization. *European Journal of Operational Research*, 260, 680–692.

Makridakis, S., Andersen, A., Carbone, R., Fildes, R., Hibon, M., Lewandowski, R., Newton, J., Parzen, E., and Winkler, R. (1982). The accuracy of extrapolation (time-series) methods: Results of a forecasting competition. *Journal of Forecasting*, 1, 111–153.

Makridakis, S., and Hibon, M. (1979). Accuracy of forecasting: Empirical investigation. *Journal of the Royal Statistical Society Series A — Statistics in Society*, 142, 97–145.

Makridakis, S, and Hibon, M. (2000). The M-3 Competition: Results, conclusions and implications. *International Journal of Forecasting*, 16, 451–476.

Marder, E. (1999). The assumptions of choice modelling: Conjoint analysis and SUMM. *Canadian Journal of Marketing Research*, 18, 1–12.

McCullough, B. D. (2009). Testing econometric software. In Palgrave Handbook of Econometrics (pp. 1293–1320). Palgrave Macmillan UK.

McNees, S. K. (1986). Forecasting accuracy of alternative techniques: A comparison of U.S. macroeconomic forecasts. *Journal of Business and Economic Statistics*, 4, 5–15.

Meade, N., and Islam, T. (2001). Forecasting the diffusion of innovations: Implications for time-series extrapolation. In J. S. Armstrong (ed.), *Principles of Forecasting: A Handbook for Researchers and Practitioners*. Boston and Dordrecht: Kluwer.

Meade, N., and Islam, T. (2006). Modelling and forecasting the diffusion of innovation — A 25-year review. *International Journal of Forecasting*, 22, 519–545.

Meade, N., and Islam, T. (2015). Forecasting in telecommunications and ICT — A review. *International Journal of Forecasting*, 31, 1105–1126.

Meeran, S., Jahanbin, S., Goodwin, P., and Quariguasi Frota Neto, J. (2017). When do changes in consumer preferences make forecasts from choice-based conjoint models unreliable? *European Journal of Operational Research*, 258, 512–524.

Mersereau, A. J. (2015). Demand Estimation from censored observations with inventory record inaccuracy. *MSOM–Manufacturing and Service Operations Management*, 17, 335–349.

Merz, J. (1991). Microsimulation: A survey of principles, developments and applications. *International Journal of Forecasting*, 7, 77–104.

Mitton, L., Shuterland, H., and Weeks, M. (2000). *Microsimulation Modelling for Policy Analysis: Challenges and Innovations*. Cambridge, UK: Cambridge University Press.

Montgomery, A. L. (2005). The implementation challenge of pricing decision support systems for retail managers. *Applied Stochastic Models in Business and Industry*, 21, 367–378.

Morwitz, V. G. (2001). Methods for forecasting with intentions data. In J. S. Armstrong (ed.), *Principles of Forecasting: A Handbook for Researchers and Practitioners*. Boston and Dordrecht: Kluwer, pp. 33–56.

Natter, M., Reutterer, T., Mild, A., and Taudes, A. (2007). An assortmentwide decision-support system for dynamic pricing and promotion planning in DIY retailing. *Marketing Science*, 26, 576–583.

Newbold, P., and Granger, C. W. J. (1974). Experience with forecasting univariate time series and the combintion of forecasts. *Journal of the Royal Statistical Society, series A*, 137, 131–164.

Nikolopoulos, K., Syntetos, A. A., Boylan, J. E., Petropoulos, F., and Assimakopoulos, V. (2011). An aggregate-disaggregate intermittent demand approach (ADIDA) to forecasting: an empirical proposition and analysis. *Journal of the Operational Research Society*, 62(3), 544–554.

Norton, J. A., and Bass, F. M. (1987). A Diffusion-Theory Model of Adoption and Substitution for Successive Generations of High-Technology Products. *Management Science*, 33, 1069–1086.

Olafsson, S., Li, X., and Wu, S. (2008). Operations research and data mining. *European Journal of Operational Research*, 187, 1429–1448.

Ord, J. K. (1988). Future developments in forecasting: The time series connexion. *International Journal of Forecasting*, 4, 389–402.

Petropoulos, F., and Kourentzes, N. (2015). Forecast combinations for intermittent demand. *Journal of the Operational Research Society*, 66(6), 914–924.

Qian, L., and Soopramanien, D. (2011). Heterogeneous consumer preferences for alternative fuel cars in China. *Transportation Research Part D: Transport and Environment*, 16, 607–613.

Sagaert, Y. R., Aghezzaf, E.-H., Kourentzes, N., and Desmet, B. (2017). Temporal big data for tire industry tactical sales forecasting. *Interfaces*, Forthcoming.

Sanders, N. R. (2001). Judgmental adjustments of statistical forecasts. In J. S. Armstrong (ed.), *Principles of Forecasting: A Handbook for Researchers and Practitioners*. Boston and Dordrecht: Kluwer, pp. 405–416.

Sanders, N. R., and Manrodt, K. B. (2003). Forecasting software in practice: Use, satisfaction, and performance. *Interfaces*, 33, 90–93.

SAS® Data mining using *SAS® Enterprise Miner™ A Case Study Approach*, Third Edition. Cary. NC Available pm: *https://support.sas.com/documentation/cdl/en/emcs/66392/PDF/default/emcs.pdf*.

Snyder, R. D., Ord, J. K., and Beaumont, A. (2012). Forecasting the intermittent demand for slow-moving inventories: A modeling approach. *International Journal of Forecasting*, 28, 485–496.

Snyder, R. D., Ord, J. K., Koehler, A. B., McLaren, K. R. and Beaumont, A. N. (2017). Forecasting compositional time series: A state space approach. *International Journal of Forecasting*, 33, 501–512.

Song, H., and Li, G. (2008). Tourism demand modelling and forecasting: A review of recent research. *Tourism Management*, 29, 203–220.

Stekler, H. O. (2007). The future of macroeconomic forecasting: Understanding the forecasting process. *International Journal of Forecasting*, 23, 237–248.

Stekler, H. O., Sendor, D., and Verlander, R. (2010). Issues in sports forecasting. *International Journal of Forecasting*, 26, 606–621.

Syntetos, A. A., and Boylan, J. E. (2005). The accuracy of intermittent demand estimates. *International Journal of Forecasting*, 21, 303–314.

Syntetos, A. A., and Boylan, J. E. (2006). On the stock control performance of intermittent demand estimators. *International Journal of Production Economics*, 103, 36–47.

Syntetos, A. A., Boylan, J. E., and Teunter, R. (2011). Classification for forecasting and inventory. *Foresight*, 20, 12–17.

Syntetos, A. A., Babai, Z., Boylan, J. E., Kolassa, S., and Nikolopoulos, K. (2016). Supply chain forecasting: Theory, practice, their gap and the future. *European Journal of Operational Research*, 252, 1–26.

Tashman, L. (Ed.). (2010). Forecast Accuracy Measurement: Pitfalls to Avoid and Practices to Adopt. *Foresight: The International Journal of Applied Forecasting, Special Issue.*

Taylor, J. W., and Espasa, A. (2008). Energy forecasting. *International Journal of Forecasting*, 24, 561–565.

Thomas, L. C. (2009). *Consumer Credit Models: Pricing, Profit and Portfolio.* Oxford, UK: Oxford University Press.

Timmermann, A., and Granger, C. W. J. (2004). Efficient market hypothesis and forecasting. *International Journal of Forecasting*, 20, 15–27.

Trapero, J. R., Kourentzes, N. and Fildes, R. (2012). Impact of information exchange on supplier forecasting performance. *Omega*, 40, 738–747.

Wallström, P., & Segerstedt, A. (2010). Evaluation of forecasting error measurements and techniques for intermittent demand. *International Journal of Production Economics*, 128(2), 625–636.

Weller, M., and Crone, S. F. (2012). Supply Chain Forecasting: Best Practices and Benchmarking Study. Lancaster Centre for Forecasting White Paper: Available on: *http://goo.gl/MPbAjz.*

Williams, D. (2007). Seasonality: Shrinkage procedures for small samples. *Foresight*, 6, 21–23.

Williams, L. V., and Stekler, H. O. (2010). Sports forecasting. *International Journal of Forecasting*, 26, 445–447.

Wind, Y., and Green, P. E. (2004) *Marketing Research and Modelling: Progress and Prospects.* New York: Springer.

Wittink, D. R. and Bergestuen, T. (2001). Forecasting with conjoint analysis. In J. S. Armstrong (ed.), *Principles of Forecasting: A Handbook for Researchers and Practitioners.* Boston and Dordrecht: Kluwer, pp. 147–170.

CHAPTER 13

Forecasting in Practice

Table of Contents

In theory there is no difference between theory and practice. In practice there is.

— Various attributions including
Yogi Berra (baseball player and coach)
and Albert Einstein (Nobel physicist)

Introduction

In this final chapter, we focus on the practical issues that may face forecasters in carrying out their job. Up to this point, we have concentrated on the many methods that can be applied to forecasting problems. But what do forecasters in organizations actually do to earn their living? And what do they need to do well? In the first section of this chapter, we look at the process forecasters go through in producing their forecasts. The process depends crucially on the nature of the problem and the data that can be used. These two factors together should lead the forecaster to consider a range of techniques. But often, only a very limited range is considered, for good reasons and for bad. To explore why that might be, we first employ the many surveys of forecasting practice to examine the techniques actually used. We then present a *forecasting method selection tree* to aid in developing a short list of approaches the forecaster can adopt. In Section 13.1.4, we discuss the issue of monitoring and evaluating forecast errors, part of the ongoing process that forecasters need to implement for many, if not all, forecasting problems. Finally, in Section 13.1.5, we review ABC-XYZ analysis as a way to decide upon the allocation of forecasting effort.

Forecasters do not work in an organizational vacuum. Far from it — they are subject to many political pressures that may affect both the process and the accuracy of their forecasts. In fact, in extreme cases, the politics of forecasting may be more important than any technical questions of accuracy. In Section 13.2, we discuss how forecasters fit into an organizational setting and the pressures they face in carrying out their job successfully.

Section 13.3 discusses two related topics: the uncertainty that remains, even after the most careful forecasting process has been carried out, and how to respond to that uncertainty. In Section 13.4, we return to what, for most practicing forecasters, is the key issue: how to improve forecasting in their organizations. Better forecasting methods are only a part of it. The chapter concludes with a final set of principles for effective forecasting.

13.1 The Process of Forecasting

In Chapter 1, we introduced PIVASE (Purpose, Information, Value, Analysis, System, and Evaluation) as a set of concepts to help understand the key elements of any forecasting problem. These elements in turn define the process adopted by the forecaster to satisfy particular organizational requirements. If this all sounds a bit abstract, let's think about a fast-moving consumer goods manufacturer selling to major supermarkets as well as to independent small retailers. What is the purpose of forecasting for this company, and, as a consequence, what variables does such an organization need to forecast? The answer to this question is a long one, and many of the variables will never be considered by the organizational forecaster. But the first purpose must be to estimate demand and the production costs associated with meeting customer service expectations and company financial requirements. The company will also need a marketing plan, to decide on its promotional and advertising expenditures, and, in addition, to consider such aspects as the desirability and effects of possible new products (see Figure 12.12). These two different forecasting tasks should be distinguished. In the first, an ongoing activity is needed to forecast demand and costs on a weekly or monthly basis. The second task requires a one-time analysis to understand and predict the success and side effects of a new product launch. Which of these two alternatives is under consideration helps to define the different tasks, as we now explain.

DISCUSSION QUESTION: *What are the important purposes behind the forecasting activities of (a) an electricity supplier and (b) a city police force?*

13.1.1 The Forecasting Task

How does a forecaster go about the process of forecasting, and what tasks are undertaken? The first task is concerned with the definition of the problem. This is rarely straightforward: One of us (RF) has twice had the experience of being asked to improve an organization's forecasting (for a manufacturer of trucks and a manufacturer of wall coverings), only to discover that the demand forecasts they produced were not at the appropriate level of detail. So, first, we need to establish precisely what needs to be forecast.

Carrying out this task requires a discussion with the clients and users of the forecasts to establish exactly what is needed, including the purpose for which the forecasts are produced and the constraints under which the forecasts have to be produced, in particular the information that could be used (PI in our notation from Chapter 1). These constraints include the resources available, such as the skill level of the forecaster and colleagues, the time required to produce the forecast, and the data and computer software available to support the task.

Figure 13.1 describes the process for producing the final forecasts to be used elsewhere in the organization. What exactly the forecasting problem is first needs to be agreed upon by the various organizational stakeholders, including those who rely on the forecasts in making their plans and decisions. This step always needs to be made for a one-time forecasting problem, but is usually bypassed with operational forecasting problems (as discussed in Chapter 12) once the process is established. Two steps are then made in parallel: data gathering and establishing the organizational assumptions from which the forecast is derived. The two tasks are harnessed in tandem in that the assumptions will include market drivers, such as the product's distribution, the marketing activities to be undertaken, and the proposed price. Equally, past data are needed on the market drivers if their impact is to be statistically estimated.

Figure 13.1 The Forecasting Process: A Task-Analytic Perspective

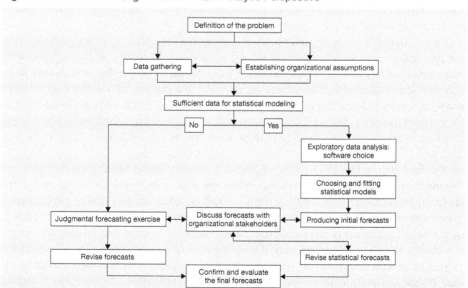

For one-off forecasting problems, data collection can be a laborious step (even through the Internet) in which the casual omission of a key variable (such as competitive activity) can lead to major forecasting errors. For those problems for which forecasts are made regularly, the core data should be readily available through the forecasting support system (FSS; see Section 12.2) — but it often is not! For the moment, we will suppose that the FSS has collated all the data available for the forecaster to use. If the database is sufficiently rich for a quantitative forecasting method to be developed, the next step is to carry out some exploratory data analysis (see Chapter 2). Where there is little to build on, the forecaster has to rely on a judgmental method of forecasting (see Chapter 11).

With a rich enough database, either an extrapolative method of forecasting or a causal model can be developed. In Chapter 9, we discussed the iterative procedure of modeling and testing the results against the data, particularly the hold-out sample. The outcome is an operational model that can be used to produce forecasts. These forecasts may include not only the market drivers or economic assumptions that will determine the actual outcomes, but also various policy decisions. Equally, though, they may not: If the method adopted is an extrapolative forecasting method (such as one of those described in Chapters 3–6), it *cannot* include such factors as novel promotions or market changes. Also, it is unlikely to include all the holidays that affect sales; moving holidays such as Easter are particularly problematic, although some forecasting systems have adjustment procedures to allow for these events (e.g., Census X-13, described briefly in Section 4.5). The forecaster, whether managing a judgmental process or a statistical method, therefore needs to consider modifying the forecast to produce a final forecast that attempts to capture these missing effects.

It is at this stage of the forecasting process that the interactions between forecasters and users are particularly important. Users must try to identify the key factors that should be incorporated into the forecasting process, and forecasters must explain to users what is (and what is not) captured by the model. This interactive process will often be iterative, with adjustments made after discussions with colleagues around the organization. Such processes can be extremely time consuming and costly, even when the Internet is used as the forum for discussion. Still, these interactions are often necessary to get the organization's stakeholders to buy into the final forecasts, for they may need to inject what they see as key pieces of information they think are relevant to the expected outcomes. When the need for such interactions is recognized and scheduled into the forecasting process, the end result is often both an overall saving in time and better results.

An additional factor to consider is what these initial forecasts, either individually or in the aggregate, imply for other parts of the organization — in particular, the organization's financial objectives (usually as exemplified by the budget). Also, if the forecasts are to be accepted, they will need to reflect the understanding that managers have of the activity. For example, a sales forecast in a drug company needs to reflect marketing's understanding of the product life cycle. The result is that senior staff may well exert their influence, leading to adjustments to the initial forecasts. These adjustments are discussed further in Section 13.2.3.

The final step in Figure 13.1, often ignored, is the evaluation of the final forecasts and the monitoring of the ongoing results. When the forecasting problem is repetitive, the standard measures we laid out in Section 2.7 will be adequate to evaluate performance. When forecasts are judgmental and lead to one-time planning decisions, the track records of individual participants can sometimes be monitored over time and feedback provided to enhance the participants' own understanding of their performance. The accumulating picture of forecast errors and the reasons behind them should lead to organizational learning. Where appropriate, these reviews should include evaluations of both the statistical forecasts and the final adjusted forecast to determine whether the adjustments lead to substantive improvements.

> **DISCUSSION QUESTION:** *How would you provide feedback to senior managers with respect to their forecasts of major one-off events?*

13.1.2 Forecasting Method Selection in Practice

In earlier chapters, we presented a large number of forecasting methods. Some of them are very simple to use with readily available commercial software (e.g., exponential smoothing), but others, such as time series neural networks are much more complex (requiring non-standard and often very expensive software). What methods do forecasters use in practice — and are they the methods we would recommend? Table 13.1 shows the results of three surveys, carried out to deliver comparable results over a time span of more than 20 years. The column headed "PS" describes the results of the most recent survey, carried out in 2006 by McCarthy, Davis, Golicic, and Mentzer. Winklhofer, Diamantopoulos, and Witt (1996) gives broader coverage, but all the surveys tell similar stories:

- Judgmental methods are used more often than quantitative methods.
- Extrapolative methods are preferred to causal methods (although there is a degree of ambiguity in the surveys — for example, whether regression has been used "causally" or to estimate a time trend).
- Simple methods are preferred to complex methods.

Table 13.1 Forecasting Techniques, Ranked in Order of Frequency of Use, by Forecast Horizon

Technique	Short Horizon < 3 Months			Mid Horizon 4 Months – 2 Years			Long Horizon > 2 Years		
	M&C	M&K	PS	M&C	M&K	PS	M&C	M&K	PS
Qualitative									
Jury of executive opinion	1	5	na	1	2	1	1	1	1
Sales force composite	1	5	2	2	2	3	8	4	3
Customer expectations	3	3	1	5	8	4	4	7	na
Quantitative									
Moving average	4	1	6	6	6	7	10	9	na
Straight-line projection	8	3	6	8	9	8	6	10	6
Exponential smoothing	4	2	3	7	1	2	9	6	5
Regression	7	5	3	2	4	6	2	2	2
Trend-line analysis	6	8	3	4	5	5	3	3	4
Simulation	11	12	na	10	13	10	6	8	na
Life cycle analysis	12	12	6	12	10	11	5	5	na
Decomposition	9	8	na	9	7	8	10	10	na
Box-Jenkins time series	10	8	na	11	11	11	11	12	na
Expert systems	nm	12	na	nm	13	11	nm	11	6
Neural networks	nm	8	na	nm	12	11	nm	13	na

Notes: M&C, Mentzer and Cox (1984), sample size = 160; M&K, Mentzer and Kahn (1995), sample size = 186; PS, present study, McCarthy *et al.* (2006), sample size = 86; nm, not measured in the study; na, not applicable (no respondents indicated use of the technique for that time horizon).

Source: Taken from McCarthy *et al.*, 2006.

A similar picture emerges if we examine forecasters' familiarity with the different techniques, although, in making the comparison, we occasionally see examples of a technique, such as Box-Jenkins (ARIMA), that is well known to respondents but not much used.

Although such surveys are valuable in giving some insight into forecasters' choice of different methods, they do not offer an explanation of the underlying reasons beyond familiarity: Of course people will often take the easy way out by selecting the method that is most familiar to them and easiest to adopt. The surveys suffer from many other weaknesses if they are to be employed as benchmarks for an organization to use in deciding which methods to consider.

DISCUSSION QUESTION: *(a) Before you accept the results of the preceding surveys at their face value, what else do you want to know?*

(b) If you wished to use survey evidence as guidance on best practice in order to help appraise your own forecasting effort, what further information would you wish to collect? (See Kolassa, 2008).

Figure 13.2 presents an explanation of some of the factors that influence how organizations select their forecasting approach.

Figure 13.2 Factors Affecting the Use of Different Forecasting Methodologies

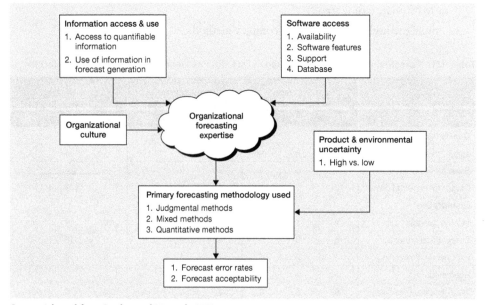

Source: Adapted from Sanders and Manrodt, 2003.

Sanders and Manrodt (2003) conducted a survey of 2,340 heads of marketing of U.S. companies (with 240 usable replies) to test elements of the model presented in Figure 13.2. The key results they identified were the importance of the product market and the perceived uncertainty in the environment, but also uncertainty in the product market. Where there was high uncertainty with rapid changes in the products and the competitive position, quantitative methods were used less frequently. Others have examined additional factors, such as the effects of organizational culture on the adoption and use of various management techniques.

An important rationale for an organization's choice of forecasting approach, which Fildes and Hastings (1994) also identified, was the lack of relevant data. In addition, the organizational culture may not be conducive to using quantitative methods. In such an organization, be it public or private, forecasting is more of a political issue, a topic we turn to in Section 13.2.3. The culture itself affects two other elements: the availability of software and relevant data, and whether the organization has set up an effective process for forecasting, including employing the necessary expertise. If an organization is antagonistic to scientific management, then spreadsheet analysis and an ad hoc process of collecting opinions might be all that can be achieved; the probable result is unnecessary forecast errors. But the key thing to note about Figure 13.2 is that the consequences of these choices affect both the forecast error rate and the acceptability of the final forecast to users within the organization.

13.1.3 Forecasting Method Selection: Which Methods Work Best Under What Circumstances?

All the methods we have described in this book have their merits. It is a question of which method proves best depending on the circumstances and the forecasting problem. Again, PIVASE captures the features we must consider in the choice: What are the problems, the forecast horizon, and the available information, and, crucially, what value is there to improving the forecast accuracy, the evaluation in PIVASE? Table 13.2 gives our personal evaluation of the different methods.

Often, the choice of method is determined by the availability of data, as we discussed in the previous section. With no directly relevant data, quantitative methods cannot be used straightforwardly. Figure 13.3 presents a decision tree that captures the choices. To avoid making the figure overly complicated, we include only the separate branches for judgmental and quantitative methods. Combinations of the two, however, as in Figure 13.1, should always be considered as a possibility. (See *www.forecastingprinciples.com* for a much more complex selection tree.)

With insufficient objective data available, two branches occur; where the task is repetitive with feedback (and learning), unaided judgment works. But this is unusual. A second split is based on whether alternative policies need to be considered. Where the answer is "no," a number of methods rely on collecting data from experts (a sales force or an expert survey) or potential customers (surveys asking whether people intend to purchase a product or service). Prediction markets take a radically different approach to obtaining a collective judgment of the likelihood of future events. There is little evidence of the respective merits of these alternative approaches, although Graefe and Armstrong (2011) suggest that Delphi is more accurate. Where alternative policies need to be considered, role-playing can be used to take into account these policies, as well as potential conflicts between actors in the situation; the aim is to understand the consequences of the different policies. The advantage arises because participants live out their assigned roles in the role-play, adopting the values and perspectives of those they represent, thereby leading to a closer simulation of their interactions. Scenarios, not a forecasting technique itself, but often a compound of many approaches, are also designed to take into account different policy options. Scenarios offer a methodology for working through alternative futures, usually based on group or expert judgments. They can therefore be used to examine the effects of alternative policies or even to predict what policies will be adopted. Again, there is currently little evidence of the effectiveness of this approach compared with alternatives. However, it is an active research area where improvements can be expected. For example, Meissner, Brands, and Wulf (2017) have proposed a method based on a structured approach to the integration of internal and expert judgment that aims to overcome the inertia common in scenario construction (i.e., participants find it difficult to think radically outside a "business-as-usual" future).

Table 13.2 Advantages and Disadvantages of Different Forecasting Methods

Method	Advantages	Disadvantages
Judgmental (see Chapter 11)		
J1 Individual Experts (Subjective)	Can be inexpensive; flexible, can forecast anything; anybody can do it. Can make use of analogies.	Accuracy is suspect (Principles 6.3 and 6.4, Armstrong, 2001), although perhaps the quality of judgments can be improved by various forms of feedback; skills are embodied in the person rather than the organization; subject to all problems of human judgment. Hogarth and Makridakis (1981) provides a still-relevant survey.
J2 Committee/ Informal Survey/ Expert Group	Brings different perspectives to bear on the problem and has the advantages listed for J1.	One loudmouth can dominate, and this person might not be the best forecaster; no one wants to disagree with the boss; more expensive than using an individual expert; problems in selecting participants, identifying expertise, and organizing a meeting.
J3 Sales Force Projects (Sales Force Composite)	Includes different opinions based on detailed knowledge of the product or region. The aggregation aims to remove individual biases.	Motivation to produce accurate forecasts is limited. Each individual is subject to the problems of J1. Takes a long time and can be expensive. Tendency to link such forecasts to sales force performance measures, thereby biasing the results.
J4 Delphi	Has the advantages of the committee or the individual expert forecaster but attempts, through anonymity, to eliminate effects of authority and group domination seen in J2. Can be carried out asynchronously, thereby reducing the time and effort involved; research evidence on both how to carry out an effective Delphi and improvements in accuracy is available in Rowe and Wright (2001).	No necessary convergence to agreed-upon forecast; reluctance to take part in more than one round; consensus does not necessarily imply accuracy, and the true expert might well not be heard.
J5 Intentions Surveys	Effective for shorter term forecasting of new products and services, and has the advantage of reflecting potential consumers' beliefs as to their future courses of action.	Expensive — and although respondents appear to give helpful answers, circumstances in the marketplace change, thereby affecting longer term forecasts. Results need to be de-biased by comparing past intentions surveys with actual results. A survey may say more about people's current attitudes and expectations than about future activities. (See Morwitz, 2001.)
Extrapolative Methods		
E1 Global Trend (Chapter 12)	Easy to learn, to use, and to understand. Can readily be programmed on a spreadsheet. Fits in with the idea of a product life cycle. In various application areas, such as telecoms, has proved useful. See Meade and Islam (2006) for a review.	Almost too easy to use and therefore encourages thoughtlessness, particularly in long term forecasting: Why should a curve depending only on time provide a suitable description of the distant future? Estimation of the saturation level is challenging.
E2 Decomposition (Chapter 4)	Incorporates trend, seasonal, and cyclical factors in an intuitively plausible model.	Limited statistical rationale; not ideally suited to forecasting, and suffers from the same problems as trend curves.
E3 Exponential Smoothing (Chapters 3-5)	Easy to computerize for large number of products; very cheap to operate; easy to set up monitoring schemes; easily understood; good performance in forecasting competitions. Widely used, particularly for short-term operational forecasting. Can be extended to give the modeler considerable flexibility.	Misses turning points. Many different variants, so a selection method is needed. Often ineffectively programmed and therefore careful attention needs to be given to its implementation, particularly the choice of smoothing parameters. Prediction intervals are likely to be miscalculated (Gardner, 2006).
E4 Box-Jenkins or ARIMA (Chapter 6)	The choice of parameterizations is wide, allowing user to identify much more subtle patterns in data than with previous methods; offers philosophy of modeling based on principle of parsimony: The simpler the model the better it is, so long as it passes range of suitable diagnostic checks.	Complex and difficult to understand, but effective automatic versions are now available in many software packages; models can become too elaborate and incorporate patterns that do not carry over into future periods.

continues

Table 13.2 Advantages and Disadvantages of Different Forecasting Methods *(continued)*

Method	Advantages	Disadvantages
Extrapolative Methods (continued)		
E5 Neural Networks (Chapter 10)	Very flexible through its nonlinear formulation and a theoretical proof that neural networks can approximate a wide range of relationships for both time series forecasting and classification. Relatively easy modeling even when underlying demand process is very complex.	Complex with no standard software implementations. Commercial software can be very expensive and is not standardized with "best practice". Statistical software (e.g., R) have limited implementations for time series forecasting. Classification is better served. Limited early evidence is given by Adya and Collopy (1998). A more positive review of recent developments is given by Crone, Hibon, and Nikolopoulos (2011).
Causal (structural)		
C1 Single-equation Regression (Chapters 7-10)	Sufficiently reliable models typically outperform alternatives (Allen and Fildes, 2001); are ideal in that they answer the question, "How does the company influence sales?"; can be used for control to establish policies (such as optimal pricing) as well as in forecasting. Intuitive interpretation of parameters. New methods such as Lasso can cope with many explanatory variables.	Models are difficult to develop, requiring expert staff and large amounts of data that organizations often fail to collect; also, there may be a problem in forecasting exogenous drivers such as *GDP* (see Ashley, 1983; 1988).
C2 VAR Models (Chapter 10)	Many economic systems do not naturally fall into the format of the single-equation model. Instead, the distinction between the dependent variables and the explanatory variables (e.g., sales and advertising) is unclear. VAR models overcome the problem of specifying the causality by modeling each of the system's variables as a lagged function of the remainder. Truly exogenous variables may also be included. The VAR approach has proved effective in forecasting compared with alternatives such as simultaneous system models (in which two or more variables are jointly, rather than sequentially determined as they are in a VAR).	Can handle only a few variables and lags; otherwise the number of parameters becomes excessive. Large data requirements; statistically complex; requires expertise and is even more time consuming to develop than regression. Methods for simplification of the initial general lag scheme are needed. Estimation of a general lag structure is problematic, although Bayesian methods seem to work well.
C3 Simulation (Section 13.3.1)	A simulation model aims to represent the processes that lead to changes in the focus variable(s). Hence, they are usually disaggregated models (compared with other causal methods). An extreme example is the global circulation models used in forecasting climate (Fildes and Kourentzes, 2011). Based on both theoretical models and participants' understanding of the problem, the models themselves can be intuitive, depending on their level of detail. Properly implemented, they can offer the decision maker substantial help and have high face validity; can be designed to be simple to use and understand; and can solve the "right" problem in focusing on policy options. With their high levels of disaggregation, it is possible to look at changes in policy where there is no history. Easy-to-use software is available.	Very expensive; often has large data requirements, although also has the flexibility to incorporate judgmental estimates; level of aggregation used in modeling is problematic; requires careful validation, which is often difficult to do in modeling the effects of new policies. Other, more aggregated causal models (such as C1 and C2) can be used as a basis for simulations, especially for what-if policy simulations.

Figure 13.3 Forecasting Method Selection Tree

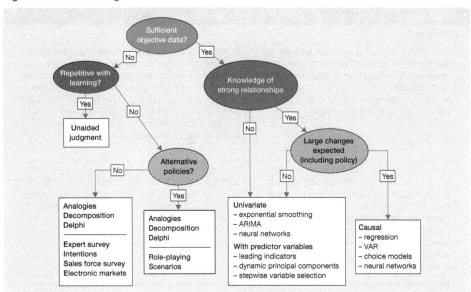

Some approaches work whether or not there are different policies to consider: analogies, making a forecast based on similarity with previous situations, decomposition of the problem into components, and Delphi, to collect and combine a variety of different expert views. All these methods were covered in Chapter 11.

Looking now at the right side of Figure 13.3, we see that when we have good objective data to use, we ask the question whether we believe that there are strong relationships between the economic or market drivers we expect to continue into the future. Also, are large changes expected in the drivers? If the answer to either question is "no," little will be gained by developing a causal model. In fact, as Allen and Fildes (2001) summarize the evidence, the overall benefits of using a causal model are, on average, slight. Only in those situations where there is good knowledge of the causal drivers, with large changes anticipated, and we expect the relationships to remain constant into the future, can a causal model reasonably deliver more accurate forecasts. Despite this cautionary note, for many business situations that are driven by promotional and marketing activities, weather, and holidays, there is very good reason to expect success (and because of the nature of academic research, the evidence on the benefits in such problems is probably underestimated).

Where there are predictor variables that collectively have substantial impact but whose individual effects are insubstantial or largely unknown, various methods can be used to include their effects. With cross-sectional data-mining approaches (including logistic regression), automatic variable selection techniques are used effectively. (See Section 9.4 and the use of such techniques in predicting computer ownership in Chapter 10; also Section 12.5.) Similar methods may be used to improve on the accuracy of time series forecasts, but here there are typically fewer observations. As a consequence, methods of combining many weakly predictive variables in time series have been developed — most recently, so-called dynamic factor models (Stock and Watson, 2002). The basic idea is that of combining a large number of predictor variables into a smaller number of factors, which are then used in regression-type models, but these methods are beyond the scope of this text. The same problem occurs in marketing where many competitive promotional variables need inclusion. In a comparison with various methods of variable reduction including factor models, a Lasso approach proved most successful (Ma, Fildes, and Huang, 2016). A similar approach was found beneficial for supply chain forecasts, permitting the incorporation of dynamics from the macroeconomic environment (Sagaert, Aghezzaf, Kourentzes, and Desmet, 2017).

In an attempt to cut through the complexities of choosing a method to fit the particularities of a forecasting problem, Green and Armstrong (2015) have edited a special issue of the *Journal of Business Research* (2015), volume 68(8), focused on evidence favoring simplicity in forecasting. Taking the argument further Armstrong, Green, and Graefe (2015) have proposed a golden rule of forecasting, "be conservative". This strategy supports simple models and specifications and they claim it is substantially better than seeking out more statistically complex alternatives. But the arguments and the evidence they present are controversial as commentators on the original article have demonstrated; see the special issue for the full discussion. Our experience and our own reading of the evidence (see, for example, Allen and Fildes, 2001) strongly suggest that for many applications, more advanced and complex modeling produces major accuracy improvements. But not always (see Principle 9.1)!

The final comparison applies to those common situations in which judgment and extrapolation are alternatives. Too many organizations rely on judgment (see Table 13.1). From a number of comparisons, it seems clear that, in general, statistical methods will beat judgment whenever the information available is shared. (See Lawrence, Goodwin, O'Connor, and Onkal, 2006, for a survey.) Statistical methods are also cheaper to operationalize on a large scale, as is found in operations. The reasons for this heavy reliance on judgmental approaches are as follows:

- The false belief that judgment provides more accurate forecasts.
- The belief that the quantitative model cannot capture all the complexity required for the forecasting problem whereas the judgmental forecast can.
- The need to justify the position of forecaster (e.g., if the model-based forecasts are sufficient, why do we employ a forecaster?).
- The exercise of ownership and control within the forecasting problem (e.g., if the demand forecaster can change the forecast, the change influences the product's availability, so, by adjusting the forecast, the forecaster controls the outcome to some extent).

However, we know from our discussion of combining in Section 12.1.2 that, generally, where we have two sets of alternative, preferably independently formulated forecasts, we usually do better by combining them. So, when a quantitative forecast is produced first and the forecaster is provided with information not already included in the model-based forecasts, she should adjust the forecast to take the additional information into account. Only when the statistical forecast has been sufficiently refined should the results be presented to decision makers, along with a clear picture of the underlying assumptions behind the model-based forecast. The decision makers can then make further (hopefully, appropriate) adjustments. As we mentioned before, such a process will usually lead to improved accuracy, although *both* statistical and final forecasts should be evaluated. Fildes and Goodwin (2007) explain in more detail how judgment can be improved in these circumstances.

■ Example 13.1: Forecasts of quarterly earnings

Forecasts based upon statistical models of quarterly earnings (often, ARIMA-based forecasts) appear to be as accurate as those made by analysts at the same point in time — that is, just after the latest earnings announcement (Brown, 1993). However, as time passes until the next announcement, no new inputs are available for the statistical model. Still, the informed analyst can build upon the statistical analysis in light of new information that emerges about the company, thereby improving upon the statistical forecast. ■

A harder task is to select the most accurate of a collection of methods, using the forecasting competition approach we described in Section 11.1.1. Of course, although carrying out a competition is sometimes a practical route forward to identifying the most accurate method, the competition must relate to the task in hand (e.g., forecasting information about all SKUs in a given sales category). Unless it is possible to consider a large number of data series and forecast origins, there is likely to remain a lot of randomness; even then, relative performance may change over time. Here again, combining is often preferable, although good software will allow the forecaster to make comparisons across individual methods and combinations to determine the best choice (see online Appendix B). Some available software attempts to carry out a competition automatically at each forecast origin. This approach, however, may lead to unstable forecasts, over-reactive to noise, because the method chosen shifts from period to period. However, in stable situations Fildes and Petropoulos (2015a) show that selection based on out-of-sample performance can be effective.

> **DISCUSSION QUESTION:** *Why might a selection approach in which the method that most recently performed best is used to forecast the next period lead to poor performance? To improved performance?*

> **DISCUSSION QUESTION:** *Putting yourself in the "shoes" of a national construction company, how would you establish a framework for forecasting for the next three months of an aggregate macroeconomic variable such as monthly housing starts? How would you go about forecasting regional housing starts in a part of the country where you operate?*

13.1.4 Forecast Evaluation and Monitoring

Throughout the book, we have emphasized the need to partition the sample, whenever possible, into estimation and hold-out samples. The reason is primarily to provide a basis for model selection and testing. When a forecasting system is already in place, the same design may be used for evaluation purposes. That is, we identify the set of time series of interest and generate corresponding forecasts over the hold-out period. The forecast performance may be measured by using the criteria first developed in Section 2.7, along with assessments of how well the prediction intervals cover the outcomes (e.g., does the 90 percent interval actually capture about 90 percent of the outcomes?). That assessment measures the statistical performance of the forecasting system and may then be used to improve it by identifying features that were previously overlooked (e.g., increases in electronic book sales that have an impact on the demand for regular books).

The second component of evaluation might be defined as whether the forecast delivers "value" to the user. Do the forecasts provide the user with sufficiently accurate information for the purpose in hand? For example, if the forecasts are used to set safety stock levels, how much does the uncertainty in demand cost the company and how much would be saved if forecasts could be improved? That is, we examine the potential value of improvements to the forecasting system. If we are willing to accept the current forecasting system, we still need to monitor its performance over time to ensure that changing conditions do not render our approach ineffective. This need requires some form of statistical process control. The original ideas on control charts are due to Walter Shewhart. His primary focus was on manufacturing processes, where production conditions might be expected to be stable over time if and when the process is in control. Typically, a small sample was taken and the process was deemed to be out of control if the sample mean was more than three standard deviations from the underlying process mean. The time between sets of readings was sufficient to ensure that successive sample means were independent and identically distributed.

We now explore how to make use of these ideas for monitoring forecast performance when the observations will be *dependent*.

Alwan and Roberts (1988) recognized the need to allow for time dependence and developed a monitoring process based upon ARIMA processes, but it is equally applicable to state-space models or any other forecasting scheme for which we can generate a predictive distribution. Alwan and Roberts also saw that it was necessary to monitor both the forecasts and the unexplained variation. They constructed charts for these two components, which they refer to as follows:

- *Common Cause Chart* (CCC): the fitted values generated by the time series model;
- *Special (or Assignable) Cause Chart* (SCC): the plot of residuals, which may be treated as a Shewhart chart when the errors are independent and identically distributed.

Alwan and Roberts (1988) urged consideration of both charts. The SCC enables the investigator to identify outliers in the usual way (as we've discussed in Section 9.7), whereas the CCC allows recognition of a potentially unacceptable trend, *even when the process is in a state of statistical control*. That is, we seek to understand the common causes leading to autocorrelated behavior, with a view to improving the process by some form of intervention. Alwan and Roberts (1995) review a number of published studies and show how the failure to allow for temporal dependence can lead to misleading conclusions.

A further point needs to be made when we consider monitoring social and economic processes. In order to calibrate the charts, we must assume that either the process is in statistical control during the calibration period, or that outliers have been successfully identified and adjusted. This outlier modification step must be approached with care; typically, the parameter estimates may not change dramatically, but the residual variance may diminish considerably, thereby narrowing the control limits. If we are overly zealous in removing outliers, we may induce a "Chicken Little" effect with too many false scares whereby excessive numbers of out-of-control signals are generated in later periods.

■ Example 13.2: Monitoring a forecast

Let us examine the SES forecasts for the WFJ sales data introduced in Chapter 2 (in *WFJ_sales.xlsx*). We may readily determine the control limits for the SCC by using the residual variance from the estimation sample, and we plot the residuals from successive one-step-ahead forecasts. Figure 13.4 shows the SCC chart for the WFJ sales series, based upon the residuals from the SES forecasts and using observations 1-40 as the estimation sample. We obtain $\alpha = 0.71$ and $RMSE = 2671$, and we plot the Z-scores for each forecast residual. The bounds are based on the standard deviation of the residuals, much like prediction intervals in Section 3.8, but now centered around zero and not around the forecasts. The unusual (out-of-control) values around the Christmas holiday periods (weeks 52–54) are clearly identified.

The CCC for the same period is shown in Figure 13.5. From this plot, the steady buildup and subsequent drop-off in sales are evident. Taken together, the two diagrams show the unusual behavior in weeks 52–54, but they also show that sales are much as expected in other time periods. If management does not like the outcomes, at least it has a clear picture of what is going on.

When the series is stationary, we may establish control limits for the CCC. However, in forecasting applications, the series being examined is often nonstationary and, consequently, does not possess a long-term mean or standard deviation. If we difference the series sufficiently to induce stationarity (Section 6.4), limits may be established for the CCC of the differenced series. ■

DISCUSSION QUESTION: *When the series is nonstationary, why is it not possible to use the CCC to construct a classical control chart with a fixed mean?*

Figure 13.4 Special Cause Chart (SCC) for WFJ Sales, Based Upon One-Step-Ahead Forecast Errors *(for periods 41–62)*

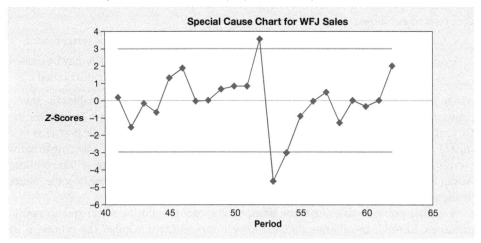

Figure 13.5 Common Cause Chart (CCC) for WFJ Sales, Based Upon One-Step-Ahead Forecasts *(for periods 41–62)*

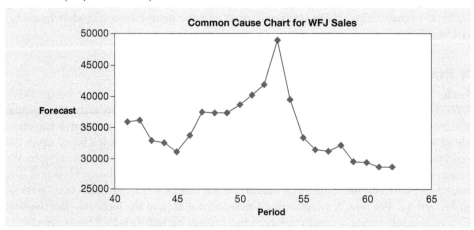

Data: WFJ_sales.xlsx

As we have shown, the SCC and CCC plots are suitable for periodic reviews of forecast performance, but the issues are somewhat different if we are checking forecasts one period ahead for what could be a large number of products. In those circumstances, we work cross-sectionally. That is, we generate the Z-scores for the latest time period for each product and then plot them on a control chart. The process is illustrated in Figure 13.6. We consider 29 costume jewelry products (all bracelets) and use SES with $\alpha = 0.3$ to generate the one-step-ahead forecasts for each product. The plot shows the Z-scores, by product, for Week 40 (when sales were fairly quiet) and Week 48 (when the Christmas rush was beginning). The plot for Week 40 indicates relatively slow sales, whereas Week 48 exhibits sales above forecast levels for all products. Only product 13 for Week 48 lies outside the control limits. Now let's define the composite Z-score across m products as

$$Z_C = \frac{(Z_1 + Z_2 + \cdots + Z_m)}{m^{1/2}}.$$

Here, the composite Z-score yields $Z_C = -3.06$ for Week 40 and $Z_C = 10.34$ for Week 48 (Christmas is coming!).

Figure 13.6 Cross-Sectional SCC Plots for 29 Jewelry Products
(for week 40:Z-40, and week 48:Z-48)

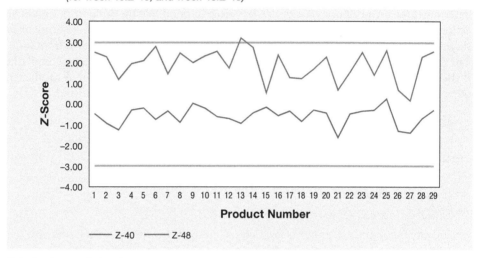

Data: Jewelry_monitoring.xlsx

The following box summarizes the key lessons when monitoring forecast errors.

TO SUCCESSFULLY MONITOR FORECASTS

- Identify forecast errors that are outside appropriate control limits and whether this signifies changes in the time series.
- Check to make sure that the system is in control over the product groups.
- Adjust the control limits to ensure that only a manageable number of products have to be examined in more detail. Identify possible out-of-control series using the Common Cause Chart.

13.1.5 ABC-XYZ Analysis

Many forecasting organizations face the problem of forecasting and monitoring the errors arising for hundreds, if not thousands, of products. It is impossible to pay attention to all of the products equally. What is required is a way of focusing on the series that are important to the business. The ABC-XYZ analysis is a popular tool in supply chain management that helps us segment the product portfolio and prioritize our efforts. The analysis has two components, the ABC part that assess the importance of a product and the XYZ part that assesses how difficult it is to forecast a product. The analysis is based on the Pareto principle that is often referred to as the 80/20 rule, implying that a small proportion of the total number of items is disproportionally important. Vilfredo Pareto, an Italian economist, in early 1900s observed that 80% of the land in Italy belonged to 20% of the population. In organizations we often observe a similar effect; relatively few products are responsible for most sales.

A standard approach is to segment the products into three classes: class A for the 20 percent or so of products that require individual attention, class B for the 30 percent of products for which an automatic monitoring scheme such as that described in the previous section would alert us to any persistent problems, and class C for the 50 percent remaining for which the forecaster looks at the errors only in response to an alert from elsewhere in the organization (e.g., an out-of-stock problem may be generating complaints). Of course, the exact proportions (and the number of segments) will always be open to debate, and what determines the importance rankings anyway? Keep in mind that the ABC setup should be actionable. For instance, using three classes A-B-C separates the product assortment in three intuitive classes: high, medium, and low importance. Nothing prohibits us from using 4 or 5 classes; however, what do these classes signify for the organization at hand? Similarly, it should not be just sales volume (i.e., the highest selling products are the A products); other factors, such as profitability and unit value, may also need to be considered.

PERFORMING AN ABC ANALYSIS

Suppose we use the value of total sales as a measure of importance and we have N products. To perform the ABC analysis we proceed as follows:

1. Order the value of sales of each product (or the chosen importance measure) from largest to smallest.

2. Calculate the cumulative ordered sales.

3. Identify the number of products for each class: A (approximately 20%), B (the next approximately 30%), with the remainder in class C. We may need to round these cut-off points.

4. Find the cumulative sales that correspond to these cut-off points. For example the cumulative sales for the top 20% of products will be the concentration (importance) for class A. Similarly for class B the concentration will be the cumulative sales up to the cut-off observation of that class ($N \times 0.5$) minus the concentration of the preceding classes: in this case class A.

DISCUSSION QUESTION: *What additional factors might prove important in deciding those products (or time series) to put into class A, the category of important products?*

The number of items under consideration and their relative importance will change over time. When the ABC analysis is updated care must be taken to avoid spurious effects caused by products being placed in different classes.

Product characteristics such as sales volume and impact on profit tell only part of the story. After all, if the forecasts of a product are always 100 percent accurate, there is no reason to monitor error. The size of the error is therefore also relevant in deciding which products fall into the various classes. The XYZ analysis focuses on how difficult is to forecast a product, with X being the class with easier items and Z the class with the more difficult ones. To perform the XYZ analysis one follows the same logic as for ABC. Therefore the important question is how to define a metric of "forecastability". Some sources have supported the use of the coefficient of variation. This is flawed, as the coefficient of variation is unable to distinguish trend and seasonality, which may inflate the variance of a time series, and therefore artificially making a time series appear more difficult to forecast. Consequently, using forecasts errors (for instance as measured by *MAPE, MAE/Mean*, or *RelMAE*) is advisable. This introduces a series of different questions: Which forecasting method to use? Which error metric? Should it be in-sample or out-of-sample errors? Again, there is no perfect answer and it depends on the problem context. Consistent with earlier discussion in this book we recommend the use of a class of exponential smoothing methods, evaluated using out-of-sample errors.

Combining both ABC and XYZ analyses allows us to evaluate products in terms of both importance and forecasting difficulty. Below are the interpretations of the extreme combinations (A-C, and X-Z):

- AX: Very important items, but relatively easy to forecast;
- CX: Relatively unimportant items that are relatively easy to forecast;
- AZ: Very important items that are hard to forecast;
- CZ: Relatively unimportant items that are hard to forecast.

In-between classes are likewise easy to interpret. This classification provides a useful way to allocate resources to the forecasting process. Suppose for instance that we have a team of experts adjusting forecasts. It is more meaningful to dedicate time to AZ products, rather than the AX products in gathering additional information to enrich statistical forecasting. Following this logic, one would expect it to be easier to have accurate forecasts for AX, BX, and CX products. If we find that we are doing poorly in terms of accuracy on AX products, we know there are problems with important products that should be relatively easy to forecast, and therefore immediate actions to improve the forecasts are required!

Typically, commercial software allows the user to categorize the time series in the FSS. New products, or products being discontinued should be excluded from the analysis, as they are qualitatively very different from established products. Similarly, intermittent demand products will tend to cluster to the CZ class, due to their nature, so it is preferable to exclude them from the analysis as well. All these excluded products can be placed in dedicated classes.

■ Example 13.3: An ABC-XYZ analysis

Let us use the data set *Jewelry.xlsx* to identify products that require special attention. We use the average sales of a product as a measure of importance. The results of the analyses are summarized in Figure 13.7.

The 20% most important products (class A) correspond to 39.3% of sales. Similarly, the next 30% of products (medium importance, class B) correspond to 30.8% of sales and last class C accounts only for 29.3% of sales, even though it includes 50% of the products.

We performed the XYZ analysis using exponential smoothing to produce the forecasts and then calculated the averages of the *RMSE* errors. The results are shown in Figure 13.7B. The first 20% of products (Z class) correspond to 29.0% of the average *RMSE* forecast errors, whereas the last 50% (class X) correspond to only 39.3%. We can combine the two analyses to classify the products both in terms of importance and forecasting difficulty, as shown in Figure 13.7C.

The forecaster may use the results summarized in Figure 13.7 to prioritize resources. There are 10 AZ products (important and difficult to forecast), which should be monitored closely and for which the forecaster may seek additional information to enrich the forecasts. The 29 AX products are important, but relatively easy to forecast, therefore close monitoring is important, but the forecasts can be automated to a large extent. On the other hand, CZ class contains 31 products, which have relatively low importance and are very difficult to forecast. Given their low importance, the forecaster may choose to dedicate limited time to this class. CX products are easy to forecast and have relatively low forecast errors. Therefore, forecasting for this class could be largely automated. In general, the lower left corner requires closer monitoring and interventions, while the top-right corner lends itself to automation. Obviously, the analysis outputs the exact products belonging to each class, allowing the forecaster to take dedicated actions. ■

Figure 13.7 ABC and XYZ Analyses for Jewelry Products:
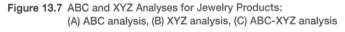
(A) ABC analysis, (B) XYZ analysis, (C) ABC-XYZ analysis

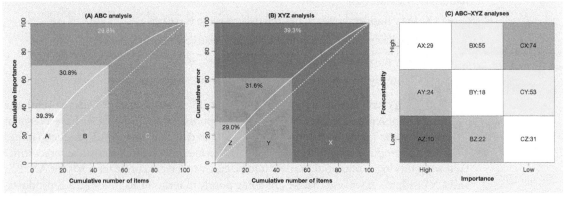

Data: Jewelry.xlsx; adapted from *Forecasting in R: Tutorial and Examples* online materials output.

13.2 The Organization of Forecasting

Forecasting takes place in many parts of an organization, private or public. In government, forecasts are needed not just for the economy as a whole, but also for the many services the government provides and at various levels of geographical and administrative disaggregation. For example, we may need to forecast such operational activities as the number of people in jail, the number passing through the court system, the number of telephone calls received, the cash required to keep the whole system running — the list is endless. In a manufacturing or retailing company, as we discussed in Chapter 12, a wide range of forecasts also is required, in both marketing and production/operations as well as in support of longer term strategic planning. For many working in such organizations, their role will require them to forecast (at the very least as part of the budgeting process), but their primary responsibility won't be the production of accurate forecasts. For others, however, this requirement will be written into their job specification and they will be evaluated on their forecasting performance. What do we know about such professional forecasters and how they perform? And what are those aspects of the job where there is most potential for improvement?

DISCUSSION QUESTION: *What do you see as the ideal educational background for a forecaster?*

13.2.1 The Forecaster

Broken down into its bare bones, the forecaster's job can be seen as taking in information and transforming it into the final forecast. This transformation process is heavily dependent on the input information. But the availability of this input information depends on the position the forecaster occupies within the organization. Figure 13.8 attempts to summarize a research project that examined the forecasting activity in a large multinational corporation with activities that ranged from manufacturing pharmaceuticals to producing paints and explosives (Fildes and Hastings, 1994). Each division included forecasters. In some divisions the forecasters talked to staff handling the marketing or sales function, while in other divisions the forecasters were closer to production and operations. The task these forecasters faced typically included the production of both medium- and long-term forecasts of demand. Elsewhere in some of the divisions, more short-term focused forecasting took place. Here, we see the forecaster sitting somewhere among planning, operations, and sales/marketing, or even finance. Alternatively, forecasting may be a separate function linked to management services.

Figure 13.8 The Market Forecaster in the Organization: Information Flows

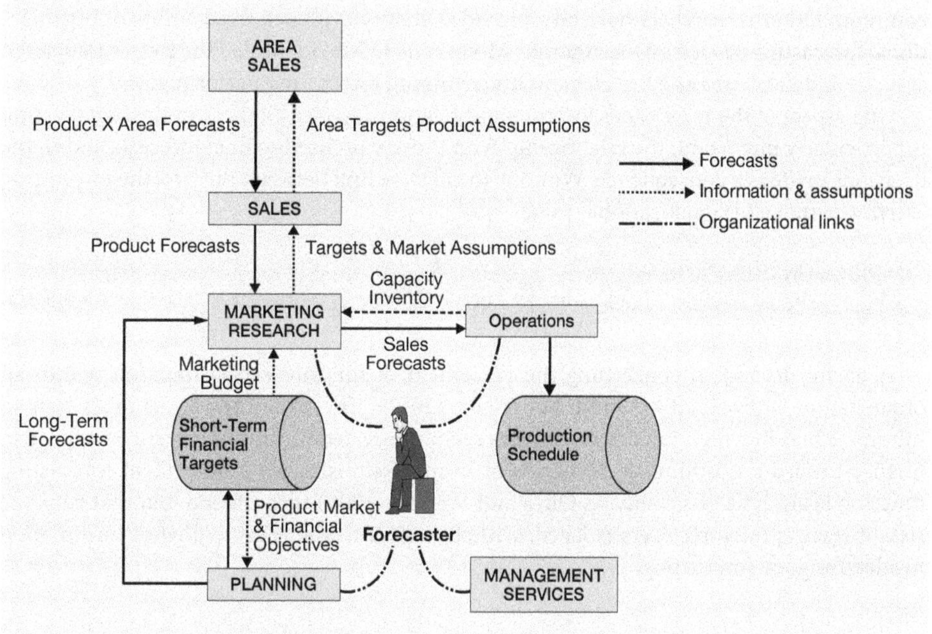

Source: Adapted from Fildes and Hastings (1994).

The information the forecaster receives on a regular basis will usually depend on their organizational location. In an ideal situation, the forecaster will be in receipt of sales information (at a geographical area or account level), but will also know the marketing plans and targets that are in place, such as the promotional schedule or sales-force activity. Competition may also be important, at both local and higher levels. A hierarchy of information is potentially available (see Section 12.2). But operational planning is also important, not least where there are capacity constraints that may limit product availability. In addition, there is the need to reconcile volume forecasts with financial forecasts (and budgets) — producing a unified set of forecast numbers across the organization, with money forecasts consistent with sales forecasts, where the methods of Section 12.3.2 to 12.3.4 should help.

> **DISCUSSION QUESTION:** *Why do many organizations (or business units) aspire to a unified set of forecast numbers that are used across the whole organization? Why is this aspiration often difficult to achieve? What are the arguments against relying on such a unified set?*

Figure 13.8 shows the ideal situation in which the forecaster is in receipt of all the information necessary to support the forecasting process. Of course, a similar picture could be drawn for the government forecaster or the financial forecaster. But in real situations, not all the links operate effectively (e.g., the forecaster may not know anything at all about the operational constraints on supply). Alternatively, marketing plans may be unavailable, either because of poorly drawn lines of responsibility or an inadequate FSS. It is the forecaster's responsibility, if only because of the need for self-preservation, to ensure that the necessary information is made available (see Minicase 13.1). In fact, in the case of the organization studied to arrive at Figure 13.8, lack of information beyond the sales history was common. Other researchers have also provided survey evidence from audits of organizational forecasting processes; for example, Moon *et al.* (2003) identified the lack of integrated systems and databases as a key element undermining forecasting performance.

One aspect of the forecaster's location and relationships with others in the organization is particularly important: the relationship with those who use the final forecasts and to the decisions made as a consequence. Without an effective link between the two, the forecasting activity cannot add organizational value.

> **DISCUSSION QUESTION:** *Why is the organizational location of the forecaster potentially important to carrying out the job effectively?*

A useful discussion concerning the placement of the forecasting function within an organization is provided by Smith and Clark (2011). The issue they focus on is how to minimize bias in which forecasters in sales seem motivated toward optimism and those in finance toward less optimistic scenarios or even pessimism. An independent forecasting function is always a possibility, as Oliva and Watson (2009) recommend, but that runs the risk of leaving the forecasters isolated, without access to the reliable flow of information needed for good forecasting.

13.2.2 The Links to the Forecast User

In many organizations, the forecaster's job is quite separate from that of the user, who will often be making decisions based on the forecast. For example, a retail demand forecast at the SKU level will be turned into an order to the supplier on the basis of the inventory on hand. Or forecasts for incoming phone calls into a call center will be turned into a staff schedule for the next month. The inventory control manager, the scheduler, the purchasing manager, the financial manager, and the account manager are usually not the forecaster. They all have different requirements of the forecasts, with different motivations. We don't in fact know much about the relationship. Anecdotally, forecasters come in for a lot of criticism for "getting it wrong," and often users will modify the final forecasts to take into account some particular aspect of the problem they believe has been inadequately dealt with. The users and their bosses have to believe the forecaster is adding value.

THE FORECASTER'S JOB

Your job as a forecaster is at risk:

- If the user of your forecasts ignores them or modifies them for unaccountable reasons.
- If the decisions made by the user do not depend on the forecasts you produce.

In an interesting (though dated) survey, Wheelwright and Clarke (1976) asked dyads composed of forecaster and user about their perceptions of each other. We give the flavor of their results in Table 13.3.

The table shows how users and forecasters differ in their perceptions; a large score indicates a major difference between the two groups. The conclusion that leaps out from the table is that neither group believes that the other has any understanding of forecasting; in particular, users don't believe that forecasters understand the problems that need to be addressed. Only on one dimension do they agree: Forecasters apparently "understand sophisticated techniques". It sounds, however, as if there is no belief on the users' part that sophistication brings success! In fact, more recent studies, such as the surveys by McCarthy *et al.* (2006) and Weller and Crone (2012), do not support this view of the technical knowledge forecasters may have: Most forecasters in organizations seem to know little about the advances in techniques that we have witnessed over the past 40 years and that are described in this book. Although we don't know much about the educational background of forecasters, there's plenty of anecdotal evidence to suggest that many, if not most, forecasters have no training in forecasting at all!

Table 13.3 Differences in Ratings Between Users' and Forecasters' Views of Each Other

	Difference Between Users and Forecasters
Forecaster's Ability	
• Understand sophisticated forecasting techniques	1%
• Understand management problems	–25%
• Produce cost-effective forecasts	–33%
• Identify best techniques	–56%
• Provide results in the time frame required	–38%
User's Ability	
• Understand essentials of forecasting	27%

The measure used for each criterion is [(% users rating the ability as good or excellent – % forecasters rating the ability as good or excellent) ÷ (% forecasters rating the ability as good or excellent)] × 100.

Source: Adapted from Wheelwright and Clarke, 1976.

Despite the limited evidence, there are some hard lessons to be drawn here. Forecasters need to understand their users' requirements and also to explain effectively to those who employ them the value that accurate forecasts add to the business. They also need to explain the importance of a business having independent forecasters who are not caught up in organizational politics, for the reasons we explain in the next section.

DISCUSSION QUESTION: *How would you organize the forecasting function within an organization to ensure both independence of the forecasters and good interactions with users?*

13.2.3 The Politics of Forecasting

DISCUSSION QUESTION: *Long-term climate forecasts have embroiled climate scientists, economists, and politicians in a major argument as to the accuracy of forecasts of global warming. Why do you think this forecast is such a political issue? Can you think of any other forecasting issues in an organizational or government setting that might prove almost as controversial?*

Research on forecasting practice has shown that forecasts are often influenced by political considerations. For evidence from government, see Deschamps (2004); from the private sector focusing primarily on financial forecasts, see Galbraith and Merrill (1996). At a company operational level, Oliva and Watson (2009) explore how the various functional biases introduced through the Sales and Operations Planning (S&OP) process of Section 12.2 can be mitigated; they recommend a coordination committee to manage the process. When we examine more disaggregated short-term forecasts, the evidence we find is more circumstantial, but forecasts at the SKU level prove to be biased and, more importantly, adjustments to statistical forecasts are most often biased upward and prove overinflated (Fildes, Goodwin, Lawrence, and Nikolopoulos, 2009). Similarly, forecasts of the completion and costs of information systems projects are also often biased upward (see Table 1 in Halkjelsvik, and Jørgensen, 2012), as they also are in new-product forecasting (Tyebjee, 1987). Likewise, many capital projects produce inflated projections of return on investment. Although there are explanations other than political influences, it seems to be that in many circumstances there is organizational pressure to produce "good news"; forecasts are just too optimistic.

DISCUSSION QUESTION: *What other explanations can you think of to explain why capital projects in both government and the private sector tend to be optimistically biased?*

In a U.S. organizational survey of the politics of forecasting, Galbraith and Merrill (1996) found that adjustments due to political reasons were widespread (with around 50 percent of forecasts adjusted to more favorable levels) by senior management. Table 13.4 gives a full picture of why adjustments were made. Overall, the aim of these senior managerial adjustments was to inflate the outcome toward a more favorable figure (Factors 1-3 in the table). The results contrast with those set forth in Fildes and Goodwin (2007), which enumerates the reasons that *forecasters* made adjustments to the statistical forecast. Here, the reasons were much more innocuous and boiled down to incorporating the additional information available to the forecasters beyond the information incorporated into the time series history.

Why did managers make such adjustments? There were a variety of reasons given, but the most important was to gain control of additional internal resources.

DISCUSSION QUESTION: *Why does an optimistic forecast lead to additional resources?*

Of course such adjustments, if appropriate, could prove beneficial, but as Figure 13.9 shows, this is not the case. In general, the political adjustments degraded the accuracy of the forecasts. They also damaged strategic decisions and investment decisions, and had an adverse impact upon forecasters' morale. These patterns of chronic mis-estimation are particularly obvious in cost estimates for public works projects. Notorious examples include the Sydney Opera House, which cost 15 times more than was originally projected. More recently, when Boston's "Big Dig" tunnel construction project was completed, the project was 275 percent over budget. Berlin's new airport, with construction costs more than 200%

over budget, (again) postponed the opening until 2018. Arguably, these projects and others like them prove worthwhile in the end!

Table 13.4 Types of Forecasting Behavior

Question	Percent of Respondents Reporting High Frequency of Behavior*
FACTOR 1. Management Requests Staff Revisions	
1. After reviewing the sales/revenue forecasts, senior management request staff to adjust revenue projections to a more favorable level.	45.1
2. After reviewing cost projections, senior management request staff to adjust cost projections to a more favorable level.	51.6
3. After reviewing pro-forma profit/loss, senior management request staff to generate revised pro-formas that are more favorable.	41.3
FACTOR 2. Management Makes Own Revisions	
4. Senior management personally revise staff's cost projections to reflect a more favorable level.	30.0
5. Senior management personally revise staff's revenue/sales forecasts to reflect a more favorable level.	23.3
FACTOR 3. Management Requests "Backcasts"	
6. Senior management predetermines an "appropriate" sales/revenue level then requests staff to generate forecasts to support this level.	41.9
7. Senior management predetermines an "appropriate" cost level then requests staff to generate cost projections to support this level.	35.5
8. Senior management predetermines an "appropriate" future financial position, then requests staff to generate pro-formas to support this decision.	36.7
FACTOR 4. Use of Incorrect Techniques and Assumptions	
9. Wrong assumptions (such as industry or economic growth) are purposely used in forecasts or models.	12.9
10. Wrong assumptions (such as industry or economic growth) are accidentally used in forecasts or models.	19.4
11. Insufficient resources are provided for the forecasting modeling effort.	35.5
12. Qualitative assessments are made when there are appropriate quantitative techniques that could also be used.	32.4
FACTOR 5. Management Ignores Models/Forecasts	
13. Staff's forecasts are simply discounted by senior management as being "unimportant."	16.1
14. Staff's forecasts are simply discounted by senior management as probably being "inaccurate."	6.6
FACTOR 6. Withholding of Information	
15. Divisions/departments withhold useful data from other departments.	25.8
16. Divisions/departments provide misleading data to other departments.	12.9
FACTOR 7. Model/Forecast Misspecification	
17. Computer models are constructed that are purposely misspecified or don't accurately reflect reality.	6.7
18. Politically sensitive variables are purposely excluded from the computer model.	20.0
19. Computer models are constructed to have a bias, to the advantage of certain departments, projects, or activities.	13.3

*Percent reported is a combination of three responses: constant[ly], almost always, and often.

Source: Results of a survey by Galbraith and Merrill (1996).

Figure 13.9 Reported Effects of Forecasting and Modeling Politics

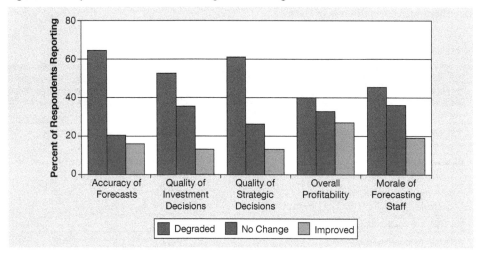

Source: Galbraith and Merrill, 1996.

How can we provide more effective forecasts without risking the loss of approval? Flyvbjerg (2008 and several earlier papers) has recommended the use of *reference class forecasting*. In essence, the forecast is calibrated against the final outcomes of similar, already completed projects; this is an example of forecasting using analogies, as discussed in Section 11.2.6. Providing such information may improve both forecasting processes and decision making.

More generally, various authors, including Galbraith and Merrill (1996), Deschamps (2005), and Oliva and Watson (2009), have discussed how to avoid the worst aspects of political forecasting — in particular, pervasive bias. The following are some of their suggestions:

- Forecasters need better training in forecasting and modeling techniques. Remember, most forecasters are not trained in forecasting!
- Guidelines need to be established for how the forecasting process should be carried out. Changes to the forecasters' forecasts should be made *only if* new evidence is brought to bear on the forecast. Such changes need to be documented (as they should be in making adjustments to statistical models in operations; see Section 12.2.1).
- Consider an independent coordination committee to manage the process.
- Make the assumptions behind the forecasts explicit.
- Aim for consensus forecasts that balance the various political interests and stand a good chance of achieving user acceptance.
- Identify bias by monitoring accuracy.
- Assign responsibility to the forecasters for their errors. Do not permit users to modify the final forecasts without accepting responsibility.

But politics are an inevitable part of the forecasting process and include information sharing, arriving at assumptions and policies, and the user group's acceptance of the forecast to use it operationally in planning and decision making.

Forecast errors remain inevitable in forecasting, even with the best process in the world. In the next section, we revisit the evaluation of forecasting in an organizational setting and touch briefly on coping with the residual unavoidable uncertainty.

DISCUSSION QUESTION: *What, if any, potentially positive effects derive from politically motivated adjustments to the forecasts?*

13.3 Dealing with Uncertainty

Through most of the book's earlier chapters, the primary focus has usually been on point forecasts, but uncertainty is of interest in its own right, because it drives much of decision making from financial investments to stock control in operations. Not only do we need a point forecast, but as we have stressed repeatedly, we need to indicate the range of possible future outcomes, for example, by estimating a prediction interval. Even better, we could hope to capture the whole distribution, which is important when the errors do not follow a normal distribution. (If the errors do follow a normal distribution, then the mean and variance serve to determine the prediction interval.) As in the volatility forecasting example of Section 6.10 it is important to remember that these intervals and distributions are themselves forecasts of *future* uncertainty. Figure 13.10 gives an example of a fan chart, which is produced by a number of central banks to capture their forecasts of uncertainty. The forecast origin is the second quarter of 2010, and the different shadings show varying degrees of uncertainty around the point forecasts as the forecast horizon lengthens.

Each color band in Figure 13.10 has the same probability of including the actual value. In addition, it is important to recognize that unlikely events do happen and the darker parts of the fan will not always capture the outcomes. However, despite the political uncertainties of the new U.S. presidency and Brexit, by the end of the first quarter of 2017, the *GDP* in the UK (similarly with the *CPI*) remained very much inside the most likely shaded area.

More generally, we might be able to predict the full error distribution, shown in Figure 13.11. Even when the histogram looks symmetrical, the distribution may have heavy tails, as shown in the probability plot, so we would underestimate the possibility of large errors. Part of the problem in the 2007-2010 financial crisis was the erroneous assumption that errors were approximately normal, so risks were systematically underestimated.

DISCUSSION QUESTION: *Identify some instances in which the extremes of the forecast error distribution are likely to have a particularly high impact, and explain why.*

Figure 13.10 The Forecast Uncertainty Around the Bank of England's GDP Forecasts from 2016 to 2020 *(fan chart published November 2016)*

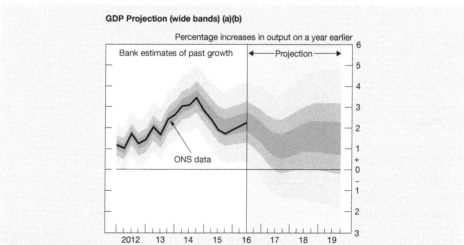

Source: http://www.bankofengland.co.uk/publications/Pages/inflationreport/2016/nov.aspx.
Reproduced with permission.

The Bank of England's Monetary Policy Committee's best collective judgement is that the mature estimate of *GDP* growth would lie within the darkest central band on only 30 occasions out of 100. The fan chart is constructed so that outturns are also expected to lie within each pair of the lighter green areas on 30 occasions. In any particular quarter of the forecast period, *GDP* growth is therefore expected to lie somewhere within the fan on 90 out of 100 occasions. And on the remaining 10 out of 100 occasions *GDP* growth can fall anywhere outside the green area of the fan chart. Over the forecast period, this has been depicted by the light gray background.

When we have an explicit statistical model, we are usually able to use past data and the model's residuals to generate an estimate of the distribution. For example, if we can assume that the distribution is normal, then the output of a regression model includes an estimate of the standard deviation of the residuals (see Chapter 8), which is used to construct prediction intervals. Alternatively, where many past out-of-sample errors have been collected, it is better to use these to estimate the empirical error distribution (see Section 2.8). But both approaches make a strong assumption that is common and almost unavoidable in all forecasting: Past errors are predictive of future errors. Nonetheless, that was not how the fan chart of Figure 13.10 was constructed. Although the errors the Bank of England had made in the past were certainly influential, the fan chart itself also takes into account the current opinions of the Bank's forecasters as to future uncertainty. In 2016, these opinions reflected the extremely uncertain global economic environment and although the short-term forecasts have tight bands, the longer term forecasts reflect this uncertainty. Thus, for major forecasts, a combination of statistical and judgmental information will typically provide improved estimates of the error distribution.

Figure 13.11 Distribution and Probability Plot of Daily Returns for the Dow-Jones Index
(from January 3rd 2011 to December 31st, 2016: n=1513.
A normal distribution is superimposed for comparison.)

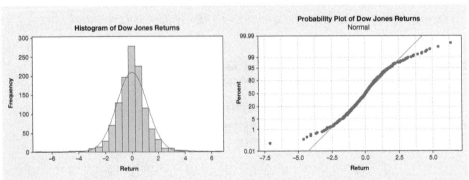

Source: Samuel H. Williamson, 'Daily Closing Value of the Dow Jones Average, 1885 to Present,' *MeasuringWorth*, 2017. *https://measuringworth.com/DJA/*.

13.3.1 Simulating Uncertainty

In any forecasting exercise, errors arise from a multitude of sources. We have examined some of these sources in Section 8.6, but we now need to develop a more extended list. Consider an underlying model of a dependent variable Y (or a set of such variables)

$$Y_t = f_t(Y_{t-1}, X_t, \varepsilon_t \mid \boldsymbol{\beta}). \tag{13.1}$$

where f_t is an function that may be time dependent and nonlinear but is often assumed to be constant and linear, X_t represents exogenous (explanatory) variables defined outside the economic system, and ε_t are random error terms. Both Y and X may be vectors; that is, multiple variables may be involved in the forecasting exercise. β is a vector of unknown parameters that are estimated from past data. Future values are generated using the relationship

$$Y_{t+k} = f_{t+k}(Y_{t+k-1}, X_{t+k}, \varepsilon_{t+k} \mid \beta).$$

Errors in producing k-periods-ahead forecasts of Y_t for period $t + k$ based on information available only up to time t arise from the following possible sources:

1. Estimation errors in estimating β

2. Randomness (originating by ε_t)

3. Errors in forecasting X_{t+k}

4. Errors in forecasting Y_{t+k-1}, $k > 1$ and any further lags in the model

5. Misspecification of the function f, including omitted variables and structural change

6. Data errors

7. Calculation errors.

The formulas of Section 8.6 cover only the first two sources of error, so we need to consider methods that incorporate at least sources 3 and 4 as well. Some progress may be made by the use of additional lags, as in Section 7.7.4, or, more generally, by means of the VAR models of Section 10.5, but complex systems may be beyond tractable analysis and we must turn to simulation methods.

The forecast function and associated error distribution can be estimated by the simulation approach shown in Figure 13.12.

Figure 13.12 Flow Chart for Simulating a Predictive Distribution

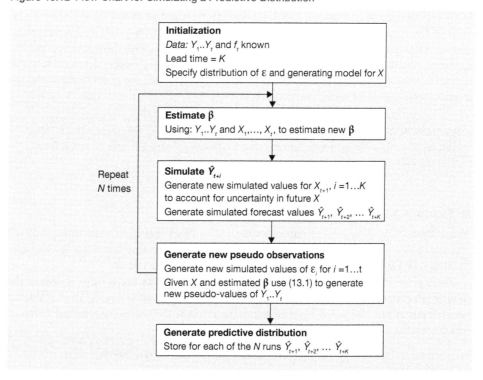

The idea behind this process is that N random draws are made from the distributions characterizing our uncertain knowledge of X and ε. By iterating through $k = 1, 2,...$ to the forecast horizon K, we generate forecasts for the next K periods based on X_{t+k} generated from the assumed distribution of Xs. This procedure is then repeated N times (where N is large) to generate a probability distribution of possible outcomes. The output from the simulation provides an estimate of the predictive distribution of the forecasts. The predictive distribution can then be used to generate prediction intervals or for other purposes, such as setting safety stocks.

Perhaps the most serious problem in the process just described is the failure to take into account the uncertainty in β, which our earlier analyses have assumed to be fixed. To gain insight into the uncertainty arising from the fact that we have estimated β, we can use our newly estimated equation to calculate the predicted values (for periods $t + 1$ to $t + K$) based on simulated Xs, which, when joined with the simulated errors, gives a new set of pseudo Y values. For the first t periods, the pseudo Ys are based on observed Xs while for the K periods ahead forecasts simulated Xs are used. With the newly simulated Ys, we can then estimate another β, and a corresponding set of Ys, both predicted and forecast. By repeatedly generating a pseudosample, we can derive a probability distribution for β, and the corresponding predictive distribution that now takes into account the uncertainties in X, ε, and β. An alternative is to assume a distribution for β, based on its estimated mean and variance, but this is difficult when there are more than one or two parameters unless we assume that these prior distributions are independent. This approach is explored in the next section.

13.3.2 Understanding the Impact of Uncertainty and Forecast Errors

Forecasting does not exist in an organizational vacuum. This observation is the very heart of this chapter. It affects many aspects of an organization's performance, from the service levels experienced by customers, its effects on cash flow and profitability, to the very survival of the organization. Similar examples occur in the not-for-profit and government sectors. An organization invests its resources in forecasting because the impact of "getting it wrong" hits the bottom-line deliverables. (Think less profit or poorer service.) In order to decide between different courses of action, the impact of both the point forecast and the forecast error should be taken into account.

> **DISCUSSION QUESTION:** *In the U.S. federal court system (in the UK, the Crown Court), what do you think are the important types of forecast error and how are these likely to affect the system's performance?*

■ Example 13.4: Cash-flow simulation study

As an illustration, Figure 13.13 shows a simple flow chart that links cash with predicted revenues and costs, which in turn depend on demand. (We assume that there is a capacity constraint of 1200 units, so demand is not always equivalent to sales.)

Here, price influences demand to generate sales (so long as the volume is within the capacity to supply it). In turn, revenue is produced, and once costs (made up of fixed and variable costs) are subtracted from revenue, the result is the corresponding net revenue, which we refer to as cash — that is,

$$Cash = Price \times Sales - (Fixed\ Cost + Unit\ Cost \times Sales).$$

Although the primary variable we wish to forecast is demand, we will also be at least as interested in the cash projections. These in turn may be used to generate an appraisal of an investment project that would service the demand and generate both fixed and variable costs. To make the whole example more realistic, we could consider two alternative investment decisions, the more expensive of which would generate lower unit operating costs with the second, cheaper alternative leading to higher operating costs in later periods. The problem then is which of the uncertain factors have the greatest effect on *Cash* and how should we set the price.

Let us suppose the demand function is

$$\ln(D_t) = \beta_0 + \lambda\ln(D_{t-1}) + \beta_1\ln(P_t) + \varepsilon_t. \tag{13.2}$$

That is to say, there is an effect of price on demand (we would expect β_1 to be negative) and a carry-over effect from the previous period's demand (we would expect λ to be positive). To complete the picture, we assume a production capacity of 1200 units.

Figure 13.13 A Simple Model of Cash as It is Affected by Demand and Costs

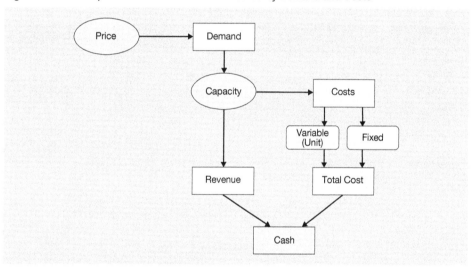

In any appraisal of investment alternatives that affect capacity, including marketing decisions, we would assess the results over a period of time. A standard method to ensure the comparability of cash flows from projects of different length is to use *net present value* (*NPV*), calculated as

$$NPV = \sum_{i=0}^{12} \frac{Cash_j}{(1+r)^j}. \tag{13.3}$$

This equation discounts future cash flows by the discount rate *r*, with the rationale that cash available now is worth more to us than future cash flows. (After all, if we have cash on hand, we could invest it and gain the interest at the very least.)

In our example, we have chosen to look at the cash flows over a 12-month period following the initial month ($j = 0$). Of course, for major investment decisions, the calculation needs to cover a number of years.

As a baseline, we can assume a constant demand of 1000 units, a capacity constraint of 1200, and a discount rate r of 1 percent per month to calculate the NPV. The result of the NPV calculation equals $120,100.

We next assume that the parameters in equation (13.2) are known exactly, with $\lambda = 0.2$, $\beta_1 = -0.5$ (characteristic of a price-inelastic product), a mean level of demand of 1000 (which determines $\beta_0 = 7.0247$), and random fluctuations in demand. (The error term, ε_t is normally distributed with zero mean and standard deviation 0.25.) The cost parameters we have assumed are also shown in Table 13.5. Each simulation of random demand leads to a new estimate of NPV. But repeating the calculations to capture demand uncertainty would be out of reach if it were done manually. We have used the @Risk software, an add-on to Excel, which makes the analysis rapid and straightforward. The results of running 10,000 simulations of demand are shown in Figure 13.14. This results in an average NPV of $118,193, less than the constant demand estimate of $120,100 because, for periods of high demand, the capacity constraint means that sales are lost. (In fact, the average demand over these simulation runs is 1020, from equation (13.1).)

Table 13.5 Assumptions Regarding the Calculation of Profit in Example 13.4

Model Parameters	Mean Demand	Price Elasticity, β_j	Carry-over λ	Standard Error, σ	Unit Costs, φ	Fixed Cost	Discount Factor	Price
Assumed distribution	Fixed	Beta	Uniform	ChiSquare	Uniform	Fixed	Fixed	Fixed
Mean Value	1000	–0.5	0.2	0.25	10	200	1%	20
Range	—	0 to -3.0	0 to 1	0 to ∞	8 to 12	—	—	—

Data and @Risk parameterization: Profit.xlsx

Figure 13.14 The Simulated Distribution of the Net Present Value as It Depends on Demand Uncertainty *(see also Exercise 13.4)*

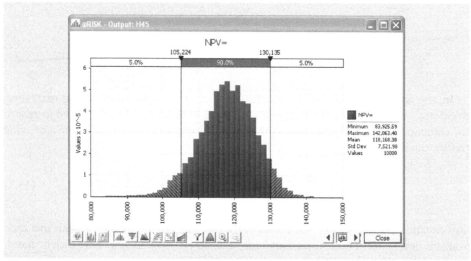

Source: Reproduced with permission from Palisade Corporation.

Figure 13.14 shows the variation possible in NPV as the sequence of random demands changes with 90 percent of runs falling within the interval from $105,000 to $130,000. But of course, the estimated NPV is even more uncertain than the figure suggests; it is based on our chosen parameter estimates. The parameters for the demand function might be estimated from past data with the use of either regression or judgment, based on our knowledge of the market, and these estimates are uncertain. So how might we take this uncertainty into account?

One easy-to-use route is through simulating uncertainty, as we described earlier. But first we have to decide on suitable probability distributions to describe our uncertainty. Figure 13.15 shows the range of probability distributions, both discrete and continuous (more precisely, probability density functions for continuous distributions), that are available in one of the well-established commercial packages, @Risk.

Figure 13.15 Distributions Available for Simulating Uncertainty in Key Model Parameters

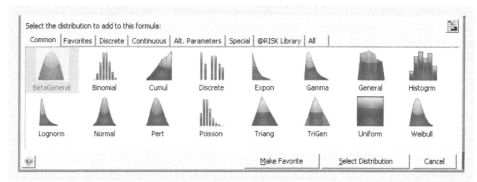

Source: Reproduced with permission from Palisade Corporation.

First let us examine the effects of uncertainty in the error variance by specifying a non-negative, strongly skewed distribution to allow for the possibility of large values. We choose the Chisq(uare) distribution, which is specified with just one parameter, again with a mean of .25, but with a range from 0 to ∞. (Of course, very large values are extremely unlikely.) We contrast the two results (the first with fixed error variance) in Figure 13.14 and the second (with uncertain variance) in Figure 13.16. The uncertainty in the standard deviation of demand has little effect on the overall mean *NPV* but considerably extends the lower tail region.

Figure 13.16 The Simulated Distribution of NPV as It Is Affected by Uncertainty in the Error Variance

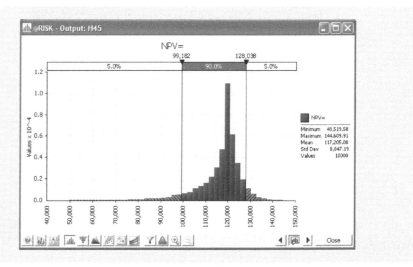

Source: Reproduced with permission from Palisade Corporation.

But of course, there are other key uncertainties we may wish to take into account. Some parameters might be quite well understood (or even known perfectly). We assume that the fixed cost is constant, as shown in Table 13.5. However, we are uncertain as to the price elasticity, believing it to lie between 0 and –1.5 on the basis of earlier research; also, we believe the lagged effect to be between 0 and 1 with a mean value of 0.5. We assume a beta distribution for the elasticity (see Fig. 13.15) and a uniform distribution for the lag parameter to capture our understanding. Other assumptions are as shown in Table 13.5. Of course, the analyst will not *know* the shape of the distribution, but typically the results are insensitive to the choice unless they are very different alternatives.

The final stage in the analysis is to pull all these uncertainties together to provide a summary of the effects on the *NPV*. @Risk also provides various charts that summarize which of the uncertainties is the most important in affecting the final value. One approach is to examine the sensitivity of the *NPV* to changes in parameters through a scatterplot of *NPV* versus the parameter in question (say, price elasticity) where the other parameters are taken as fixed. Figure 13.17 compares the results from the uncertainty in the price elasticity with that from the carry-over effect.

Figure 13.17 Scattergrams of NPV versus Uncertainty in Model Parameters

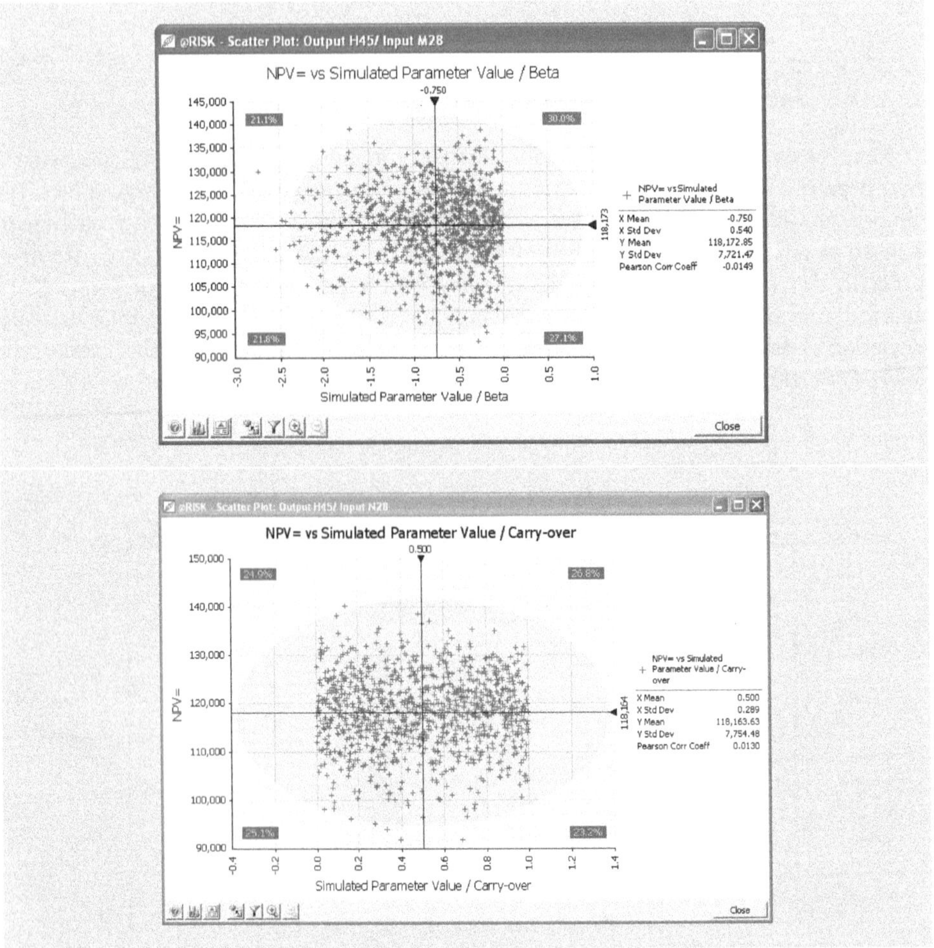

Source: Reproduced with permission from Palisade Corporation.

Comparing the two scatterplots, we see that there is little difference from uncertainty in the two parameters (carry-over and price elasticity) on the variation in *NPV* (with a similar standard deviation of around 8800). The *NPV* distribution is also similar, with a comparable range. ■

The scatterplots show the relationship between a selected output variable and an uncertain parameter in the model and are calculated with other parameters in the model fixed at their base level. This approach neglects the possibility of a correlation between the uncertain parameters. For example, if elasticity was high, perhaps unit costs would also have a higher mean due to the higher costs of meeting the increased fluctuations in demand. These simulation models (and software) can also incorporate this feature of the problem.

An alternative to scatterplots is to use a tornado diagram, which attempts to explain the variation in *NPV* (or another simulated output) by changes in the various parameter values on the basis of a regression model. A tornado diagram can be constructed from the input and output of the simulation runs. Each run has a set of input parameters (e.g., carry-over λ, elasticity β_1, unit costs) characterizing the distributions, and these inputs then lead to a corresponding output, here *NPV*. The regression model is of the form $NPV = f(\beta_1, \lambda, \phi)$, where the model could include interaction effects between the parameters (e.g., a term $\lambda\phi$ in the regression model).

DISCUSSION QUESTION: *In a final examination on a business forecasting course, how many additional points out of 100 would you expect to gain from six additional hours of study? What distribution would you use to describe your uncertainty?*

DISCUSSION QUESTION: *In the airline industry, revenue management is used to fill the planes and get the best financial return from a flight. Discuss how you might model a two-price-class flight in which the cheaper tickets are not refundable, and what uncertainties arise around the cash the flight generates?*

Simulation models that aim to capture the key interactions in complex systems are also used as forecasting models, as we have shown in Example 13.4. Although the parameters in the model may be estimated by the techniques of earlier chapters, the dependent variable we focus on, net present value, is estimated through the simulation model. Such methods have been used to model the effects of demand uncertainty and forecast error in manufacturing (Fildes and Kingsman, 2011), in defense (Gardner, 1990), and in services (Sanders and Graman, 2009). But they can also be used to forecast the effects of complex policy changes such as those arising in government. For example, changes in a government's health care policy (such as Medicare) lead to individual decisions with consequences for the hospital system and government finances. The simulation model would then be based on demographic knowledge of potential patients, their likely illnesses, and patient pathways through the health-care system. The output variables would include such items as the costs of treatment and the average time for a patient's stay in hospital.

The final example in this brief overview of simulation models for forecasting is modeling climate, a topic we touched on in Section 12.7. Climate models (developed in research institutes around the world) are based on physical flows of air, water, CO_2, etc., over time through a world broken down into geographical cubes over land and sea. The flows obey physical laws, so the model is based on mathematical equations. The aim is to predict meteorological phenomena, such as temperature, rainfall, and ocean currents, across the globe and how they are affected by greenhouse gas (CO_2) concentrations and emissions. In particular, the press and politicians pay considerable attention to such headline forecasts as the predicted increase in global average temperature over the next 100 years. More detailed local forecasts are also produced by these global circulation models, and such forecasts can affect localized planning decisions. Similar simulation models are used in the short term, for day-to-day weather forecasting.

In sum, by simulating the system (be it a business process, a government policy, or the world's climate), it is possible to generate forecasts, estimate their uncertainty, and evaluate policies. The models themselves need not be statistically based, although they will often include components that rely on the methods we have described here. Their validation is subject to all the forecast accuracy concerns we have discussed; therefore, the principles we have laid out hold equally for these simulation models as they do for their statistical or naïve alternatives. For an example in climate modeling of how these two approaches can usefully be compared and combined to produce better understanding and improved forecast accuracy, see Fildes and Kourentzes (2011).

13.3.3 Scenarios as a Means of Understanding Uncertainty

Sometimes, particularly in longer term strategic decision making, there are many components of uncertainty. They interact in complicated ways, and it would be difficult, if not impossible, to lay out the complete system of social, economic, and market interactions in a form like that shown in Figure 13.13. To deal with this type of messy or so-called *wicked problem*, scenarios have been developed. The idea of a scenario as a consistent story was introduced in Section 11.5. Such stories get increasingly complex as the time scales we need to consider lengthen and there are more and more decision points and greater environmental uncertainty. Although, in our organization, we will have control over some of these decisions and their outcomes, other actors in the system we are analyzing will in turn respond to our decisions in essentially unpredictable ways. More and more branches sprout and develop, potentially overwhelming the possibility of considering every alternative. Instead, we may choose to consider a limited number of these scenarios, which consist of a mixture of our organizational decisions, decisions by other actors (such as competitors or governments), and environmental events. Section 11.6 discussed how a limited number of scenarios should be selected from the large number of possibilities.

Because scenarios have no probabilistic interpretation, they cannot be used to provide a probabilistic summary of key variables, as in the risk analysis we described in the previous section.[1] However, they can be used to examine the robustness of different organizational decisions, as shown in Figure 13.18. Here, two scenarios have been developed and the policies that best fit the particular environmental and competitive futures they embody have been translated into a set of outcomes: policy set 1 designed to meet the circumstances in scenario 1, policy 2 matching scenario 2. (Note that these outcomes should aim to represent equilibrium states rather than capturing transitory fluctuations.) Of course, three or more scenarios could be considered along with any number of organizational policies.

But perhaps the organization adopts policy set 1 while scenario 2 (or something like it) develops, or vice versa. The *Risk Summary* aims to capture what would be lost in such circumstances. A robust policy in the face of the complex uncertainties captured by the scenarios is a policy in which the loss in both financial terms and strategic position is small when the policy is tested over all the scenarios. In general, of course such a policy would

---

1   While most scenario researchers explicitly deny there is (or should be) a probabilistic interpretation of a set of scenarios, of course a subjective assignment of probabilities is always possible and may often be forced on the analyst.

always lose out compared with the policy chosen to fit a particular scenario (such as policy 1 for Scenario 1 in Figure 13.18).

Figure 13.18 Using Scenarios to Identify Robust Policies

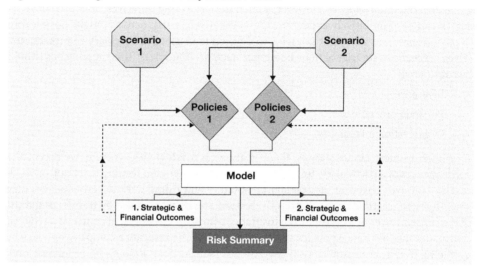

SCENARIOS AND RISK

A *risk summary* compares the loss from alternative policies arising from different future scenarios.

A *robust policy* is a policy in which the likely loss is small over a wide range of scenarios (relative to the policy that would have been selected if the future was known with certainty — the *perfect information* policy).

DISCUSSION QUESTION OR GROUP PROJECT: *In 2016/17, political changes in Europe (Brexit and major elections in France and Germany), and the U.S. and Mexico (President Trump's proposed trade policies) were starting to affect the car industry. Taking the role of analyst for GM or Nissan, state what you see as the major sources of uncertainty in maintaining and improving profitability over the next five years. Develop two scenarios that capture some of these key uncertainties. Who would you wish to participate in a professional scenario development activity for a car manufacturer?*

In sum, multiple scenarios offer an approach to capturing the uncertainty inherent in complex (often longer term) environmental, political, technological, and demographic developments. Such scenarios aim to capture the interactive effects of key drivers that affect the problem being analyzed. But they are unable to offer a probabilistic summary of possible outcomes. Instead, they are best used to identify applicable policies that are robust to as wide a range as possible of alternative futures as well as any outstanding major risks. In fact, some have argued that so-called "black swan" events (Taleb, 2007), that is events that are outside the range seen in the past, and totally outside the experience and expectations of forecasters, cannot be dealt with by conventional forecasting methods. But like the Great Recession of 2007/8, they may have dramatic consequences. Such low levels of predictability require different responses beyond conventional forecasting (Makridakis and Taleb, 2009), some of which we discuss in the next section.

13.3.4 Dealing with Irreducible Uncertainty

Uncertainty costs organizations money, and it can even threaten their very existence. Unfortunately, we can't do away with it. In the previous sections, we examined ways we could estimate uncertainty and develop policies that are optimal or, at the very least, robust while lowering the risk level. However, sometimes protecting ourselves from extreme outcomes can be prohibitively expensive. Or, alternatively a risk activity might not be core to our business and we might not wish to develop the expertise necessary to protect ourselves (exchange-rate transactions being just such an example). Three approaches should be considered:

- Insurance
- Portfolio procedures
- Organizational flexibility.

Insurance: In most circumstances, there is always a residual risk whereby we accept the consequences of a particularly unlikely event (e.g., high demand leading to an out-of-stock result). However, covering the residual uncertainty and riding out the consequences may sometimes be regarded as too dangerous. Instead, the risk is reduced by transferring most of the consequences of a disaster to an insurance company. The effect, of course, is a reduced return, because insurance policies always cost money. The insurance company operates by averaging over a set of similar risky investments (see *Portfolio Procedures*, to follow), only some of which will lead to a claim. From the insurance company's perspective these investments should have limited correlation.

A variant of the same notion consists of using futures markets or forward contracting to purchase an option now in order to purchase a fixed amount at a fixed price in the future. For example, raw materials (and foreign currency) can be purchased through futures markets so that the amount to be paid for a future need is known now. In marketing, long-term contracts can be made with large purchasers, even when futures markets do not exist. Although all of these devices cost money, they do meet the aim of reducing uncertainty.

A subtler variation of this idea has been described by Quinn (1989) as *logical incrementalism*. Simply put, it is the recommendation that where outcomes may prove costly and uncertainty is high, only those decisions are contemplated that are viable over a wide range of possible futures — the robustness analysis we discussed in the previous section. For example, in planning a power station, the decision regarding which fuel to use may be postponed, with plans based on coal, oil, or natural gas as the power source. Designing the power station to operate with any of these fuel sources is another alternative. Though costly, such duplications overcome the very high uncertainty in fuel price forecasts. As the forecasting (and planning) lead time decreases, uncertainty is also decreased and more definite choices can be made. Decisions here are made sequentially rather than being executed only once. The cost derives from the alternative courses of action being kept open for a longer period than they would if the decision had been made once and for all. Such an approach also demands sophisticated planning.

Portfolio Procedures: It has long been known that if two alternative investments can be found with similar returns but with outcomes negatively or only slightly positively correlated, a portfolio investment in both decreases the risk level, leaving the return unchanged. The same idea can be used in examining whether diversification (of products or businesses) can lead to decreased risk. In effect, the forecaster needs to forecast not just the returns from different projects but their interrelationships as well. The problem remains one of identifying alternative investments that are not strongly positively correlated with your own. The difficulties associated with the portfolio approach do not negate the usefulness of seeking out countercyclical investments. The financial crisis of 2007–2008 was partially caused by the failure to recognize that asset returns would have stronger positive correlations than was historically the case.

Organizational Flexibility: The time horizon of a forecast is made up of a number of distinct components: the time to gain information (the *information lead time*), the time to plan and execute a course of action (the *planning lead time*), and the time during which the action reaps its consequences (the *action lead time*). The first two of these are under the control of the organization. By increasing the speed at which internal information is made available and by increasing the organization's responsiveness to a problem, the need to forecast is minimized. Modern manufacturing has tried hard to cut lead times and improve flexibility, although outsourcing supply from the U.S. and Europe to distant countries such as China (for cost reasons) has had the opposite effect, increasing the need for forecasting. For research-based organizations such as pharmaceutical firms, organizational flexibility is only of limited help, in that the action lead time associated with patents is very long.

> **DISCUSSION QUESTION:** *Energy prices are expected to fluctuate considerably over the next 20 years or longer. What are the major factors in U.S. (alternatively, German) energy markets, and what approaches should the government consider to mitigate the associated risks? What actions should household consumers living in upstate New York (alternatively, southern England) consider to mitigate their risk?*

In the end, in most organizational settings, none of these risk-controlling concepts overcomes the need to forecast; mostly they aim to lessen the risk of the endeavor without costing too much. Without accepting some degree of risk, there is usually little reward, so we turn now to how organizations should go about improving their forecasting performance.

13.4 Improving Forecasting

The ultimate purpose of this book is to improve an organization's forecasting activities. This purpose includes as a primary objective making the forecasts more accurate through the approaches we have summarized in Section 13.1. But there are many additional issues to consider before improvements can be implemented within an organization, and there are many barriers to improvement to be overcome. Fildes and Hastings (1994) asked forecasters two key questions in their survey of company forecasters: What barriers did they see to improving forecasting (in their organization)? and What were their priorities for making such improvements? Tables 13.6 and 13.7 address these two points. Table 13.6 shows the respondents' level of agreement (agree, neutral, disagree) with the various statements given in column 1. For example, for statement 1, the typical response was to agree, with 72 percent of respondents falling into that class.

One important issue to note is the concern the respondents (all industry forecasters) had with their lack of training! The results are illustrative only of a particular organization at a point in time. But, linked to various current pieces of evidence including a more recent survey (Fildes and Petropoulos, 2015b), they support the view that at the heart of any improvements lies a forecast support system (which is available in principle but may not be in practice) that can deliver data together with easy-to-use techniques that combine judgment with statistical methods (Fildes and Hastings, 1994, Table 7). The use of a forecasting audit approach led to much the same set of priorities (Moon *et al.*, 2003). In the respondents' terminology, what is needed is improved functional integration (across marketing, finance, and operations), improved approaches (better methods of forecasting beyond the naïve ones), and better systems, as indicated in Table 13.7. Fildes and Goodwin (2013) provide a more recent discussion of what is needed for a forecasting support system to be effective while Petropoulos (2015, followed by a discussion) looks at future developments including the role of open source software such as R.

But there remain some major barriers to implementing improved approaches and systems, not to mention the perennial organizational problem of better functional integration. Barriers to innovation, particularly in the context of information systems, have been a major research area, so we can draw on the findings. Also, some authors have paid particular attention to improving forecasting practice (Schultz, 1984).

Table 13.6 Barriers to Adopting Formal Forecasting Methods: Respondents' Attitudes

Statement	Qualitative Response in Median Class	Response in Median Class
1. I do not have sufficient training in the use of formalized forecasting.	Agree	72%
2. The data available for forecasting are limited in detail or history.	Disagree	63%
3. No suitable database currently exists that is directly usable.	Disagree	63%
4. Judgmental techniques are more accurate than quantitative ones in my business.	Agree	56%
5. I tried formal techniques, but they failed to produce more accurate results.	Neutral	53%
6. There is no help available to provide assistance in generating forecasts.	Neutral	44%
7. I am satisfied with the standard (or results) obtained by my existing methods.	Disagree	38%
8. I do not have sufficient time and/or resources to develop formal techniques.	Agree	38%

Source: Fildes and Hastings, 1994.

Table 13.7 Possible Actions Contributing to Improved Forecasting: Percentage of Respondents Scoring the Action as Important or Very Important *(47 respondents)*

Action	Percent Agreeing
Availability of internal data	78%
Motivation to produce better quality forecasts	72%
Measuring the accuracy/value of the forecasting activity	74%
Quality of judgmental interventions made by the forecasting team	74%
Quality of Forecasting software	62%
Lack of training	57%

Source: Fildes and Petropoulos, 2015b.

Since we have identified the fact that new systems and better integrated databases across functional areas are priorities, we can refer to the work of Rogers (1995) and his many successors. In most companies, there are already systems (and forecasting support systems of a sort) in place. So, compatibility with existing practices (and systems) is one factor affecting the potential for improvement. Reliance on Excel as the forecasting vehicle, while meeting this need, runs a major risk of processes that are error prone, because of both programming errors and the over-reliance on a restrictive set of software tools. A range of Excel add-ins is available to provide extended functionality, often at very modest cost. The ability to test out a new forecasting process in a part of the organizational forecasting activity lessens the risk. The ability to communicate the essence of a new system and its complexity, both in learning to use it and in everyday operation, proves important. And crucially, there is the ability to demonstrate the value of the new systems and processes to deliver improved decision making.

But this list alone has often proved insufficient. We still rely on senior management to start the process of change: There needs to be an understanding at the top of the organization that improvements can be achieved with a consequential need to motivate and train the forecasting team. It seems to us that senior managers may be all too aware of the inadequacies of their forecasting systems but do not appreciate the fact that improvements are possible. Sometimes, however, the dissatisfaction is transformed into action by environmental events outside the forecasting activity. A common example is a situation in which changes in the information systems area, such as the implementation of a new enterprise resources planning (ERP) system, necessitate reconsideration of the FSS as well. The final point, communication, is concerned more with the success of the implementation; that success will depend on continuing support from senior management, but also on their relationship with the designers of the new system and on the implementation strategy that is pursued so that the organization's forecasters get the most from the new system.

IMPLEMENTING IMPROVEMENTS IN FORECASTING

Implementing improved forecasting processes and systems requires that the new system:

- Be compatible with existing practices if possible.
- Has its risks managed by incremental adoption. Ideally, the system can be introduced sequentially in the organization.
- Be comprehensible, with its features easily communicated to those who will use it.
- Add demonstrable value above the current system.

Changes in practice require:

- A trained and motivated forecasting team.
- Key performance indicators (such as accuracy) that make sense for both the organization and the forecasters.

13.5 Principles for Improving Forecasting

The rationale for the principles that follow has been established in the course of this chapter, so we do not elaborate further upon the supporting arguments.

[13.1] When planning a forecasting activity, work through the PIVASE stages (Purpose, Information, Value, Analysis, System and Evaluation) to establish an appropriate framework.

[13.2] Where quantitative methods are a practical alternative to judgmental approaches, use the quantitative approach.

[13.3] Where there is additional information available to the forecaster, adjust the quantitative forecast to take this information into account.

[13.4] Evaluate the performance of both quantitative forecasts and the finally adjusted forecast to determine both forecast quality and the value-added effectiveness of the adjustments.

[13.5] Where there is a range of plausible forecasts, consider the use of a combined method to produce the final forecast.

[13.6] For an ongoing forecasting problem, monitor forecast errors in the important class-A series.

[13.7] Establish a base of operations for the forecasting team that enables it both to produce forecasts free of political pressure and to communicate effectively with decision makers and forecast users in other functional areas.

[13.8] As a forecaster, make sure that your organizational links are reliable in supplying you with key pieces of information. Also, make sure those who use your forecasts are aware of their value.

A key issue for forecasters is how well connected they are to other parts of the organization. In particular, the boss of the forecasting unit needs to be fully aware of the value of improved forecasting.

[13.9] Identify key risks through simulation or scenario analysis.

[13.10] Identify robust strategies for high-risk problems.

[13.11] Consider adopting insurance, portfolio approaches, and organizational flexibility in situations of high risk.

[13.12] Identify the barriers to improving forecasting practice when working in an organizational setting.

Key barriers include lack of consistent data, poorly designed and implemented software, and lack of adequate training for the forecasting staff. Employ trained forecasters (or develop suitable training programs based on the information presented in this book!).

Summary

The focus of this book is on forecasting methods and the principles that lead to their effective application. However, the book would be incomplete without a discussion of forecasting practice and why organizational practice is often far removed from the idealized view frequently presented in more mathematical textbooks. In Section 13.1, we discussed the process most forecasters go through to produce their forecasts, from gathering relevant data to the last step of evaluating the final forecast. A crucial step in the journey is the selection of the appropriate forecasting method from the array of possible approaches we described in earlier chapters. Surveys show that organizational practice is too reliant on unstructured judgment. In Section 13.1, we discussed the methods forecasters in fact use and we summarized the strengths and weaknesses of those methods to aid in selection. The principle to remember is that different methods are appropriate in different applications. Often, the only route is through careful evaluation followed by monitoring forecast errors, the final topic of the section.

Section 13.2 took us further into the organizational issues surrounding forecasting — in particular, the biases that can result from political pressures and the importance of linking forecasting accuracy to the value of the forecasts to the decision maker.

Despite the advances in forecasting methodology over the past 30 years, residual uncertainty remains high for many important forecasting problems, so methods are needed to understand the consequences of uncertainty and develop policies to mitigate the worst effects of those consequences. Simulating the effects of uncertainty and developing robust strategies in the light of a range of scenarios was proposed. But that still leaves the case where risk remains high and better forecasting does not offer a way out. Here, various organizational strategies, including insurance, may be helpful. The chapter concluded with a discussion of how organizationally-based forecasting can be improved in practice. After all, the best methods in the world will never prove sufficient if people in organizations fail to put them to work.

Exercises

13.1   Putting yourself in the shoes of a new manager in charge of a call center forecasting activity, how would you establish a framework for forecasting incoming calls for a forecast horizon of eight weeks?

13.2   We developed several models for Netflix sales in Chapter 3. Use these fitted models to establish SCC and CCC charts for each model, and evaluate model performance in each case.

13.3   Monitoring and, if necessary, adjusting the forecast for a product in CleanCare, a producer of cleaning products, takes an hour of management time. Using the data set *Manufact.xlsx*, which contains monthly data on the initial statistical forecasts, the final management-adjusted forecasts, and the actual outcomes, devise an ABC-XYZ categorization that, on average, would take no more than a week (35 hours) of a forecaster's time to monitor.

13.4   Using the model and data in *Profit.xlsx* and risk analysis software, evaluate two different policies: (i) a policy wherein the price is decreased 10 percent if demand in the previous period is below 950 and increased by 10 percent if demand is above 1050 and (ii) a policy of an increased capacity of an additional 100 units, which is bought at an additional unit cost of $5. If the carry-over effect lies between 0.5 and 0.9, does that affect your views of these different policies?

13.5   Using the model in *Profit.xlsx*, comment on the comparative sensitivity of the *NPV* to the uncertain parameters. Make a reasonable assumption as to the uncertainty around the unit cost. Does this assumption affect our choice between a fixed price of $20 and policy (i) in Exercise 13.4?

Minicase 13.1 The Management of Call-Center Forecasting

In CreditBank, a new manager has recently been put in charge of the call center's forecasting support function. She is an accountant by background, and forecasting is just one part of her managerial responsibilities. However, there is pressure from senior management to improve accuracy. The new manager made some preliminary inquiries which suggested that the accuracy level for the core business of forecasting incoming account inquiries as measured by *MAPE* a week ahead was 22 percent. Her view from looking at cross-industry benchmarking studies was that 10 percent was a more satisfactory level, and she was confident that her manager would find that percentage acceptable. So she gave the forecasting group a month in which to improve its performance. Within the group, Mark A. had the responsibility of forecasting these calls, which was done with an industry standard package (based on exponential smoothing and weekly profiles of calls). The accuracy figure was calculated automatically from within the software. Data on the calls are given in the data set *Credit_call.xlsx*. What would you recommend that Mark A. do?

References

Adya, M., and Collopy, F. (1998). How effective are neural networks at forecasting and prediction? A review and evaluation. *Journal of Forecasting*, 17, 481–495.

Allen, P. G. and Fildes, R. (2001). Econometric forecasting. In J. S. Armstrong (ed.), *Principles of Forecasting: A Handbook for Researchers and Practitioners*. Boston and Dordrecht: Kluwer, pp. 303–362.

Alwan, L. C., and Roberts, H. V. (1988). Time-series modeling for statistical process control. *Journal of Business and Economic Statistics*, 6, 87–95.

Alwan, L. C., and Roberts, H. V. (1995). The problem of misplaced control limits. *Applied Statistics*, 44, 269–278.

Armstrong, J. S. (2001). Standards and practices in forecasting. In J. S. Armstrong (ed.), *Principles of Forecasting: A Handbook for Researchers and Practitioners*. Boston and Dordrecht: Kluwer.

Ashley, R. (1983). On the usefulness of macroeconomic forecasts as inputs to forecasting models. *Journal of Forecasting*, 2, 211–223.

Ashley, R. (1988). On the relative worth of recent macroeconomic forecasts. *International Journal of Forecasting*, 4, 363–376.

Brown, L. D. (1993). Earnings forecasting research: Its implications for capital markets research. *International Journal of Forecasting*, 9, 295–320.

Crone, S. F., Hibon, M., and Nikolopoulos, K. (2011). Advances in forecasting with neural networks? Empirical evidence from the NN3 competition on time series prediction. *International Journal of Forecasting*, 27, 635–660.

Deschamps, E. (2004). The impact of institutional change on forecast accuracy: A case study of budget forecasting in Washington state. *International Journal of Forecasting*, 20, 647–657.

Deschamps, E. (2005). Six steps to overcome bias in the forecast process. *Foresight: The International Journal of Applied Forecasting*, 2, 5–11.

Fildes, R., and Goodwin, P. (2007). Against your better judgment? How organizations can improve their use of management judgment in forecasting. *Interfaces*, 37, 570–576.

Fildes, R., and Goodwin, P. (2013). Forecasting support systems: What we know, what we need to know. *International Journal of Forecasting*, 29, 290–294.

Fildes, R., Goodwin, P., Lawrence, M., and Nikolopoulos, K. (2009). Effective forecasting and judgmental adjustments: An empirical evaluation and strategies for improvement in supply-chain planning. *International Journal of Forecasting*, 25, 3–23.

Fildes, R., and Hastings, R. (1994). The organization and improvement of market forecasting. *Journal of the Operational Research Society*, 45, 1–16.

Fildes, R., and Kingsman, B. (2011). Incorporating demand uncertainty and forecast error in supply chain planning models. *Journal of the Operational Research Society*, 62, 483–500.

Fildes, R., and Kourentzes, N. (2011). Validation and forecasting accuracy in models of climate change. *International Journal of Forecasting*, 27, 968–995.

Fildes, R., and Petropoulos, F. (2015a). Simple versus complex selection rules for forecasting many time series. *Journal of Business Research*, 68, 1692–1701.

Fildes, R., and Petropoulos, F. (2015b). Improving forecast quality in practice. *Foresight: International Journal of Applied Forecasting*, 36, 5–12.

Flyvbjerg, B, (2008). Curbing optimism bias and strategic misrepresentation in planning: Reference class forecasting in practice. *European Planning Studies*, 16, 3–21.

Galbraith, C. S., and Merrill, G. B. (1996). The politics of forecasting: Managing the truth. *California Management Review*, 38, 29–43.

Gardner, E. S. (1990). Evaluating forecast performance in an inventory control system. *Management Science*, 36, 490–499.

Gardner, E. S., Jr. (2006). Exponential smoothing: The state of the art — Part II. *International Journal of Forecasting*, 22, 637–666.

Graefe, A., and Armstrong, J. S. (2011). Comparing face-to-face meetings, nominal groups, Delphi and prediction markets on an estimation task. *International Journal of Forecasting*, 27, 183–195.

Green, K. C., and Armstrong, J. S. (2015). Simple versus complex forecasting: The evidence. *Journal of Business Research*, 68(8): 1678–1685.

Halkjelsvik, T., and Jørgensen, M. (2012). From origami to software development: A review of studies on judgment-based predictions of performance time. *Psychological Bulletin*, 138, 238–271.

Hogarth, R. M., and Makridakis, S. (1981). Forecasting and planning: An evaluation. *Management Science*, 27, 115–138.

Kolassa, S. (2008). Can we obtain valid benchmarks from published surveys of forecast accuracy? *Foresight: The International Journal of Applied Forecasting*, 11, 6–14.

Lawrence, M., Goodwin, P., O'Connor, M., and Onkal, D. (2006). Judgmental forecasting: A review of progress over the last 25 years. *International Journal of Forecasting*, 22, 493–518.

Ma, S., Fildes, R., and Huang, T. (2016). Demand forecasting with high dimensional data: The case of SKU retail sales forecasting with intra- and inter-category promotional information. *European Journal of Operational Research*, 249, 245–257.

Makridakis, S., and Taleb, N. (2009). Decision making and planning under low levels of predictability. Introduction. *International Journal of Forecasting*, 25, 716–733.

McCarthy, T. M., Davis, D. F., Golicic, S. L., and Mentzer, J. T. (2006). The evolution of sales forecasting management: A 20-year longitudinal study of forecasting practices. *Journal of Forecasting*, 25, 303–324.

Meade, N., and Islam, T. (2006). Modelling and forecasting the diffusion of innovation: A 25-year review. *International Journal of Forecasting*, 22, 519–545.

Meissner, P., Brands, C. and Wulf, T. (2017) Quantifying blind spots and weak signals in executive judgment: A structured integration of expert judgment into the scenario development process. *International Journal of Forecasting*, 33, 244–253.

Moon, M. A., Mentzer, J. T., and Smith, C. D. (2003). Conducting a sales forecasting audit. *International Journal of Forecasting*, 19, 5–25.

Morwitz, V. G. (2001). Methods for forecasting with intentions data. In J. S. Armstrong (ed.), *Principles of Forecasting: A Handbook for Researchers and Practitioners*. Boston and Dordrecht: Kluwer, pp. 33–56.

Petropoulos, F. (2015). Forecasting support systems: ways forward. *Foresight: The International Journal of Applied Forecasting*, 39, 5–11.

Oliva, R. and Watson, N. (2009). Managing functional biases in organizational forecasts: A case study of consensus forecasting in supply chain planning. *Production and Operations Management*, 18, 138–151.

Quinn, J. B. (1989). Strategic change: Logical incrementalism (reprint). *Sloan Management Review*, 30 (4), 45–60.

Rogers, E. M. (1995). *Diffusion of Innovations*. New York: Free Press.

Rowe, G., and Wright, G. (2001). Expert opinion in forecasting: The role of the Delphi technique. In J. S. Armstrong (ed.), *Principles of Forecasting: A Handbook for Researchers and Practitioners*. Boston and Dordrecht: Kluwer, pp. 125–144.

Sagaert, Y. R., Aghezzaf E-H., Kourentzes N. and Desmet B. (2017). Temporal big data for tire industry tactical sales forecasting. *Interfaces* (to appear).

Sanders, N. R. and Graman, G. A. (2009). Quantifying costs of forecast errors: A case study of the warehouse environment. *Omega*, 37(1), 116–125.

Sanders, N. R. and Manrodt, K. B. (2003). Forecasting software in practice: Use, satisfaction, and performance. *Interfaces*, 33, 90–93.

Schultz, R. L. (1984). The implementation of forecasting models. *Journal of Forecasting*, 3, 43–55.

Smith, J., and Clark, S. (2011). Who should own the business forecasting function? *Foresight: The International Journal of Applied Forecasting*, 20, 4–9.

Stock, J. H., and Watson, M. W. (2002). Forecasting using principal components from a large number of predictors. *Journal of the American Statistical Association*, 97, 1167–1179.

Taleb, N. N. (2007). *The Black Swan: The Impact of the Highly Improbable*. New York: Random House.

Tyebjee, T. T. (1987). Behavioral biases in new product forecasting. *International Journal of Forecasting*, 3, 393–404.

Weller, M., and Crone, S. F. (2012). *Supply Chain Forecasting: Best Practices & Benchmarking Study*. Lancaster Centre for Forecasting White Paper, Lancaster University, UK: Downloadable: *http://goo.gl/MPbAjz*.

Wheelwright, S. C., and Clarke, D. G. (1976). Corporate forecasting: Promise and reality. *Harvard Business Review*, 54 (6), 40–64, 198.

Winklhofer, H., Diamantopoulos, A., and Witt, S. F. (1996). Forecasting practice: A review of the empirical literature and an agenda for future research. *International Journal of Forecasting*, 12, 193–221.

GLOSSARY

ABC Analysis: Segmentation of products into three classes: class A for the 20 percent or so of products that require individual attention, class B for the 30 percent of products for which an automatic monitoring scheme is acceptable, and class C for the 50 percent remaining for which the forecaster looks at the errors only in response to an alert from elsewhere in the organization (e.g., an out-of-stock problem may be generating complaints); see Section 13.1.5.

ABC-XYZ Analysis: In addition to being classified into A, B, or C, each series is classified into X, Y, or Z depending on the difficulty of forecasting the series with X having the lowest errors (measured appropriately, e.g., *RelMAE*), to Z having the highest errors; see Section 13.1.5.

Absolute Error: The value of the *forecast error*, ignoring its sign.

Accuracy Measures: Alternative measures of forecasting accuracy based on the forecast error; see Section 2.7.

Additive Model: A model whereby its components are added together to describe the observations; see Section 4.1.

Additive Outlier: A single extreme value, after which the series reverts to its previous pattern; see Section 5.5.

Agent-Based Model: A micro-simulation model that adopts a highly-disaggregate perspective, based on the interactions of actors in the system being modeled and how they are affected by proposed policies.

Akaike's Information Criterion (AIC): An *information criterion* designed to select the best forecasting model (as measured by *MSE* penalized by the number of parameters in the model); see Section 5.4.2.

Algorithm: An explicit numerical routine that automatically calculates an output (forecast) given the inputs, with no human intervention.

Alternative Hypothesis (H_A): The statement that is used as the logical alternative of the *null hypothesis*. Frequently, the alternative hypothesis states that there is a relationship between the dependent variable and one or more explanatory variables; see online Appendix A.5.

Analogies: Forecasts (often made for new products or in conflict situations) that are based upon comparisons with similar past events (e.g., forecasting the demand for tablet computers on the basis of laptop sales patterns); see Section 11.2.6.

Analysis of Variance (ANOVA): A statistical procedure for testing whether or not a *regression model* (or a set of variables) has any predictive power. Failure to reject the *null*

hypothesis implies that the model (or set of variables) has no predictive value; see Section 8.3.2.

ARCH Model: A statistical model for the variance of a time series that has an *autoregressive*-like structure; see Section 6.10.

Area Under the Curve (AUC): The AUC (or Area Under the ROC – AUROC) summarizes the *Receiver Operating Characteristics* (ROC) by computing how much of the plot is under the curve for a classifier; see Section 10.4.1.

ARIMA Model: A model for a time series that involves *autoregressive* and *moving average components* and may also require *differencing* to remove *nonstationary* components; see Chapter 6.

Arithmetic Mean: See *mean*.

Autocorrelation: The *correlation* between current and past, or *lagged*, values of a time series; see Section 6.1.

Autocorrelation Function (ACF): The plot of the *autocorrelations* versus the order of the *lag*; see Section 6.1.

Automatic Model Selection: The process of choosing a model directly by an automated search using either an *information criterion* or an *out-of-sample* accuracy measure.

Autoregressive Conditional Heteroscedasticity: See *ARCH* and *GARCH models*.

Autoregressive Integrated Moving Average Model: See *ARIMA model*.

Autoregressive Model: A model that describes the dependence of a time series on its own past in terms of lagged values of that series; see Section 6.2

Backward Selection: A method of selecting a regression model; see also *forward selection, stepwise regression, best subsets regression*, and Section 9.4.2.

Bayesian Information Criterion (BIC): An *information criterion* designed to maximize the probability of selecting the correct underlying statistical model. It penalizes additional parameters more strongly than *AIC* does; see Section 5.4.2.

Best Subsets Regression: An approach to selecting a regression model that considers all possible subsets of the variables and so guarantees the largest possible R^2 (or some other preselected criterion, such as *AIC*). This approach is computationally more expensive than other selection methods; see Section 9.4.2.

Black Swan Event: An event totally unexpected outside the observed comparable history that would have been very hard if not impossible to predict.

Box–Cox Transformation: A transformation based upon a power of the original variable; see Section 3.7.3.

Box–Jenkins Models: See *ARIMA models*.

Brier Score: A proper score function that measures the accuracy of probabilistic predictions; see Section 11.5.4.

Brown's Method: A special case of *linear exponential smoothing*; see Section 3.6.1.

Bullwhip Effect: An effect that occurs when forecasts are not coordinated, whereby variations in demand at the retailer level are amplified at the manufacturer level and further amplified at the supplier level; see Section 12.3.1.

Causal Model: A model that purports to explain the variations in the *dependent variable* by *explanatory variables* that are assumed to have a causal relationship; see also *regression model*.

Census X-13: Also Census X-12. Methods of seasonal adjustment that are widely used for macroeconomic series; see Section 4.5.

Centered Moving Average (CMA): A *centered moving average* associates a *moving average* exactly with a time period in the observed series, i.e., it shifts the *moving average* to the middle-period of the observations on which it is calculated. When K is odd the *CMA* is the same as *MA*, but when K is even the *CMA* is defined by taking the average of successive pairs of *moving averages so* that the time period associated with the average corresponds exactly to a time period in the observed series; see Section 4.4.

Central Limit Theorem: The theorem which states that, as the sample size increases, the *sampling distribution* of the *sample mean* approaches the *normal distribution*. This result is the cornerstone upon which much of *statistical inference* is built; see online Appendix A.3.

CHAID: The Chi-Squared Automatic Interaction Detection approach to *pruning* a *classification tree;* see Section 10.2.2.

Choice Model: A model used to predict a consumer's choice (e.g., the choice of a brand within a product class) based upon the consumer's demographics and preferences; see Section 12.4.4.

Chow Test: A test that uses two distinct samples to test the equality of the slopes in a regression model; see Section 9.9.

Churn: The phenomenon that occurs when a customer then cancels the service provided to him or her by a particular organization (such as a mobile phone company).

Classification Table: A table that summarizes the numbers (or percentages) of correctly and incorrectly classified cases for a *predictive classification* procedure; see Section 10.2.

Classification Tree: A diagram that shows the successive partitions of a data set by classifying observations into distinct groups in order to improve the prediction of cases (e.g., distinguishing those who "buy" from those who "don't buy"); see Section 10.2.

Coefficient of Determination (R^2): Measures the proportion of the variation in the dependent variable explained by the regression model; see Section 7.4.2.

Coefficient of Multiple Correlation (R): The correlation between the observed and fitted values, which may be computed as the square root of the *coefficient of determination*; see Section 7.4.2.

Collaborative Planning, Forecasting, and Replenishment (CPFR): The practice of the partial sharing of information on retail sales and their forecasts, inventories and planned orders between a retailer and its suppliers with a view to improving service and mitigating any *bullwhip effects*. In its fullest extent it embraces a close relationship to jointly managing stocks and service between the two parties.

Cointegration: Two first-order, or $I(1)$, *nonstationary* variables are said to be cointegrated if there is a *stationary* linear relationship between them; see Appendix 10D.

Combining Forecasts: Two or more forecasts may be combined, usually by taking some form of weighted average. Properly chosen, such combinations often outperform even the single method selected as "best"; see Section 12.1.2.

Common Cause Chart (CCC): The chart of the fitted values generated by a time series model; see Section 13.1.4.

Conditional Forecast: A forecast that uses the actual values of the explanatory variables, even if these would not have been known at the time the forecast was made.

Conditional Variance: The variance of a future observation, given the past history of the time series; see Section 6.10.1.

Confidence Interval: When a confidence interval for an unknown *parameter* is constructed appropriately, this interval will include the true value of the parameter on the proportion of occasions set by the *confidence level*; see online Appendix A.4.1.

Confidence Level: A prespecified value that determines the proportion of occasions on which the *confidence interval* will include the true value of the parameter. This level is often chosen to be 0.90, 0.95 or 0.99.

Conjoint Model: See *choice model*.

Cook's Distance (D): A measure of the influence of an observation on the set of regression coefficients. Influential observations may be *leverage points* or *outliers*, or both.

Correlation Coefficient: A measure of association between two variables that is unaffected by changes in the origin or changes of scale. A value of +1 (−1) indicates a perfect positive (negative) linear association; see Section 2.5.

Critical Region: The set of values of the sample statistic for which the *null hypothesis* will be rejected; see online Appendix A.5.

CRM (Customer Relationship Management) Model: A class of models that aim to help establish and maintain a mutually valuable relationship between an organization and its customers by establishing *causal* (or indicative) relationships between customer behavior and various customer and product characteristics.

Cross-sectional Data: Data for which all observations are collected over the same relatively short time period.

Crowd-based forecasting: A crowd of potential experts is used to provide individual forecasts which are then aggregated; see Section 11.2.2.

Customer Surveys: Forecasts developed using intentions-to-buy surveys of potential customers; see Section 11.2.5.

Cutoff Percentage: See *threshold value.*

Cutoff Value: See *threshold value.*

Cyclical Component: A time series is said to have a cyclical component if it displays random fluctuations around the trend but those fluctuations have a periodicity with constant mean.

Damped Trend: A modification to *linear exponential smoothing* whereby the forecast trend line flattens out over time; see Section 3.5.

Data Generating Process: A statistical model that is assumed to correctly represent the economic or social system in which data are generated. It can only be known to be correct in artificial systems.

Decomposition: The breaking down of a problem into its constituent parts; for example, the partition of a time series into cyclical, seasonal, trend, and random components; see Sections 4.4 and 11.5.2.

Degrees of Freedom (DF): The net number of observations available for the estimation of the population variance, typically equal to the sample size minus the number of other parameters estimated.

Delphi Method: A method for developing forecasts that employs a panel of experts who do not meet but provide their inputs anonymously. The process consists of several rounds where information and forecasts are shared, leading to a distribution of forecast outcomes in the final round. The summary forecast may be the mean, median, or mode of these revised expert forecasts as well as the distribution of outcomes. It can also be used for qualitative forecasting; see Section 11.3.

Dependent Variable: The variable of interest in a *regression analysis.*

Deseasonalized Series: A time series from which the *seasonal component* has been removed.

Deviation: The observed value minus the *arithmetic mean.*

Diagnostic Tests: Statistical tests employed to check the assumptions underlying a model; see Section 8.5.

Difference (first): In a time series, the value of the current observation minus the value that immediately precedes it, i.e., $Y_t - Y_{t-1}$; see Section 2.6.1.

Differencing: The operation of subtracting a previous value in a time series from the current value in order to remove *nonstationarity* due to either the trend or the seasonal pattern; see Section 2.6.1.

Diffusion Curve: A *growth curve* underpinned by a model for the growth of demand; see Section 12.4.3.

Double Exponential Smoothing: See *linear exponential smoothing.*

Dummy Variable: See *indicator variable.*

Durbin–Watson Test: A test statistic used to determine whether the errors in a regression model have any residual first-order *autocorrelation*; see Appendix 8A.

Econometric Model: A set of *regression* equations developed to describe an economic system.

Elasticity: The proportionate change in the dependent variable relative to a given proportionate change in an *explanatory variable*; see Section 7.6.2.

Empirical Prediction Interval: A prediction interval based upon the empirical error distribution; see Section 2.8.2.

Error: See *forecast error* and *random error.*

Error Correction Form: Where a *forecast function* is expressed in terms of an adjustment to the most recent *forecast error.*

Error Correction Model (ECM): A *vector autoregressive model* that has cross-equation constraints on the parameters, formulated in terms of a *cointegrating* relationship; see Appendix 10D.

Estimation Sample: The subset of the data that is used to estimate the unknown *parameters* in a statistical model.

ETS Classification Scheme: Summary description of state space models that specifies the Error, Trend, and Seasonal structure; see Section 5.1.3.

Ex ante Forecast: See *unconditional forecast.*

Exogenous Variable: A variable determined outside the system being modeled. It may be known (such as the indicator variable for a known event) or its value assumed for a what-if *conditional forecast*. Potentially it would require forecasting when producing an *unconditional forecast.*

Expected Value: The average value for a sample statistic when (conceptually) a large number of such samples is taken. Thus, the expected value of the sample mean is the population mean. A *random variable* taking discrete values has an expected value that is a (probability) weighted average of the possible values; see online Appendix A.1.

Expert (Group) Opinion: A judgment based forecast produced by a single "expert" or a group of experts.

Explanatory Variables: The variables used to explain variations in the *dependent variable* in a *regression analysis.*

Exponential Curve: See *growth curve* and *diffusion curve.*

Exponentially Weighted Moving Average (EWMA): See *simple exponential smoothing* and Section 3.3.

Ex post Forecast: See *conditional forecast.*

Extrapolation: Using past values of a series to forecast the likely future path of that series.

Extrapolative Forecast: A forecast based on the past values of the series.

Extreme Observation: See *outlier.*

F-Test: See *analysis of variance.*

Fan Chart: A graphical representation of the uncertainty in a forecast over the forecast horizon.

Final Forecast: The forecast made available to forecast users, often based on a statistical forecast that is judgmentally adjusted.

Fitting Sample: See *estimation sample*.

Focus Group: A facilitated discussion group focused on an interactive exploration to establish the dimensions of a particular (forecasting) question rather than the forecast itself; see Section 11.2.2

Forecast: A prediction or estimate of an actual outcome expected in a future time period or for another situation.

Forecast Adjustment: Modification to a (usually) quantitative forecast, using subjective information; see Section 12.4.6.

Forecast Error: The difference between the actual observation and the *forecast*.

Forecast Function: A mathematical expression for deriving forecasts over the *forecast horizon*.

Forecast Horizon: The number of time periods ahead for which the forecast is made.

Forecast Origin: The point in time from which forecasts are made.

Forecasting Competition: A comparative evaluation of forecasting methods using multiple time series, typically across multiple time *horizons* and evaluated by a variety of different *accuracy measures*.

Forecasting Method: A procedure for generating a forecast. Where a quantitative *algorithm* is used to estimate a *forecast function* that is not based upon an underlying statistical model, it is termed *heuristic*; see Section 3.1.

Forecasting Model: See *statistical model*.

Forecasting Support System (FSS): A set of (typically computer-based) procedures that facilitate interactive forecasting of key variables in a given organizational context. An FSS enables users to combine relevant information, analytical models, and judgments, as well as visualizations, to produce (or create) forecasts and monitor their accuracy; see Section 12.2.

Forward Selection: A method of selecting a regression model; see also *backward selection, stepwise regression, best subsets regression*, and Section 9.4.

GARCH Model: A statistical model for the variance of a time series that has both *autoregressive*-like and *moving average*–like structures; see Section 6.10.

Geodemographic Segmentation System (GSS): A classification of neighborhoods (e.g., census tracts) into segments by grouping tracts with similar demographic characteristics. The basic premise of a GSS is that people tend to gravitate toward communities populated with people of similar backgrounds, interests, and means; see Section 12.5.

Geometric Mean (of observations): Defined as the *n*-th root of the product of the *n* observations, it is particularly appropriate for summarizing a set of percentages or ratios (such as occur in error calculations, e.g., the *MAPE* or *RelMAE* for a number of data series).

Gini coefficient: See *Area Under the Curve*.

Goodness-of-fit: A measure of the closeness of a model's predictions to the observations, e.g., *MSE*.

Gompertz Curve: A particular example of a *growth curve* and *diffusion curve*; see Section 12.4.2.

Group-think: A characteristic of an expert group forecast where those inside the group accept only like views: their predictions cannot be challenged and conflicting views and information are rejected.

Growth Curve: Usually a nonlinear equation describing demand for a product as a function of time. If the curve has a finite upper limit, that limit is often known as the *market potential* of the product; see Section 12.4.2.

Heteroscedasticity: The assumption that the *random error* in a *statistical model* does not have a constant variance.

Hidden Layer: A layer of *hidden nodes* that make up a *neural network*; see Section 10.4.

Hidden Node: A component of a *neural network* that is made up from a single neuron; see Section 10.4.

Hierarchical Forecasting: Forecasting either from the top down (disaggregation), from the bottom up (aggregation), or by hierarchical combination, so that forecasts at different levels are consistent (i.e., the total amount forecast at one level of the hierarchy matches the amount at the next higher level); see Section 12.3.3.

Hold-Out Sample: Set of data withheld from the end of a series; to be compared with the forecast values in assessing a forecasting model; see Section 3.3.3.

Holt's Method: See *linear exponential smoothing*.

Holt–Winters Methods: A method for forecasting series with both trend and seasonal components. The *forecast function* may involve purely *additive* level, trend, and seasonal components, or it may have a *mixed additive-multiplicative* form; see Sections 4.6 and 4.7.

Homoscedasticity: The assumption that the *random error* in a *statistical* model has a constant variance.

Horizon: See *forecast horizon*.

Hyperparameter: A parameter that characterizes a class of model that must be pre-selected before the model can be estimated.

Indicator Variable: When observations fall into one of a number of categories, we distinguish the observations by defining *dummy variables*, each of which is set equal to 1 if the observation falls into one category and 0 if it falls into any other (e.g., two categories: Female = 1, Male = 0; the months of the year January = 1, other months = 0, similarly for the other 11 months); see Section 9.1.

Information Criterion: An overall performance criterion that combines a goodness-of-fit measure (e.g., the *mean square error*) with a *penalty function* to make allowances for extra parameters being included in a statistical model; see Section 5.3.2.

In-sample: The data in the *estimation sample*. Where there is a three-fold split in the data set into *training*, *validation*, and test, the *validation data* form a part of the *in-sample* data; see Section 10.4.

Integrated Series: A time series is integrated if it is *nonstationary* and requires differencing to induce *stationarity*; see Chapter 6 and also Appendix 10B.

Intermittent Demand: Demand for a product that may be zero in many periods and such that any nonzero demand may be highly variable; see Section 12.3.5.

Intervention Analysis: A method of making adjustments to a model to take into account possible changes in structure, either permanent or temporary; see Section 9.8.

Invertibility: A time series model is invertible if the coefficients in the *moving average model* decay over time such that the sum of their absolute values is finite. This property is required for the estimation of *ARIMA models*.

Irregular Component: The remaining fluctuations in a time series after the trend, seasonal (and *cyclical*) components have been removed; see *random error*.

Judgmental Forecasting: The process of producing forecasts based on integrating information based on subjective beliefs. The integration may be made informally or through a structured process. For example, the forecast may be obtained by aggregating the subjective forecasts of a number of individuals. Such forecasts may also involve subjective adjustments to quantitative forecasts; see Chapter 11.

Jury of Expert Opinion: Forecasts developed by a panel of experts who participate in an actual or virtual meeting; see Section 11.2.3.

Lag: The time difference between two observations in a time series (e.g., April is at lag 3 relative to July in monthly observations); see Section 6.1.

Lasso Regression: A method of estimation of a regression (type) model that minimizes the *MSE* subject to constraining the model's parameters. The effect is a simpler model, forcing some parameters towards zero; see Section 9.5.2.

Leading Indicator: A variable that changes in advance of the changes in the dependent variable of interest and that is therefore useful for forecasting. A leading indicator ideally has a *causal* relationship with the dependent variable; see Section 7.8.

Level Shift: A permanent, long-term change in the level of a time series.

Leverage Point: An observation that is not "close" to the rest of the observations in the sample. Such data points may distort the estimates of the regression parameters; see Section 9.7.1.

Linear Exponential Smoothing: A forecasting method that generates *locally linear forecasts* by smoothing past observations in the time series, adjusted by the most recent *forecast error*; see Section 3.4.

Linear Model: A regression model that is linear in the parameters; see Section 7.5.1.

Linear Moving Average: A form of *moving average* that estimates a local trend line; see Section 3.6.4.

Locally Constant Forecasts: A series is locally constant from the forecast origin if the mean level is not forecast to change over time.

Locally Linear Forecasts: A series is locally linear if the mean level is expected to increase (or decrease) linearly over time. When a new observation is recorded, estimates of the intercept and *trend* are updated.

Logarithmic Transformation: A transformation of a variable from the original scale to a logarithmic scale; see Section 2.6.2.

Logistic Curve: See *growth curve* and *diffusion curve*.

Logistic Regression: A method of *regression analysis* in which the dependent variable defines membership in two (or more) distinct classes, typically coded as 0 and 1; see Section 10.3.

Macroeconomics: The study of aggregate economic activity at the regional or national level.

Market Potential: The total expected size of the future market for a product or service; see Section 12.4.4.

Market Response Model: A model for predicting the market demand for a product at brand or *SKU* level that takes into account explanatory variables, including price, promotions, and competitors' actions; see Section 12.4.5.

Matrix plot: An array of *scatterplots*; see Section 2.3.

Mean: The average of a set of observations; see Section 2.4.2.

Mean Absolute Deviation: See *mean absolute error*.

Mean Absolute Error (MAE): The average value of the *absolute errors*; see Section 2.7.2.

Mean Absolute Percentage Error (MAPE): The average value of the *absolute percentage errors*; see Section 2.7.2.

Mean Absolute Scaled Error (MASE): A measure of forecasting performance given by scaling the *mean absolute error* out-of-sample for the current method by the *mean absolute error* from the random walk errors in the estimation sample; see Section 2.7.2.

Mean Error (ME): The average value of the forecast errors; see Section 2.7.1.

Mean Percentage Error (MPE): The average value of the *percentage errors*; see Section 2.7.1.

Mean Reverting: A time series is mean reverting if the optimal forecasts of its long-term behavior converge to the mean value of the series; see Section 6.2.1.

Mean Square Error (MSE): The average value of the squares of the *forecast errors*; see Section 2.7.2.

Median: The middle value in a set of observations that is ordered from smallest to largest; see Section 2.4.2.

Method Selection Tree: A decision tree designed to assist the process of selecting a forecasting method; see Section 13.1.3.

Mixed Additive–Multiplicative Model: A model in which the trend and seasonal components are multiplied together and the error term is added to the product; see Section 4.1.

Modified Exponential Curve: See *growth curve* and *diffusion curve* and Section 12.4.2.

Monitoring: The process of checking forecasts to ensure that changing conditions do not render the current forecasting system inadequate; see Section 13.1.4.

Moving Average: A (simple) *moving average* of order K is the average of K terms in a time series, taken over successive observations.

Moving Average Model: A model that describes the dependence of a time series on its own past in terms of lagged values of random errors; see Section 6.2.

Multicollinearity: A phenomenon that occurs when (some of) the explanatory variables of a regression model are highly correlated. Multicollinearity can lead to unstable or unrealistic estimates of regression parameters. Multicollinearity may be causal, data based, or definitional; see Section 9.5.

Multiple Regression: *Regression analysis* with more than one input (*explanatory) variable*; see Section 8.2.

Multiple Temporal Aggregation (MTA): A modeling approach that combines forecasts from different *temporal aggregations* of the data (e.g., daily, weekly, monthly (4 weeks)); see Section 12.3.4.

Multiplicative Model: A model in which the components are multiplied together; see Section 4.1.

Naïve Forecast: A forecast that uses the current value of a time series as the forecast for the next and subsequent periods.

Natural Logarithm: Logarithm to base $e = 2.71828\ldots$; see Section 2.6.2.

Net Present Value (NPV): The value of future net cash flows (receipts minus expenditures), discounted over time by an appropriate discount rate.

Neural Network: A system of inputs, intermediate unobservable (latent) variables (known as *hidden nodes*), and outputs that provides a general framework for nonlinear model building; see Section 10.4.

Noise: See *random error*.

Neuron: A building block of a *neural network*; see Section 10.4.

Nonlinear Model: A model that is nonlinear in the *parameters*; see Section 9.6.

Nonlinear Trend Curve: See *growth curve* and *diffusion curve*.

Nonstationarity: A *time series* is nonstationary if any of the *mean*, *variance*, and *autocorrelations* change over time.

Normal Distribution: The probability distribution that is most commonly assumed to describe the error terms in a statistical model. The density function is a bell-shaped curve; see online Appendix A.2.

Normal Interval: A *prediction interval* based upon the *normal distribution*.

Normal Probability Plot: A plot of the observed *order statistics* against their *expected values* when the underlying distribution is *normal*; see online Appendix A.6.

Null Hypothesis (H_0): The statement that is used as the benchmark for a *significance test*; it hypothesizes a specific value (or range of values) for the parameter under consideration. Frequently, in regression analysis, the null hypothesis states that there is no relationship between the dependent variable and one or more explanatory variables. The null hypothesis is compared against the *alternative hypothesis*; see online Appendix A.5.

Observation Equation: An equation that relates the observations to underlying *state variable(s)* (such as the trend and seasonal); see Section 5.1.2.

Order Statistics: The kth *order statistic* of a sample is equal to its kth-smallest value. Important special cases are the minimum, maximum and *median*; see Section 2.4.2.

Ordinary Least Squares (OLS): The method used to estimate unknown parameters in a statistical model by minimizing the *sum of squared errors*; see Section 7.2.1.

Origin: See *forecast origin*.

Outlier: An observation (or residual from a statistical model) that lies far away from its expected or forecast value and, if not adjusted, may cause serious estimation or forecast errors; see Section 5.5.

Out-of-Sample: The data in the *hold-out sample*.

Panel Data: Cross-sectional measurements that are repeated over time, such as individual monthly expenditures for a sample of consumers.

Parameter: In a statistical model a parameter (or parameters) embody the relationship between variables in the model, (e.g., the relationship between the dependent variable and an explanatory variable in a regression model). When a single random variable is under consideration, the parameters specify its probability distribution (e.g. population *mean* and *variance)*.

Partial Autocorrelation: The *correlation* between the current and *lagged values* of a time series after allowing for the dependence on intermediate values; see Section 6.3.

Partial Autocorrelation Function (PACF): The plot of the *partial autocorrelations* versus the order of the *lag*; see Section 6.3.1.

Pearson Product Moment Correlation Coefficient: See *correlation coefficient*.

Pegels' Classification Scheme: See *ETS Classification*, also Section 5.1.3.

Penalty Function: A term that is added to a goodness-of-fit measure for a statistical model (e.g., *mean square error*) in an *information criterion* to make allowances for the parameters in the model.

Percentage Error: The difference between the actual and forecast values, expressed as a percentage of the actual value; see Section 2.7.1.

PIVASE: The six fundamental components of any forecasting activity: Purpose, Information, Value (of forecasting), Analysis (and forecasting), System, and Evaluation; see Section 1.1.

Planning: The steps an organization takes in response to its forecasts to move toward its objectives.

Point Forecast: See *forecast*.

Pollyanna Effect: A result that looks too good to be true.

Polynomial Regression Scheme: A regression model that includes quadratic and possibly higher-order powers of the explanatory variables.

Population: The set of all possible outcomes in a statistical study. For studies of human populations, this set consists of actual people; in time series studies, the "population" may be a purely conceptual set of possible values of the series.

Prediction Interval: A statement that a future observation will lie within a prespecified range of values with a probability derived from the *predictive distribution;* see Section 2.8.

Prediction Markets: An electronic market set up to trade "shares" that represent two or more distinct outcomes of a future activity (e.g., a Democratic or Republican victory in a presidential election). Participants trade the shares at prices that reflect traders' expectations about the final outcome; see Section 11.4.

Predictive Classification: Set of statistical methods that classify cases into two or more distinct categories (e.g., potential consumers into those who "buy" and those who "don't buy"); see Section 10.1.

Predictive (or Prediction) Distribution: The *probability distribution* for a future observation, derived from a *forecasting model*; see Section 2.8.

Probability Distribution: The specification of the possible values that a *random variable* may take, together with the associated set of probabilities.

Product Life Cycle: The different stages of consumer demand for a product: launch, growth, maturity, and finally, decline.

Pruning Rule: A method of simplifying a *classification tree* so that only the important subdivisions are retained.

P-Value: The observed significance level that is used in hypothesis testing. If the *P*-value is less than the *significance level*, the *null hypothesis* is rejected; see Section 7.6.1.

Quantitative Forecasting: Forecasting based on the application of a prescribed explicit (algorithmic) analysis of numerically coded data. This kind of forecasting may be *causal, extrapolative*, or a blend of both; see Section 11.1.

Random Error: The unexplained difference between the *expected* and observed values in a statistical model. In a valid model, the random error for a particular observation is completely unpredictable.

Random Variable: A variable that may take on one of a number of possible values, according to a specified *probability distribution*.

Random Walk: A naïve model that uses the previous observation as the forecast for the current period; see Section 6.3.1.

Range: The difference between the largest and smallest values in the sample; see Section 2.4.3.

Receiver Operating Characteristic (ROC): Plot of *Sensitivity* against (1 – *Specificity*) for different *Threshold Values*; see Section 10.1.1.

Regression Analysis: A statistical model-building procedure that relates the variable of interest (the *dependent variable*) to one or more *explanatory variables*; see Section 7.1.1.

RelMAE: The Relative Mean Absolute Error is the ratio of the *MAE* for one forecasting method, relative to the *MAE* for the *random walk* (or some other benchmark); see Section 2.7.2.

Residual: The estimate of the *random error* (= observed – fitted).

Risk Summary: A comparison of the loss from alternative policies arising from different future *scenarios*. The selected policy is robust if the likely loss is small over a wide range of scenarios.

Role-playing: Forecasts based upon a *scenario* that describes a conflict situation. Participants adopt particular roles of either individuals or organizations engaged in the conflict and endeavor to achieve their objectives (such as a negotiated outcome); see Section 11.6.1.

Rolling Horizon: The repeated estimation and evaluation of the forecast error by advancing the *estimation sample* one observation at a time and repeating the error calculations.

Rolling Origin Evaluation: See *rolling horizon*.

Rolling Regression: The estimation of a regression model which is progressively updated from an initial *estimation sample*, either by adding data incrementally or by using a moving window with a fixed number of observations. Both lead to a sequence of parameter estimates that give insight into the model's stability over time; see Section 9.9.1.

Root Mean Square(d) Error (RMSE): The square root of the *mean square error*.

Safety Stock: The amount of stock held at *SKU* level above the forecast level of sales to allow for errors in the forecast.

Sales Force Projections: Aggregate forecasts developed from information and forecasts supplied by a company's sales force; see Section 11.2.4.

Sample: The set of individuals or outcomes actually observed; a subset of the *population*.

Sampling Distribution: The probability distribution for a sample statistic; see online Appendix A.3.

Scatterplot (or Scattergram): A plot of the dependent variable (Y) against an input variable (X); see Section 2.3.

Scenarios: A consistent set of statements about possible future events and trends and their dependencies, tracing the progression of the present to the future through a descriptive narrative. Scenarios are often used to motivate people and solicit information from them, rather than directly for forecasting; see Section 11.6.

Seasonal Adjustment: Process of removing seasonality from time series data so that underlying trends may be examined; see Chapter 4.

Seasonal Component: A time series is said to have a seasonal component if it displays a recurrent pattern with a fixed and known duration.

Seasonal Decomposition: The partition of a time series into *trend, seasonal,* and *irregular components*; see Section 4.4.

Seasonal Plot: A diagram with the seasons (e.g., months) on the horizontal axis and with overlaid plots for multiple seasons (e.g., years).

Seasonality: A recurrent pattern of fixed and known duration (e.g., months within a year).

Sensitivity: The proportion of target events in a *predictive classification* problem that are correctly predicted.

Signal: The predictable component of a statistical model.

Significance Level: The probability that a *null hypothesis* would be rejected when it is true; see online Appendix A.5.

Simple Exponential Smoothing: A *forecast function* based upon a weighted average of the most recent observation and the previous *forecast error*; see Section 3.3.

Simple Linear Regression: *Regression analysis* with a single *explanatory variable*; see Section 7.1.

Simulated Distribution: A distribution (usually for forecasting errors) developed by running a large number of simulations of the forecasting process and then calculating the forecast errors from each run; see Section 13.3.1.

Single Expert (Unaided Judgment): Forecasts based upon the (expert) knowledge of a single individual; see Section 11.2.1.

SKU: See *stock keeping unit.*

Smoothing Constants (Parameters): The parameters that determine the extent of the adjustment to the local level (and local trend) in *exponential smoothing.*

Special (or Assignable) Cause Chart (SCC): The plot of residuals, which may be treated as a Shewhart chart, given independent, identically distributed errors.

Specificity: The proportion of nontarget events that are correctly predicted in a *predictive classification* problem; see Section 10.1.1.

Standard Deviation: The square root of the *variance.*

Standard Error: The *standard deviation* of a parameter estimate.

Standard Error of Estimate (S): The square root of the *sum of squared errors,* divided by the residual *degrees of freedom.* The standard error of estimate is a key measure of the accuracy of a model and is used in the construction of *prediction intervals*; see Section 7.4.1.

Standardized Score: The value of the *deviation* of an observation about the mean, divided by its *standard deviation*; see Section 2.4.4.

State Equation: An equation that describes how a *state variable* or component changes over time; see Section 5.1.2.

State Variable: A variable that describes a component (e.g., *trend, seasonal*) of a time series. State variables are not necessarily directly observable.

State-Space Model: A model that consists of an *observation equation* and one or more *state equations*; see Chapter 5.

Stationarity: A time series is stationary if it has a constant mean and variance and its autocorrelations depend only on the relative time between the observations; see Section 6.1.1.

Statistic: A function calculated from the sample data, e.g., the *sample mean.*

Statistical Forecast: Forecast made from a statistical model.

Statistical Inference: The process of using a random sample to draw conclusions about the population of interest.

Statistical Model: A statistical description of the *data-generating process* from which a forecasting method may be derived. Forecasts are made with the use of a *forecast function* derived from the model. A statistical model is a necessary foundation for the construction of prediction intervals.

Stepwise Regression: A method of selecting a model that proceeds by alternately adding and dropping variables that aims to find a model that explains the highest possible proportion of the variation in the *dependent variable*; see also *backward selection.*

Stochastic Process: A random process in which outcomes are generated according to a set of probabilistic rules.

Stock Keeping Unit (SKU): A specific and well-defined item at the lowest level of aggregation (potentially including its location). Used in inventory control.

Studentized Residual: A residual divided by an estimate of its particular standard deviation.

Student's *t*-Distribution: The probability distribution that describes the distribution of the sample mean and sample regression coefficients when the variance is unknown.

Sum of Squared Errors (SSE): The sum of squares of the *errors (residuals)*; see Section 7.2.1.

Supply Chain Forecasting: The forecasting activities of retailers, manufacturers, and their upstream suppliers, which may or may not be coordinated. A lack of coordination leads to the so-called *bullwhip effect*; see Section 12.3.2.

Target: Estimate of what might be achieved by implementing a plan. A target should be based upon the corresponding forecast.

Target Class: The particular category of interest in a *predictive classification* study (e.g., the defaulters on a loan).

Target Marketing: Promotional activities aimed at particular consumer groups and based upon predictions of their likely interest in the product or service offered (compared to other groups).

Target Variable: The variable of interest in a *predictive classification* that describes the different categorical outcomes, e.g., a "good" customer and a "bad" customer.

Temporal Aggregation: Aggregates a *time series* into a lower sampling frequency. For example, a monthly time series aggregated over 3 months to transform it to quarterly time series; see Section 12.3.4.

Test Sample: See *hold-out sample*; see Section 10.4.

Theil's U: A measure of forecasting performance, given by scaling the *root mean square error* for the current method by the *root mean square error* for *naïve forecasts*.

Threshold Value: Used in *predictive classification* to assign predicted outcomes of the *target variable* to the *target class*. After ranking the observations in the sample under analysis (using the training, validation or test samples), the observations that are predicted as falling above the cut-off are assigned to the target class. If the value is defined as a percentage (say x%), the highest x% of the ranked observations are predicted to fall into the target class; see Section 10.1.

Time Series: A set of comparable measurements on a variable recorded at points in time.

Total Sum of Squares (SST): Sum of squared deviations (measured about the overall mean) for the dependent variable; see Section 7.4.

Tracking Signal: A method for monitoring the forecast errors to identify if recent errors are "out of control" (i.e., have become unexpectedly biased or large). A version of *simple exponential smoothing* uses the tracking signal by adjusting the smoothing constant on the basis of the most recent errors; see Section 3.6.3.

Training Sample: See *estimation sample*; see Section 10.4.

Transformation: The mathematical conversion of an equation or a variable into an equivalent entity (e.g., the conversion of a *multiplicative model* that uses logarithms to give a linear equation).

Trend: A systematic change (up or down) in the mean level of a time series.

Type I Error: See *significance level.*

Unconditional Forecast: A forecast which uses only the information available at the time the forecast is made (i.e., at the *forecast origin*).

Validation Sample: Part of the in-sample data used to choose *hyperparameters* or between different models; see Section 10.4.

Variance: The average of the squared deviations about the arithmetic mean; see Section 2.4.3.

Variance Inflation Factor (VIF): A measure of the extent to which the variance of a regression estimate is increased because of multicollinearity among the explanatory variables; see Section 9.5.

Vector Autoregressive (VAR) Models: A set of two or more autoregressive equations that represents all the variables as linear functions of the lagged values of all variables in the model; see Section 10.5.

What-if Forecast: A forecast that uses assumed values of the explanatory variables to determine the potential outcomes of different policy alternatives or different possible futures.

Wisdom-of-crowds: See *crowd-based forecasting.*

Z-Score: See *standardized score.*

INDEX

Page numbers with an *f* refer to a figure; a *t* refers to a table; an *n* refers to a footnote. Bolded page numbers indicate the page range for an entire chapter.

CPSIA information can be obtained
at www.ICGtesting.com
Printed in the USA
FFHW011142281018
49004987-53270FF